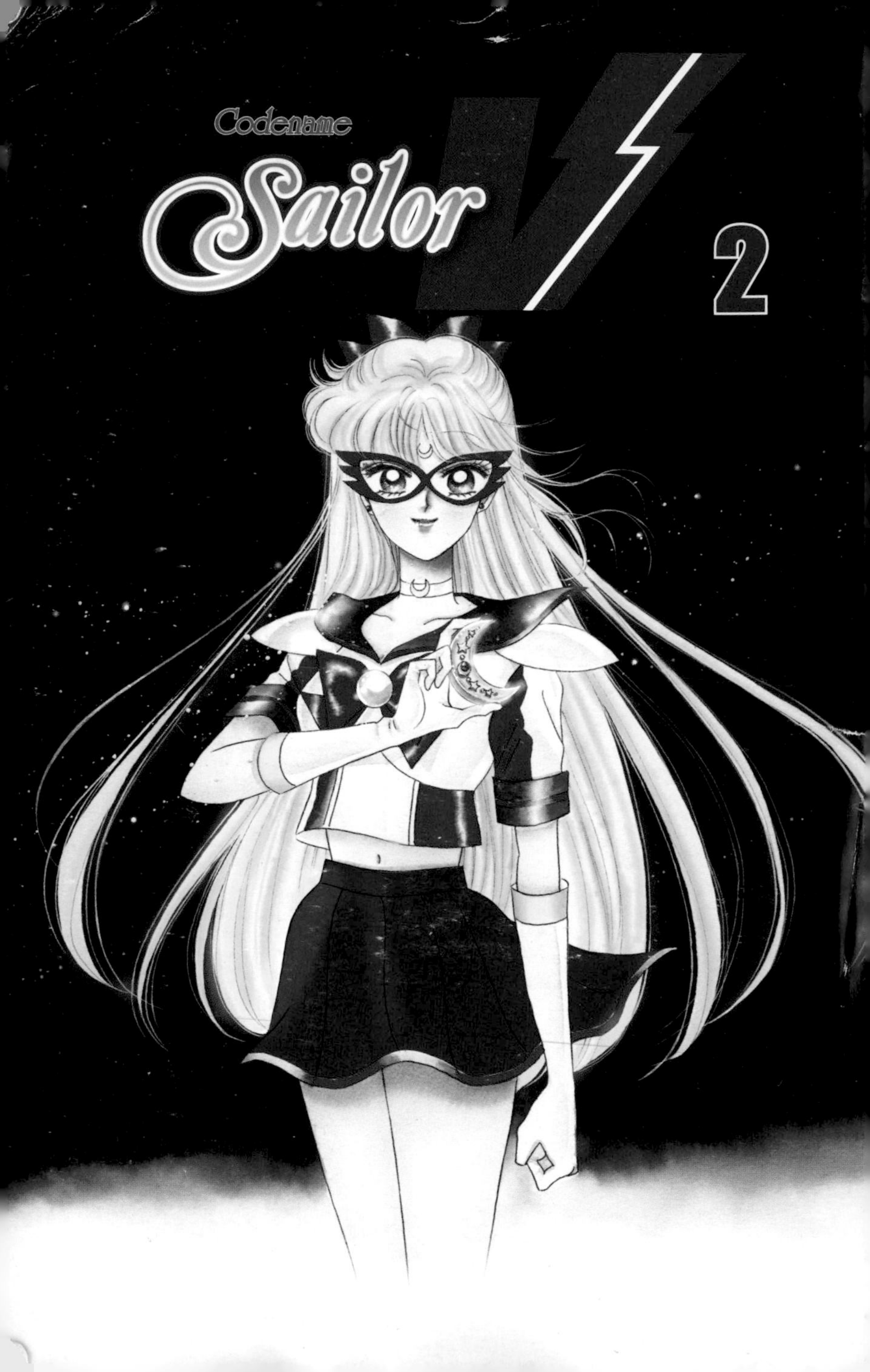
Codename
Sailor V
2

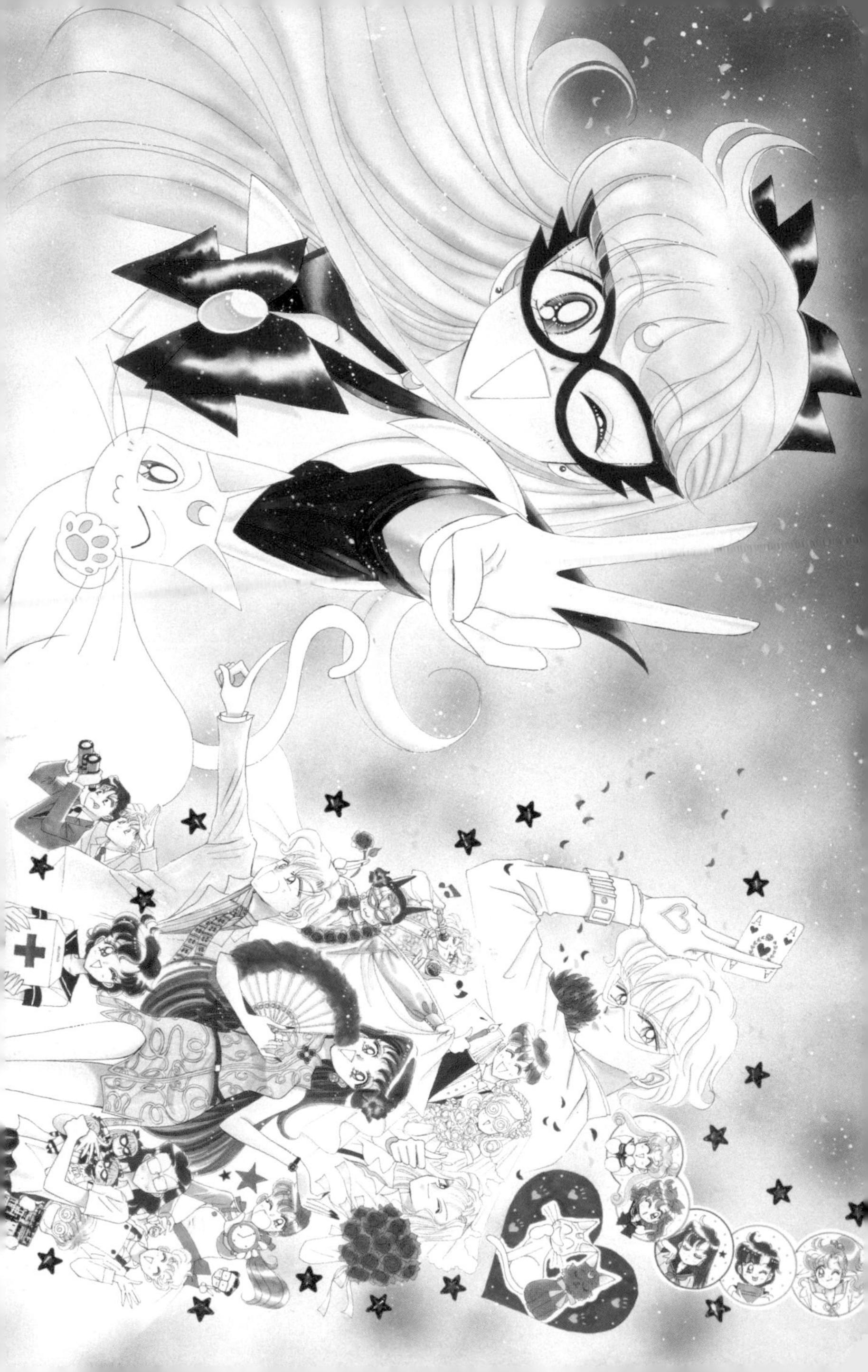

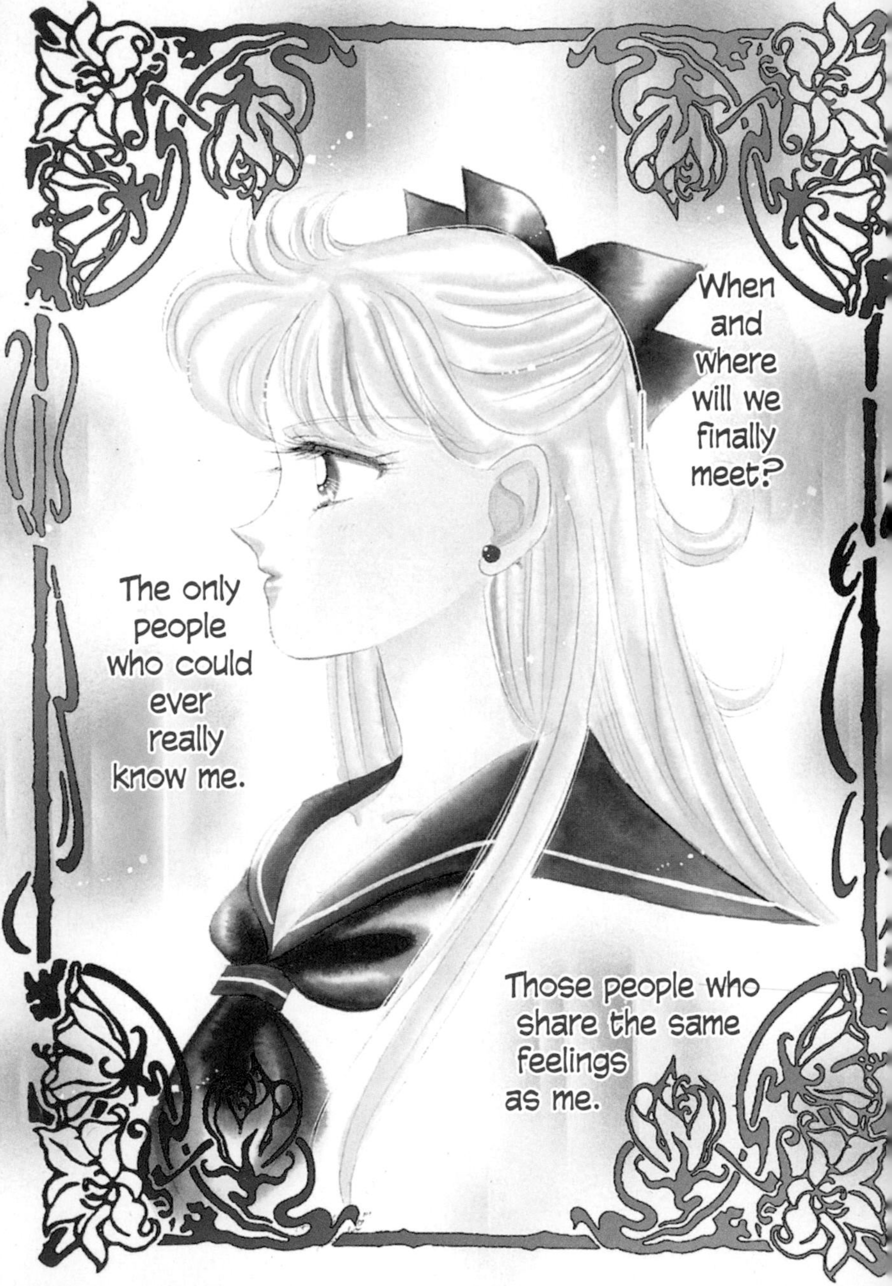
When and where will we finally meet?
The only people who could ever really know me.
Those people who share the same feelings as me.

Vol.9 Sailor V vs. deVleene

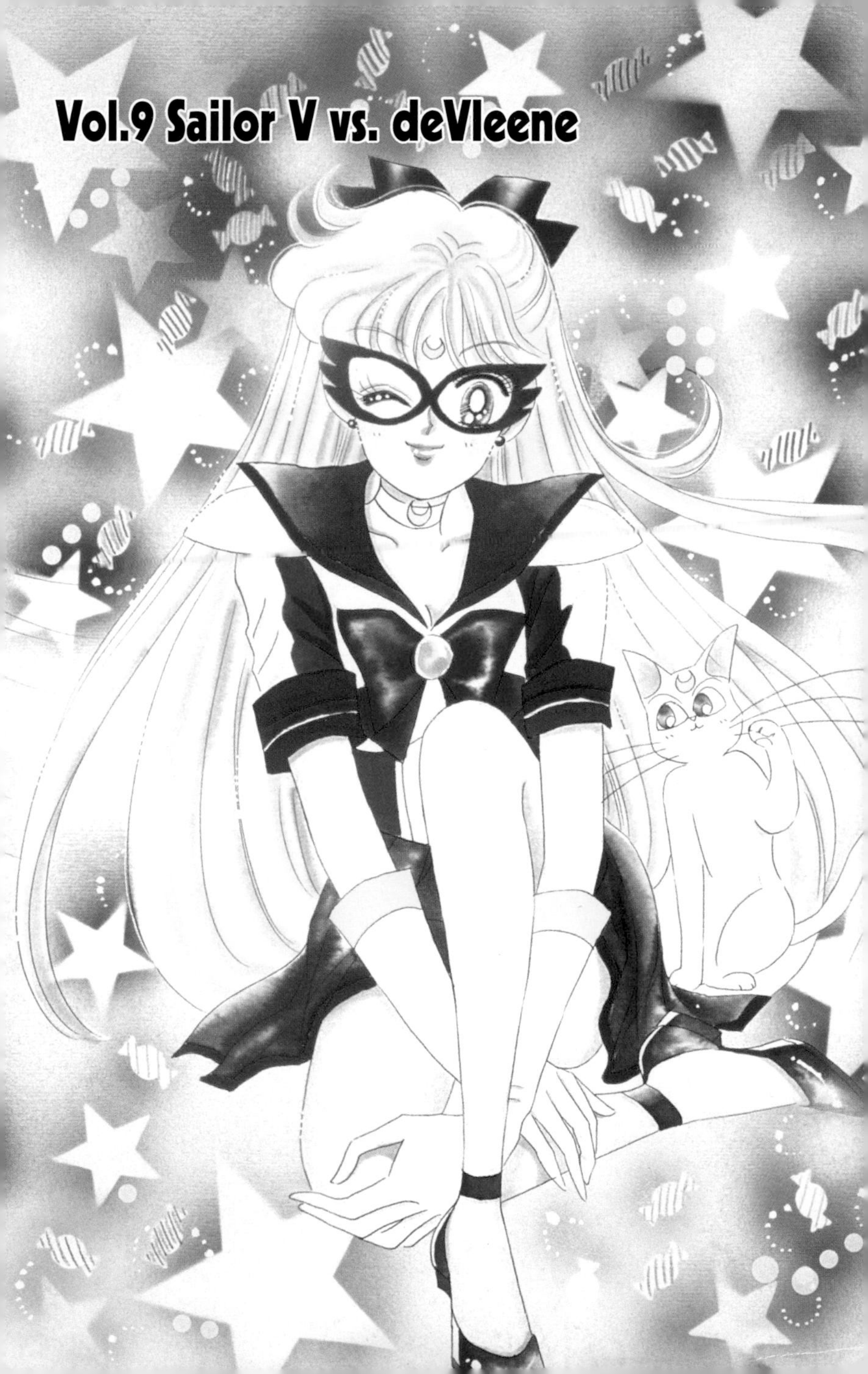

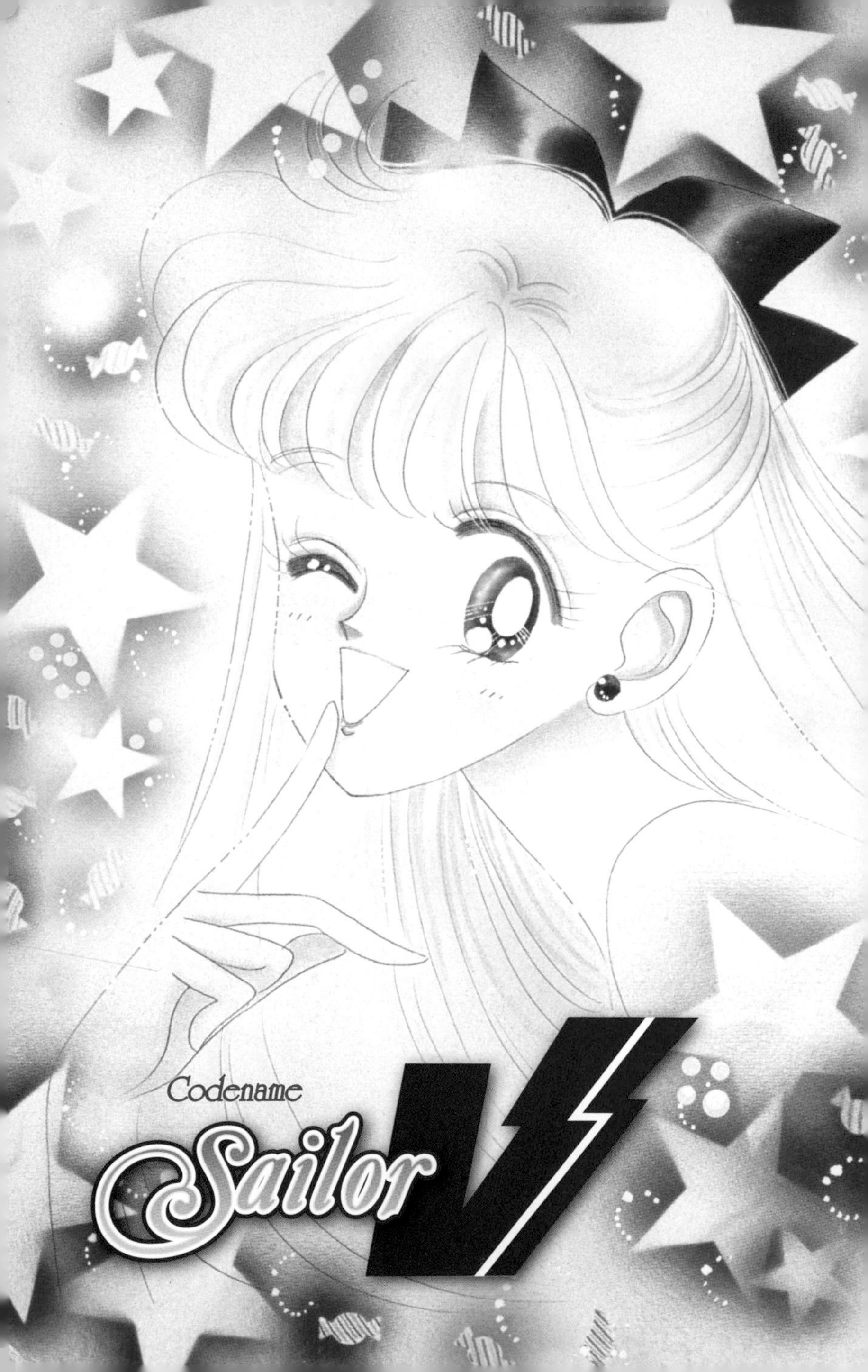
Codename
Sailor V

CONTENTS

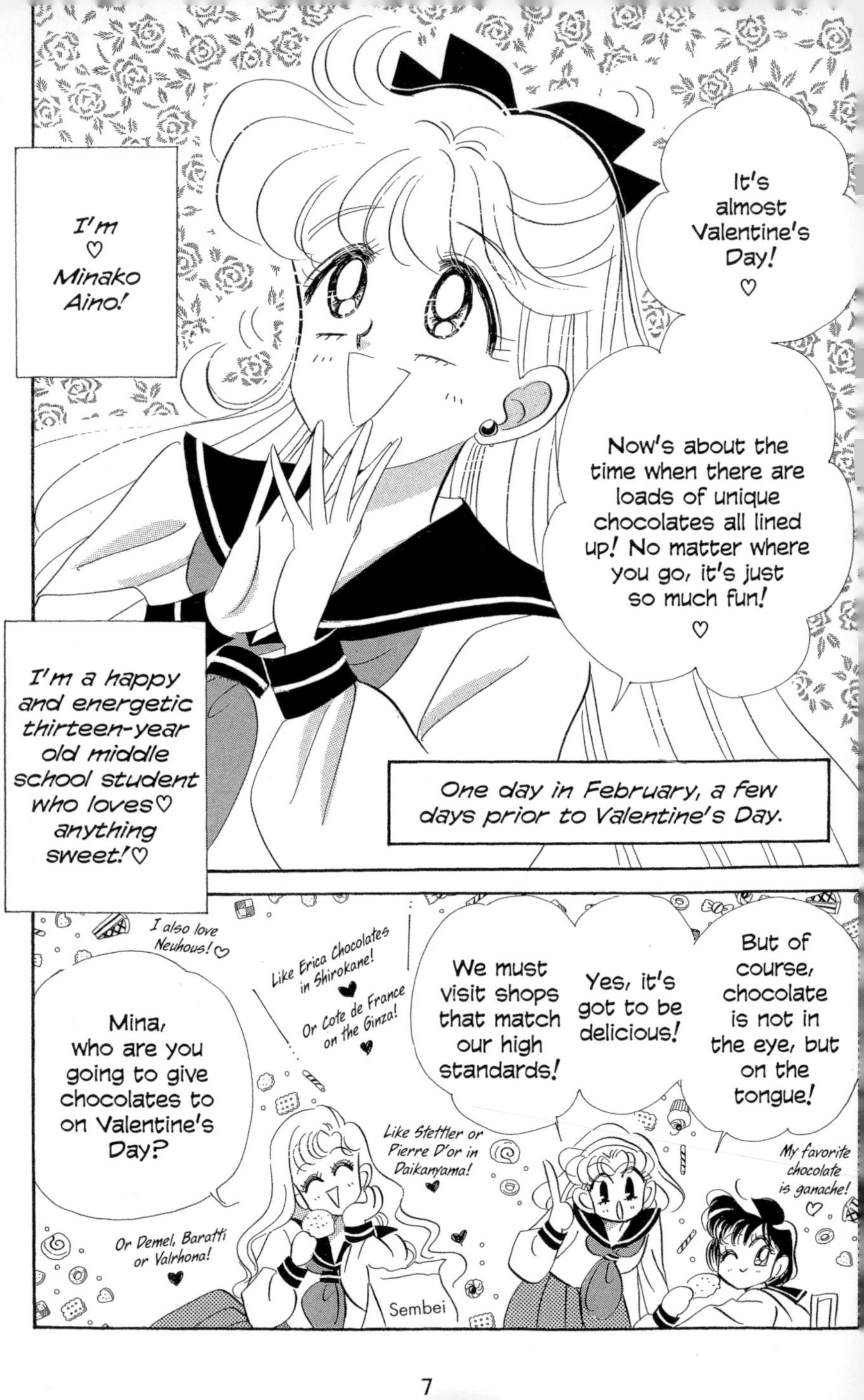
It's almost Valentine's Day! ♡
I'm ♡ Minako Aino!
Now's about the time when there are loads of unique chocolates all lined up! No matter where you go, it's just so much fun! ♡
I'm a happy and energetic thirteen-year old middle school student who loves♡ anything sweet!♡
One day in February, a few days prior to Valentine's Day.
But of course, chocolate is not in the eye, but on the tongue!
Yes, it's got to be delicious!
We must visit shops that match our high standards!
Like Erica Chocolates in Shirokane! ♥
Or Cote de France on the Ginza! ♥
I also love Neuhous! ♡
Mina, who are you going to give chocolates to on Valentine's Day?
My favorite chocolate is ganache! ♡
Like Stettler or Pierre D'or in Daikanyama! ♥
Or Demel, Baratti or Valrhona! ♥
Sembei

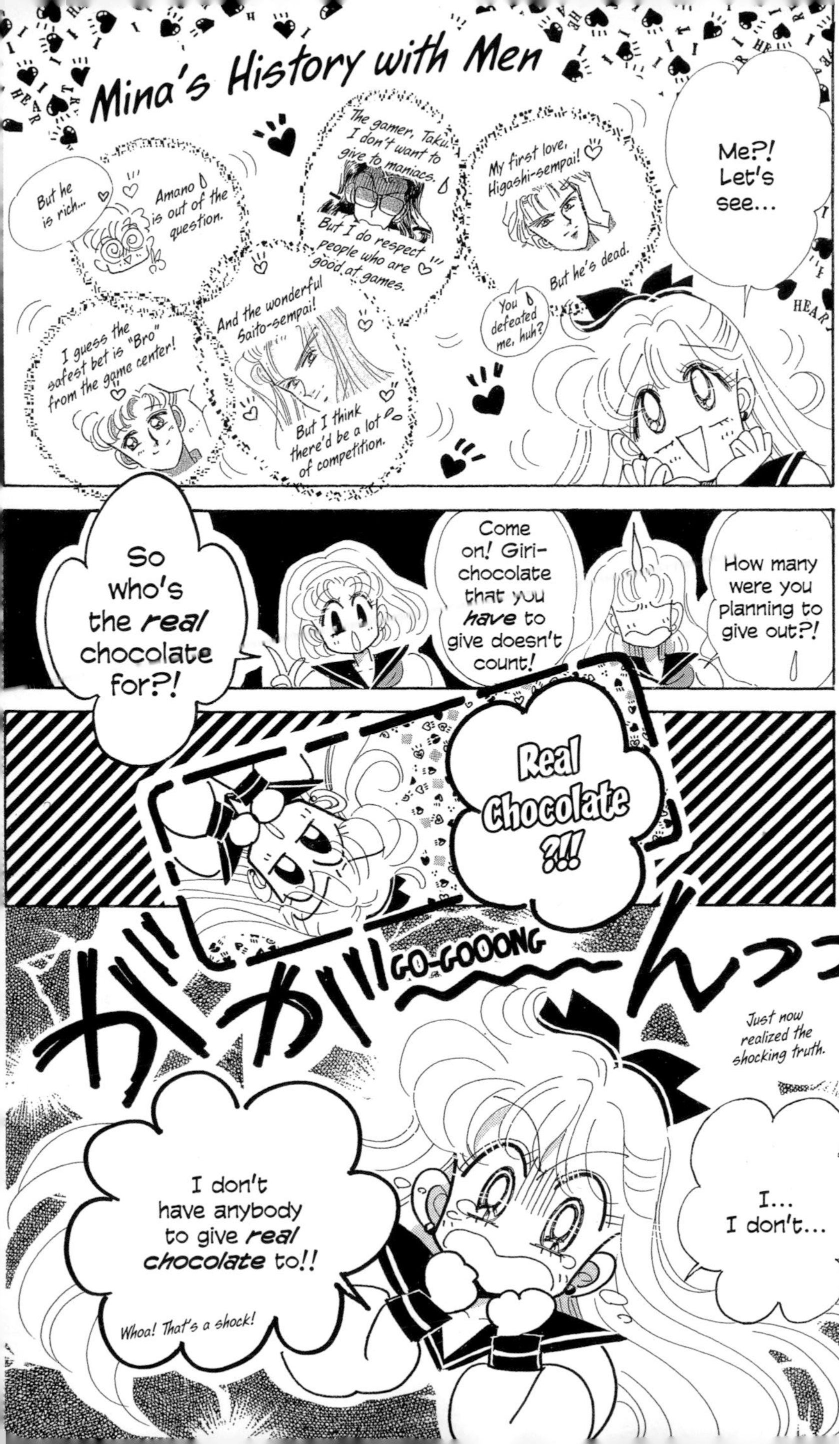

Mina's History with Men
Me?! Let's see...
My first love, Higashi-sempai!
But he's dead.
You defeated me, huh?
The gamer, Taku. I don't want to give to maniacs.
But I do respect people who are good at games.
Amano is out of the question.
But he is rich...
And the wonderful Saito-sempai!
But I think there'd be a lot of competition.
I guess the safest bet is "Bro" from the game center!
How many were you planning to give out?!
Come on! Giri-chocolate that you *have* to give doesn't count!
So who's the *real* chocolate for?!
Real Chocolate ?!!
GO-GOOONG
Just now realized the shocking truth.
I... I don't...
I don't have anybody to give *real chocolate* to!!
Whoa! That's a shock!

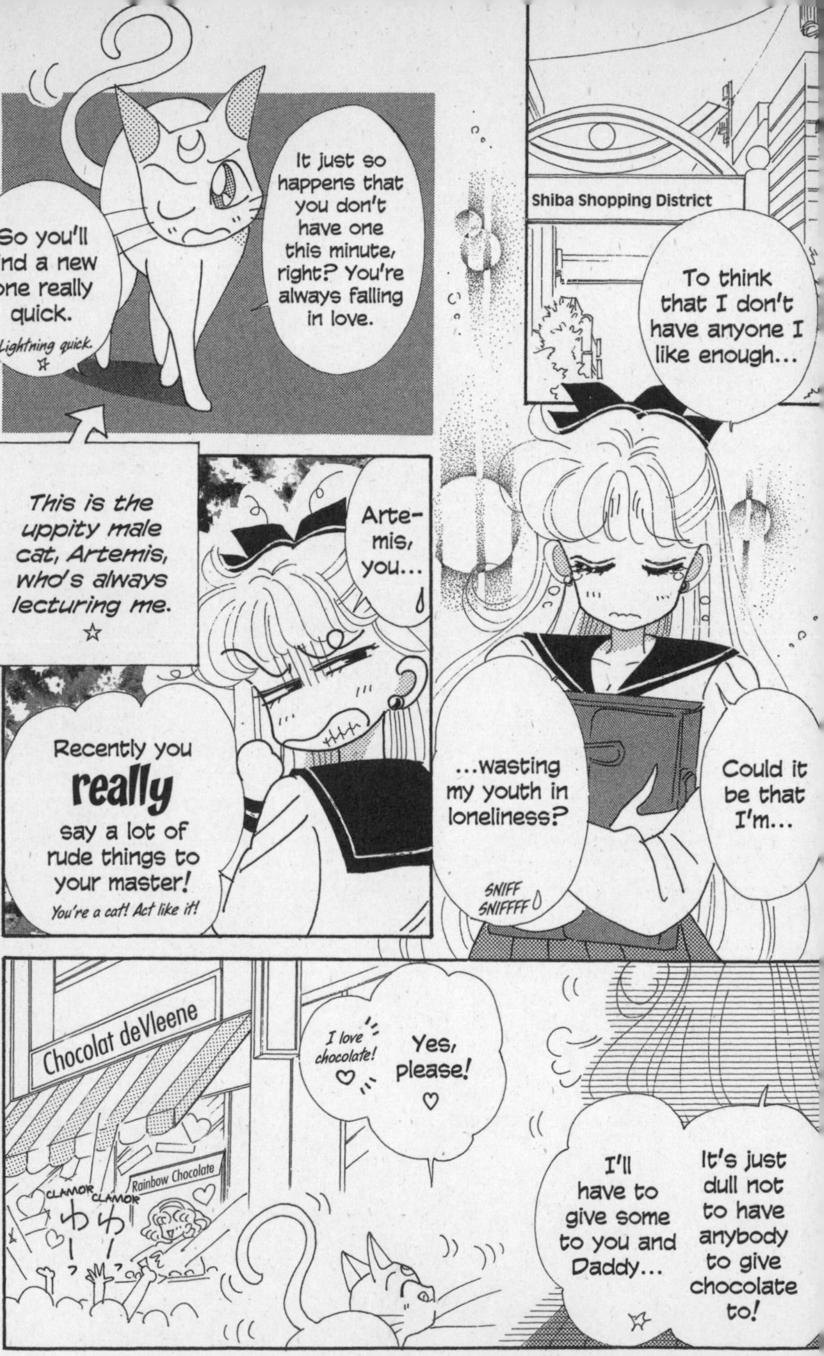

Shiba Shopping District
To think that I don't have anyone I like enough...
Could it be that I'm...
...wasting my youth in loneliness?
SNIFF SNIFFFF
It just so happens that you don't have one this minute, right? You're always falling in love.
So you'll find a new one really quick.
Lightning quick. ☆
This is the uppity male cat, Artemis, who's always lecturing me. ☆
Arte-mis, you...
Recently you **really** say a lot of rude things to your master!
You're a cat! Act like it!
It's just dull not to have anybody to give chocolate to!
I'll have to give some to you and Daddy...
Yes, please! ♡
I love chocolate! ♡
Chocolat deVleene
Rainbow Chocolate
CLAMOR CLAMOR

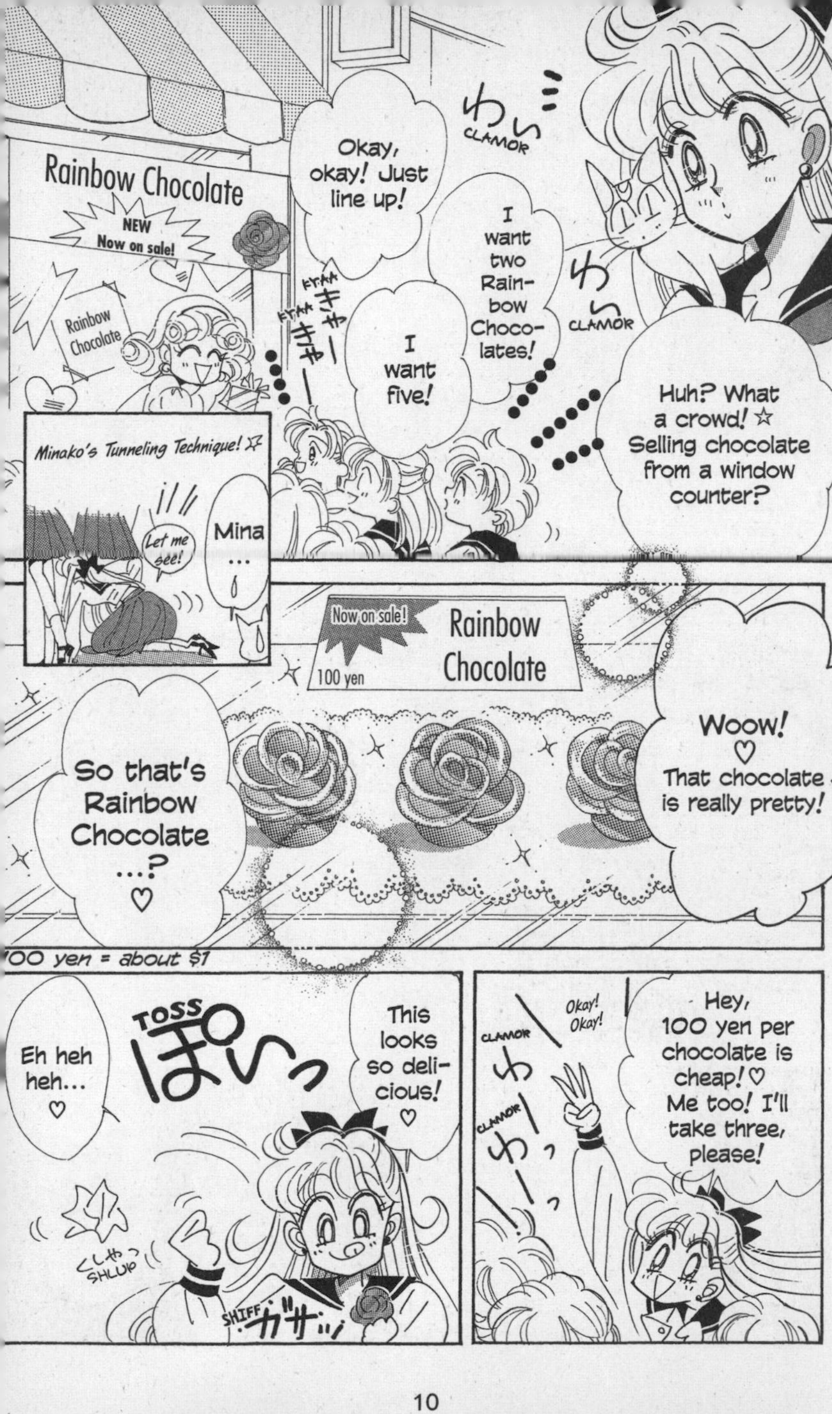
CLAMOR
CLAMOR
Huh? What a crowd! ☆ Selling chocolate from a window counter?
Okay, okay! Just line up!
I want two Rainbow Chocolates!
KYAA
KYAA
I want five!
Rainbow Chocolate
NEW Now on sale!
Rainbow Chocolate
Minako's Tunneling Technique! ☆
Mina ...
Let me see!
Woow! ♡ That chocolate is really pretty!
Now on sale!
Rainbow Chocolate
100 yen
So that's Rainbow Chocolate ...? ♡
00 yen = about $1
Hey, 100 yen per chocolate is cheap! ♡ Me too! I'll take three, please!
Okay! Okay!
CLAMOR
CLAMOR
This looks so deli-cious! ♡
TOSS
Eh heh heh... ♡
SHLUP
SHIFF

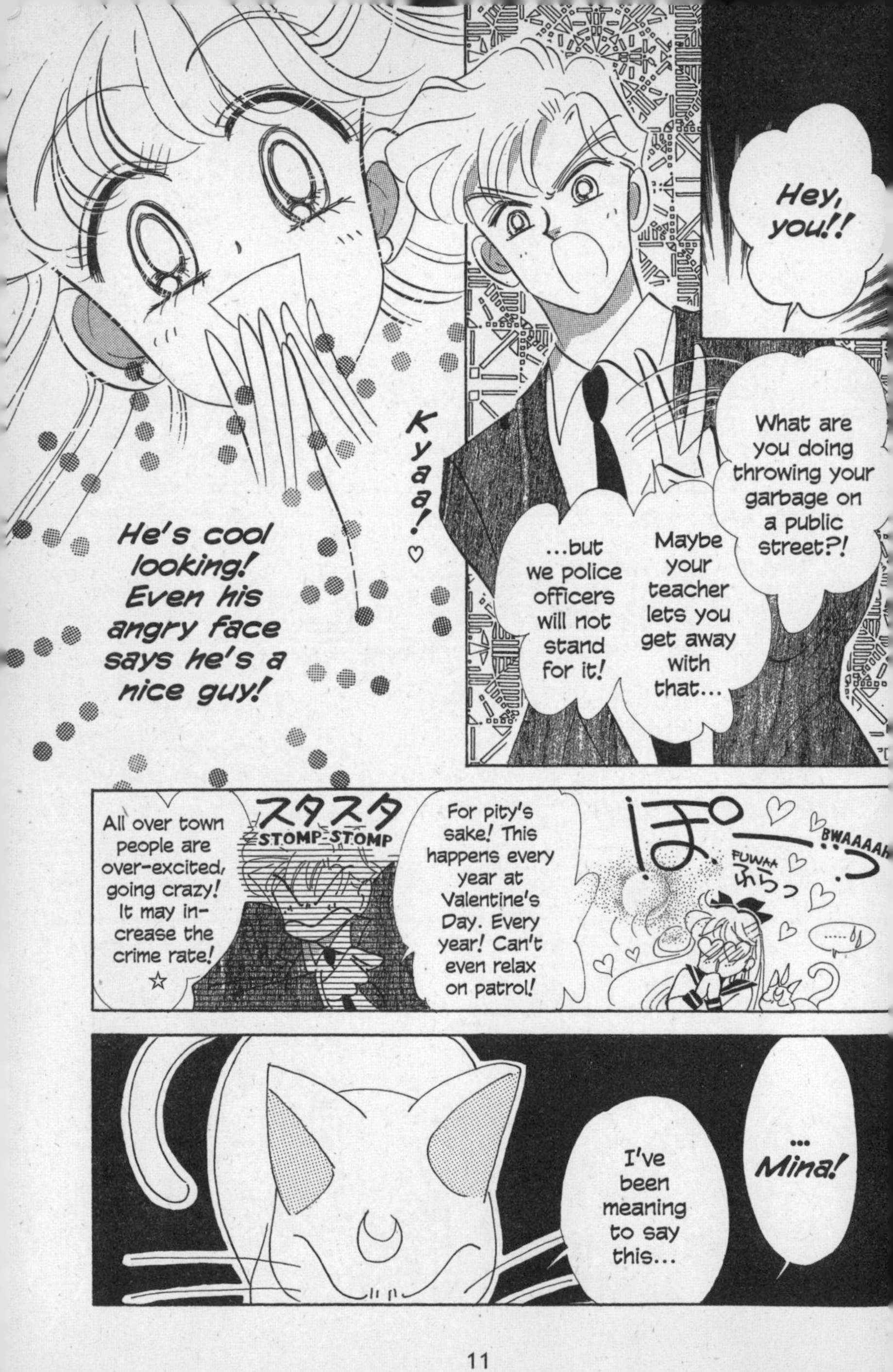
Hey, you!!
What are you doing throwing your garbage on a public street?!
Maybe your teacher lets you get away with that...
...but we police officers will not stand for it!
Kyaa! ♡
He's cool looking! Even his angry face says he's a nice guy!
ぽー
BWAAAAH
FUWAA ふらっ
.....
For pity's sake! This happens every year at Valentine's Day. Every year! Can't even relax on patrol!
スタスタ
STOMP-STOMP
All over town people are over-excited, going crazy! It may increase the crime rate! ☆
...Mina!
I've been meaning to say this...

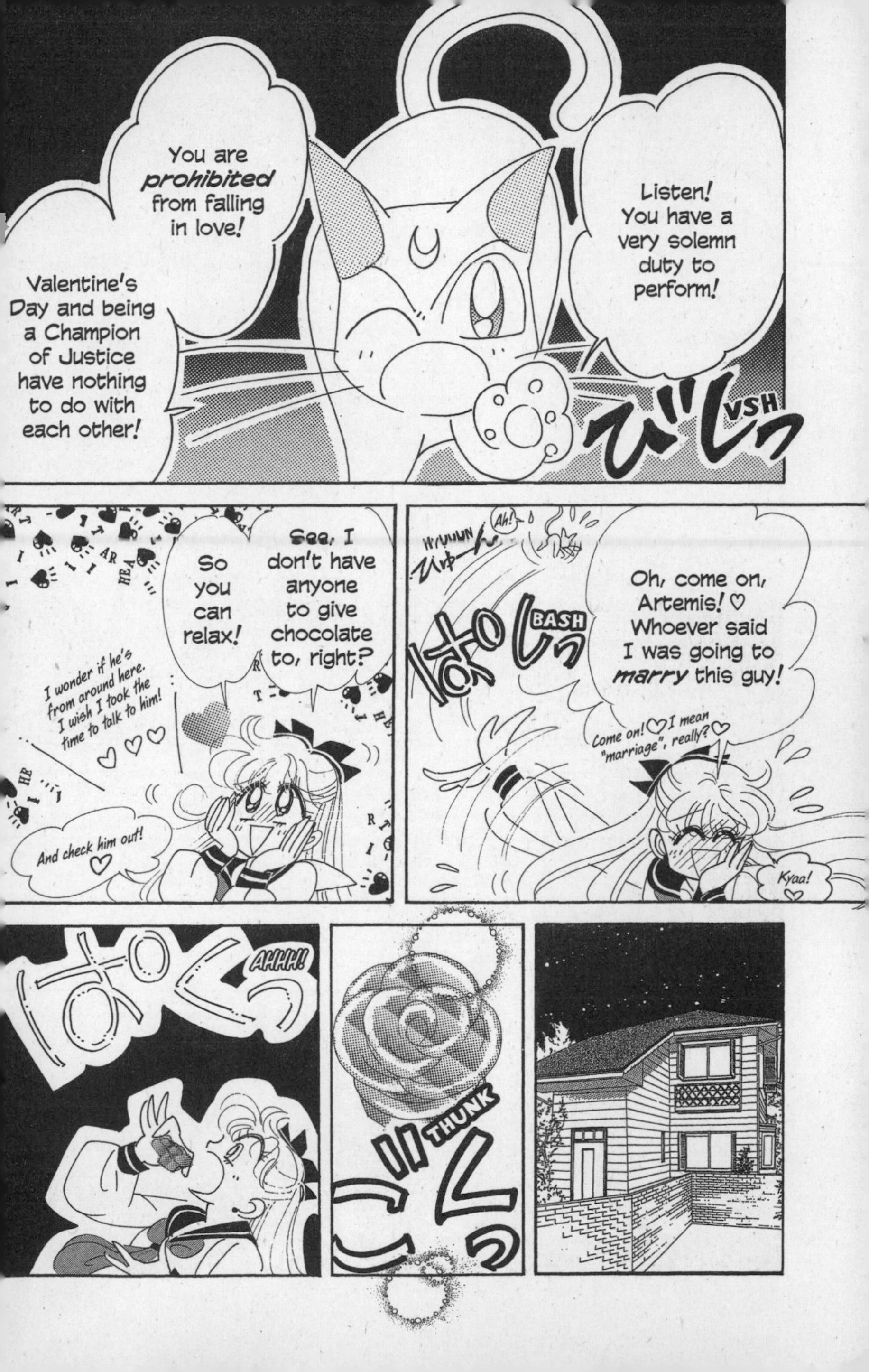
Listen! You have a very solemn duty to perform!
You are *prohibited* from falling in love!
Valentine's Day and being a Champion of Justice have nothing to do with each other!
VSH
Ah!
Oh, come on, Artemis! ♡ Whoever said I was going to *marry* this guy!
BASH
Come on! ♡ I mean "marriage", really? ♡
Kyaa! ♡
See, I don't have anyone to give chocolate to, right?
So you can relax!
I wonder if he's from around here. I wish I took the time to talk to him!
And check him out! ♡
THUNK
AHHH!

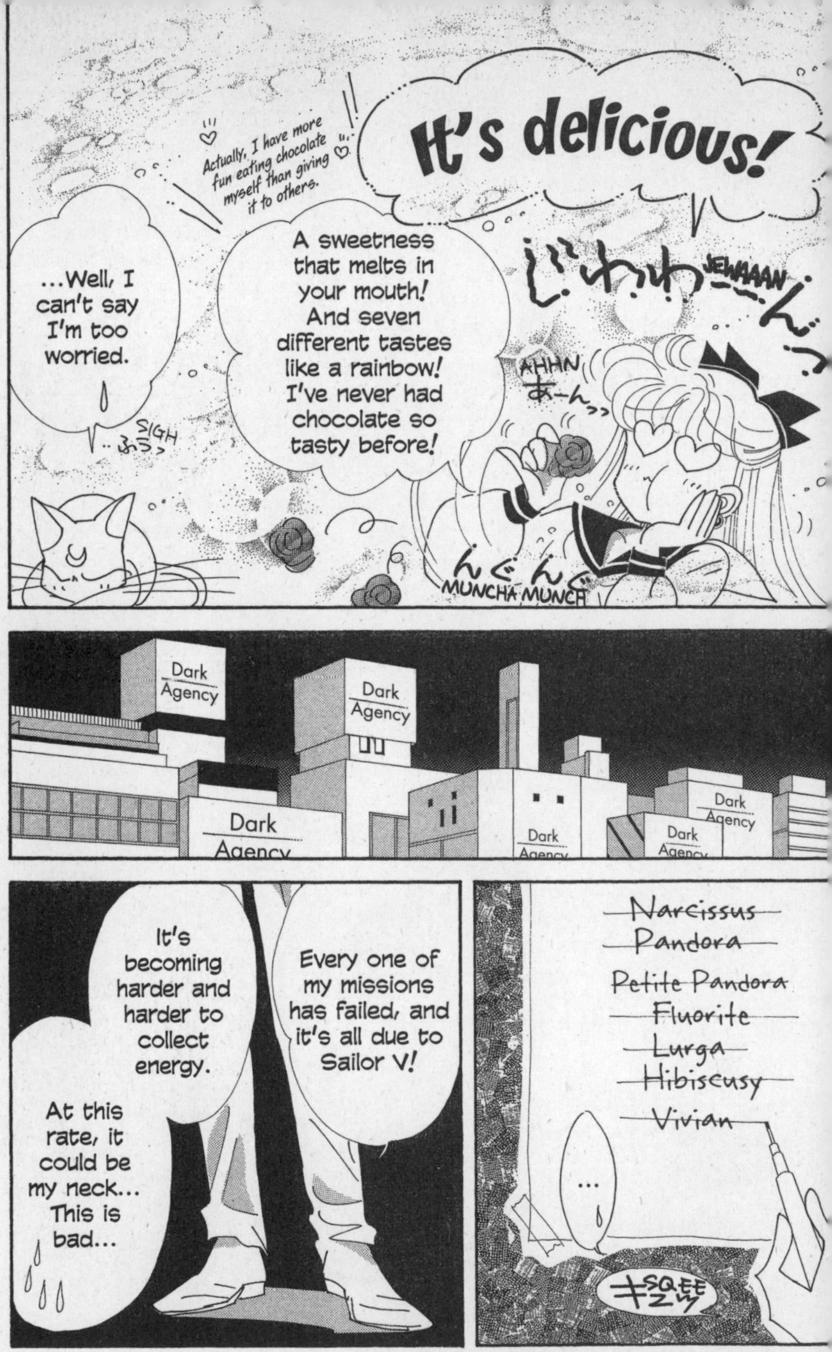
It's delicious!
Actually, I have more fun eating chocolate myself than giving it to others.
じわわ～ん JEWAAAN
A sweetness that melts in your mouth! And seven different tastes like a rainbow! I've never had chocolate so tasty before!
AHHN あ～ん
...Well, I can't say I'm too worried.
SIGH ふぅ
んぐんぐ MUNCHA MUNCH
Dark Agency
Dark Agency
Dark Agency
Dark Agency
Dark
Dark
Narcissus
Pandora
Petite Pandora
Fluorite
Lurga
Hibiscusy
Vivian
...
キュッ SQEE
Every one of my missions has failed, and it's all due to Sailor V!
It's becoming harder and harder to collect energy.
At this rate, it could be my neck... This is bad...

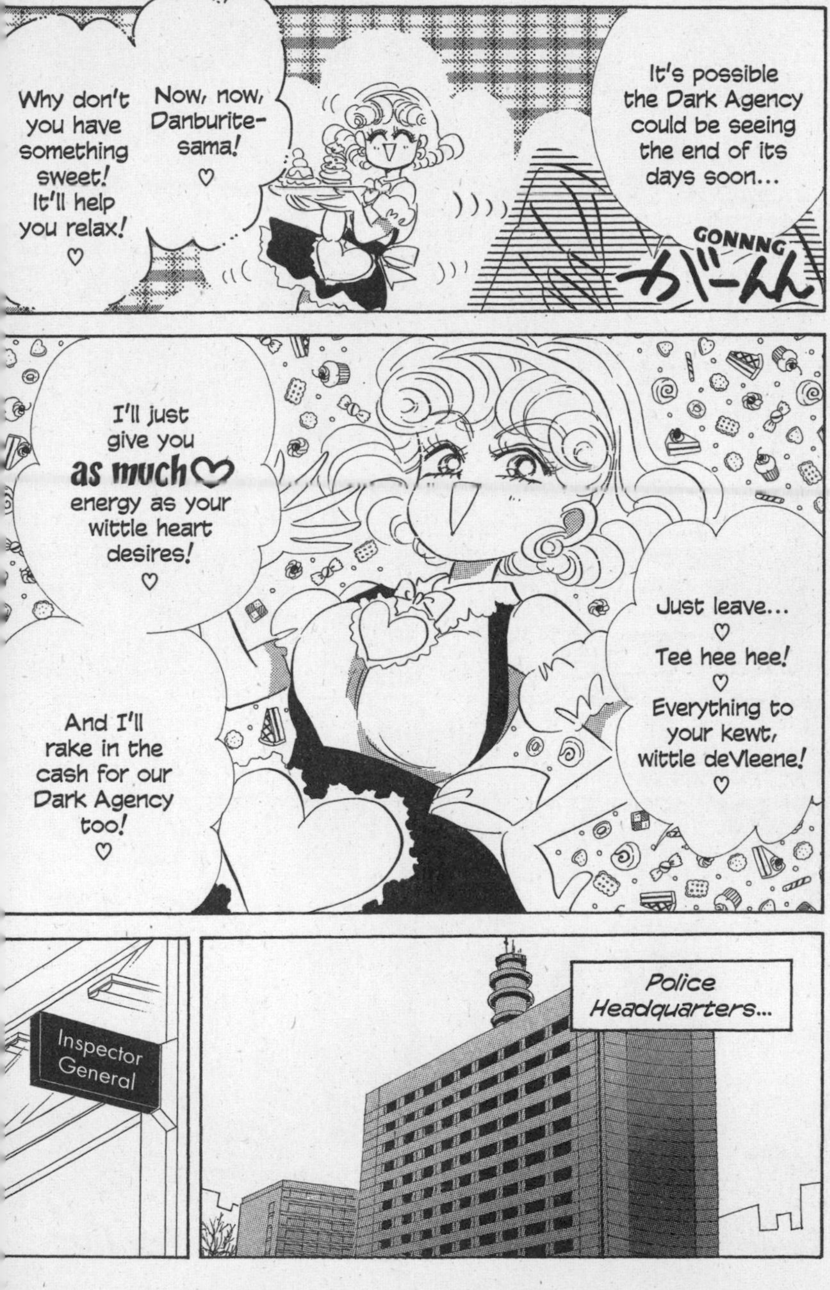
It's possible the Dark Agency could be seeing the end of its days soon...
GONNNG
がーん
Now, now, Danburite-sama! ♡
Why don't you have something sweet! It'll help you relax! ♡
I'll just give you as much ♡ energy as your wittle heart desires! ♡
Just leave... ♡ Tee hee hee! ♡ Everything to your kewt, wittle deVleene! ♡
And I'll rake in the cash for our Dark Agency too! ♡
Police Headquarters...
Inspector General

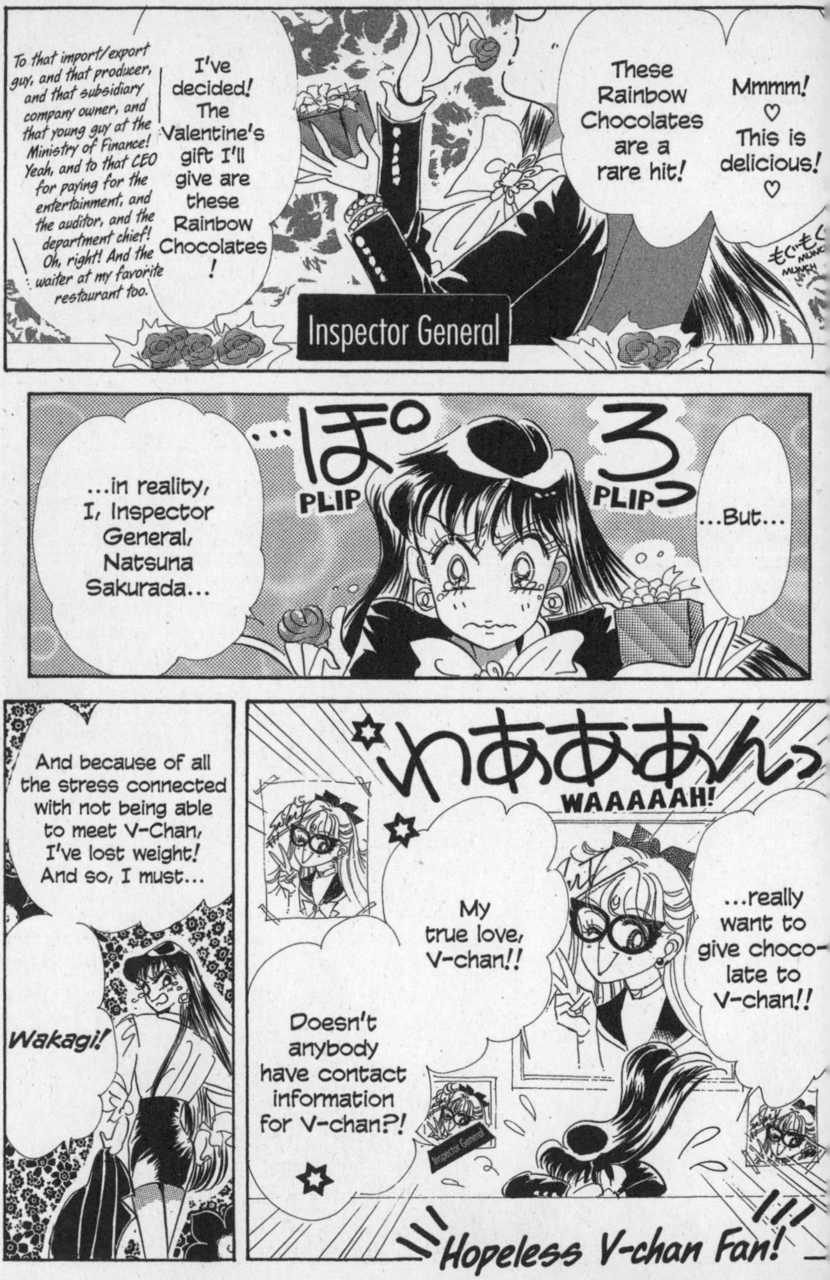
Mmmm! ♡ This is delicious! ♡
もぐもぐ MUNCH MUNCH
These Rainbow Chocolates are a rare hit!
Inspector General
I've decided! The Valentine's gift I'll give are these Rainbow Chocolates!
To that import/export guy, and that producer, and that subsidiary company owner, and that young guy at the Ministry of Finance! Yeah, and to that CEO for paying for the entertainment, and the auditor, and the department chief! Oh, right! And the waiter at my favorite restaurant too.
...But...
ろっ PLIP
…ぽ PLIP
...in reality, I, Inspector General, Natsuna Sakurada...
わあああんっ WAAAAAH!
...really want to give choco-late to V-chan!!
My true love, V-chan!!
Doesn't anybody have contact information for V-chan?!
Inspector General
Hopeless V-chan Fan!
And because of all the stress connected with not being able to meet V-Chan, I've lost weight! And so, I must...
Wakagi!

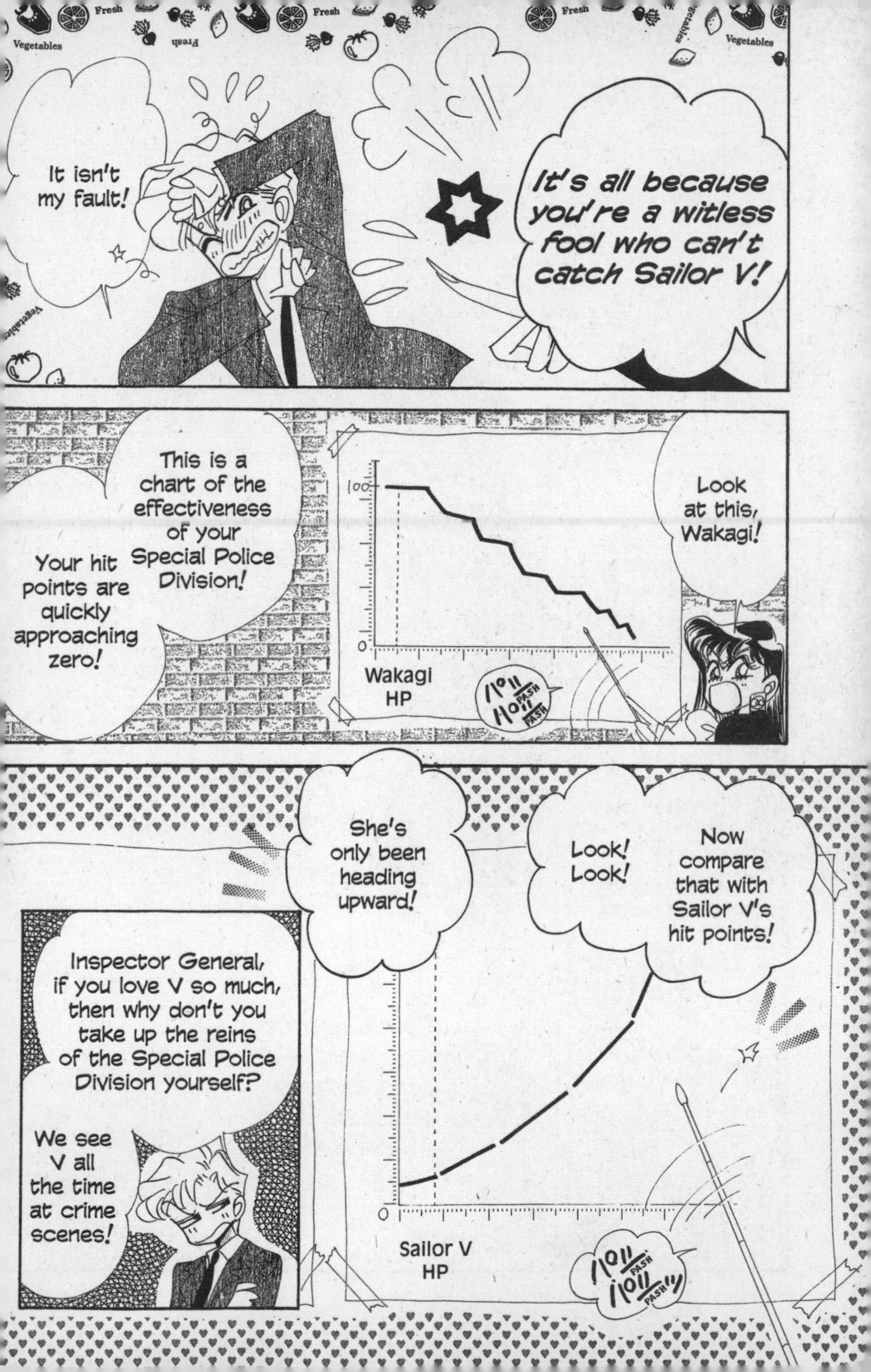

It's all because you're a witless fool who can't catch Sailor V!
It isn't my fault!
Look at this, Wakagi!
This is a chart of the effectiveness of your Special Police Division!
Your hit points are quickly approaching zero!
100
0
Wakagi HP
PASH PASH
Now compare that with Sailor V's hit points!
Look! Look!
She's only been heading upward!
0
Sailor V HP
PASH PASH
Inspector General, if you love V so much, then why don't you take up the reins of the Special Police Division yourself?
We see V all the time at crime scenes!

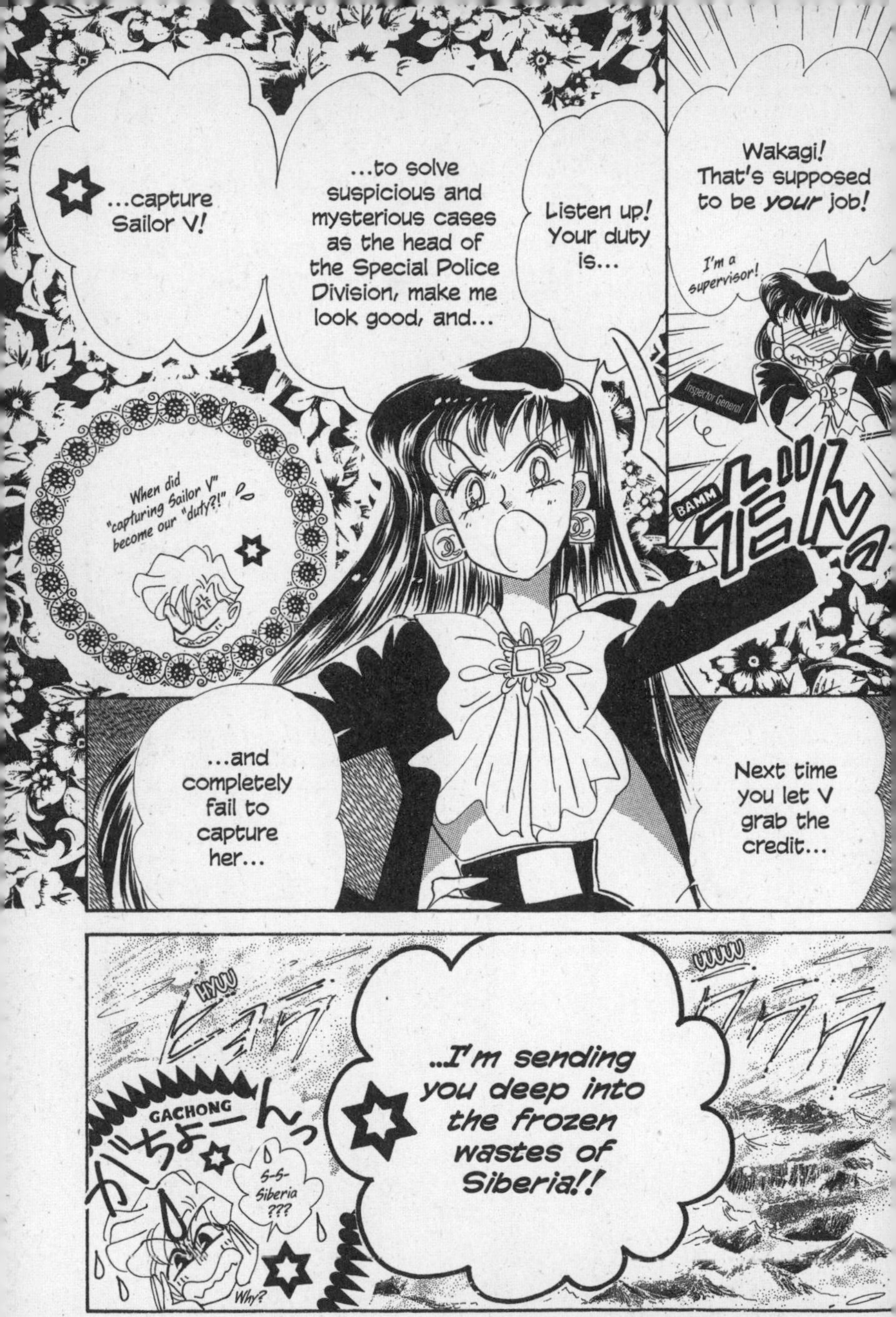
Wakagi! That's supposed to be *your* job!
I'm a supervisor!
Inspector General
BAMM
Listen up! Your duty is...
...to solve suspicious and mysterious cases as the head of the Special Police Division, make me look good, and...
...capture Sailor V!
When did "capturing Sailor V" become our "duty?!"
...and completely fail to capture her...
Next time you let V grab the credit...
UUUU
HYUU
...I'm sending you deep into the frozen wastes of Siberia!!
GACHONG
S-S-Siberia ???
Why?

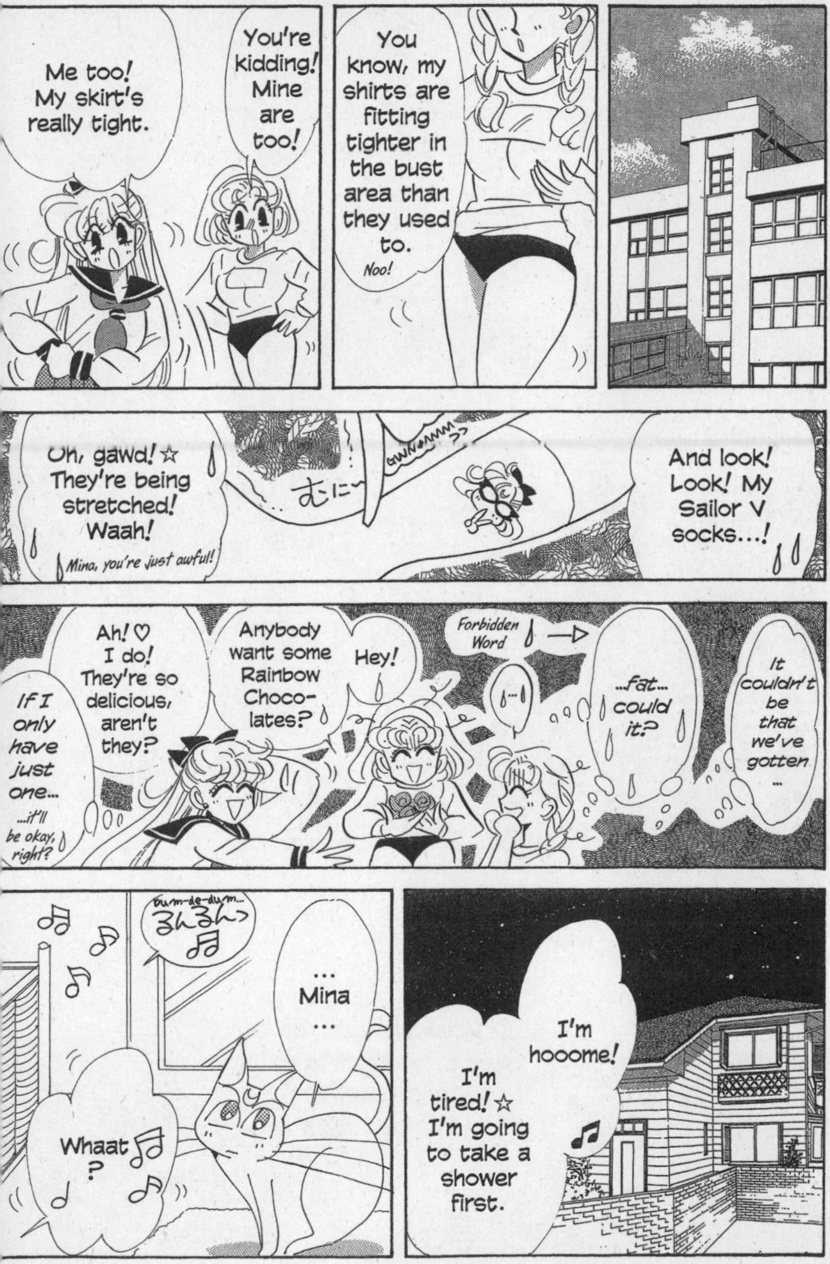
You know, my shirts are fitting tighter in the bust area than they used to.
Noo!
You're kidding! Mine are too!
Me too! My skirt's really tight.
And look! Look! My Sailor V socks...!
むに～
Oh, gawd!☆ They're being stretched! Waah!
Mina, you're just awful!
It couldn't be that we've gotten ...
...fat... could it?
Forbidden Word
Hey!
Anybody want some Rainbow Chocolates?
Ah!♡ I do! They're so delicious, aren't they?
If I only have just one...
...it'll be okay, right?
I'm hooome!
I'm tired!☆ I'm going to take a shower first.
dum-de-dum...
ふんふん
... Mina ...
Whaat?

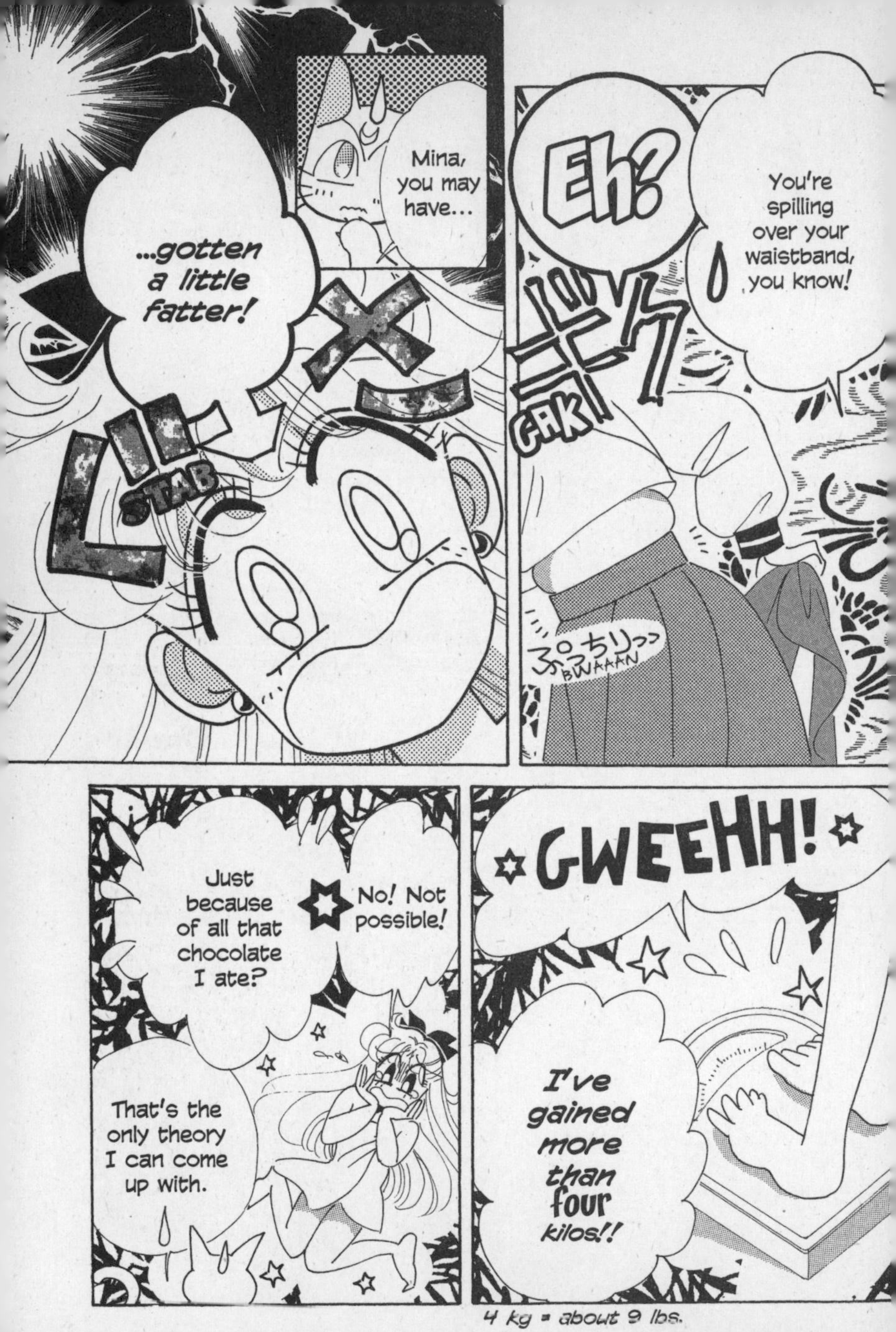
Eh?
You're spilling over your waistband, you know!
CRK
BWAAAN
Mina, you may have...
...gotten a little fatter!
STAB
GWEEHH!
I've gained more than four kilos!!
No! Not possible!
Just because of all that chocolate I ate?
That's the only theory I can come up with.

4 kg = about 9 lbs.

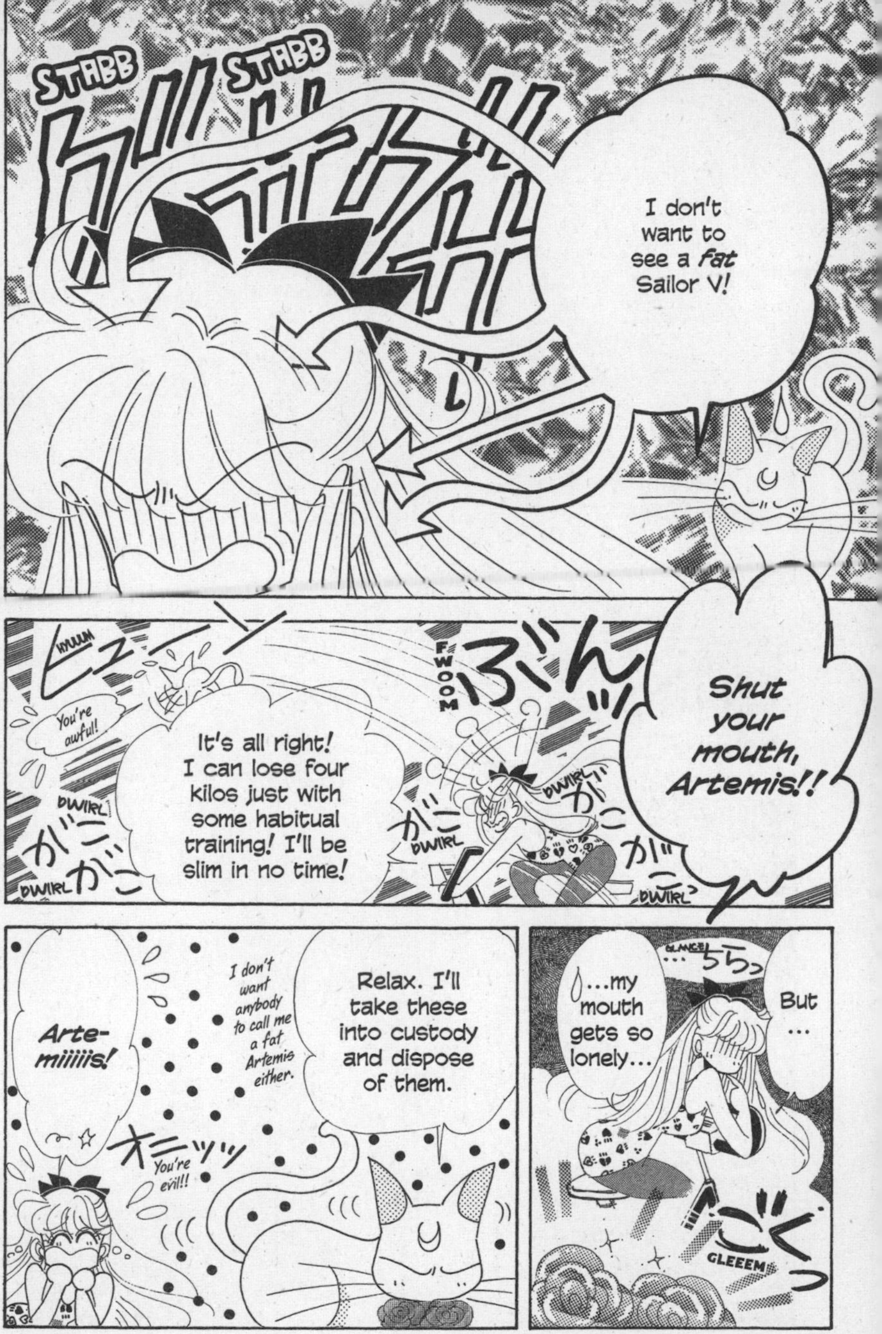
I don't want to see a *fat* Sailor V!
STABB STABB
Shut your mouth, Artemis!!
FWOOM
It's all right! I can lose four kilos just with some habitual training! I'll be slim in no time!
HYUUUN
You're awful!
DWIRL
DWIRL
DWIRL
DWIRL
But ...
GLANCE
...my mouth gets so lonely...
GLEEEM
Relax. I'll take these into custody and dispose of them.
I don't want anybody to call me a fat Artemis either.
Arte-miiiiis!
You're evil!!

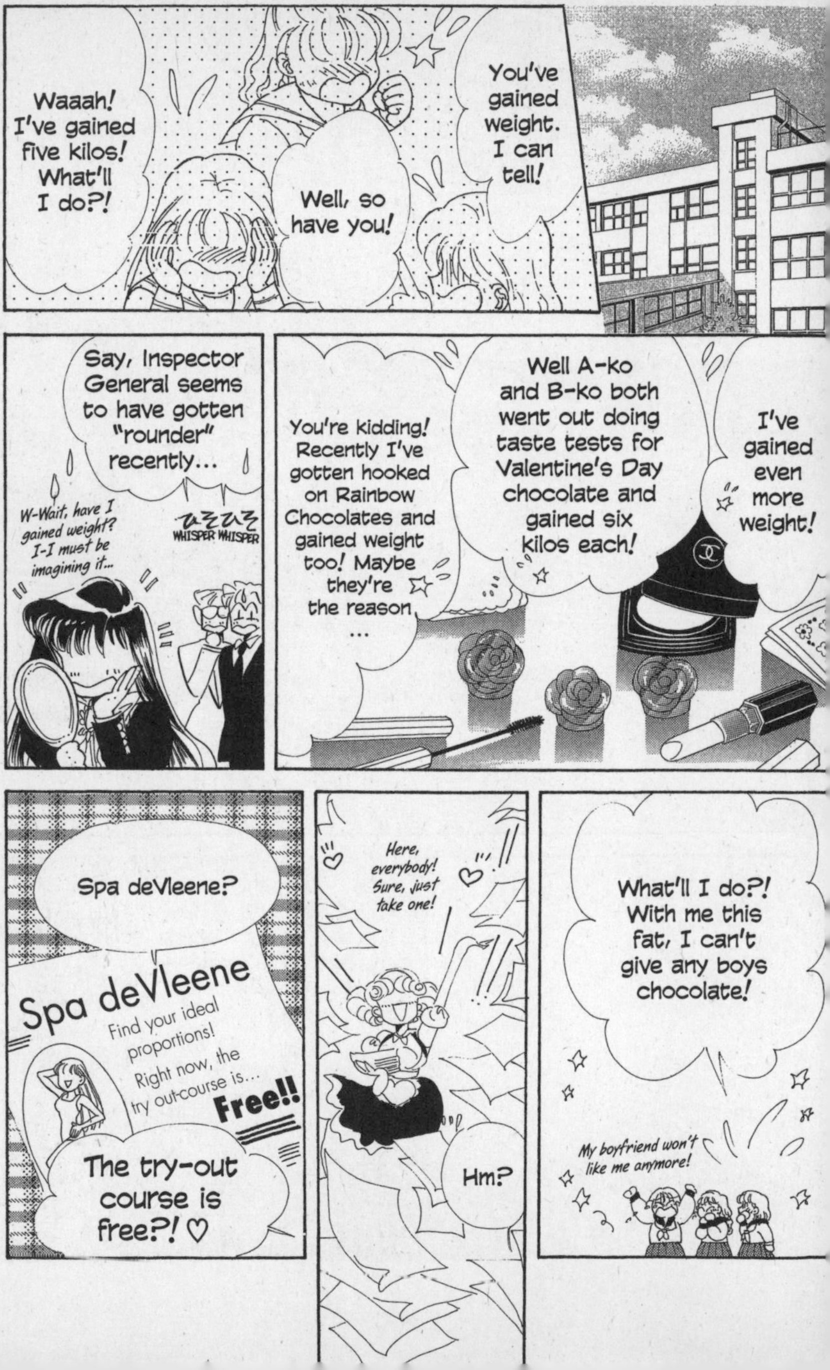
You've gained weight. I can tell!
Well, so have you!
Waaah! I've gained five kilos! What'll I do?!
I've gained even more weight!
Well A-ko and B-ko both went out doing taste tests for Valentine's Day chocolate and gained six kilos each!
You're kidding! Recently I've gotten hooked on Rainbow Chocolates and gained weight too! Maybe they're the reason...
Say, Inspector General seems to have gotten "rounder" recently...
ひそひそ
WHISPER WHISPER
W-Wait, have I gained weight? I-I must be imagining it...
What'll I do?! With me this fat, I can't give any boys chocolate!
My boyfriend won't like me anymore!
Here, everybody! Sure, just take one!
Hm?
Spa deVleene?
Spa deVleene
Find your ideal proportions!
Right now, the try out-course is...
Free!!
The try-out course is free?! ♡

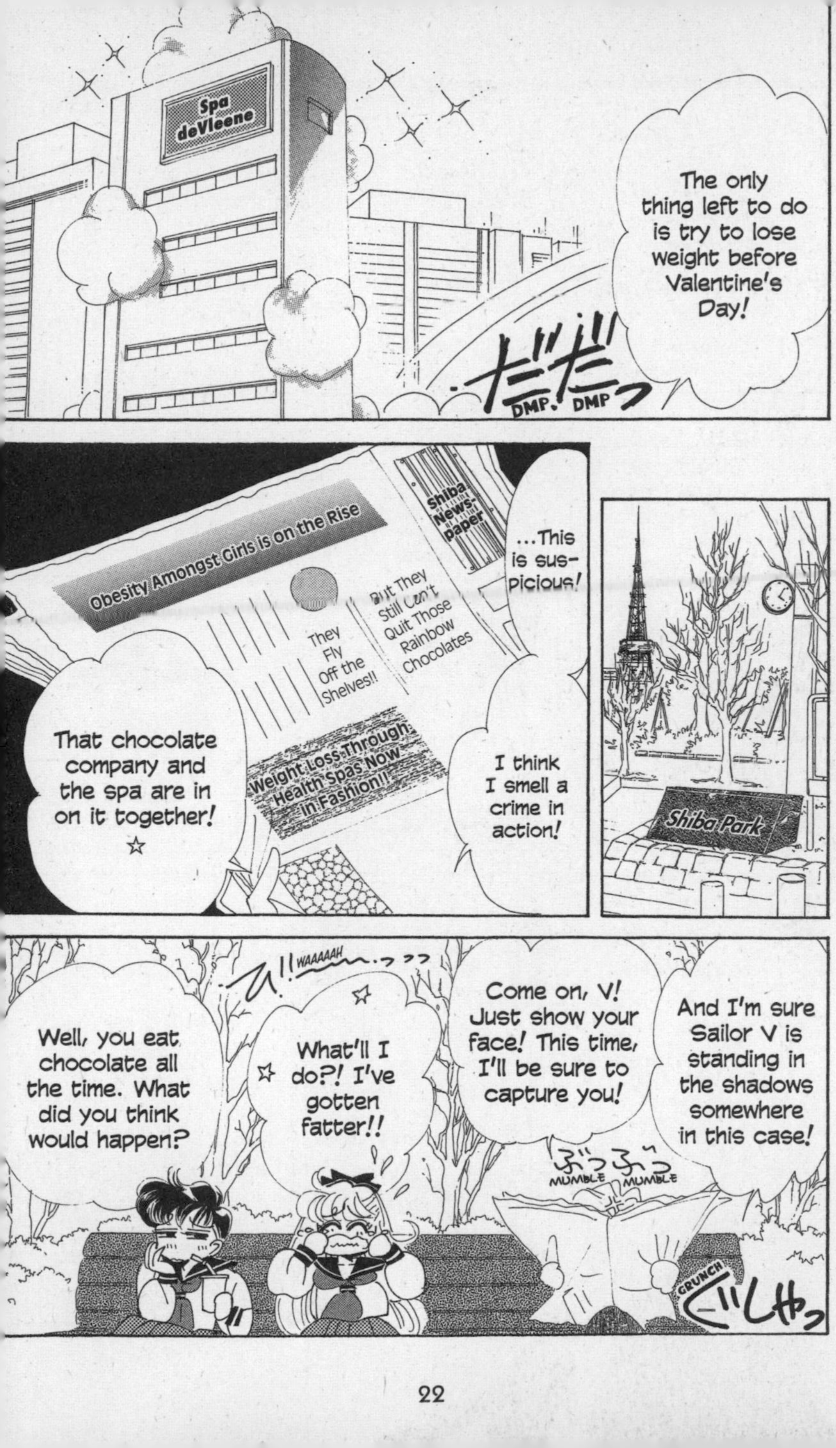
Spa deVleene
The only thing left to do is try to lose weight before Valentine's Day!
DMP. DMP
Shiba Park
...This is suspicious!
Shiba Newspaper
Obesity Amongst Girls is on the Rise
But They Still Can't Quit Those Rainbow Chocolates
They Fly Off the Shelves!!
I think I smell a crime in action!
Weight Loss Through Health Spas Now in Fashion!!
That chocolate company and the spa are in on it together! ☆
And I'm sure Sailor V is standing in the shadows somewhere in this case!
Come on, V! Just show your face! This time, I'll be sure to capture you!
MUMBLE MUMBLE
GRUNCH
WAAAAAH
What'll I do?! I've gotten fatter!!
Well, you eat chocolate all the time. What did you think would happen?

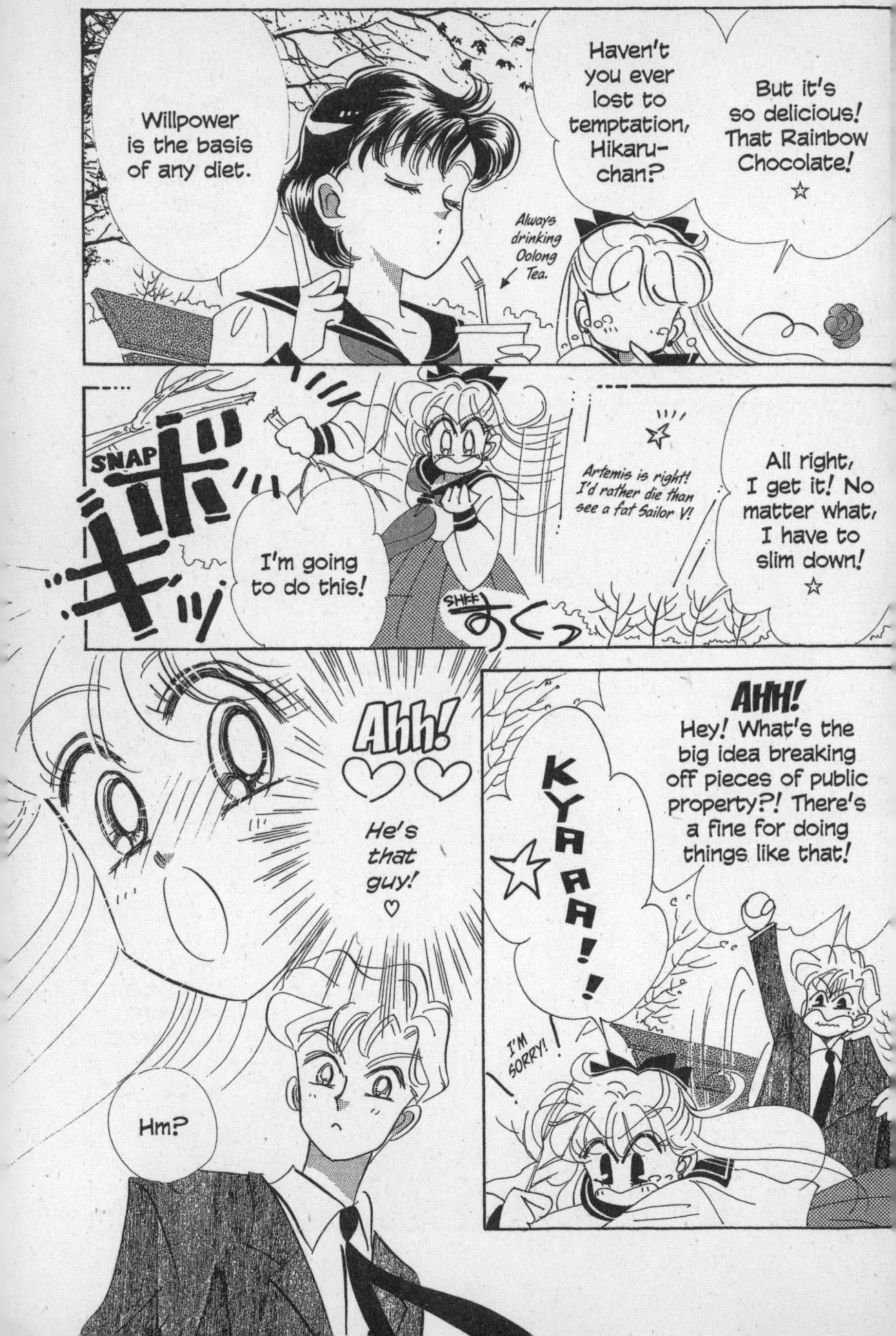
But it's so delicious! That Rainbow Chocolate! ☆
Haven't you ever lost to temptation, Hikaru-chan?
Always drinking Oolong Tea.
Willpower is the basis of any diet.
All right, I get it! No matter what, I have to slim down! ☆
Artemis is right! I'd rather die than see a fat Sailor V!
SHFF すくっ
I'm going to do this!
SNAP ボギッ
AHH! Hey! What's the big idea breaking off pieces of public property?! There's a fine for doing things like that!
KYAAA!!
I'M SORRY!
Ahh! ♡ ♡
He's that guy! ♡
Hm?

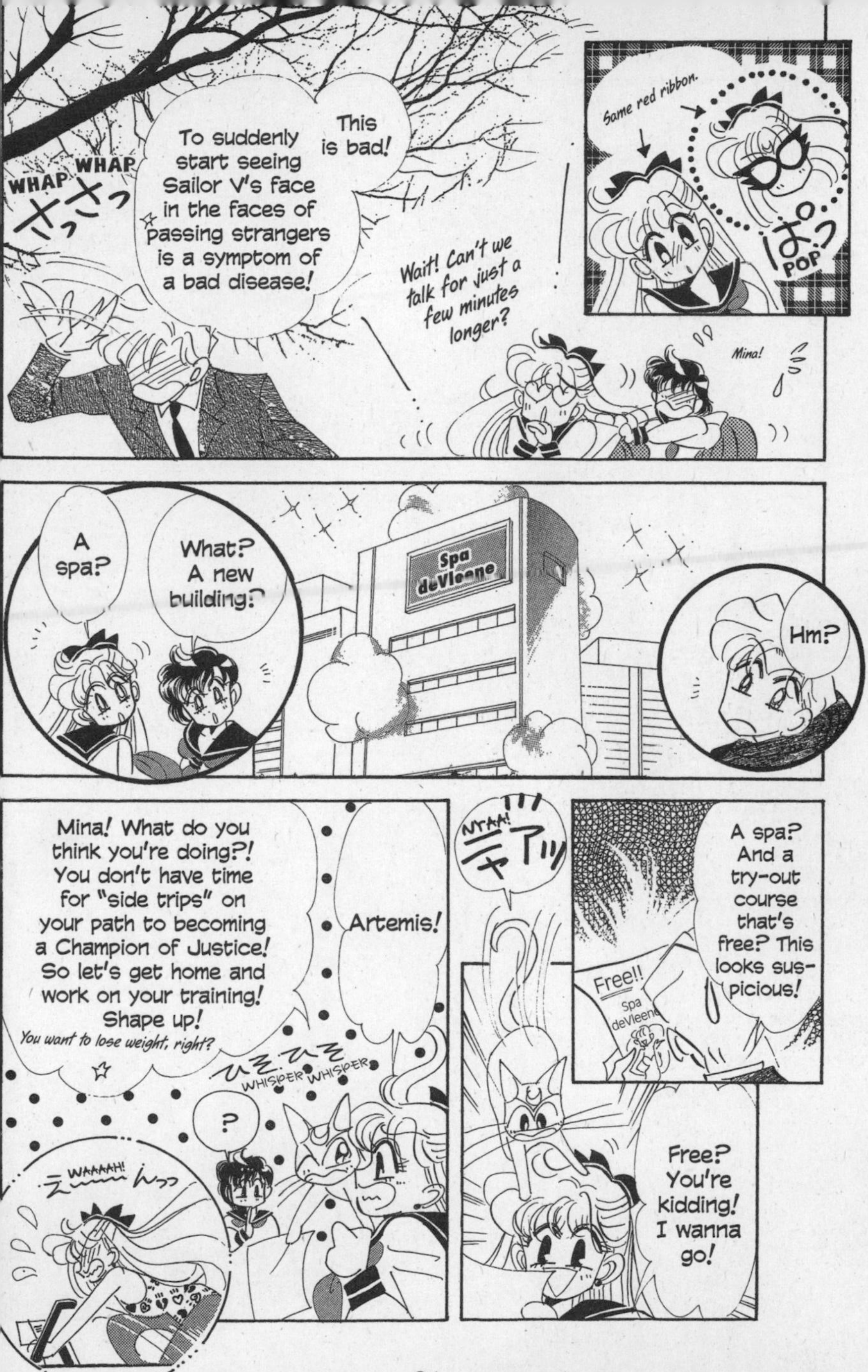

Same red ribbon.
ぱっ POP
This is bad!
To suddenly start seeing Sailor V's face in the faces of passing strangers is a symptom of a bad disease!
WHAP WHAP
さっさっ
Wait! Can't we talk for just a few minutes longer?
Mina!
Hm?
Spa deVleene
What? A new building?
A spa?
A spa? And a try-out course that's free? This looks suspicious!
Free!!
Spa deVleene
Free? You're kidding! I wanna go!
NYAAA!
ニャアッ
Artemis!
Mina! What do you think you're doing?! You don't have time for "side trips" on your path to becoming a Champion of Justice! So let's get home and work on your training! Shape up!
You want to lose weight, right?
ひそひそ WHISPER WHISPER
?
えーんっ WAAAAH!

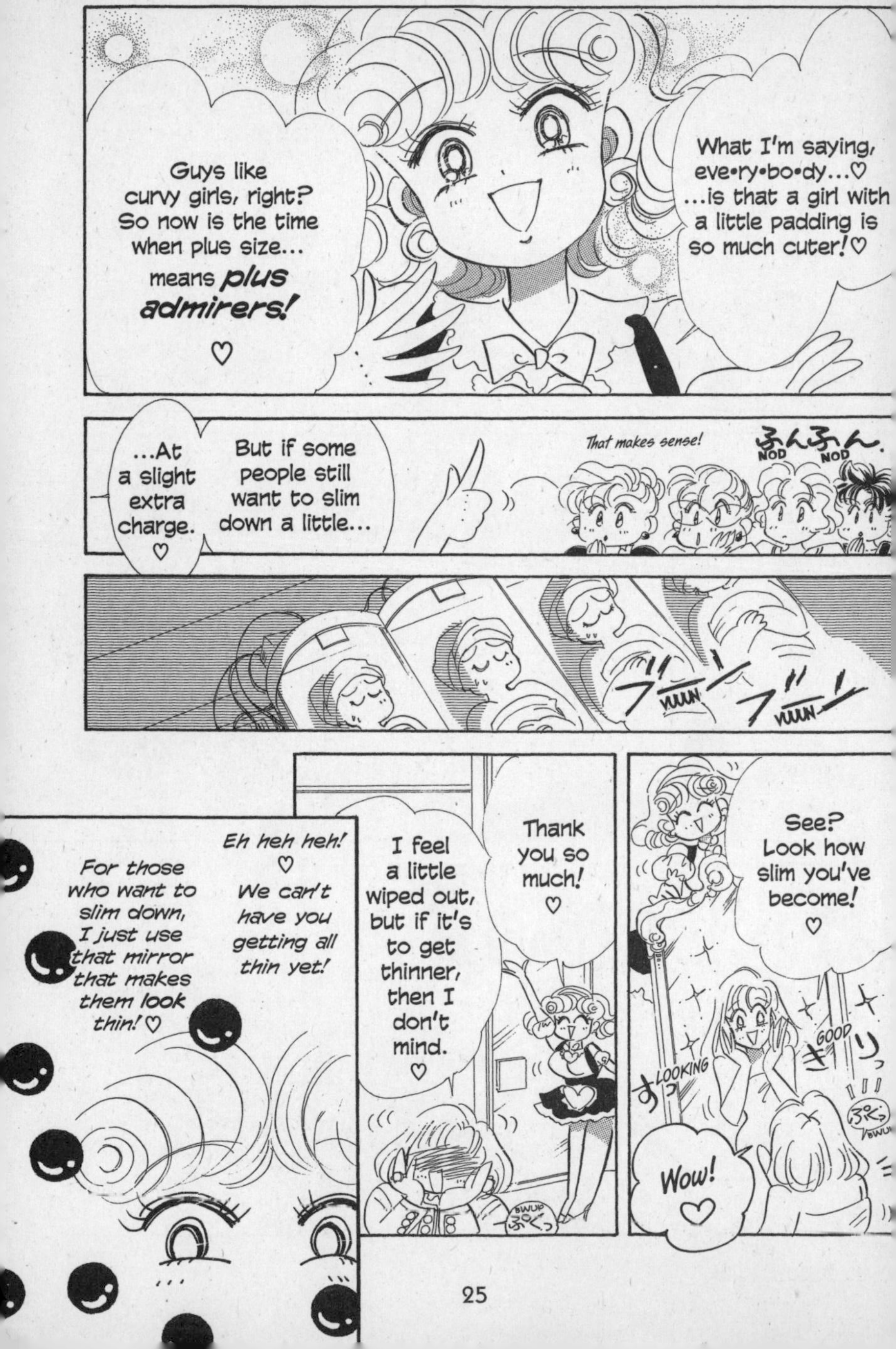
What I'm saying, eve•ry•bo•dy...♡ ...is that a girl with a little padding is so much cuter!♡
Guys like curvy girls, right? So now is the time when plus size... means **plus admirers!** ♡
That makes sense!
ふんふん NOD NOD
But if some people still want to slim down a little...
...At a slight extra charge. ♡
VUUN VUUN
See? Look how slim you've become! ♡
LOOKING
GOOD
BWUP
Wow! ♡
Thank you so much! ♡
I feel a little wiped out, but if it's to get thinner, then I don't mind. ♡
BWUP
Eh heh heh! ♡ We can't have you getting all thin yet!
For those who want to slim down, I just use that mirror that makes them look thin! ♡

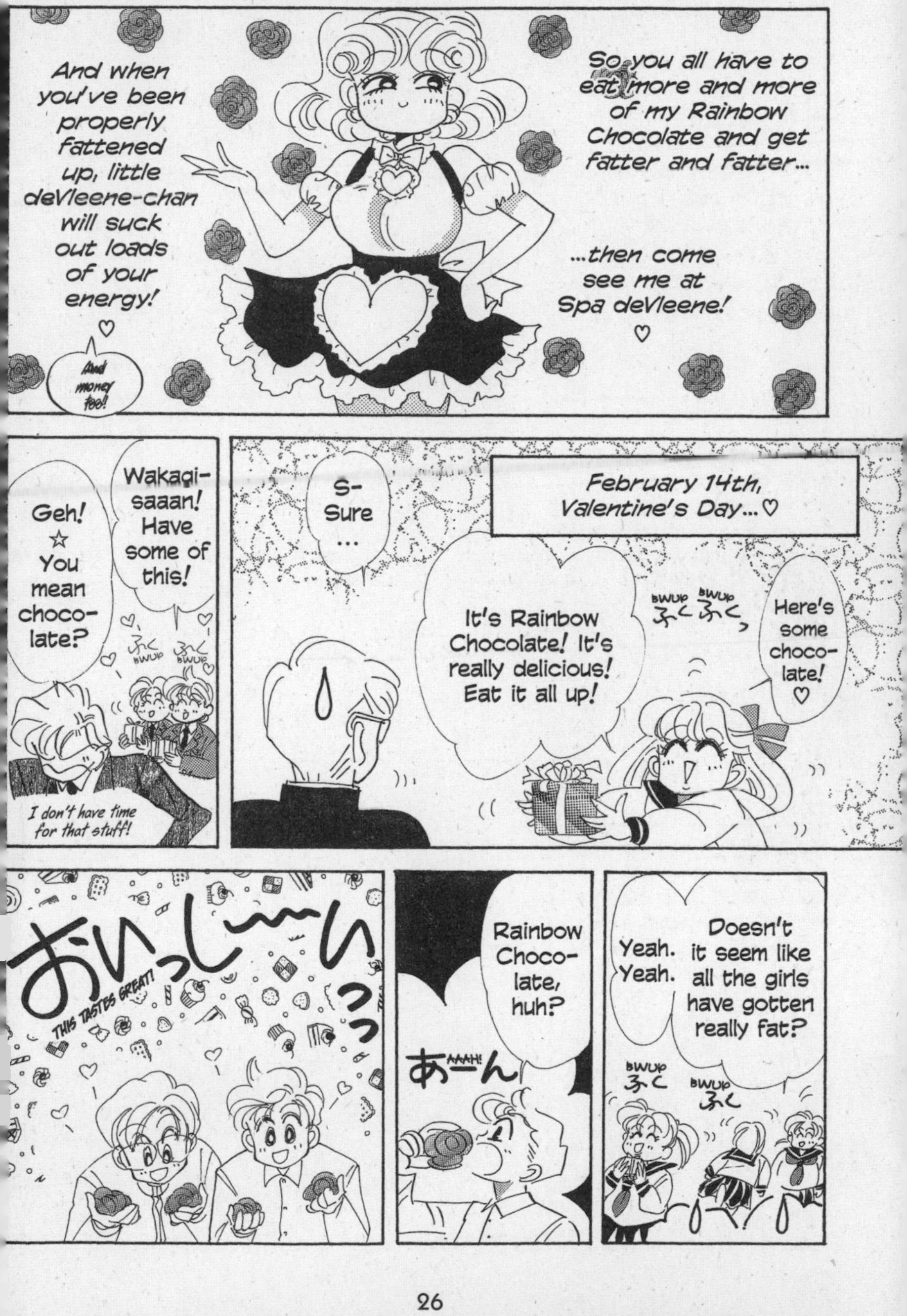

So you all have to eat more and more of my Rainbow Chocolate and get fatter and fatter...
...then come see me at Spa deVleene! ♡
And when you've been properly fattened up, little deVleene-chan will suck out loads of your energy! ♡
And money too!
February 14th, Valentine's Day...♡
Here's some chocolate! ♡
ふくふく BWUP BWUP
It's Rainbow Chocolate! It's really delicious! Eat it all up!
S-Sure...
Wakagi-saaan! Have some of this!
Geh! ☆ You mean chocolate?
ふく ふく BWUP BWUP
I don't have time for that stuff!
Doesn't it seem like all the girls have gotten really fat?
Yeah. Yeah.
ふく BWUP ふく BWUP
Rainbow Chocolate, huh?
あーん AAAH!
おいっし〜〜いっっ
THIS TASTES GREAT!

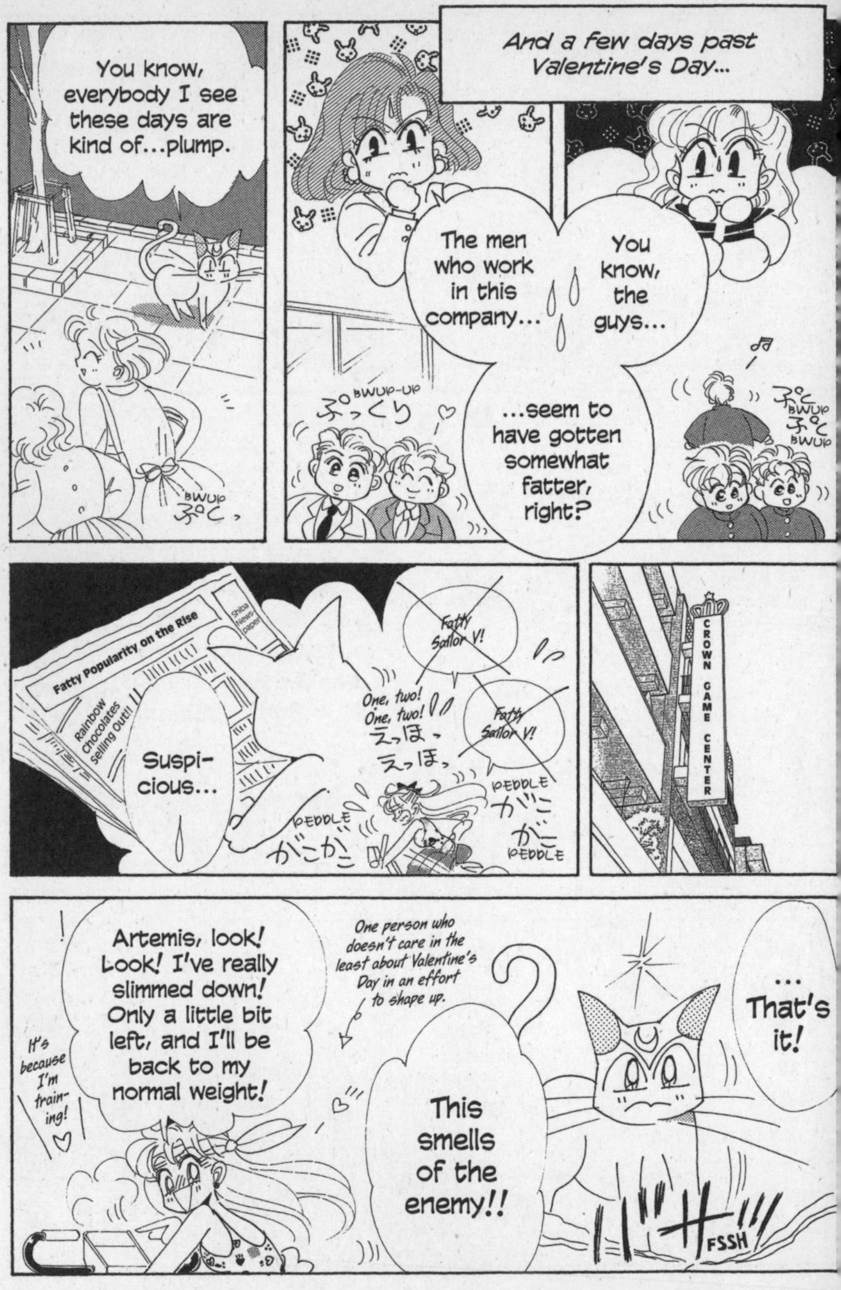
And a few days past Valentine's Day...
You know, the guys...
The men who work in this company...
...seem to have gotten somewhat fatter, right?
ぷく BWUP ぷく BWUP
ぷっくり BWUP-UP
You know, everybody I see these days are kind of...plump.
ぷく BWUP
CROWN GAME CENTER
Shiba Newspaper
Fatty Popularity on the Rise
Rainbow Chocolates Selling Out!!
Fatty Sailor V!
Fatty Sailor V!
One, two! One, two!
えっほ、えっほ、
がこがこ PEDDLE
がこがこ PEDDLE
Suspicious...
...That's it!
This smells of the enemy!!
FSSH
One person who doesn't care in the least about Valentine's Day in an effort to shape up.
Artemis, look! Look! I've really slimmed down! Only a little bit left, and I'll be back to my normal weight!
It's because I'm training!

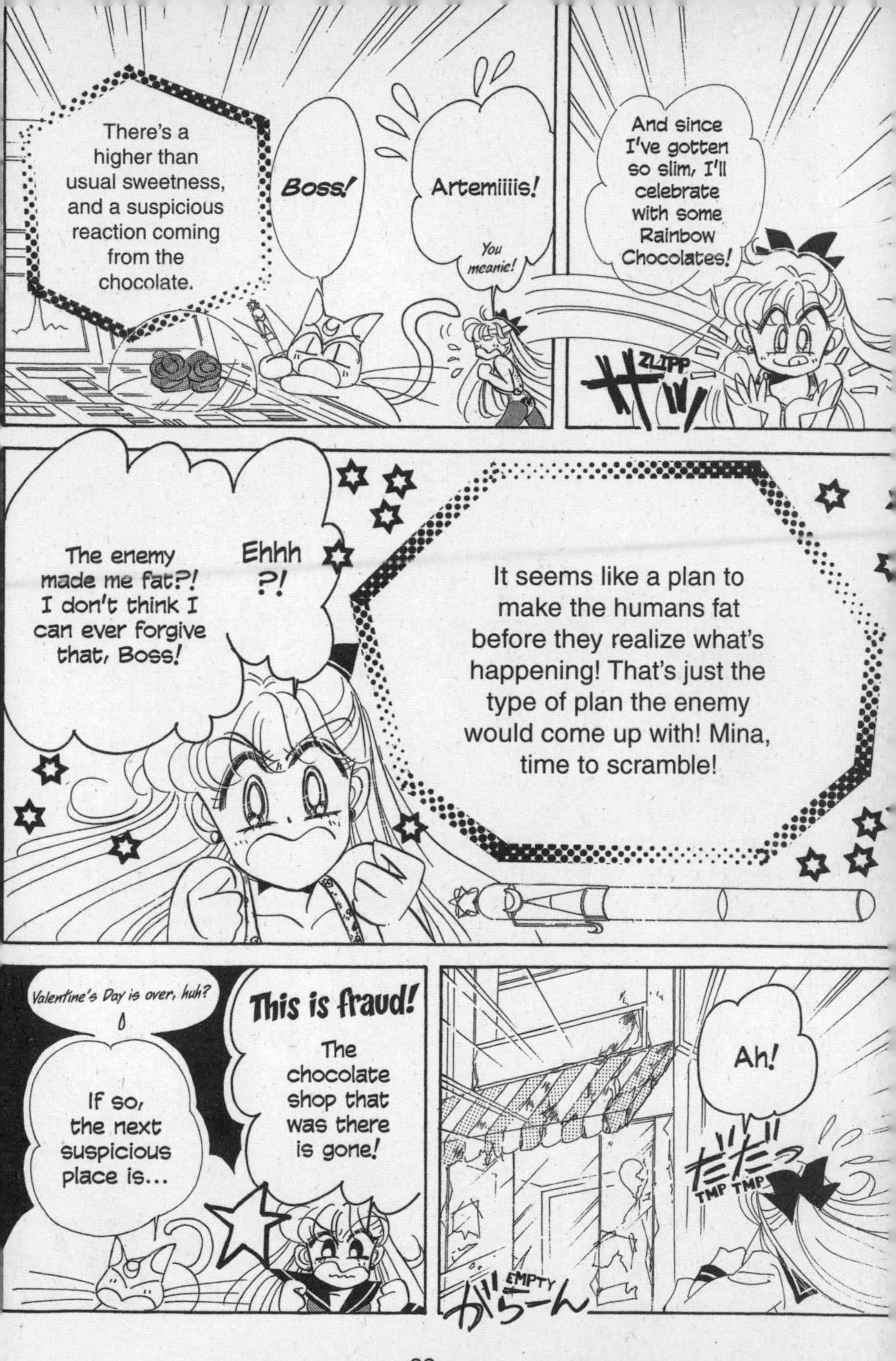
And since I've gotten so slim, I'll celebrate with some Rainbow Chocolates!
ZLIPP
Artemiiiis!
You meanie!
Boss!
There's a higher than usual sweetness, and a suspicious reaction coming from the chocolate.
It seems like a plan to make the humans fat before they realize what's happening! That's just the type of plan the enemy would come up with! Mina, time to scramble!
Ehhh ?!
The enemy made me fat?! I don't think I can ever forgive that, Boss!
Ah!
だだっ
TMP TMP
EMPTY
がらーん
This is fraud!
The chocolate shop that was there is gone!
Valentine's Day is over, huh?
If so, the next suspicious place is...

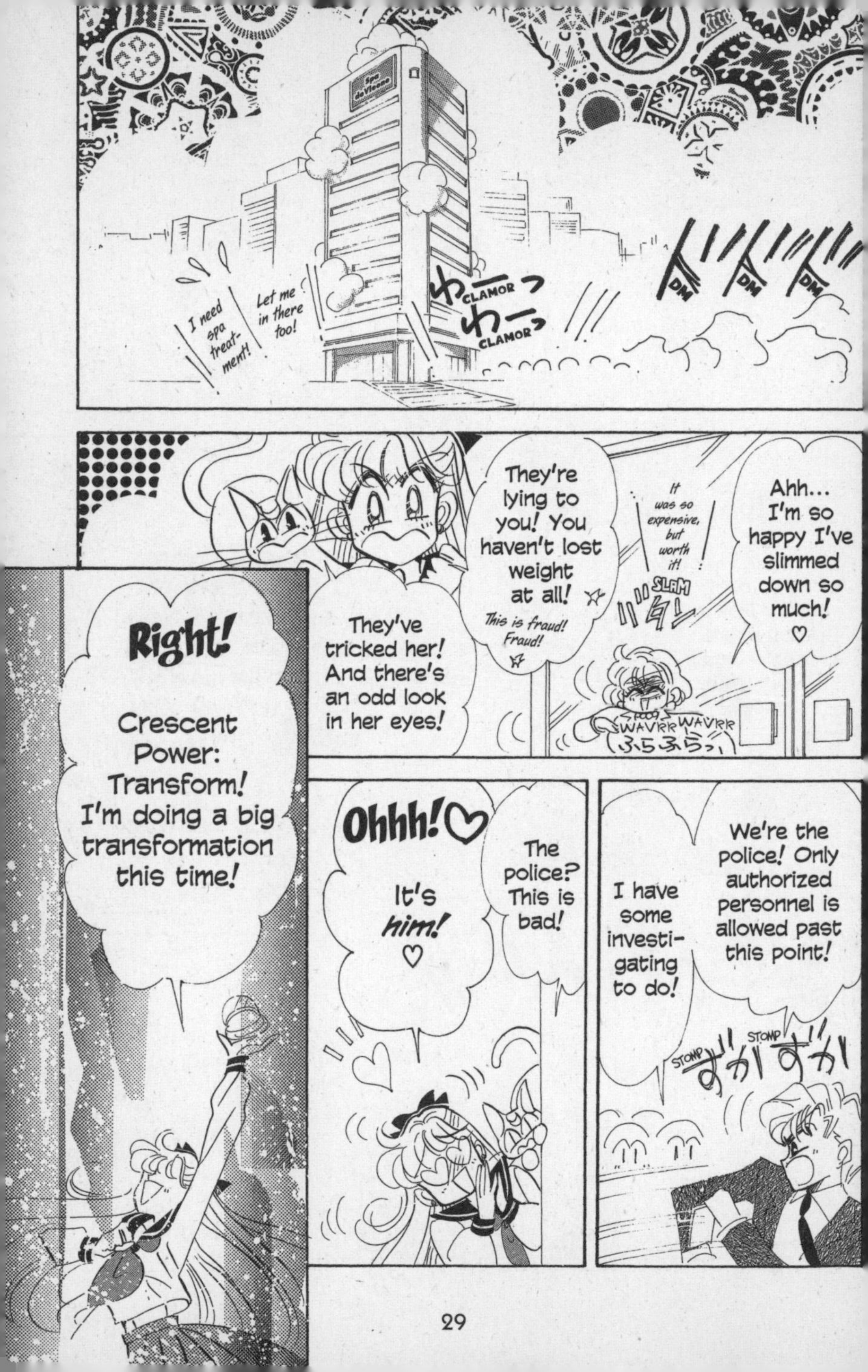
DM DM DM
わー CLAMOR
わー CLAMOR
Let me in there too!
I need spa treatment!
Ahh... I'm so happy I've slimmed down so much! ♡
It was so expensive, but worth it!
SLAM
WAVRR WAVRR
ふらふらっ
They're lying to you! You haven't lost weight at all!
This is fraud! Fraud!
They've tricked her! And there's an odd look in her eyes!
We're the police! Only authorized personnel is allowed past this point!
I have some investigating to do!
STOMP STOMP
ずかずか
The police? This is bad!
Ohhh! ♡
It's him! ♡
Right!
Crescent Power: Transform! I'm doing a big transformation this time!

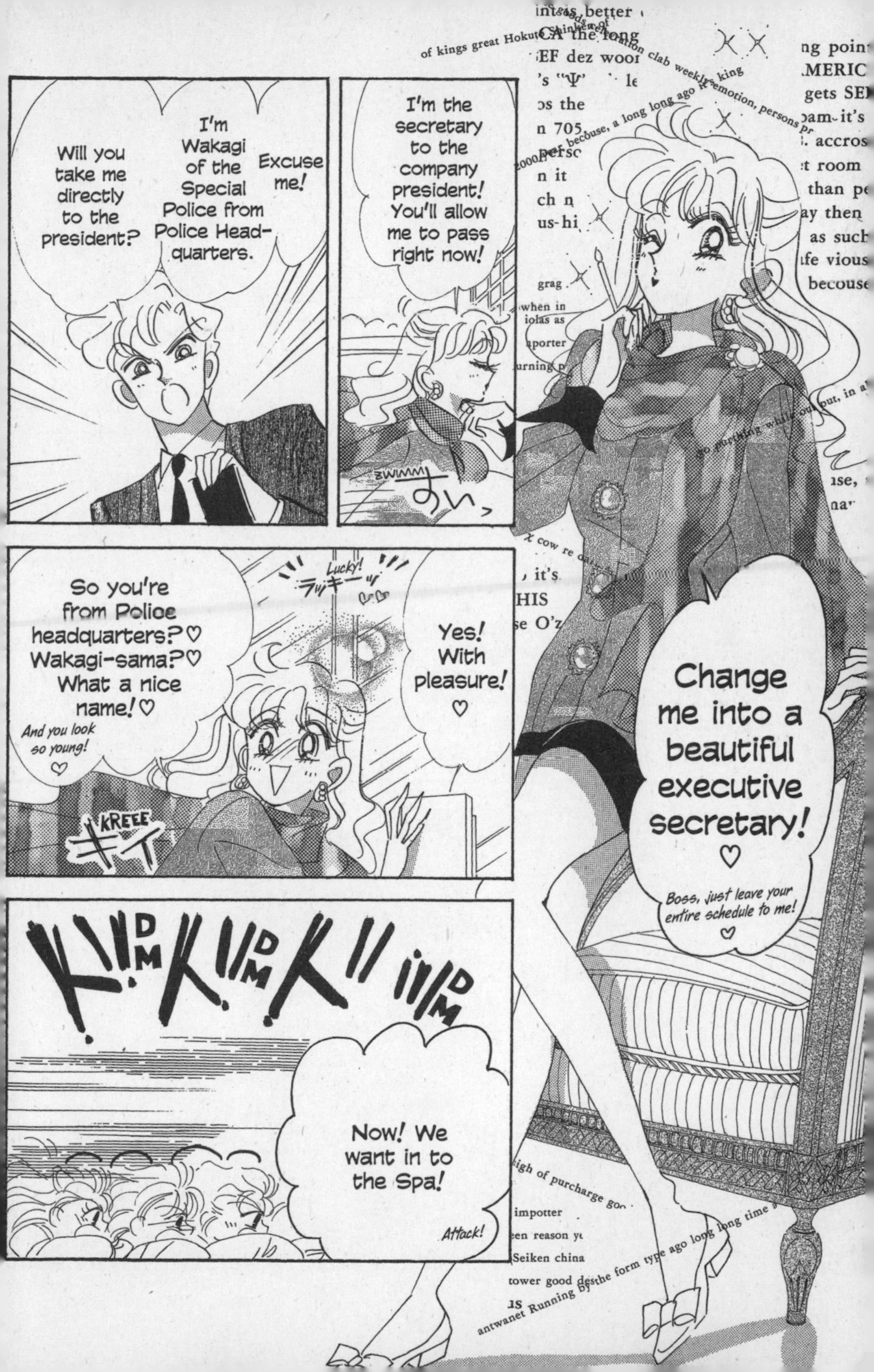
Change me into a beautiful executive secretary! ♡
Boss, just leave your entire schedule to me! ♡
I'm the secretary to the company president! You'll allow me to pass right now!
ZWIMM
Excuse me!
I'm Wakagi of the Special Police from Police Headquarters.
Will you take me directly to the president?
Yes! With pleasure! ♡
Lucky!
So you're from Police headquarters?♡ Wakagi-sama?♡ What a nice name!♡
And you look so young! ♡
KREEE
KDM KDM KDM
Now! We want in to the Spa!
Attack!

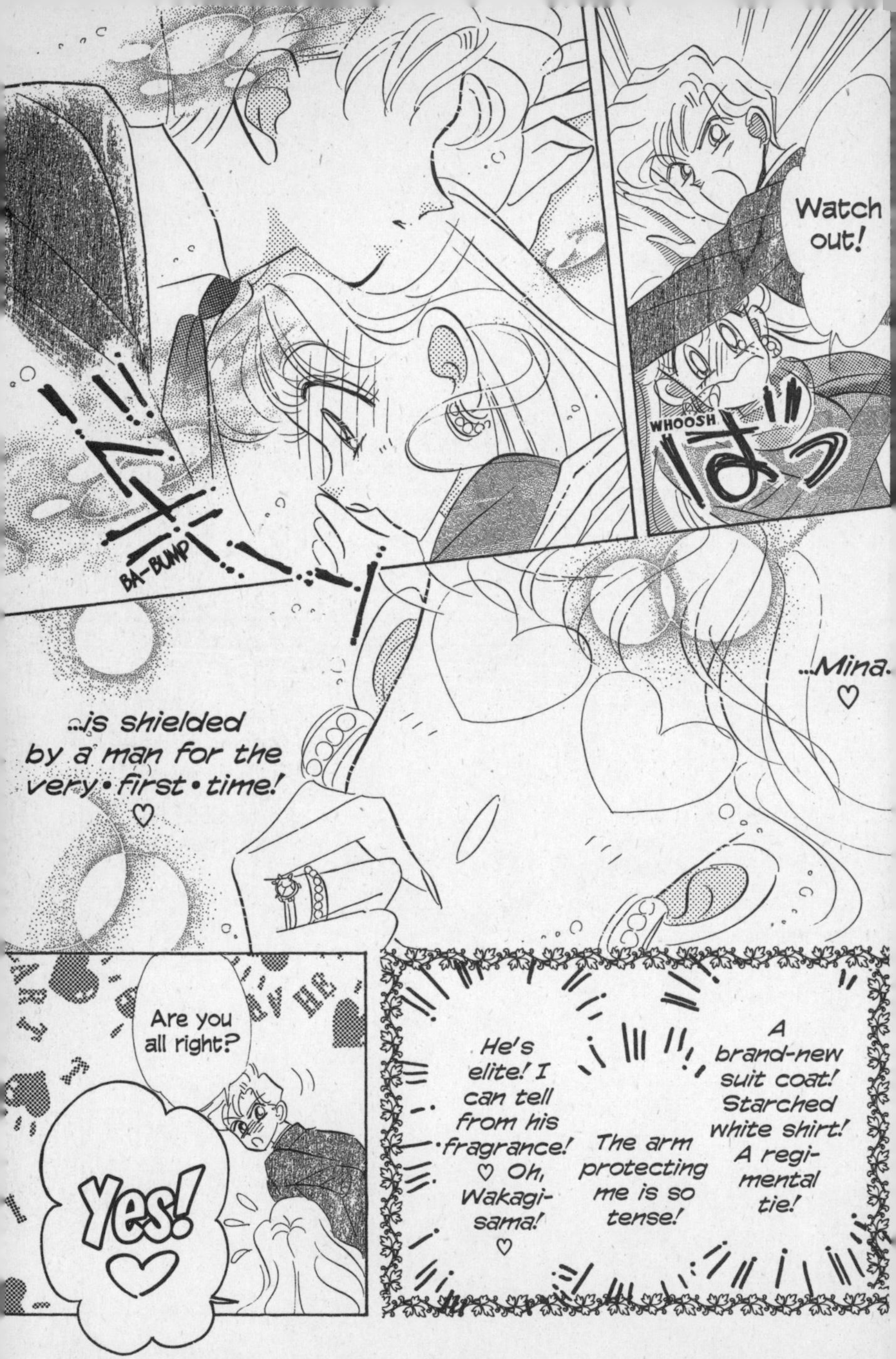
Watch out!
WHOOSH
はっ
BA-BUMP
...Mina. ♡
...is shielded by a man for the very • first • time! ♡
A brand-new suit coat! Starched white shirt! A regi-mental tie!
The arm protecting me is so tense!
He's elite! I can tell from his fragrance! ♡ Oh, Wakagi-sama! ♡
Are you all right?
Yes! ♡

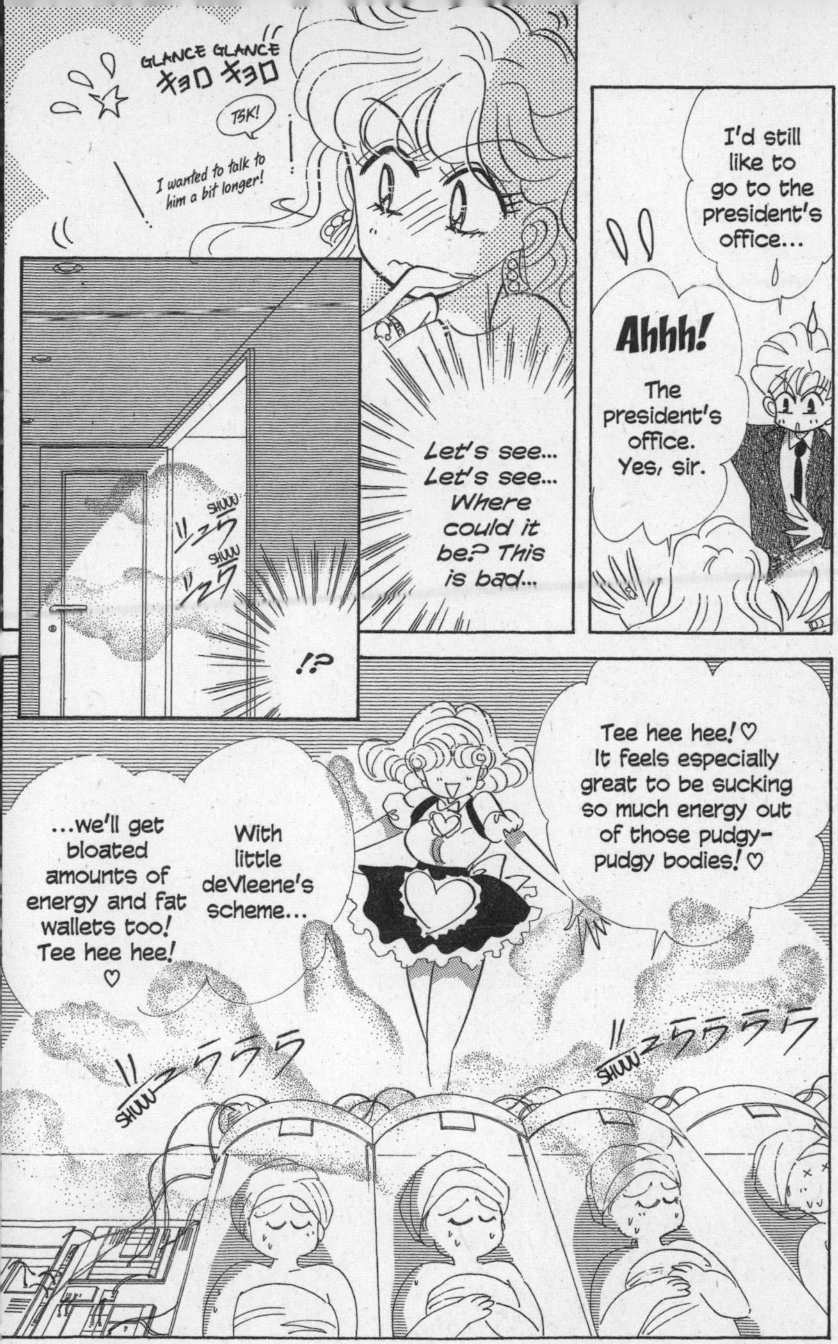
I'd still like to go to the president's office...
Ahhh!
The president's office. Yes, sir.
GLANCE GLANCE
キョロ キョロ
TSK!
I wanted to talk to him a bit longer!
Let's see... Let's see... Where could it be? This is bad...
SHUUU
SHUUU
!?
Tee hee hee! ♡ It feels especially great to be sucking so much energy out of those pudgy-pudgy bodies! ♡
With little deVleene's scheme...
...we'll get bloated amounts of energy and fat wallets too! Tee hee hee! ♡
SHUUU
SHUUU

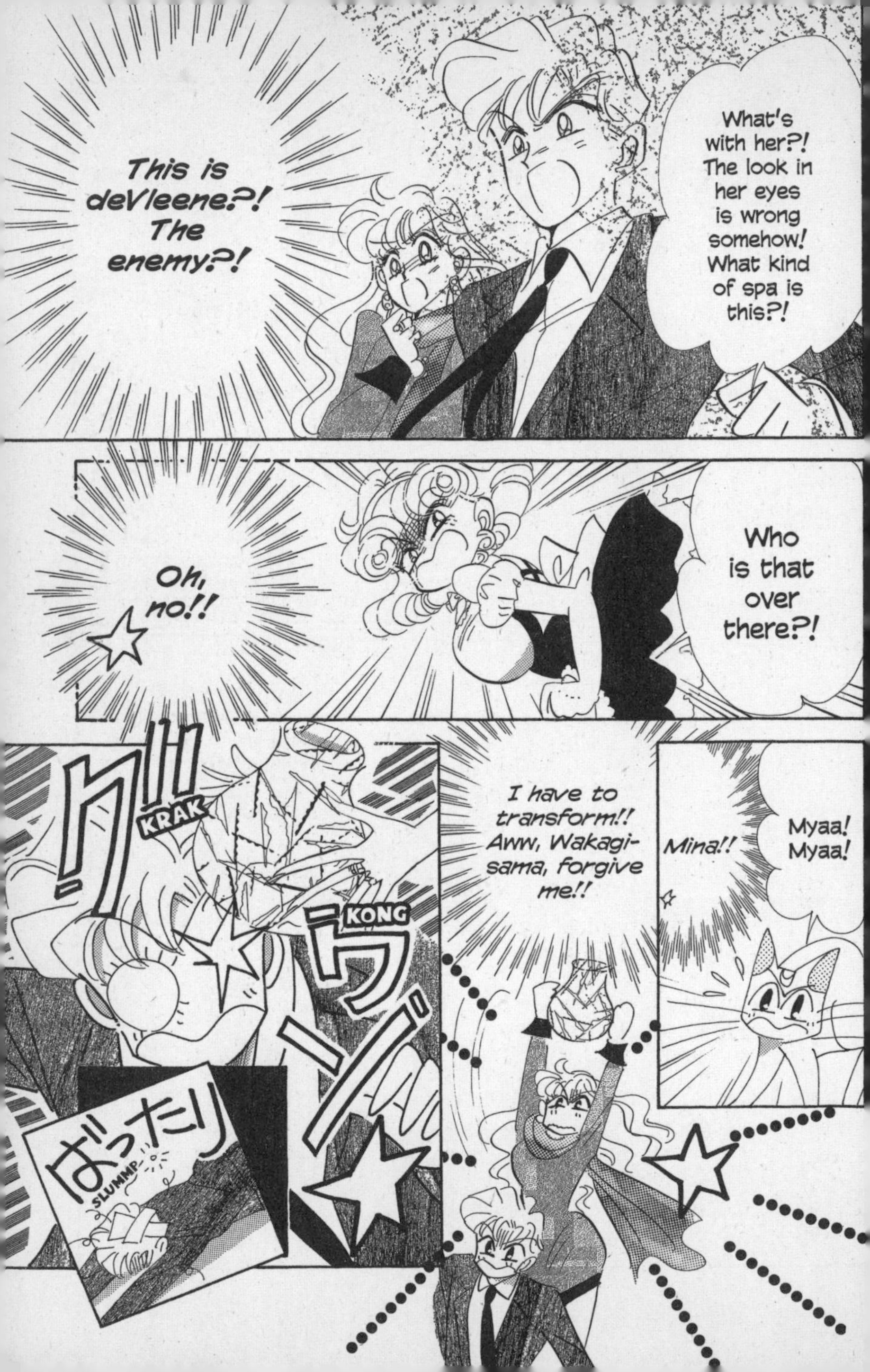
What's with her?! The look in her eyes is wrong somehow! What kind of spa is this?!
This is deVleene?! The enemy?!
Who is that over there?!
Oh, no!!
Myaa! Myaa!
Mina!!
I have to transform!! Aww, Wakagi-sama, forgive me!!
KRAK
KONG
ぱったり
SLUMMP

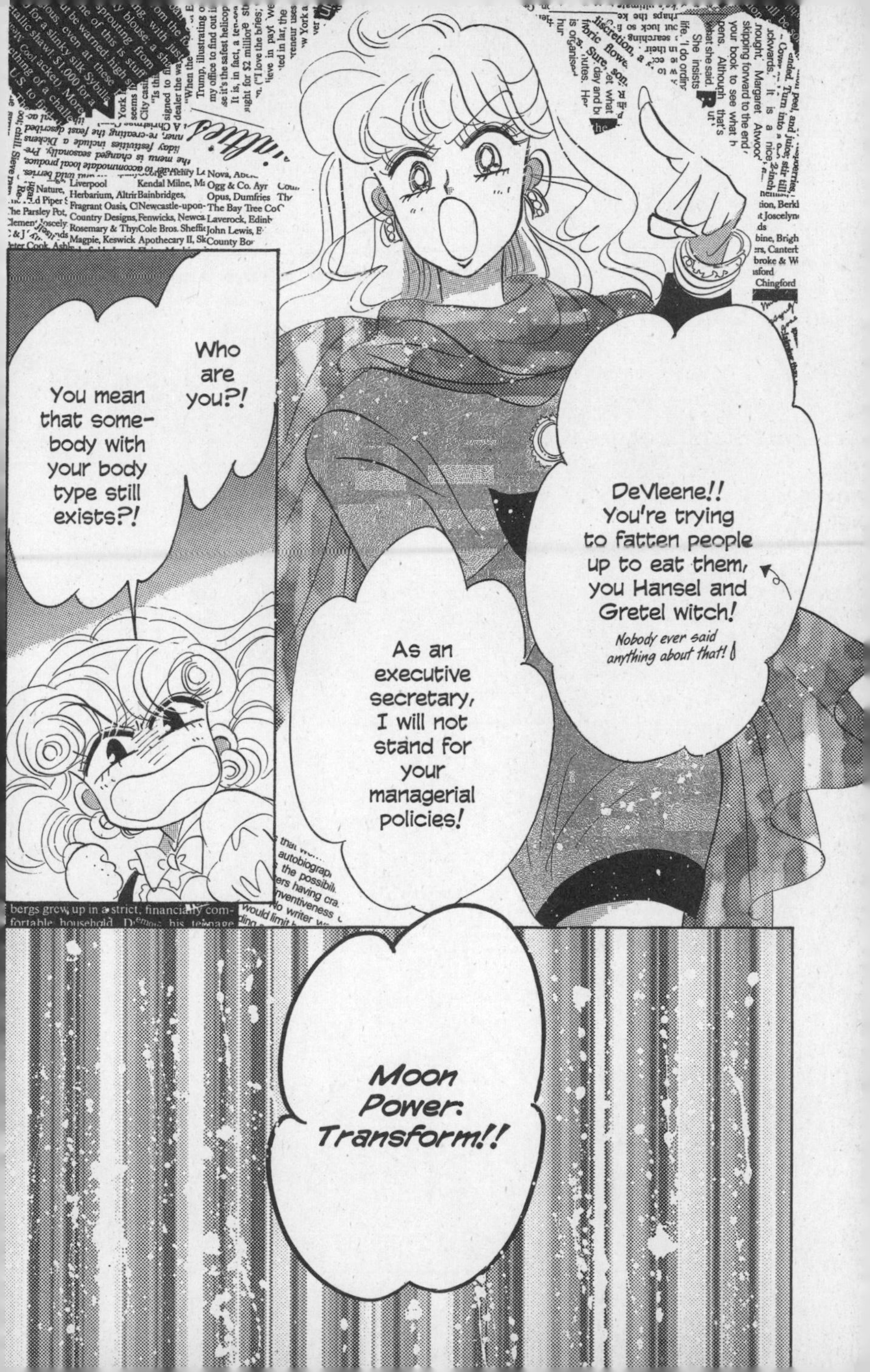

DeVleene!! You're trying to fatten people up to eat them, you Hansel and Gretel witch!
Nobody ever said anything about that!
As an executive secretary, I will not stand for your managerial policies!
Who are you?!
You mean that some-body with your body type still exists?!
Moon Power: Transform!!

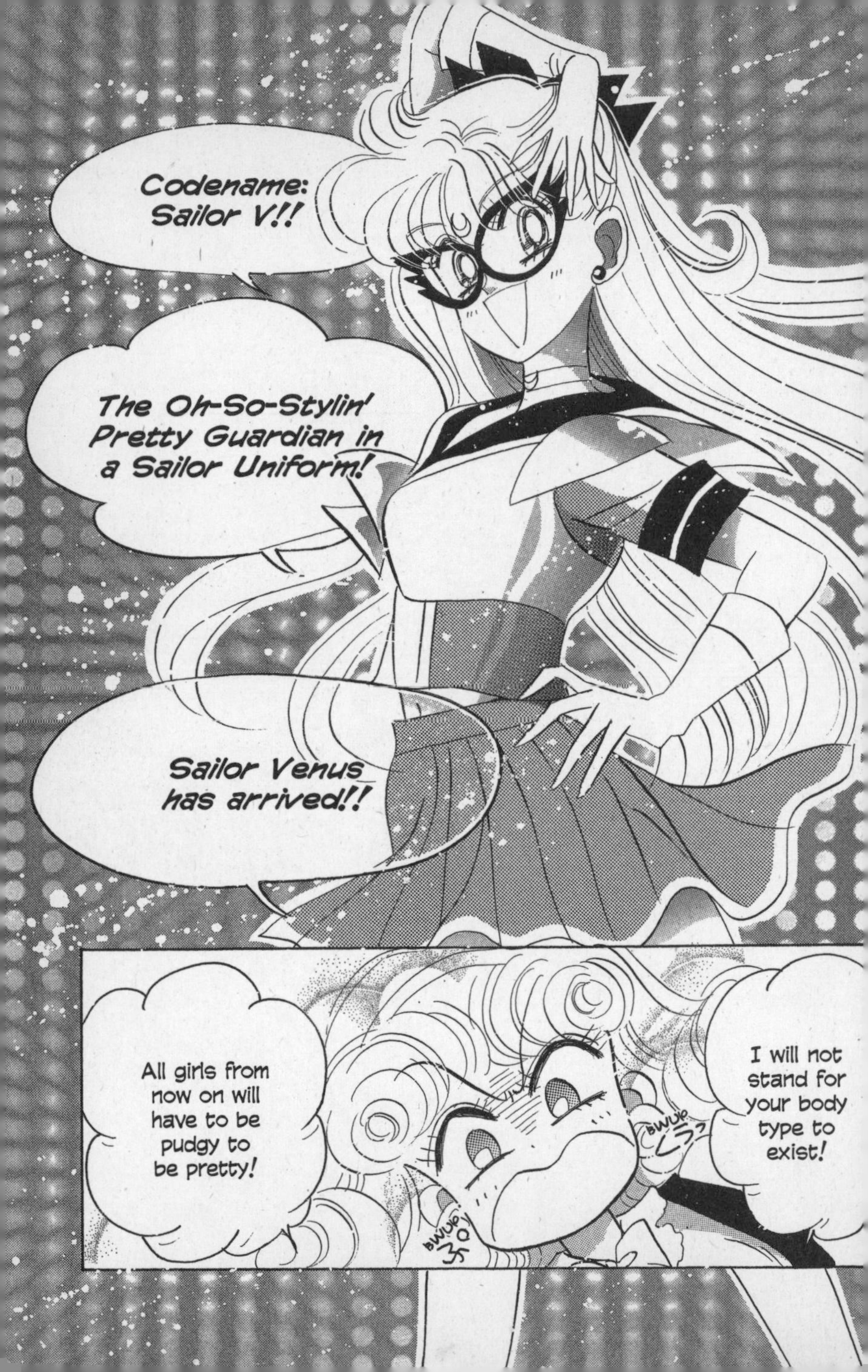
Codename: Sailor V!!
The Oh-So-Stylin' Pretty Guardian in a Sailor Uniform!
Sailor Venus has arrived!!
I will not stand for your body type to exist!
BWUP
All girls from now on will have to be pudgy to be pretty!
BWUP

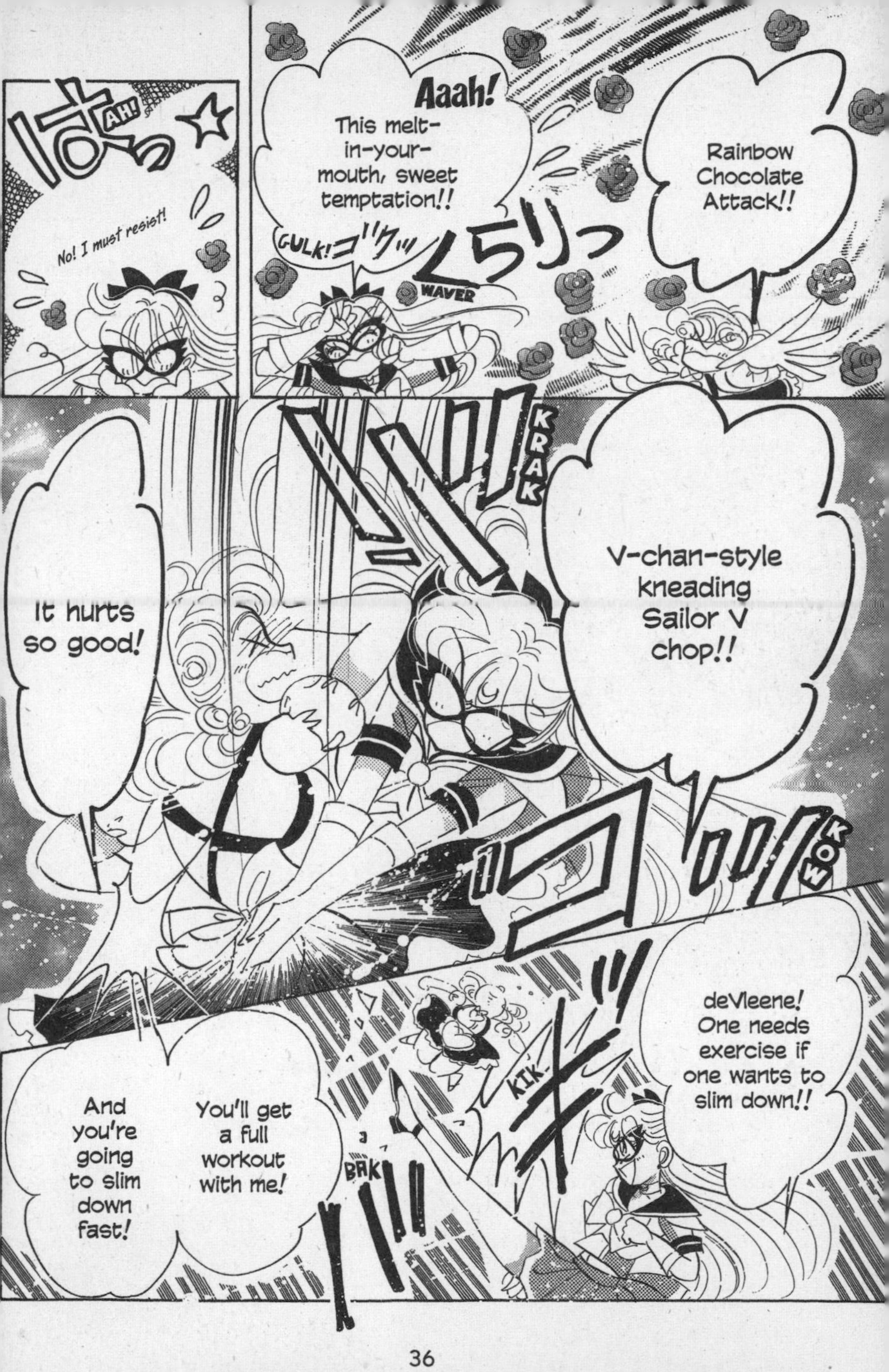
Rainbow Chocolate Attack!!
Aaah! This melt-in-your-mouth, sweet temptation!!
GULK! ゴクッ
くらりっ
WAVER
はっ
AH!
No! I must resist!
KRAK
V-chan-style kneading Sailor V chop!!
It hurts so good!
KOW
deVleene! One needs exercise if one wants to slim down!!
KIK
BAK
You'll get a full workout with me!
And you're going to slim down fast!

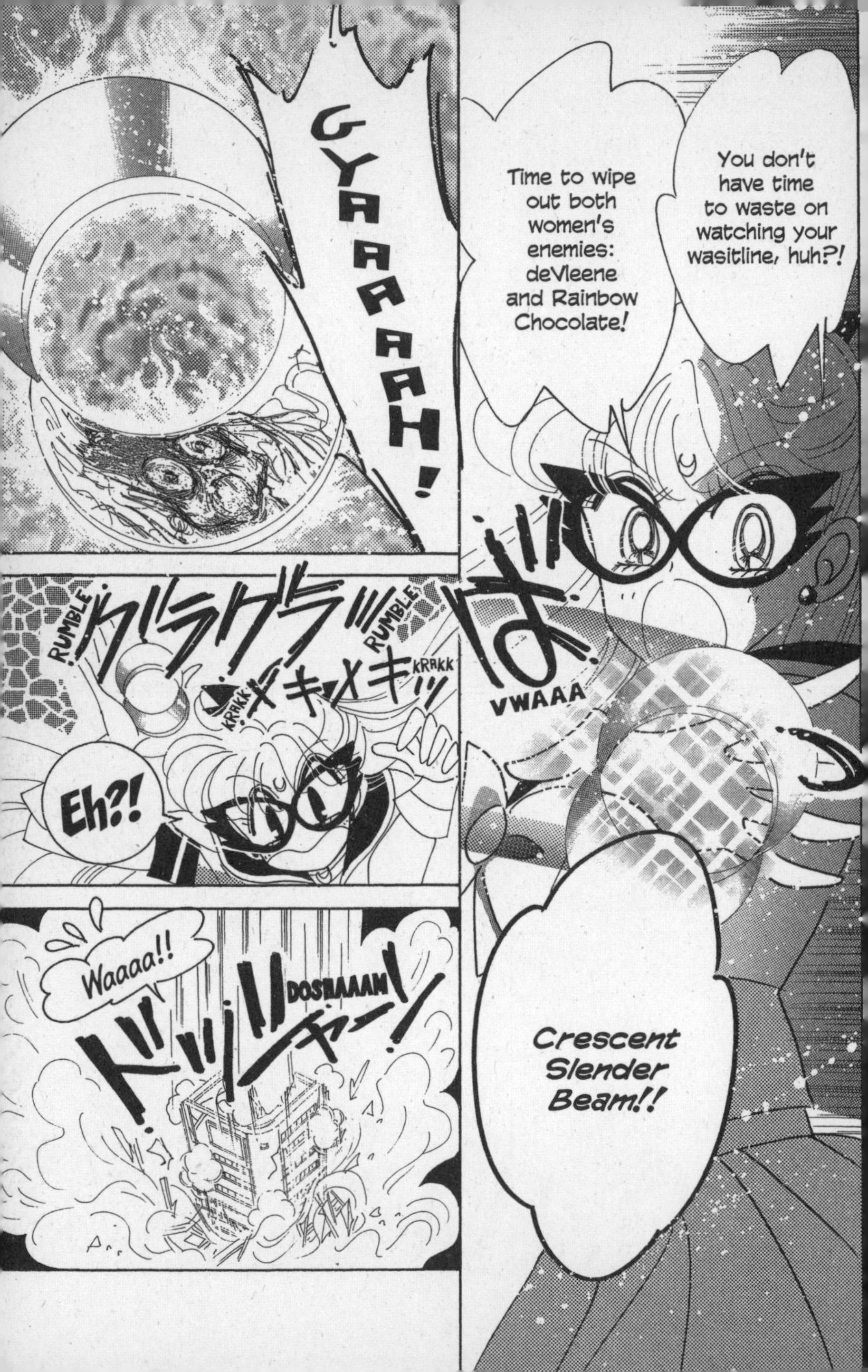

You don't have time to waste on watching your wasitline, huh?!
Time to wipe out both women's enemies: deVleene and Rainbow Chocolate!
VWAAA
Crescent Slender Beam!!
GYAAAAAH!
RUMBLE
グラグラ
RUMBLE
KRAKK
メキメキッ
KRAKK
Eh?!
Waaaa!!
DOSHAAAM

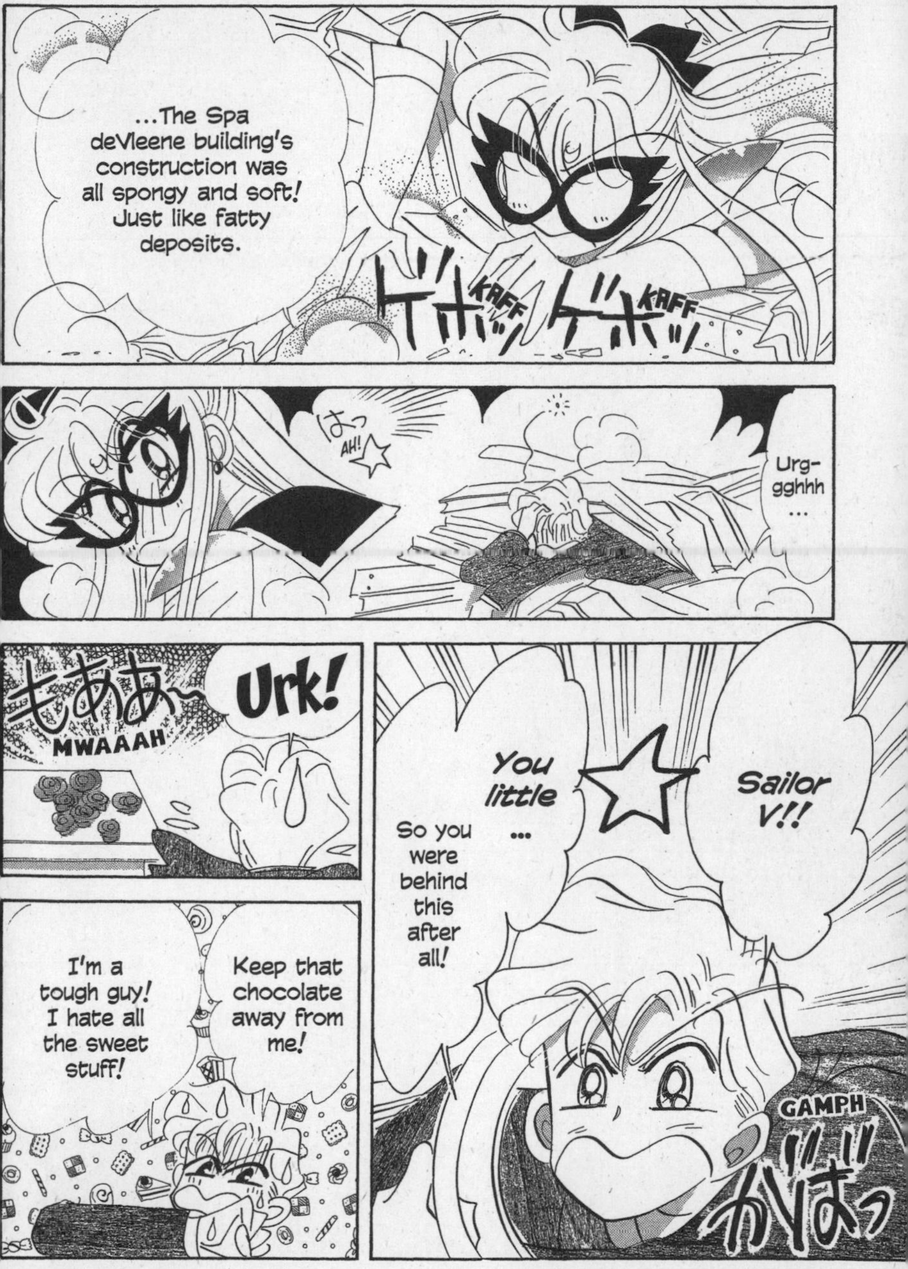
...The Spa deVleene building's construction was all spongy and soft! Just like fatty deposits.
ゲホッ KAFF
ゲホッ KAFF
Urg-gghhh ...
はっ AH!
Sailor V!!
You little ...
So you were behind this after all!
GAMPH
がばっ
Urk!
もあぁ～ MWAAAH
Keep that chocolate away from me!
I'm a tough guy! I hate all the sweet stuff!

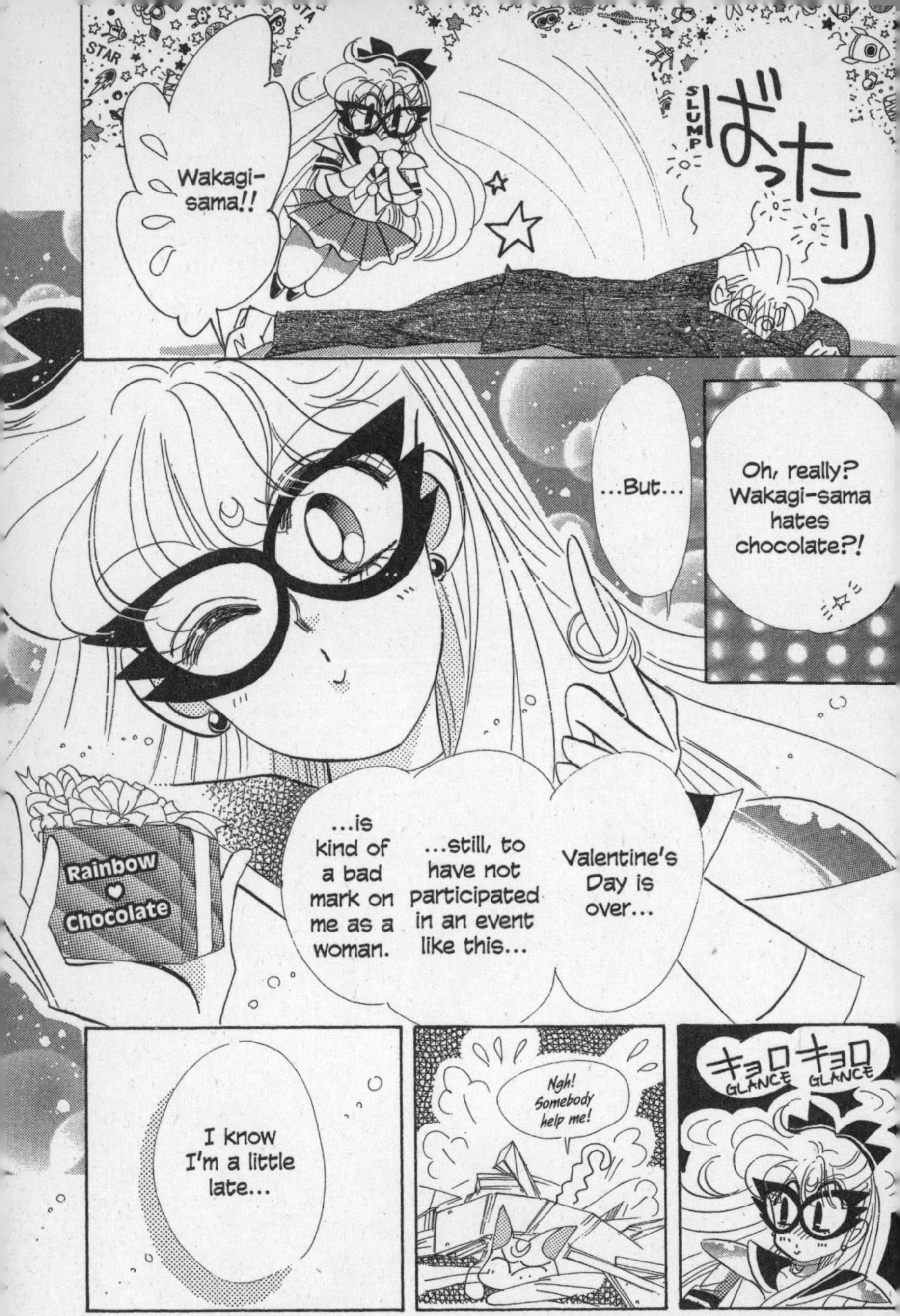
ばったり
SLUMP
Wakagi-sama!!
Oh, really? Wakagi-sama hates chocolate?!
...But...
Valentine's Day is over...
...still, to have not participated in an event like this...
...is kind of a bad mark on me as a woman.
Rainbow ♥ Chocolate
キョロ キョロ
GLANCE GLANCE
Ngh! Somebody help me!
I know I'm a little late...

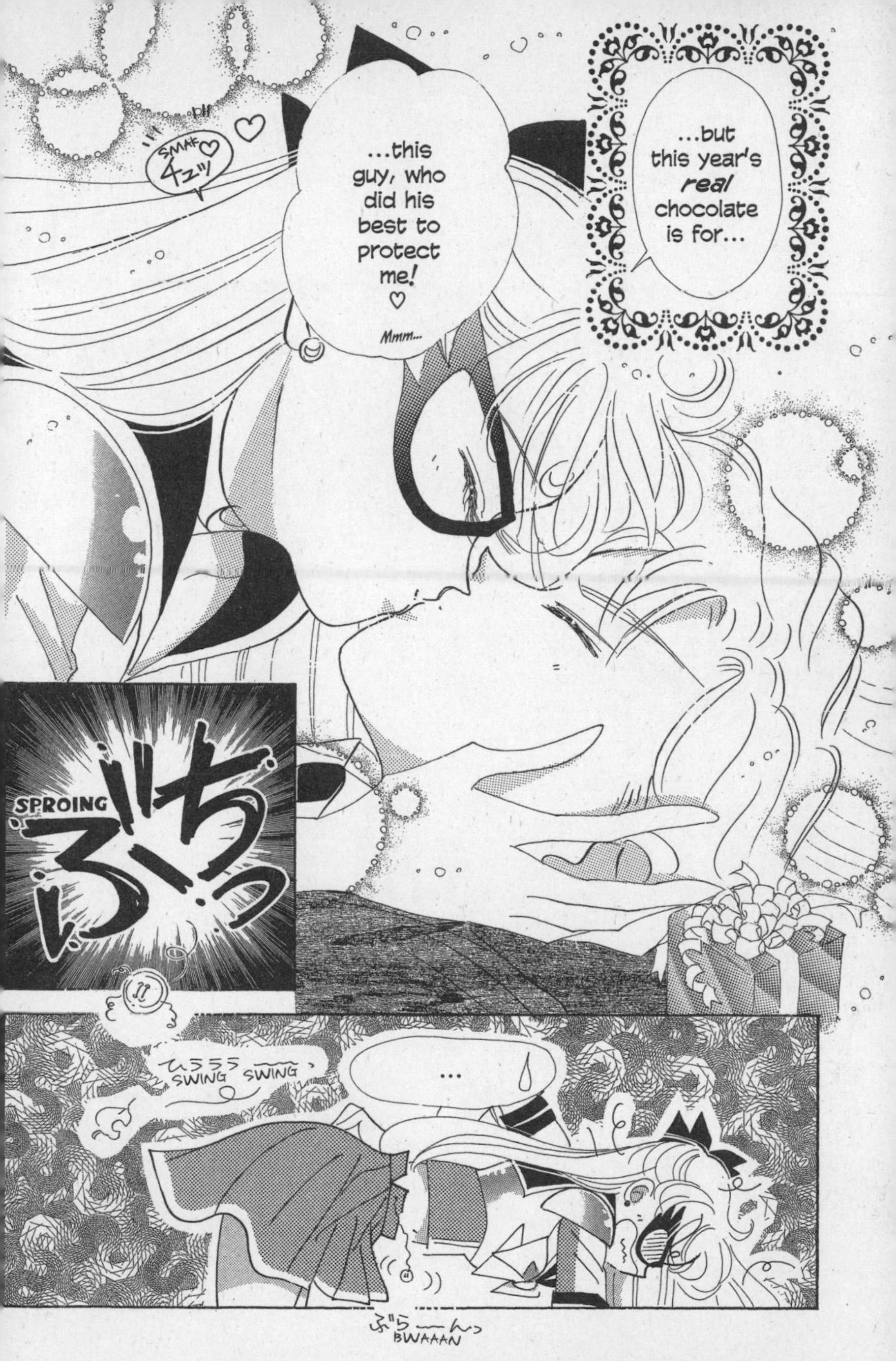
...but this year's *real* chocolate is for...
...this guy, who did his best to protect me! ♡
Mmm...
SMAK
チュッ
SPROING
ぶちっ
...
SWING SWING
BWAAAN

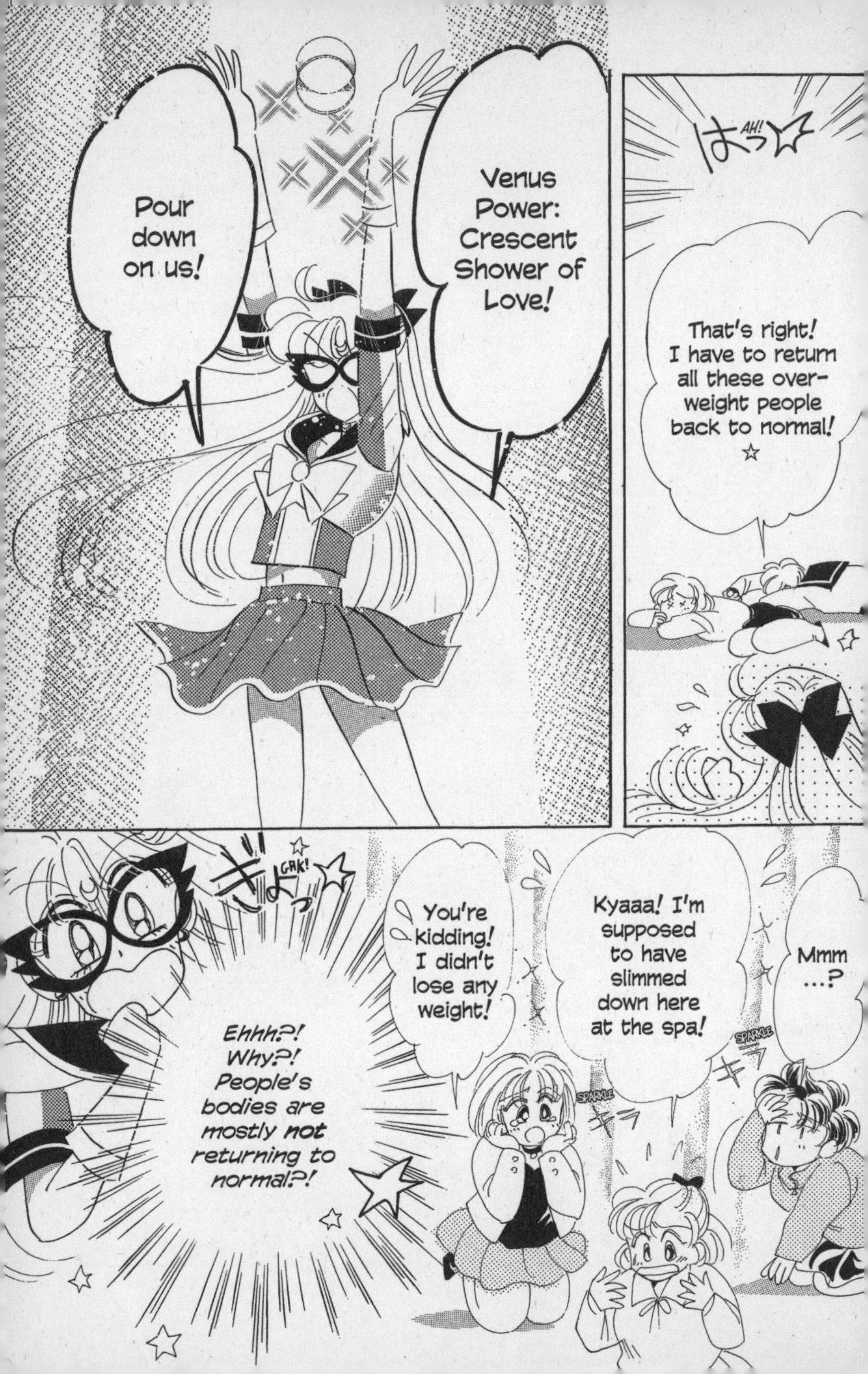

はっ
AH!
That's right! I have to return all these over-weight people back to normal! ☆
Venus Power: Crescent Shower of Love!
Pour down on us!
Mmm ...?
キラ
SPARKLE
Kyaaa! I'm supposed to have slimmed down here at the spa!
キラ
SPARKLE
You're kidding! I didn't lose any weight!
ぎょっ
GAK!
Ehhh?! Why?! People's bodies are mostly **not** returning to normal?!

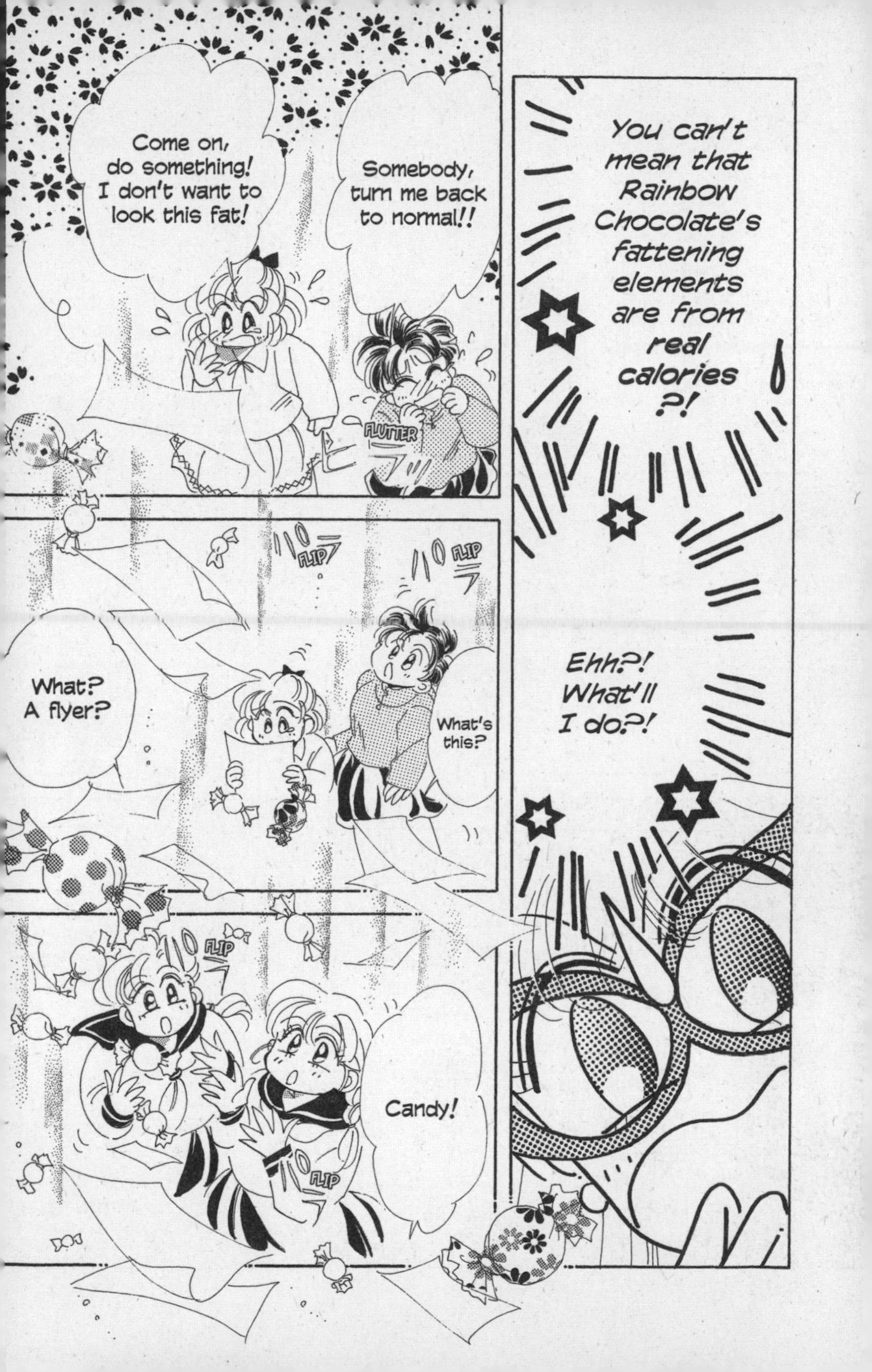
You can't mean that Rainbow Chocolate's fattening elements are from real calories?!
Ehh?! What'll I do?!
Somebody, turn me back to normal!!
Come on, do something! I don't want to look this fat!
FLUTTER
FLIP
FLIP
What's this?
What? A flyer?
Candy!
FLIP
FLIP

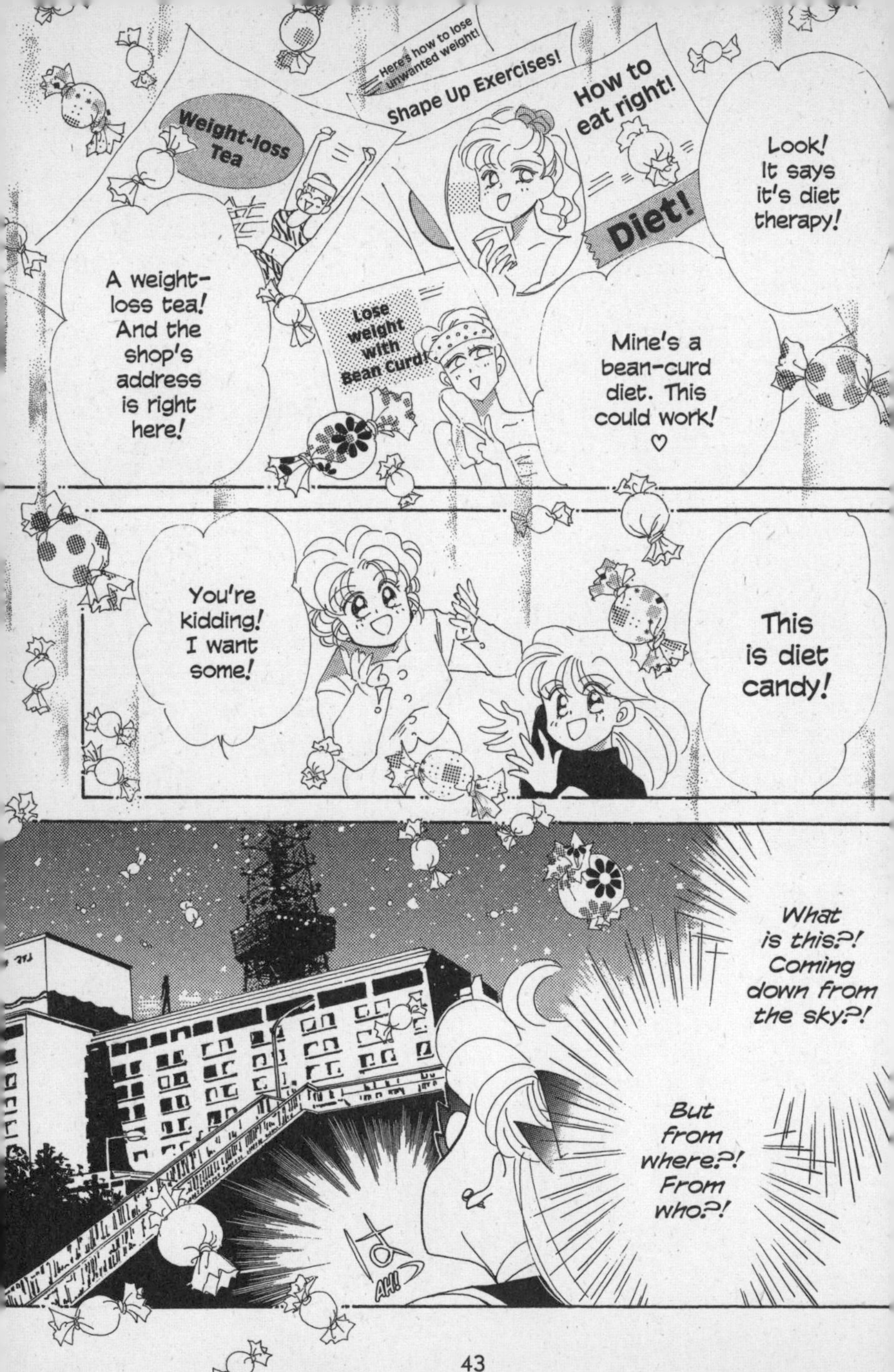
Look! It says it's diet therapy!
How to eat right!
Diet!
Here's how to lose unwanted weight!
Shape Up Exercises!
Weight-loss Tea
Lose weight with Bean Curd!
Mine's a bean-curd diet. This could work! ♡
A weight-loss tea! And the shop's address is right here!
This is diet candy!
You're kidding! I want some!
What is this?! Coming down from the sky?!
But from where?! From who?!
AH!

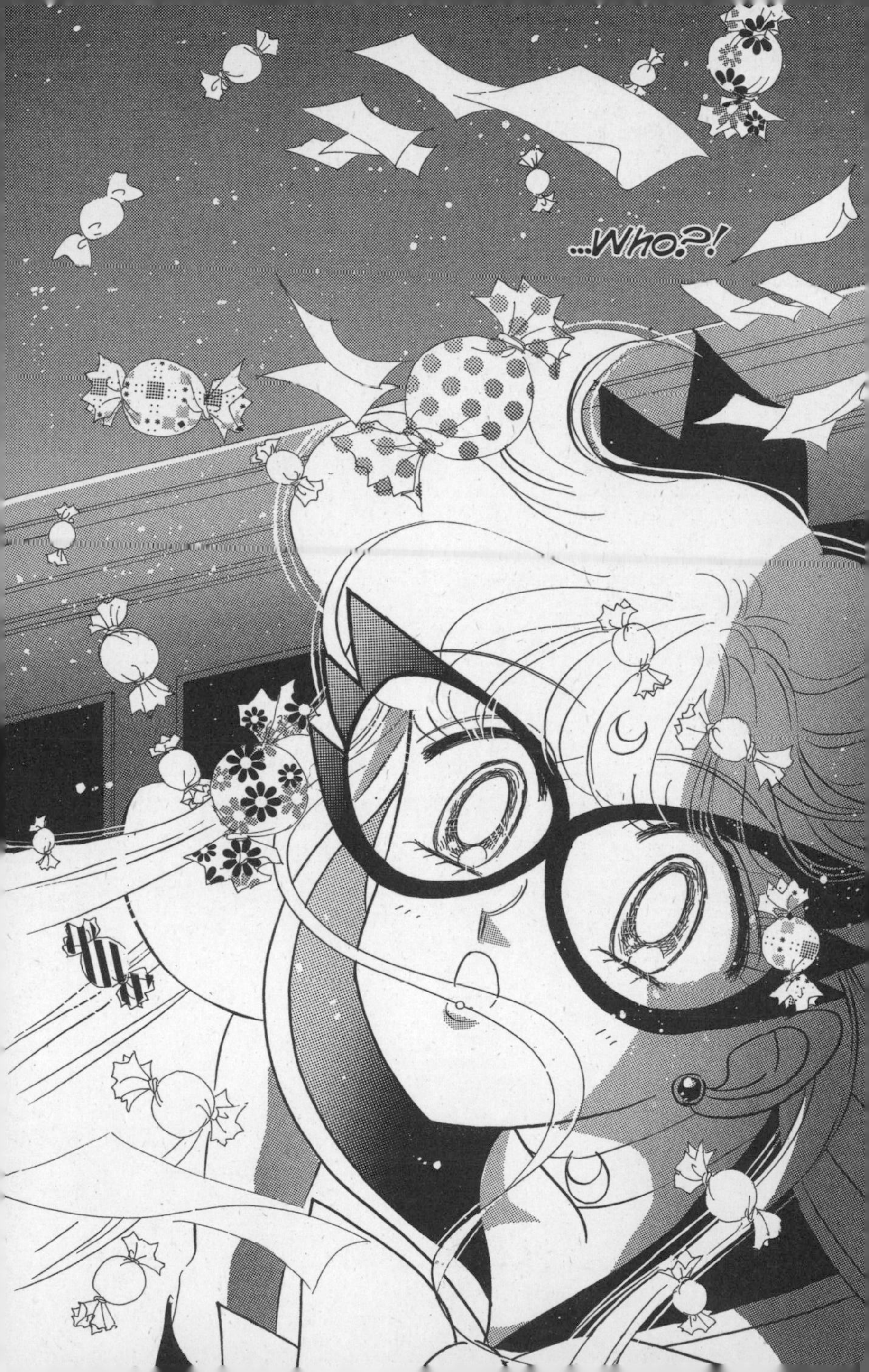
...Who?!

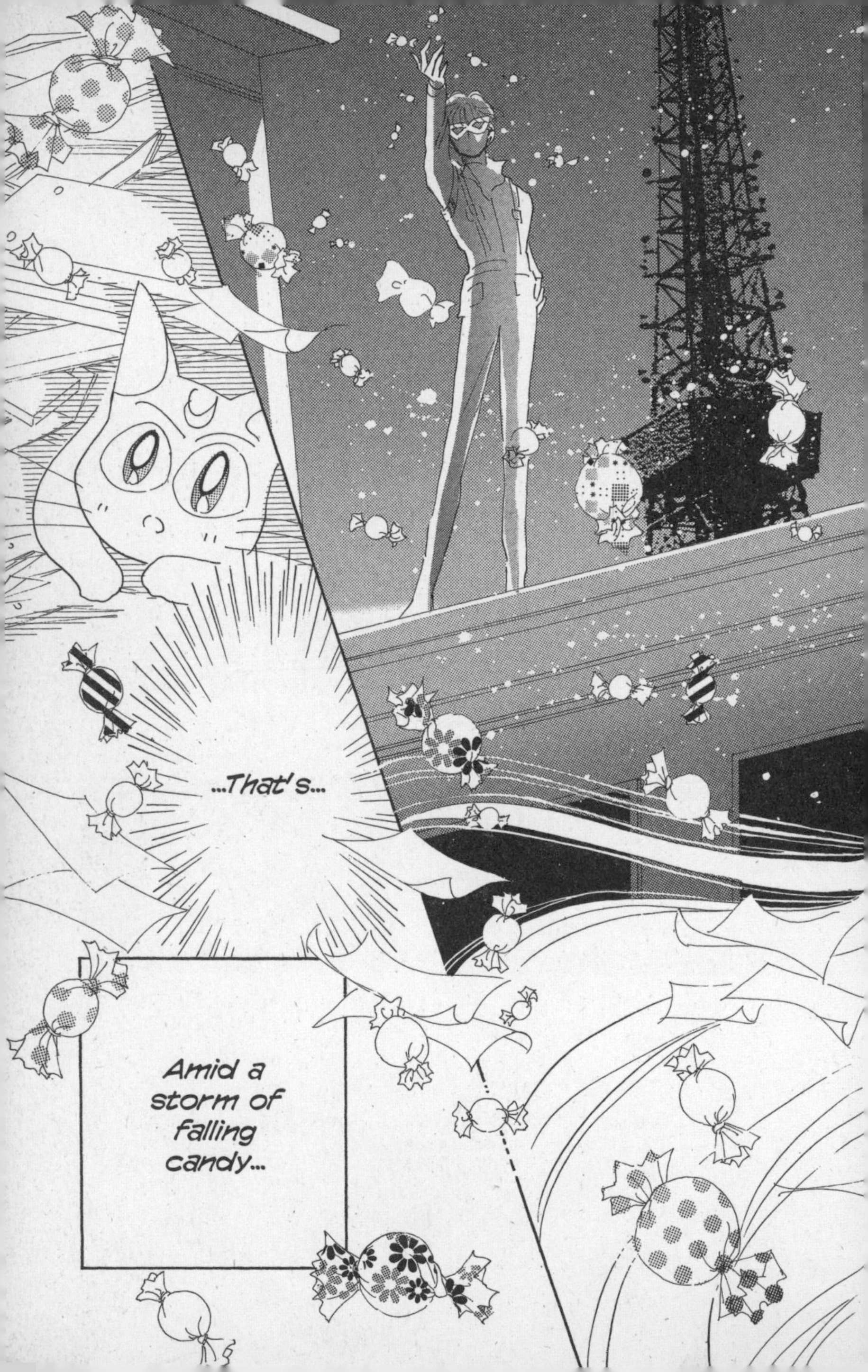
...That's...
Amid a storm of falling candy...

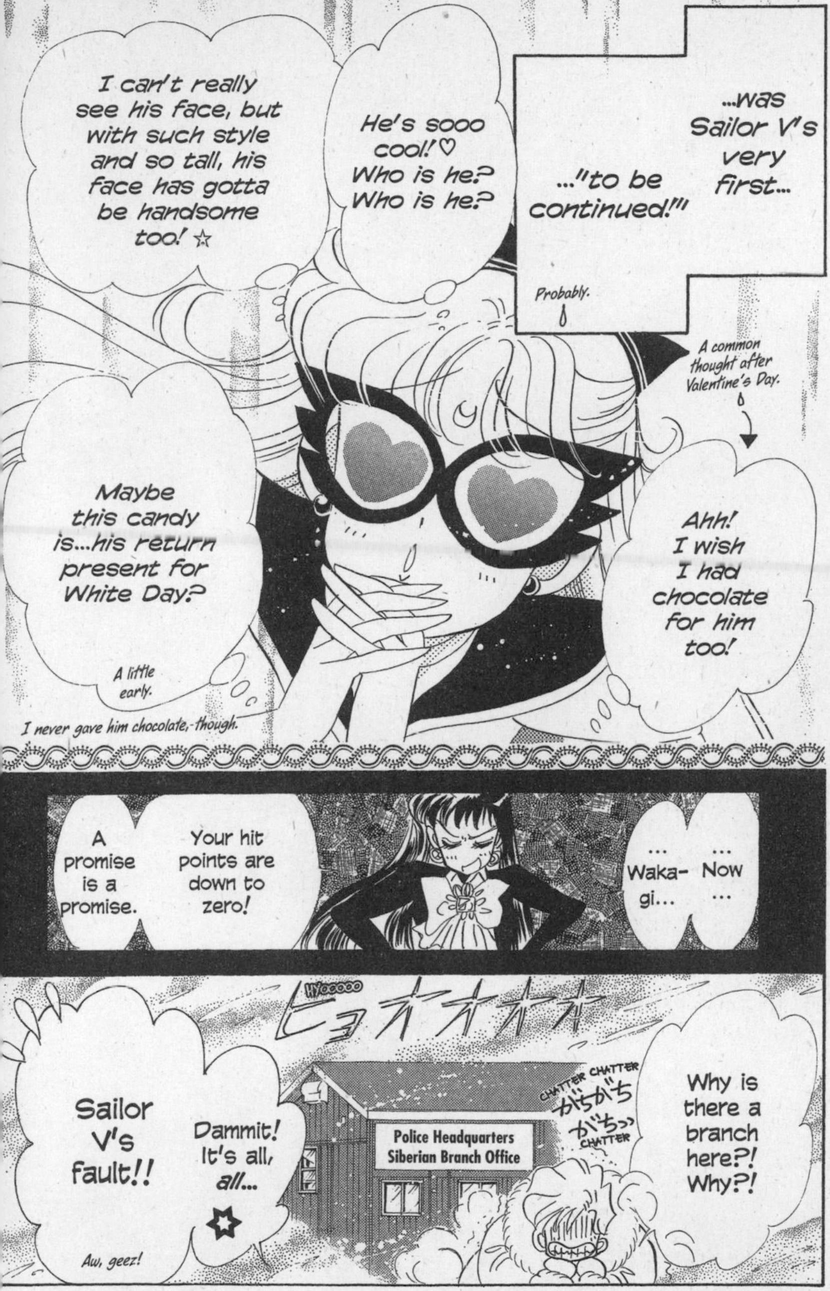
...was Sailor V's very first...
..."to be continued!"
Probably.
A common thought after Valentine's Day.
He's sooo cool!♡ Who is he? Who is he?
I can't really see his face, but with such style and so tall, his face has gotta be handsome too! ☆
Ahh! I wish I had chocolate for him too!
Maybe this candy is...his return present for White Day?
A little early.
I never gave him chocolate, though.
... Now ...
... Waka-gi...
Your hit points are down to zero!
A promise is a promise.
HYOOOOO
ヒョオオオオ
Why is there a branch here?! Why?!
CHATTER CHATTER
がちがち
がちっっ
CHATTER
Police Headquarters Siberian Branch Office
Dammit! It's all, all...
Sailor V's fault!!
Aw, geez!

• The End •

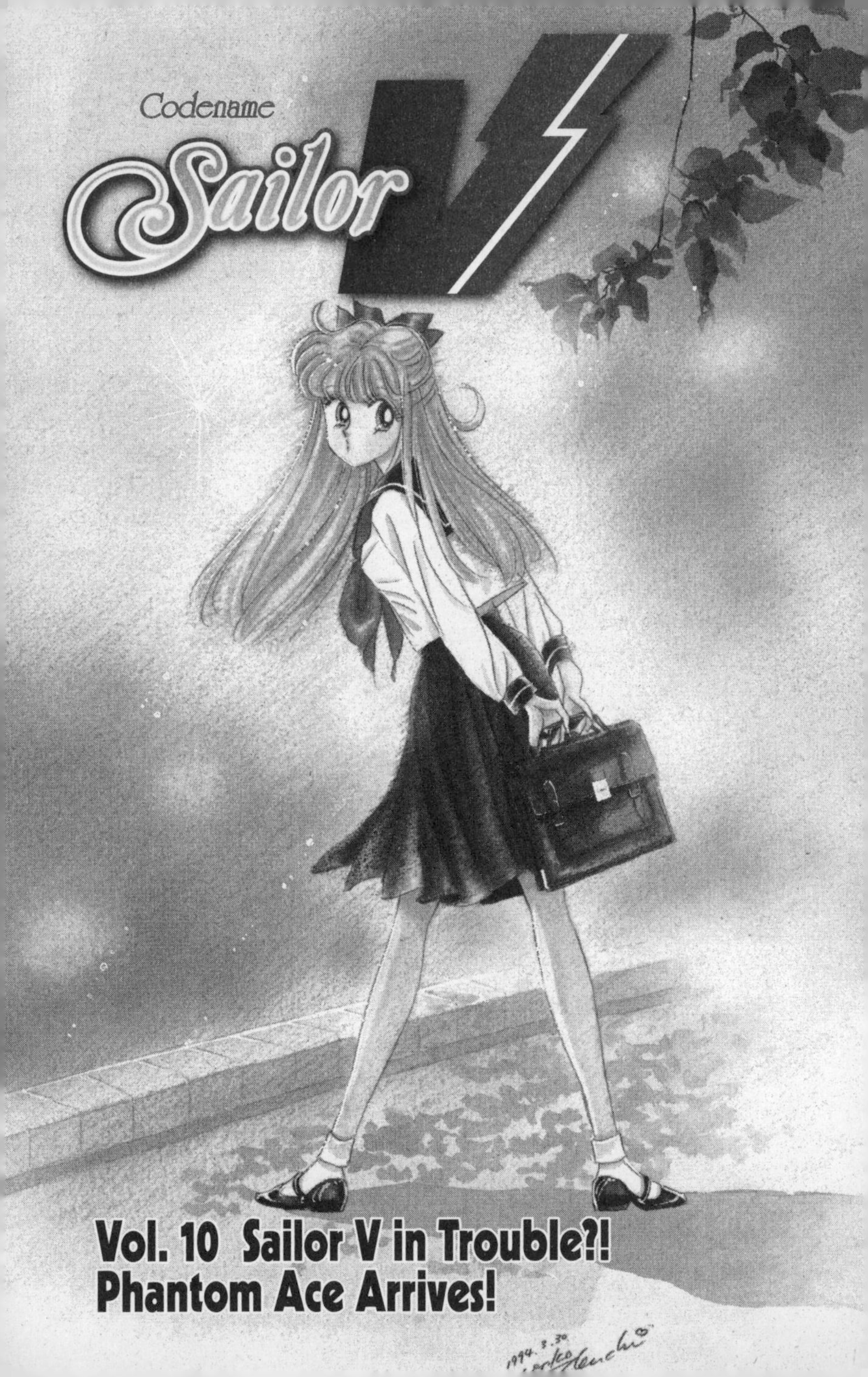
Codename
Sailor V
Vol. 10 Sailor V in Trouble?!
Phantom Ace Arrives!

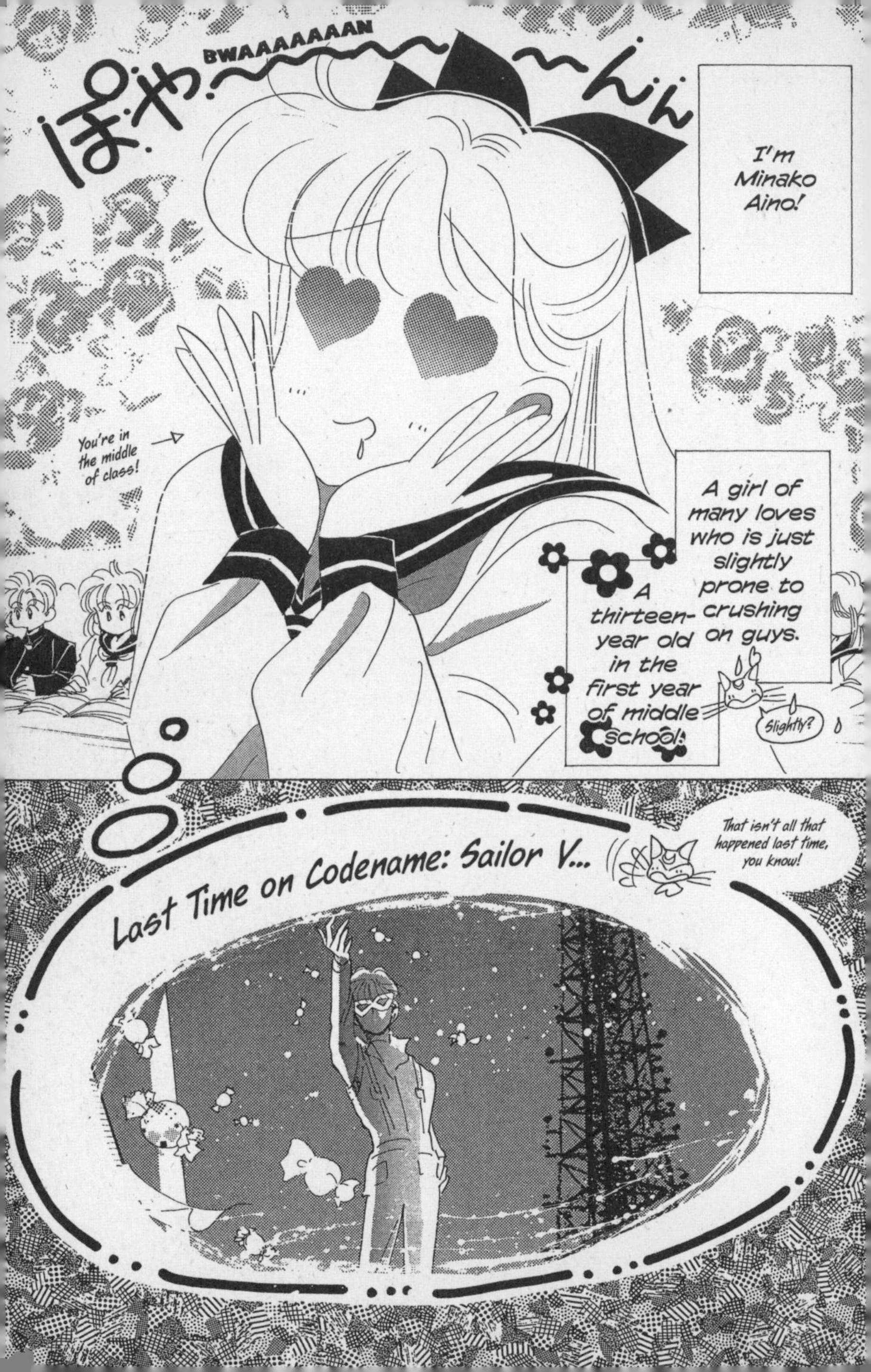

BWAAAAAAAN
ぽや〜〜〜〜〜んん
I'm Minako Aino!
A girl of many loves who is just slightly prone to crushing on guys.
A thirteen-year old in the first year of middle school!
Slightly?
You're in the middle of class!
That isn't all that happened last time, you know!
Last Time on Codename: Sailor V...

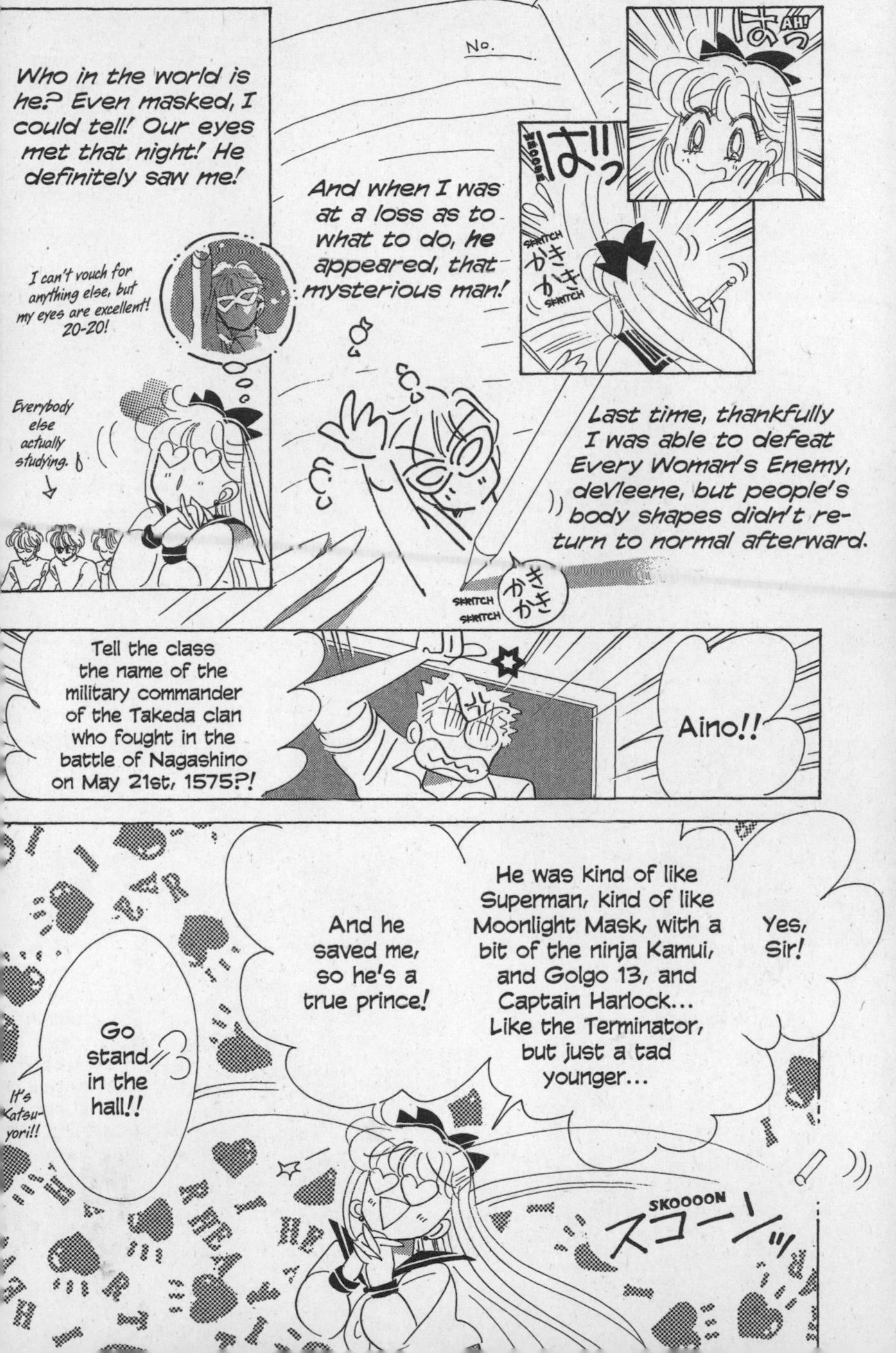

はっ
AH!
はっ
かきかき
SKRITCH
SKRITCH
Last time, thankfully I was able to defeat Every Woman's Enemy, deVleene, but people's body shapes didn't return to normal afterward.
かきかき
SKRITCH
SKRITCH
And when I was at a loss as to what to do, he appeared, that mysterious man!
No.
Who in the world is he? Even masked, I could tell! Our eyes met that night! He definitely saw me!
I can't vouch for anything else, but my eyes are excellent! 20-20!
Everybody else actually studying.
Aino!!
Tell the class the name of the military commander of the Takeda clan who fought in the battle of Nagashino on May 21st, 1575?!
Yes, Sir!
He was kind of like Superman, kind of like Moonlight Mask, with a bit of the ninja Kamui, and Golgo 13, and Captain Harlock... Like the Terminator, but just a tad younger...
And he saved me, so he's a true prince!
Go stand in the hall!!
It's Katsuyori!!
SKOOOON
スコーン

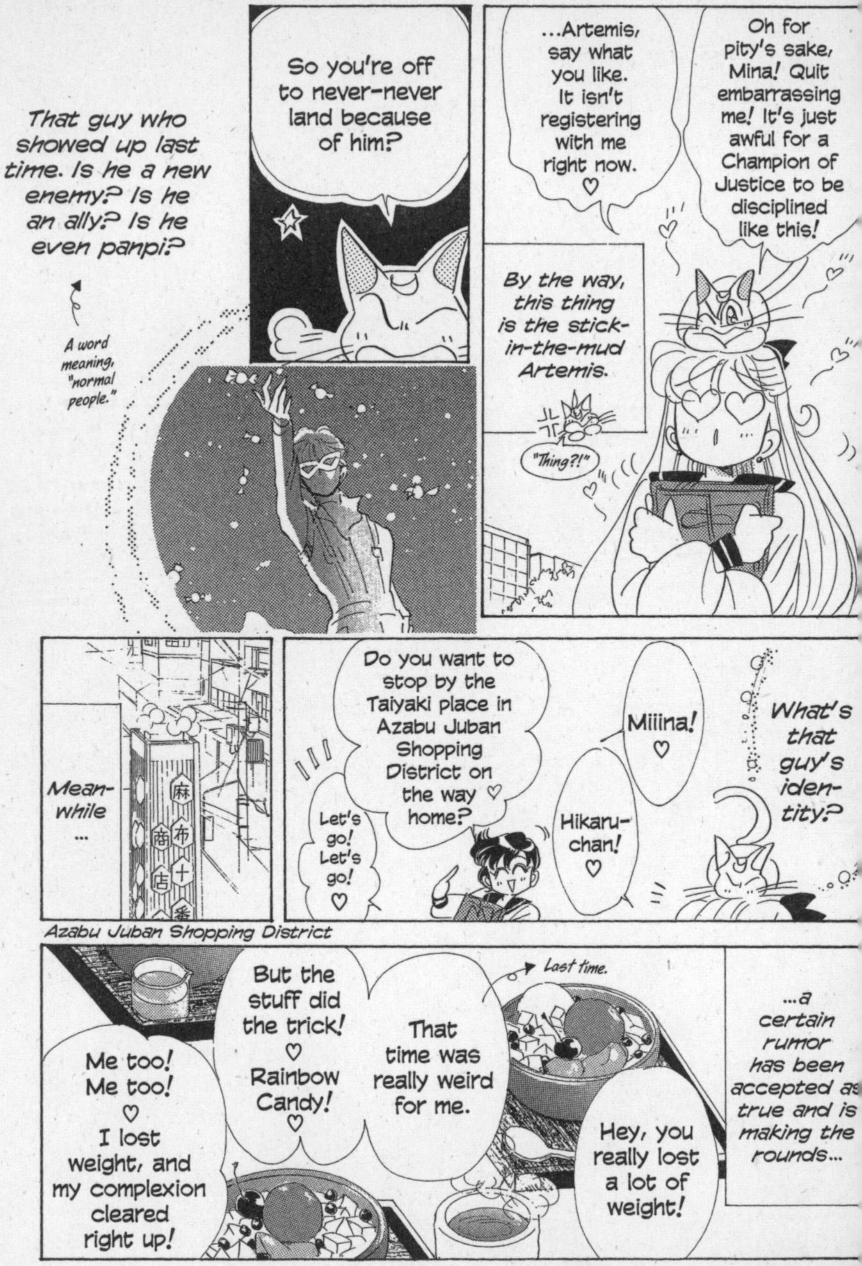

Oh for pity's sake, Mina! Quit embarrassing me! It's just awful for a Champion of Justice to be disciplined like this!
...Artemis, say what you like. It isn't registering with me right now. ♡
By the way, this thing is the stick-in-the-mud Artemis.
"Thing?!"
So you're off to never-never land because of him?
That guy who showed up last time. Is he a new enemy? Is he an ally? Is he even panpi?
A word meaning, "normal people."
What's that guy's identity?
Miiina! ♡
Hikaru-chan! ♡
Do you want to stop by the Taiyaki place in Azabu Juban Shopping District on the way home? ♡
Let's go! Let's go! ♡
Meanwhile...
麻布十番商店
Azabu Juban Shopping District
...a certain rumor has been accepted as true and is making the rounds...
Hey, you really lost a lot of weight!
That time was really weird for me.
Last time.
But the stuff did the trick! ♡ Rainbow Candy! ♡
Me too! Me too! ♡ I lost weight, and my complexion cleared right up!

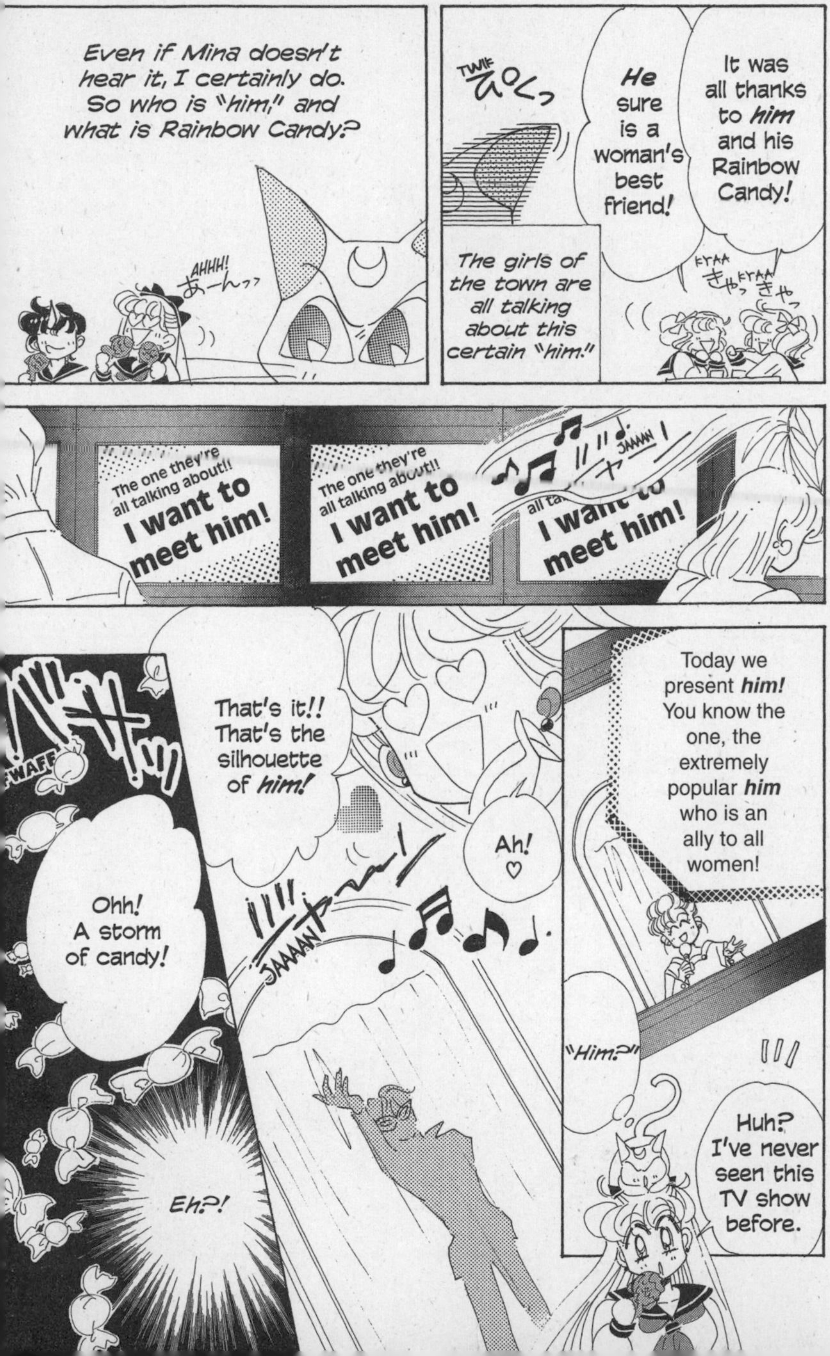
It was all thanks to *him* and his Rainbow Candy!
He sure is a woman's best friend!
TWIP
ぴくっ
The girls of the town are all talking about this certain "*him*."
KYAA
きゃっ
KYAA
きゃっ
Even if Mina doesn't hear it, I certainly do. So who is "*him*," and what is Rainbow Candy?
AHHH!
あーんっっ
JAAAN
The one they're all talking about!!
I want to meet him!
The one they're all talking about!!
I want to meet him!
I want to meet him!
Today we present *him!* You know the one, the extremely popular *him* who is an ally to all women!
"*Him?*"
Huh? I've never seen this TV show before.
That's it!! That's the silhouette of *him!*
Ah! ♡
JAAAAN
FWAFF
Ohh! A storm of candy!
Eh?!

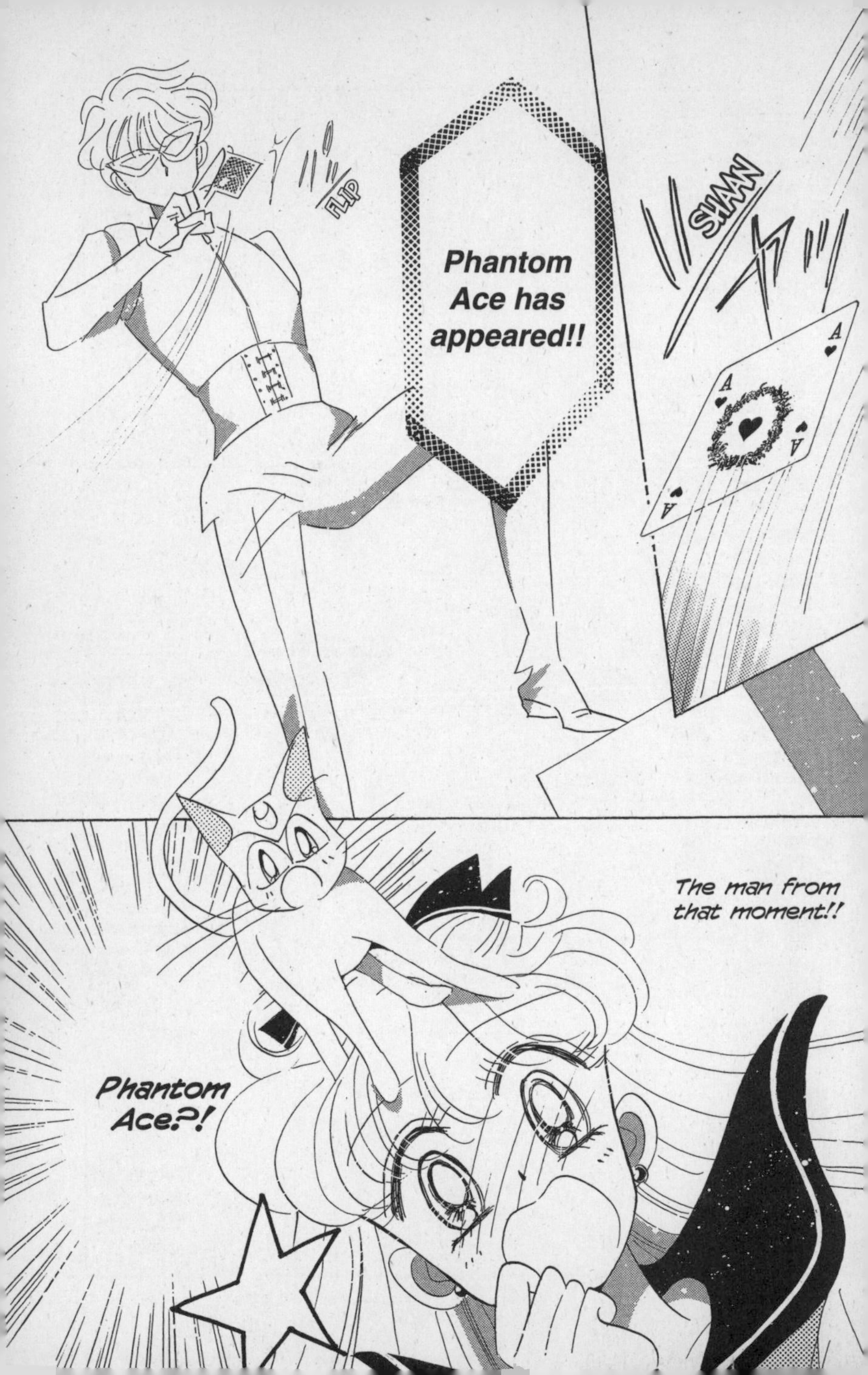
SHAAN
Phantom Ace has appeared!!
FLIP
The man from that moment!!
Phantom Ace?!

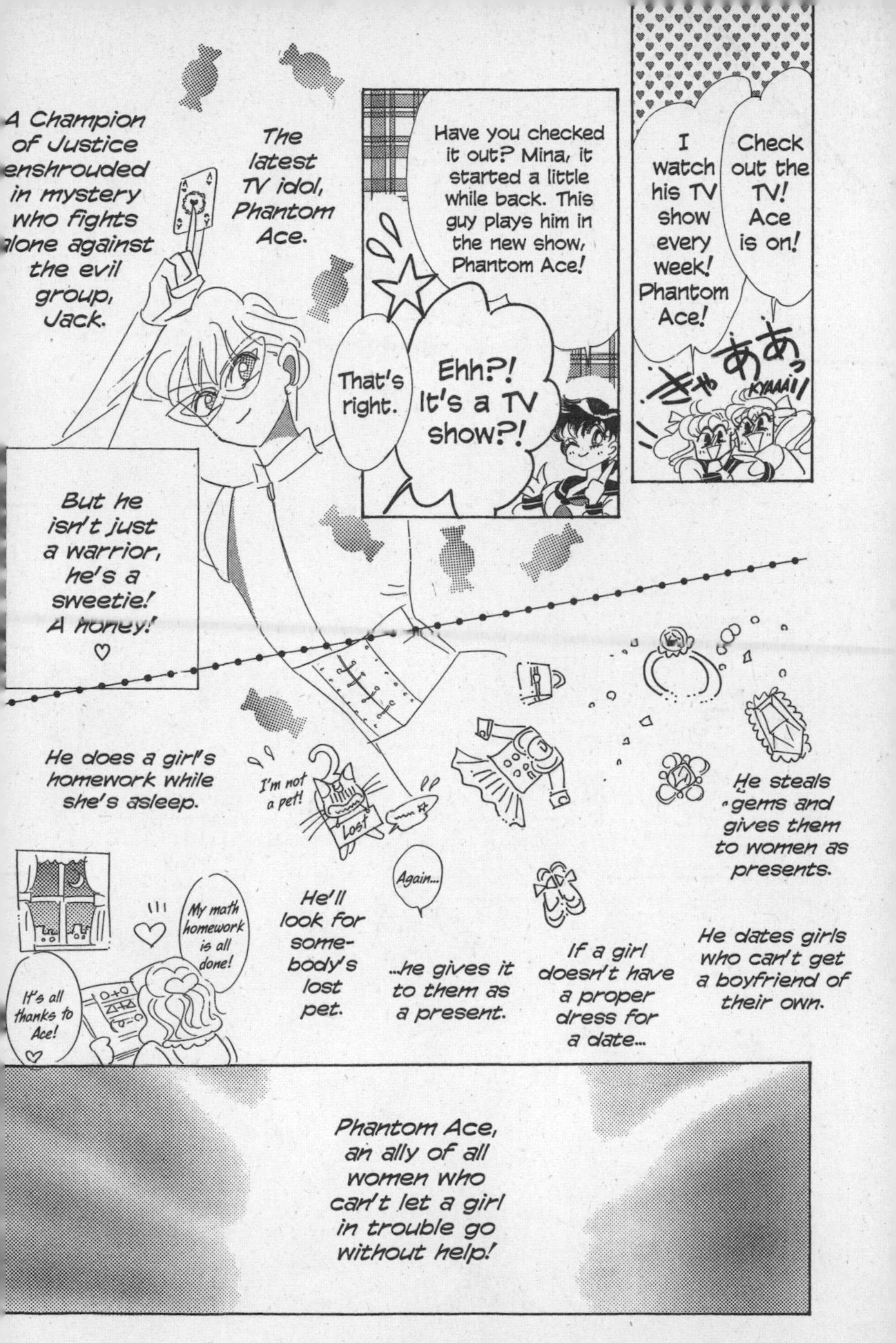
Check out the TV! Ace is on!
I watch his TV show every week! Phantom Ace!
きゃああっ
KYAAA!!
Have you checked it out? Mina, it started a little while back. This guy plays him in the new show, Phantom Ace!
Ehh?! It's a TV show?!
That's right.
The latest TV idol, Phantom Ace.
A Champion of Justice enshrouded in mystery who fights alone against the evil group, Jack.
But he isn't just a warrior, he's a sweetie! A honey! ♡
He steals gems and gives them to women as presents.
He dates girls who can't get a boyfriend of their own.
If a girl doesn't have a proper dress for a date...
...he gives it to them as a present.
Again...
He'll look for somebody's lost pet.
I'm not a pet!
Lost
He does a girl's homework while she's asleep.
My math homework is all done!
It's all thanks to Ace! ♡
Phantom Ace, an ally of all women who can't let a girl in trouble go without help!

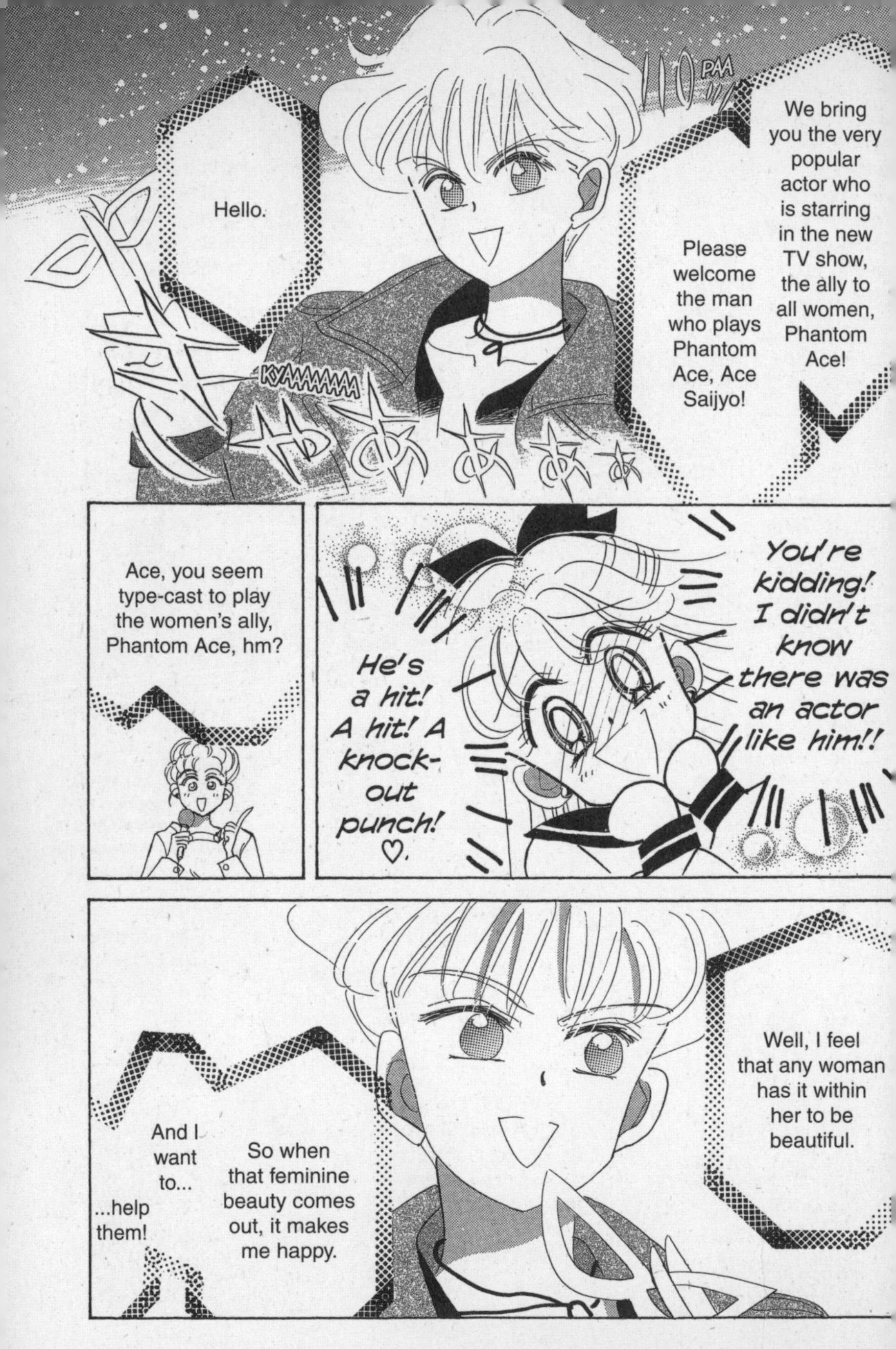
PAA
We bring you the very popular actor who is starring in the new TV show, the ally to all women, Phantom Ace!
Please welcome the man who plays Phantom Ace, Ace Saijyo!
Hello.
KYAAAAAAA
You're kidding! I didn't know there was an actor like him!!
He's a hit! A hit! A knock-out punch! ♡.
Ace, you seem type-cast to play the women's ally, Phantom Ace, hm?
Well, I feel that any woman has it within her to be beautiful.
So when that feminine beauty comes out, it makes me happy.
And I want to...
...help them!

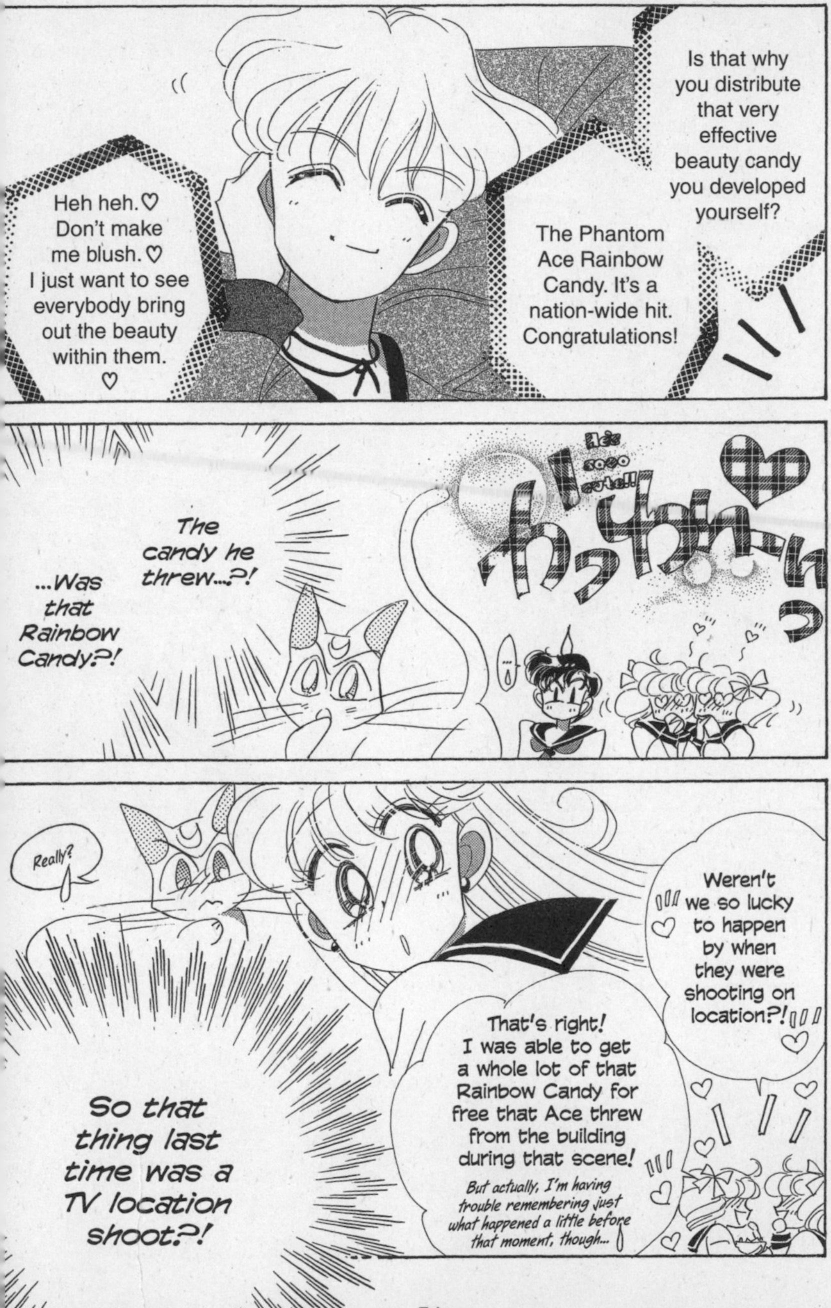
Is that why you distribute that very effective beauty candy you developed yourself?
The Phantom Ace Rainbow Candy. It's a nation-wide hit. Congratulations!
Heh heh.♡ Don't make me blush.♡ I just want to see everybody bring out the beauty within them. ♡
He's sooo cute!!
The candy he threw...?!
...Was that Rainbow Candy?!
Weren't we so lucky to happen by when they were shooting on location?!
That's right! I was able to get a whole lot of that Rainbow Candy for free that Ace threw from the building during that scene!
But actually, I'm having trouble remembering just what happened a little before that moment, though...
Really?
So that thing last time was a TV location shoot?!

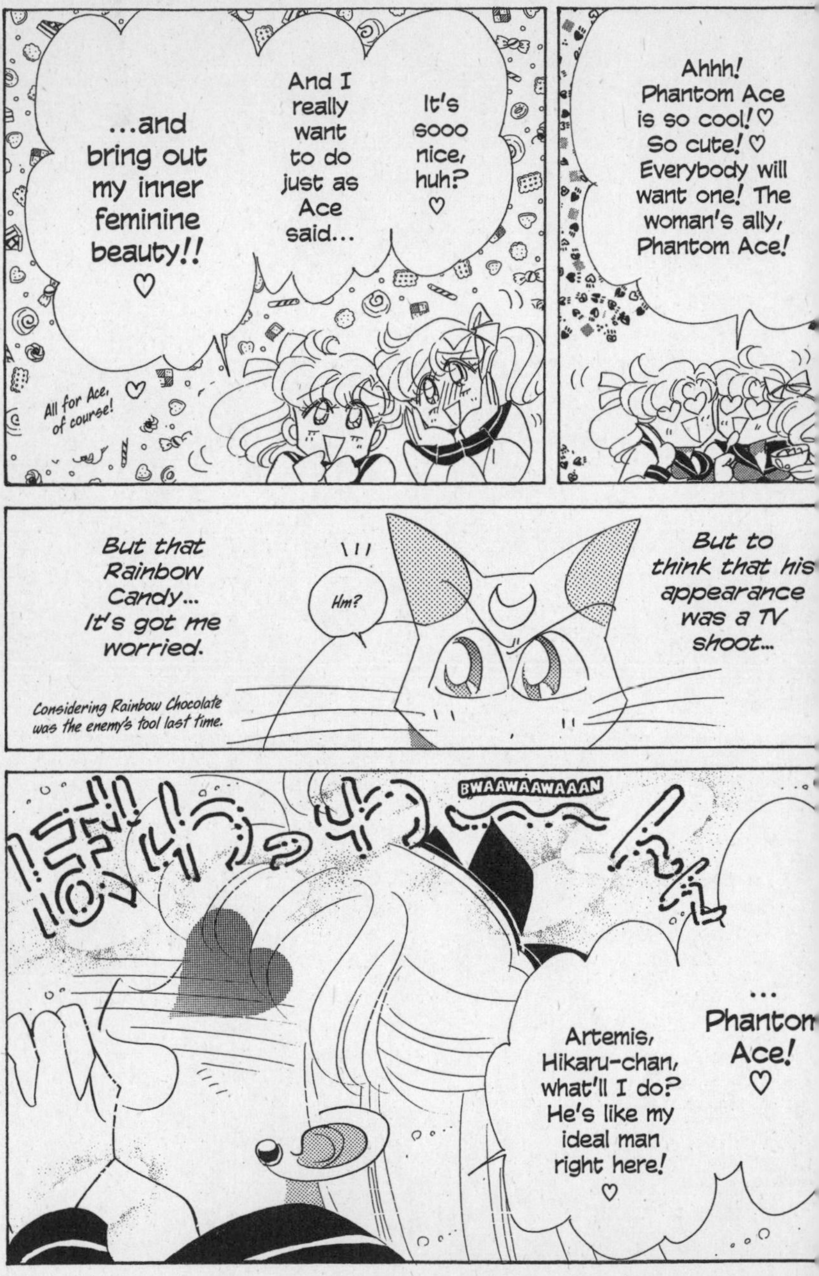
Ahhh! Phantom Ace is so cool! ♡ So cute! ♡ Everybody will want one! The woman's ally, Phantom Ace!
It's sooo nice, huh? ♡
And I really want to do just as Ace said...
...and bring out my inner feminine beauty!! ♡
All for Ace, of course! ♡
But to think that his appearance was a TV shoot...
Hm?
But that Rainbow Candy... It's got me worried.
Considering Rainbow Chocolate was the enemy's tool last time.
BWAAWAAWAAAN
...Phantom Ace! ♡
Artemis, Hikaru-chan, what'll I do? He's like my ideal man right here! ♡

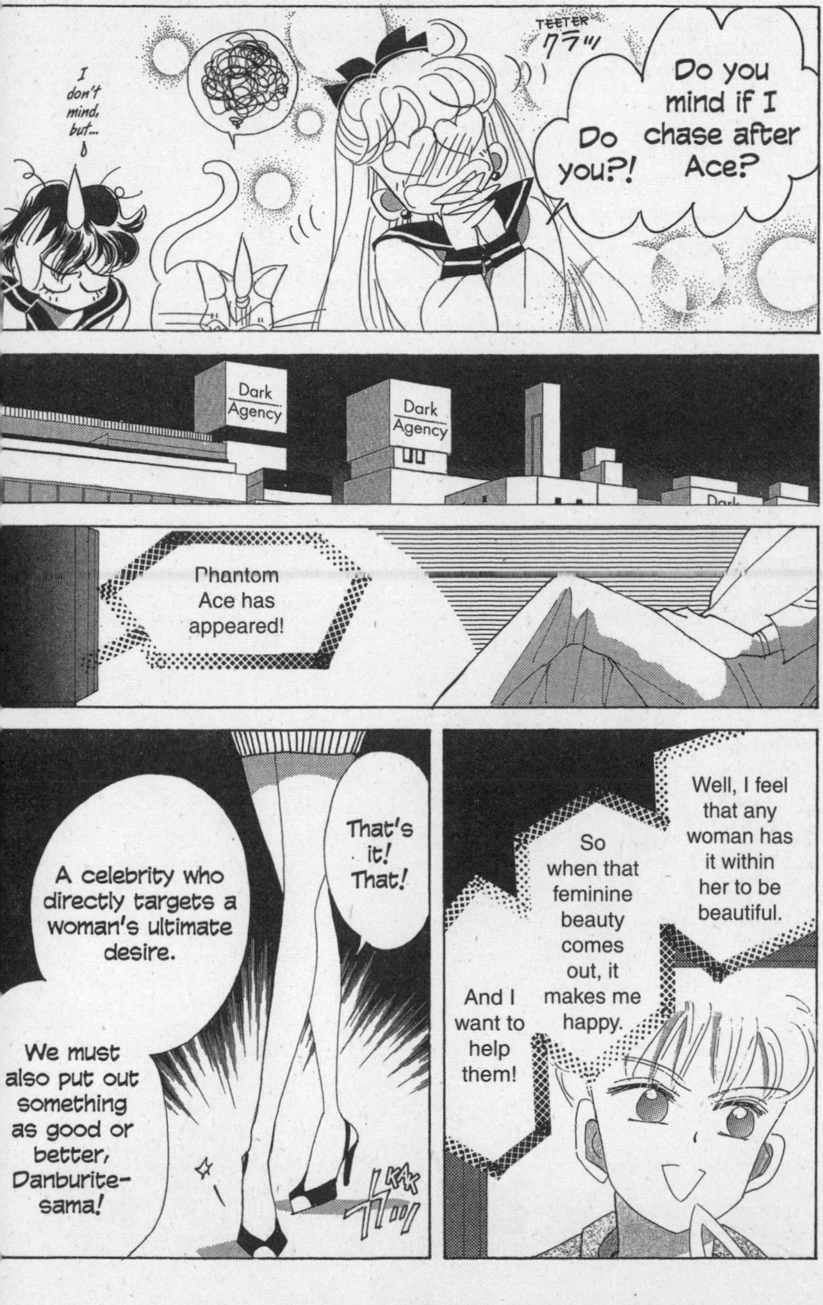

Do you mind if I chase after Ace?
Do you?!
TEETER
クラッ
I don't mind, but...
Dark Agency
Dark Agency
Phantom Ace has appeared!
Well, I feel that any woman has it within her to be beautiful.
So when that feminine beauty comes out, it makes me happy.
And I want to help them!
That's it! That!
A celebrity who directly targets a woman's ultimate desire.
We must also put out something as good or better, Danburite-sama!
KAK

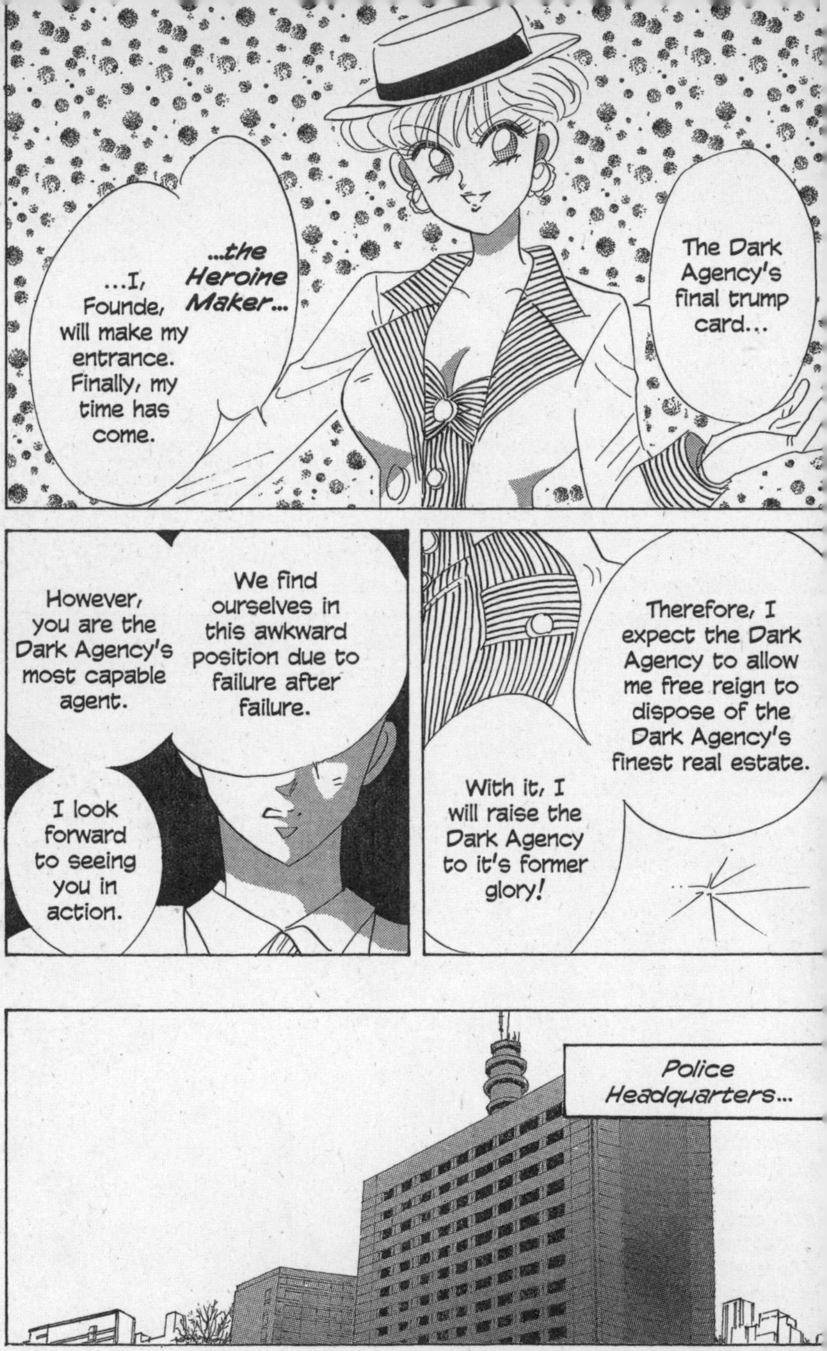
The Dark Agency's final trump card...
...the Heroine Maker...
...I, Founde, will make my entrance. Finally, my time has come.
Therefore, I expect the Dark Agency to allow me free reign to dispose of the Dark Agency's finest real estate.
With it, I will raise the Dark Agency to it's former glory!
We find ourselves in this awkward position due to failure after failure.
However, you are the Dark Agency's most capable agent.
I look forward to seeing you in action.
Police Headquarters...

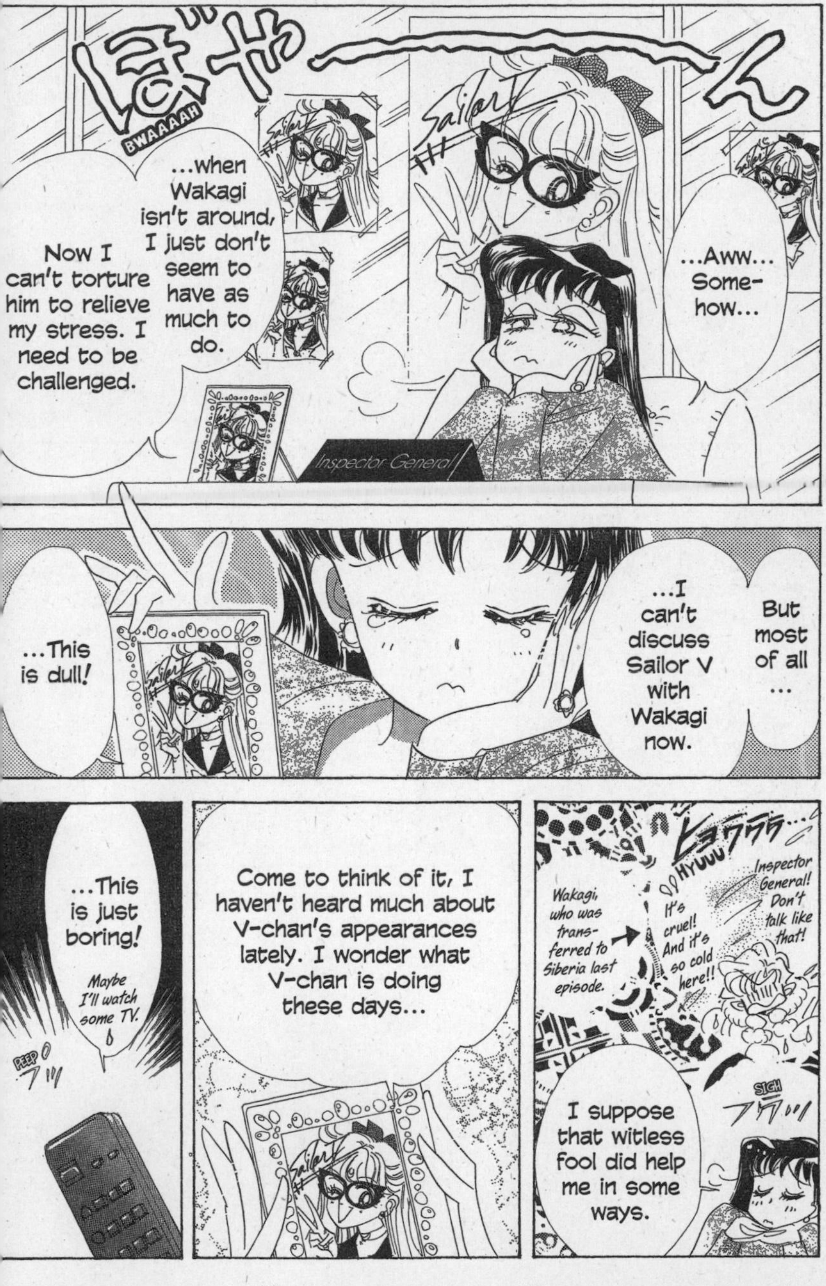
ぼやーーーん
BWAAAAH
...Aww... Somehow...
...when Wakagi isn't around, I just don't seem to have as much to do.
Now I can't torture him to relieve my stress. I need to be challenged.
Inspector-General
But most of all ...
...I can't discuss Sailor V with Wakagi now.
...This is dull!
ヒョワララ...
HYUUU
Inspector General! Don't talk like that!
It's cruel! And it's so cold here!!
Wakagi, who was transferred to Siberia last episode.
SIGH
I suppose that witless fool did help me in some ways.
Come to think of it, I haven't heard much about V-chan's appearances lately. I wonder what V-chan is doing these days...
...This is just boring!
Maybe I'll watch some TV.
PEEP

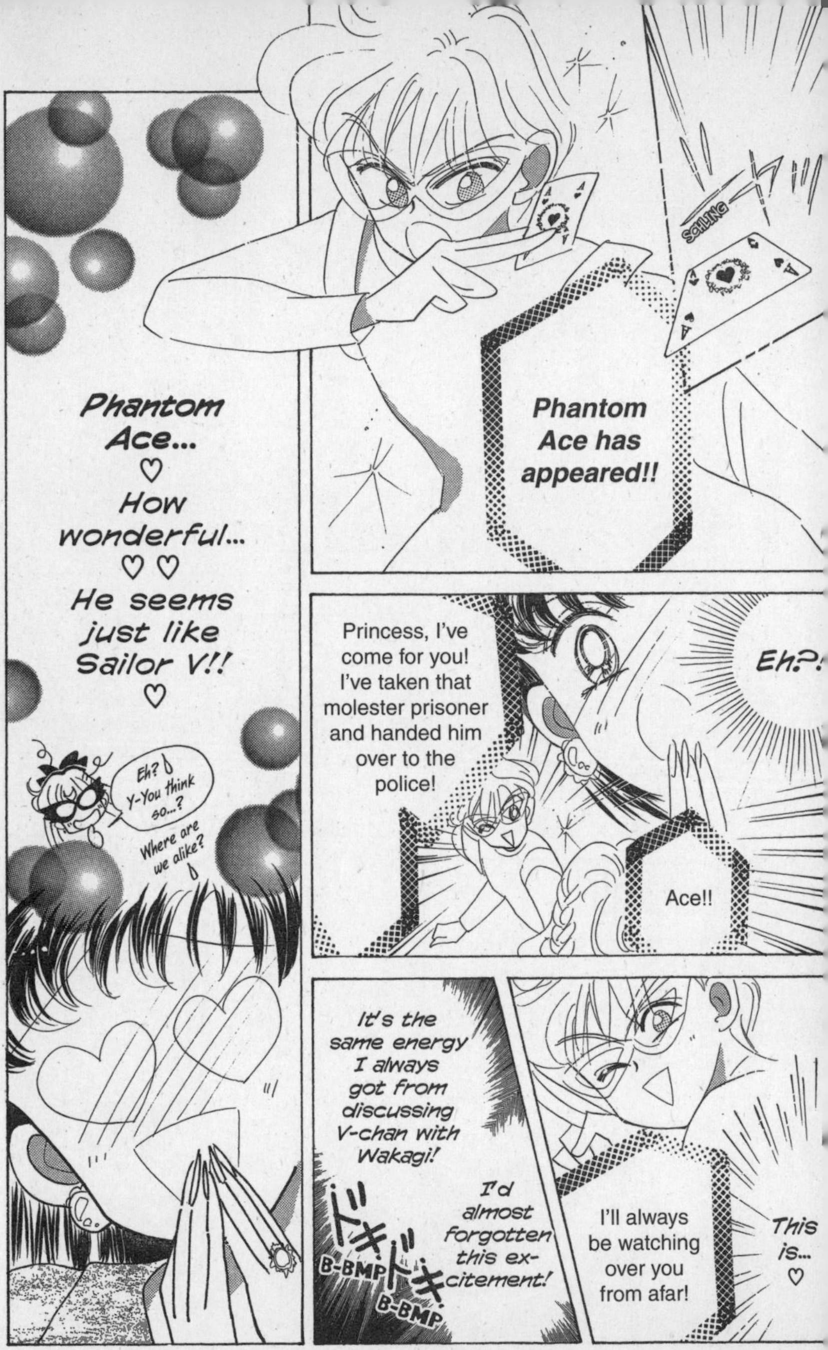
SCHLING
Phantom Ace has appeared!!
Princess, I've come for you! I've taken that molester prisoner and handed him over to the police!
Eh?!
Ace!!
This is... ♡
I'll always be watching over you from afar!
It's the same energy I always got from discussing V-chan with Wakagi!
I'd almost forgotten this ex-citement!
ドキドキ
B-BMP
B-BMP
Phantom Ace... ♡ How wonderful... ♡ ♡ He seems just like Sailor V!! ♡
Eh? Y-You think so...?
Where are we alike?

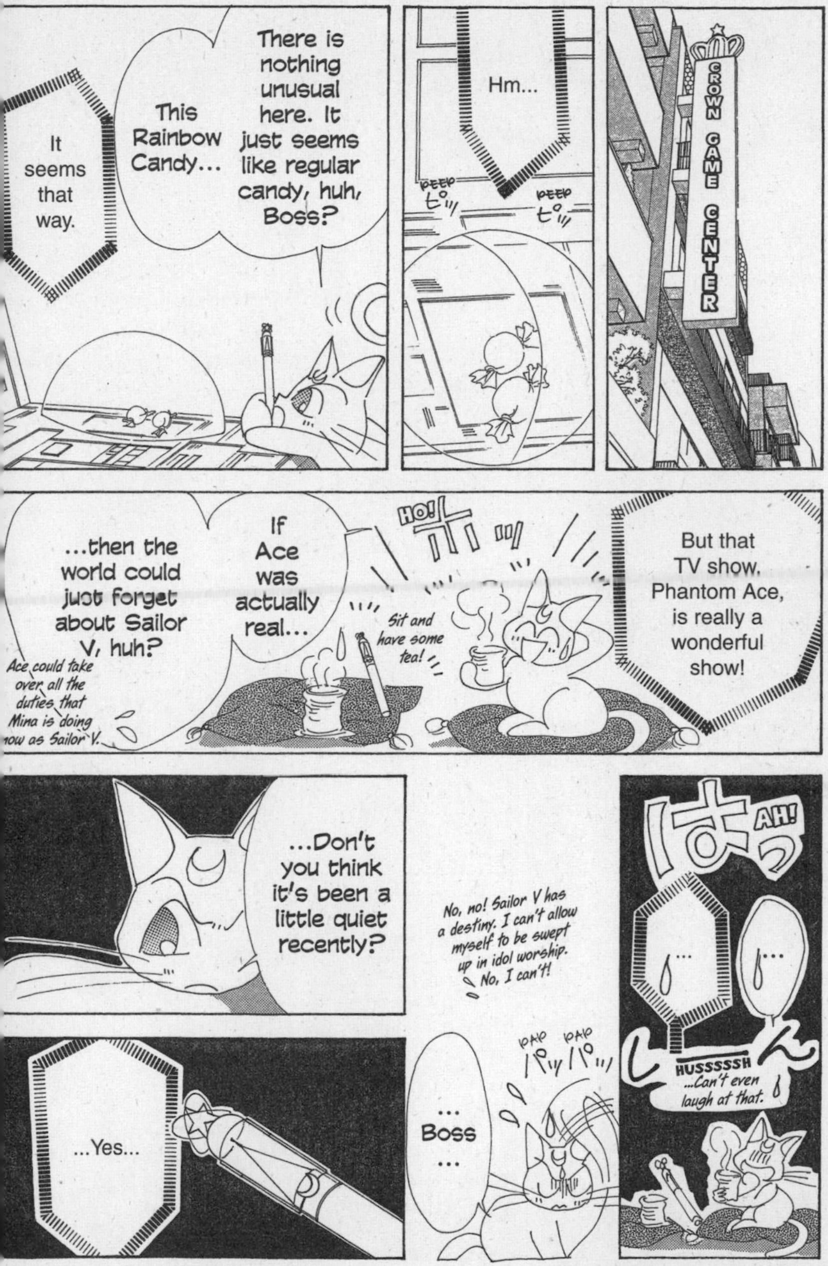
CROWN GAME CENTER
Hm...
PEEP
PEEP
There is nothing unusual here. It just seems like regular candy, huh, Boss?
This Rainbow Candy...
It seems that way.
But that TV show, Phantom Ace, is really a wonderful show!
HO!
Sit and have some tea!
If Ace was actually real...
...then the world could just forget about Sailor V, huh?
Ace could take over all the duties that Mina is doing now as Sailor V.
AH!
...
...
HUSSSSSH
...Can't even laugh at that.
...Don't you think it's been a little quiet recently?
No, no! Sailor V has a destiny. I can't allow myself to be swept up in idol worship. No, I can't!
PAP PAP
... Boss ...
...Yes...

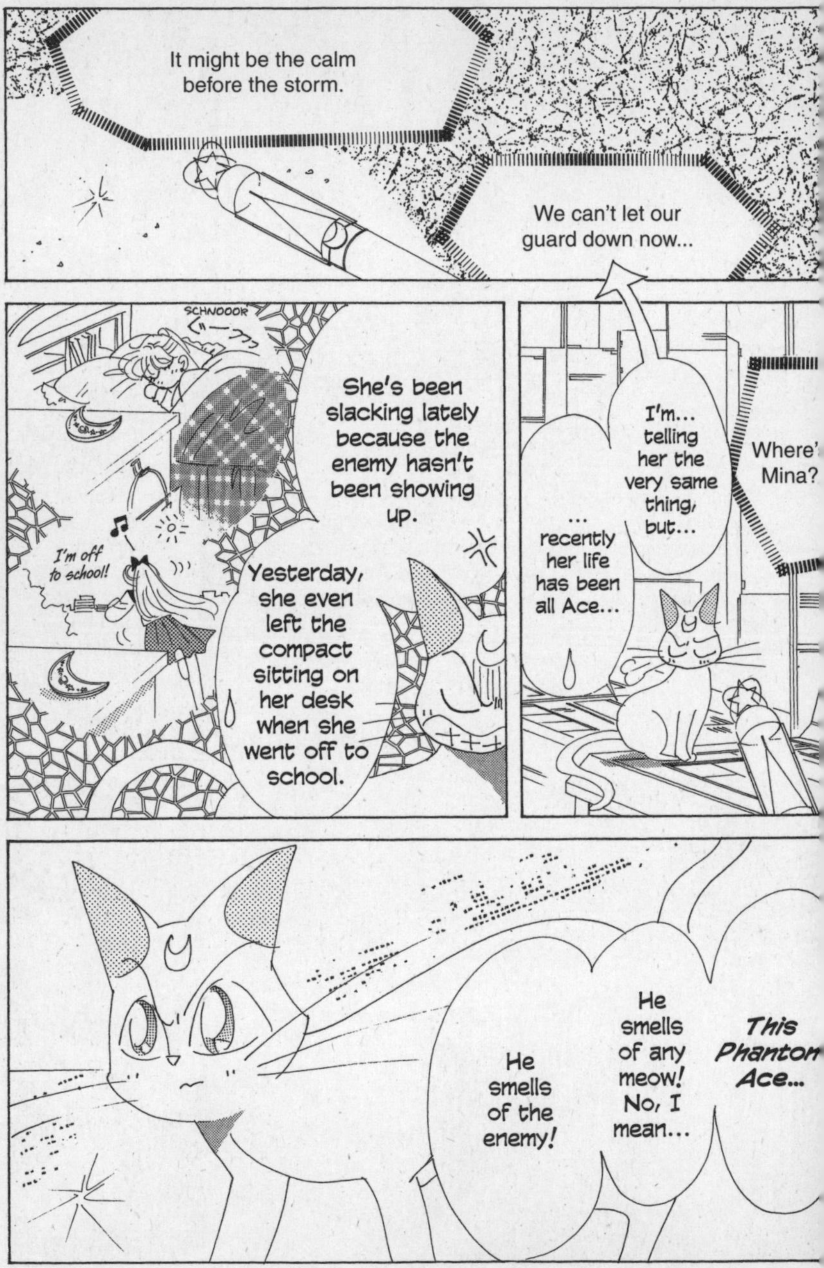

It might be the calm before the storm.
We can't let our guard down now...
Where'
Mina?
I'm... telling her the very same thing, but...
... recently her life has been all Ace...
SCHNOOOR
She's been slacking lately because the enemy hasn't been showing up.
I'm off to school!
Yesterday, she even left the compact sitting on her desk when she went off to school.
This Phanton Ace...
He smells of any meow! No, I mean...
He smells of the enemy!

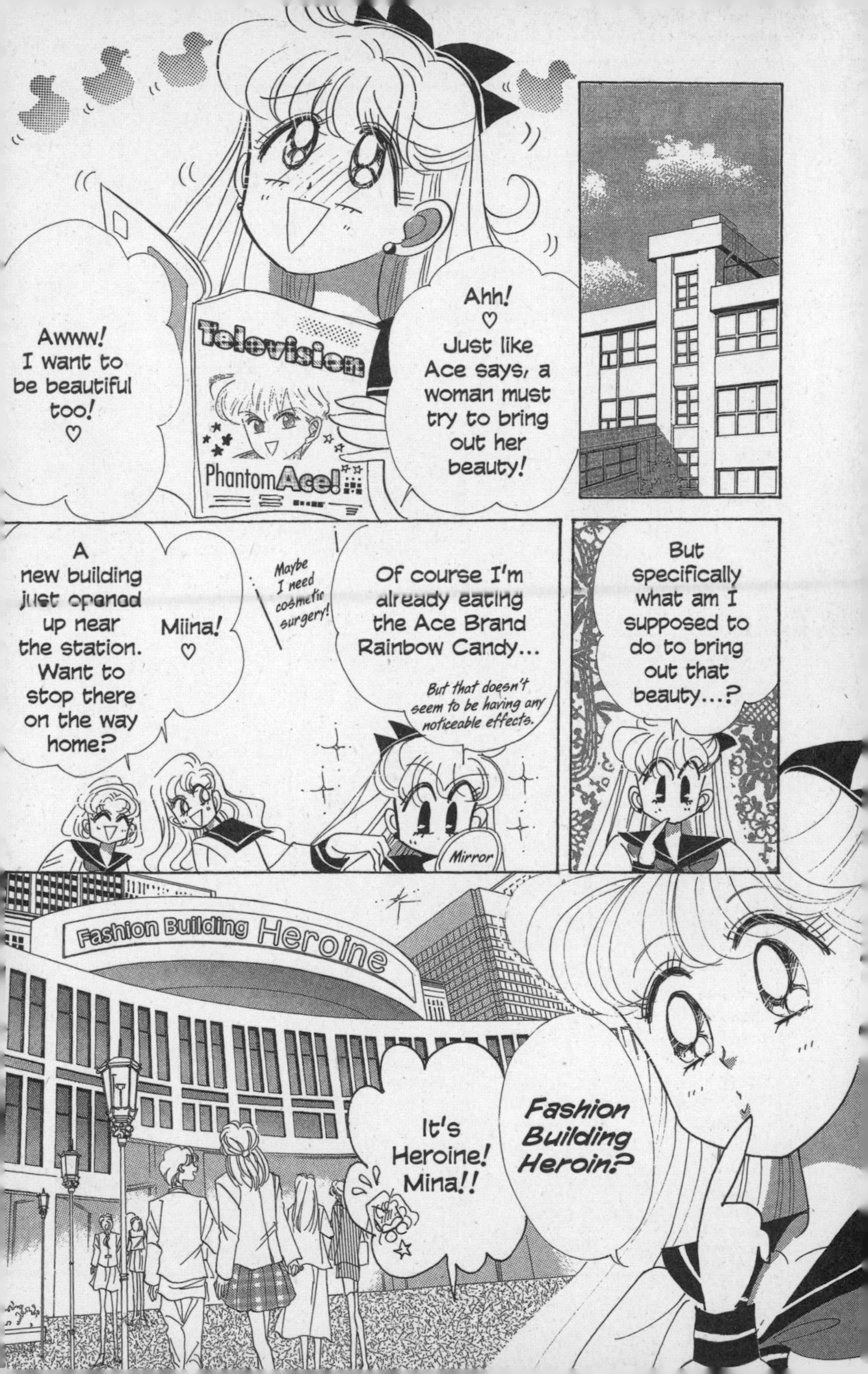
Ahh! ♡ Just like Ace says, a woman must try to bring out her beauty!
Television
Phantom Ace!
Awww! I want to be beautiful too! ♡
But specifically what am I supposed to do to bring out that beauty...?
Of course I'm already eating the Ace Brand Rainbow Candy...
But that doesn't seem to be having any noticeable effects.
Mirror
Maybe I need cosmetic surgery!
Miina! ♡
A new building just opened up near the station. Want to stop there on the way home?
Fashion Building Heroine
Fashion Building Heroin?
It's Heroine! Mina!!

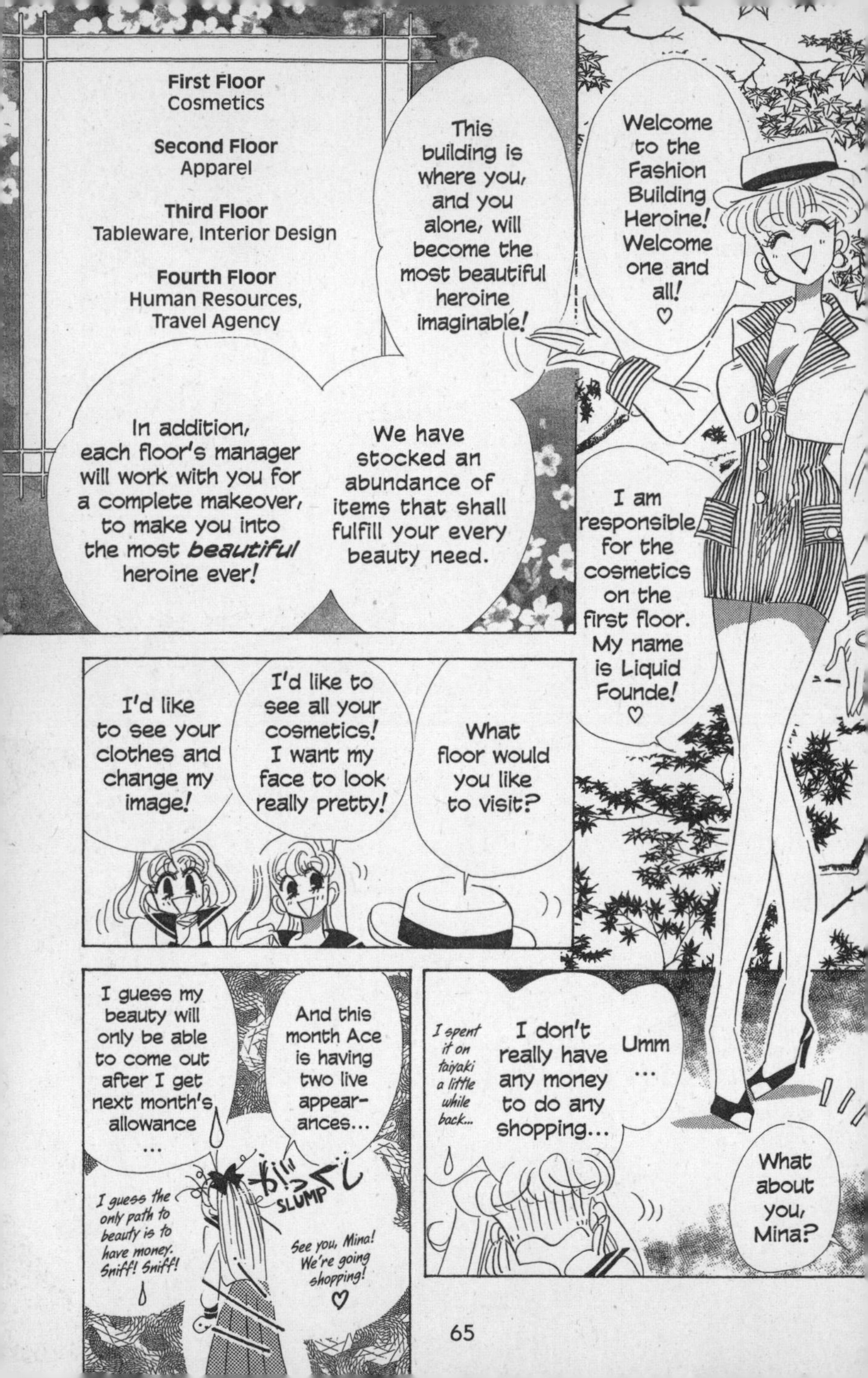
Welcome to the Fashion Building Heroine! Welcome one and all! ♡
I am responsible for the cosmetics on the first floor. My name is Liquid Founde! ♡
What about you, Mina?
This building is where you, and you alone, will become the most beautiful heroine imaginable!
We have stocked an abundance of items that shall fulfill your every beauty need.
In addition, each floor's manager will work with you for a complete makeover, to make you into the most *beautiful* heroine ever!
First Floor Cosmetics
Second Floor Apparel
Third Floor Tableware, Interior Design
Fourth Floor Human Resources, Travel Agency
What floor would you like to visit?
I'd like to see all your cosmetics! I want my face to look really pretty!
I'd like to see your clothes and change my image!
Umm ...
I don't really have any money to do any shopping...
I spent it on taiyaki a little while back...
And this month Ace is having two live appear-ances...
I guess my beauty will only be able to come out after I get next month's allowance ...
SLUMP
See you, Mina! We're going shopping! ♡
I guess the only path to beauty is to have money. Sniff! Sniff!

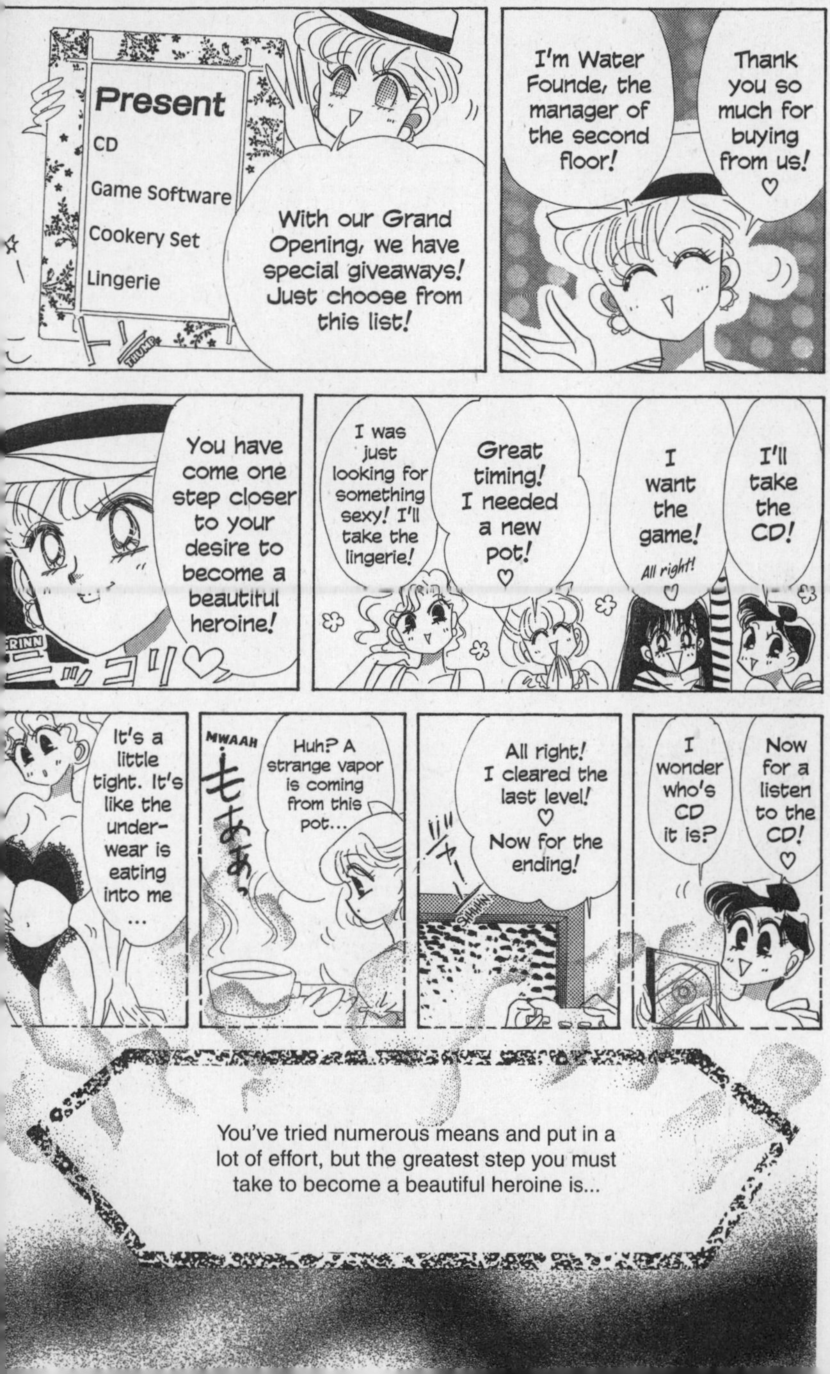
Thank you so much for buying from us! ♡
I'm Water Founde, the manager of the second floor!
Present
CD
Game Software
Cookery Set
Lingerie
With our Grand Opening, we have special giveaways! Just choose from this list!
THUMP
I'll take the CD!
I want the game!
All right! ♡
Great timing! I needed a new pot! ♡
I was just looking for something sexy! I'll take the lingerie!
You have come one step closer to your desire to become a beautiful heroine!
RINN
Now for a listen to the CD! ♡
I wonder who's CD it is?
All right! I cleared the last level! ♡ Now for the ending!
SHIIIIN
Huh? A strange vapor is coming from this pot...
MWAAH
It's a little tight. It's like the under-wear is eating into me ...
You've tried numerous means and put in a lot of effort, but the greatest step you must take to become a beautiful heroine is...

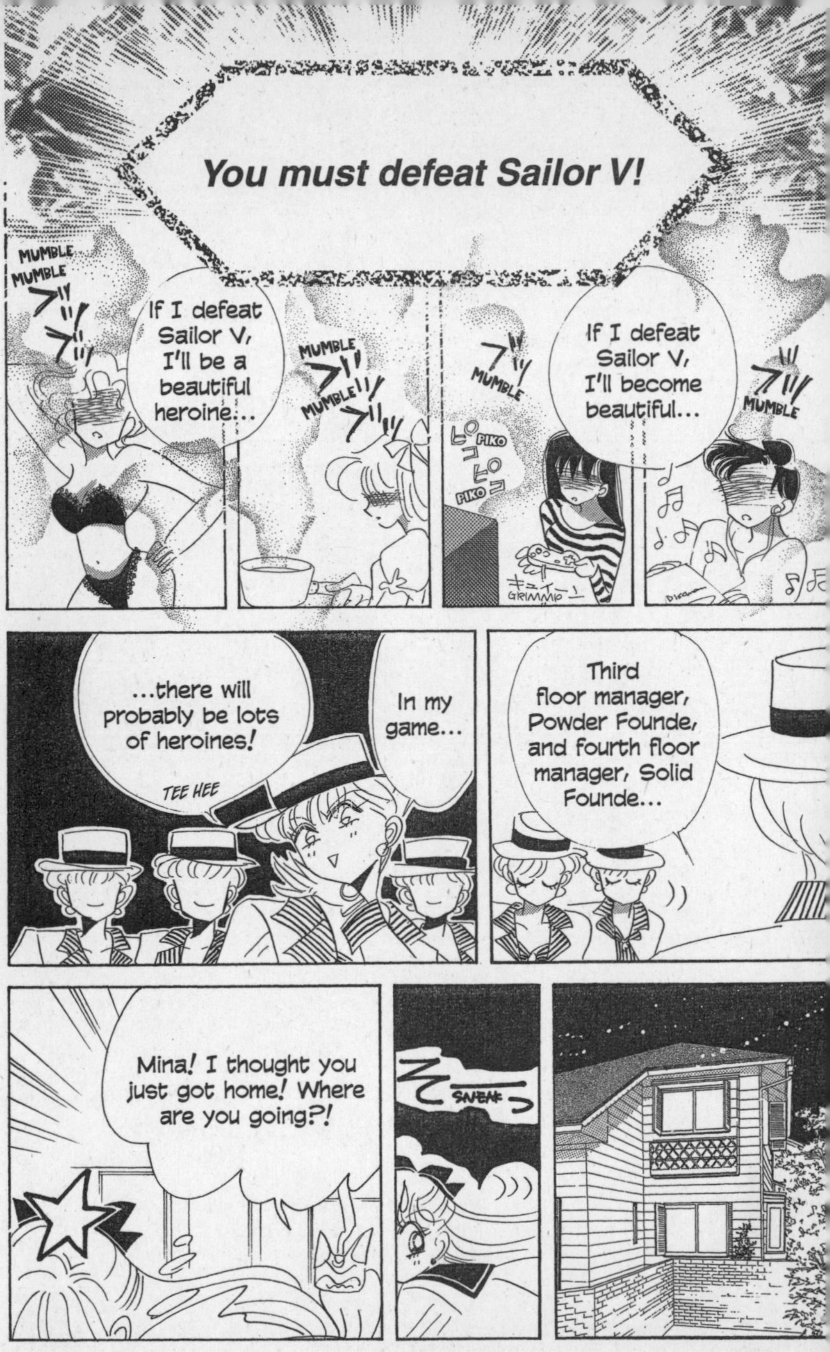
You must defeat Sailor V!
MUMBLE
If I defeat Sailor V, I'll become beautiful...
PIKO
PIKO
GRIMMP
MUMBLE
MUMBLE
MUMBLE
If I defeat Sailor V, I'll be a beautiful heroine...
MUMBLE
MUMBLE
Third floor manager, Powder Founde, and fourth floor manager, Solid Founde...
In my game...
...there will probably be lots of heroines!
TEE HEE
SNEAK
Mina! I thought you just got home! Where are you going?!

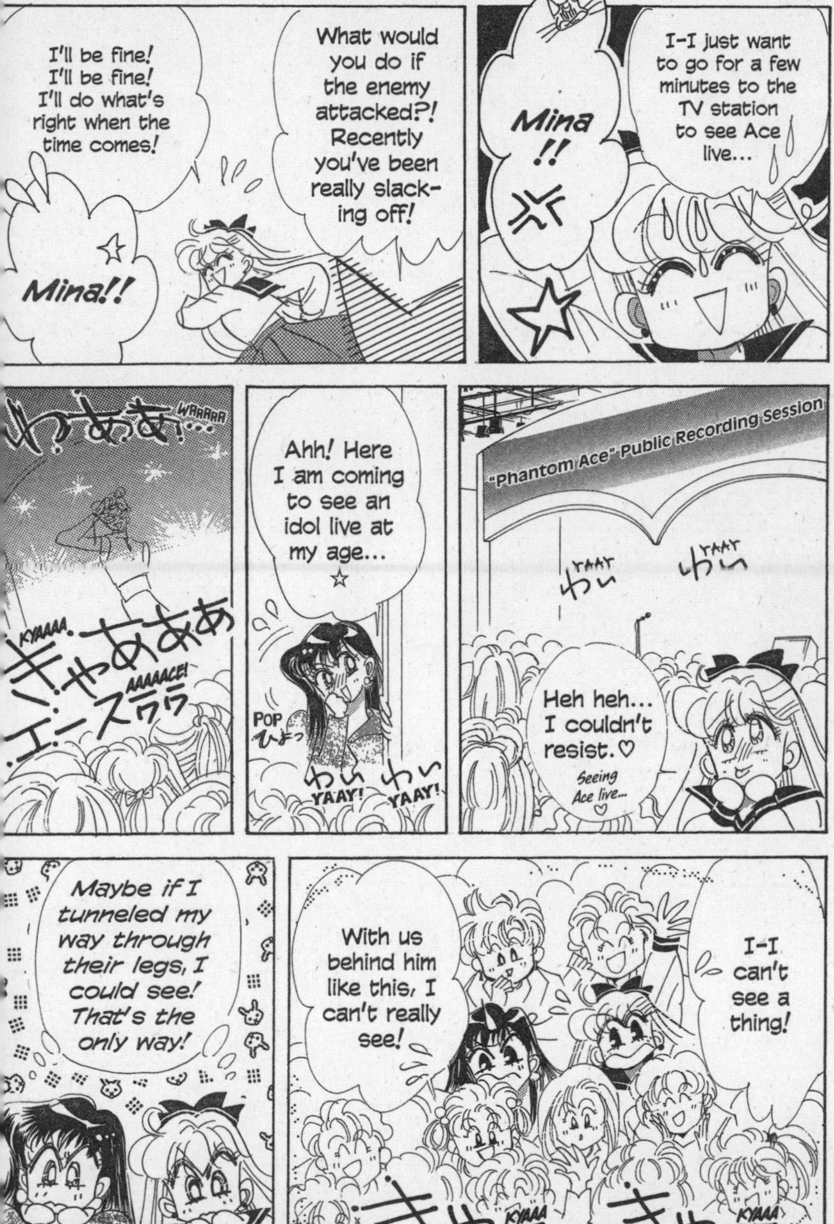

I-I just want to go for a few minutes to the TV station to see Ace live...
Mina!!
What would you do if the enemy attacked?! Recently you've been really slacking off!
I'll be fine! I'll be fine! I'll do what's right when the time comes!
Mina!!
"Phantom Ace" Public Recording Session
YAAY
YAAY
Heh heh... I couldn't resist. ♡
Seeing Ace live... ♡
Ahh! Here I am coming to see an idol live at my age... ☆
POP
YAAY!
YAAY!
WAAAAA
KYAAAA
AAAAACE!
I-I can't see a thing!
With us behind him like this, I can't really see!
KYAAA
KYAAA
Maybe if I tunneled my way through their legs, I could see! That's the only way!

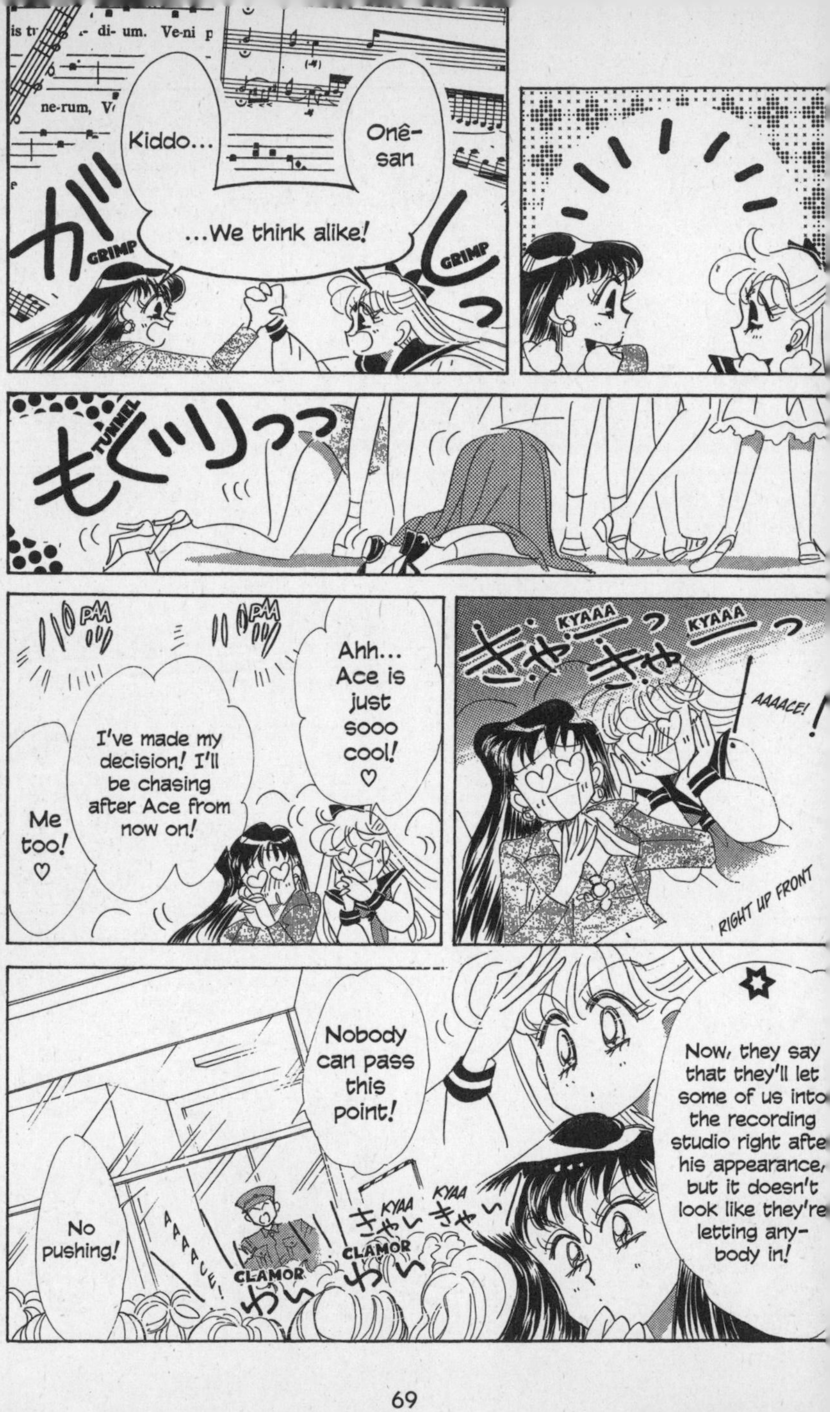
Onê-san
Kiddo...
...We think alike!
GRIMP
GRIMP
TUNNEL
もぐりっっ
KYAAA
きゃーっ
KYAAA
きゃーっ
AAAACE!
RIGHT UP FRONT
Ahh... Ace is just sooo cool! ♡
PAA
PAA
I've made my decision! I'll be chasing after Ace from now on!
Me too! ♡
Now, they say that they'll let some of us into the recording studio right afte his appearance, but it doesn't look like they'r letting any-body in!
Nobody can pass this point!
KYAA
きゃいきゃい
CLAMOR
わいわい
CLAMOR
AAAACE!
No pushing!

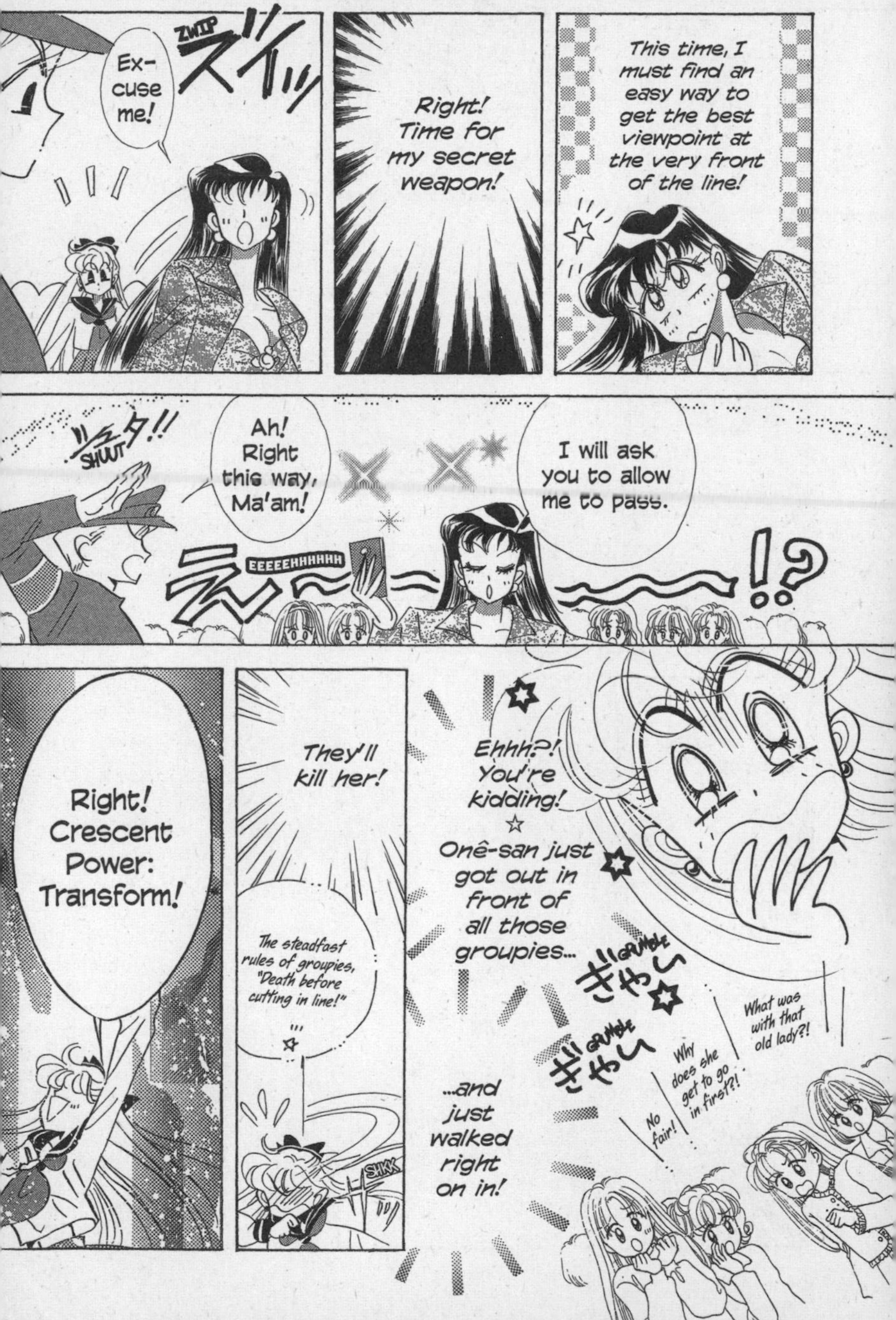
This time, I must find an easy way to get the best viewpoint at the very front of the line!
Right! Time for my secret weapon!
ZWIP
Ex-cuse me!
I will ask you to allow me to pass.
EEEEEHHHHHH
!?
Ah! Right this way, Ma'am!
SHUUT
Ehhh?! You're kidding! ☆ Onê-san just got out in front of all those groupies...
...and just walked right on in!
GRUMBLE
GRUMBLE
What was with that old lady?!
Why does she get to go in first?!
No fair!
They'll kill her!
The steadfast rules of groupies, "Death before cutting in line!"
SHKK
Right! Crescent Power: Transform!

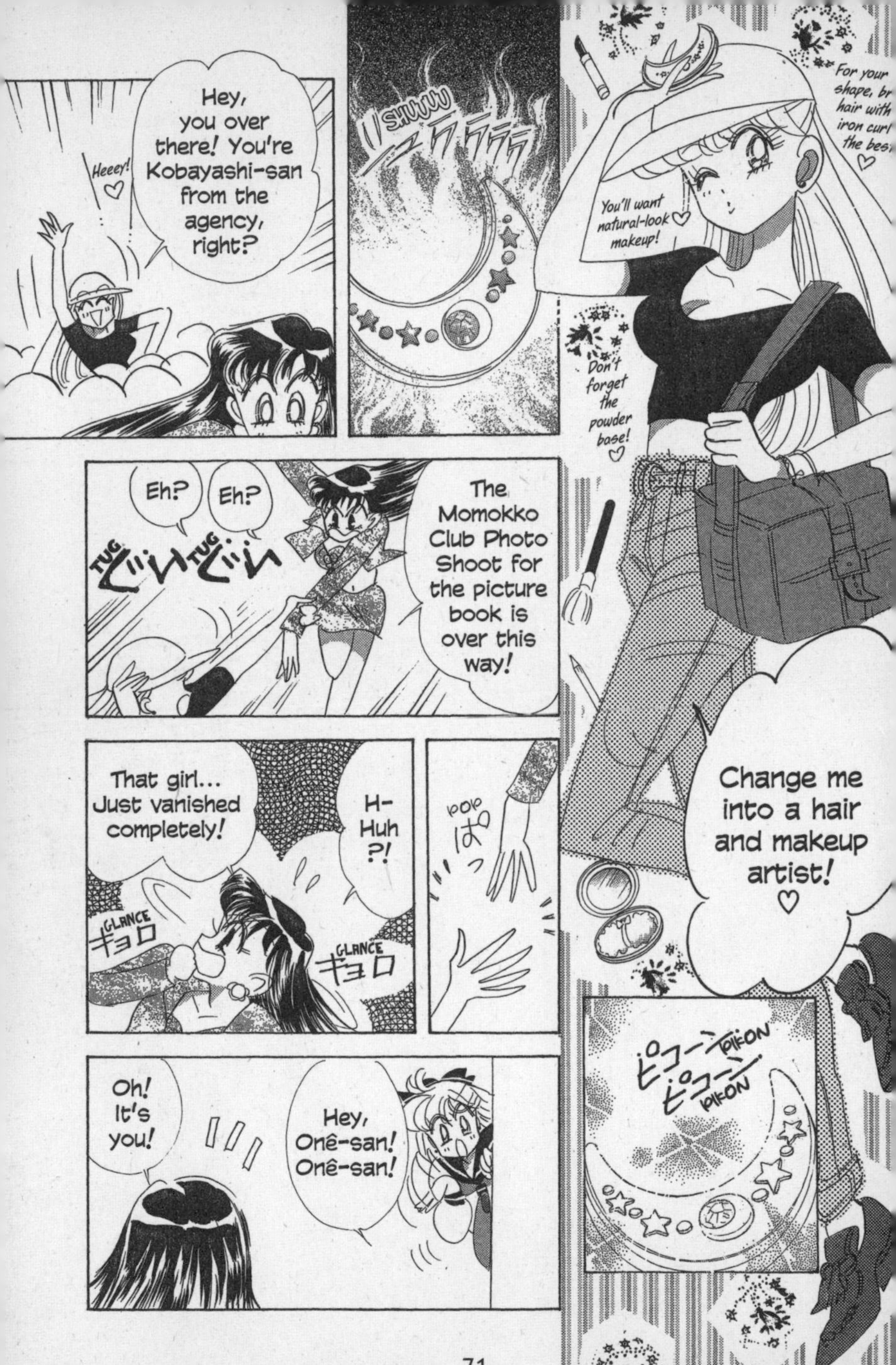
For your shape, br hair with iron curl the bes ♡
You'll want natural-look makeup! ♡
Don't forget the powder base! ♡
Change me into a hair and makeup artist! ♡
PIKON
PIKON
SHUUUU
Hey, you over there! You're Kobayashi-san from the agency, right?
Heeey! ♡
The Momokko Club Photo Shoot for the picture book is over this way!
Eh?
Eh?
TUG TUG
POP
H-Huh?!
That girl... Just vanished completely!
GLANCE
GLANCE
Hey, Onê-san! Onê-san!
Oh! It's you!

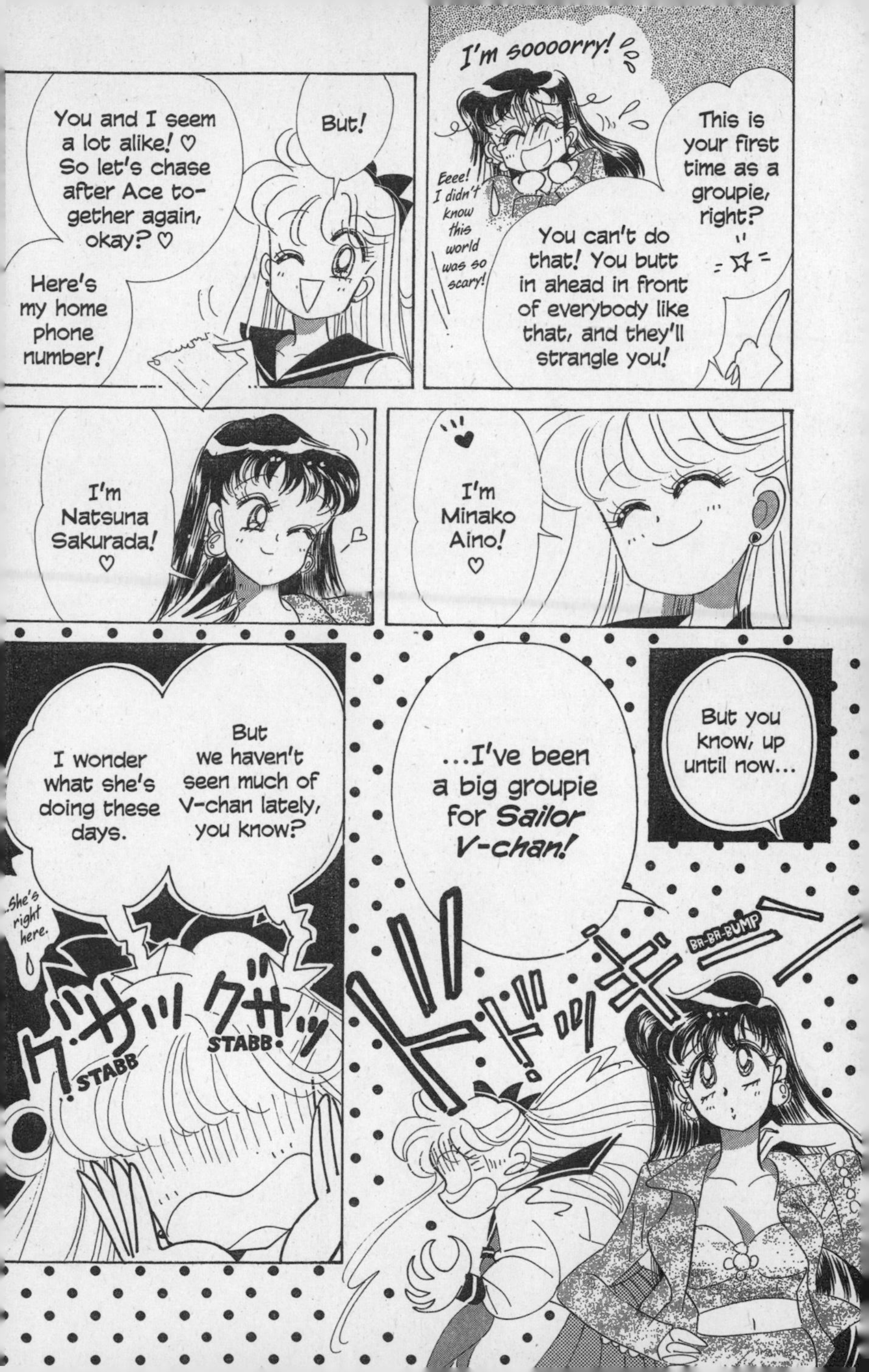
This is your first time as a groupie, right?
You can't do that! You butt in ahead in front of everybody like that, and they'll strangle you!
I'm soooorry!
Eeee! I didn't know this world was so scary!
But!
You and I seem a lot alike! ♡ So let's chase after Ace together again, okay? ♡
Here's my home phone number!
I'm Minako Aino! ♡
I'm Natsuna Sakurada! ♡
But you know, up until now...
...I've been a big groupie for Sailor V-chan!
BA-BA-BUMP
But we haven't seen much of V-chan lately, you know?
I wonder what she's doing these days.
...She's right here.
グサッ
STABB
グサッ
STABB

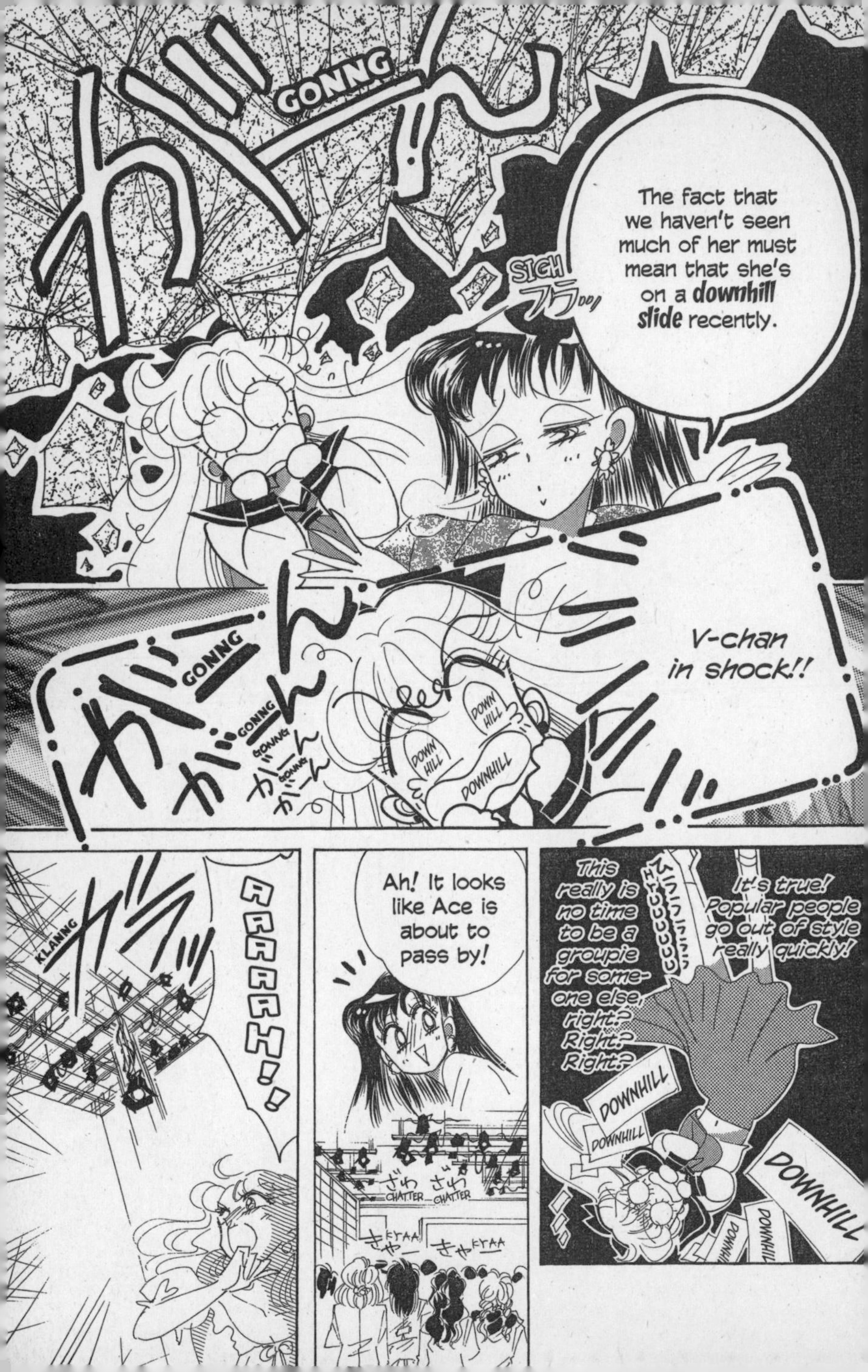
The fact that we haven't seen much of her must mean that she's on a **downhill slide** recently.
SIGH フラ
GONNG
V-chan in shock!!
GONNG
GONNG
GONNG
GONNG
DOWN HILL
DOWN HILL
DOWNHILL
It's true! Popular people go out of style really quickly!
This really is no time to be a groupie for some-one else, right? Right? Right?
DOWNHILL
DOWNHILL
DOWNHILL
DOWNHILL
DOWNHILL
Ah! It looks like Ace is about to pass by!
CHATTER CHATTER
KYAA KYAA
AAAAAAH!!
KLANNG

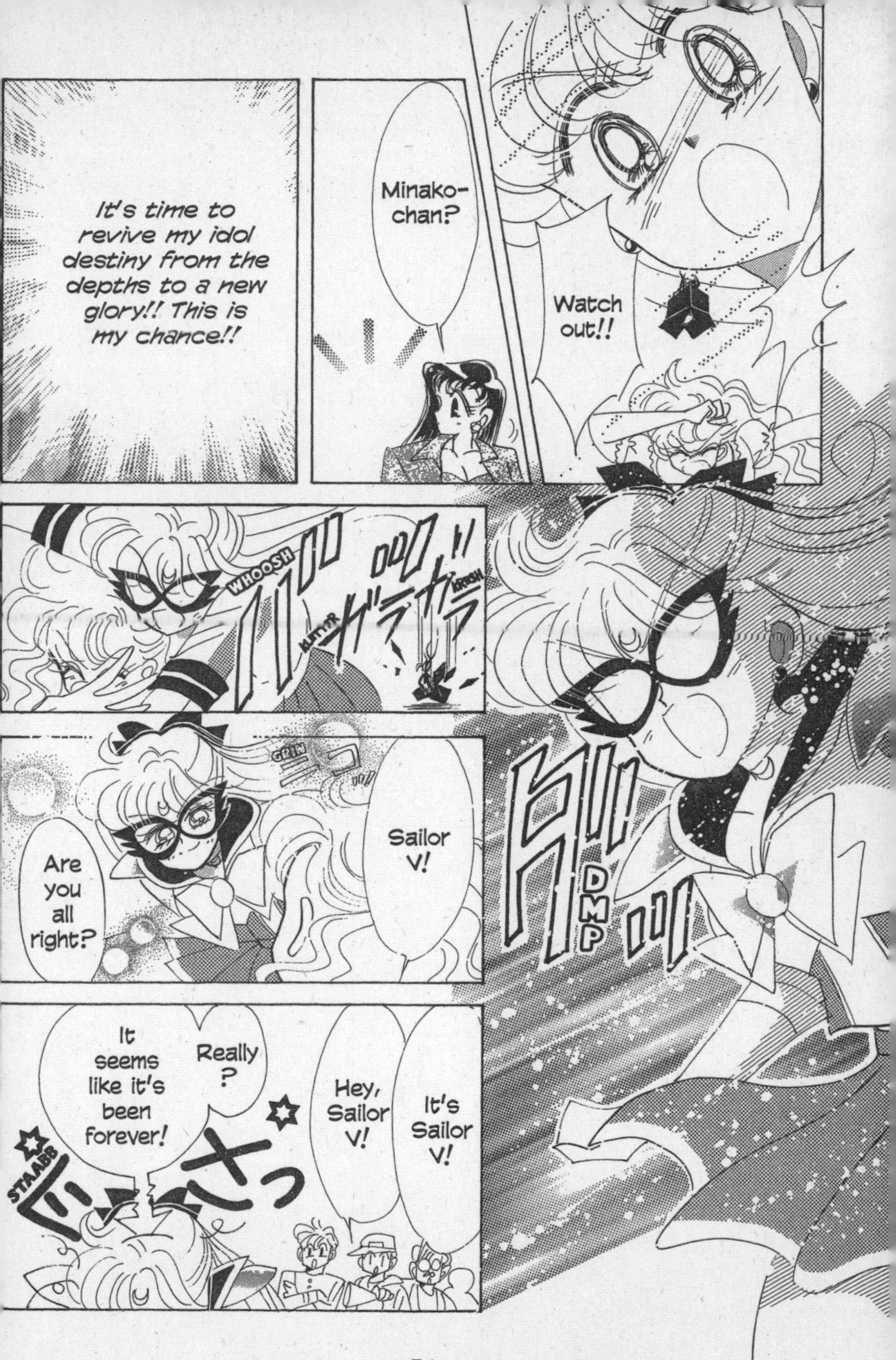
Watch out!!
Minako-chan?
It's time to revive my idol destiny from the depths to a new glory!! This is my chance!!
DMP
WHOOSH
KRRSH
ガラガラ
Sailor V!
GRIN
Are you all right?
It's Sailor V!
Hey, Sailor V!
Really?
It seems like it's been forever!
STAABB

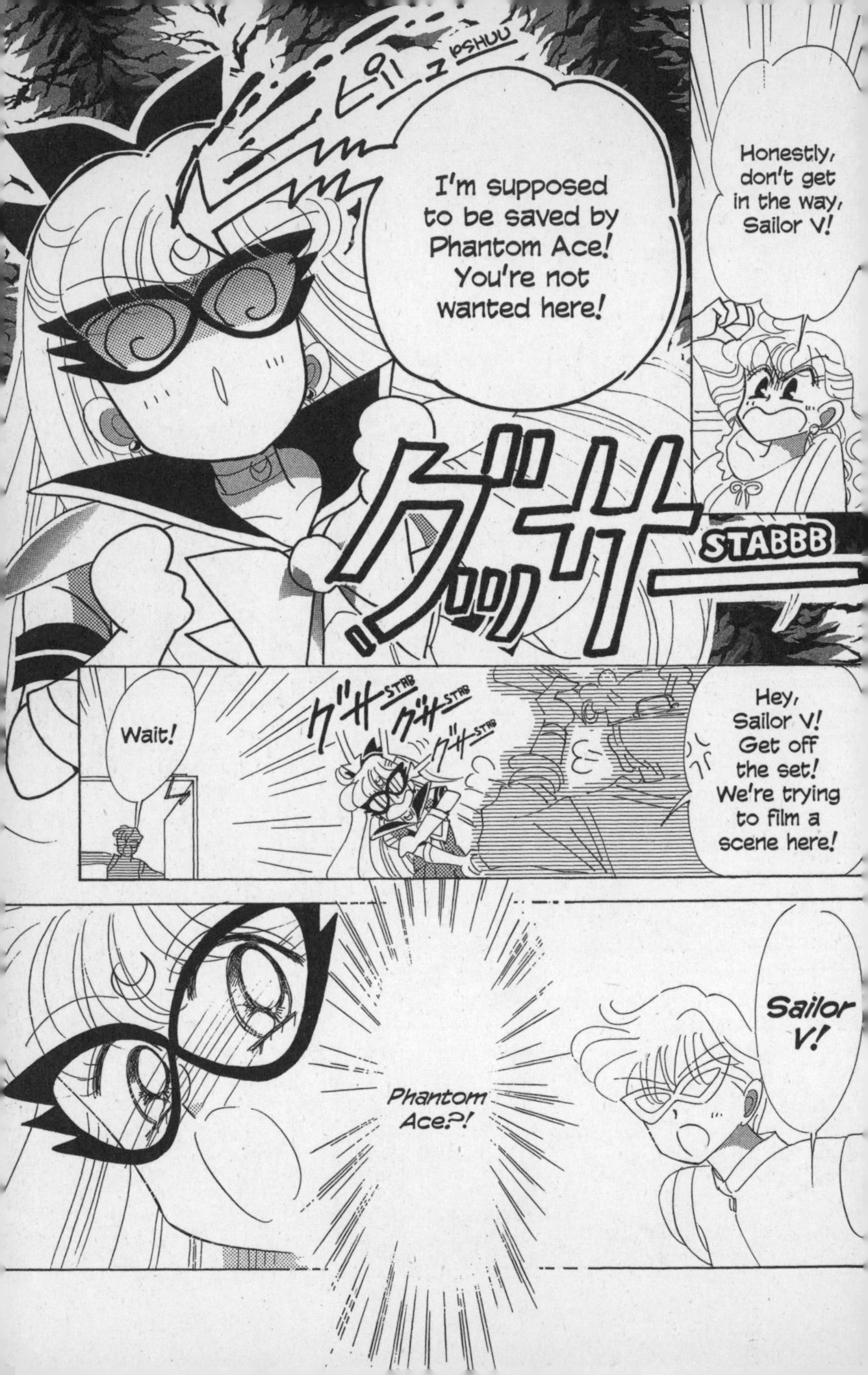
Honestly, don't get in the way, Sailor V!
PSHUU
I'm supposed to be saved by Phantom Ace! You're not wanted here!
STABBB
Hey, Sailor V! Get off the set! We're trying to film a scene here!
STAB
STAB
STAB
Wait!
Sailor V!
Phantom Ace?!

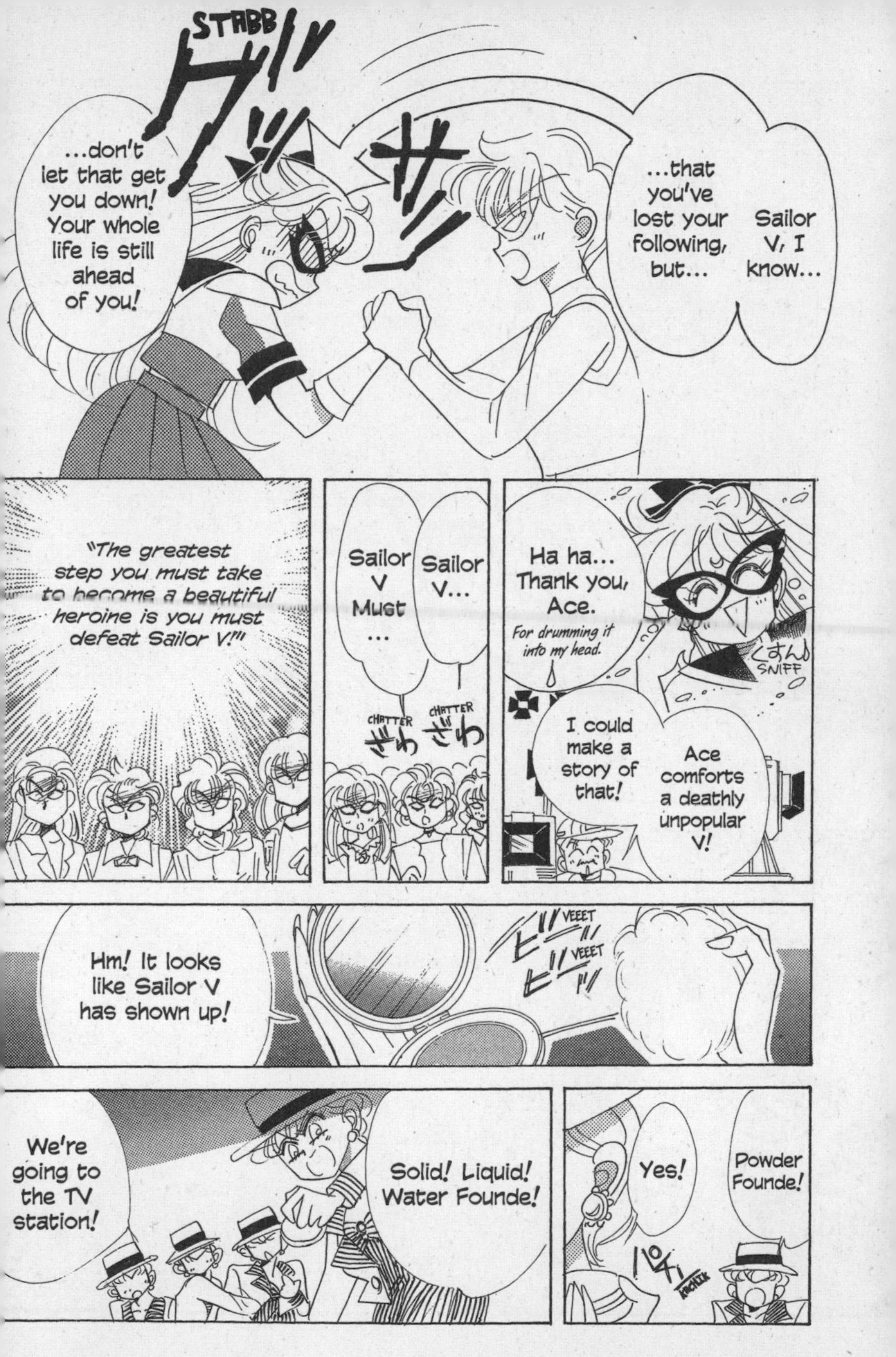
STABB
Sailor V, I know...
...that you've lost your following, but...
...don't let that get you down! Your whole life is still ahead of you!
Ha ha... Thank you, Ace.
For drumming it into my head.
くすん
SNIFF
Ace comforts a deathly unpopular V!
I could make a story of that!
Sailor V...
Sailor V Must ...
CHATTER
CHATTER
ざわ ざわ
"The greatest step you must take to become a beautiful heroine is you must defeat Sailor V!"
VEEET
VEEET
Hm! It looks like Sailor V has shown up!
Powder Founde!
Yes!
Solid! Liquid! Water Founde!
We're going to the TV station!

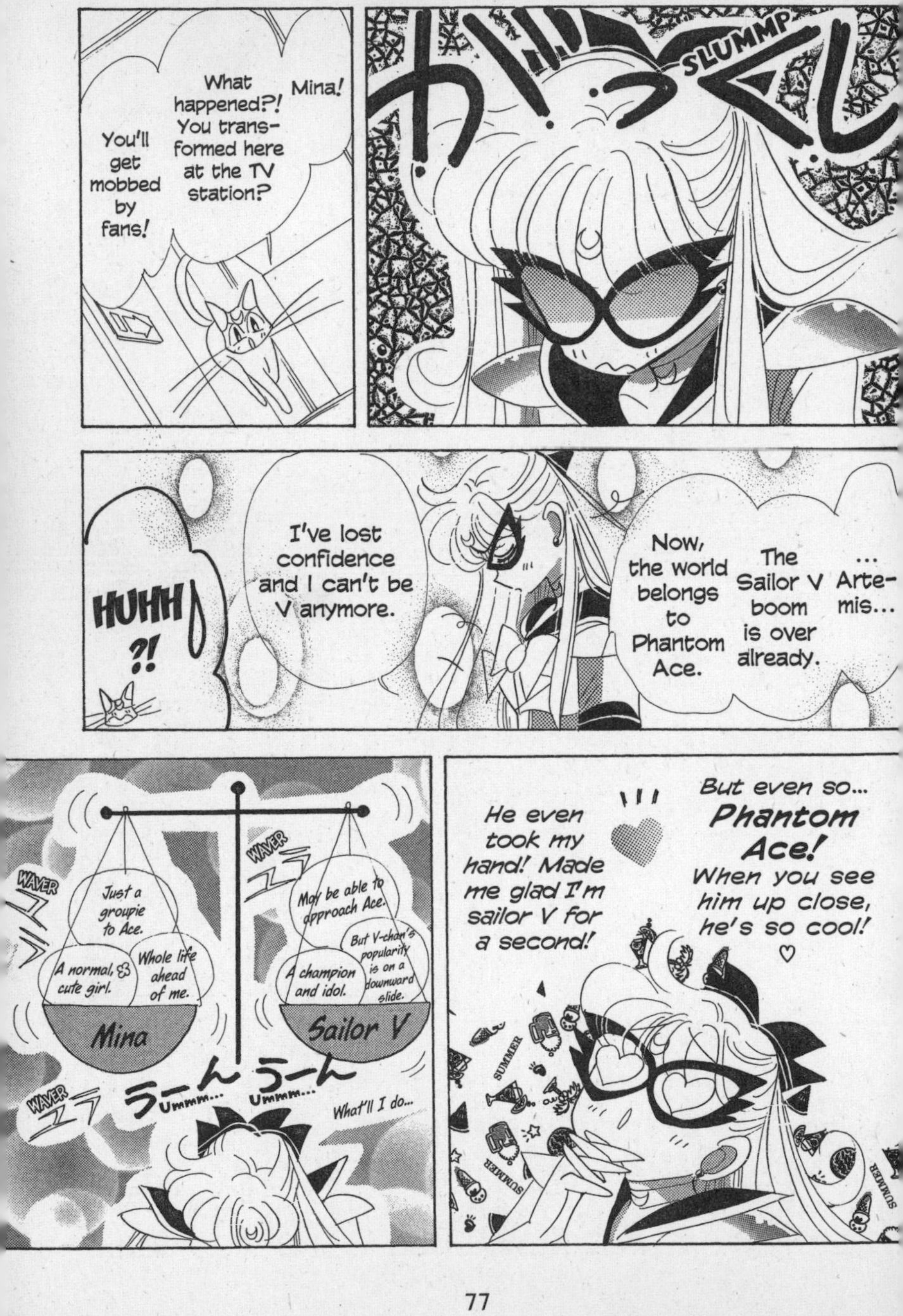

SLUMMP
Mina!
What happened?! You transformed here at the TV station?
You'll get mobbed by fans!
...Artemis...
The Sailor V boom is over already.
Now, the world belongs to Phantom Ace.
I've lost confidence and I can't be V anymore.
HUHH ?!
But even so... Phantom Ace! When you see him up close, he's so cool! ♡
He even took my hand! Made me glad I'm sailor V for a second!
SUMMER
SUMMER
SUMMER
WAVER
WAVER
WAVER
Sailor V
May be able to approach Ace.
But V-chan's popularity is on a downward slide.
A champion and idol.
Mina
Just a groupie to Ace.
Whole life ahead of me.
A normal, cute girl.
Ummm...
Ummm...
What'll I do...

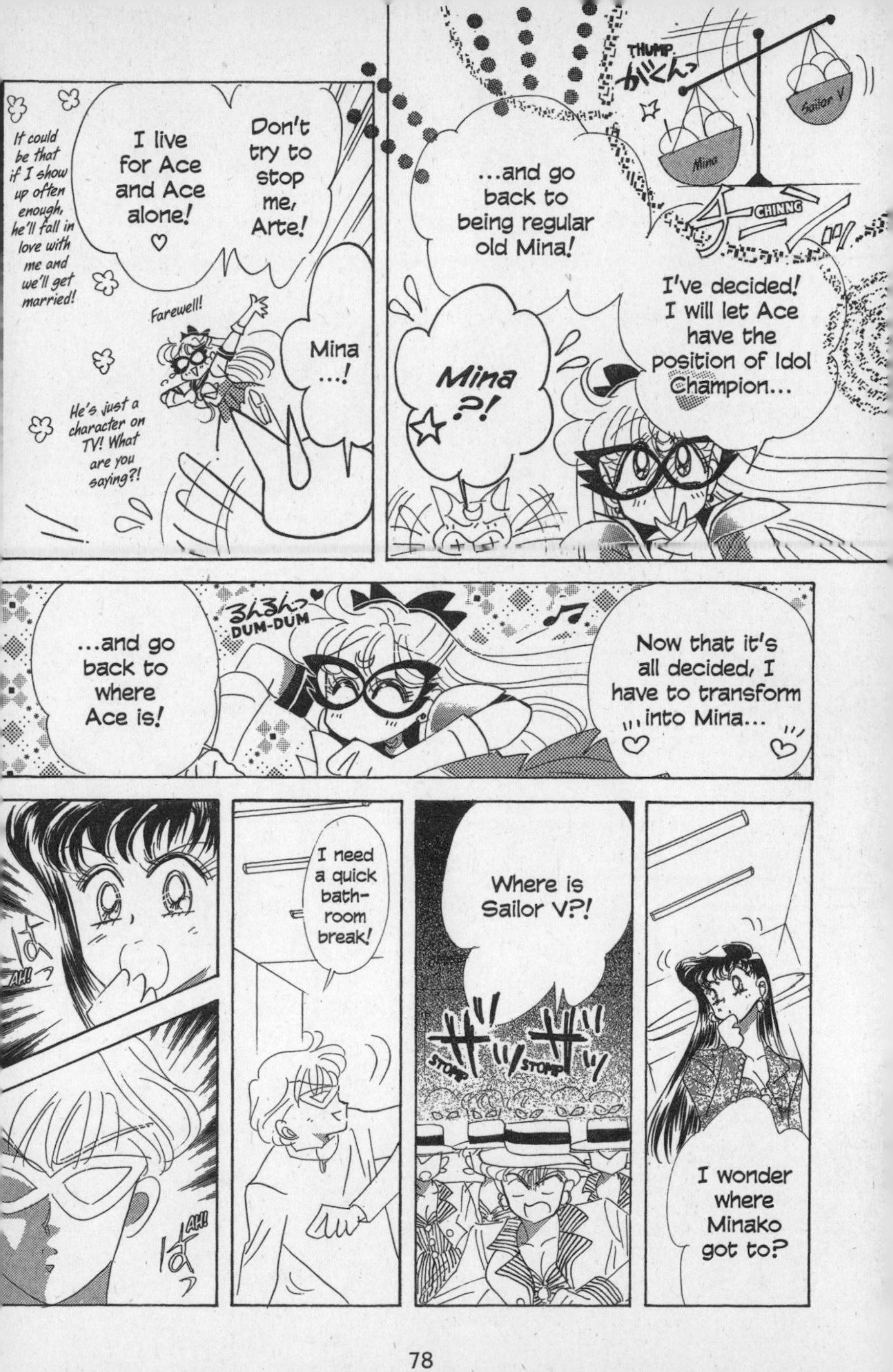
THUMP
がくんっ
Sailor V
Mina
CHINNG
I've decided! I will let Ace have the position of Idol Champion...
...and go back to being regular old Mina!
Mina ?!
Don't try to stop me, Arte!
I live for Ace and Ace alone!
Mina ...!
Farewell!
It could be that if I show up often enough, he'll fall in love with me and we'll get married!
He's just a character on TV! What are you saying?!
Now that it's all decided, I have to transform into Mina...
るんるんっ
DUM-DUM
...and go back to where Ace is!
I wonder where Minako got to?
Where is Sailor V?!
STOMP
STOMP
I need a quick bathroom break!
AH!
AH!

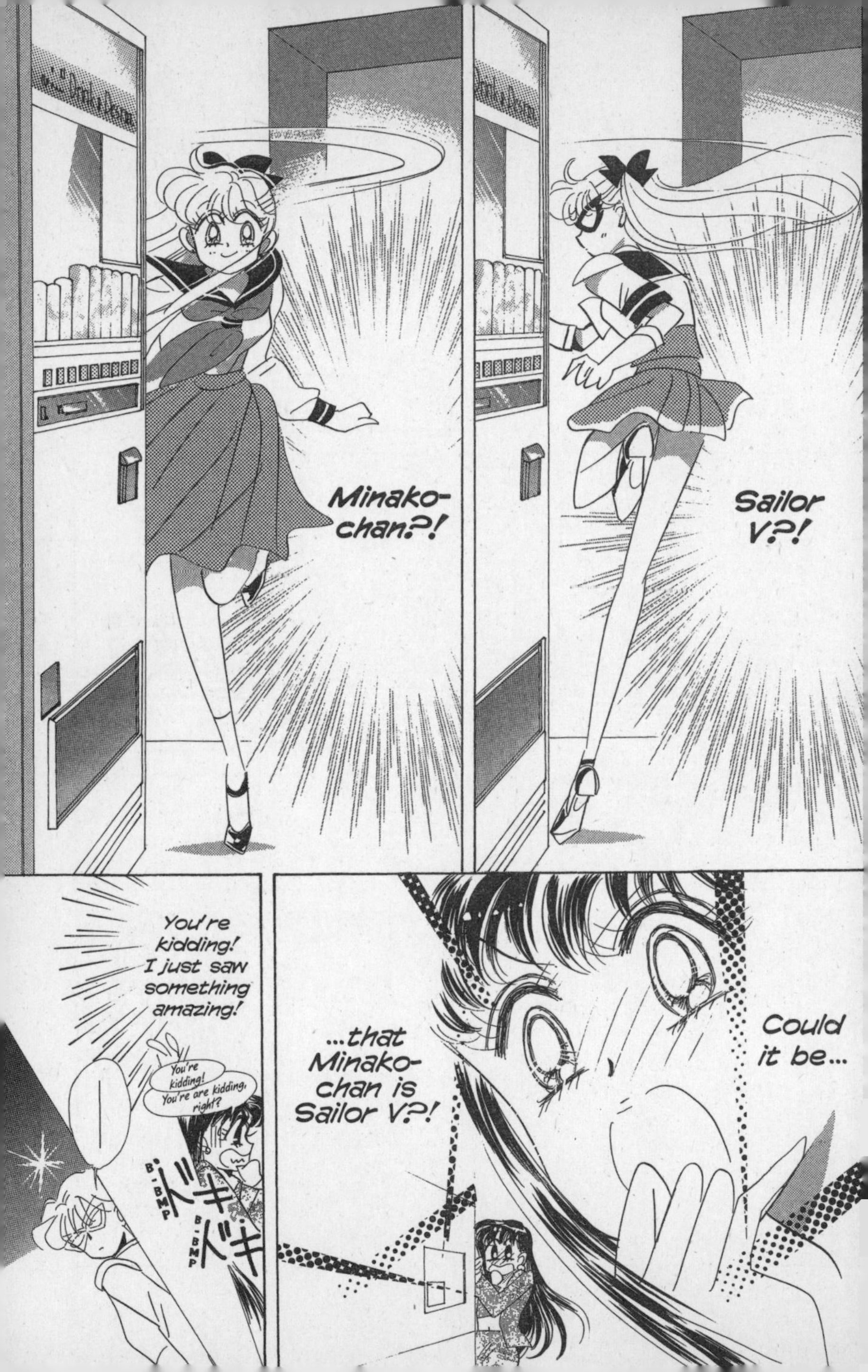
Sailor V?!
Minako-chan?!
Could it be...
...that Minako-chan is Sailor V?!
You're kidding! I just saw something amazing!
You're kidding! You're are kidding, right?
B-BMP
B-BMP

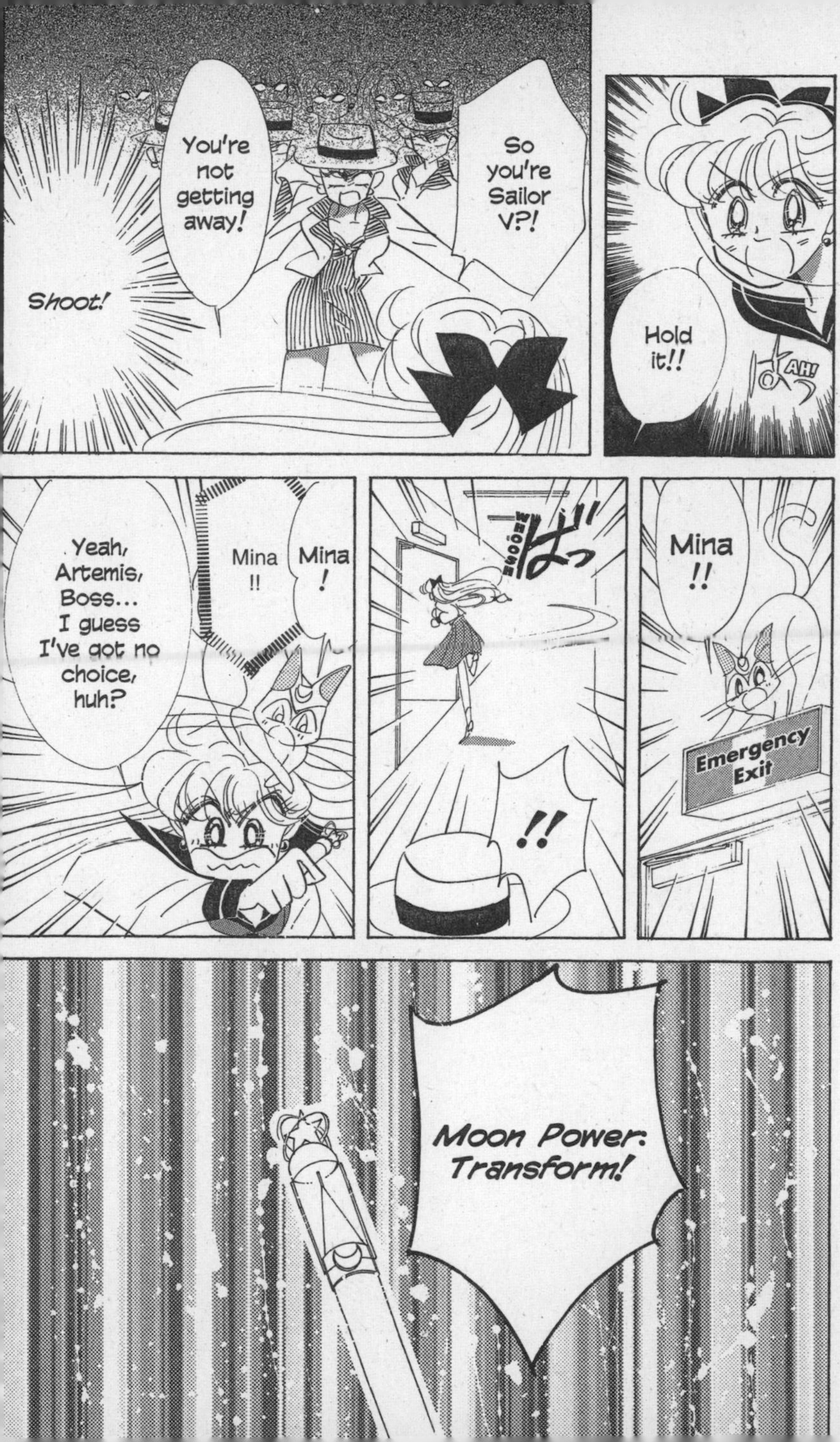
Hold it!!
はっ
AH!
So you're Sailor V?!
You're not getting away!
Shoot!
Mina !!
ばっ
WHOOSH
!!
Mina !
Mina !!
Yeah, Artemis, Boss... I guess I've got no choice, huh?
Moon Power: Transform!

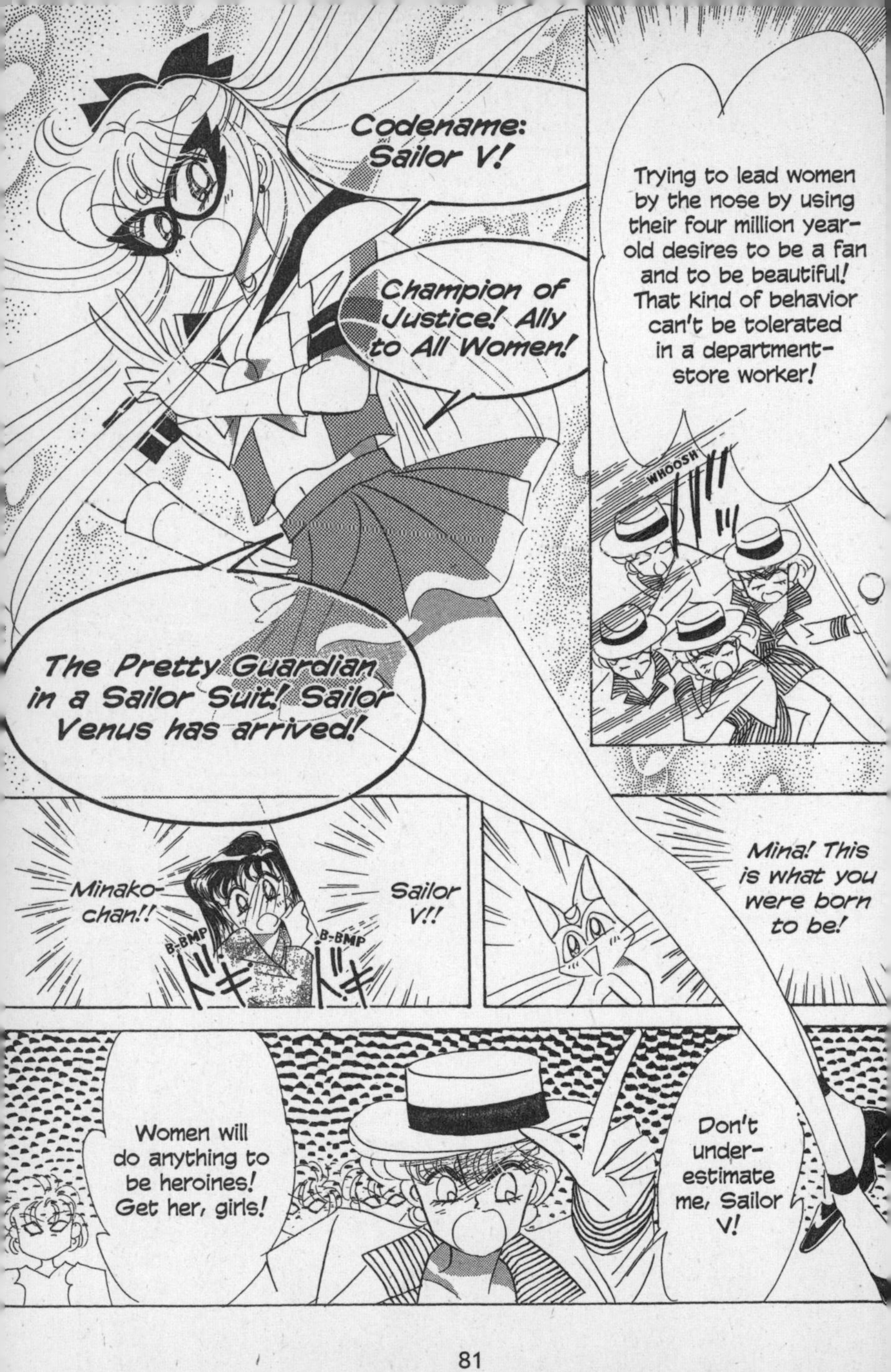
Trying to lead women by the nose by using their four million year-old desires to be a fan and to be beautiful! That kind of behavior can't be tolerated in a department-store worker!
WHOOSH
Codename: Sailor V!
Champion of Justice! Ally to All Women!
The Pretty Guardian in a Sailor Suit! Sailor Venus has arrived!
Mina! This is what you were born to be!
Sailor V!!
Minako-chan!!
B-BMP ドキ
B-BMP ドキ
Don't under-estimate me, Sailor V!
Women will do anything to be heroines! Get her, girls!

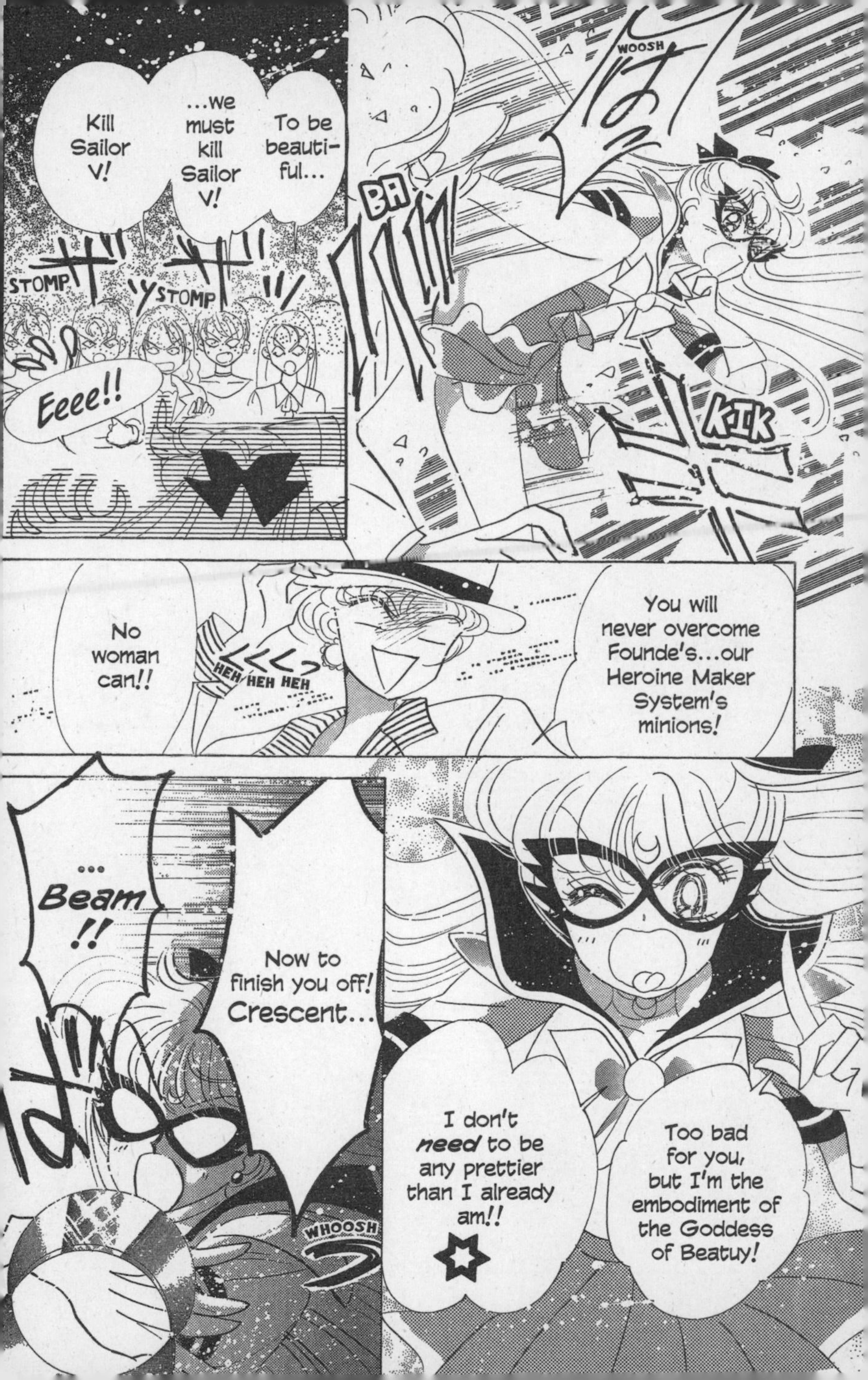
WOOSH
BA
KIK
To be beautiful...
...we must kill Sailor V!
Kill Sailor V!
STOMP
STOMP
Eeee!!
You will never overcome Founde's...our Heroine Maker System's minions!
HEH HEH HEH
No woman can!!
Too bad for you, but I'm the embodiment of the Goddess of Beatuy!
I don't *need* to be any prettier than I already am!!
Now to finish you off! Crescent...
... Beam!!
WHOOSH

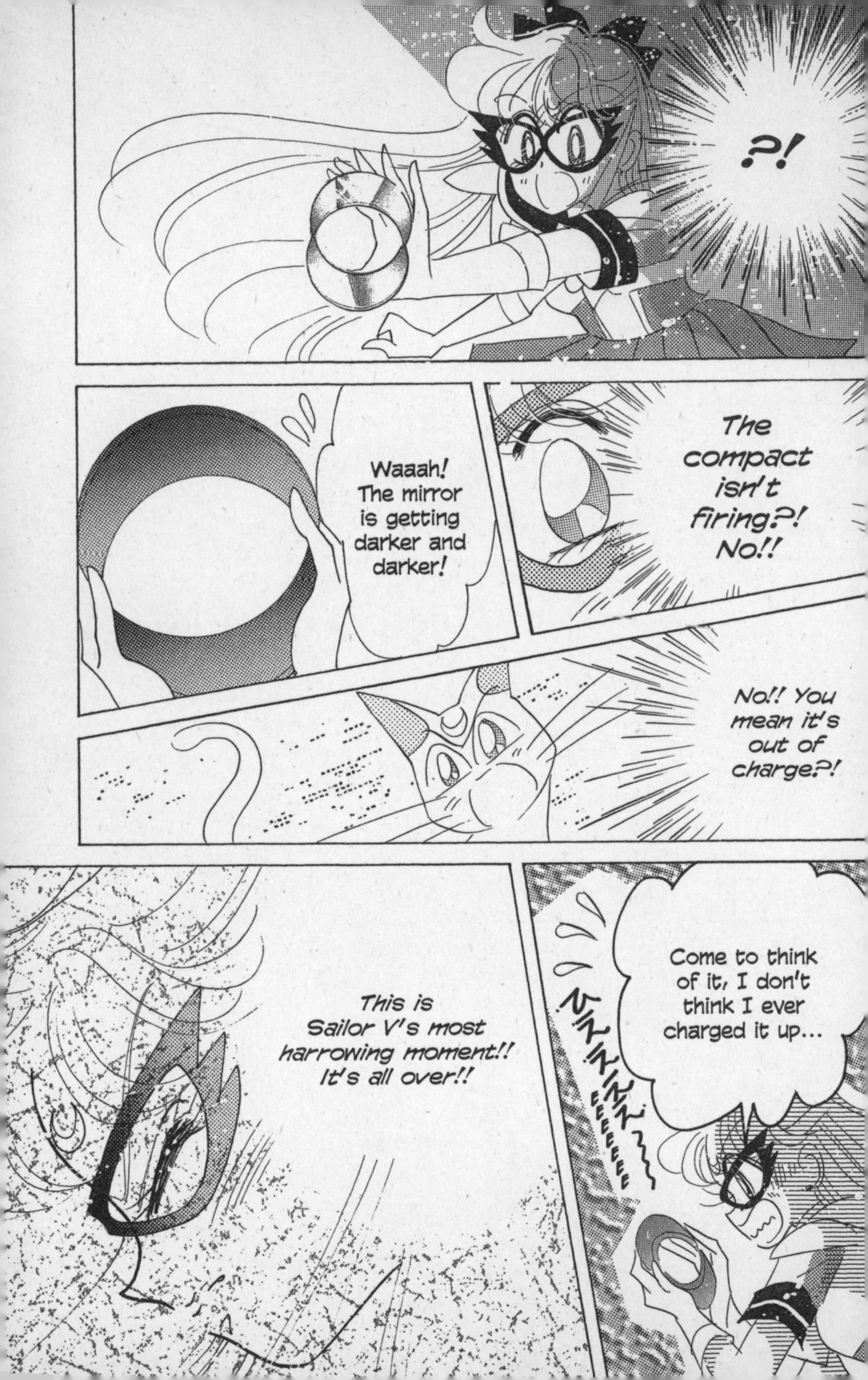
?!
The compact isn't firing?! No!!
Waaah! The mirror is getting darker and darker!
No!! You mean it's out of charge?!
Come to think of it, I don't think I ever charged it up...
This is Sailor V's most harrowing moment!! It's all over!!

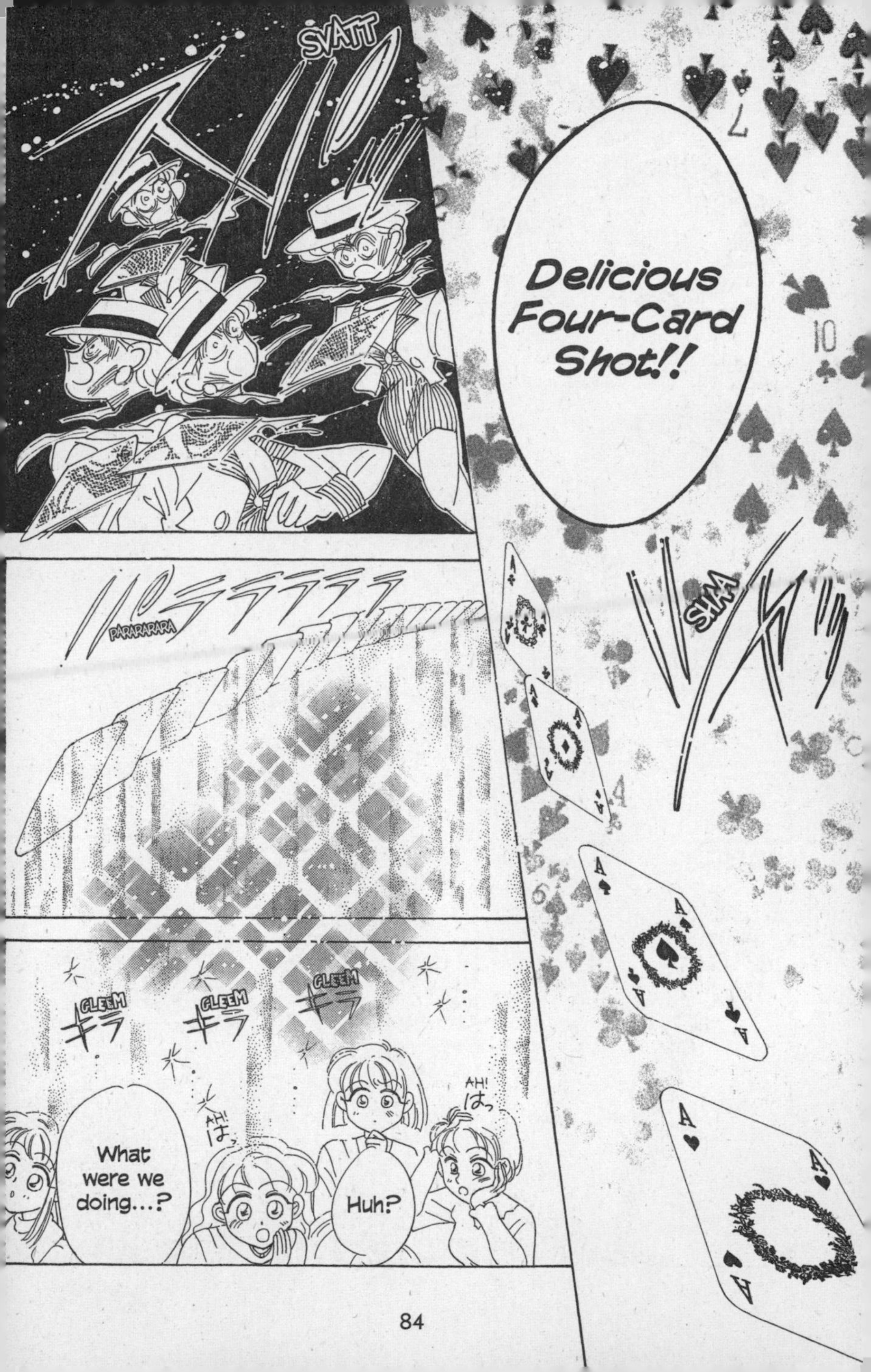
Delicious Four-Card Shot!!
SHAA
SVATT
PARARARARA
GLEEM
GLEEM
GLEEM
AH!
Huh?
AH!
What were we doing...?

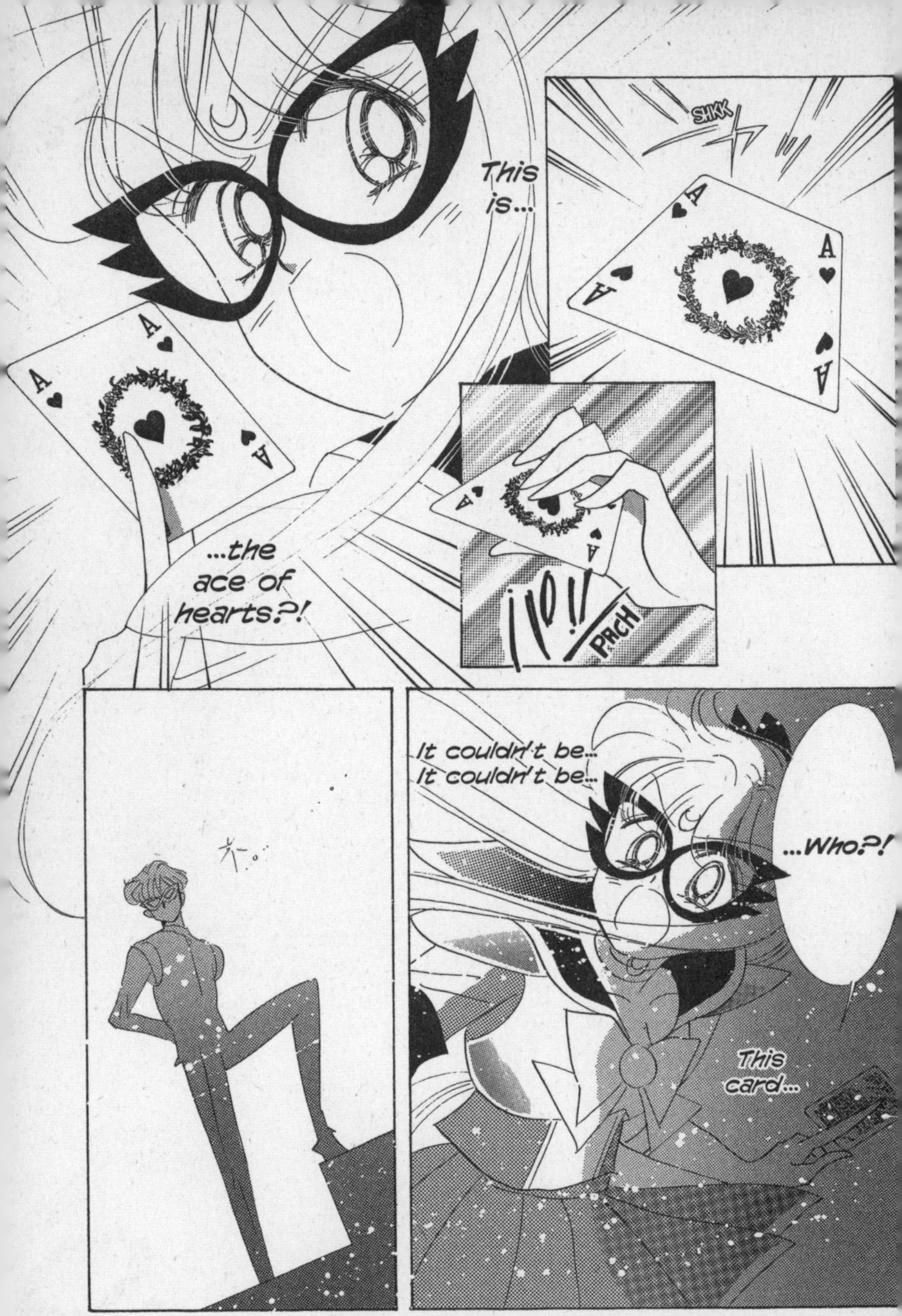
SHKK
PACH
This is...
...the ace of hearts?!
It couldn't be... It couldn't be...
...Who?!
This card...

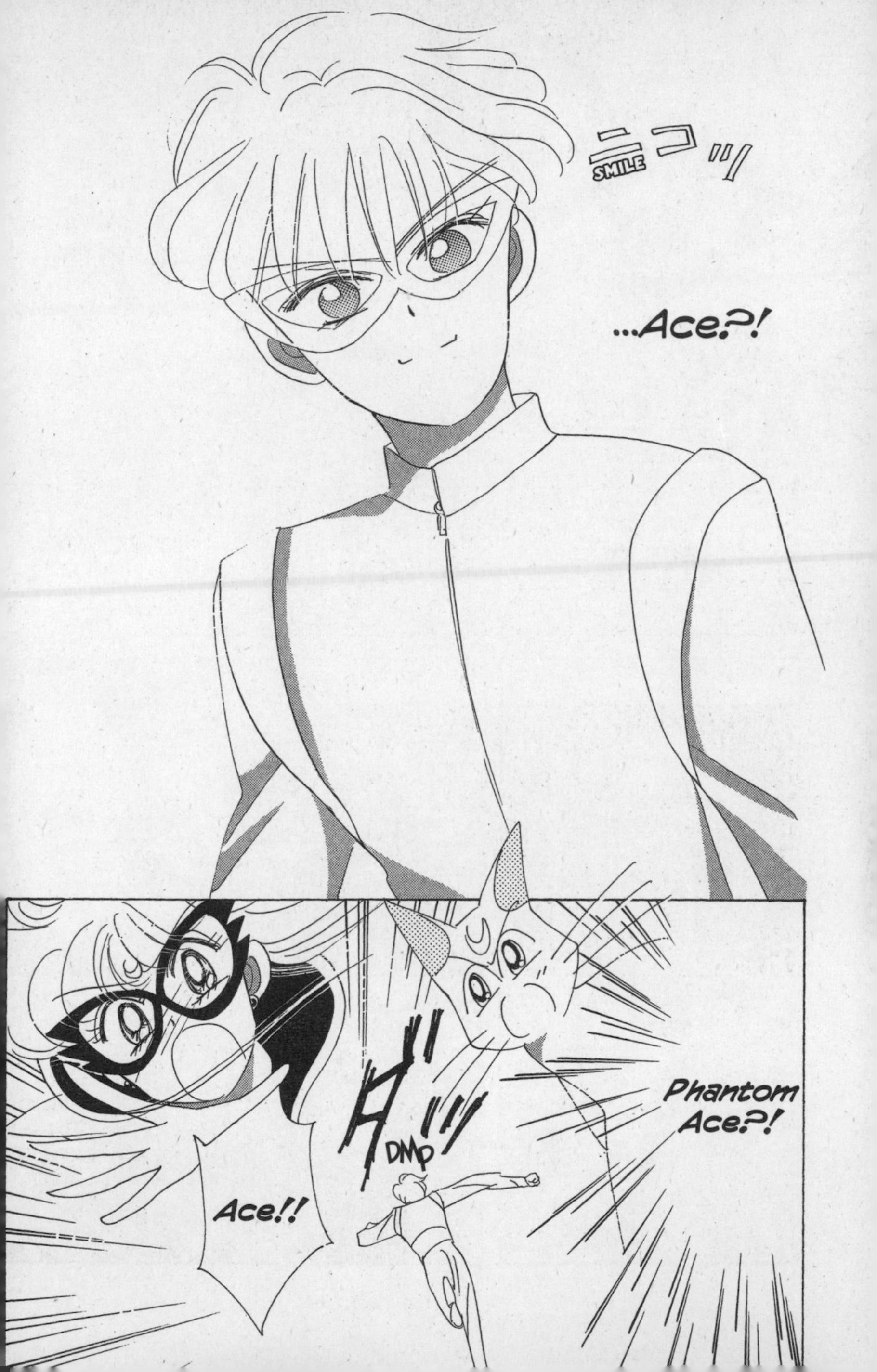
ニコッ
SMILE
...Ace?!
Phantom Ace?!
DMP
Ace!!

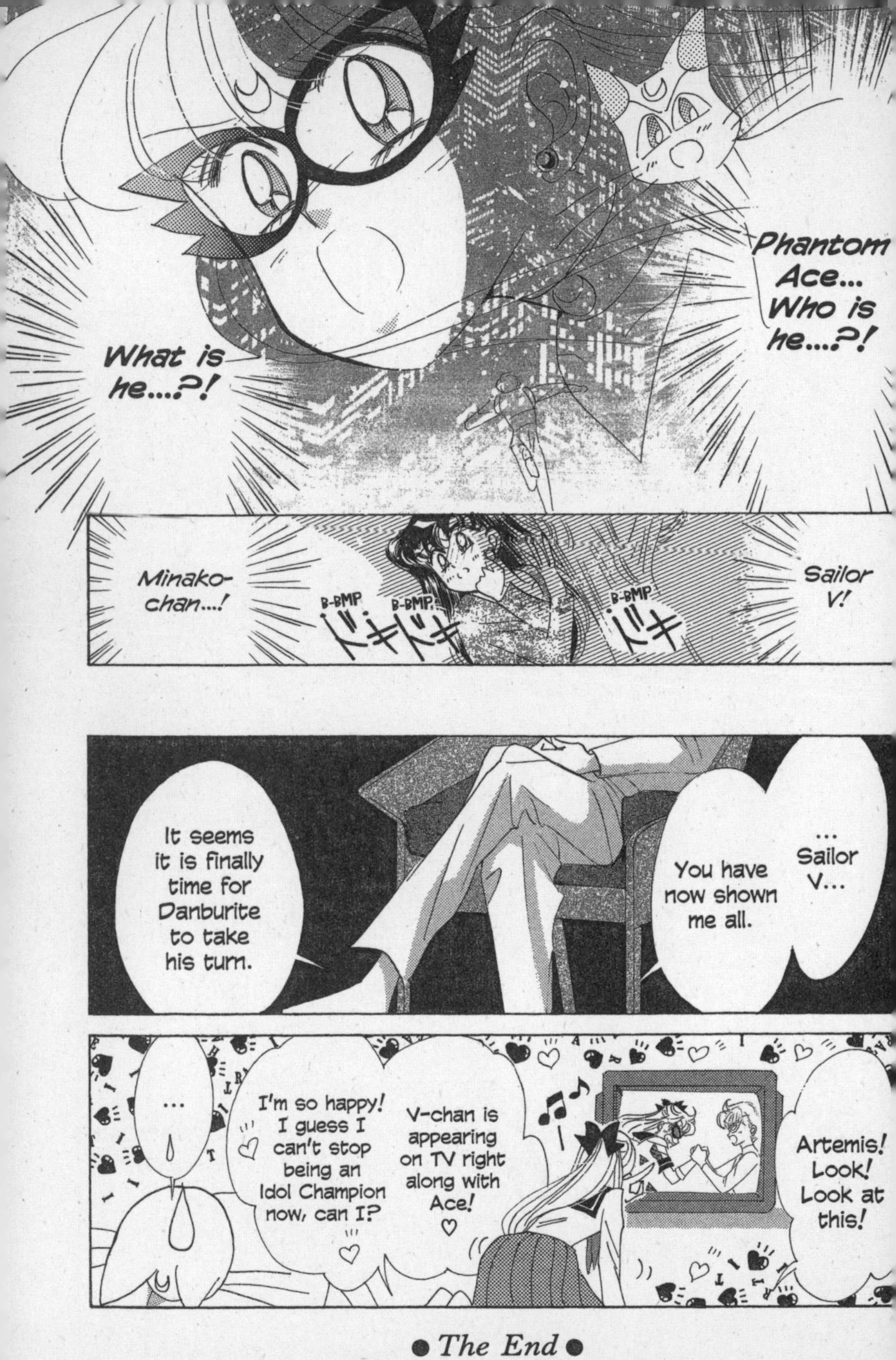
Phantom Ace... Who is he...?!
What is he...?!
Sailor V!
B-BMP
B-BMP
B-BMP
Minako-chan...!
... Sailor V...
You have now shown me all.
It seems it is finally time for Danburite to take his turn.
Artemis! Look! Look at this!
V-chan is appearing on TV right along with Ace!
I'm so happy! I guess I can't stop being an Idol Champion now, can I?
...

●*The End*●

Vol. 11 Pet Chapter 1, Nyan-Nyan's Schemes!

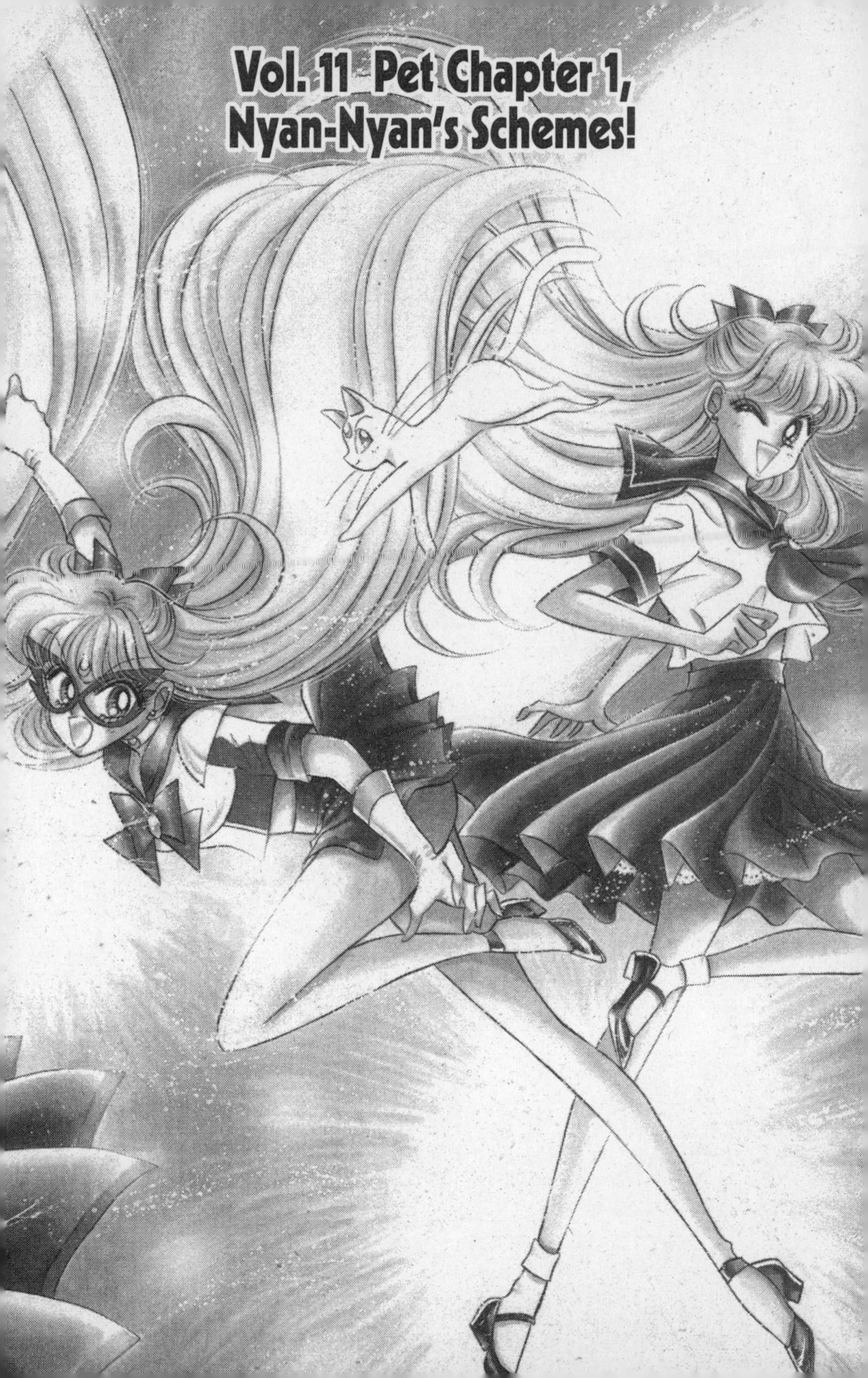

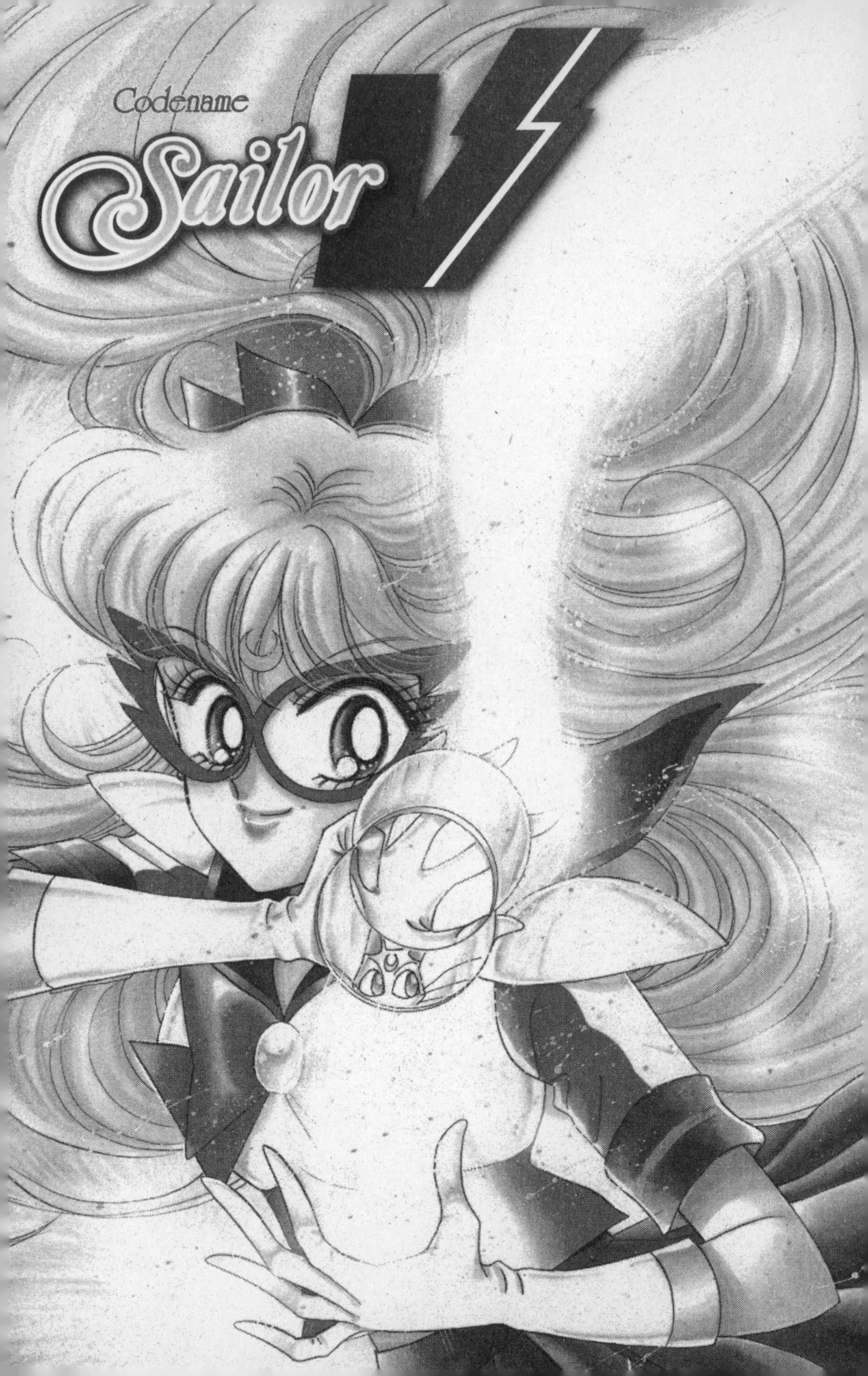
Codename
Sailor V

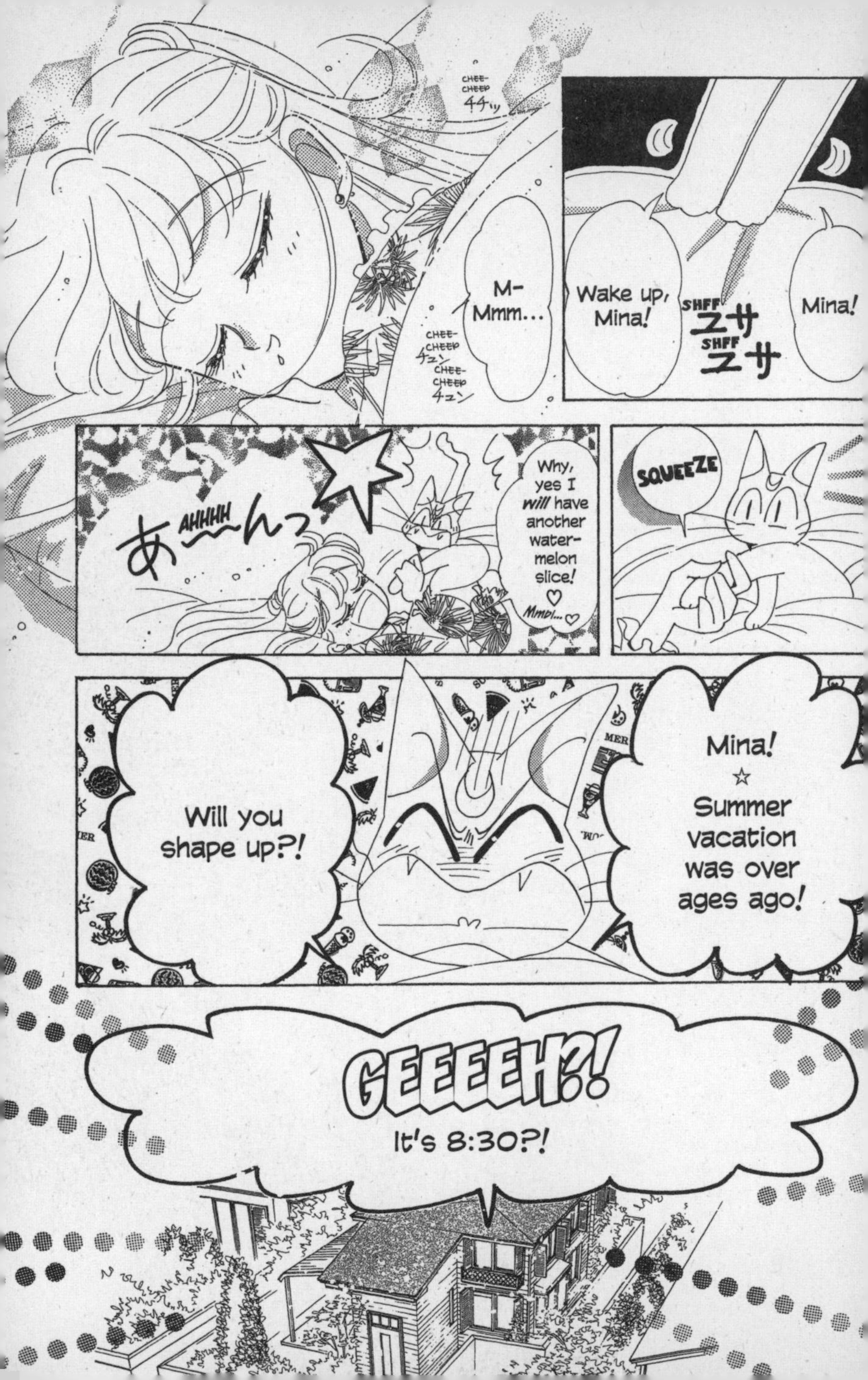
Mina!
SHFF ユサ
SHFF ユサ
Wake up, Mina!
CHEE-CHEEP チチッ
M-Mmm...
CHEE-CHEEP チュン
CHEE-CHEEP チュン
SQUEEZE
Why, yes I *will* have another water-melon slice! ♡
Mmm!...♡
AHHHH あ〜んっ
Mina! ☆ Summer vacation was over ages ago!
Will you shape up?!
GEEEEH?!
It's 8:30?!

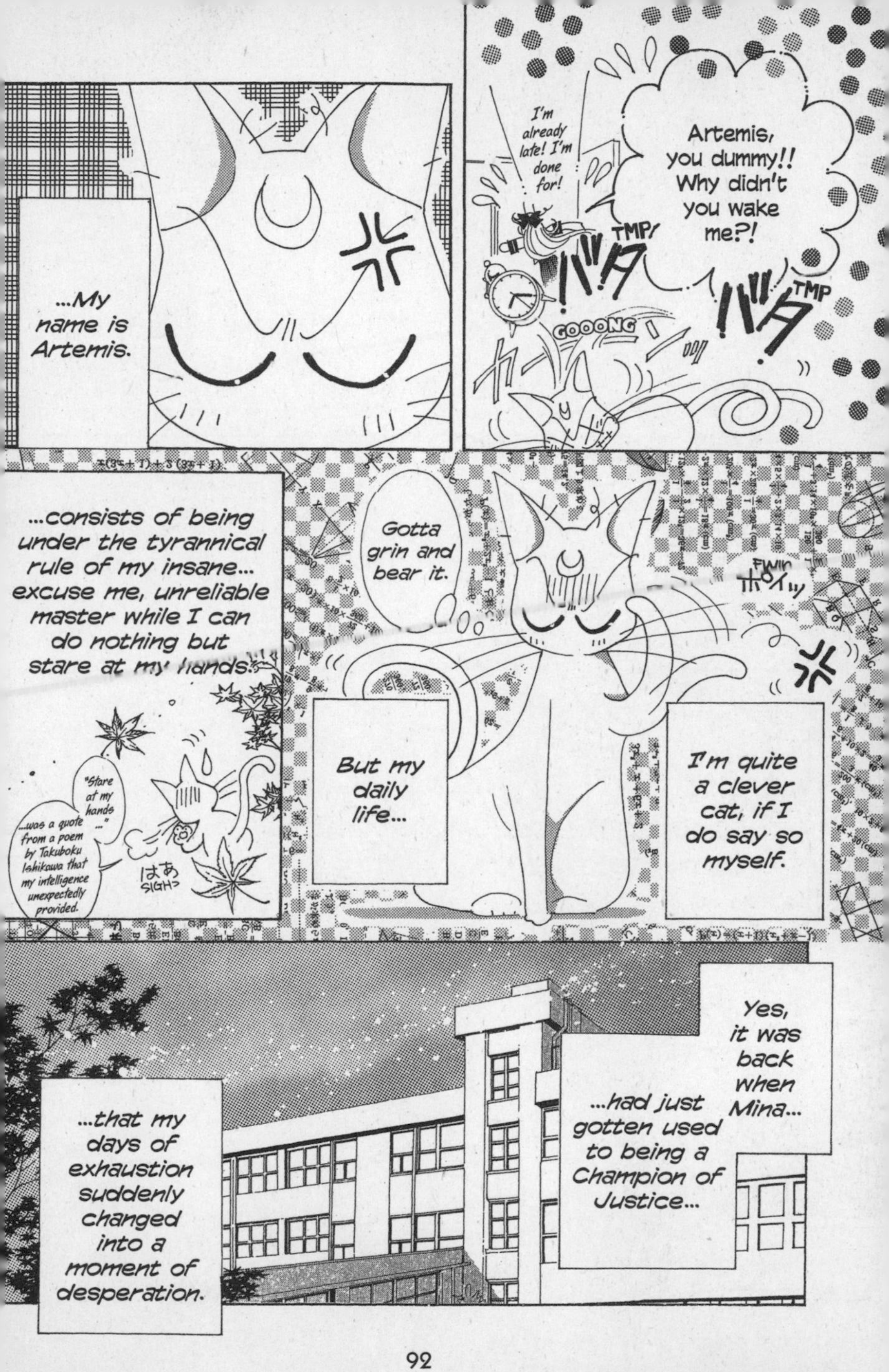
Artemis, you dummy!! Why didn't you wake me?!
I'm already late! I'm done for!
TMP
バタ
TMP
バタ
GOOONG
カーン
...My name is Artemis.
FWIP
ポイッ
Gotta grin and bear it.
I'm quite a clever cat, if I do say so myself.
But my daily life...
...consists of being under the tyrannical rule of my insane... excuse me, unreliable master while I can do nothing but stare at my hands.
"Stare at my hands..."
...was a quote from a poem by Takuboku Ishikawa that my intelligence unexpectedly provided.
はあ SIGH
Yes, it was back when Mina...
...had just gotten used to being a Champion of Justice...
...that my days of exhaustion suddenly changed into a moment of desperation.

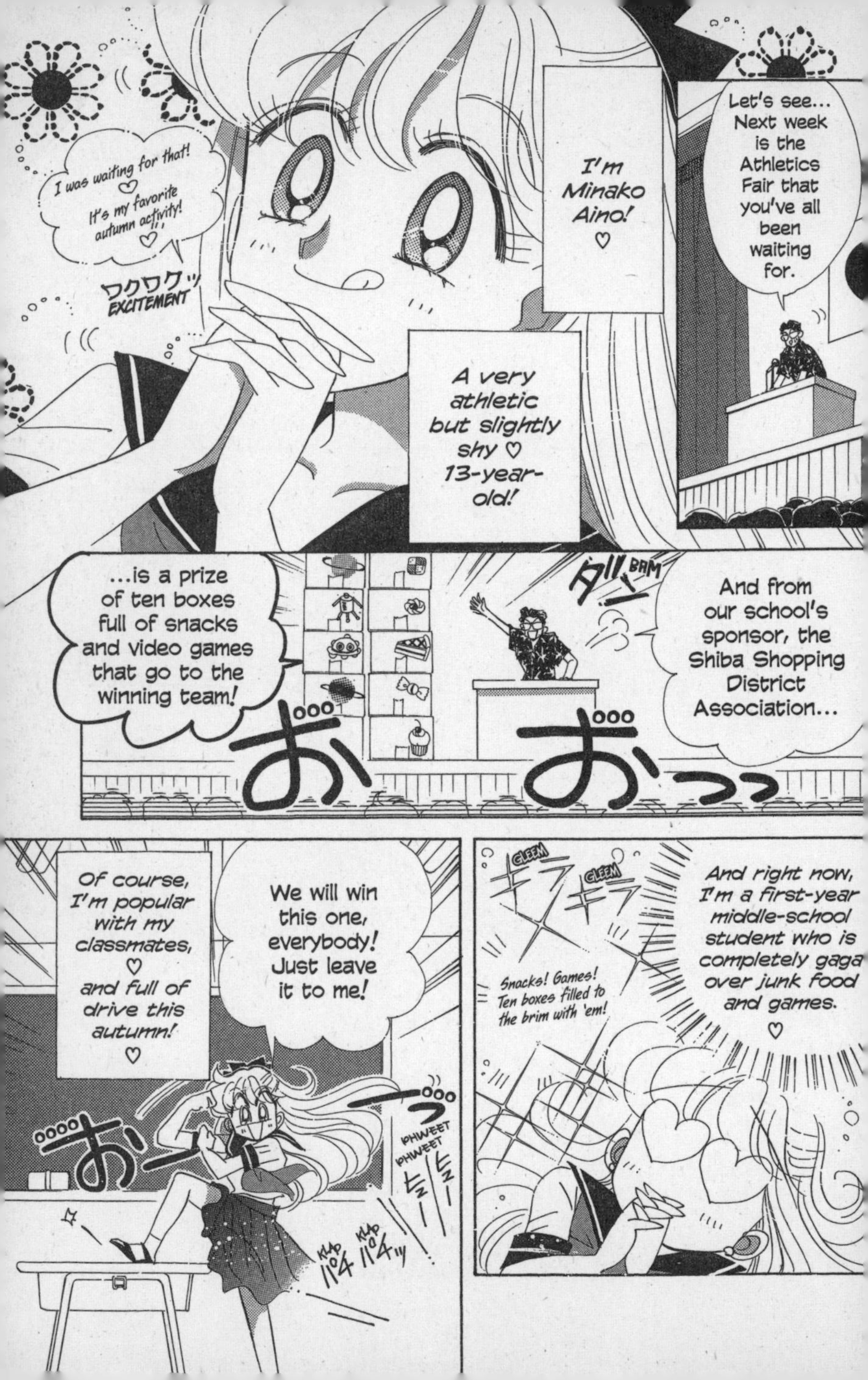
Let's see... Next week is the Athletics Fair that you've all been waiting for.
I'm Minako Aino! ♡
A very athletic but slightly shy ♡ 13-year-old!
I was waiting for that! ♡ It's my favorite autumn activity! ♡
ワクワクッ EXCITEMENT
And from our school's sponsor, the Shiba Shopping District Association...
BAM
...is a prize of ten boxes full of snacks and video games that go to the winning team!
And right now, I'm a first-year middle-school student who is completely gaga over junk food and games. ♡
GLEEM GLEEM
Snacks! Games! Ten boxes filled to the brim with 'em!
Of course, I'm popular with my classmates, ♡ and full of drive this autumn! ♡
We will win this one, everybody! Just leave it to me!
PHWEET PHWEET
KLAP KLAP

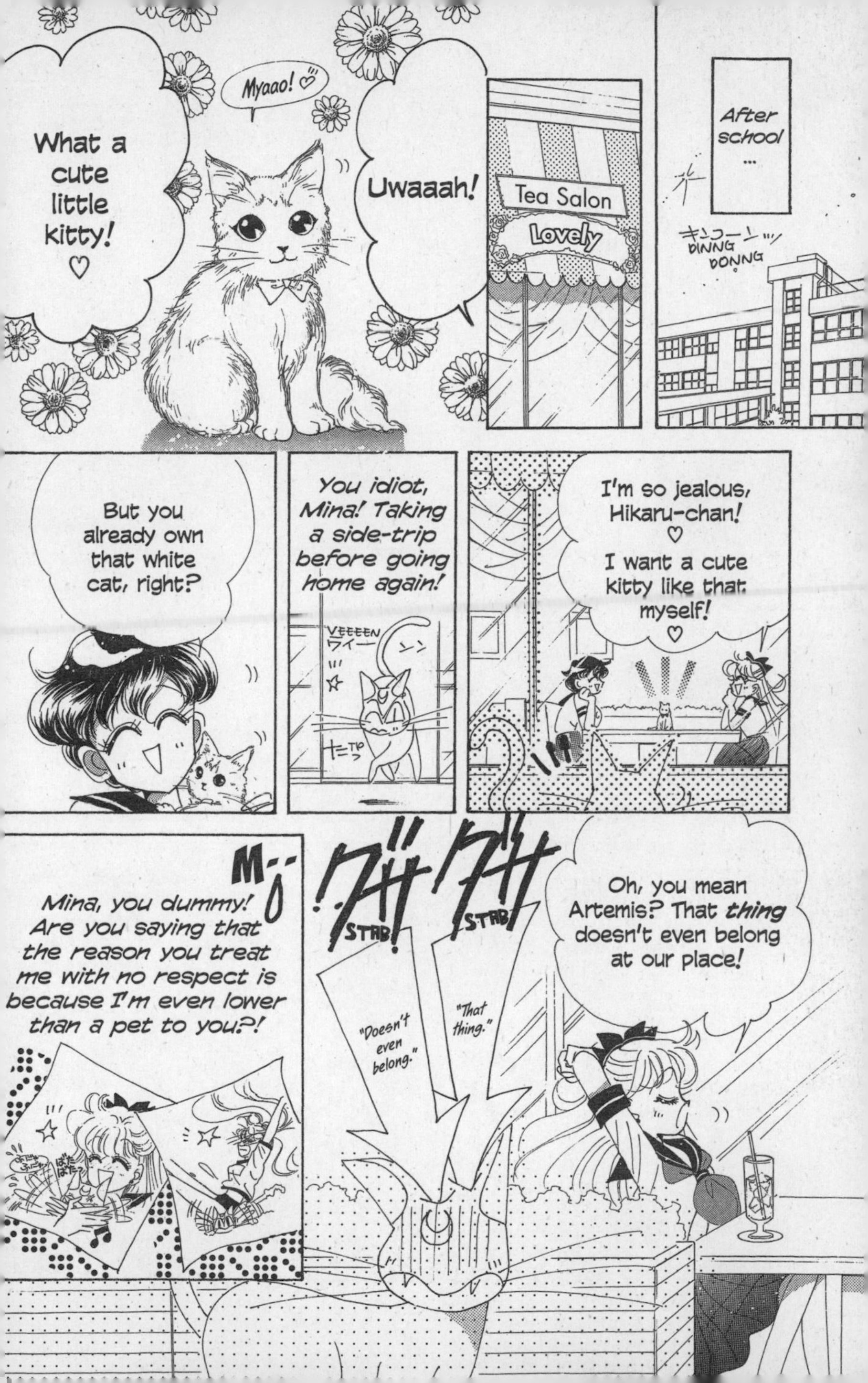

After school ...
DINNG DONNG
Tea Salon
Lovely
Uwaaah!
Myaao! ♡
What a cute little kitty! ♡
I'm so jealous, Hikaru-chan! ♡ I want a cute kitty like that myself! ♡
You idiot, Mina! Taking a side-trip before going home again!
VEEEEN
TIP
But you already own that white cat, right?
Oh, you mean Artemis? That *thing* doesn't even belong at our place!
STAB
STAB
"That thing."
"Doesn't even belong."
M--
Mina, you dummy! Are you saying that the reason you treat me with no respect is because I'm even lower than a pet to you?!

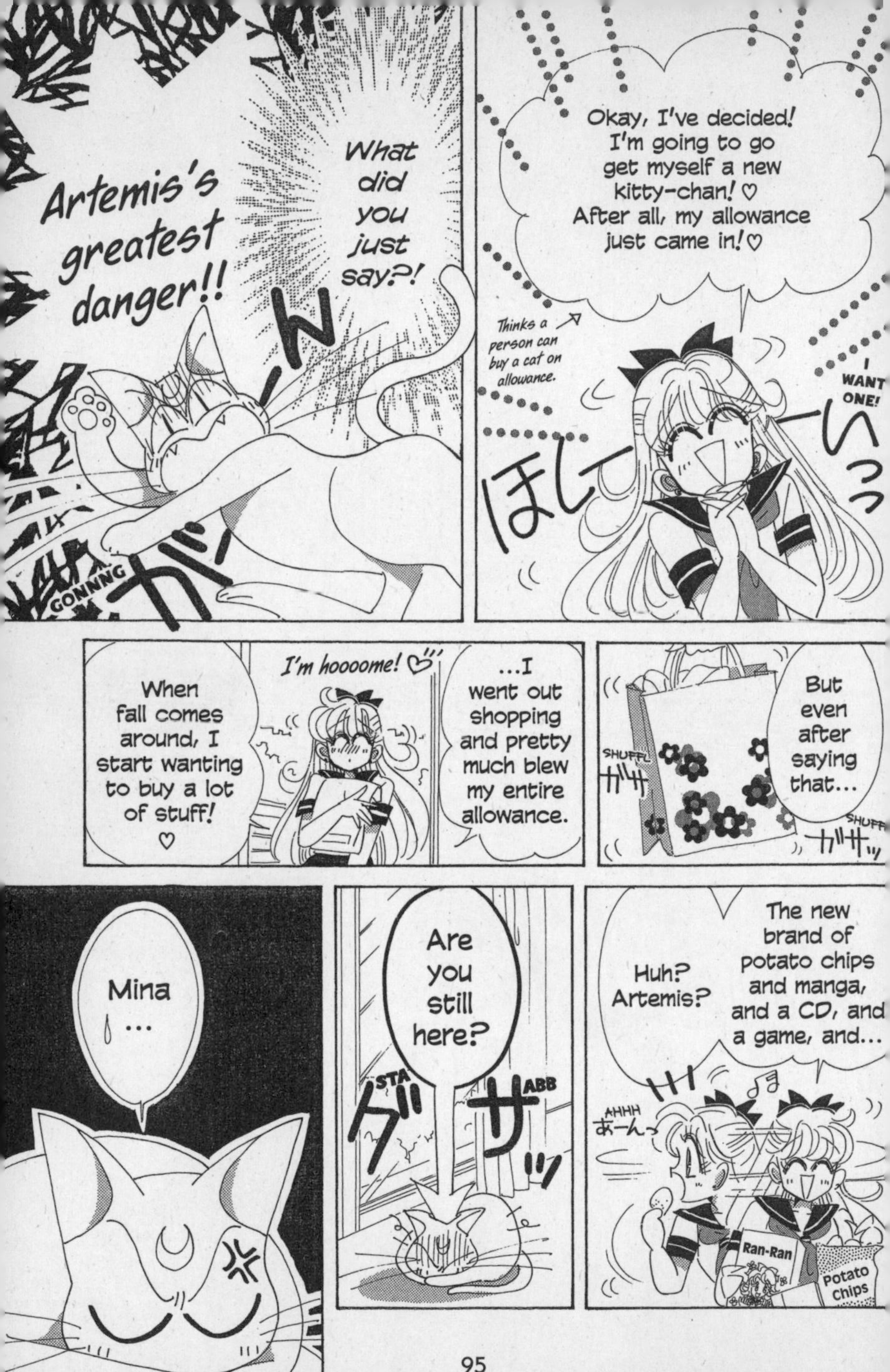

Okay, I've decided! I'm going to go get myself a new kitty-chan! ♡ After all, my allowance just came in! ♡
I WANT ONE!
ほしーいっ
Thinks a person can buy a cat on allowance.
What did you just say?!
Artemis's greatest danger!!
ガーン
GONNNG
But even after saying that...
SHUFFL
ガサ
SHUFFL
ガサッ
...I went out shopping and pretty much blew my entire allowance.
I'm hoooome! ♡
When fall comes around, I start wanting to buy a lot of stuff! ♡
The new brand of potato chips and manga, and a CD, and a game, and...
Huh? Artemis?
AHHH
あーんっ
Ran-Ran
Potato Chips
Are you still here?
STA
ガ
ABB
サッ
Mina...

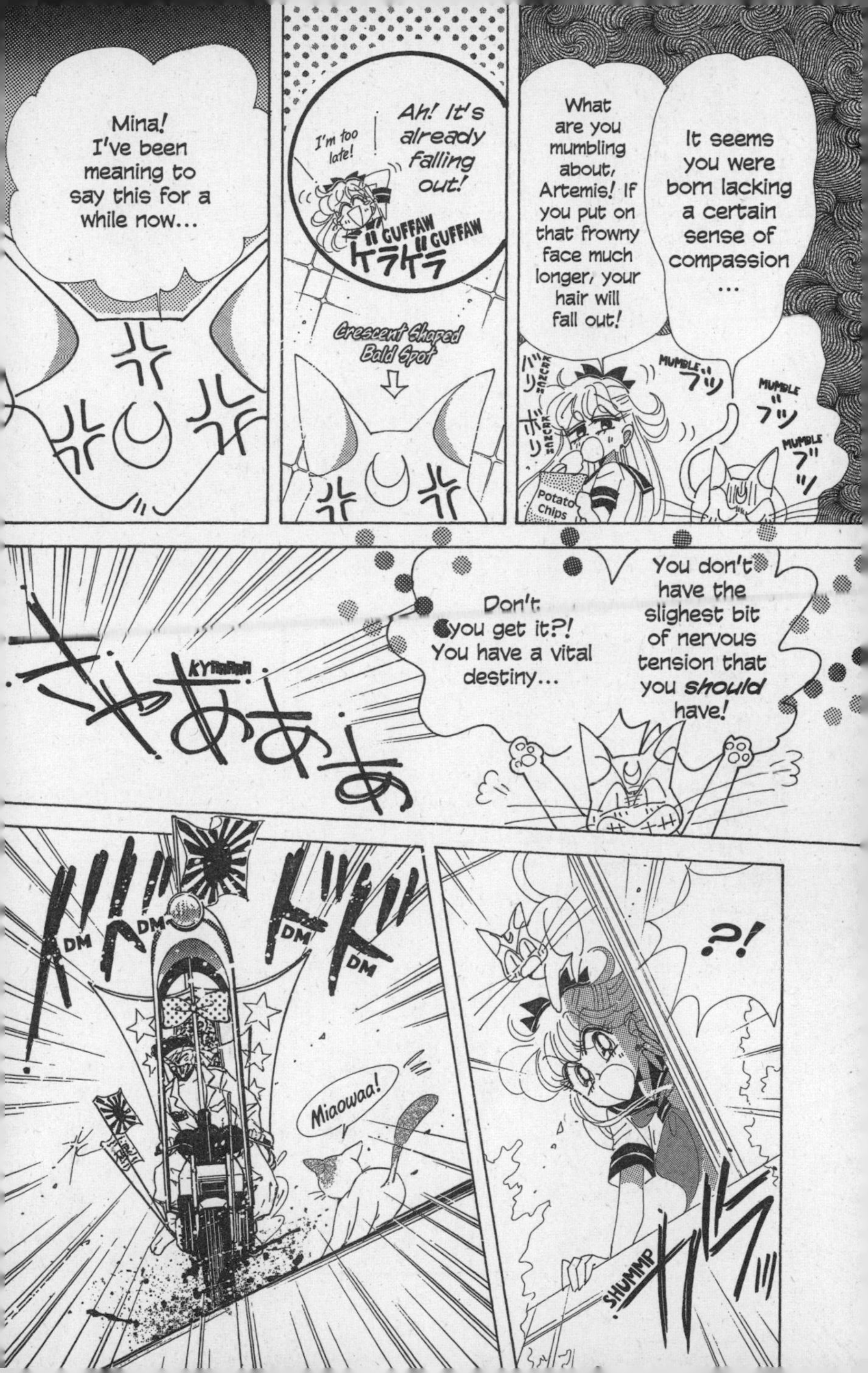

It seems you were born lacking a certain sense of compassion ...
What are you mumbling about, Artemis! If you put on that frowny face much longer, your hair will fall out!
MUMBLE
MUMBLE
MUMBLE
Potato Chips
Ah! It's already falling out!
I'm too late!
GUFFAW GUFFAW
Crescent Shaped Bald Spot
Mina! I've been meaning to say this for a while now...
You don't have the slighest bit of nervous tension that you *should* have!
Don't you get it?! You have a vital destiny...
?!
SHUMMP
DM
DM
DM
DM
Miaowaa!

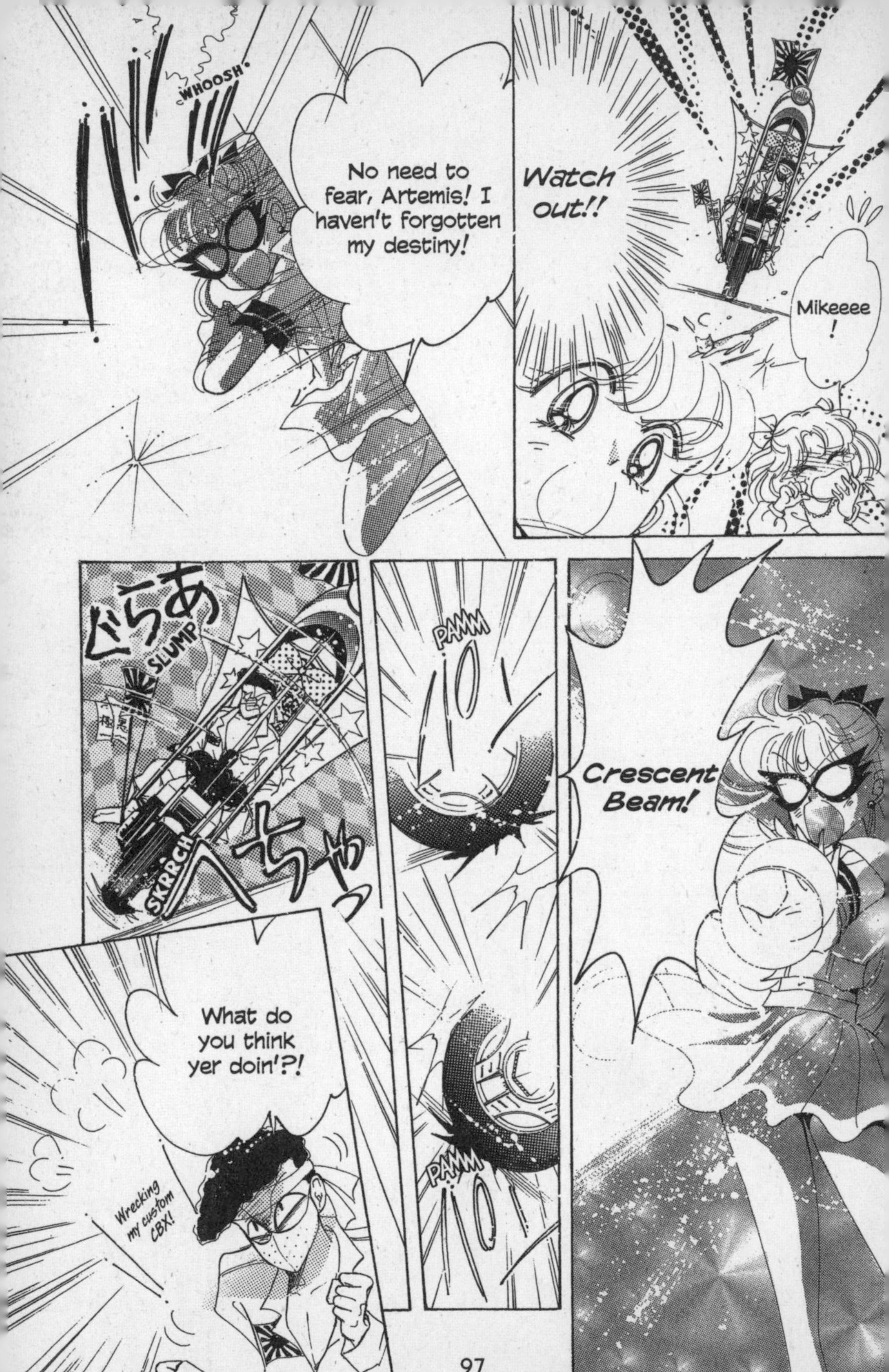
Watch out!!
Mikeeee!
WHOOSH
No need to fear, Artemis! I haven't forgotten my destiny!
Crescent Beam!
PAMM
PAMM
ぐらあ
SLUMP
へちゃっ
SKRRCH
What do you think yer doin'?!
Wrecking my custom CBX!

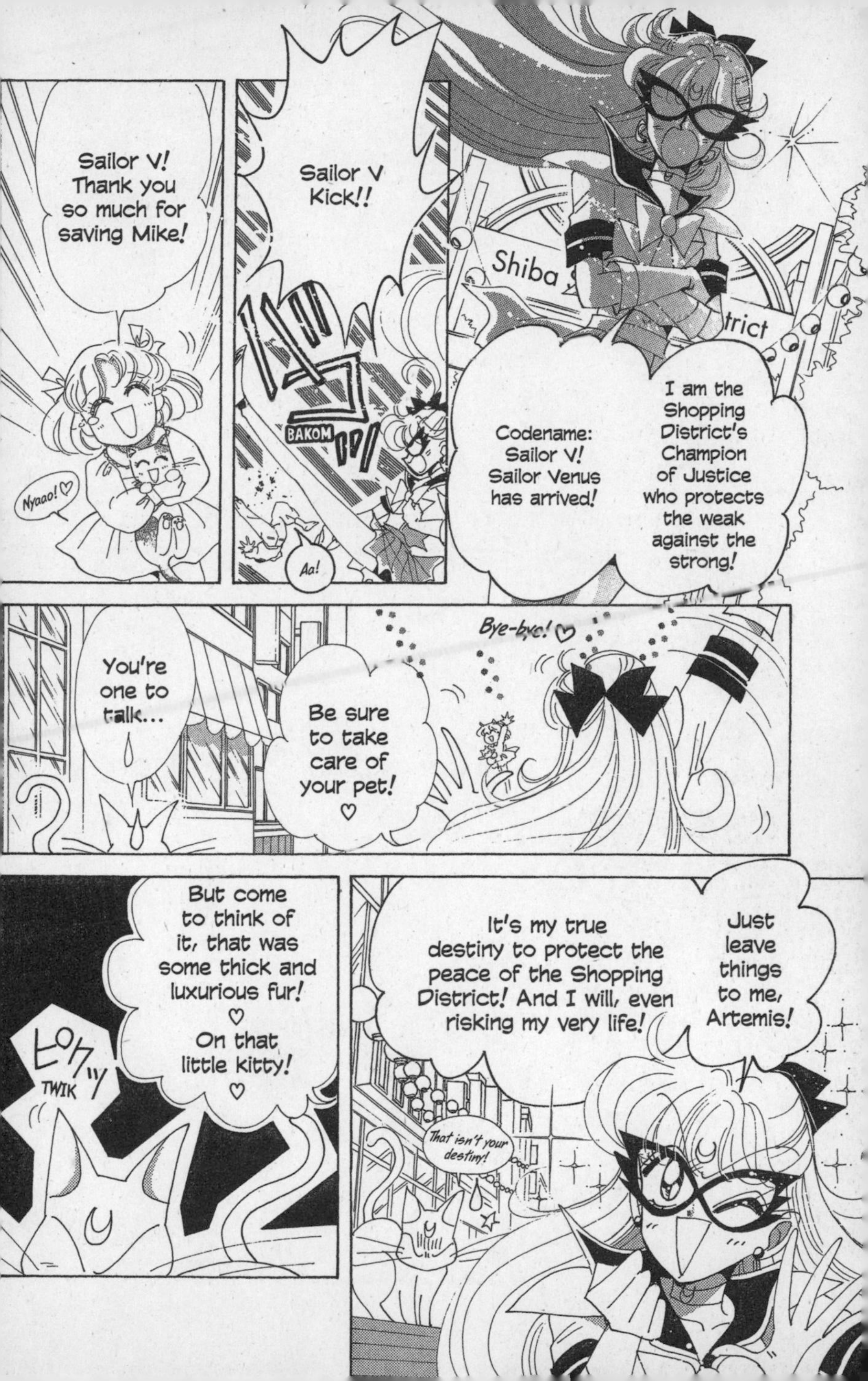
Shiba
trict
I am the Shopping District's Champion of Justice who protects the weak against the strong!
Codename: Sailor V! Sailor Venus has arrived!
Sailor V Kick!!
BAKOM
Aa!
Sailor V! Thank you so much for saving Mike!
Nyaao! ♡
Bye-bye! ♡
Be sure to take care of your pet! ♡
You're one to talk...
Just leave things to me, Artemis!
It's my true destiny to protect the peace of the Shopping District! And I will, even risking my very life!
That isn't your destiny!
But come to think of it, that was some thick and luxurious fur! ♡ On that little kitty! ♡
ピクッ
TWIK

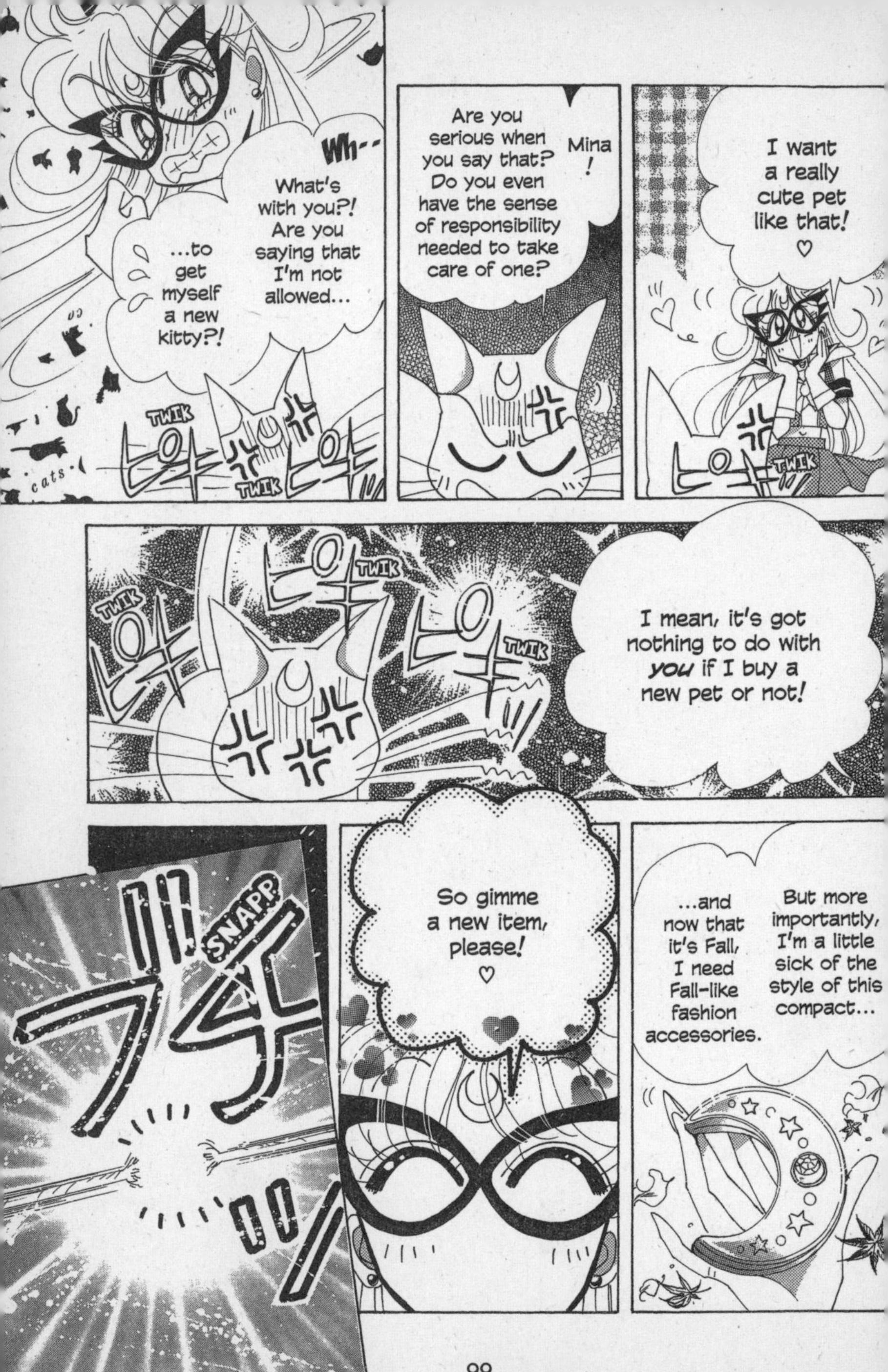
I want a really cute pet like that! ♡
TWIK
Mina!
Are you serious when you say that? Do you even have the sense of responsibility needed to take care of one?
Wh--
What's with you?! Are you saying that I'm not allowed...
...to get myself a new kitty?!
TWIK
TWIK
cats
I mean, it's got nothing to do with *you* if I buy a new pet or not!
TWIK
TWIK
TWIK
But more importantly, I'm a little sick of the style of this compact...
...and now that it's Fall, I need Fall-like fashion accessories.
So gimme a new item, please! ♡
SNAPP

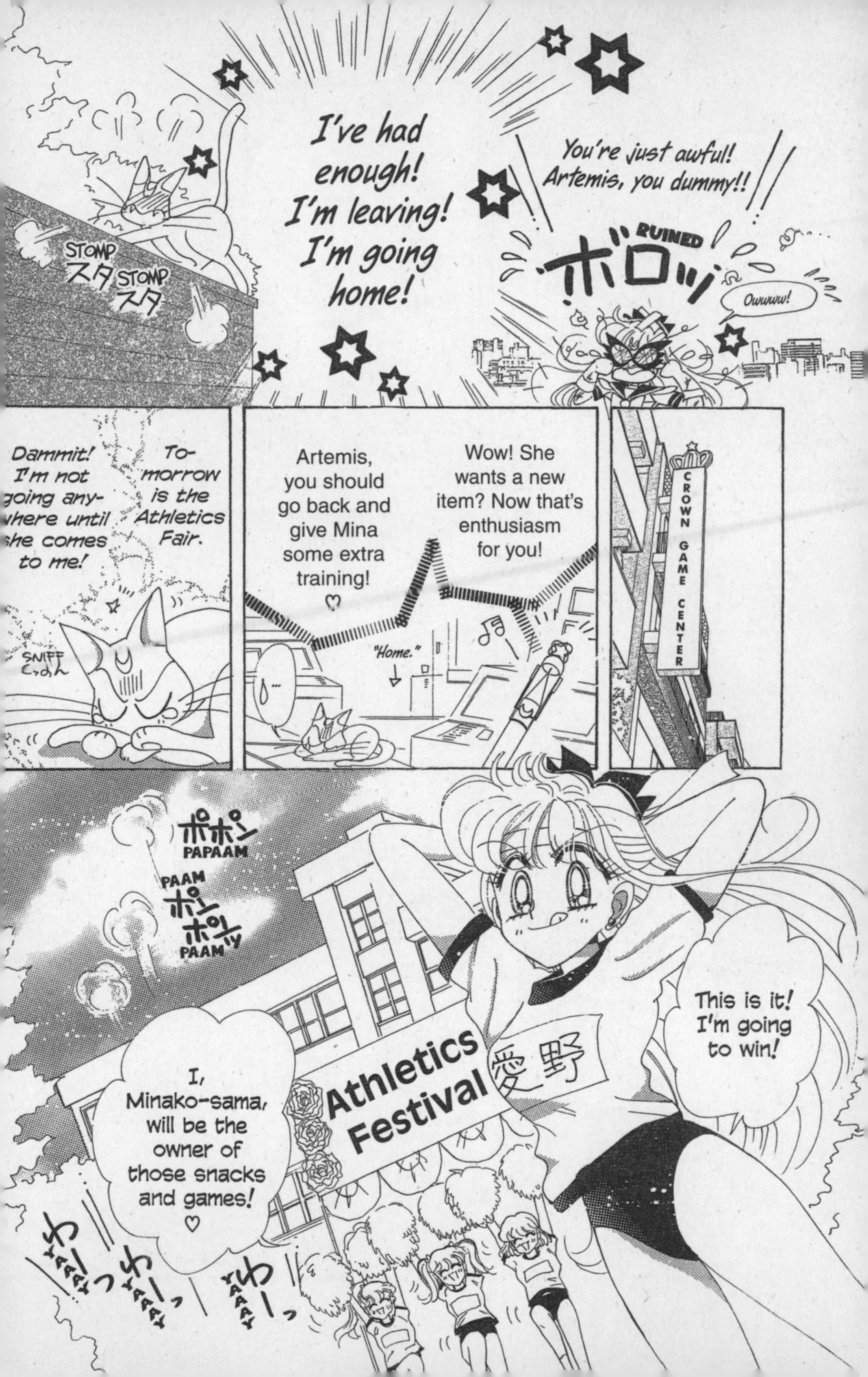

You're just awful! Artemis, you dummy!!
RUINED
ボロッ
Owwww!
I've had enough! I'm leaving! I'm going home!
STOMP スタ
STOMP スタ
CROWN GAME CENTER
Wow! She wants a new item? Now that's enthusiasm for you!
Artemis, you should go back and give Mina some extra training! ♡
"Home."
...
To-morrow is the Athletics Fair.
Dammit! I'm not going anywhere until she comes to me!
SNIFF くすん
This is it! I'm going to win!
Athletics Festival 愛野
PAPAAM ポポン
PAAM ポン ポンッ PAAM
I, Minako-sama, will be the owner of those snacks and games! ♡
YAAAY わーっ
YAAAY わーっ
YAAAY わーっ

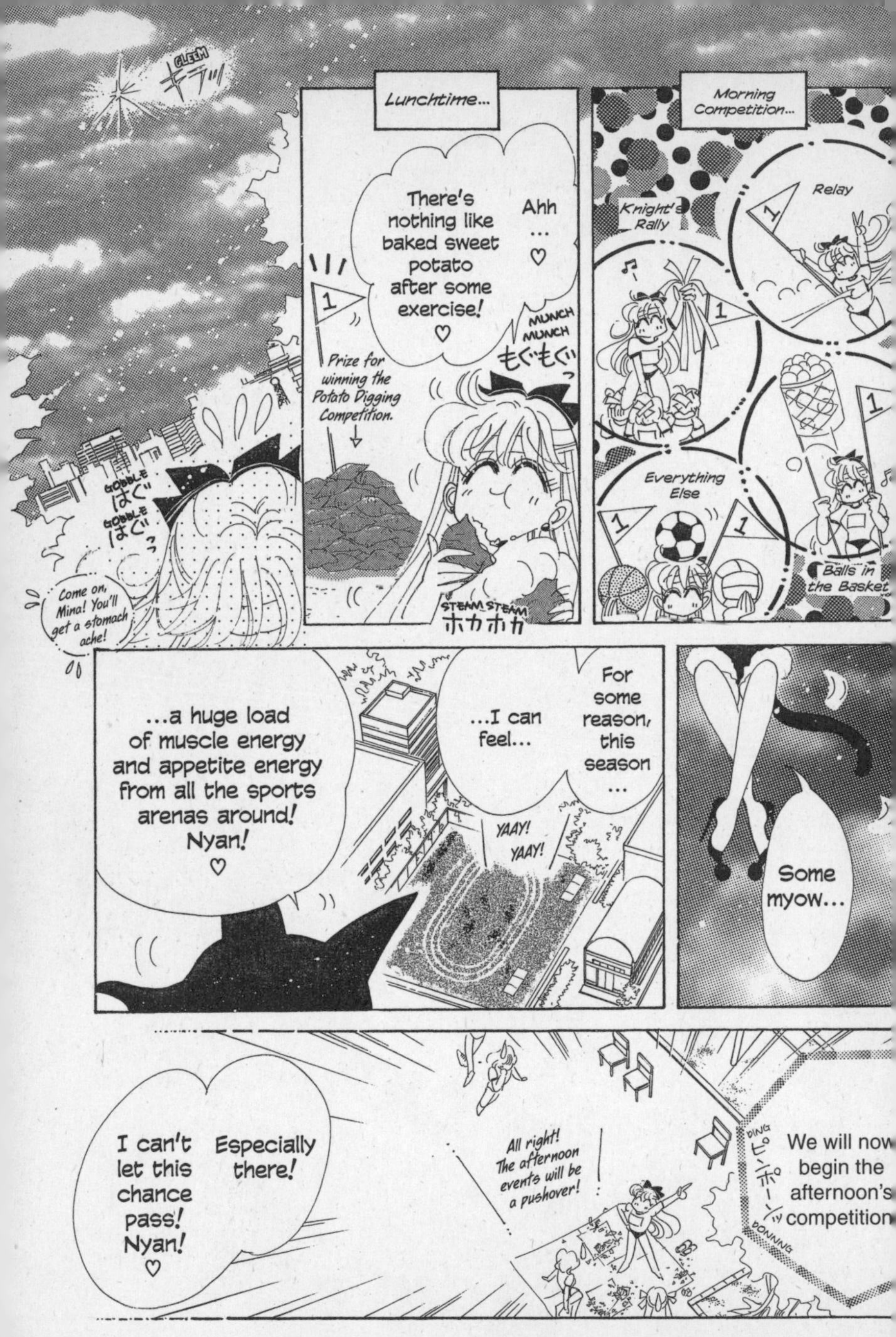

Morning Competition...
Relay
Knight's Rally
Balls in the Basket
Everything Else
Lunchtime...
Ahh ... ♡
There's nothing like baked sweet potato after some exercise! ♡
MUNCH MUNCH
もぐもぐっ
Prize for winning the Potato Digging Competition.
STEAM STEAM
ホカホカ
GLEEM
キラッ
GOBBLE
はぐ
GOBBLE
はぐっ
Come on, Mina! You'll get a stomach ache!
Some myow...
For some reason, this season ...
...I can feel...
YAAY! YAAY!
...a huge load of muscle energy and appetite energy from all the sports arenas around! Nyan! ♡
We will now begin the afternoon's competition
DING
ピンポーン
DONNNG
All right! The afternoon events will be a pushover!
Especially there!
I can't let this chance pass! Nyan! ♡

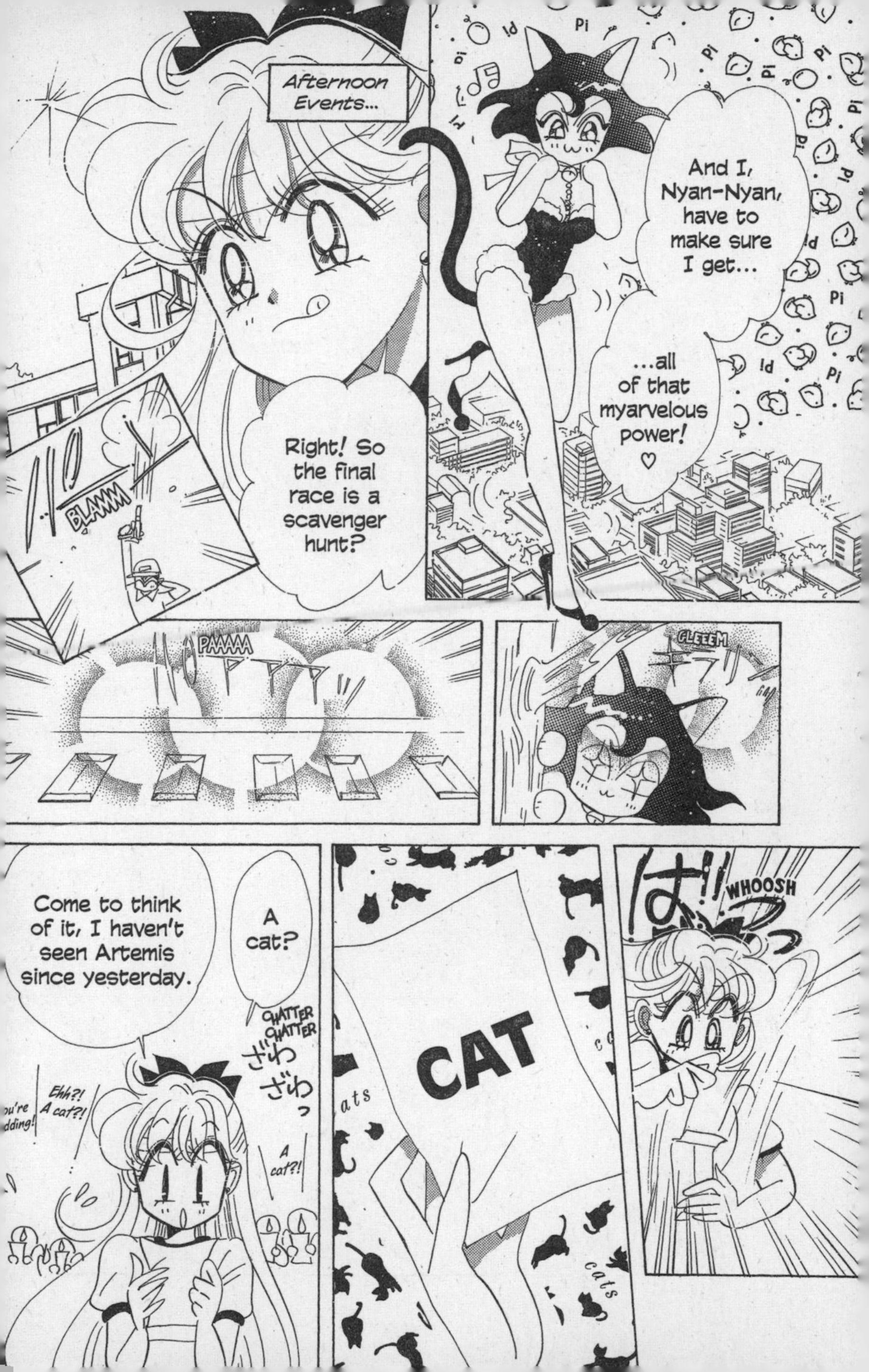
And I, Nyan-Nyan, have to make sure I get...
...all of that myarvelous power! ♥
Afternoon Events...
Right! So the final race is a scavenger hunt?
BLAMM
GLEEEM
PAAAAA
WHOOSH
CAT
cats
A cat?
Come to think of it, I haven't seen Artemis since yesterday.
CHATTER CHATTER
Ehh?! A cat?!
A cat?!

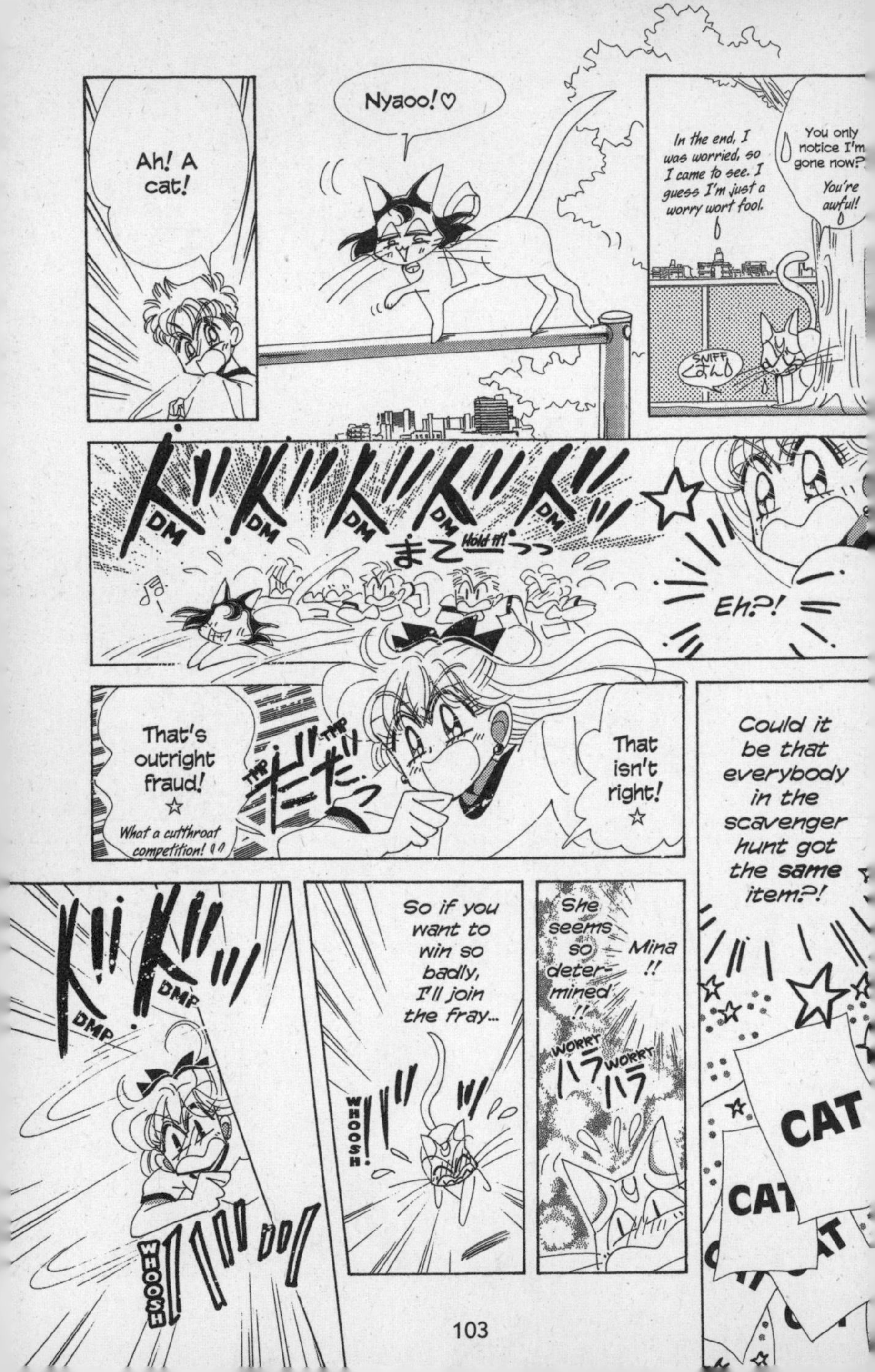
You only notice I'm gone now?
You're awful!
In the end, I was worried, so I came to see. I guess I'm just a worry wort fool.
SNIFF くすん
Nyaoo!♡
Ah! A cat!
Eh?!
DM DM DM DM DM
まて Hold it!
Could it be that everybody in the scavenger hunt got the same item?!
CAT
CAT
CAT
That isn't right! ☆
TMP TMP
That's outright fraud! ☆
What a cutthroat competition!
Mina!!
She seems so determined!!
WORRY ハラ WORRY ハラ
So if you want to win so badly, I'll join the fray...
WHOOSH
DMP DMP
WHOOSH

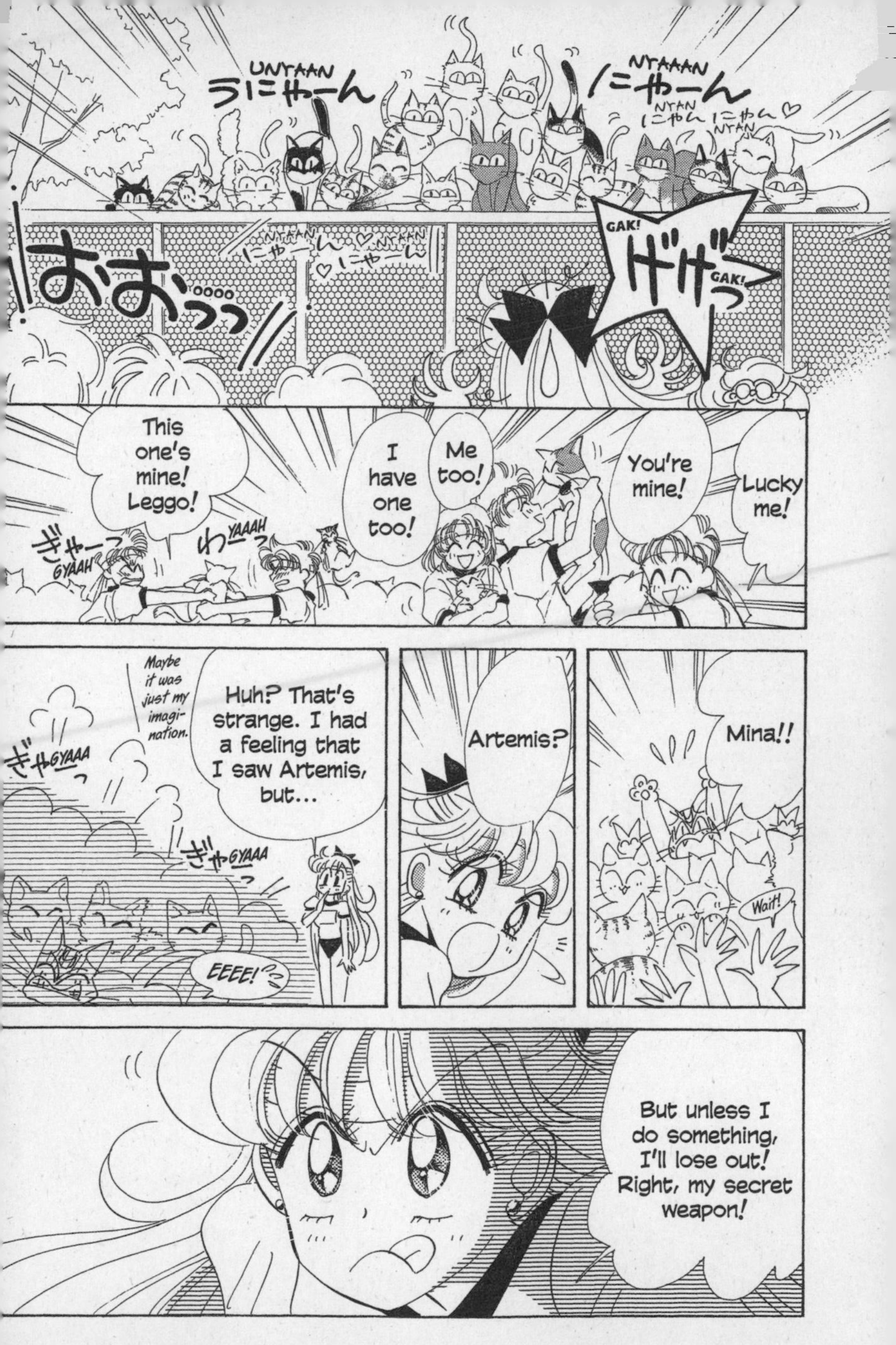
にゃーん
NYAAAN
にゃん にゃん♡
NYAN NYAN
ザザっ
GAK!
GAK!
うにゃーん
UNYAAN
にゃーん♡にゃーん
NYAAN NYAAN
おおっっ
OOOO
Lucky me!
You're mine!
Me too!
I have one too!
This one's mine! Leggo!
わーっ
YAAAH
ぎゃーっ
GYAAH
Mina!!
Wait!
Artemis?
Huh? That's strange. I had a feeling that I saw Artemis, but...
Maybe it was just my imagination.
ぎゃ
GYAAA
ぎゃ
GYAAA
EEEE!
But unless I do something, I'll lose out! Right, my secret weapon!

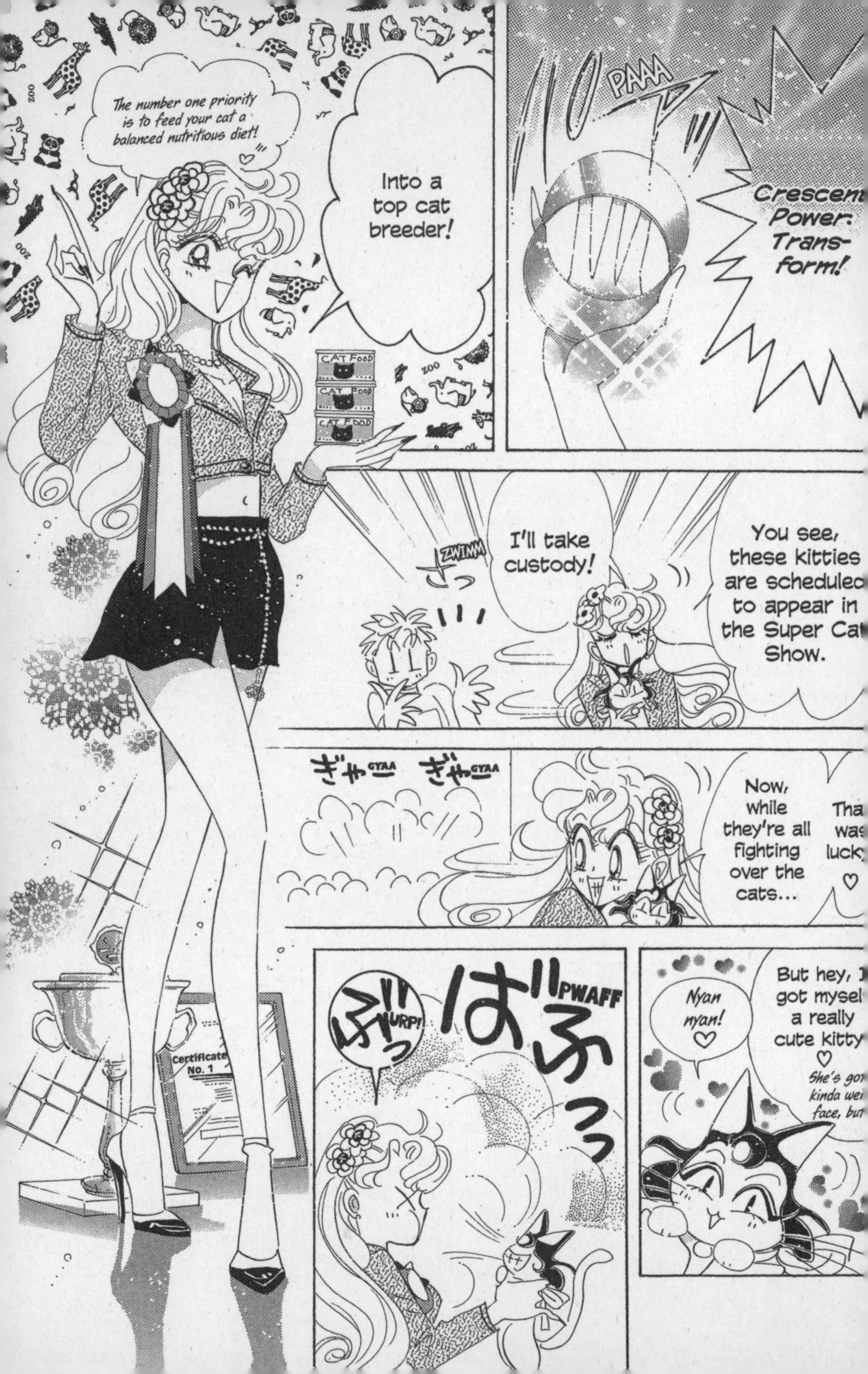
PAAA
Crescen
Power:
Trans-
form!
Into a top cat breeder!
The number one priority is to feed your cat a balanced nutritious diet!
CAT FOOD
CAT FOOD
CAT FOOD
ZOO
Certificate No. 1
You see, these kitties are schedule to appear in the Super Ca Show.
I'll take custody!
ZWIMM
Tha was luck ♡
Now, while they're all fighting over the cats...
ぎゃGYAA ぎゃGYAA
But hey, I got mysel a really cute kitty ♡
She's go kinda wei face, bu
Nyan nyan! ♡
はふっPWAFF
ふっURP!

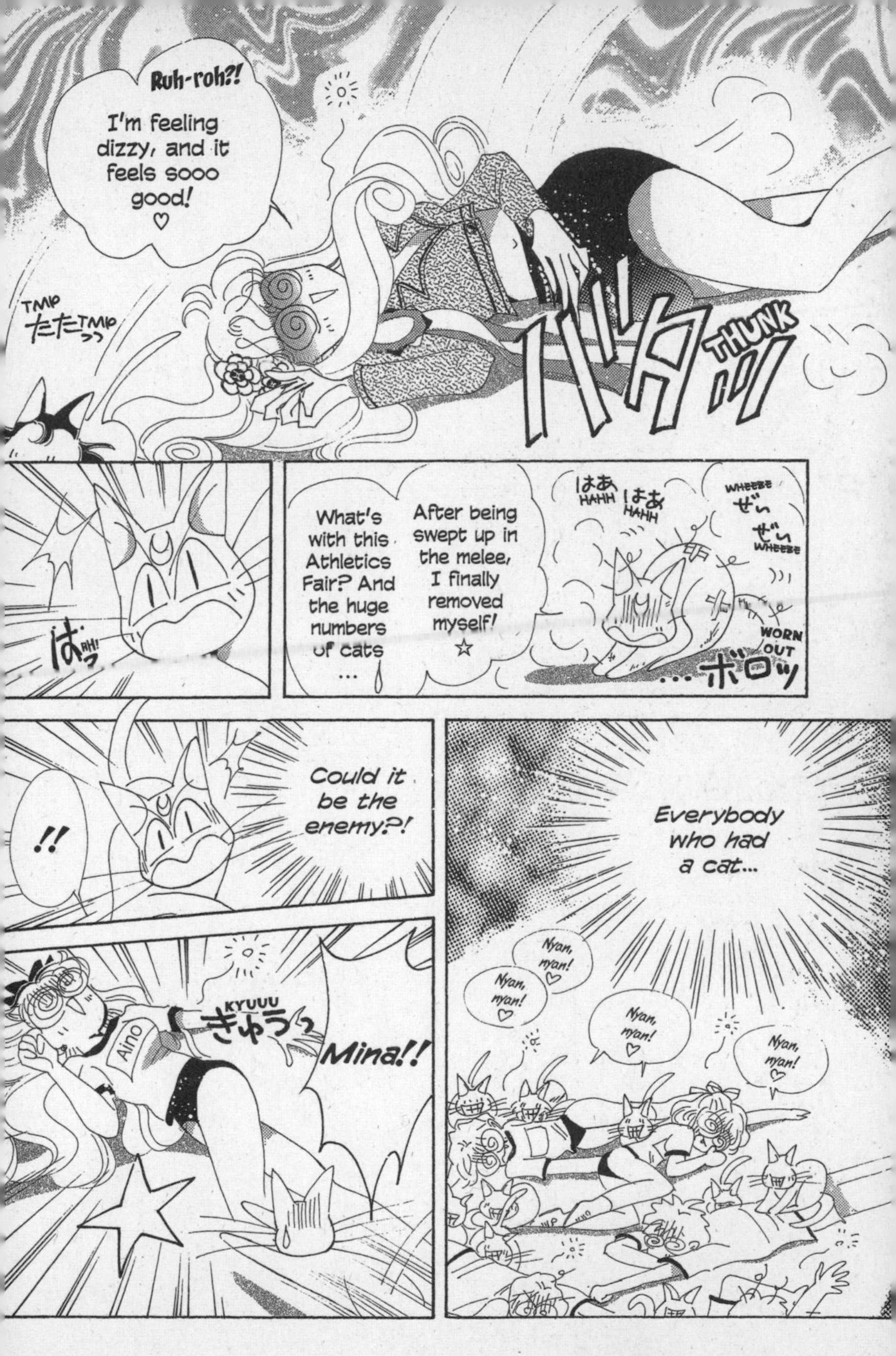
Ruh-roh?!
I'm feeling dizzy, and it feels sooo good! ♡
バタッ THUNK
TMP たた TMP っっ
ぜい WHEEZE ぜい WHEEZE
はあ HAHH はあ HAHH
WORN OUT ...ボロッ
After being swept up in the melee, I finally removed myself! ☆
What's with this Athletics Fair? And the huge numbers of cats ...
はっ RH!
Everybody who had a cat...
Nyan, nyan! ♡
Nyan, nyan! ♡
Nyan, nyan! ♡
Nyan, nyan! ♡
Could it be the enemy?!
!!
Mina!!
KYUUU きゅう

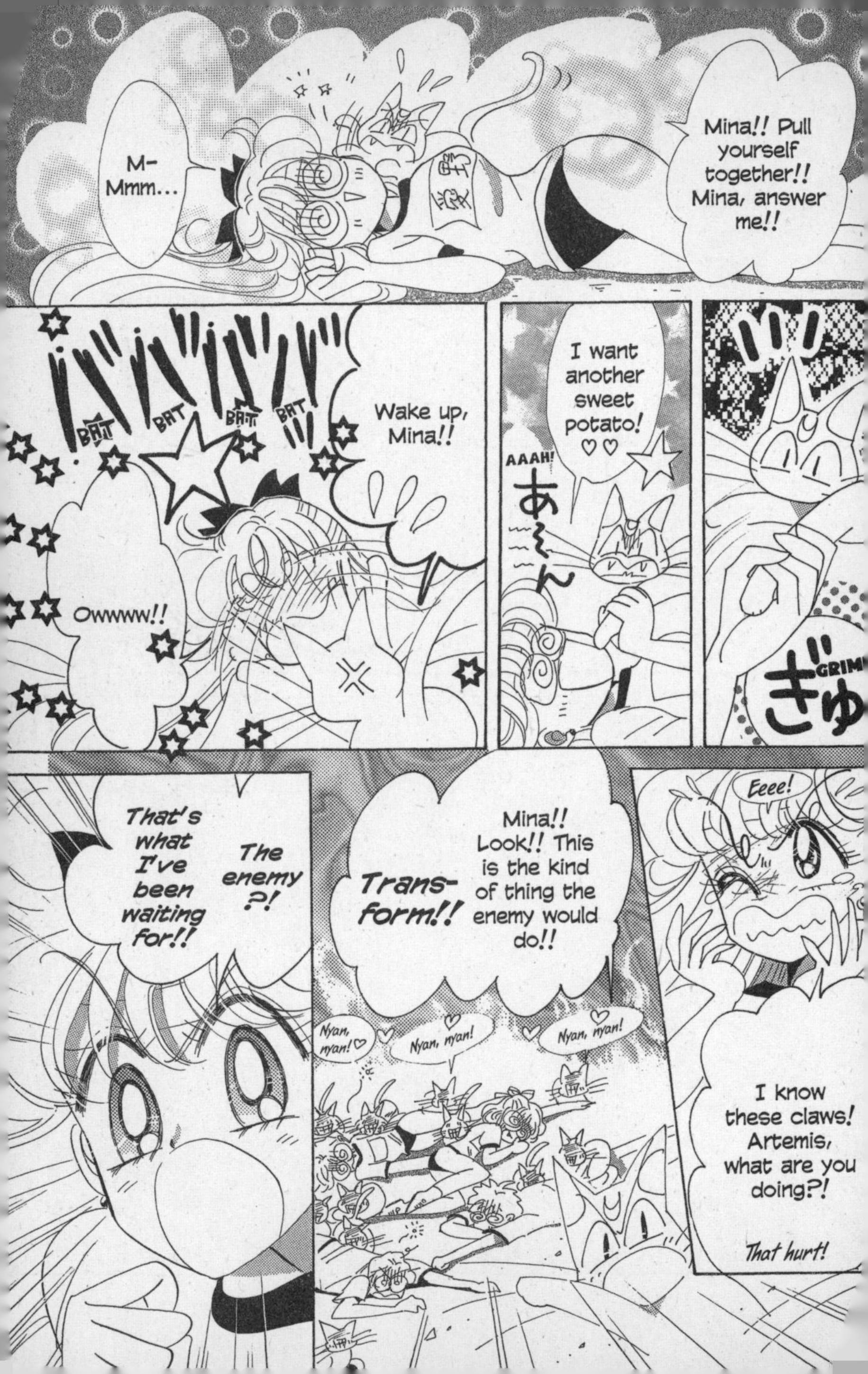
Mina!! Pull yourself together!! Mina, answer me!!
M-Mmm...
ぎゅ
GRIM
I want another sweet potato! ♡♡
あ〜ん
AAAH!
Wake up, Mina!!
BAT BAT BAT BAT
Owwww!!
Eeee!
I know these claws! Artemis, what are you doing?!
That hurt!
Mina!! Look!! This is the kind of thing the enemy would do!!
Transform!!
Nyan, nyan!
Nyan, nyan!
Nyan, nyan! ♡
The enemy ?!
That's what I've been waiting for!!

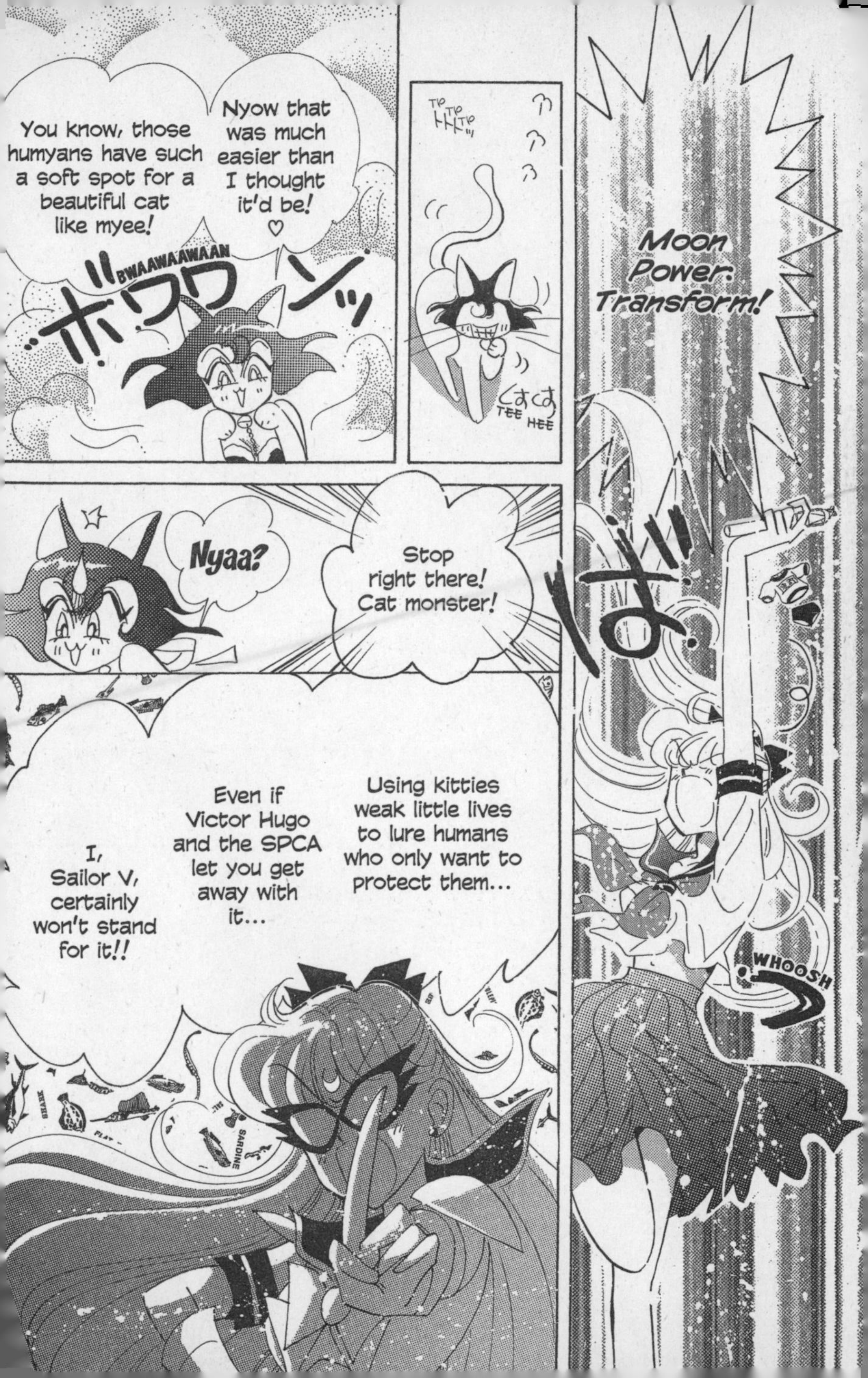

Moon Power: Transform!
ばっ
WHOOSH
トトトト
TIP TIP TIP TIP
くすくす
TEE HEE
Nyow that was much easier than I thought it'd be! ♡
You know, those humyans have such a soft spot for a beautiful cat like myee!
ボワワンッ
BWAAWAAWAAN
Stop right there! Cat monster!
Nyaa?
Using kitties weak little lives to lure humans who only want to protect them...
Even if Victor Hugo and the SPCA let you get away with it...
I, Sailor V, certainly won't stand for it!!
SARDINE

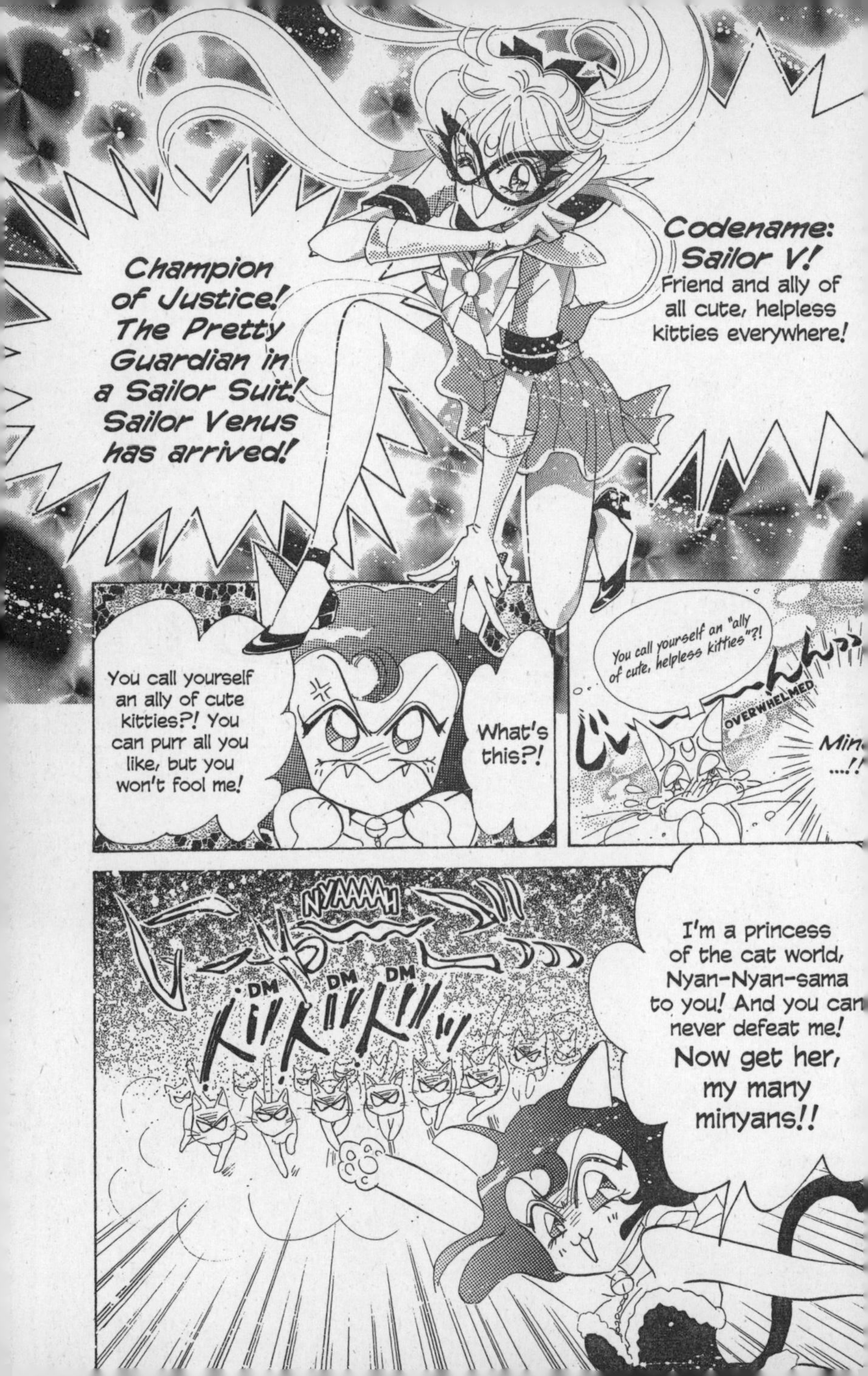
Codename: Sailor V!
Friend and ally of all cute, helpless kitties everywhere!
Champion of Justice! The Pretty Guardian in a Sailor Suit! Sailor Venus has arrived!
You call yourself an "ally of cute, helpless kitties"?!
OVERWHELMED
Min...!!
What's this?!
You call yourself an ally of cute kitties?! You can purr all you like, but you won't fool me!
I'm a princess of the cat world, Nyan-Nyan-sama to you! And you can never defeat me!
Now get her, my many minyans!!
NYAAAAH
DM
DM
DM

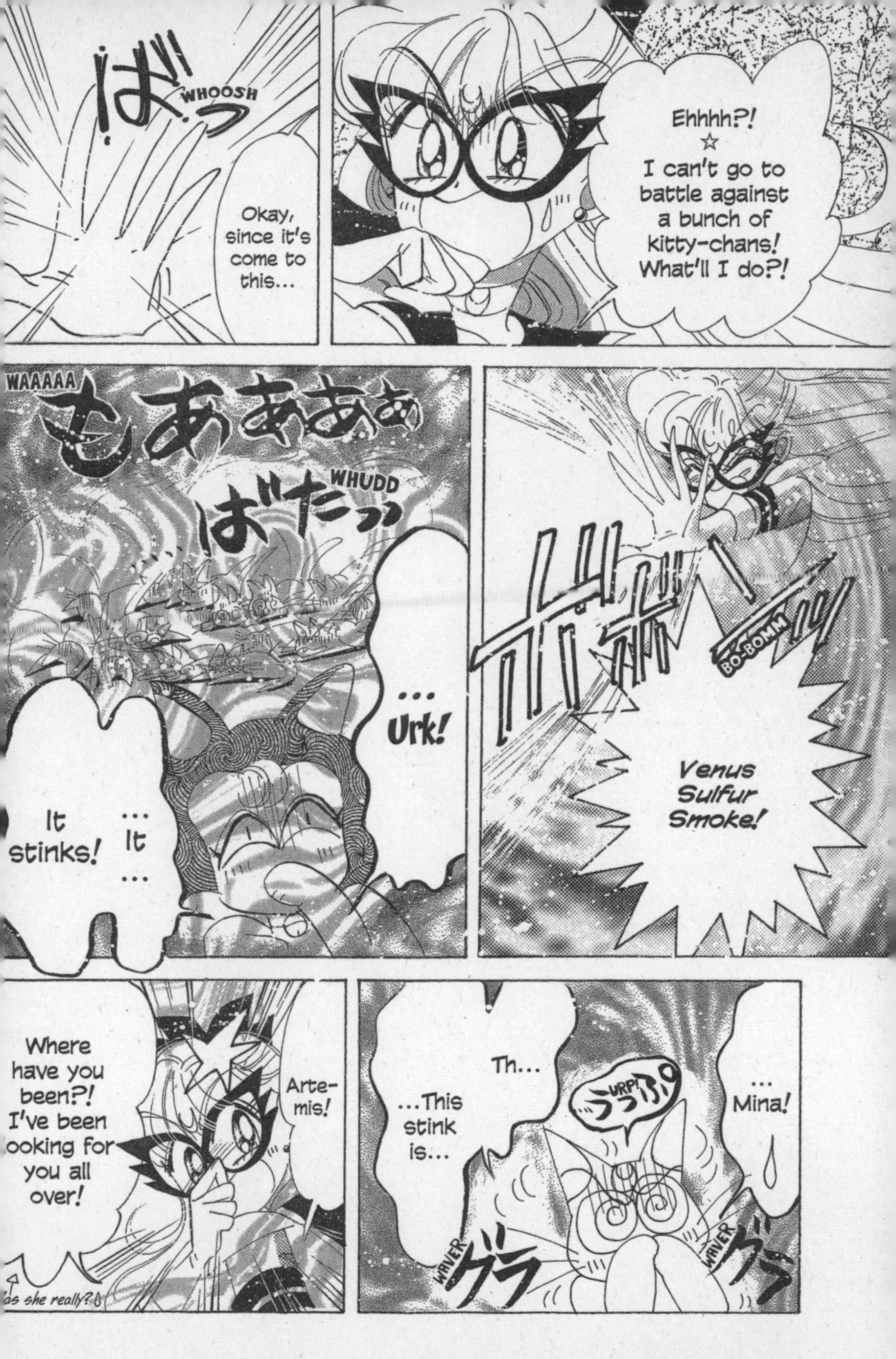
Ehhhh?! ☆ I can't go to battle against a bunch of kitty-chans! What'll I do?!
WHOOSH
Okay, since it's come to this...
BO-BOMM
Venus Sulfur Smoke!
WAAAAA
WHUDD
... Urk!
... It ...
It stinks!
... Mina!
URP!
Th...
...This stink is...
WAVER
WAVER
Arte-mis!
Where have you been?! I've been looking for you all over!

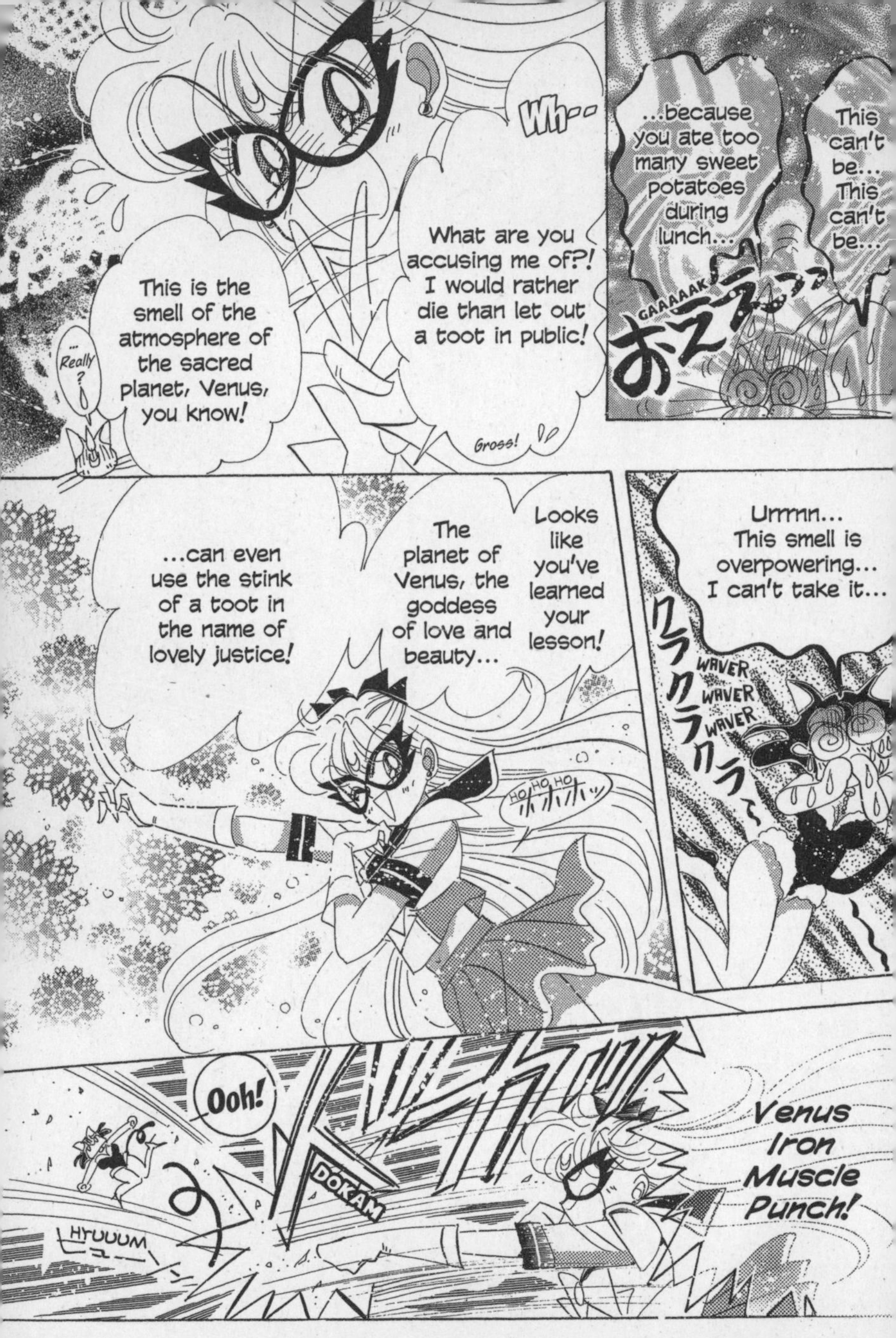
This can't be... This can't be...
...because you ate too many sweet potatoes during lunch...
GAAAAAK
おえええっ
Wh--
What are you accusing me of?! I would rather die than let out a toot in public!
This is the smell of the atmosphere of the sacred planet, Venus, you know!
...Really?
Gross!
Urrmn... This smell is overpowering... I can't take it...
WAVER WAVER WAVER
Looks like you've learned your lesson!
The planet of Venus, the goddess of love and beauty...
...can even use the stink of a toot in the name of lovely justice!
HO HO HO
ホホホッ
Venus Iron Muscle Punch!
DOKAM
Ooh!
HYUUUM

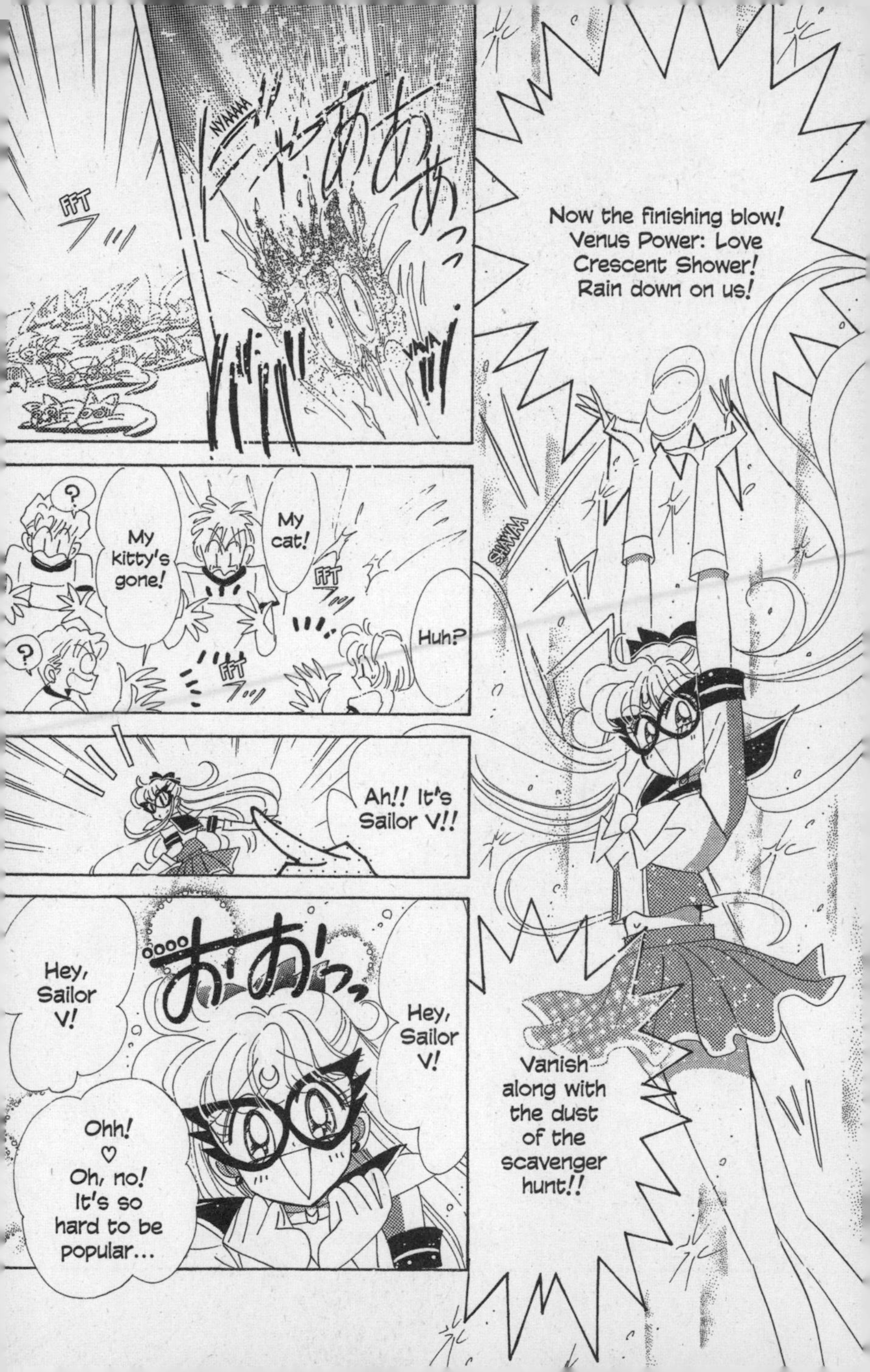
Now the finishing blow! Venus Power: Love Crescent Shower! Rain down on us!
Vanish along with the dust of the scavenger hunt!!
NYAAAA
FFT
Huh?
My cat!
FFT
FFT
My kitty's gone!
Ah!! It's Sailor V!!
Hey, Sailor V!
OOOO
Hey, Sailor V!
Ohh! ♡ Oh, no! It's so hard to be popular...

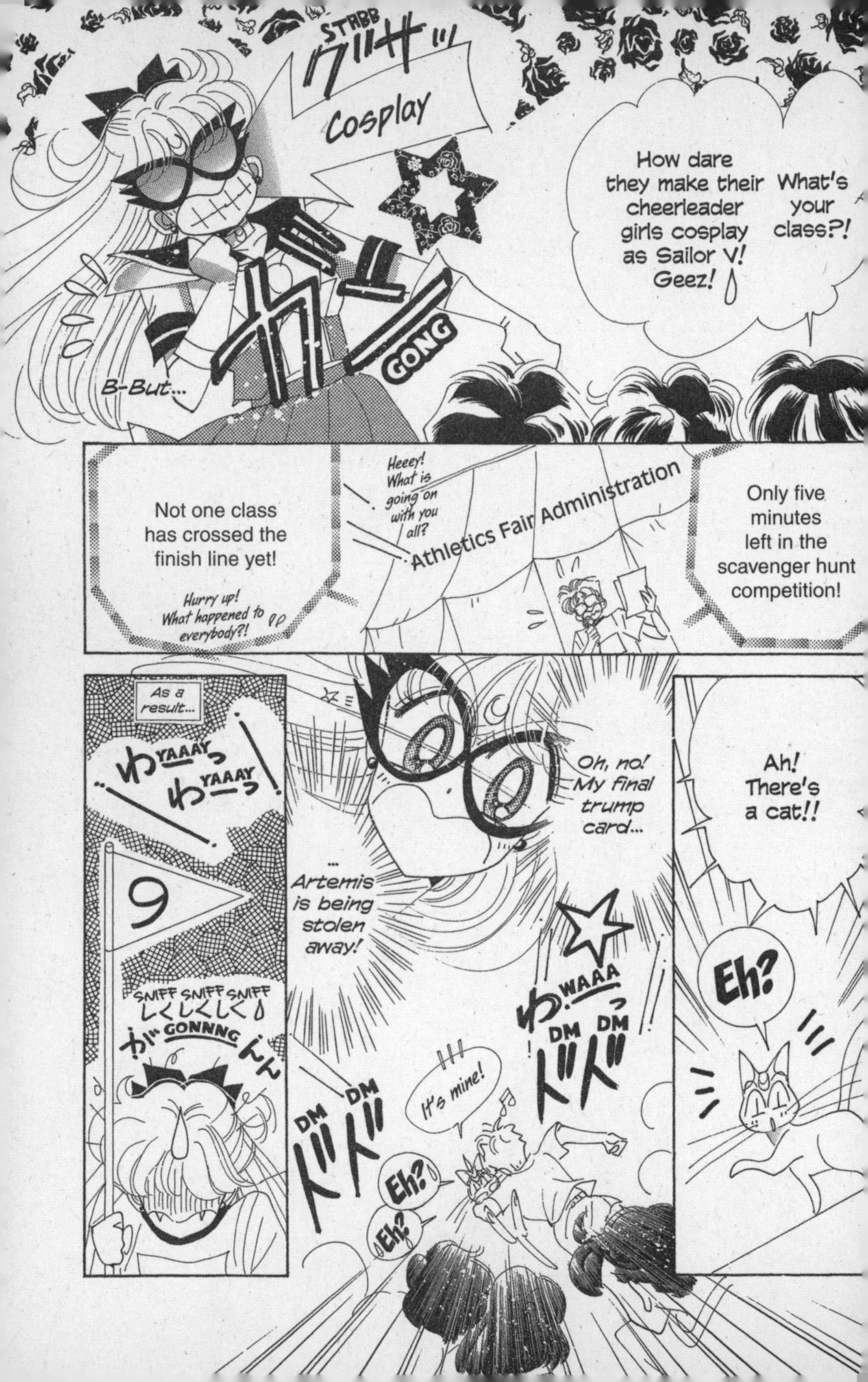

What's your class?!
How dare they make their cheerleader girls cosplay as Sailor V! Geez!
STABB
グサッ
Cosplay
GONG
ガーン
B-But...
Only five minutes left in the scavenger hunt competition!
Athletics Fair Administration
Heeey! What is going on with you all?
Not one class has crossed the finish line yet!
Hurry up! What happened to everybody?!
Ah! There's a cat!!
Eh?
Oh, no! My final trump card...
...Artemis is being stolen away!
WAAA
わっ
DM DM
ドド
It's mine!
Eh?
Eh?
DM DM
ドド
As a result...
YAAAY わーっ
YAAAY わーっ
9
SNIFF SNIFF SNIFF
しくしくしく
GONNNG
がーん

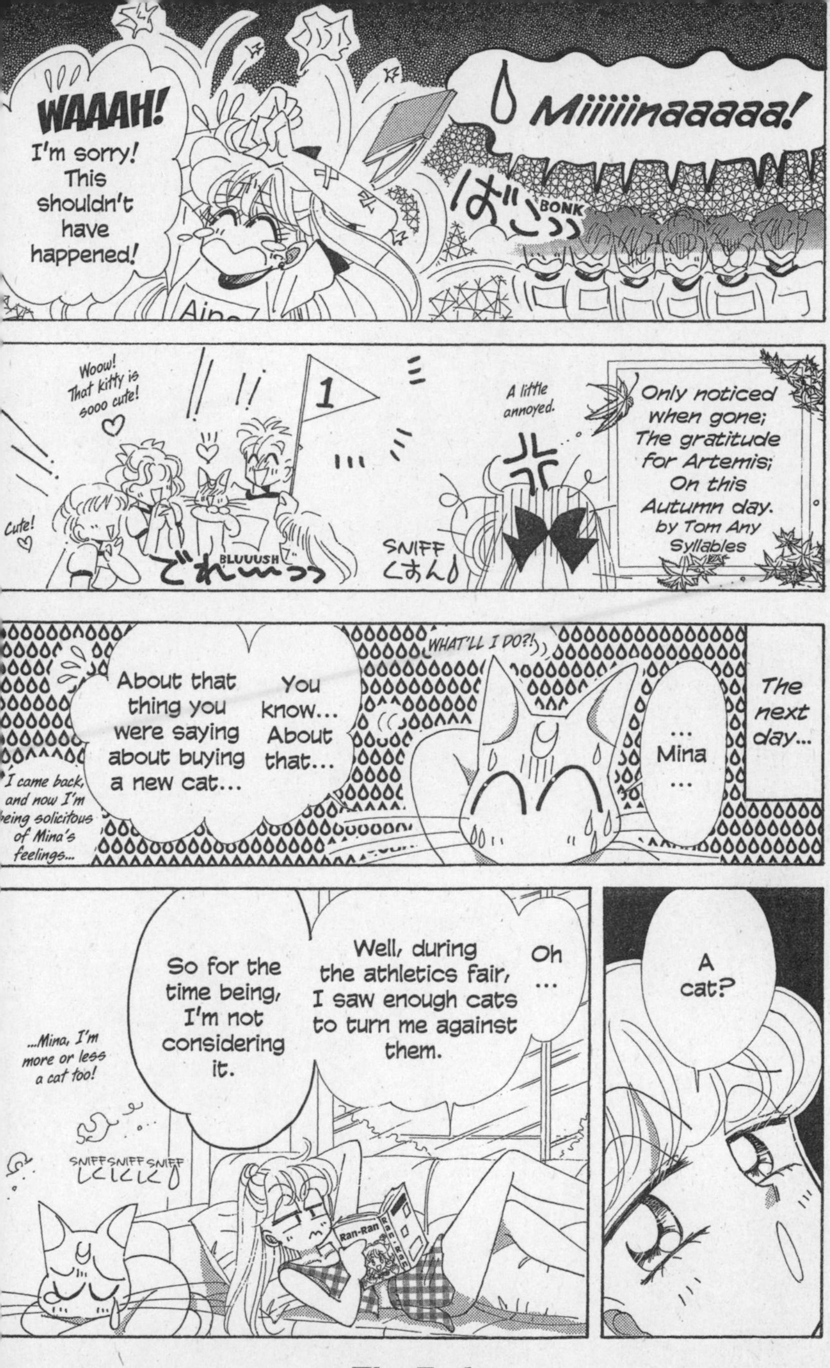

Miiiiinaaaaa!
ばごっ BONK
WAAAH!
I'm sorry! This shouldn't have happened!
Only noticed when gone; The gratitude for Artemis; On this Autumn day.
by Tom Any Syllables
A little annoyed.
SNIFF くおん
Woow! That kitty is sooo cute!
BLUUUSH でれ〜っ
Cute!
The next day...
... Mina ...
WHAT'LL I DO?!
You know... About that...
About that thing you were saying about buying a new cat...
I came back, and now I'm being solicitous of Mina's feelings...
A cat?
Oh ...
Well, during the athletics fair, I saw enough cats to turn me against them.
So for the time being, I'm not considering it.
...Mina, I'm more or less a cat too!
SNIFFSNIFFSNIFF しくしく
Ran-Ran

• *The End* •

Vol. 12 Pet Chapter 2, Wan-Wan's Schemes!

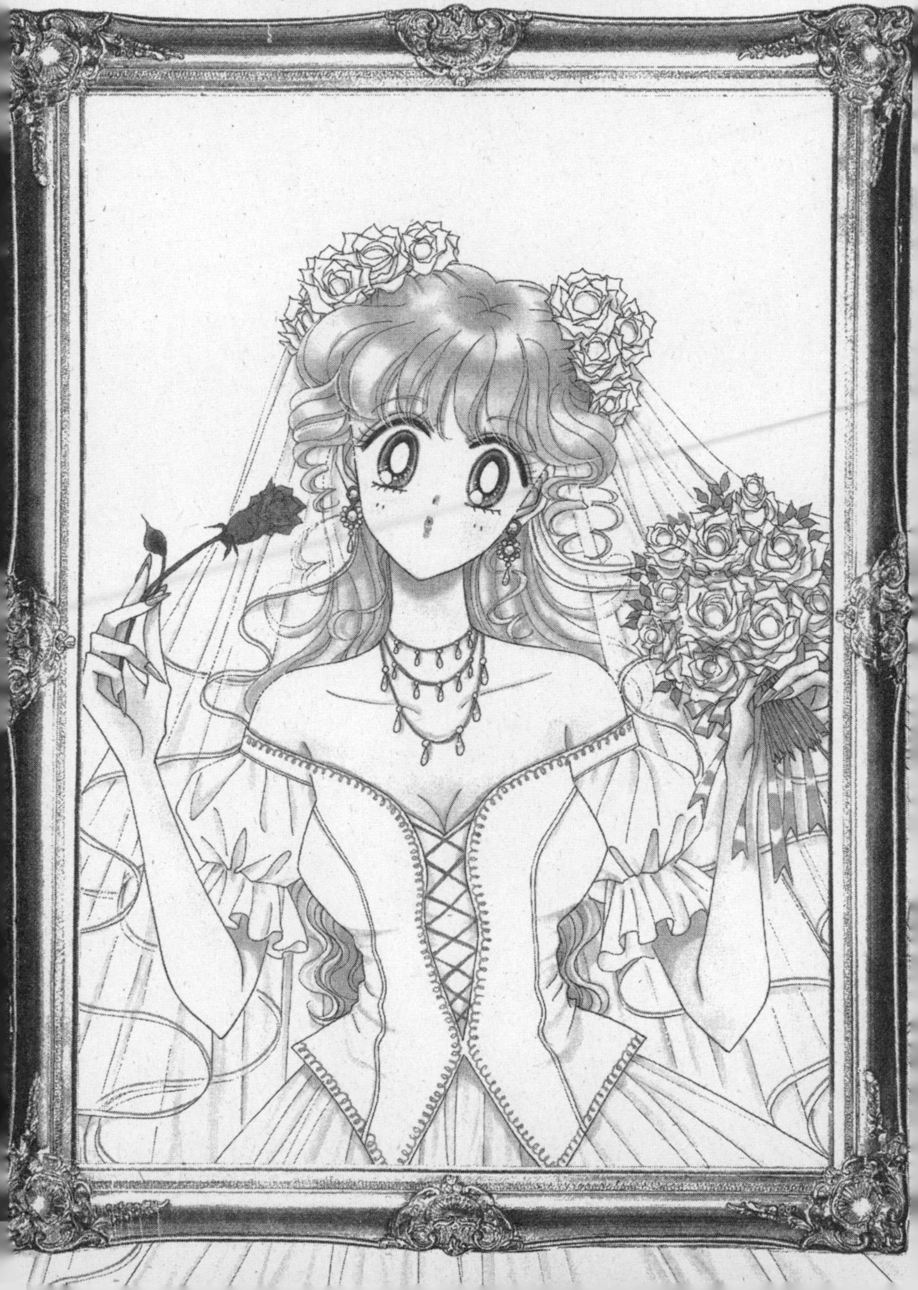

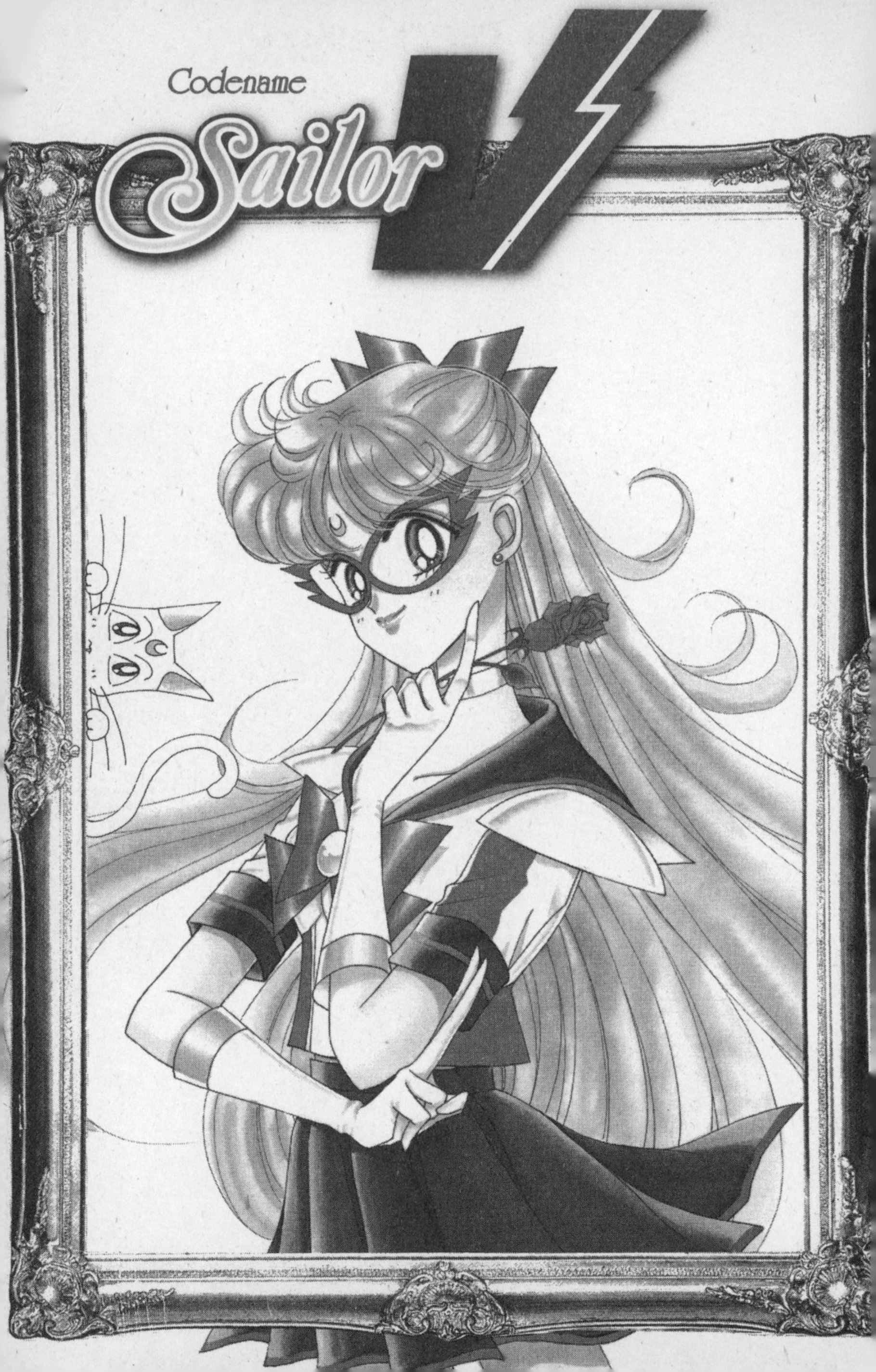
Codename
Sailor V

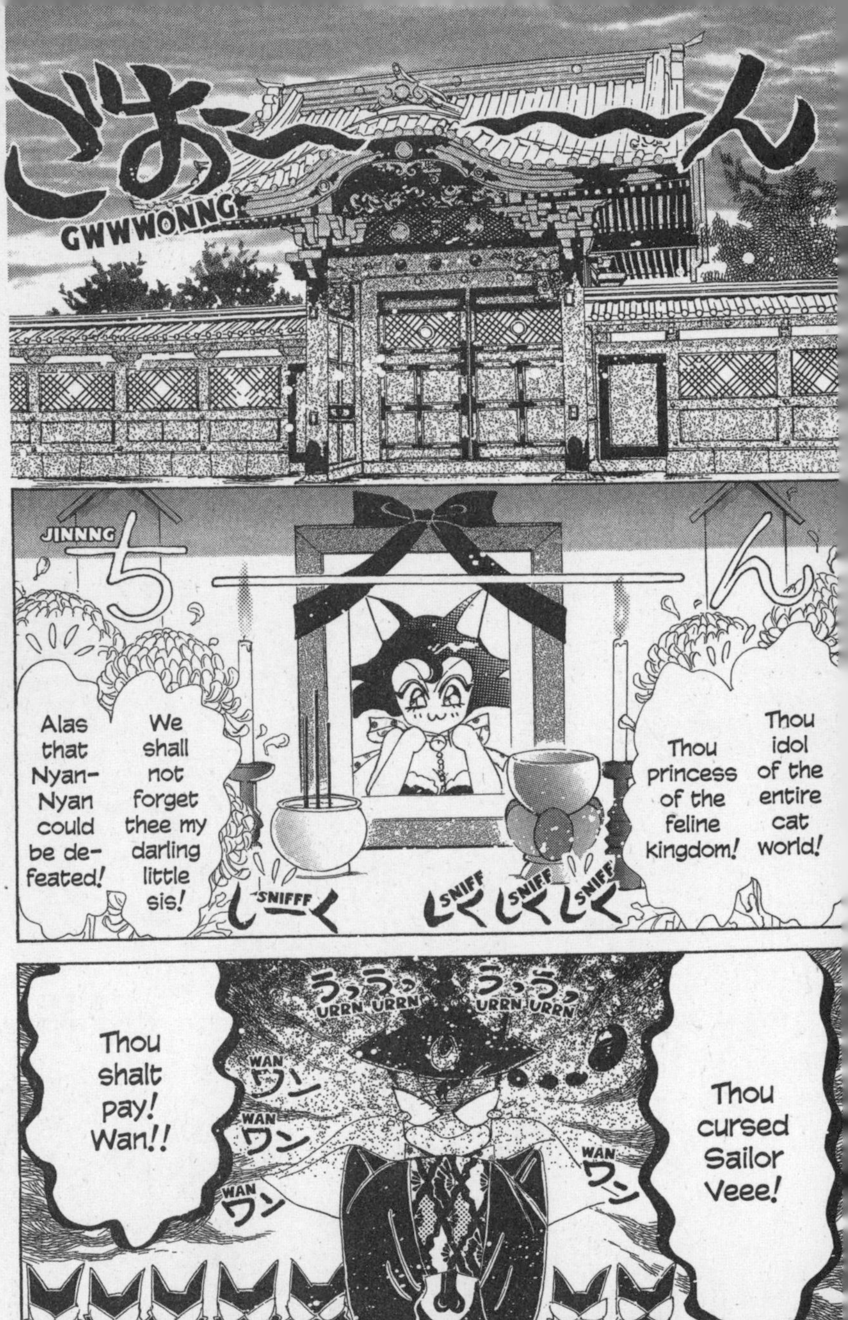
ごお〜〜〜ん
GWWWONNG
ちーん
JINNNG
Thou idol of the entire cat world!
Thou princess of the feline kingdom!
We shall not forget thee my darling little sis!
Alas that Nyan-Nyan could be defeated!
しくしくしく
SNIFF SNIFF SNIFF
しーく
SNIFFF
うっうっ
URRN URRN
うっうっ
URRN URRN
Thou cursed Sailor Veee!
ワン
WAN
ワン
WAN
ワン
WAN
ワン
WAN
Thou shalt pay! Wan!!

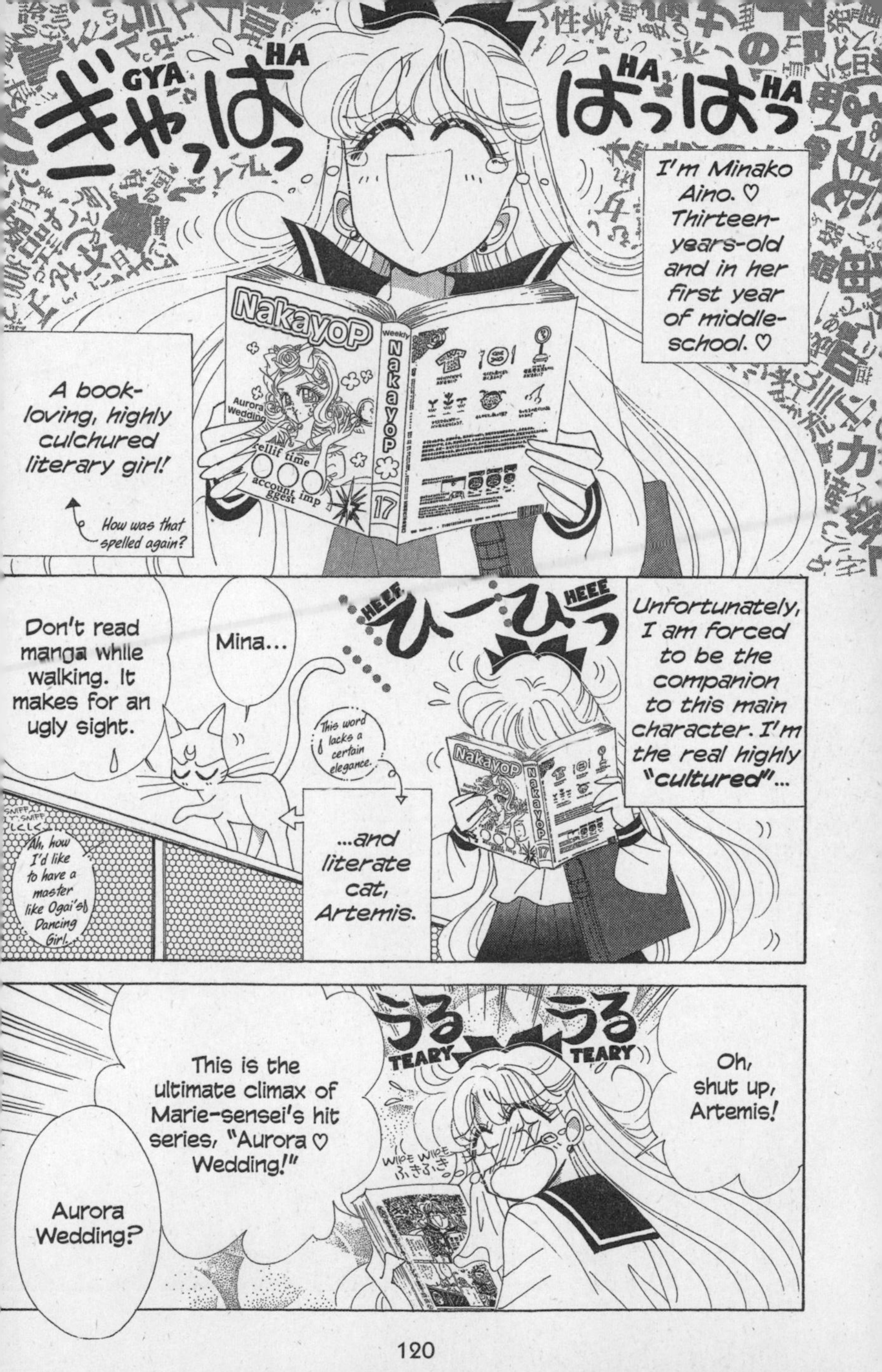
GYA HA
HA HA
I'm Minako Aino. ♡ Thirteen-years-old and in her first year of middle-school. ♡
A book-loving, highly culchured literary girl!
How was that spelled again?
HEEE HEEE
Unfortunately, I am forced to be the companion to this main character. I'm the real highly "cultured"...
Mina...
Don't read manga while walking. It makes for an ugly sight.
This word lacks a certain elegance.
...and literate cat, Artemis.
SNIFF SNIFF
Ah, how I'd like to have a master like Ogai's Dancing Girl.
TEARY TEARY
Oh, shut up, Artemis!
WIPE WIPE
This is the ultimate climax of Marie-sensei's hit series, "Aurora ♡ Wedding!"
Aurora Wedding?

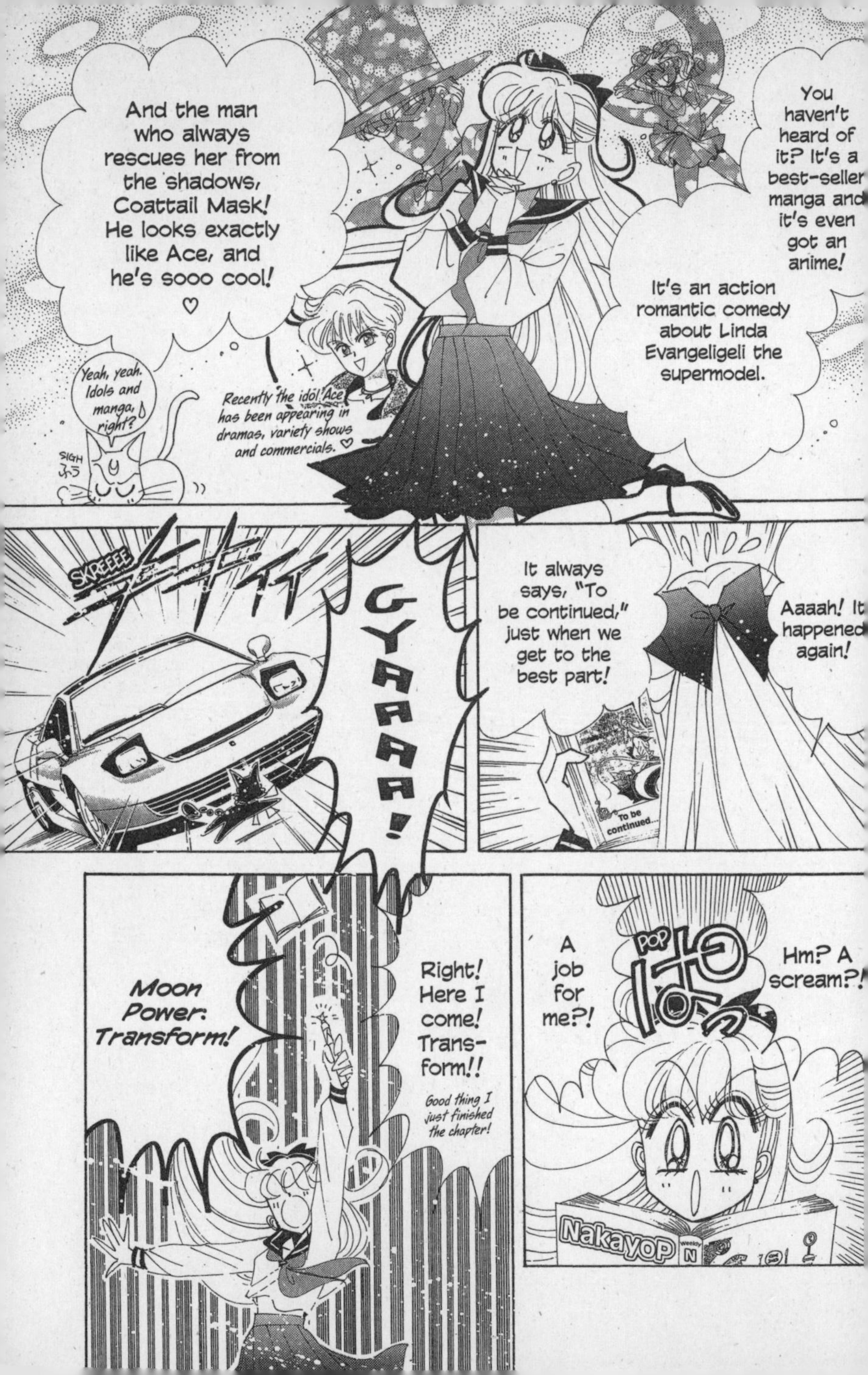
You haven't heard of it? It's a best-seller manga and it's even got an anime!
It's an action romantic comedy about Linda Evangeligeli the supermodel.
And the man who always rescues her from the shadows, Coattail Mask! He looks exactly like Ace, and he's sooo cool! ♡
Recently the idol Ace has been appearing in dramas, variety shows and commercials. ♡
Yeah, yeah. Idols and manga, right?
SIGH
Aaaah! It happened again!
It always says, "To be continued," just when we get to the best part!
To be continued...
SKREEEE
GYAAAA!
Hm? A scream?!
POP
A job for me?!
Nakayop
Weekly
N
Right! Here I come! Trans-form!!
Good thing I just finished the chapter!
Moon Power: Transform!

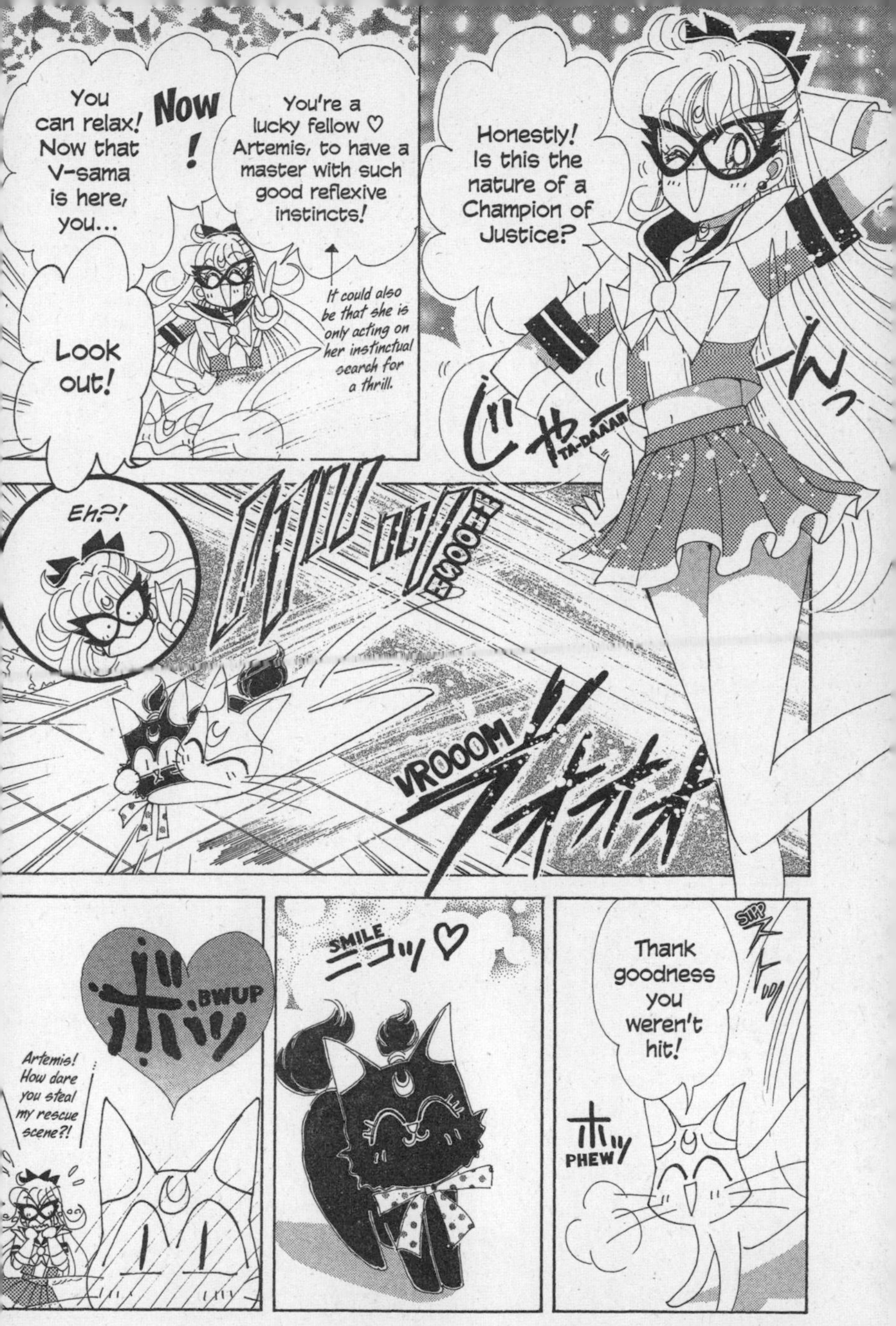
Honestly! Is this the nature of a Champion of Justice?
じゃ〜ん
TA-DAAAH
You're a lucky fellow ♡ Artemis, to have a master with such good reflexive instincts!
Now!
You can relax! Now that V-sama is here, you...
It could also be that she is only acting on her instinctual search for a thrill.
Look out!
Eh?!
WHOOSH
VROOOM!!
Thank goodness you weren't hit!
SIPP
ホッ
PHEW
ニコッ ♡
SMILE
ボッ
BWUP
Artemis! How dare you steal my rescue scene?!

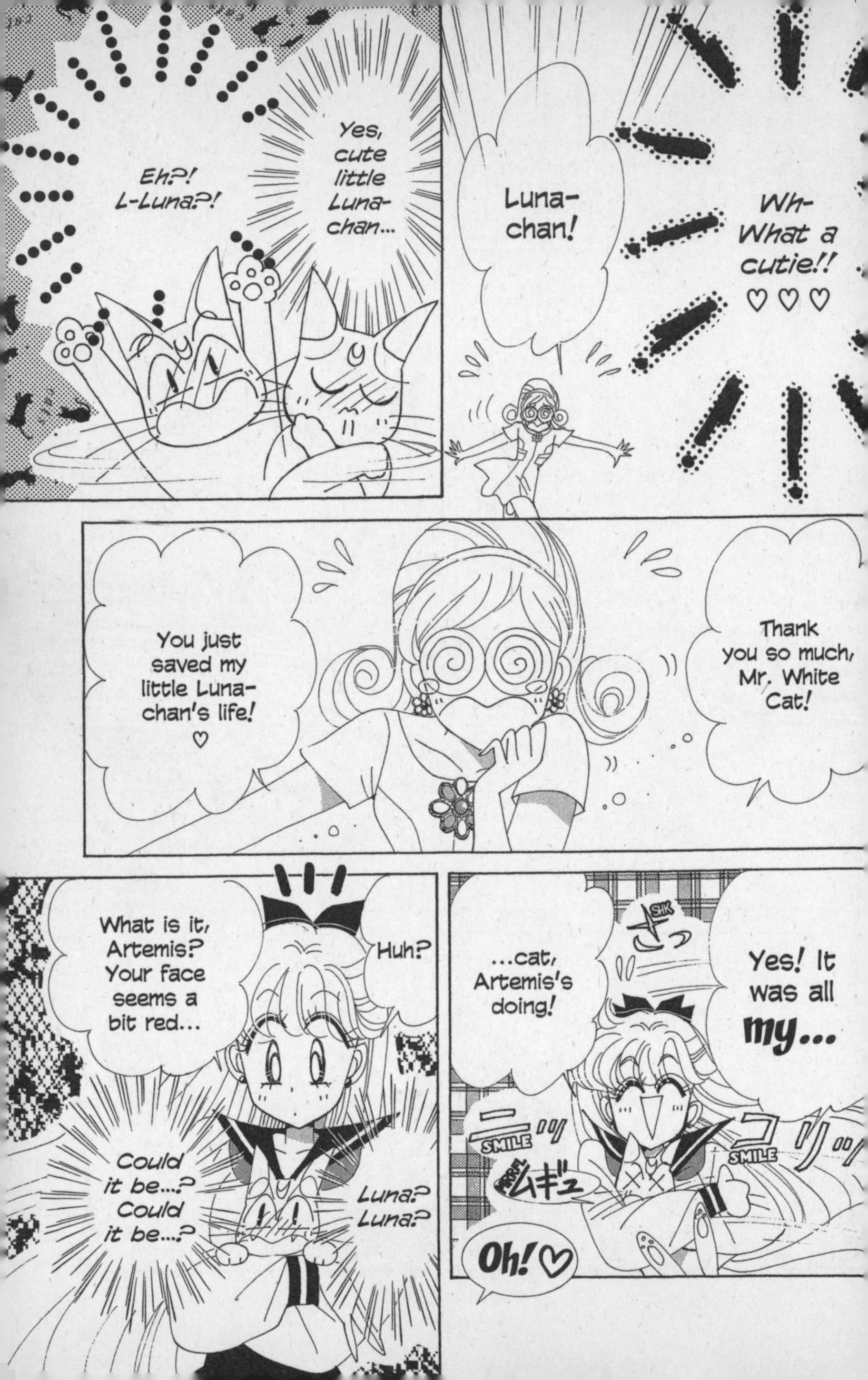
Wh- What a cutie!! ♡ ♡ ♡
Luna-chan!
Yes, cute little Luna-chan...
Eh?! L-Luna?!
Thank you so much, Mr. White Cat!
You just saved my little Luna-chan's life! ♡
Yes! It was all my...
SHK
...cat, Artemis's doing!
SMILE
SMILE
Oh! ♡
Huh?
What is it, Artemis? Your face seems a bit red...
Luna? Luna?
Could it be...? Could it be...?

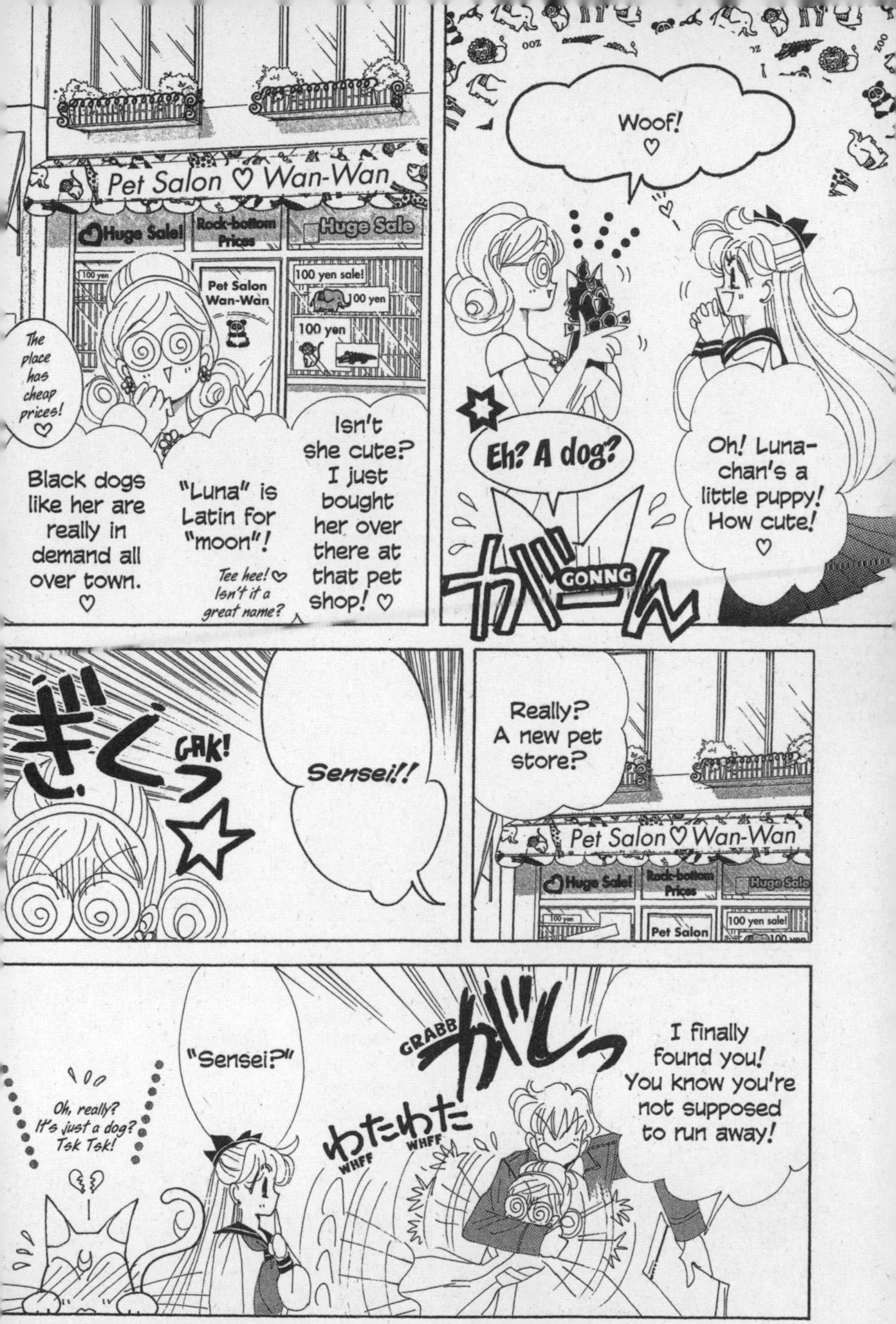

Woof! ♡
Oh! Luna-chan's a little puppy! How cute! ♡
Eh? A dog?
GONNG
Isn't she cute? I just bought her over there at that pet shop! ♡
"Luna" is Latin for "moon"!
Tee hee! ♡ Isn't it a great name?
Black dogs like her are really in demand all over town. ♡
The place has cheap prices! ♡
Pet Salon ♡ Wan-Wan
Huge Sale!
Rock-bottom Prices
Huge Sale
100 yen
Pet Salon Wan-Wan
100 yen sale!
100 yen
100 yen
Really? A new pet store?
Pet Salon ♡ Wan-Wan
Huge Sale!
Rock-bottom Prices
Huge Sale
100 yen
Pet Salon
100 yen sale!
Sensei!!
GAK!
I finally found you! You know you're not supposed to run away!
GRABB
わたわた
WHFF
WHFF
"Sensei?"
Oh, really? It's just a dog? Tsk Tsk!

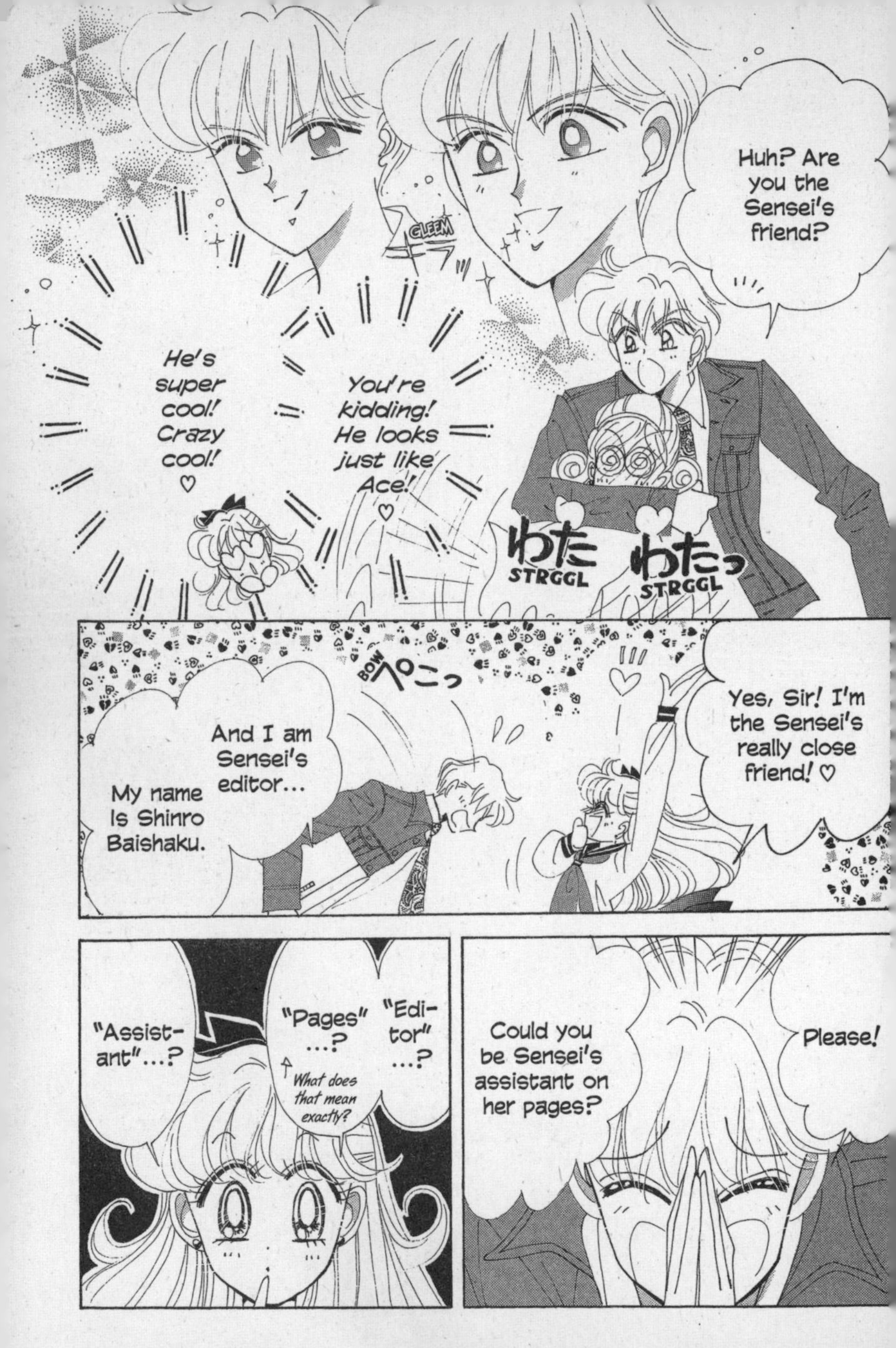
Huh? Are you the Sensei's friend?
GLEEM
You're kidding! He looks just like Ace! ♡
He's super cool! Crazy cool! ♡
わたっ STRGGL
わた STRGGL
Yes, Sir! I'm the Sensei's really close friend! ♡
ぺこっ BOW
And I am Sensei's editor...
My name is Shinro Baishaku.
Please!
Could you be Sensei's assistant on her pages?
"Editor"...?
"Pages"...?
What does that mean exactly?
"Assistant"...?

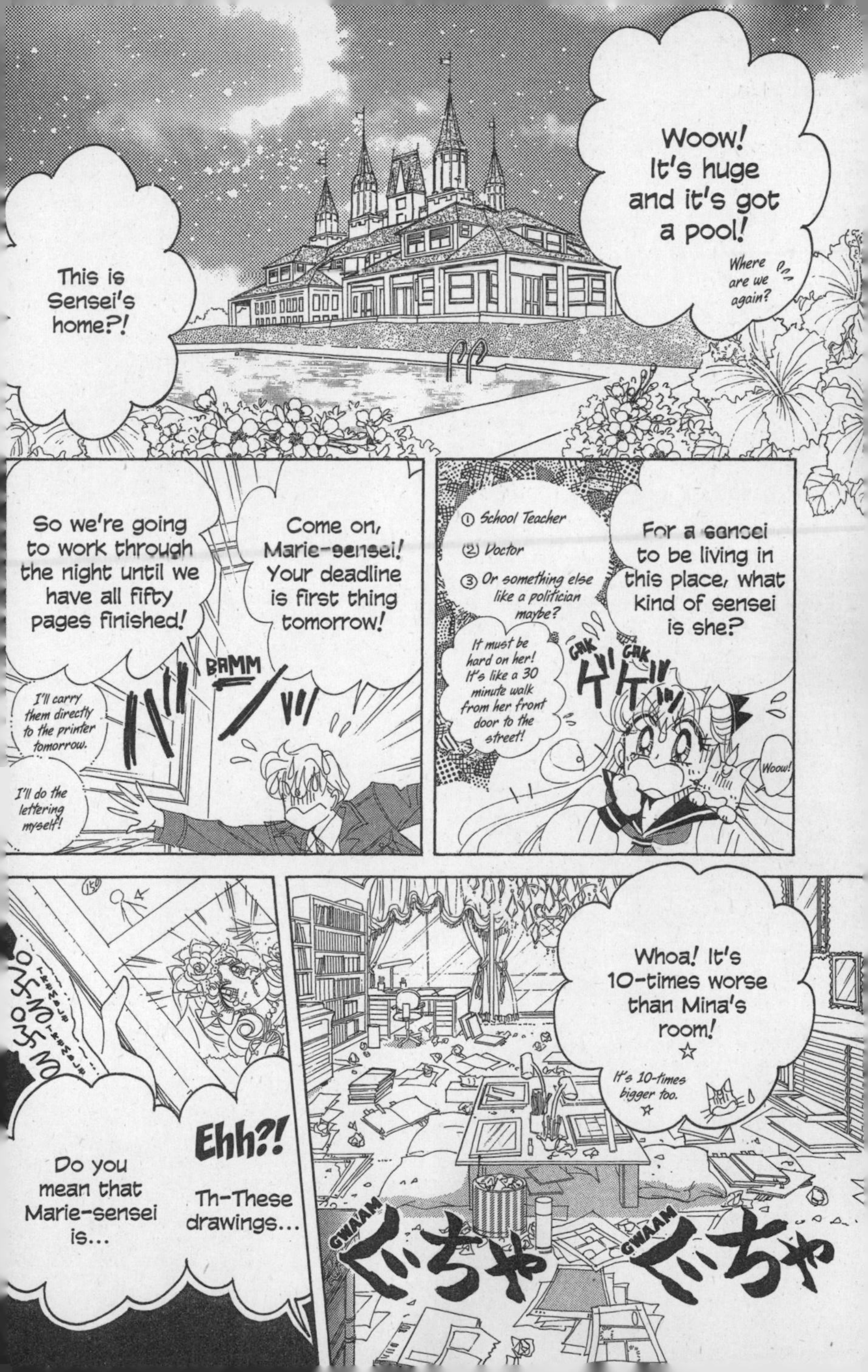
Woow! It's huge and it's got a pool!
Where are we again?
This is Sensei's home?!
For a sensei to be living in this place, what kind of sensei is she?
① School Teacher
② Doctor
③ Or something else like a politician maybe?
It must be hard on her! It's like a 30 minute walk from her front door to the street!
GAK GAK
Woow!
Come on, Marie-sensei! Your deadline is first thing tomorrow!
So we're going to work through the night until we have all fifty pages finished!
BAMM
I'll carry them directly to the printer tomorrow.
I'll do the lettering myself!
Whoa! It's 10-times worse than Mina's room! ☆
It's 10-times bigger too. ☆
GWAAM ぐちゃ
GWAAM ぐちゃ
Ehh?!
Th-These drawings...
Do you mean that Marie-sensei is...

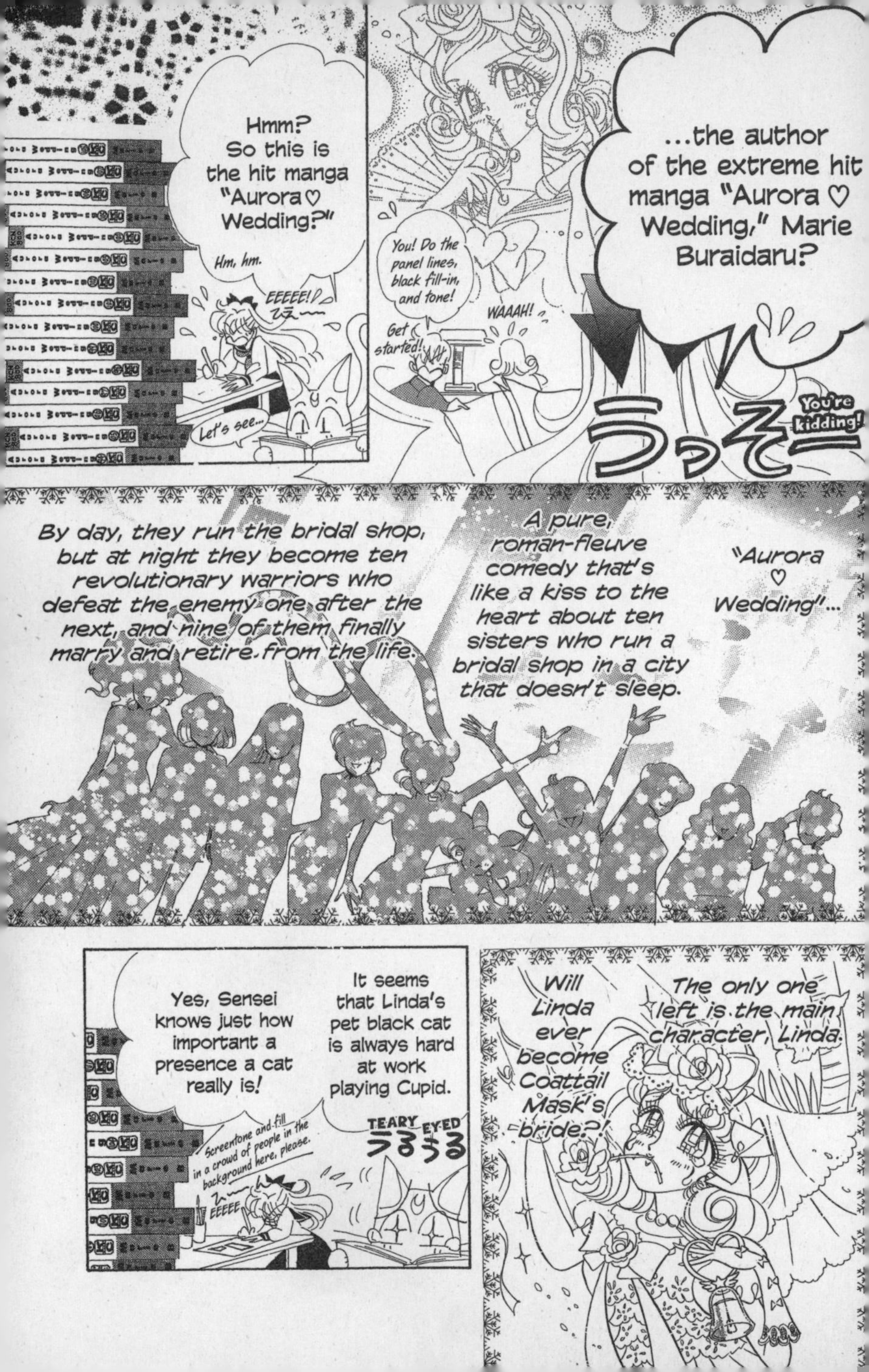
...the author of the extreme hit manga "Aurora ♡ Wedding," Marie Buraidaru?
You! Do the panel lines, black fill-in, and tone!
WAAAH!
Get started!
You're kidding!
うっそー
Hmm? So this is the hit manga "Aurora ♡ Wedding?"
Hm, hm.
EEEEE! ひえ〜
Let's see...
"Aurora ♡ Wedding"...
A pure, roman-fleuve comedy that's like a kiss to the heart about ten sisters who run a bridal shop in a city that doesn't sleep.
By day, they run the bridal shop, but at night they become ten revolutionary warriors who defeat the enemy one after the next, and nine of them finally marry and retire from the life.
The only one left is the main character, Linda.
Will Linda ever become Coattail Mask's bride?!
It seems that Linda's pet black cat is always hard at work playing Cupid.
Yes, Sensei knows just how important a presence a cat really is!
TEARY EYED
うるうる
Screentone and fill in a crowd of people in the background here, please.
EEEEE

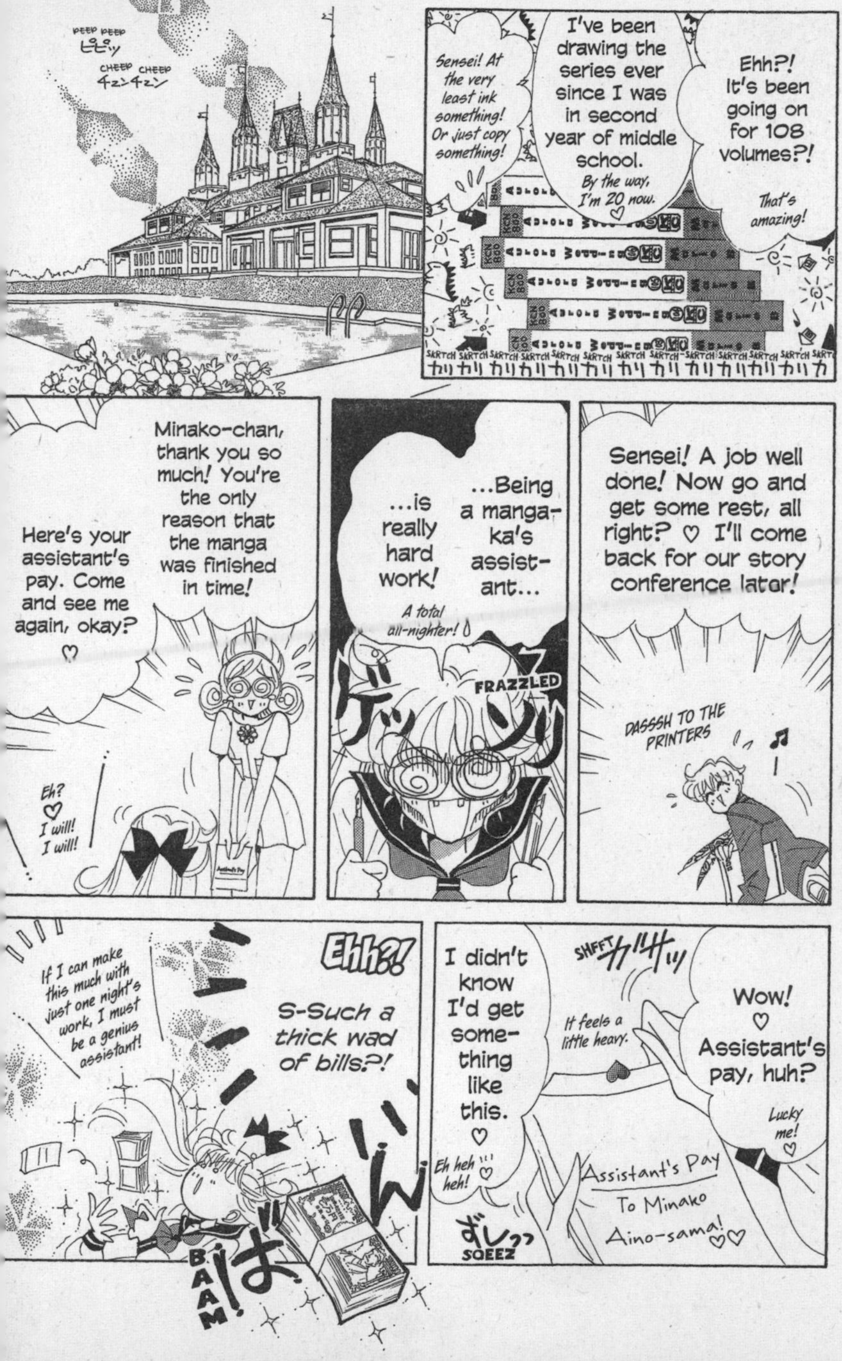
Ehh?! It's been going on for 108 volumes?!
That's amazing!
I've been drawing the series ever since I was in second year of middle school.
By the way, I'm 20 now. ♡
Sensei! At the very least ink something! Or just copy something!
SKRTCH SKRTCH SKRTCH SKRTCH SKRTCH SKRTCH SKRTCH SKRTCH SKRTCH SKRTCH SKRTCH SKRTCH
カリカリカリカリカリカリカリカリカリカリカリカリカ
PEEP PEEP
ピピッ
CHEEP CHEEP
チュンチュン
Sensei! A job well done! Now go and get some rest, all right? ♡ I'll come back for our story conference later!
DASSSH TO THE PRINTERS
...Being a manga-ka's assistant...
...is really hard work!
A total all-nighter!
FRAZZLED
Minako-chan, thank you so much! You're the only reason that the manga was finished in time!
Here's your assistant's pay. Come and see me again, okay? ♡
Eh? ♡ I will! I will!
Wow! ♡ Assistant's pay, huh?
Lucky me! ♡
SHFFT
It feels a little heavy.
I didn't know I'd get something like this. ♡
Assistant's Pay To Minako Aino-sama! ♡♡
Eh heh heh! ♡
SQEEZ
Ehh?!
S-Such a thick wad of bills?!
If I can make this much with just one night's work, I must be a genius assistant!
BAAM!

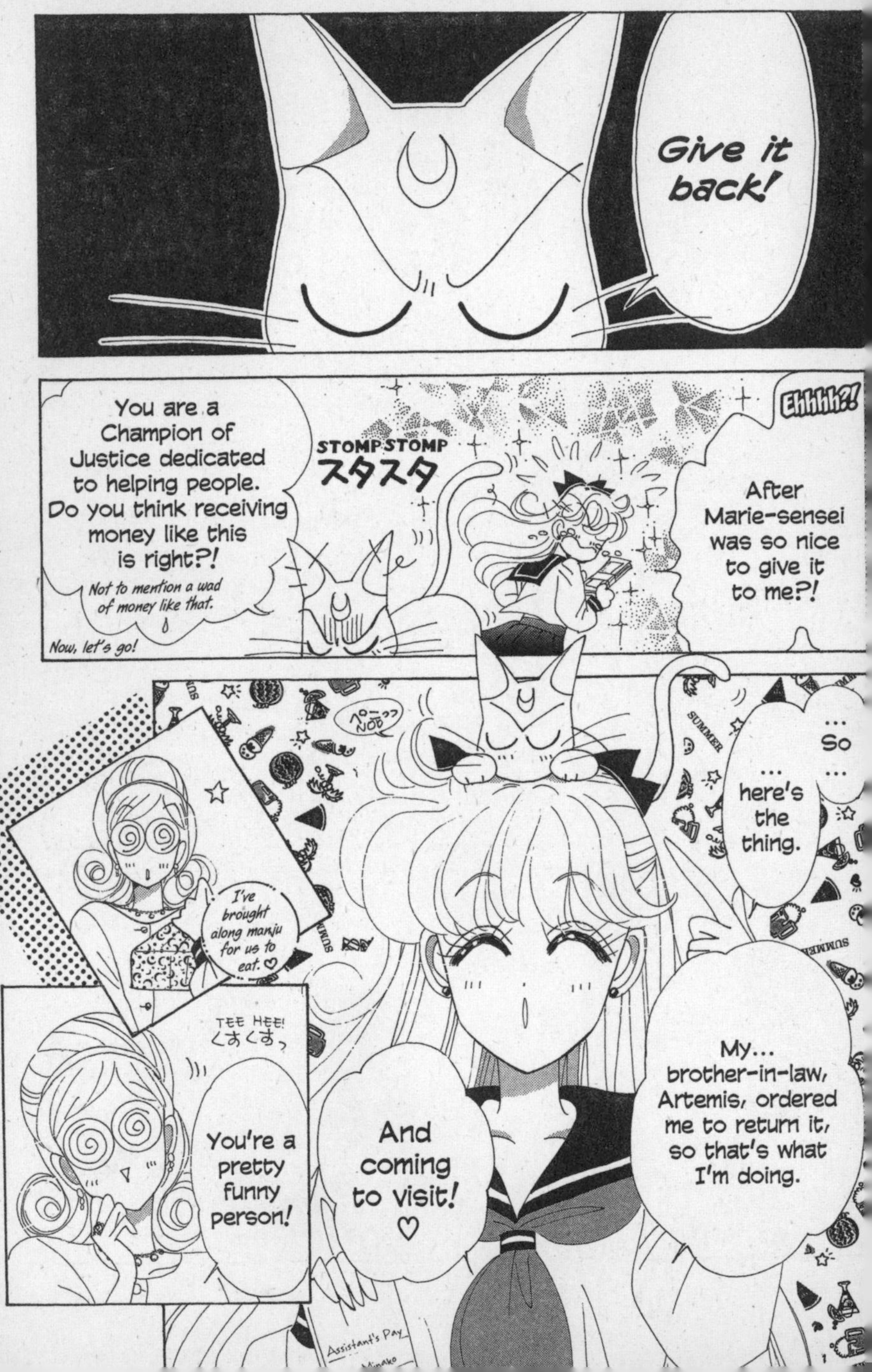
Give it back!
Ehhhh?!
After Marie-sensei was so nice to give it to me?!
STOMP STOMP スタスタ
You are a Champion of Justice dedicated to helping people. Do you think receiving money like this is right?!
Not to mention a wad of money like that.
Now, let's go!
... So ... here's the thing.
My... brother-in-law, Artemis, ordered me to return it, so that's what I'm doing.
And coming to visit! ♡
I've brought along manju for us to eat. ♡
TEE HEE! くすくすっ
You're a pretty funny person!
Assistant's Pay

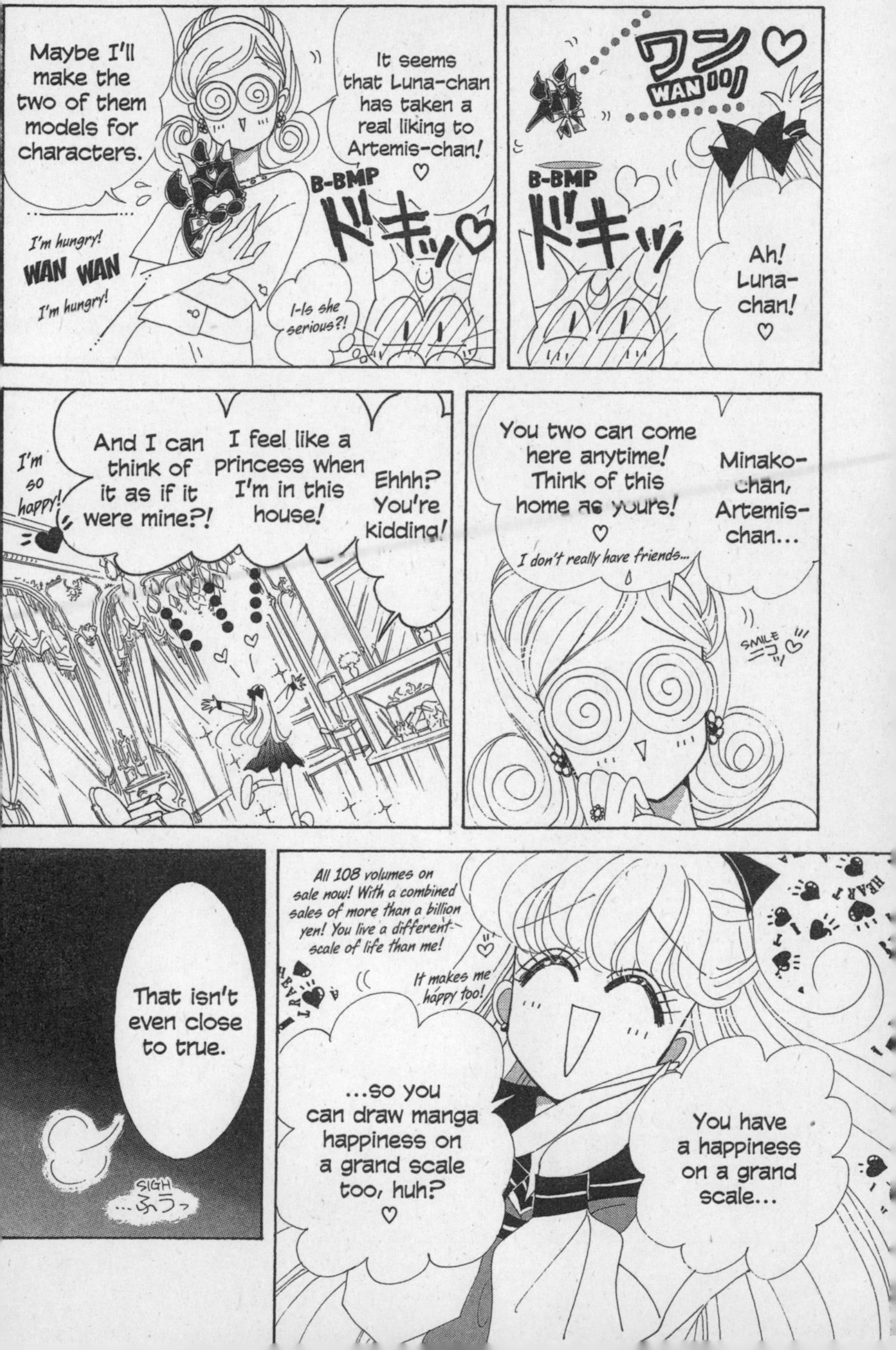
ワン♡
WAN
B-BMP
ドキッ
Ah! Luna-chan! ♡
It seems that Luna-chan has taken a real liking to Artemis-chan! ♡
B-BMP
ドキッ♡
Maybe I'll make the two of them models for characters.
I-Is she serious?!
I'm hungry!
WAN WAN
I'm hungry!
Minako-chan, Artemis-chan...
You two can come here anytime! Think of this home as yours! ♡
I don't really have friends...
SMILE
ニコッ♡
Ehhh? You're kidding!
I feel like a princess when I'm in this house!
And I can think of it as if it were mine?!
I'm so happy!
You have a happiness on a grand scale...
...so you can draw manga happiness on a grand scale too, huh? ♡
It makes me happy too!
All 108 volumes on sale now! With a combined sales of more than a billion yen! You live a different scale of life than me!
That isn't even close to true.
SIGH
...ふうっ

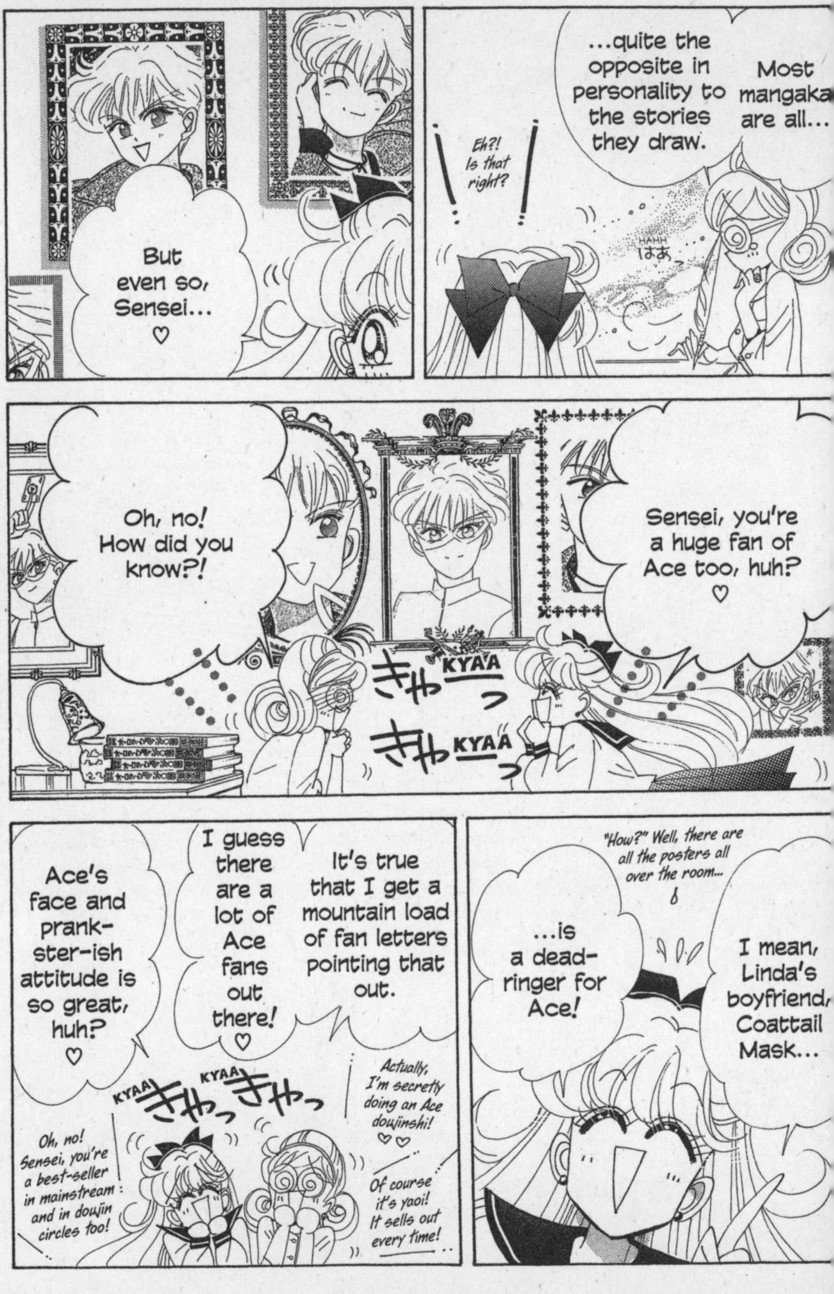

Most mangaka are all...
...quite the opposite in personality to the stories they draw.
HAHH はあっ
Eh?! Is that right?
But even so, Sensei... ♡
Sensei, you're a huge fan of Ace too, huh? ♡
KYAA きゃーっ
KYAA きゃっ
Oh, no! How did you know?!
I mean, Linda's boyfriend, Coattail Mask...
...is a dead-ringer for Ace!
"How?" Well, there are all the posters all over the room...
It's true that I get a mountain load of fan letters pointing that out.
I guess there are a lot of Ace fans out there! ♡
Ace's face and prank-ster-ish attitude is so great, huh? ♡
KYAA きゃっ
KYAA きゃっ
Actually, I'm secretly doing an Ace doujinshi! ♡♡
Of course it's yaoi! It sells out every time!
Oh, no! Sensei, you're a best-seller in mainstream and in doujin circles too!

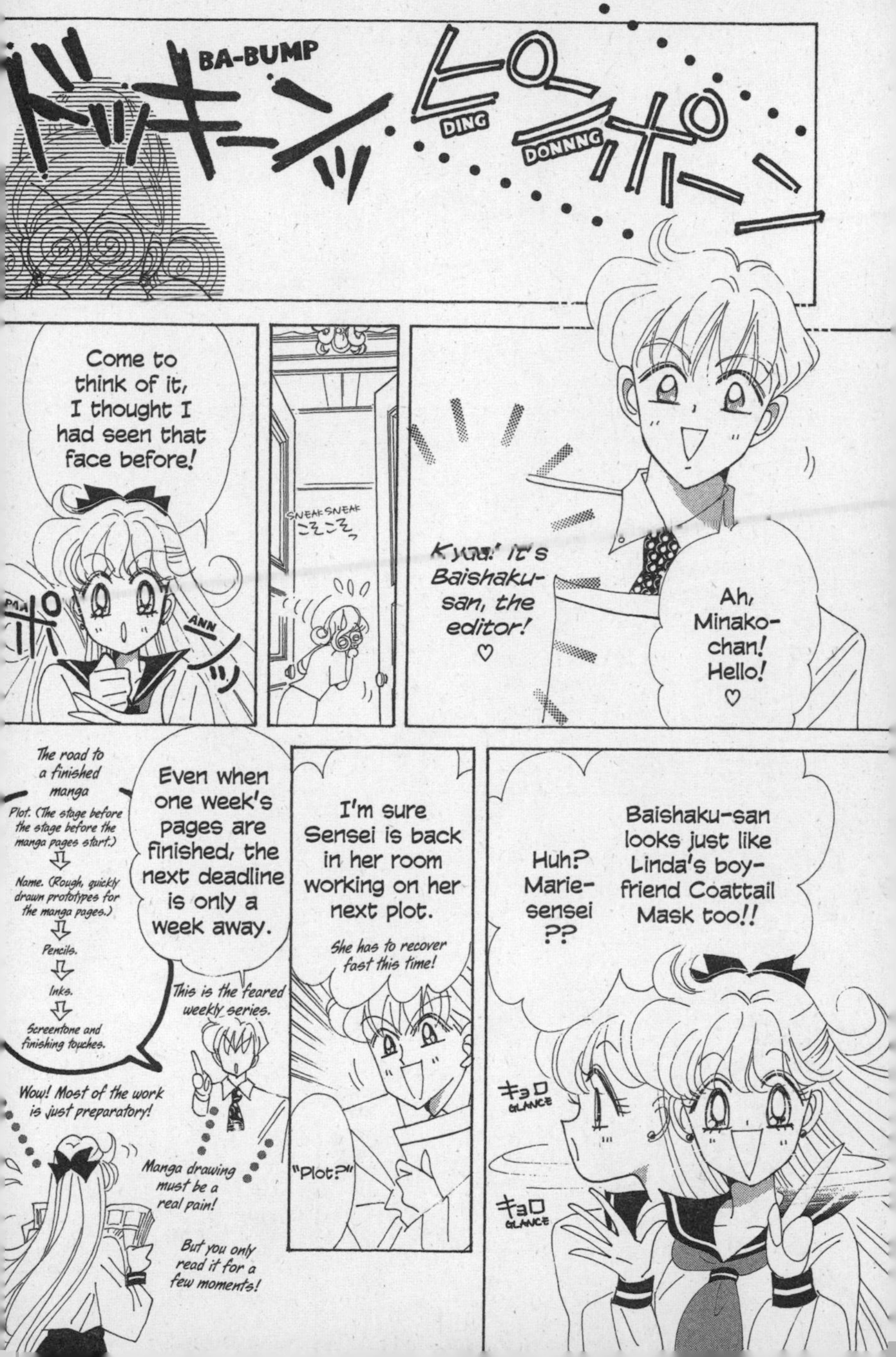
DING
DONNNG
BA-BUMP
Ah, Minako-chan! Hello! ♡
Kyaa! It's Baishaku-san, the editor! ♡
SNEAKSNEAK
こそこそっ
Come to think of it, I thought I had seen that face before!
PAA
ANN
Baishaku-san looks just like Linda's boyfriend Coattail Mask too!!
Huh? Marie-sensei ??
キョロ GLANCE
キョロ GLANCE
I'm sure Sensei is back in her room working on her next plot.
She has to recover fast this time!
"Plot?"
Even when one week's pages are finished, the next deadline is only a week away.
The road to a finished manga
Plot. (The stage before the stage before the manga pages start.)
Name. (Rough, quickly drawn prototypes for the manga pages.)
Pencils.
Inks.
Screentone and finishing touches.
This is the feared weekly series.
Wow! Most of the work is just preparatory!
Manga drawing must be a real pain!
But you only read it for a few moments!

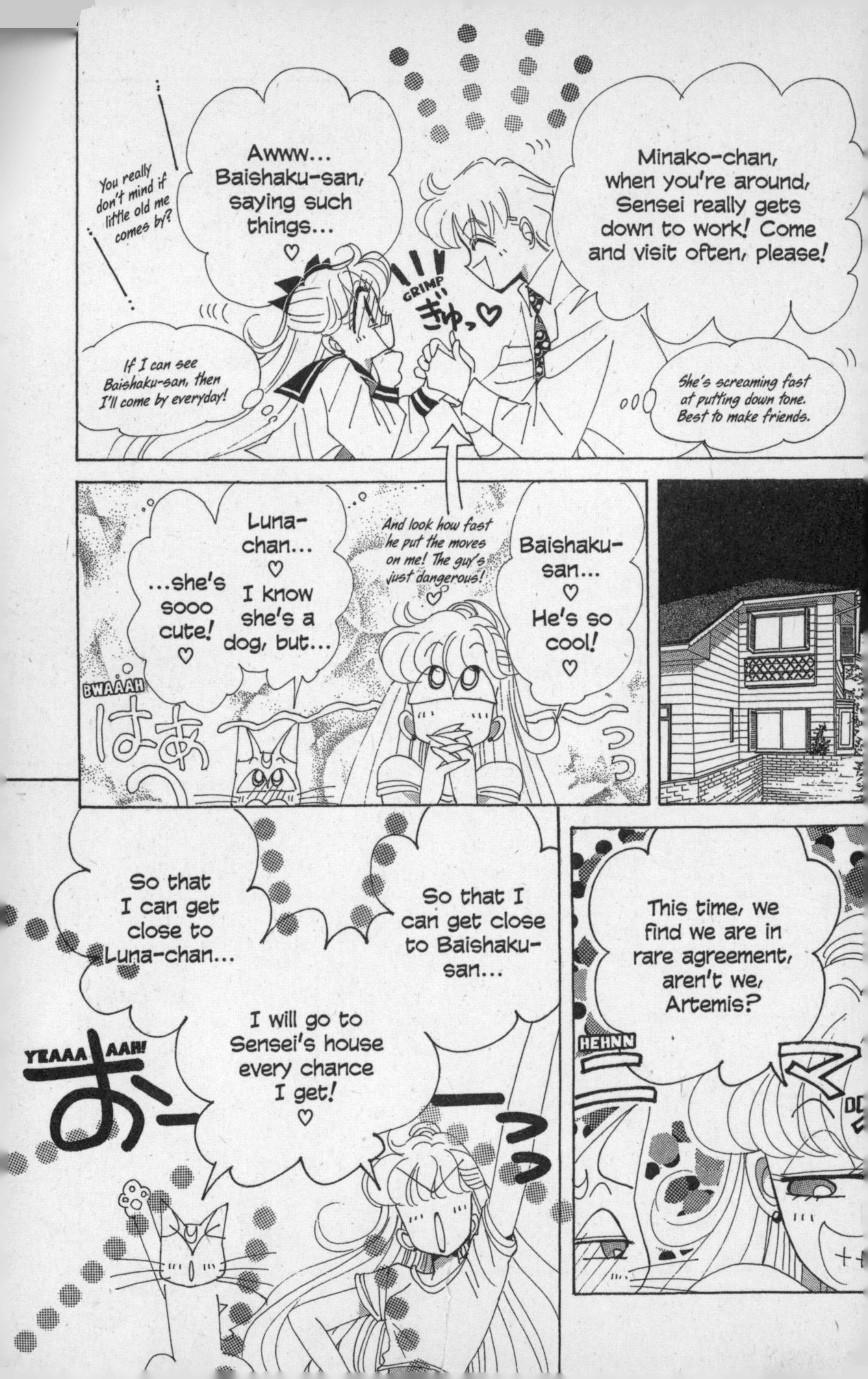
Minako-chan, when you're around, Sensei really gets down to work! Come and visit often, please!
Awww... Baishaku-san, saying such things... ♡
You really don't mind if little old me comes by?
GRIMP
ぎゅっ ♡
She's screaming fast at putting down tone. Best to make friends.
If I can see Baishaku-san, then I'll come by everyday!
Baishaku-san... ♡ He's so cool! ♡
And look how fast he put the moves on me! The guy's just dangerous! ♡
Luna-chan... ♡ I know she's a dog, but...
...she's sooo cute! ♡
BWAAAH
はぁっ
This time, we find we are in rare agreement, aren't we, Artemis?
HEHNN
So that I can get close to Baishaku-san...
So that I can get close to Luna-chan...
I will go to Sensei's house every chance I get! ♡
YEAAAAAH!
おーっ

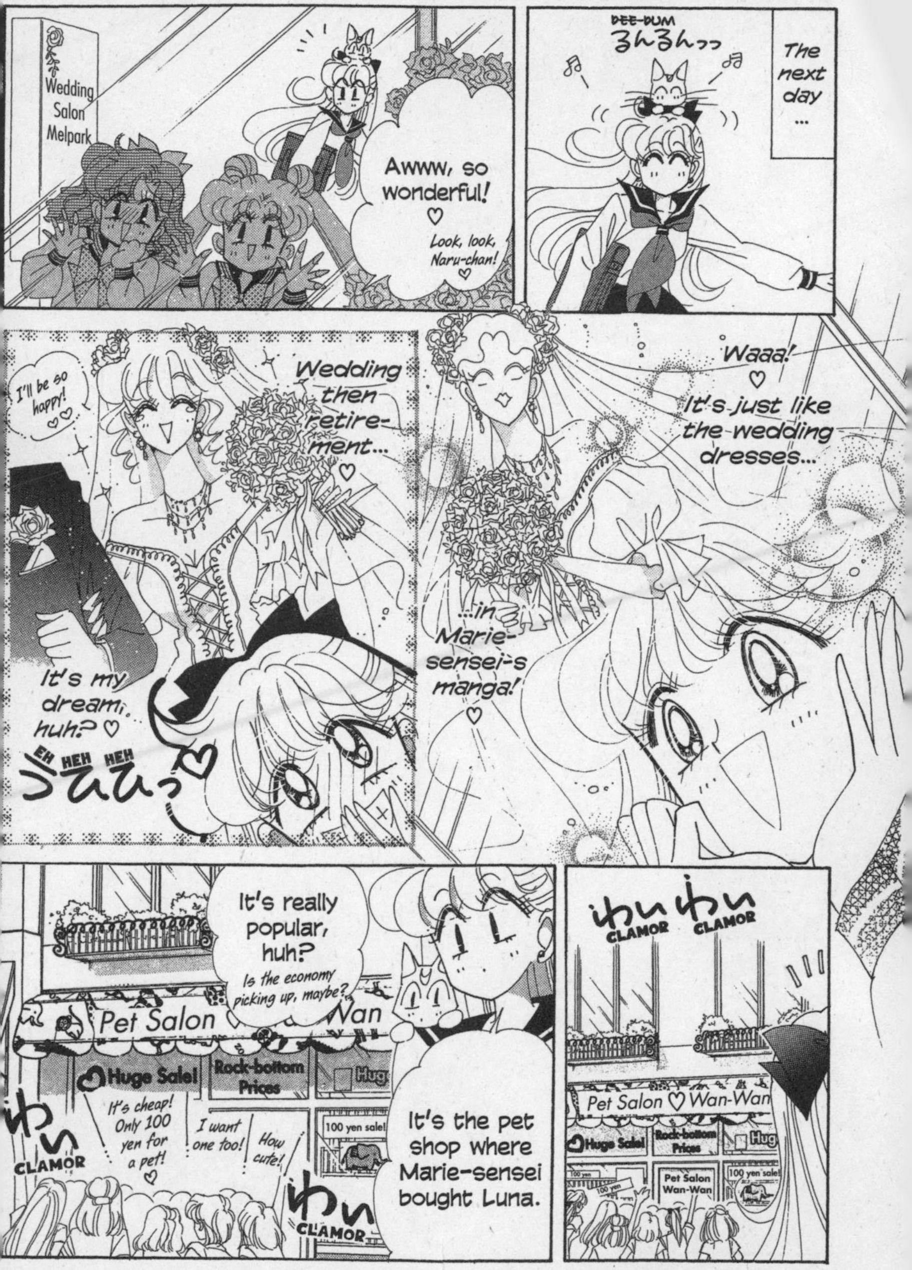
The next day ...
DEE-DUM
るんるんっっ
Awww, so wonderful! ♡
Look, look, Naru-chan! ♡
Wedding Salon Melpark
Waaa! ♡
It's just like the wedding dresses...
...in Marie-sensei's manga! ♡
Wedding then retirement... ♡
I'll be so happy! ♡♡
It's my dream, huh? ♡
EH HEH HEH
うひひっ
わいわい
CLAMOR CLAMOR
Pet Salon ♡ Wan-Wan
Huge Sale!
Rock-bottom Prices
100 yen sale!
Pet Salon Wan-Wan
It's really popular, huh?
Is the economy picking up, maybe?
It's the pet shop where Marie-sensei bought Luna.
Pet Salon
Huge Sale!
Rock-bottom Prices
100 yen sale!
It's cheap! Only 100 yen for a pet! ♡
I want one too!
How cute!
わい
CLAMOR
わい
CLAMOR

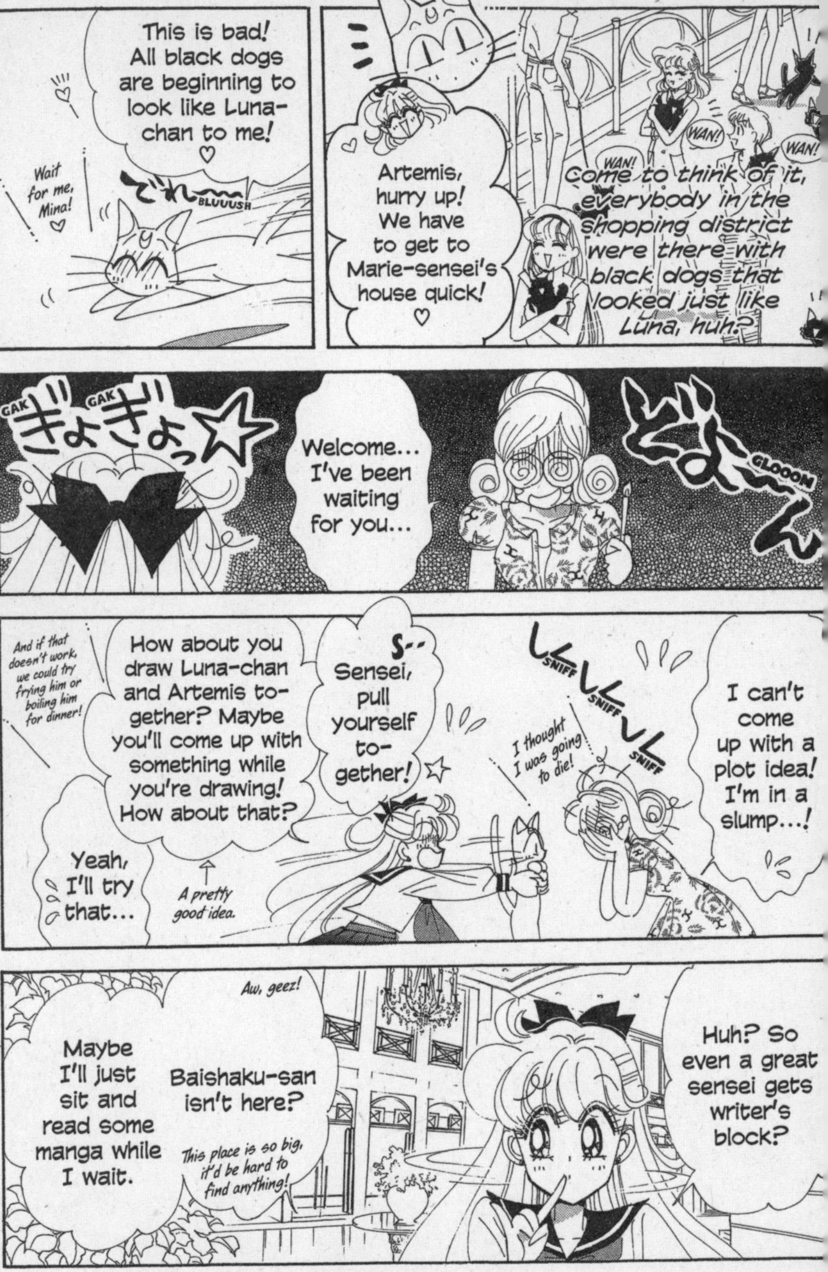
WAN!
WAN!
WAN!
Come to think of it, everybody in the shopping district were there with black dogs that looked just like Luna, huh?
Artemis, hurry up! We have to get to Marie-sensei's house quick! ♡
This is bad! All black dogs are beginning to look like Luna-chan to me! ♡
でれ〜 BLUUUSH
Wait for me, Mina! ♡
どよ〜ん GLOOOM
Welcome... I've been waiting for you...
ぎょぎょっ☆ GAK GAK
I can't come up with a plot idea! I'm in a slump...!
し く SNIFF
し く SNIFF
し く SNIFF
I thought I was going to die!
S-- Sensei, pull yourself together!
How about you draw Luna-chan and Artemis together? Maybe you'll come up with something while you're drawing! How about that?
And if that doesn't work, we could try frying him or boiling him for dinner!
A pretty good idea.
Yeah, I'll try that...
Huh? So even a great sensei gets writer's block?
Baishaku-san isn't here?
Aw, geez!
This place is so big, it'd be hard to find anything!
Maybe I'll just sit and read some manga while I wait.

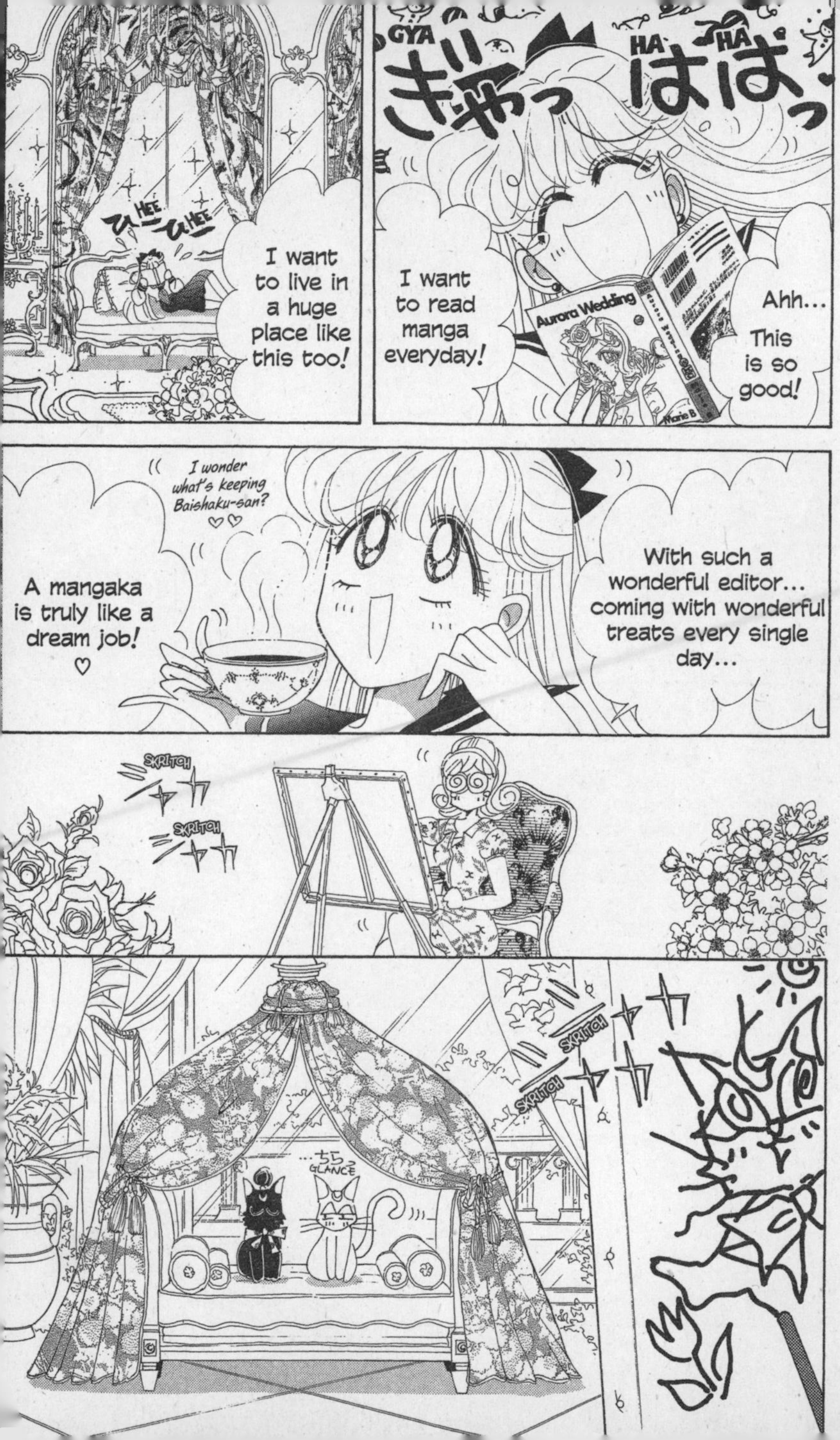

GYA
ぎゃっ
HA HA
はぱっ
Ahh... This is so good!
Aurora Wedding
Marie B
I want to read manga everyday!
ひー HEE ひー HEE
I want to live in a huge place like this too!
With such a wonderful editor... coming with wonderful treats every single day...
I wonder what's keeping Baishaku-san? ♡♡
A mangaka is truly like a dream job! ♡
SKRITCH
SKRITCH
SKRITCH
SKRITCH
...ちら GLANCE

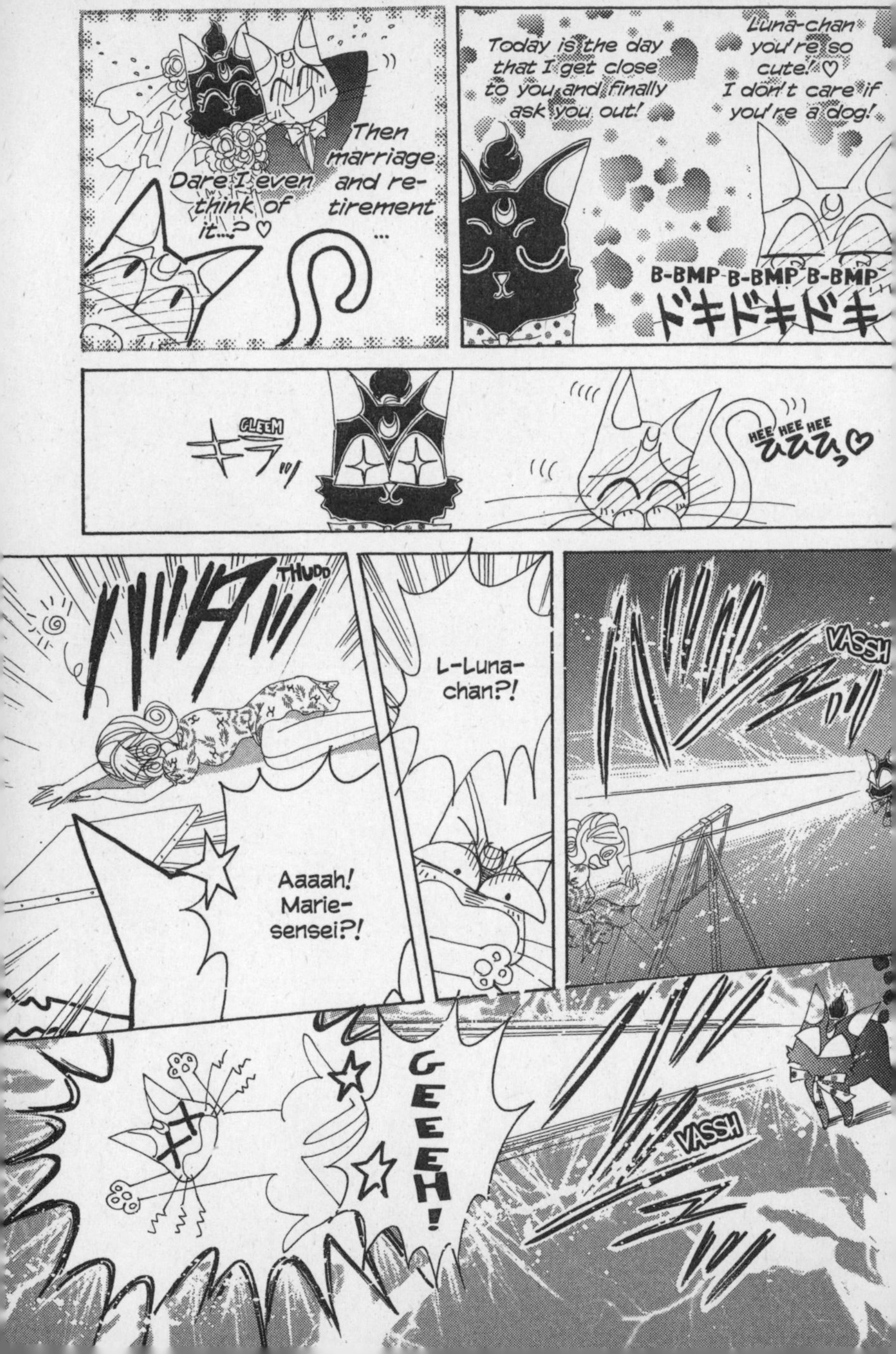
Luna-chan you're so cute! ♡ I don't care if you're a dog!
Today is the day that I get close to you and finally ask you out!
B-BMP B-BMP B-BMP
ドキドキドキ
Then marriage and re-tirement ...
Dare I even think of it...? ♡
HEE HEE HEE
ひひひっ♡
GLEEM
キラッ
VASSH
L-Luna-chan?!
THUDD
バタッ
Aaaah! Marie-sensei?!
VASSH
GEEEEH!

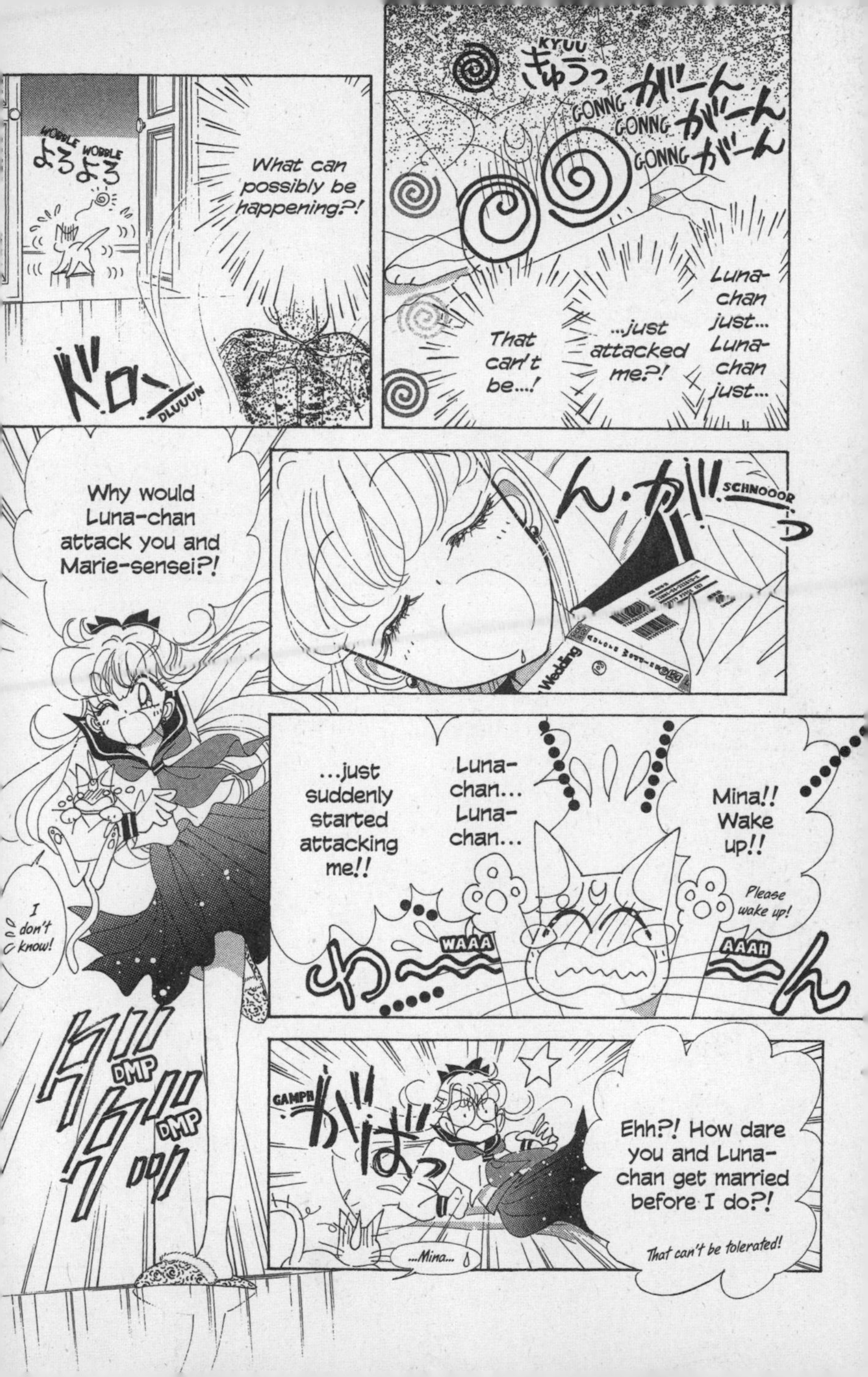
KYUU
きゅうっ
GONNG がーん
GONNG がーん
GONNG がーん
Luna-chan just... Luna-chan just...
...just attacked me?!
That can't be...!
What can possibly be happening?!
WOBBLE WOBBLE
よろよろ
ドローン
DLUUUN
SCHNOOOR
Mina!! Wake up!!
Please wake up!
AAAH
Luna-chan... Luna-chan...
...just suddenly started attacking me!!
WAAA
Ehh?! How dare you and Luna-chan get married before I do?!
That can't be tolerated!
GAMPH
がばっ
...Mina...
Why would Luna-chan attack you and Marie-sensei?!
I don't know!
DMP
DMP

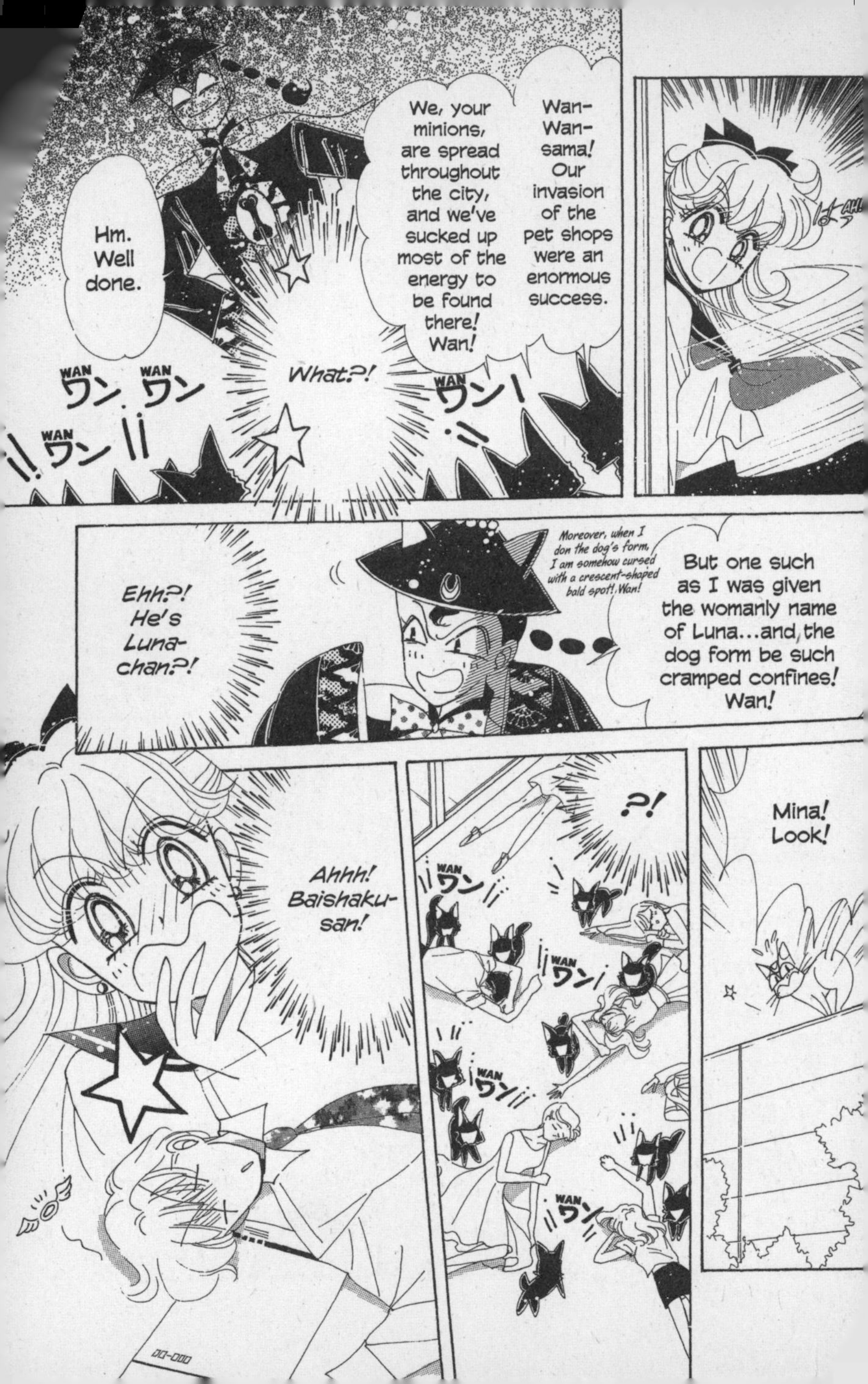
はっ AH!
Wan-Wan-sama! Our invasion of the pet shops were an enormous success.
We, your minions, are spread throughout the city, and we've sucked up most of the energy to be found there! Wan!
Hm. Well done.
WAN ワン
What?!
WAN ワン
WAN ワン
WAN ワン
But one such as I was given the womanly name of Luna...and the dog form be such cramped confines! Wan!
Moreover, when I don the dog's form, I am somehow cursed with a crescent-shaped bald spot! Wan!
Ehh?! He's Luna-chan?!
Mina! Look!
?!
WAN ワン
WAN ワン
WAN ワン
WAN ワン
Ahhh! Baishaku-san!

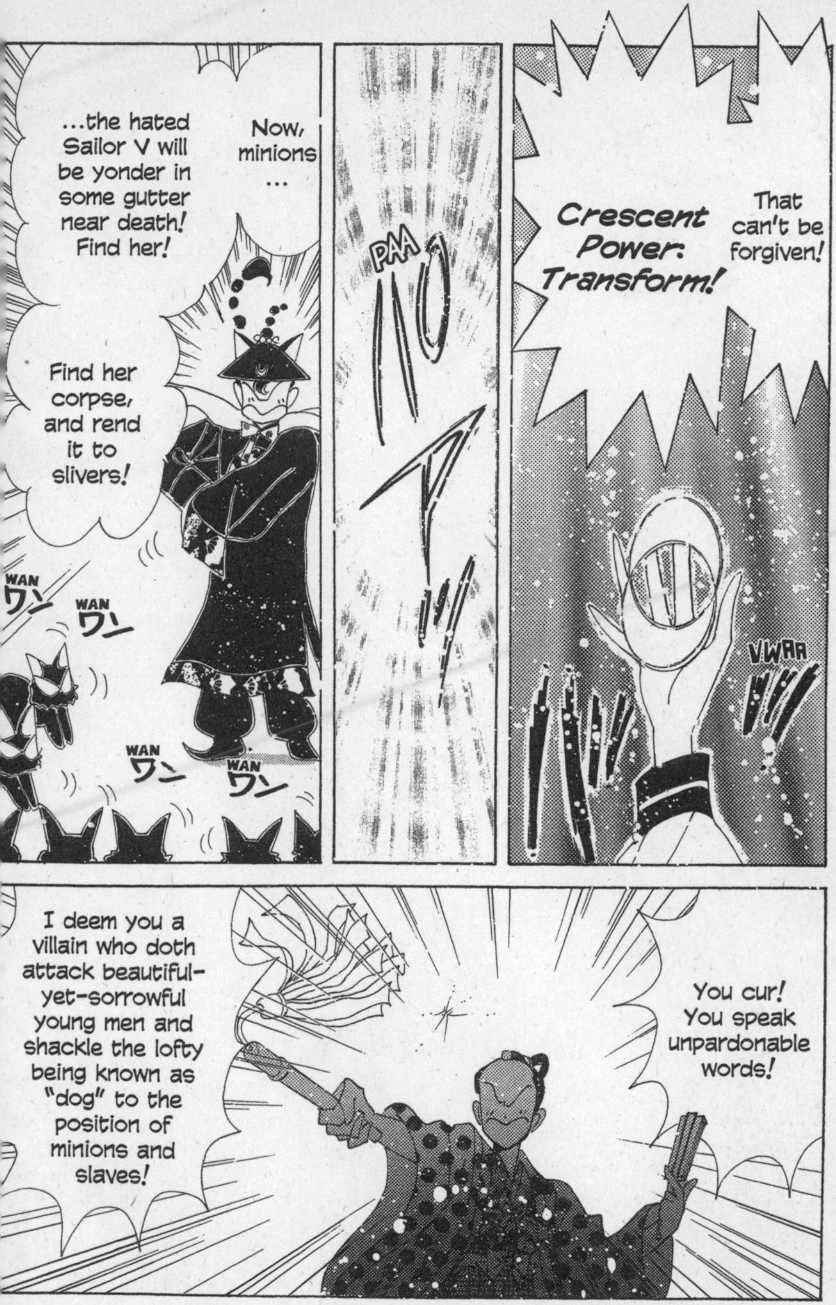
That can't be forgiven!
Crescent Power: Transform!
VWAA
PAA
Now, minions ...
...the hated Sailor V will be yonder in some gutter near death! Find her!
Find her corpse, and rend it to slivers!
WAN ワン
WAN ワン
WAN ワン
WAN ワン
You cur! You speak unpardonable words!
I deem you a villain who doth attack beautiful-yet-sorrowful young men and shackle the lofty being known as "dog" to the position of minions and slaves!

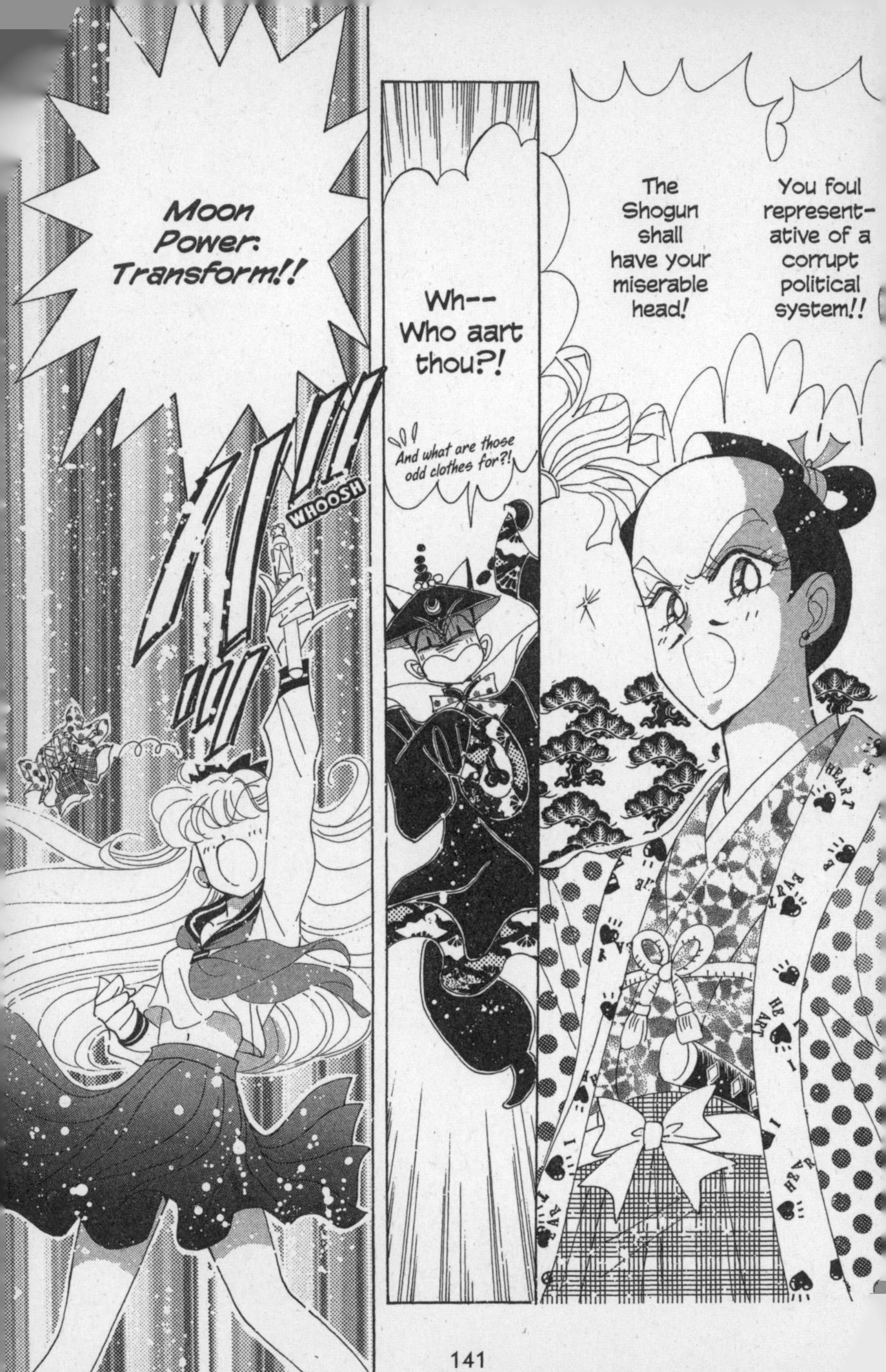
You foul representative of a corrupt political system!!
The Shogun shall have your miserable head!
Wh-- Who aart thou?!
And what are those odd clothes for?!
Moon Power: Transform!!
WHOOSH

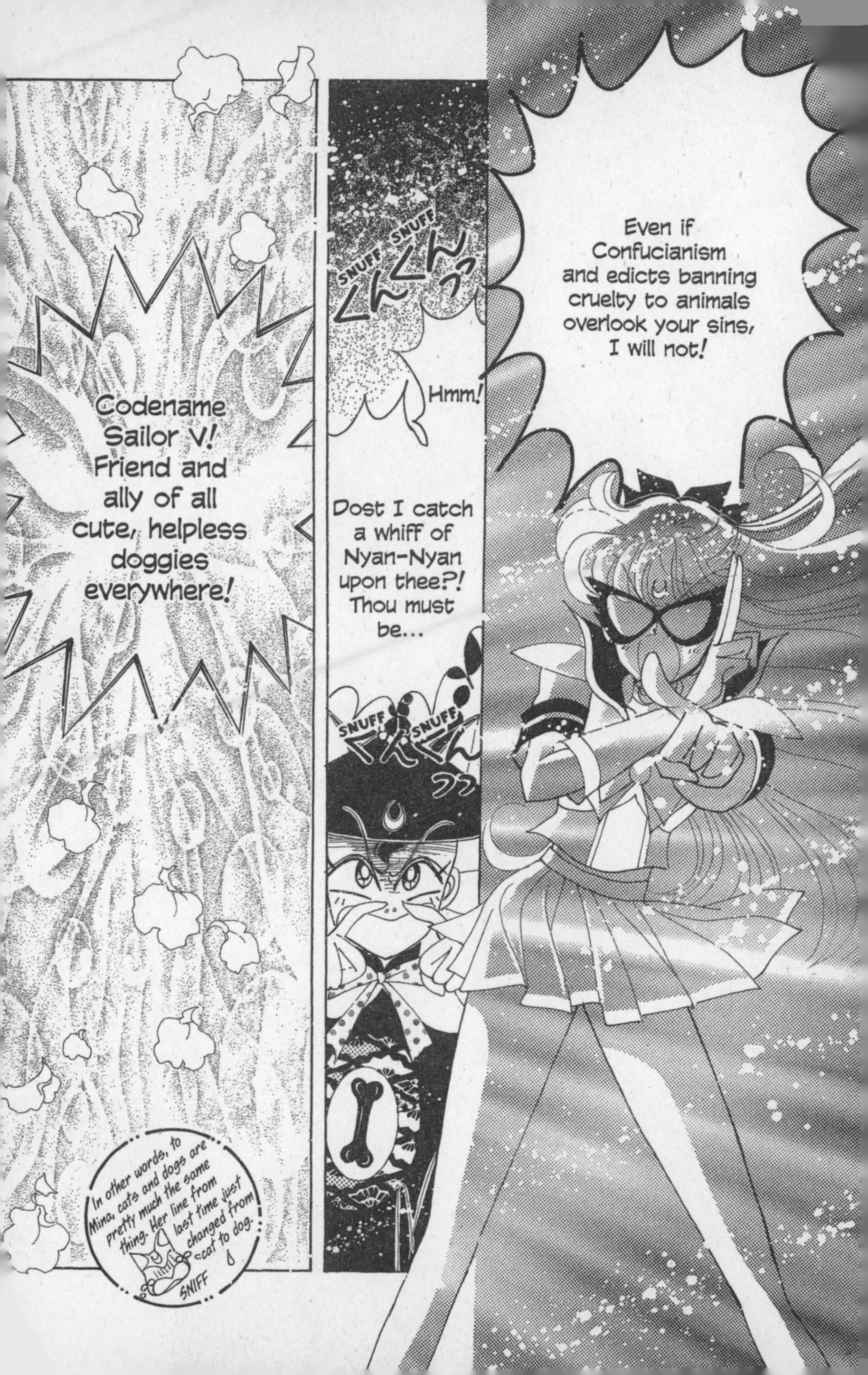
Even if Confucianism and edicts banning cruelty to animals overlook your sins, I will not!
SNUFF SNUFF
Hmm!
Dost I catch a whiff of Nyan-Nyan upon thee?! Thou must be...
SNUFF SNUFF
Codename Sailor V! Friend and ally of all cute, helpless doggies everywhere!
In other words, to Mina, cats and dogs are pretty much the same thing. Her line from last time just changed from cat to dog.
SNIFF

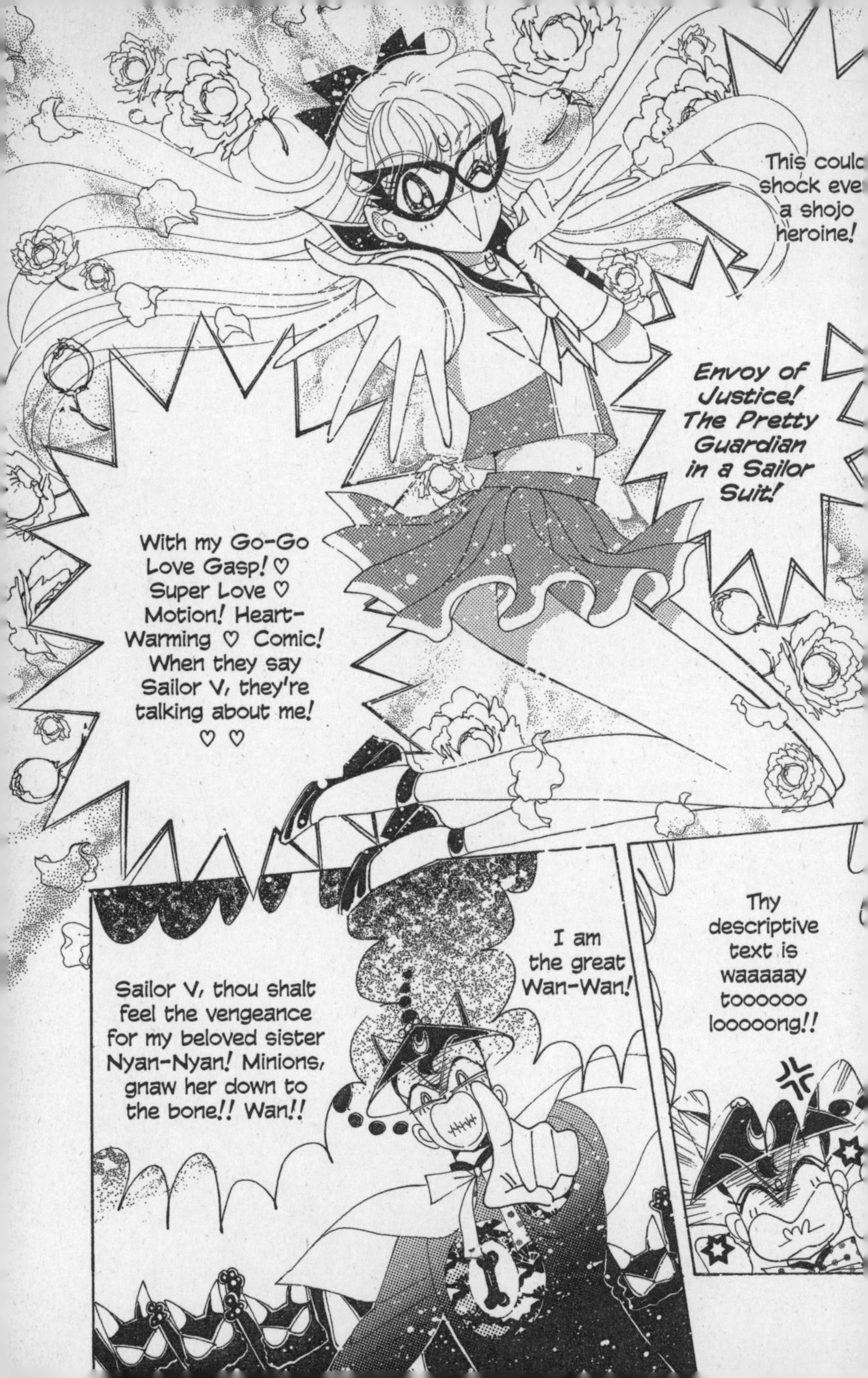
This coul shock eve a shojo heroine!
Envoy of Justice! The Pretty Guardian in a Sailor Suit!
With my Go-Go Love Gasp! ♡ Super Love ♡ Motion! Heart-Warming ♡ Comic! When they say Sailor V, they're talking about me! ♡ ♡
Thy descriptive text is waaaaay tooooo loooong!!
I am the great Wan-Wan!
Sailor V, thou shalt feel the vengeance for my beloved sister Nyan-Nyan! Minions, gnaw her down to the bone!! Wan!!

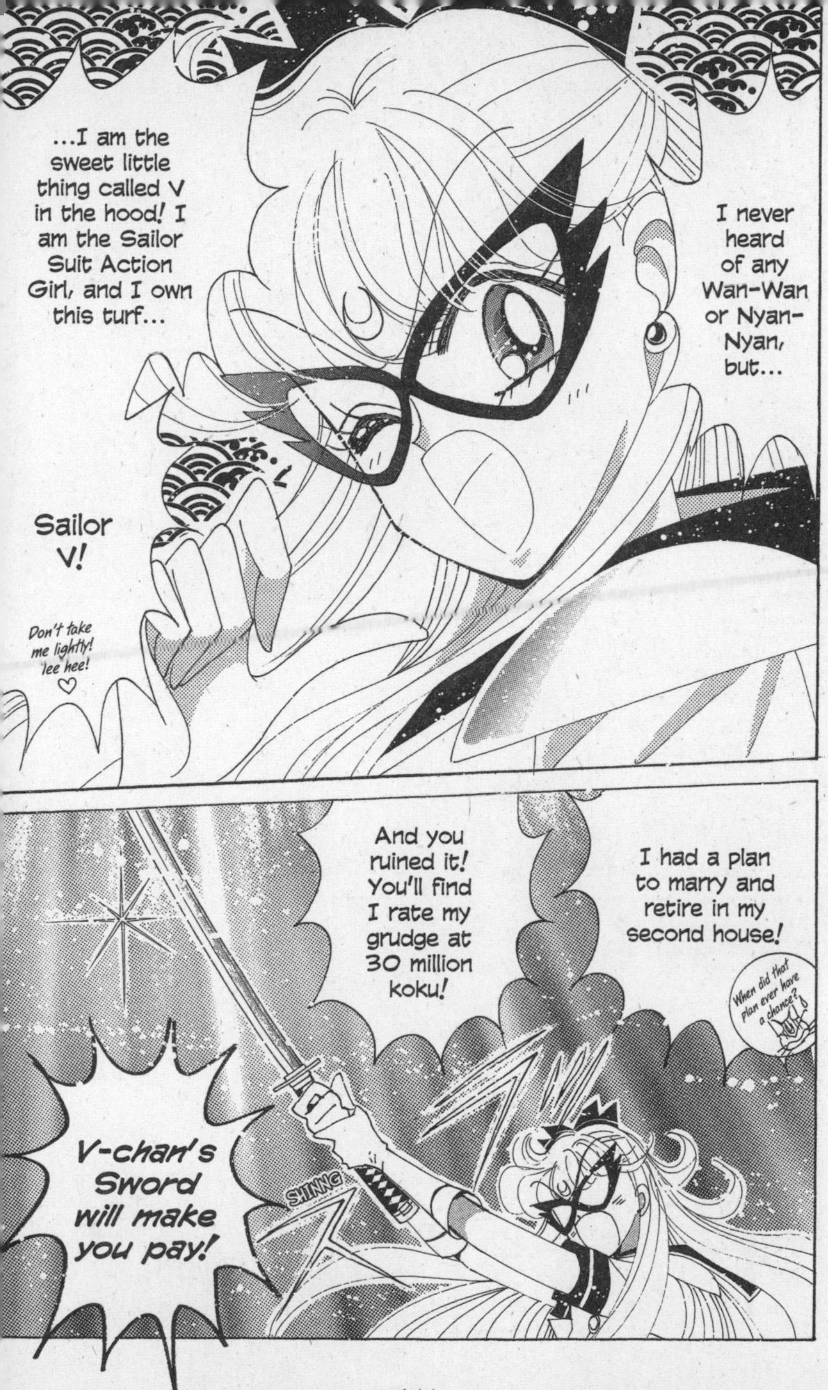
I never heard of any Wan-Wan or Nyan-Nyan, but...
...I am the sweet little thing called V in the hood! I am the Sailor Suit Action Girl, and I own this turf...
Sailor V!
Don't take me lightly! Iee hee! ♡
I had a plan to marry and retire in my second house!
When did that plan ever have a chance?
And you ruined it! You'll find I rate my grudge at 30 million koku!
SHING
V-chan's Sword will make you pay!

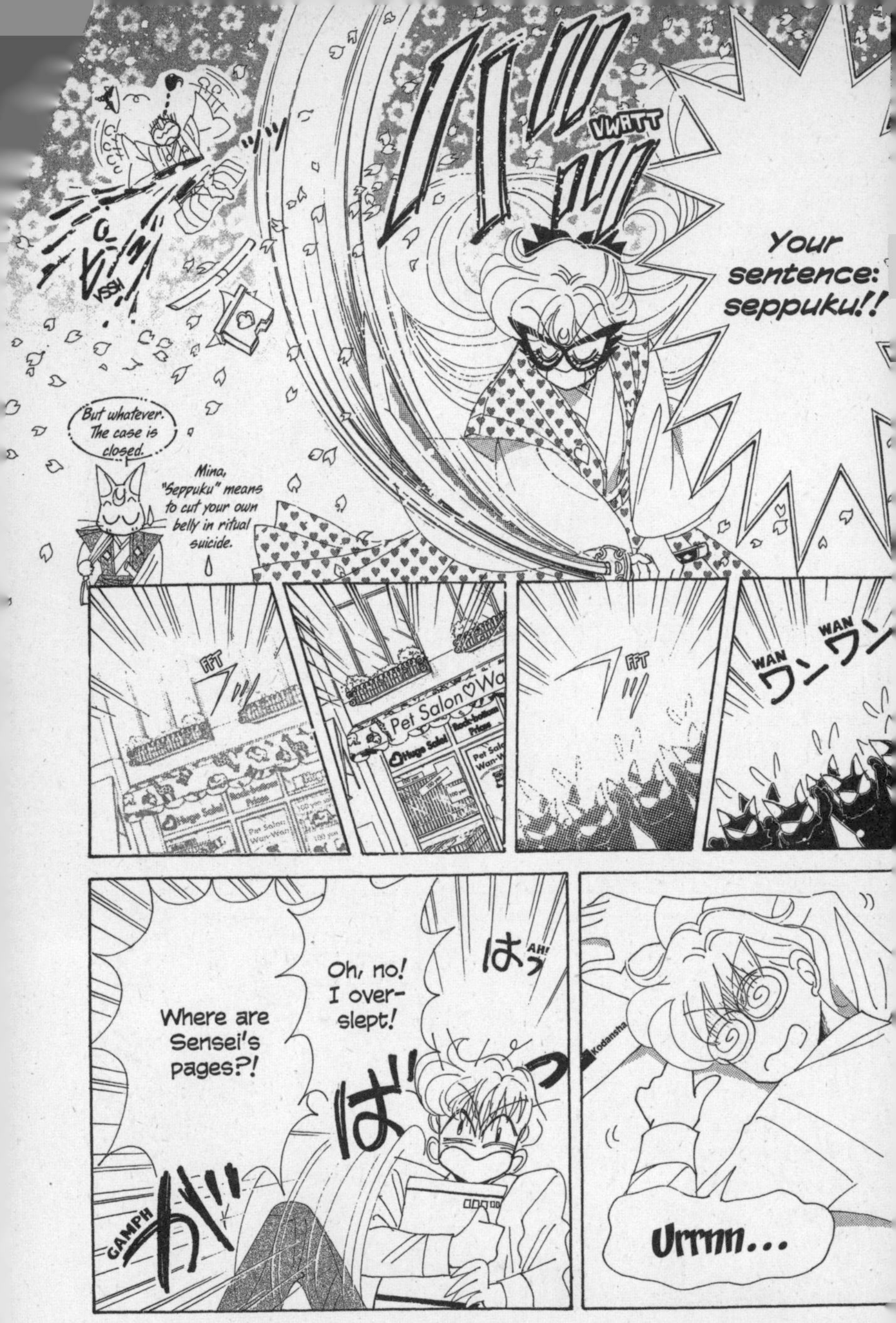
VWATT
Your sentence: seppuku!!
VSSH
But whatever. The case is closed.
Mina, "Seppuku" means to cut your own belly in ritual suicide.
WAN WAN
ワンワン
FFT
Pet Salon♡Wa
Huge Sale!
Rock-bottom Prices
FFT
Urrnn...
AH!
は
Oh, no! I over-slept!
Where are Sensei's pages?!
ばっ
GAMPH
がばっ

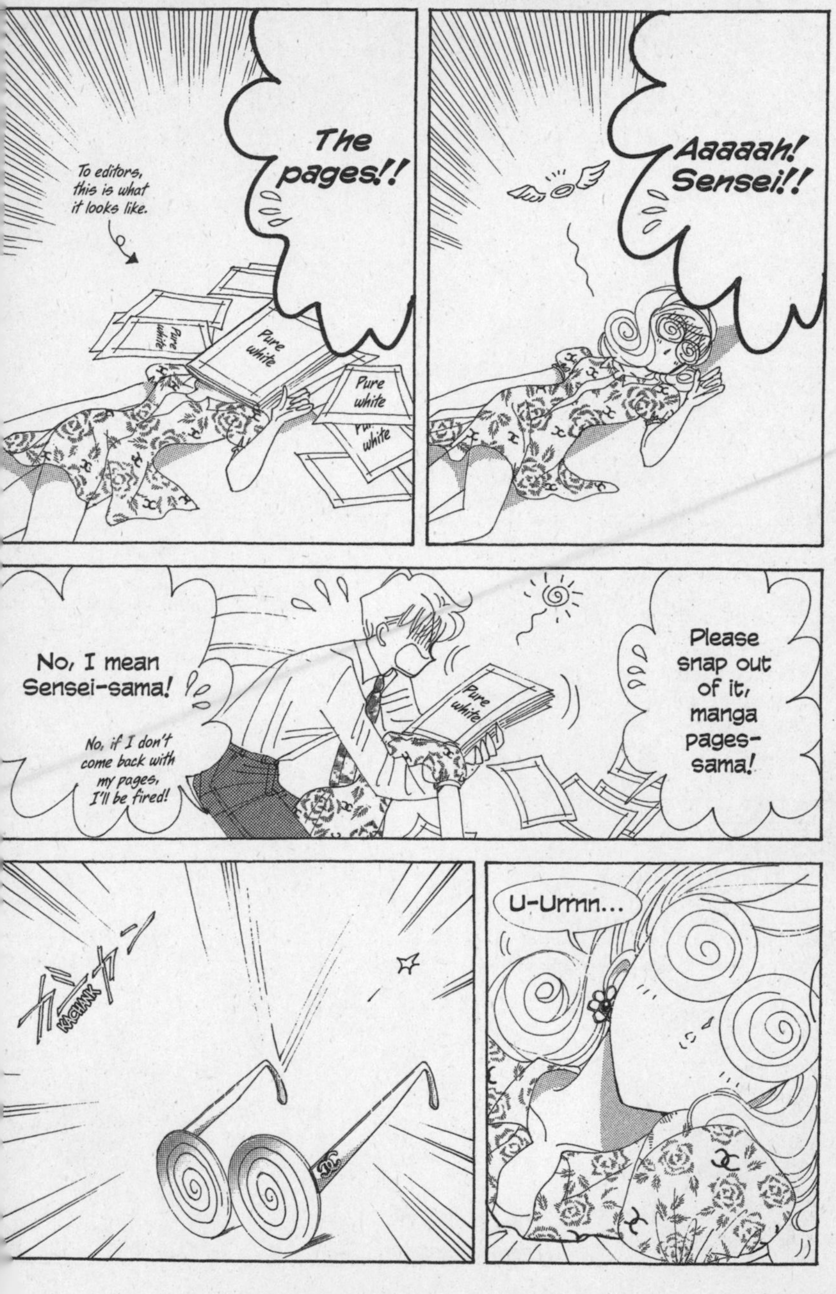
Aaaaah! Sensei!!
The pages!!
To editors, this is what it looks like.
Pure white
Pure white
Pure white
Pure white
Please snap out of it, manga pages-sama!
Pure white
No, I mean Sensei-sama!
No, if I don't come back with my pages, I'll be fired!
U-Urmn...
KACHANK

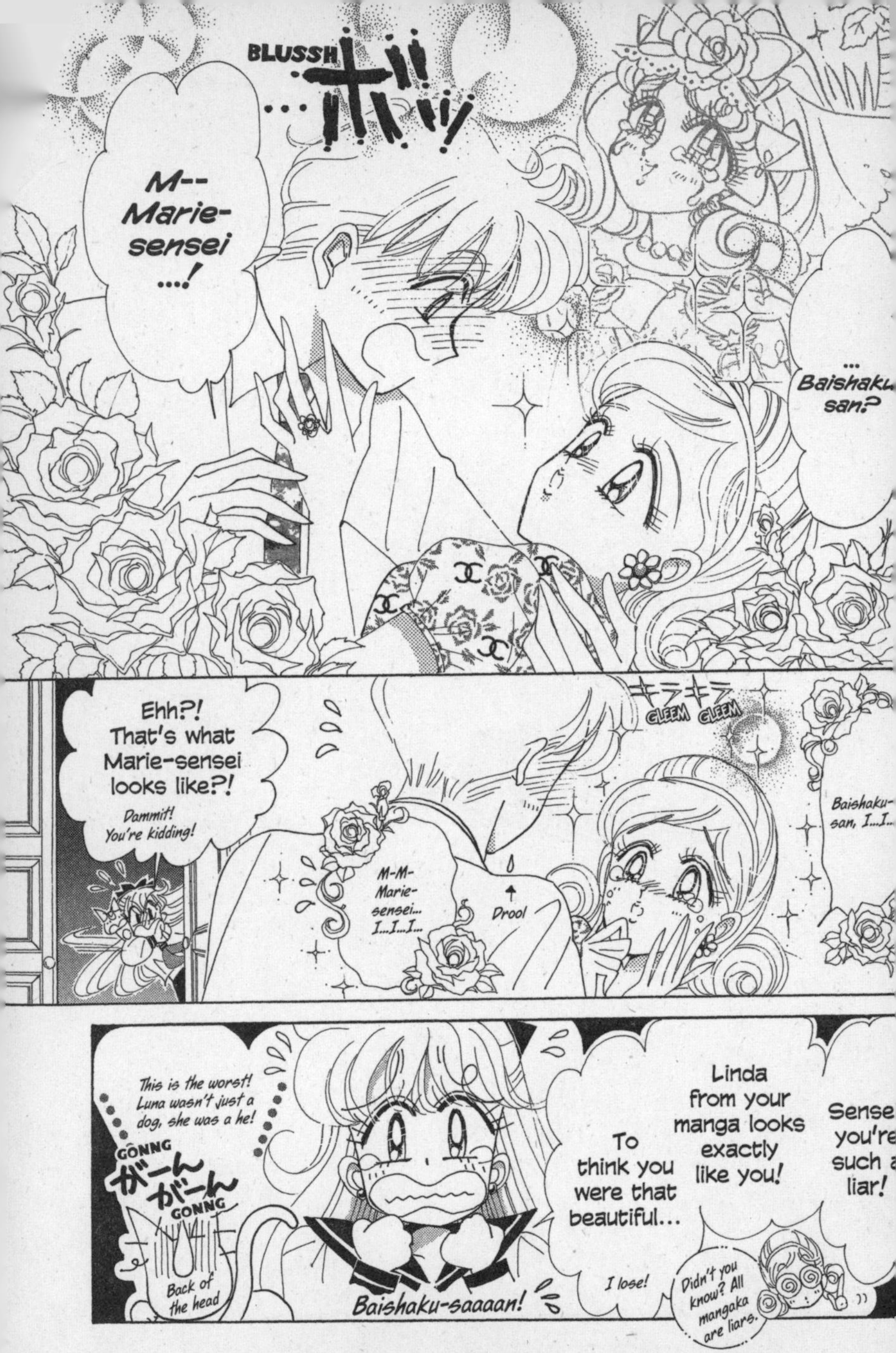
... Baishaku-san?
BLUSSH
...ホッ
M-- Marie-sensei ...!
Baishaku-san, I...I...
キラキラ GLEEM GLEEM
M-M-Marie-sensei... I...I...I...
Drool
Ehh?! That's what Marie-sensei looks like?!
Dammit! You're kidding!
Sense you're such a liar!
Linda from your manga looks exactly like you!
To think you were that beautiful...
I lose!
Didn't you know? All mangaka are liars.
Baishaku-saaaan!
This is the worst! Luna wasn't just a dog, she was a he!
GONNG がーん がーん GONNG
Back of the head

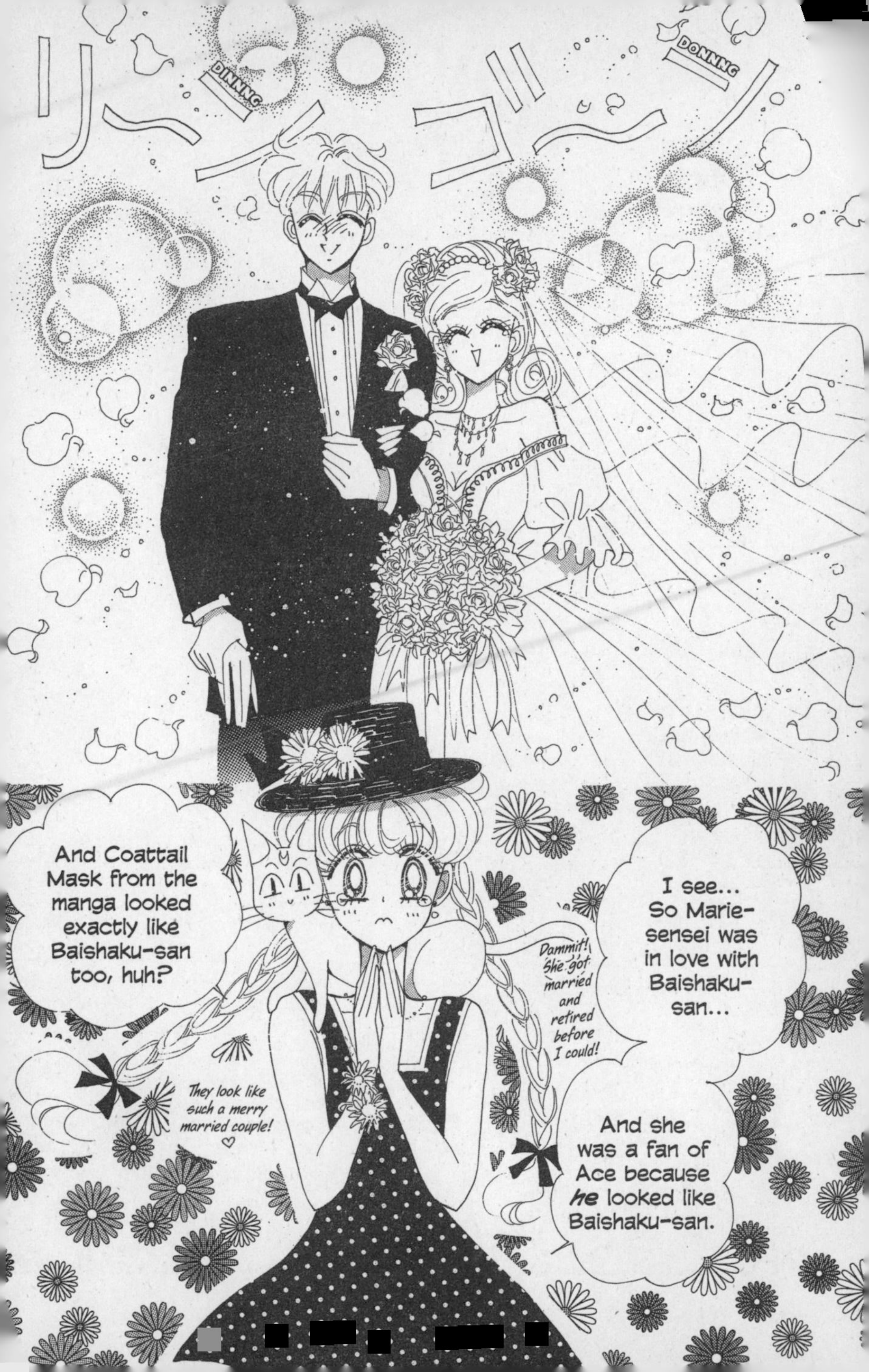
DONNNG
DINNG
I see... So Marie-sensei was in love with Baishaku-san...
And she was a fan of Ace because **he** looked like Baishaku-san.
Dammit! She got married and retired before I could!
And Coattail Mask from the manga looked exactly like Baishaku-san too, huh?
They look like such a merry married couple! ♡

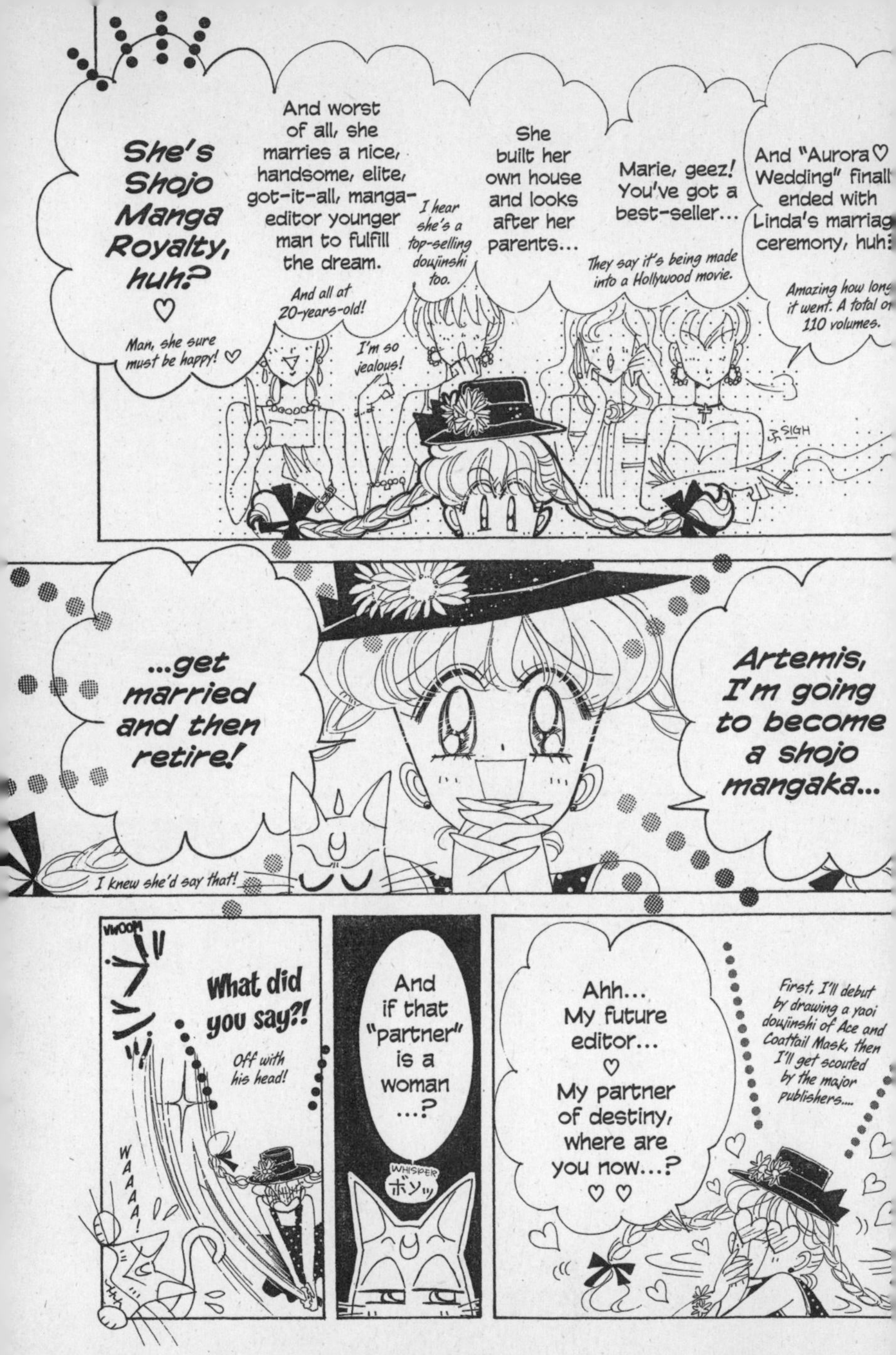
And "Aurora♡ Wedding" finall ended with Linda's marriag ceremony, huh?
Amazing how long it went. A total o 110 volumes.
SIGH
Marie, geez! You've got a best-seller...
They say it's being made into a Hollywood movie.
She built her own house and looks after her parents...
I hear she's a top-selling doujinshi too.
And worst of all, she marries a nice, handsome, elite, got-it-all, manga-editor younger man to fulfill the dream.
And all at 20-years-old!
I'm so jealous!
She's Shojo Manga Royalty, huh? ♡
Man, she sure must be happy! ♡
Artemis, I'm going to become a shojo mangaka...
...get married and then retire!
I knew she'd say that!
First, I'll debut by drawing a yaoi doujinshi of Ace and Coattail Mask, then I'll get scouted by the major publishers....
Ahh... My future editor... ♡ My partner of destiny, where are you now...? ♡ ♡
And if that "partner" is a woman ...?
WHISPER
ボソッ
VWOOM
What did you say?!
Off with his head!
WAAAAA!

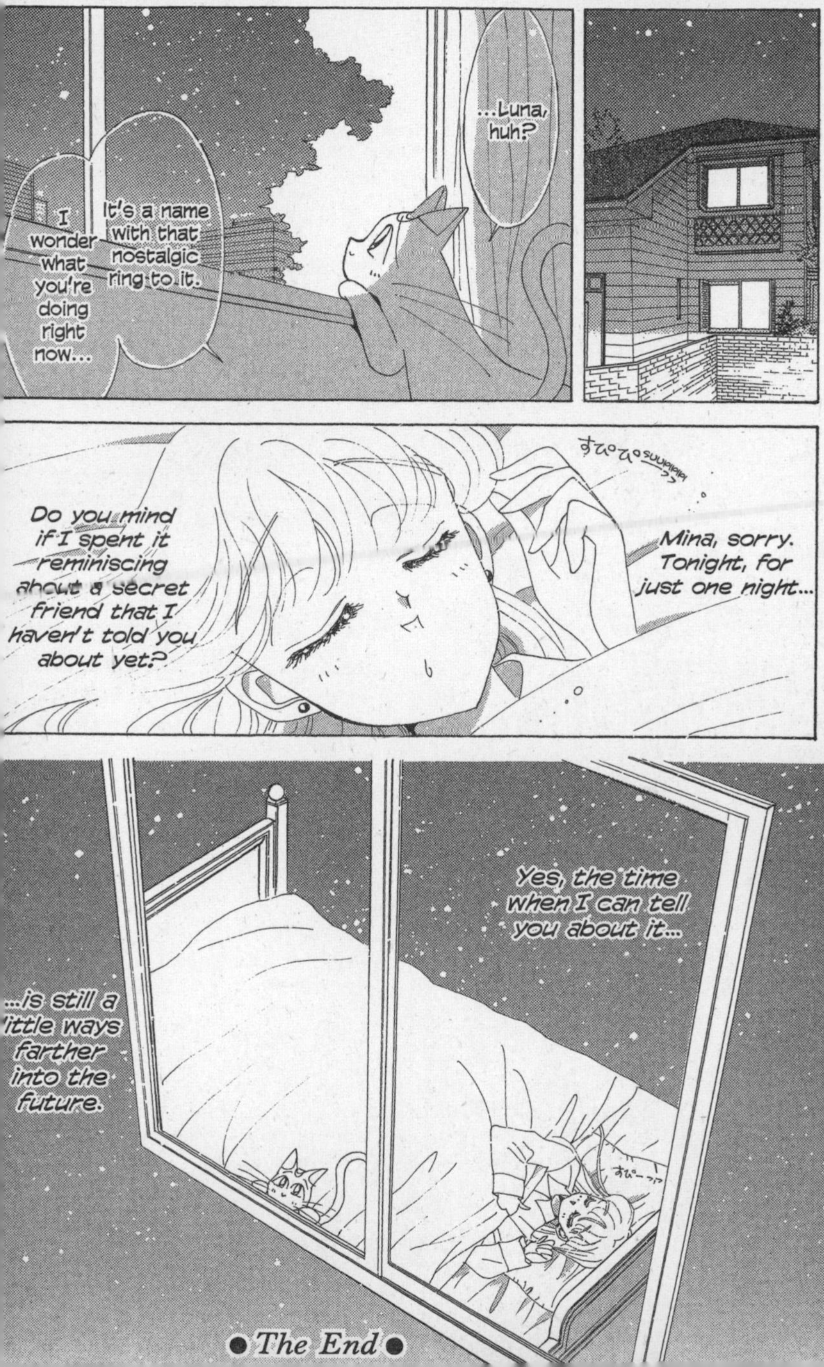
...Luna, huh?
It's a name with that nostalgic ring to it.
I wonder what you're doing right now...
Mina, sorry. Tonight, for just one night...
Do you mind if I spent it reminiscing about a secret friend that I haven't told you about yet?
Yes, the time when I can tell you about it...
...is still a little ways farther into the future.
• The End •

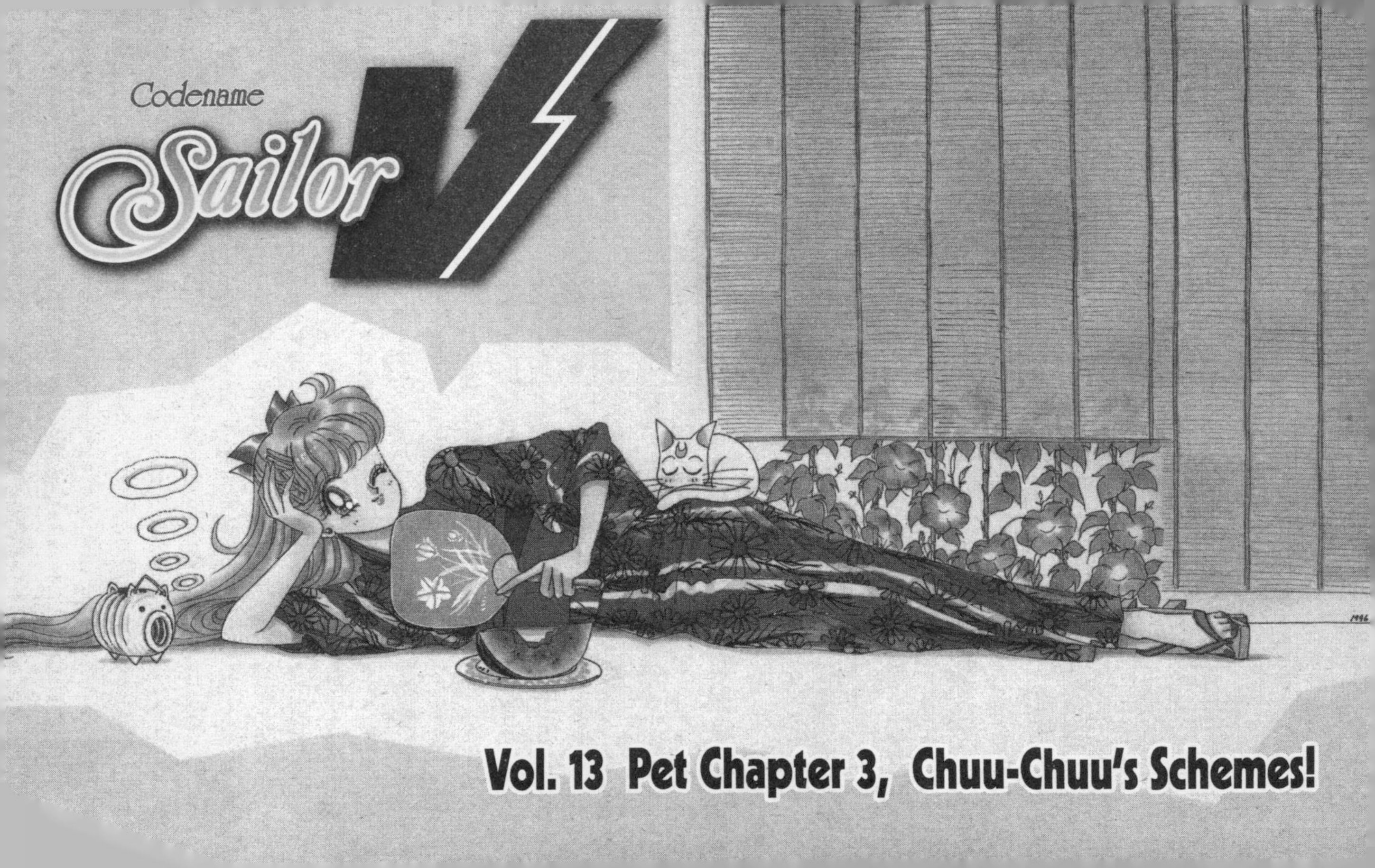
Codename
Sailor V
1996

Vol. 13 Pet Chapter 3, Chuu-Chuu's Schemes!

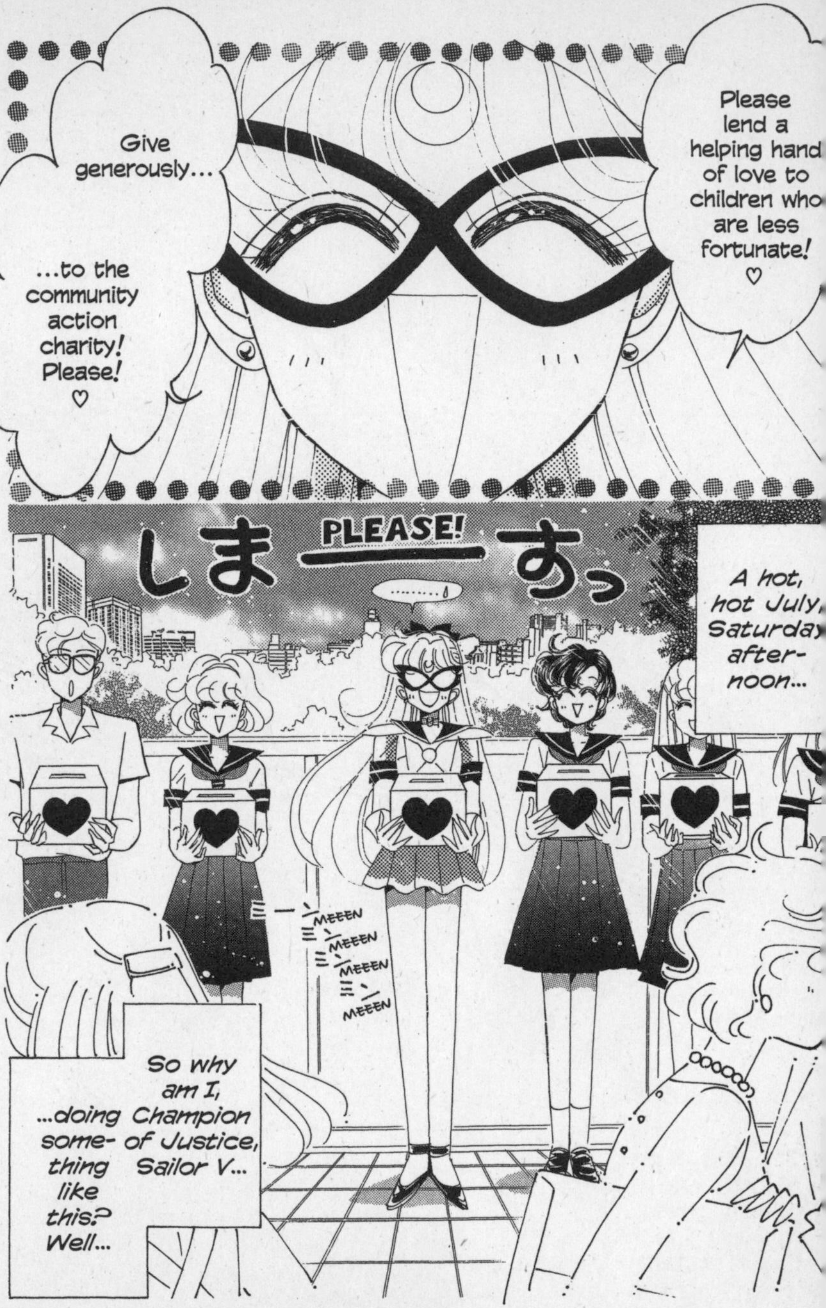
Please lend a helping hand of love to children who are less fortunate! ♡
Give generously...
...to the community action charity! Please! ♡
A hot, hot July, Saturday afternoon...
しまーすっ PLEASE!
........!
MEEEN MEEEN MEEEN MEEEN
So why am I, Champion of Justice, Sailor V...
...doing something like this? Well...

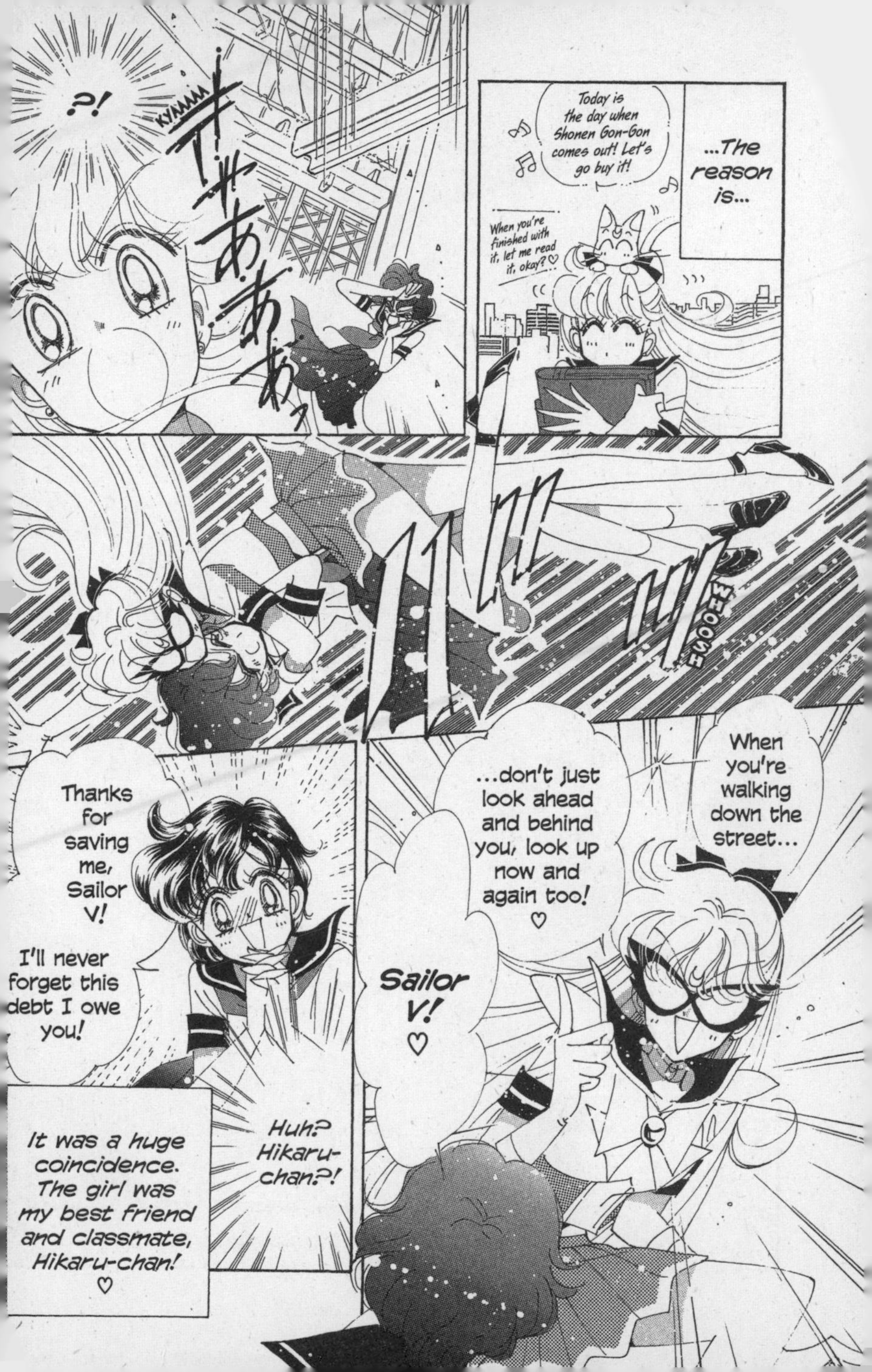
...The reason is...
Today is the day when Shonen Gon-Gon comes out! Let's go buy it!
When you're finished with it, let me read it, okay? ♡
KYAAAAA
?!
WHOOSH
When you're walking down the street...
...don't just look ahead and behind you, look up now and again too! ♡
Sailor V! ♡
Huh? Hikaru-chan?!
Thanks for saving me, Sailor V!
I'll never forget this debt I owe you!
It was a huge coincidence. The girl was my best friend and classmate, Hikaru-chan! ♡

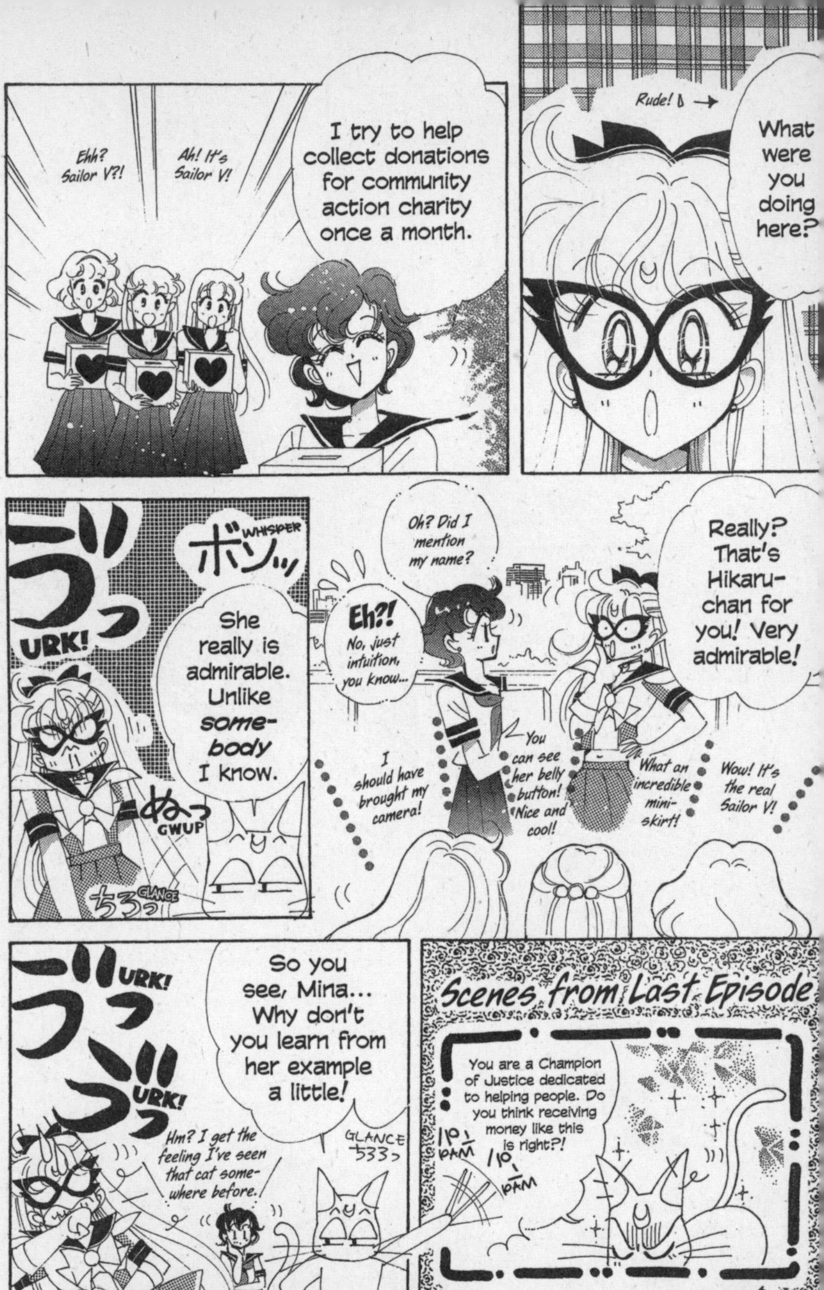

What were you doing here?
Rude!
I try to help collect donations for community action charity once a month.
Ah! It's Sailor V!
Ehh? Sailor V?!
Really? That's Hikaru-chan for you! Very admirable!
Oh? Did I mention my name?
Eh?! No, just intuition, you know...
Wow! It's the real Sailor V!
What an incredible mini-skirt!
You can see her belly button! Nice and cool!
I should have brought my camera!
ボソッ WHISPER
She really is admirable. Unlike *somebody* I know.
うっ URK!
ぬっ GWUP
ちろっ GLANCE
Scenes from Last Episode
You are a Champion of Justice dedicated to helping people. Do you think receiving money like this is right?!
PAM
PAM
The most important panel from last time.
So you see, Mina... Why don't you learn from her example a little!
うっ URK!
うっ URK!
GLANCE
Hm? I get the feeling I've seen that cat somewhere before.

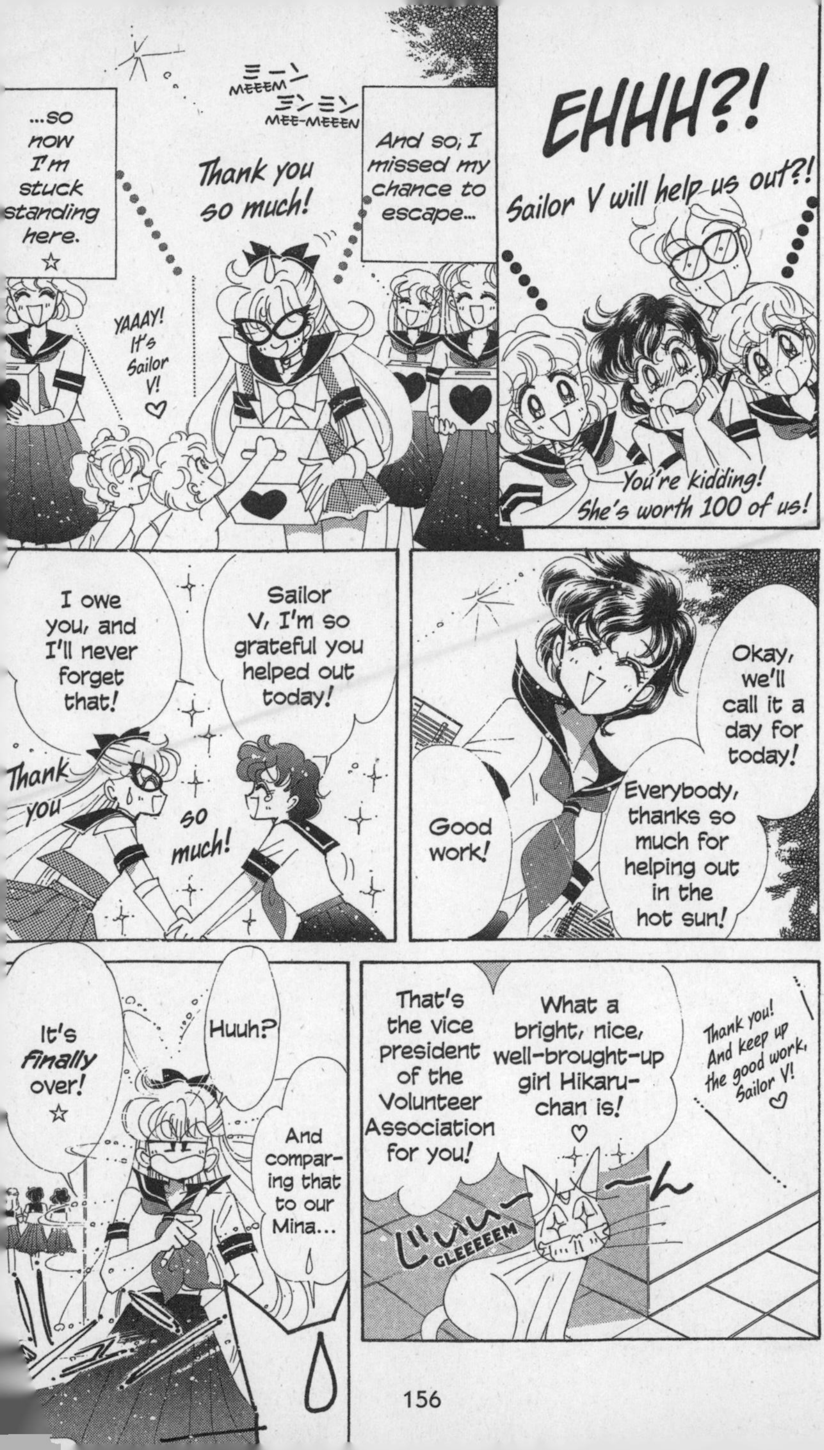
EHHH?!
Sailor V will help us out?!
You're kidding! She's worth 100 of us!
And so, I missed my chance to escape...
ミーン MEEEM
ミンミン MEE-MEEEN
Thank you so much!
...so now I'm stuck standing here. ☆
YAAAY! It's Sailor V! ♡
Okay, we'll call it a day for today!
Everybody, thanks so much for helping out in the hot sun!
Good work!
Sailor V, I'm so grateful you helped out today!
I owe you, and I'll never forget that!
Thank you so much!
Thank you! And keep up the good work, Sailor V! ♡
What a bright, nice, well-brought-up girl Hikaru-chan is! ♡
That's the vice president of the Volunteer Association for you!
じぃぃ〜ん GLEEEEEM
Huuh?
It's *finally* over! ☆
And comparing that to our Mina...

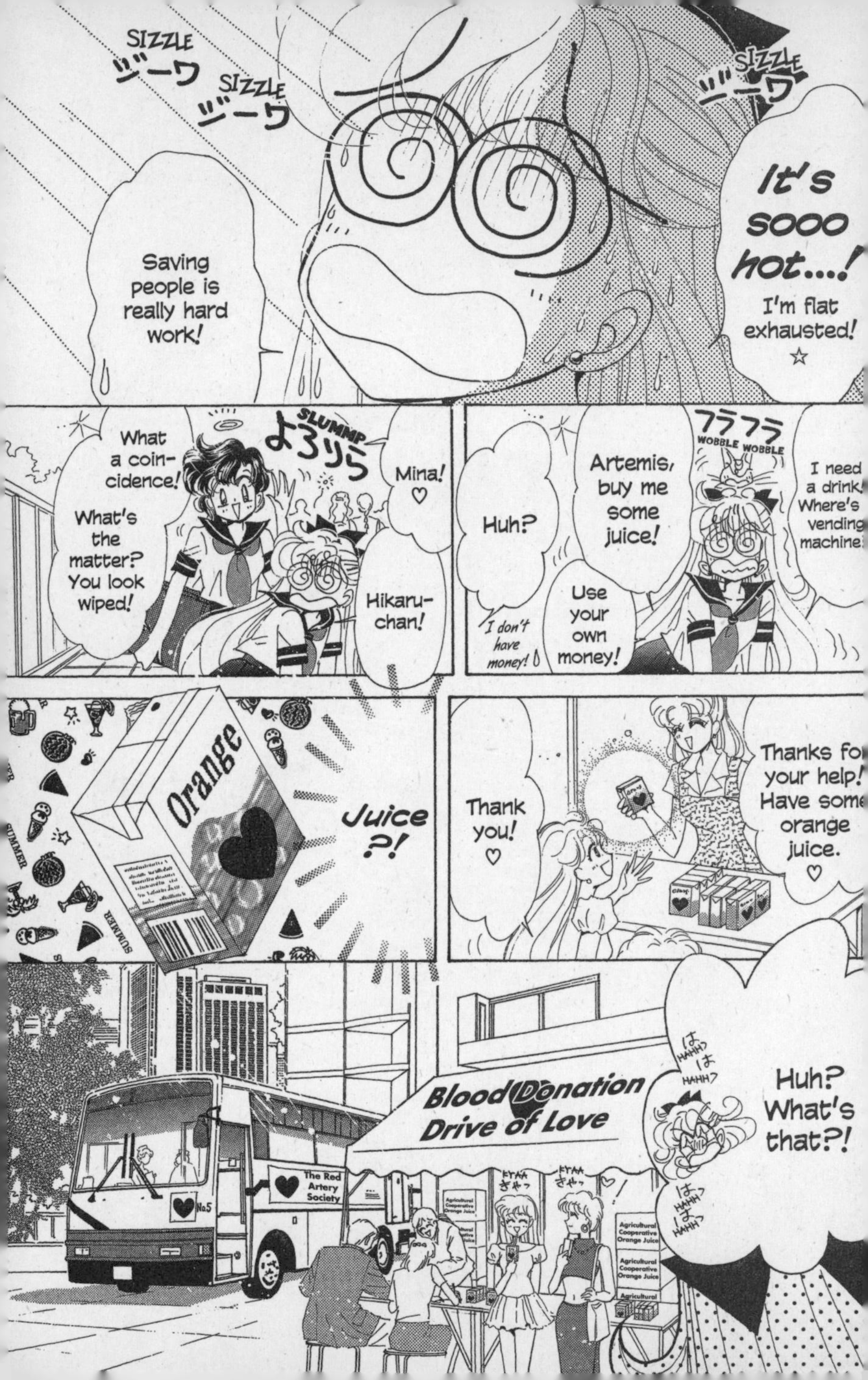
SIZZLE
ジーワ
It's sooo hot...!
I'm flat exhausted! ☆
SIZZLE
ジーワ
SIZZLE
ジーワ
Saving people is really hard work!
I need a drink! Where's vending machine
フラフラ
WOBBLE WOBBLE
Artemis, buy me some juice!
Huh?
Use your own money!
I don't have money!
Mina! ♡
SLUMMP
よろりら
What a coincidence!
What's the matter? You look wiped!
Hikaru-chan!
Thanks fo your help! Have som orange juice. ♡
Thank you! ♡
Juice ?!
Orange
SUMMER
Huh? What's that?!
はっ HAHH
はっ HAHH
はっ HAHH
はっ HAHH
Blood Donation Drive of Love
KYAA きゃっ
KYAA きゃっ
Agricultural Cooperative Orange Juice
Agricultural Cooperative Orange Juice
Agricultural Cooperative Orange Juice
The Red Artery Society
No.5

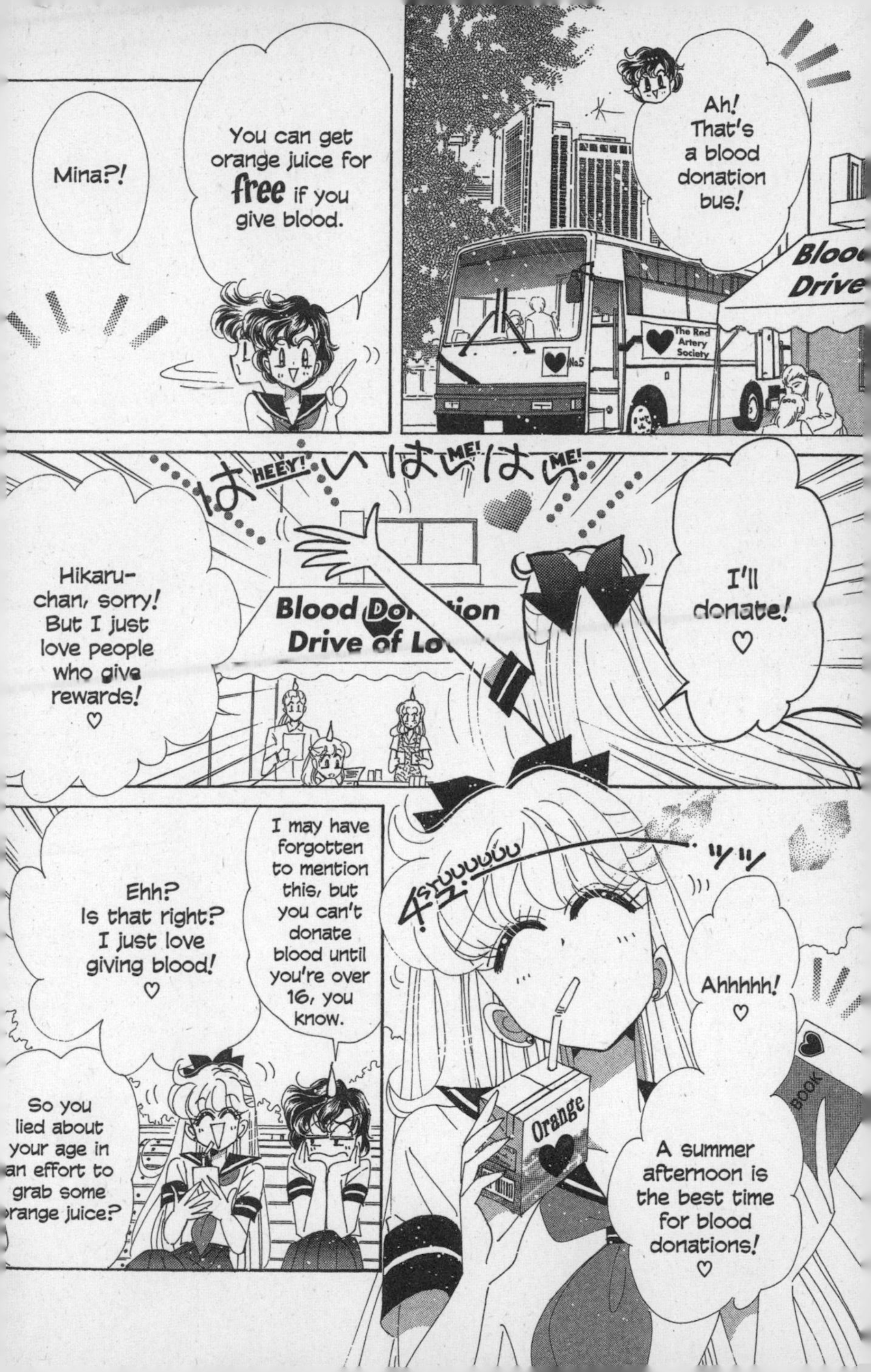
Ah! That's a blood donation bus!
Blood Drive
The Red Artery Society
No.5
You can get orange juice for free if you give blood.
Mina?!
HEEY!
ME!
ME!
I'll donate! ♡
Hikaru-chan, sorry! But I just love people who give rewards! ♡
Ahhhhh! ♡
A summer afternoon is the best time for blood donations! ♡
Orange
BOOK
I may have forgotten to mention this, but you can't donate blood until you're over 16, you know.
Ehh? Is that right? I just love giving blood! ♡
So you lied about your age in an effort to grab some orange juice?

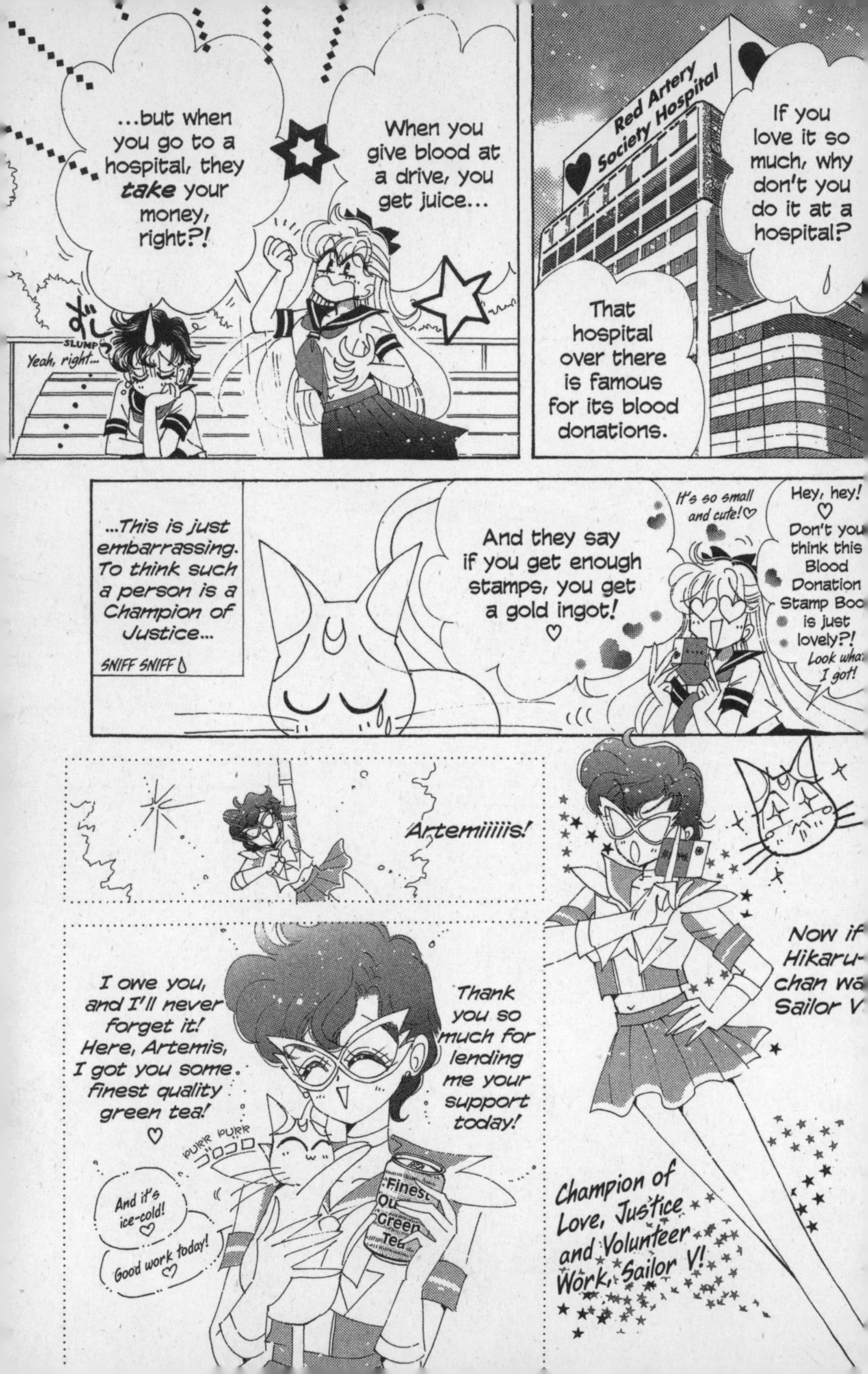
Red Artery Society Hospital
If you love it so much, why don't you do it at a hospital?
That hospital over there is famous for its blood donations.
When you give blood at a drive, you get juice...
...but when you go to a hospital, they *take* your money, right?!
ずし
SLUMP
Yeah, right...
Hey, hey! ♡ Don't you think this Blood Donation Stamp Boo is just lovely?!
Look what I got!
It's so small and cute! ♡
And they say if you get enough stamps, you get a gold ingot! ♡
...This is just embarrassing. To think such a person is a Champion of Justice...
SNIFF SNIFF
Now if Hikaru-chan wa Sailor V
Champion of Love, Justice and Volunteer Work, Sailor V!
Artemiiiiis!
Thank you so much for lending me your support today!
I owe you, and I'll never forget it! Here, Artemis, I got you some finest quality green tea! ♡
PURR PURR
ゴロゴロ
And it's ice-cold! ♡
Good work today! ♡
Finest Qu Green Tea

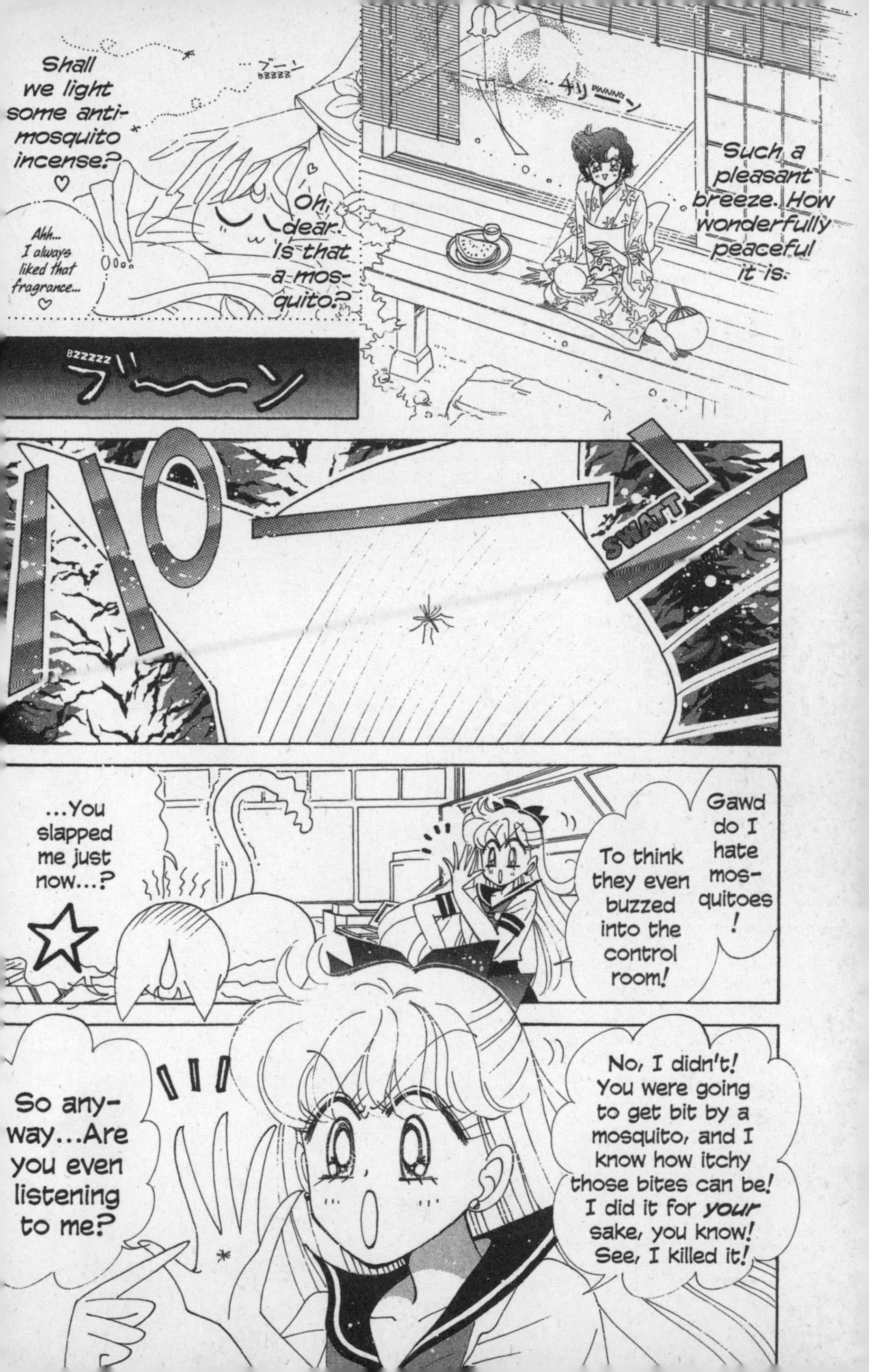

…チリーン DINNNG
Such a pleasant breeze. How wonderfully peaceful it is.
…ブーン BZZZZ
Shall we light some anti-mosquito incense? ♡
Oh, dear. Is that a mosquito?
Ahh... I always liked that fragrance... ♡
BZZZZZ ブーーン
SWATT
Gawd do I hate mosquitoes!
To think they even buzzed into the control room!
...You slapped me just now...?
No, I didn't! You were going to get bit by a mosquito, and I know how itchy those bites can be! I did it for *your* sake, you know! See, I killed it!
So anyway...Are you even listening to me?

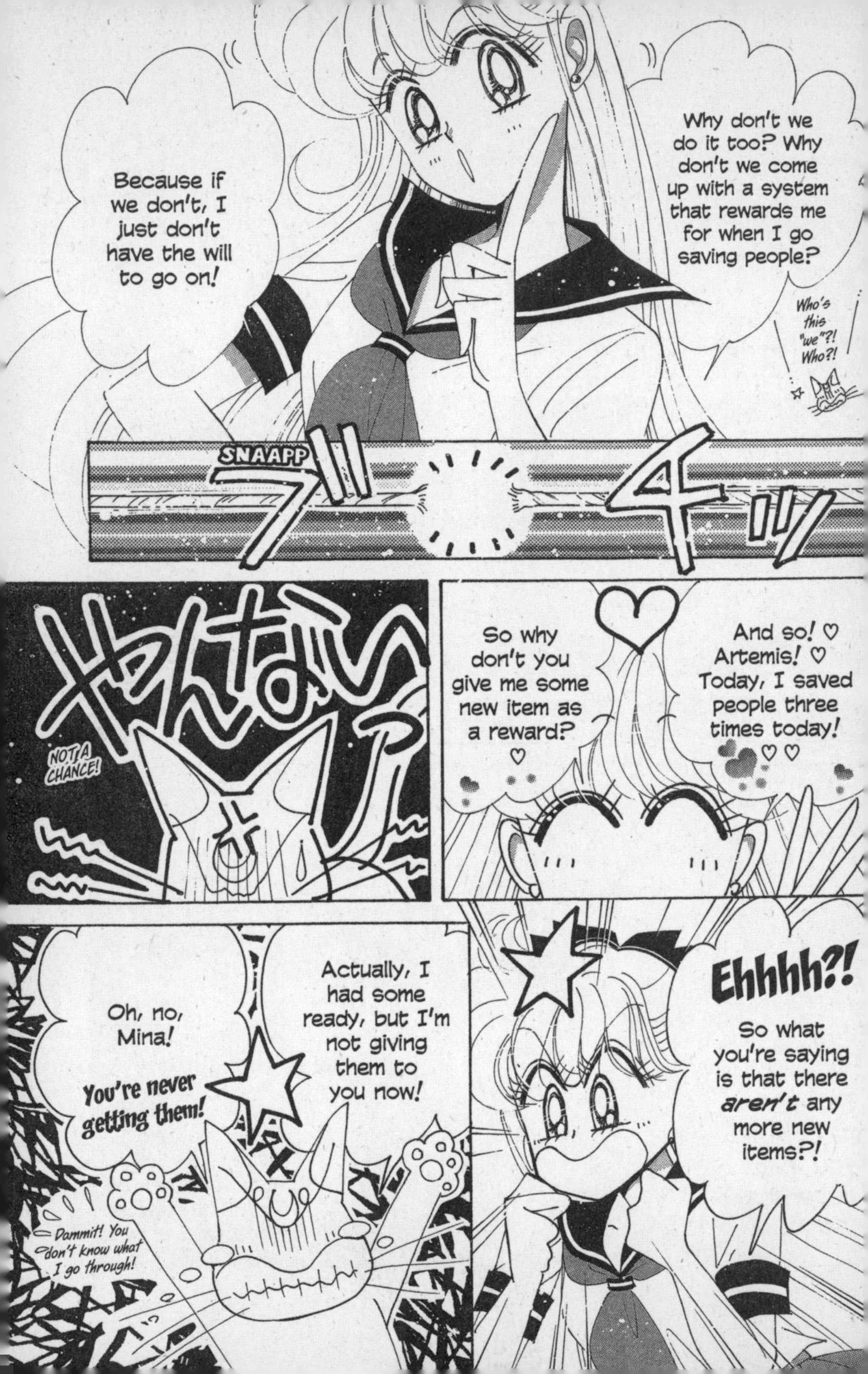
Why don't we do it too? Why don't we come up with a system that rewards me for when I go saving people?
Who's this "we"?! Who?!
Because if we don't, I just don't have the will to go on!
SNAAPP
And so! ♡ Artemis! ♡ Today, I saved people three times today! ♡ ♡
So why don't you give me some new item as a reward? ♡
NOT A CHANCE!
Ehhhh?!
So what you're saying is that there *aren't* any more new items?!
Actually, I had some ready, but I'm not giving them to you now!
Oh, no, Mina!
You're never getting them!
Dammit! You don't know what I go through!

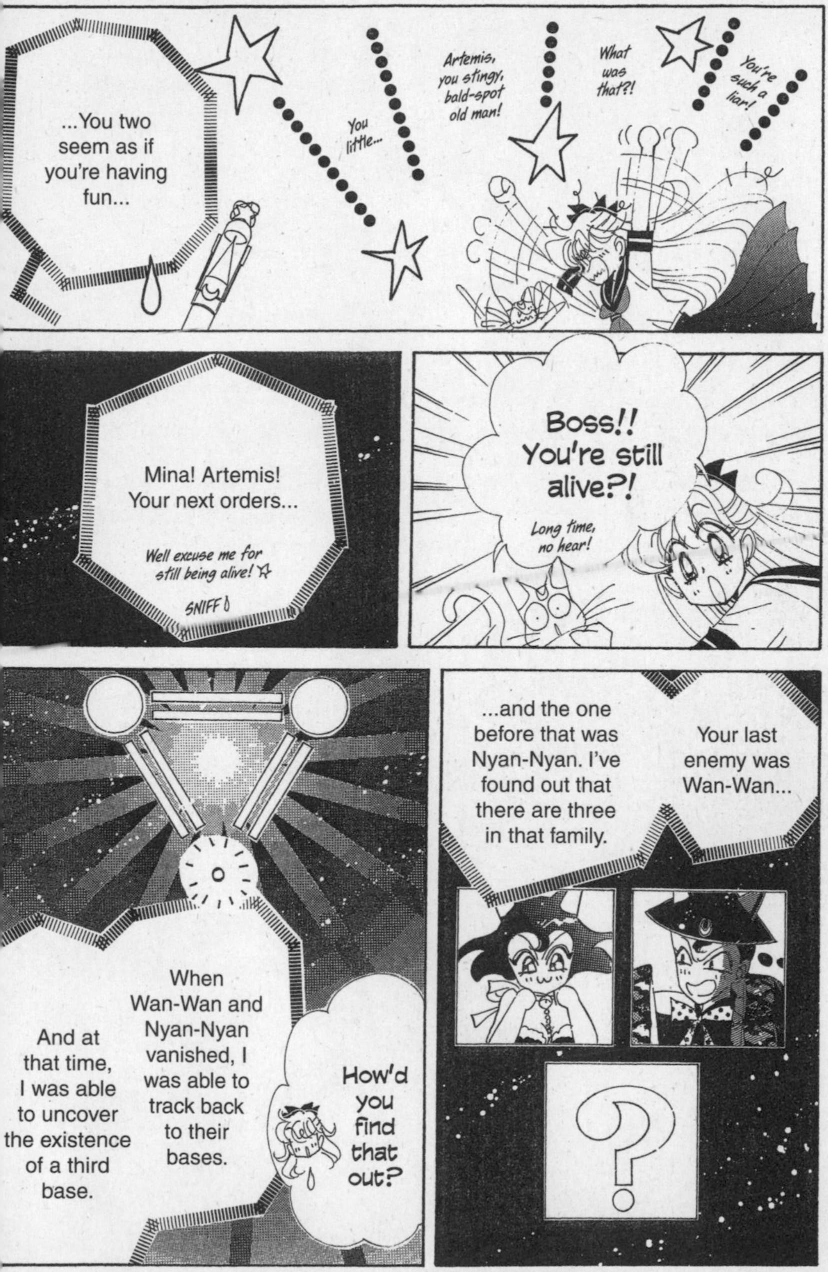
You're such a liar!
What was that?!
Artemis, you stingy, bald-spot old man!
You little...
...You two seem as if you're having fun...
Boss!! You're still alive?!
Long time, no hear!
Mina! Artemis! Your next orders...
Well excuse me for still being alive!
SNIFF
Your last enemy was Wan-Wan...
...and the one before that was Nyan-Nyan. I've found out that there are three in that family.
?
How'd you find that out?
When Wan-Wan and Nyan-Nyan vanished, I was able to track back to their bases.
And at that time, I was able to uncover the existence of a third base.

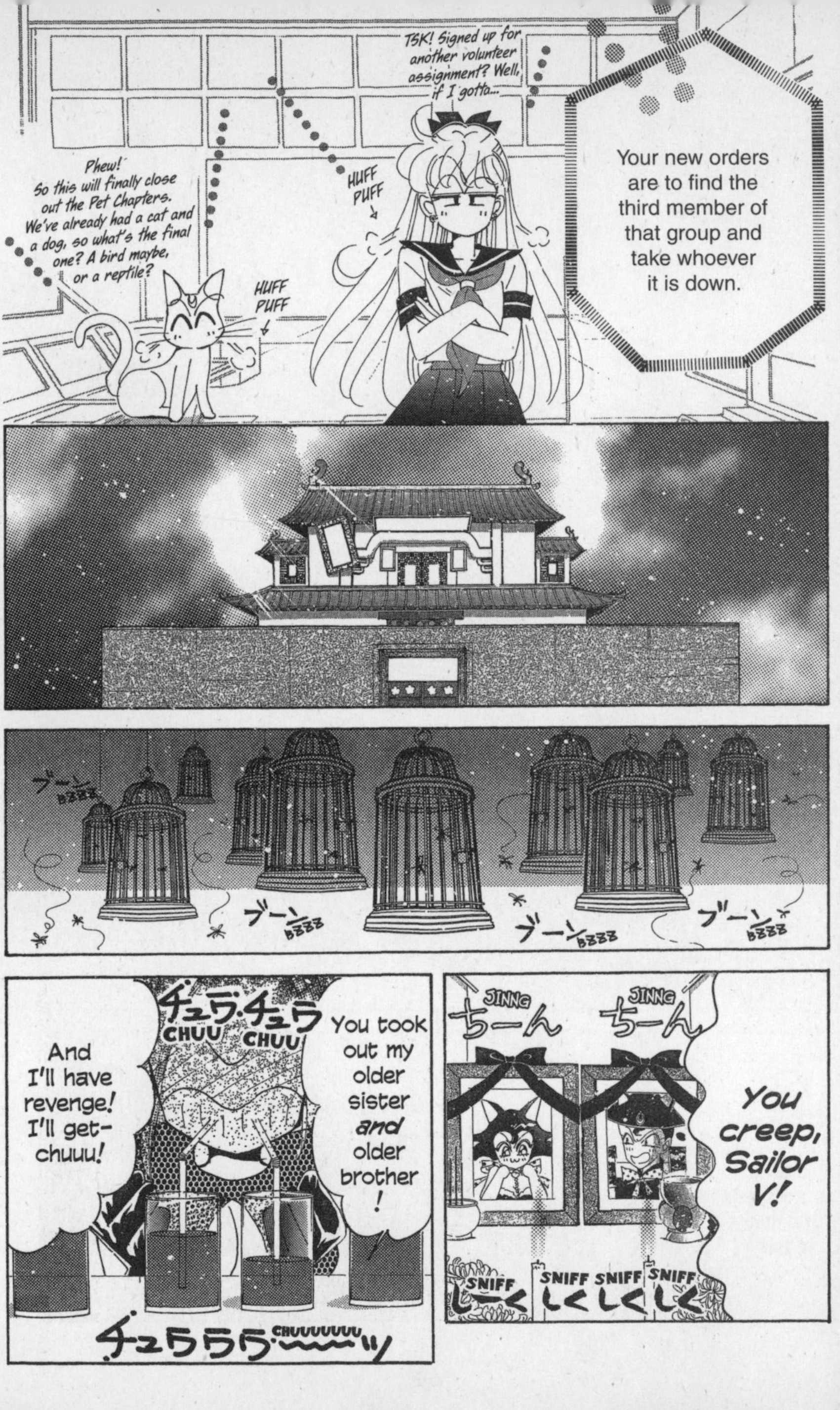
Your new orders are to find the third member of that group and take whoever it is down.
TSK! Signed up for another volunteer assignment? Well, if I gotta...
HUFF PUFF
Phew! So this will finally close out the Pet Chapters. We've already had a cat and a dog, so what's the final one? A bird maybe, or a reptile?
HUFF PUFF
ブーン BZZZ
ブーン BZZZ
ブーン BZZZ
ブーン BZZZ
ちーん JINNG ちーん JINNG
You creep, Sailor V!
SNIFF SNIFF SNIFF SNIFF
しくしくしく
チュラ・チュラ CHUU CHUU
You took out my older sister and older brother!
And I'll have revenge! I'll get-chuuu!
チュラララ CHUUUUUUU

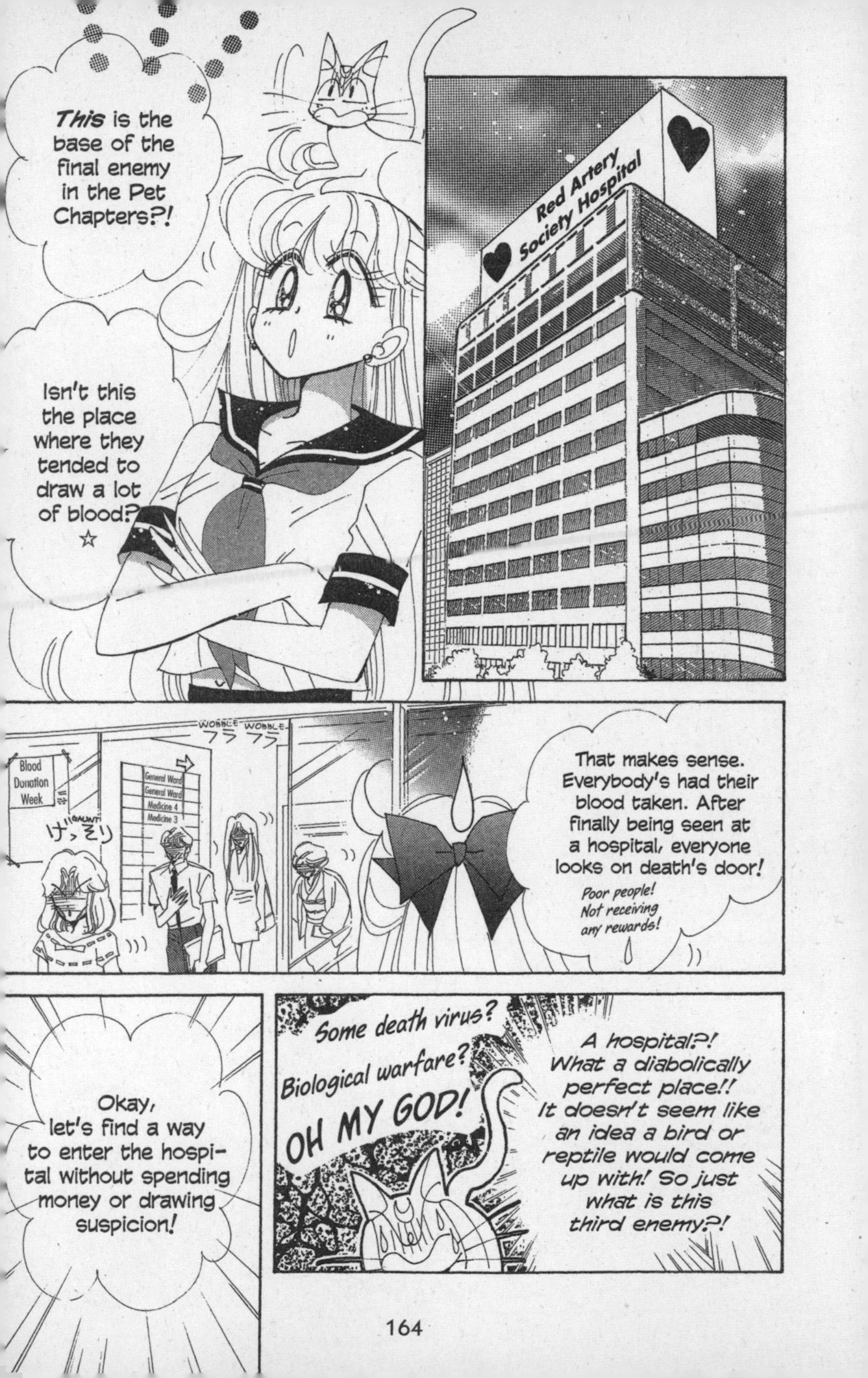

Red Artery Society Hospital
This is the base of the final enemy in the Pet Chapters?!
Isn't this the place where they tended to draw a lot of blood? ☆
That makes sense. Everybody's had their blood taken. After finally being seen at a hospital, everyone looks on death's door!
Poor people! Not receiving any rewards!
WOBBLE WOBBLE
フラ フラ
General Ward
General Ward
Medicine 4
Medicine 3
Blood Donation Week
GAUNT
げっそり
A hospital?! What a diabolically perfect place!! It doesn't seem like an idea a bird or reptile would come up with! So just what is this third enemy?!
Some death virus?
Biological warfare?
OH MY GOD!
Okay, let's find a way to enter the hospital without spending money or drawing suspicion!

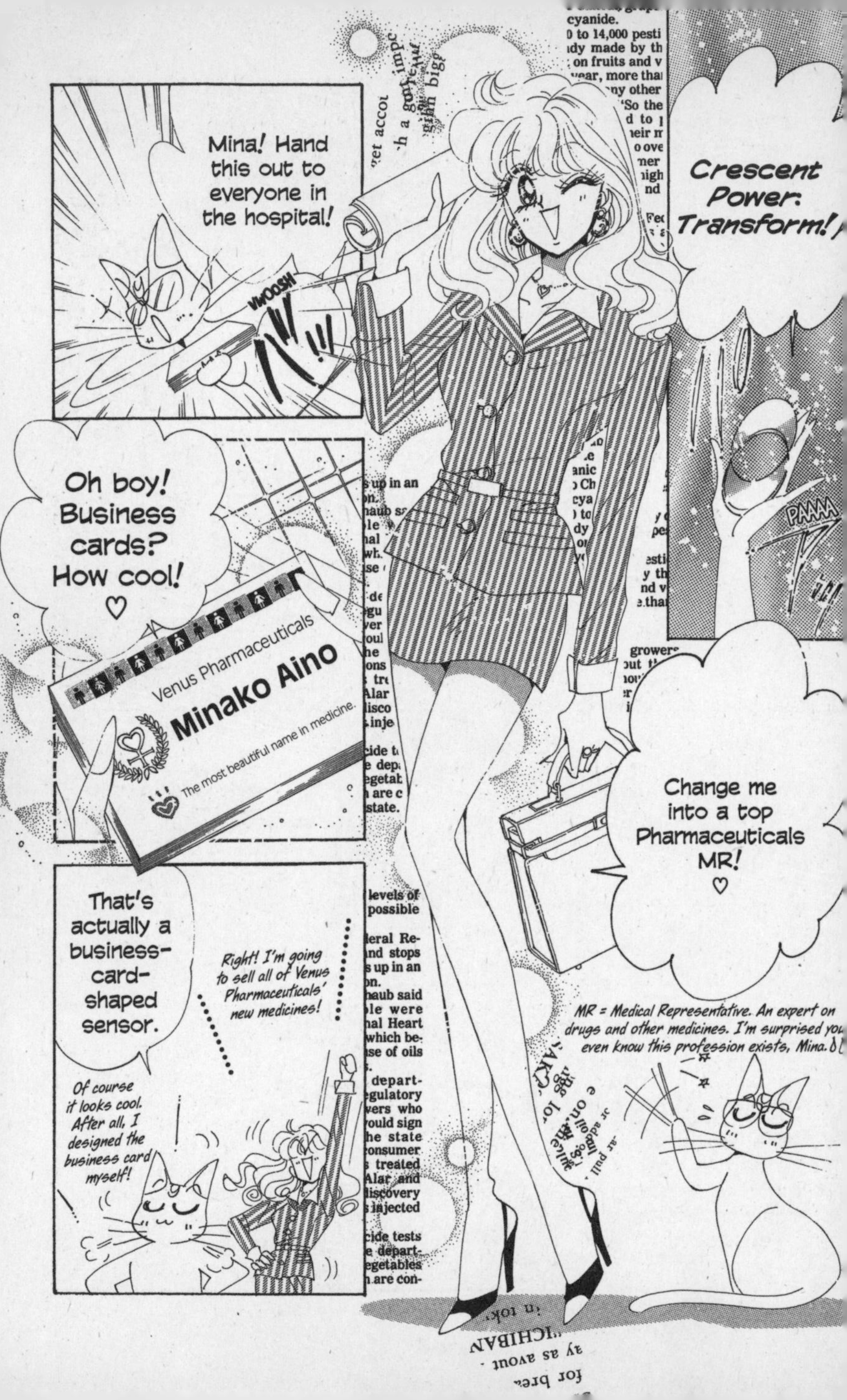
Crescent Power: Transform!
Change me into a top Pharmaceuticals MR! ♡
MR = Medical Representative. An expert on drugs and other medicines. I'm surprised you even know this profession exists, Mina.
Mina! Hand this out to everyone in the hospital!
VWOOSH
Oh boy! Business cards? How cool! ♡
Venus Pharmaceuticals
Minako Aino
The most beautiful name in medicine.
That's actually a business-card-shaped sensor.
Right! I'm going to sell all of Venus Pharmaceuticals' new medicines!
Of course it looks cool. After all, I designed the business card myself!

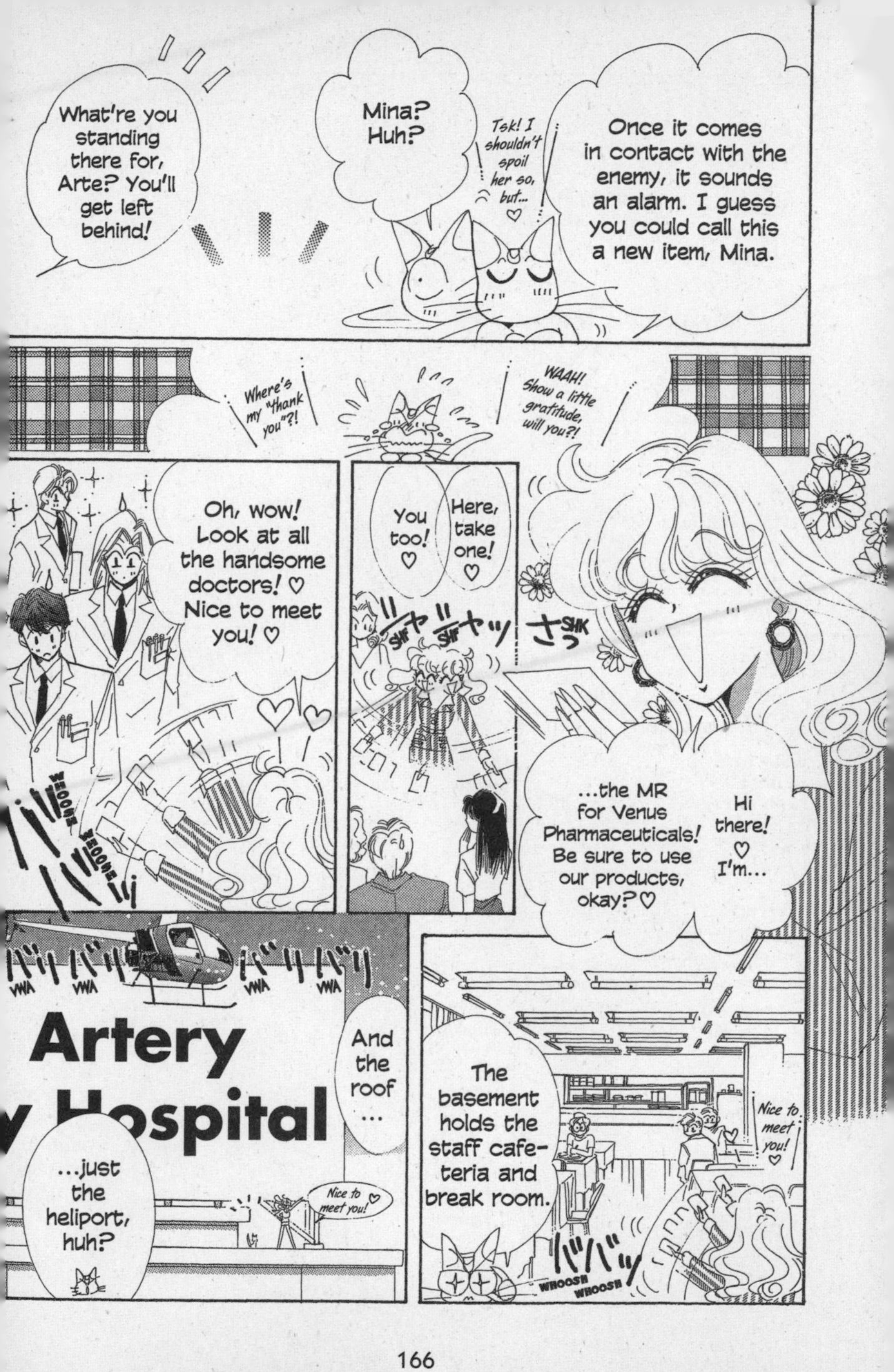
Once it comes in contact with the enemy, it sounds an alarm. I guess you could call this a new item, Mina.
Tsk! I shouldn't spoil her so, but... ♡
Mina? Huh?
What're you standing there for, Arte? You'll get left behind!
WAAH! Show a little gratitude, will you?!
Where's my "thank you"?!
Hi there! ♡ I'm...
...the MR for Venus Pharmaceuticals! Be sure to use our products, okay? ♡
SHK
Here, take one! ♡
You too! ♡
SHF
SHF
Oh, wow! Look at all the handsome doctors! ♡ Nice to meet you! ♡
WHOOSH
WHOOSH
The basement holds the staff cafeteria and break room.
Nice to meet you! ♡
WHOOSH
WHOOSH
And the roof...
VWA
VWA
VWA
VWA
Artery
y Hospital
Nice to meet you! ♡
...just the heliport, huh?

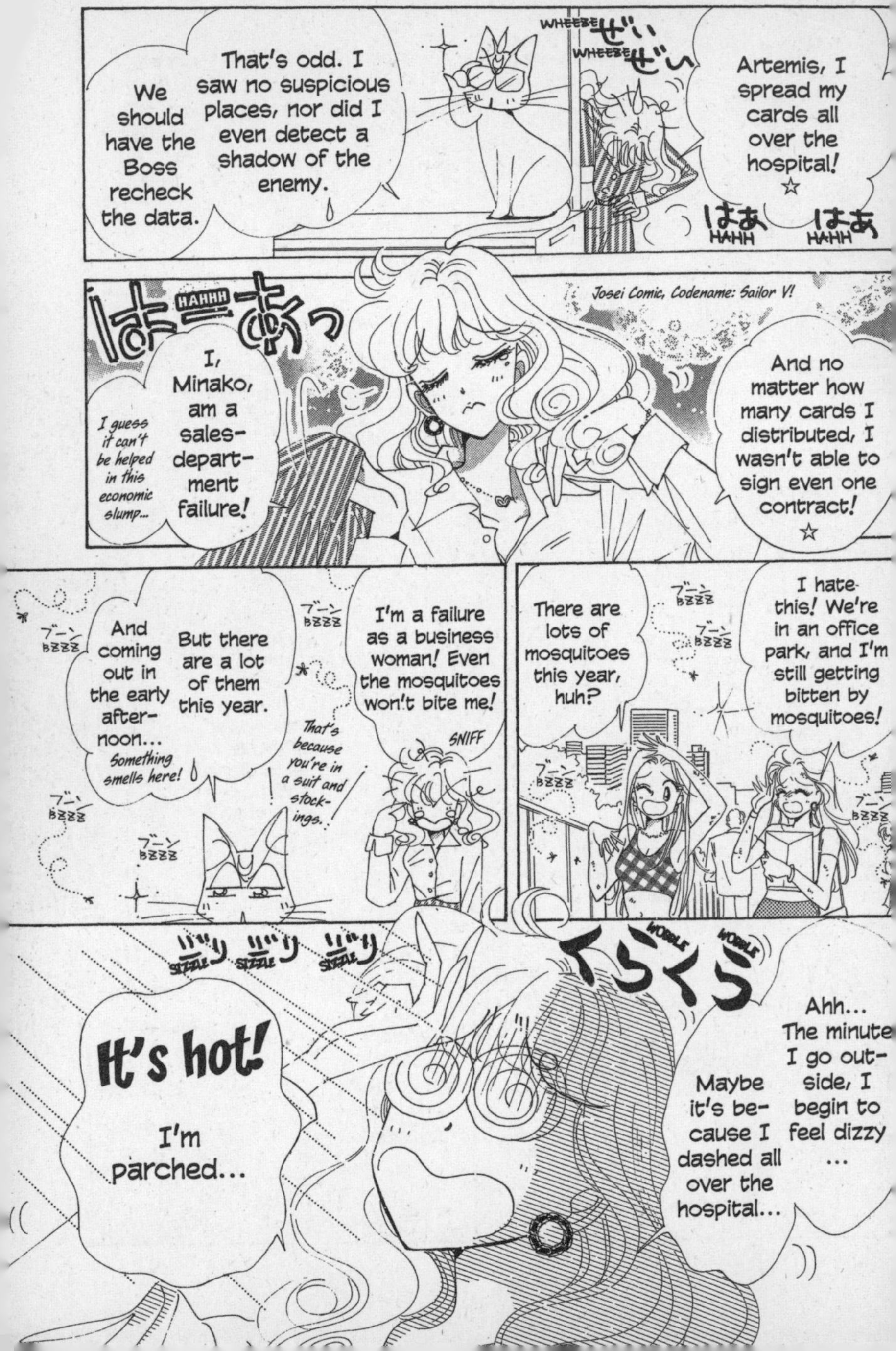
Artemis, I spread my cards all over the hospital! ☆
WHEEBE ぜい WHEEBE ぜい
はあ HAHH はあ HAHH
That's odd. I saw no suspicious places, nor did I even detect a shadow of the enemy.
We should have the Boss recheck the data.
Josei Comic, Codename: Sailor V!
And no matter how many cards I distributed, I wasn't able to sign even one contract! ☆
はーあっ HAHHH
I, Minako, am a sales-department failure!
I guess it can't be helped in this economic slump...
I hate this! We're in an office park, and I'm still getting bitten by mosquitoes!
There are lots of mosquitoes this year, huh?
ブーン BZZZ
I'm a failure as a business woman! Even the mosquitoes won't bite me!
SNIFF
That's because you're in a suit and stockings.
But there are a lot of them this year.
And coming out in the early afternoon... Something smells here!
Ahh... The minute I go outside, I begin to feel dizzy...
Maybe it's because I dashed all over the hospital...
くらくら WOBBLE WOBBLE
ジリ SIZZLE ジリ SIZZLE ジリ SIZZLE
It's hot!
I'm parched...

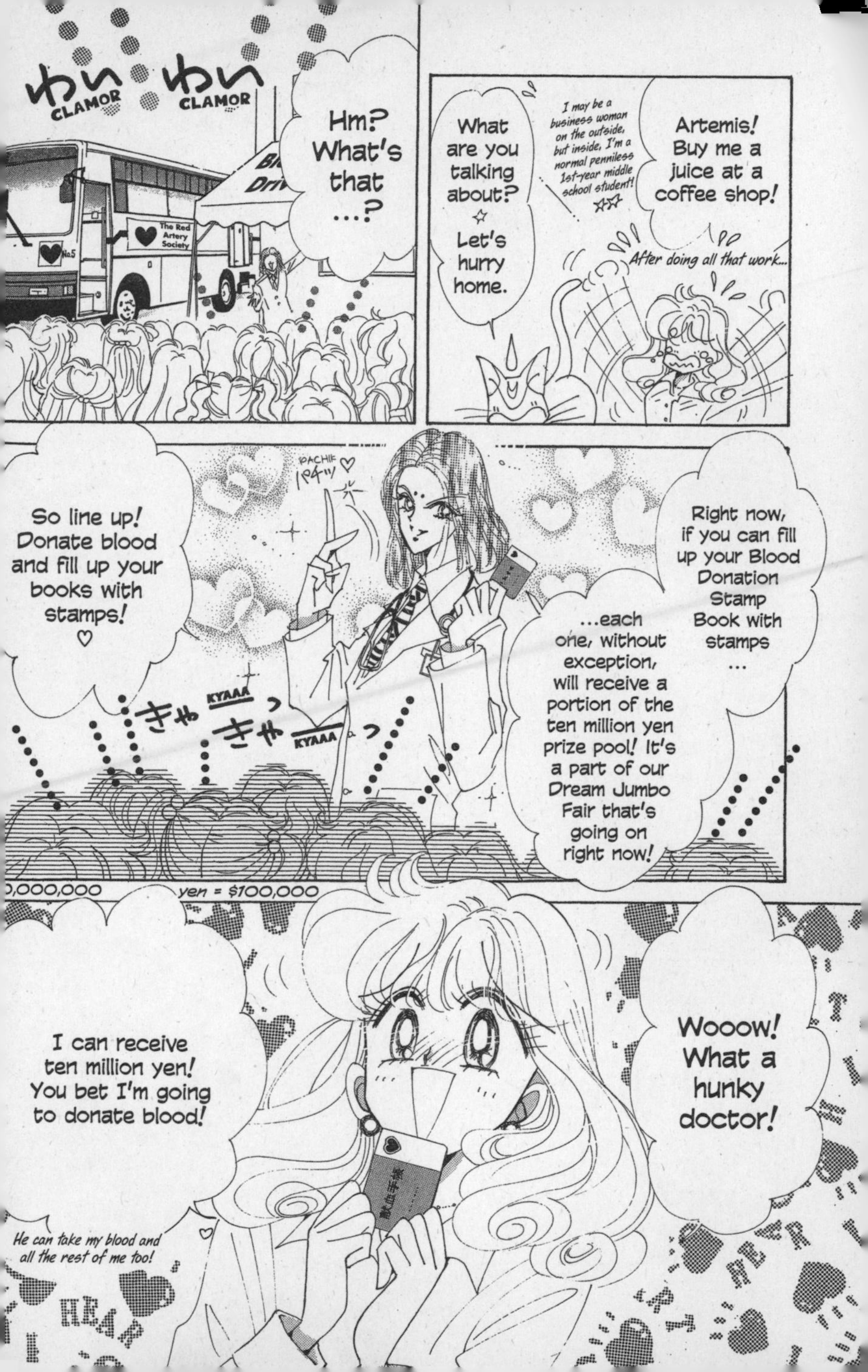
Artemis! Buy me a juice at a coffee shop!
I may be a business woman on the outside, but inside, I'm a normal penniless 1st-year middle school student! ☆☆
What are you talking about? ☆ Let's hurry home.
After doing all that work...
Hm? What's that ...?
わい CLAMOR わい CLAMOR
The Red Artery Society
No.5
Right now, if you can fill up your Blood Donation Stamp Book with stamps ...
...each one, without exception, will receive a portion of the ten million yen prize pool! It's a part of our Dream Jumbo Fair that's going on right now!
パチッ PACHI! ♡
So line up! Donate blood and fill up your books with stamps! ♡
きゃ KYAAA きゃ KYAAA
0,000,000 yen = $100,000
Wooow! What a hunky doctor!
I can receive ten million yen! You bet I'm going to donate blood!
He can take my blood and all the rest of me too!

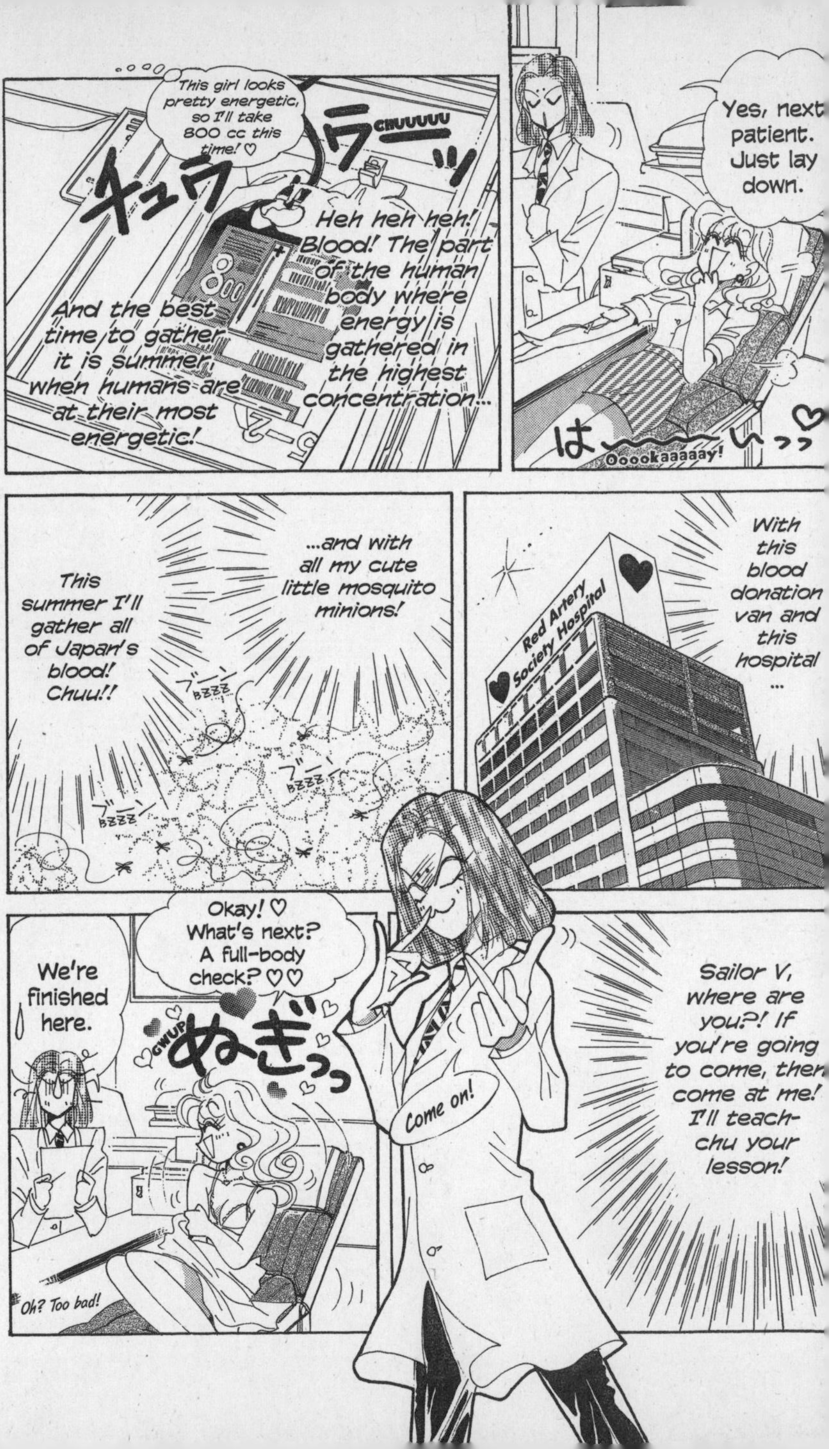
Yes, next patient. Just lay down.
Ooookaaaaay!
This girl looks pretty energetic, so I'll take 800 cc this time! ♡
CHUUUUU
Heh heh heh! Blood! The part of the human body where energy is gathered in the highest concentration...
And the best time to gather it is summer, when humans are at their most energetic!
With this blood donation van and this hospital ...
Red Artery Society Hospital
...and with all my cute little mosquito minions!
This summer I'll gather all of Japan's blood! Chuu!!
BZZZ
BZZZ
BZZZ
Sailor V, where are you?! If you're going to come, then come at me! I'll teach-chu your lesson!
Come on!
Okay! ♡ What's next? A full-body check? ♡♡
We're finished here.
GWUP
Oh? Too bad!

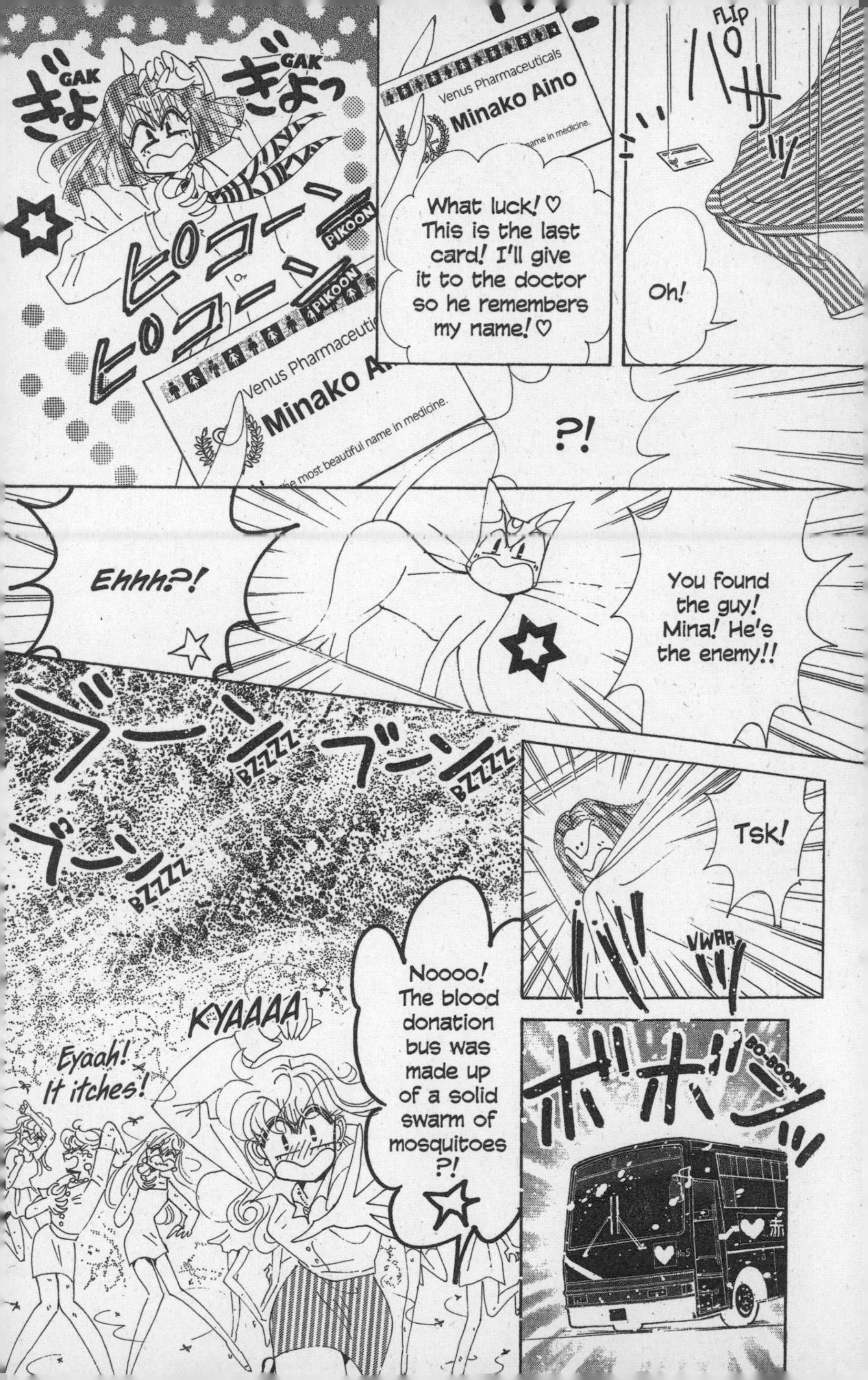
FLIP
Oh!
Venus Pharmaceuticals
Minako Aino
name in medicine.
What luck! ♡ This is the last card! I'll give it to the doctor so he remembers my name! ♡
GAK
GAK
PIKOON
PIKOON
Venus Pharmaceutic
Minako Ai
the most beautiful name in medicine.
?!
You found the guy! Mina! He's the enemy!!
Ehhh?!
Tsk!
VWAA
BO-BOOM
BZZZZ
BZZZZ
BZZZZ
Noooo! The blood donation bus was made up of a solid swarm of mosquitoes ?!
KYAAAA
Eyaah! It itches!

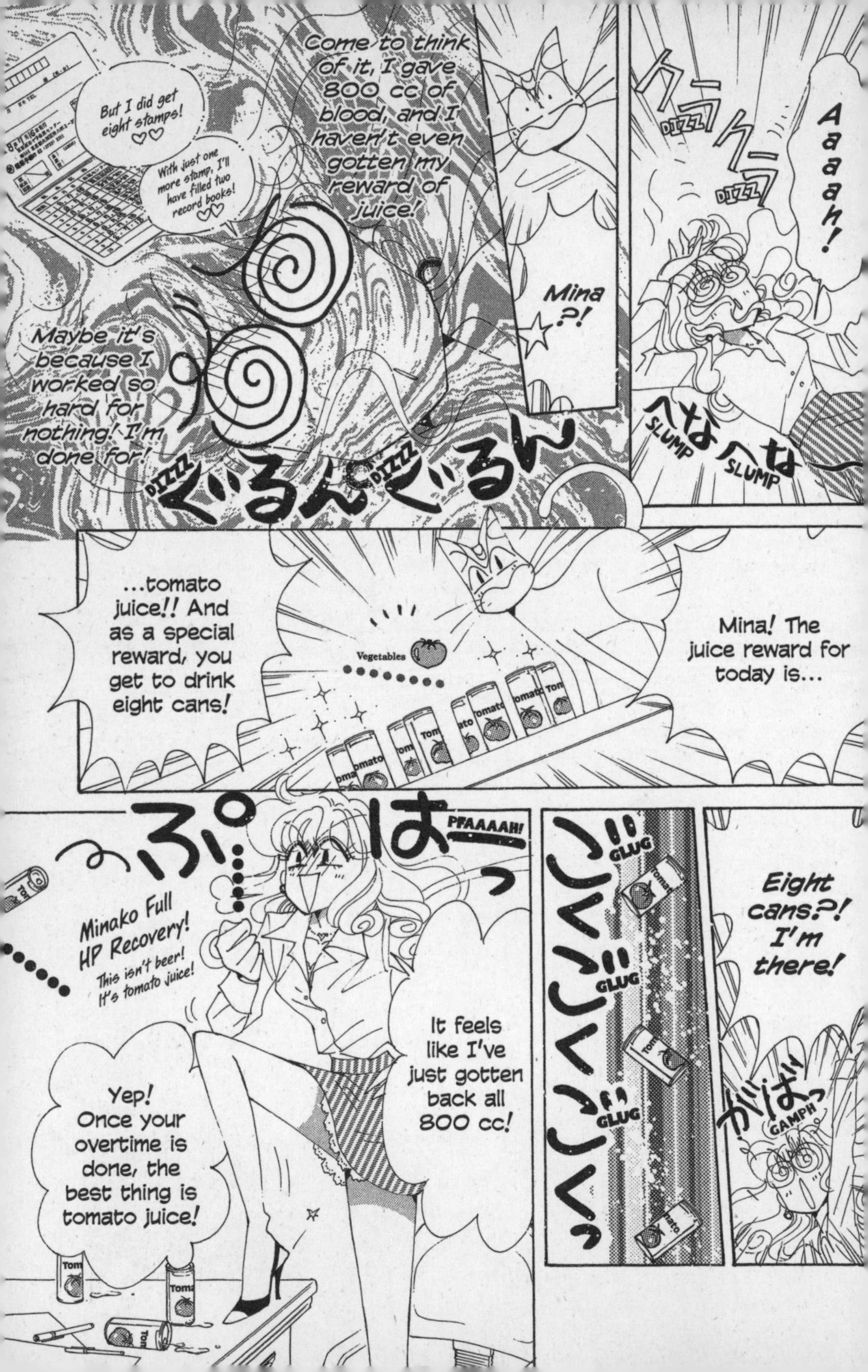

Aaaah!
くらくら DIZZ DIZZ
へなへな SLUMP SLUMP
Mina?!
Come to think of it, I gave 800 cc of blood, and I haven't even gotten my reward of juice!
But I did get eight stamps! ♡♡
With just one more stamp, I'll have filled two record books! ♡♡
Maybe it's because I worked so hard for nothing! I'm done for!
ぐるんぐるん DIZZ DIZZ
Mina! The juice reward for today is...
...tomato juice!! And as a special reward, you get to drink eight cans!
Vegetables
Eight cans?! I'm there!
がばっ GAMPH
ごくごくごくっ GLUG GLUG GLUG
ぷはーっ PFAAAAH!
It feels like I've just gotten back all 800 cc!
Minako Full HP Recovery!
This isn't beer! It's tomato juice!
Yep! Once your overtime is done, the best thing is tomato juice!

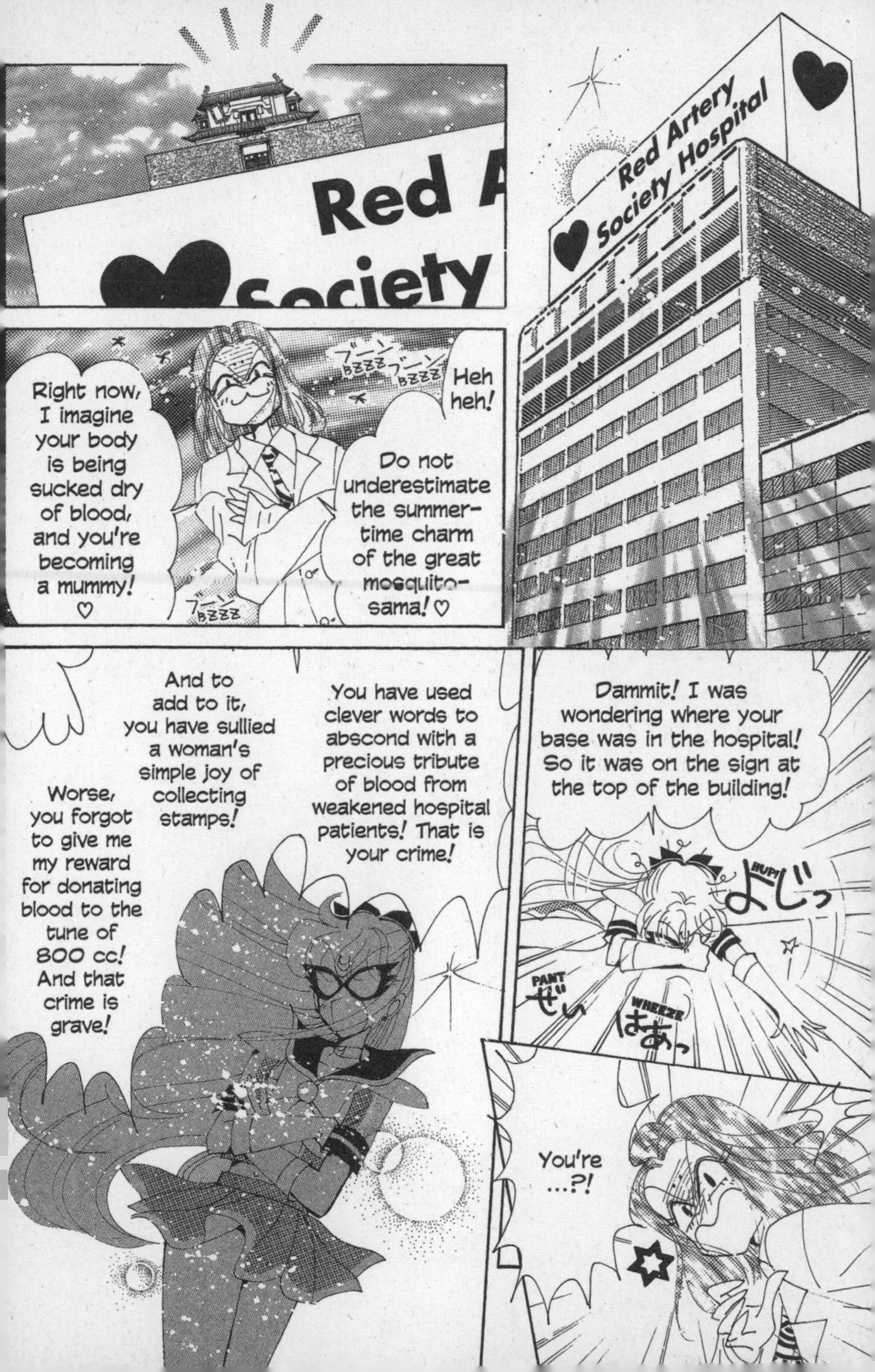
Red Artery Society Hospital
Red A
Society
ブーン BZZZ ブーン BZZZ
Heh heh!
Do not underestimate the summer-time charm of the great mosquito-sama! ♡
Right now, I imagine your body is being sucked dry of blood, and you're becoming a mummy! ♡
ブーン BZZZ
Dammit! I was wondering where your base was in the hospital! So it was on the sign at the top of the building!
HUP! よじっ
PANT ぜい
WHEEZE はあっ
You're ...?!
You have used clever words to abscond with a precious tribute of blood from weakened hospital patients! That is your crime!
And to add to it, you have sullied a woman's simple joy of collecting stamps!
Worse, you forgot to give me my reward for donating blood to the tune of 800 cc! And that crime is grave!

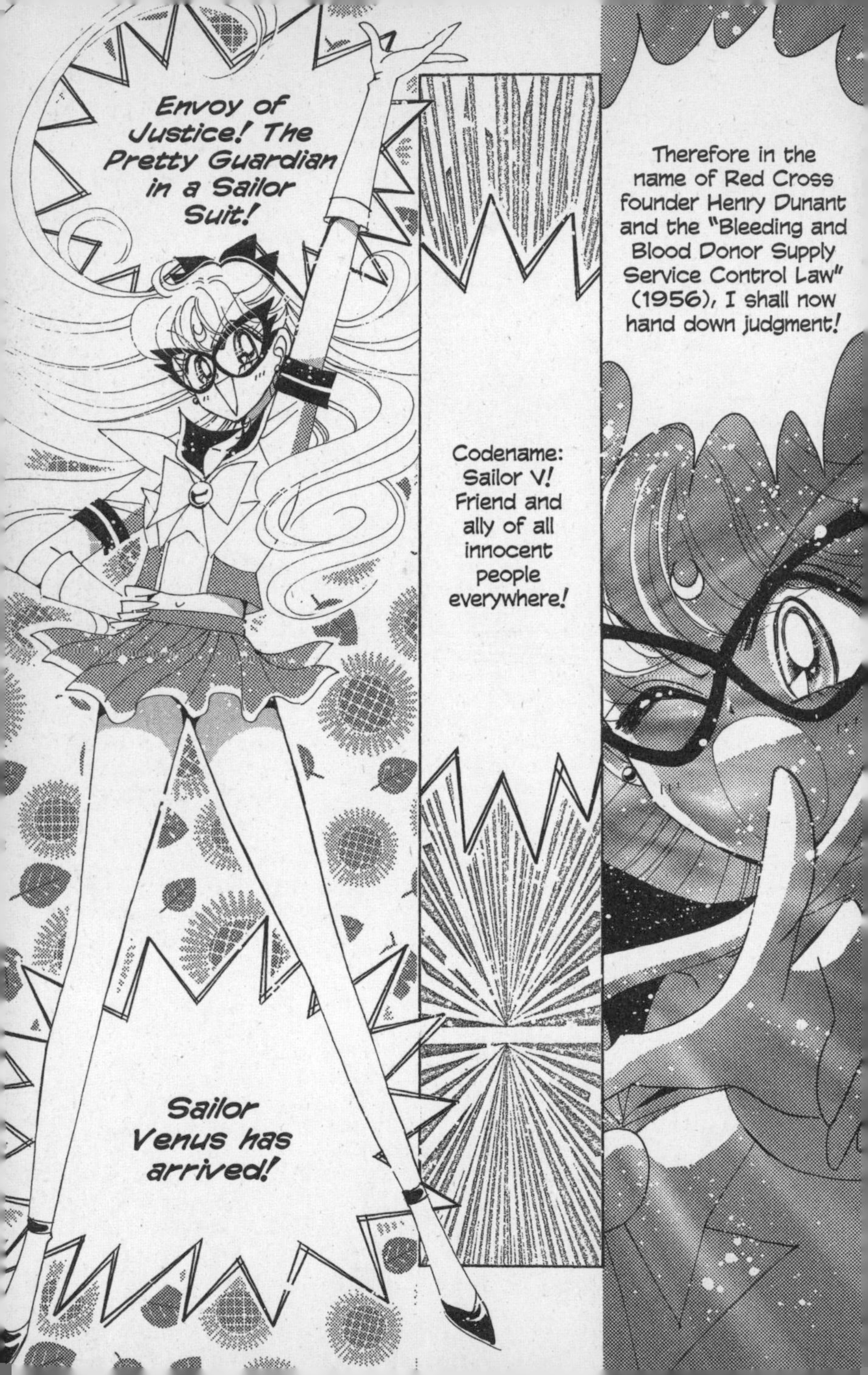
Therefore in the name of Red Cross founder Henry Dunant and the "Bleeding and Blood Donor Supply Service Control Law" (1956), I shall now hand down judgment!
Codename: Sailor V! Friend and ally of all innocent people everywhere!
Envoy of Justice! The Pretty Guardian in a Sailor Suit!
Sailor Venus has arrived!

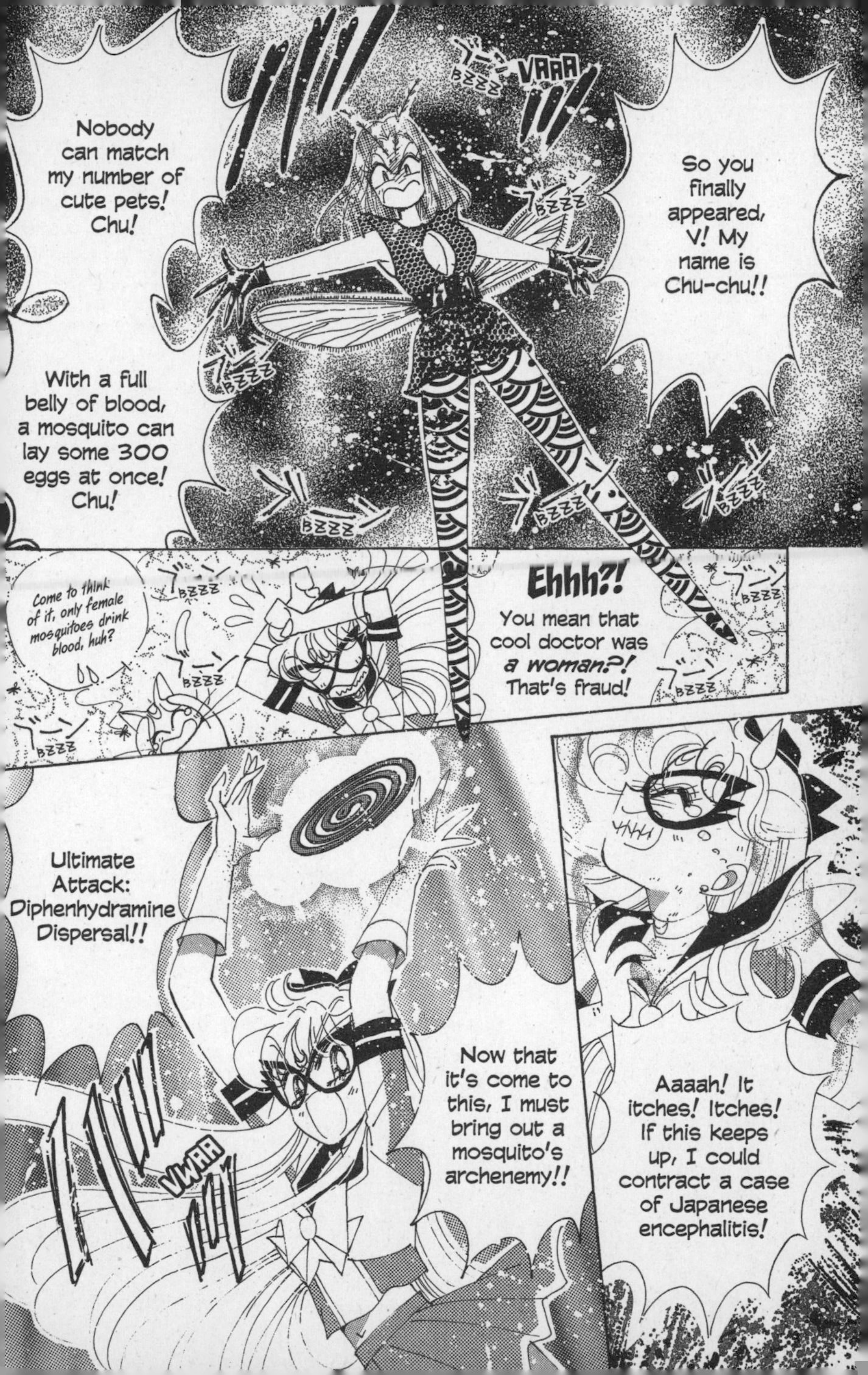
VAAA
BZZZ
So you finally appeared, V! My name is Chu-chu!!
Nobody can match my number of cute pets! Chu!
With a full belly of blood, a mosquito can lay some 300 eggs at once! Chu!
BZZZ
Ehhh?! You mean that cool doctor was a woman?! That's fraud!
Come to think of it, only female mosquitoes drink blood, huh?
BZZZ
Aaaah! It itches! Itches! If this keeps up, I could contract a case of Japanese encephalitis!
Now that it's come to this, I must bring out a mosquito's archenemy!!
Ultimate Attack: Diphenhydramine Dispersal!!
VWAA

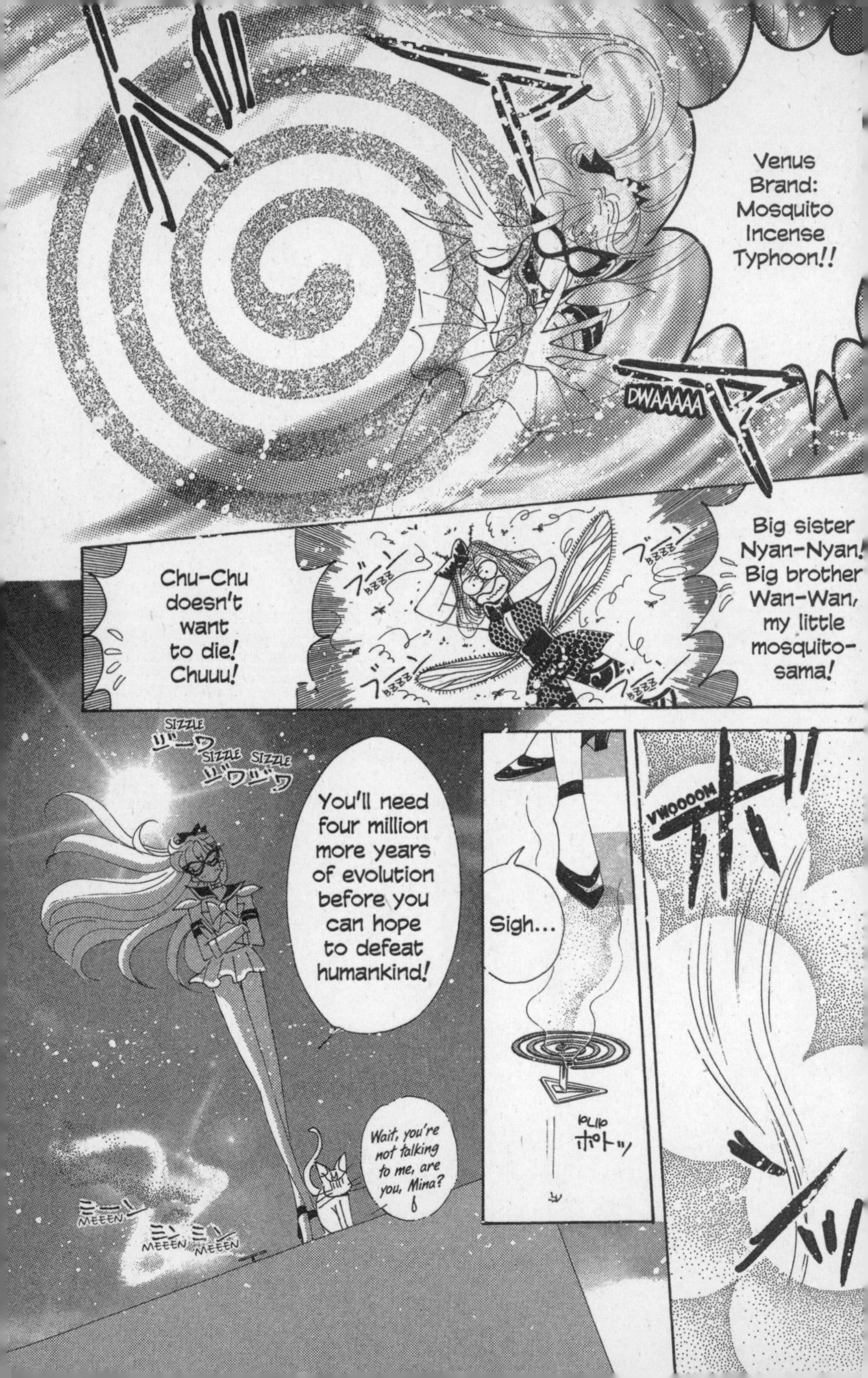
Venus Brand: Mosquito Incense Typhoon!!
DWAAAAA
Big sister Nyan-Nyan! Big brother Wan-Wan, my little mosquito-sama!
BZZZ
BZZZ
BZZZ
BZZZ
Chu-Chu doesn't want to die! Chuuu!
VWOOOOM
Sigh...
PLIP
SIZZLE
SIZZLE SIZZLE
You'll need four million more years of evolution before you can hope to defeat humankind!
Wait, you're not talking to me, are you, Mina?
MEEEN
MEEEN MEEEN

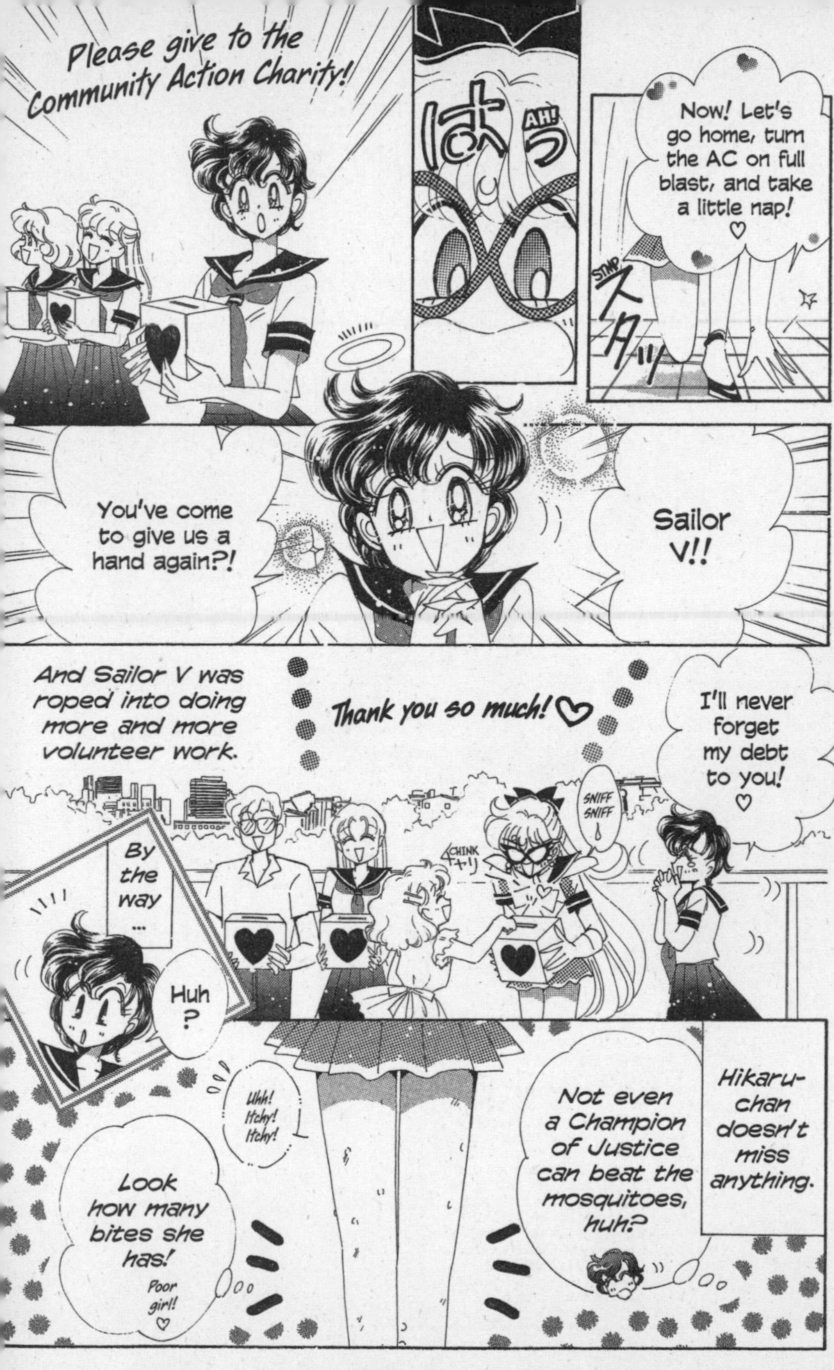
Now! Let's go home, turn the AC on full blast, and take a little nap! ♡
STMP
スタッ
はう
AH!
Please give to the Community Action Charity!
Sailor V!!
You've come to give us a hand again?!
I'll never forget my debt to you! ♡
SNIFF SNIFF
CHINK
チャリ
Thank you so much! ♡
And Sailor V was roped into doing more and more volunteer work.
By the way ...
Huh?
Hikaru-chan doesn't miss anything.
Not even a Champion of Justice can beat the mosquitoes, huh?
Uhh! Itchy! Itchy!
Look how many bites she has!
Poor girl! ♡

• The End •

About Blood Donation

Blood can be donated by just about
anyone, and is collected for when transfusion
becomes necessary, such as during surgery.
Blood donation takes place on donation
buses and donation rooms located
around town. In Japan, the Japanese Red
Cross conducts all blood donation drives.
Healthy folks 16 to 64 years-old are eligible
to become donors. In this story, Minako
donated 800 cc of blood, but in reality
blood is donated in units of 400 mL or
200 mL of whole blood. Or, if a patient
needs a certain portion of the blood
(such as platelets), Apheresis donation
may extract up to a maximum of 600 mL.
Just to make sure it is understood, this
story has absolutely nothing to do with
the Japanese Red Cross.

Vol. 14 The Young Man Who Bet on the Headband Stone

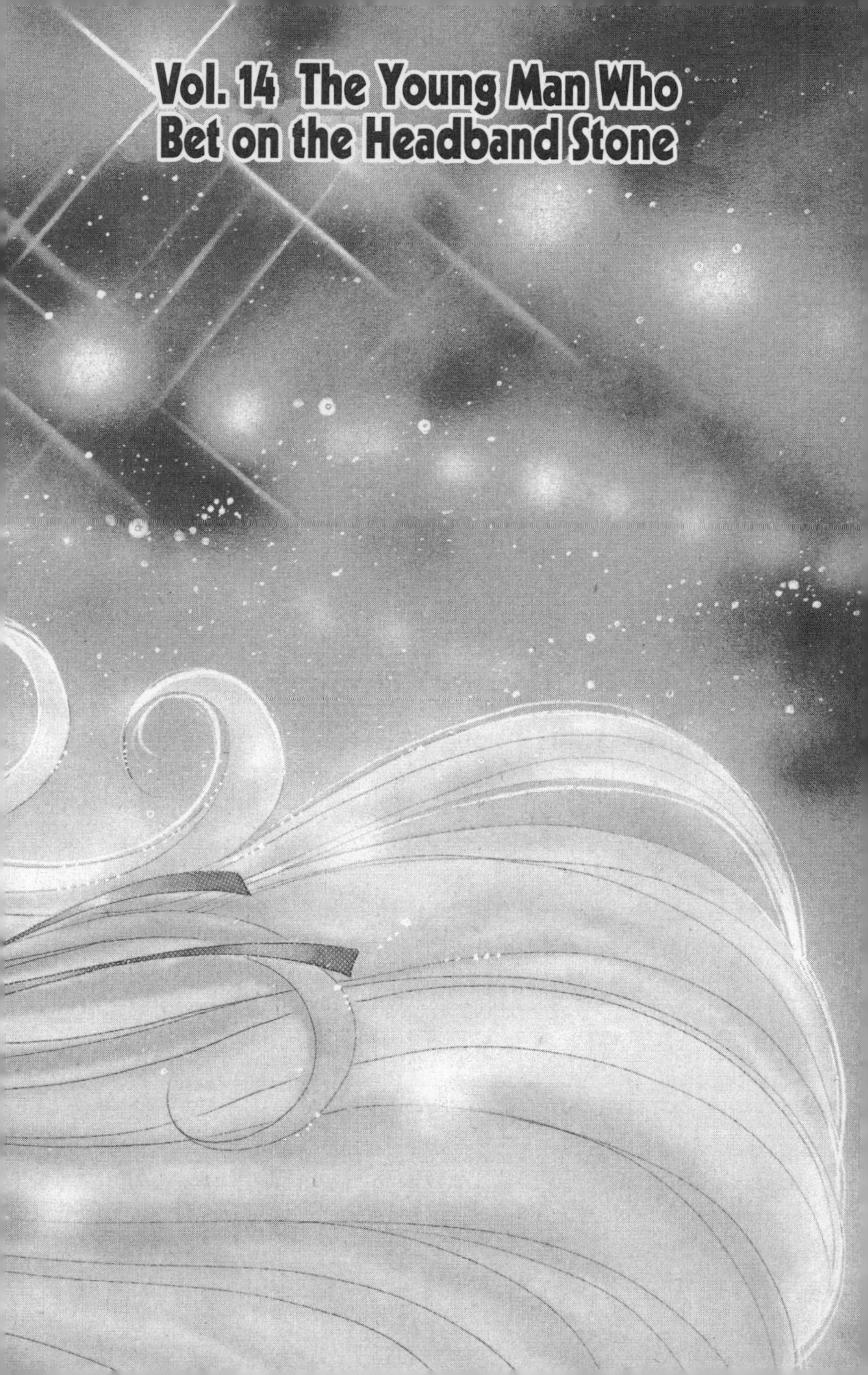

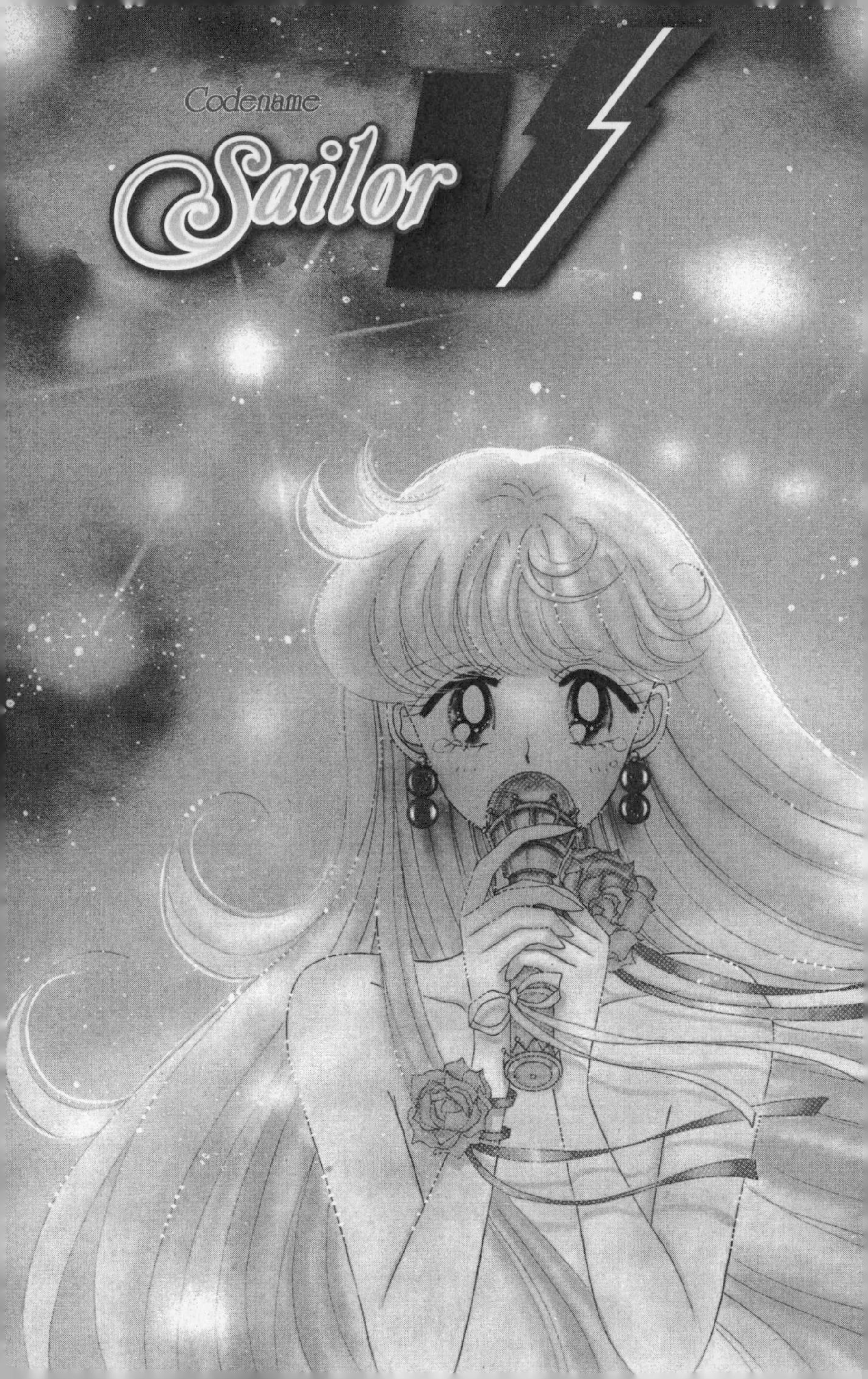
Codename
Sailor V

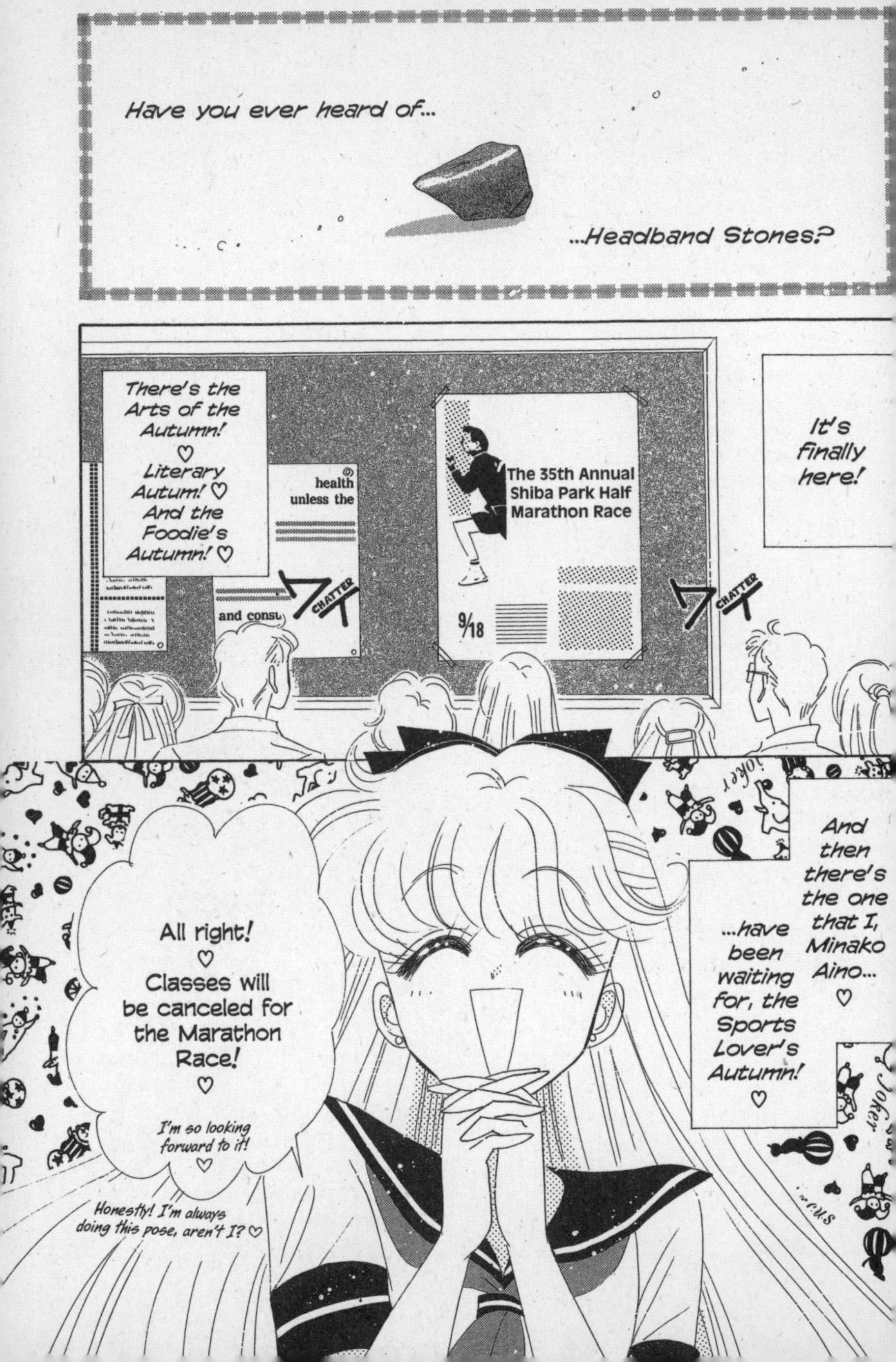
Have you ever heard of...
...Headband Stones?
It's finally here!
CHATTER
The 35th Annual Shiba Park Half Marathon Race
9/18
CHATTER
There's the Arts of the Autumn! ♡ Literary Autum! ♡ And the Foodie's Autumn! ♡
health unless the
and consu
And then there's the one that I, Minako Aino... ♡
...have been waiting for, the Sports Lover's Autumn! ♡
All right! ♡ Classes will be canceled for the Marathon Race! ♡
I'm so looking forward to it! ♡
Honestly! I'm always doing this pose, aren't I? ♡
Joker
Joker

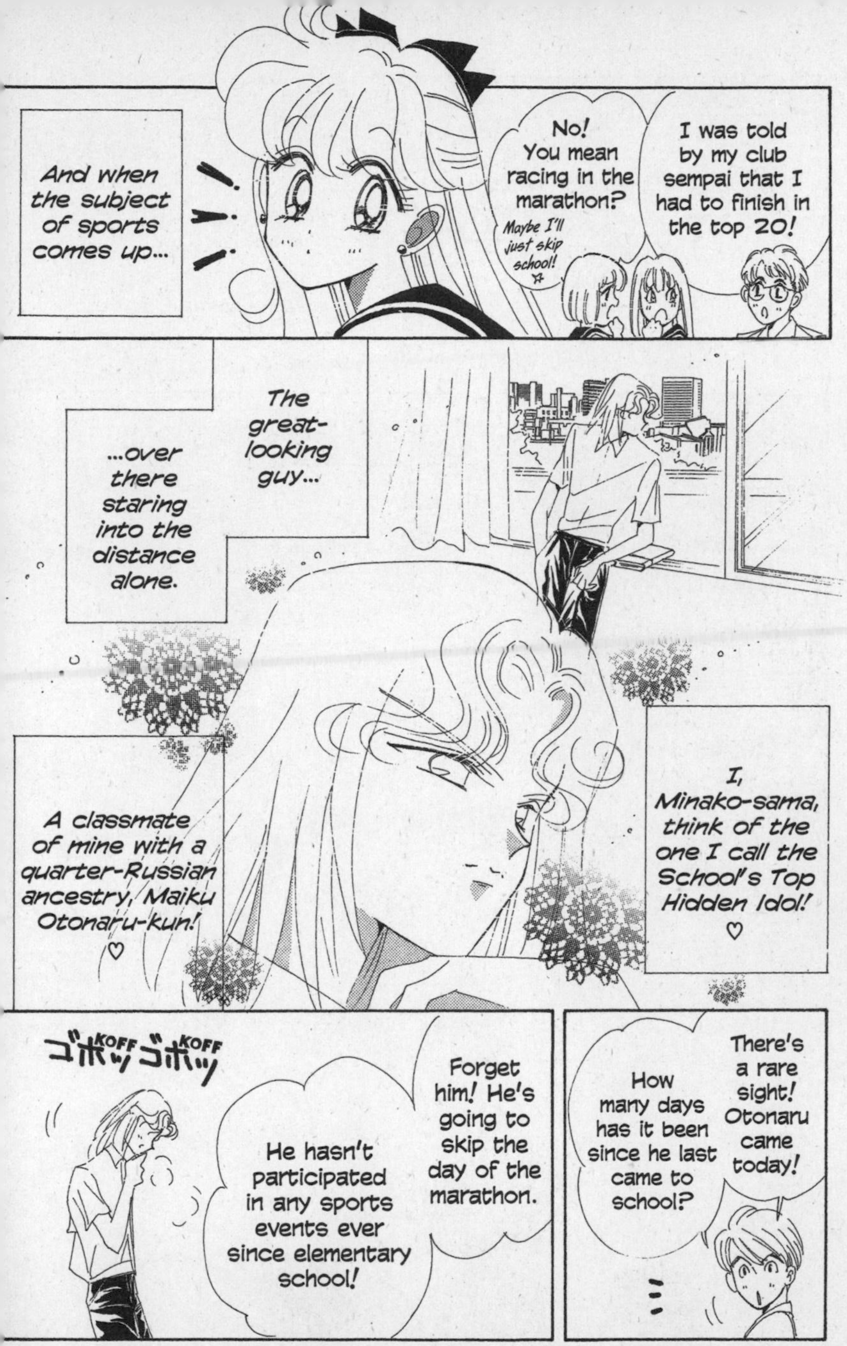
I was told by my club sempai that I had to finish in the top 20!
No! You mean racing in the marathon?
Maybe I'll just skip school! ☆
And when the subject of sports comes up...
The great-looking guy...
...over there staring into the distance alone.
I, Minako-sama, think of the one I call the School's Top Hidden Idol! ♡
A classmate of mine with a quarter-Russian ancestry, Maiku Otonaru-kun! ♡
There's a rare sight! Otonaru came today!
How many days has it been since he last came to school?
Forget him! He's going to skip the day of the marathon.
He hasn't participated in any sports events ever since elementary school!
ゴボッ KOFF ゴボッ KOFF

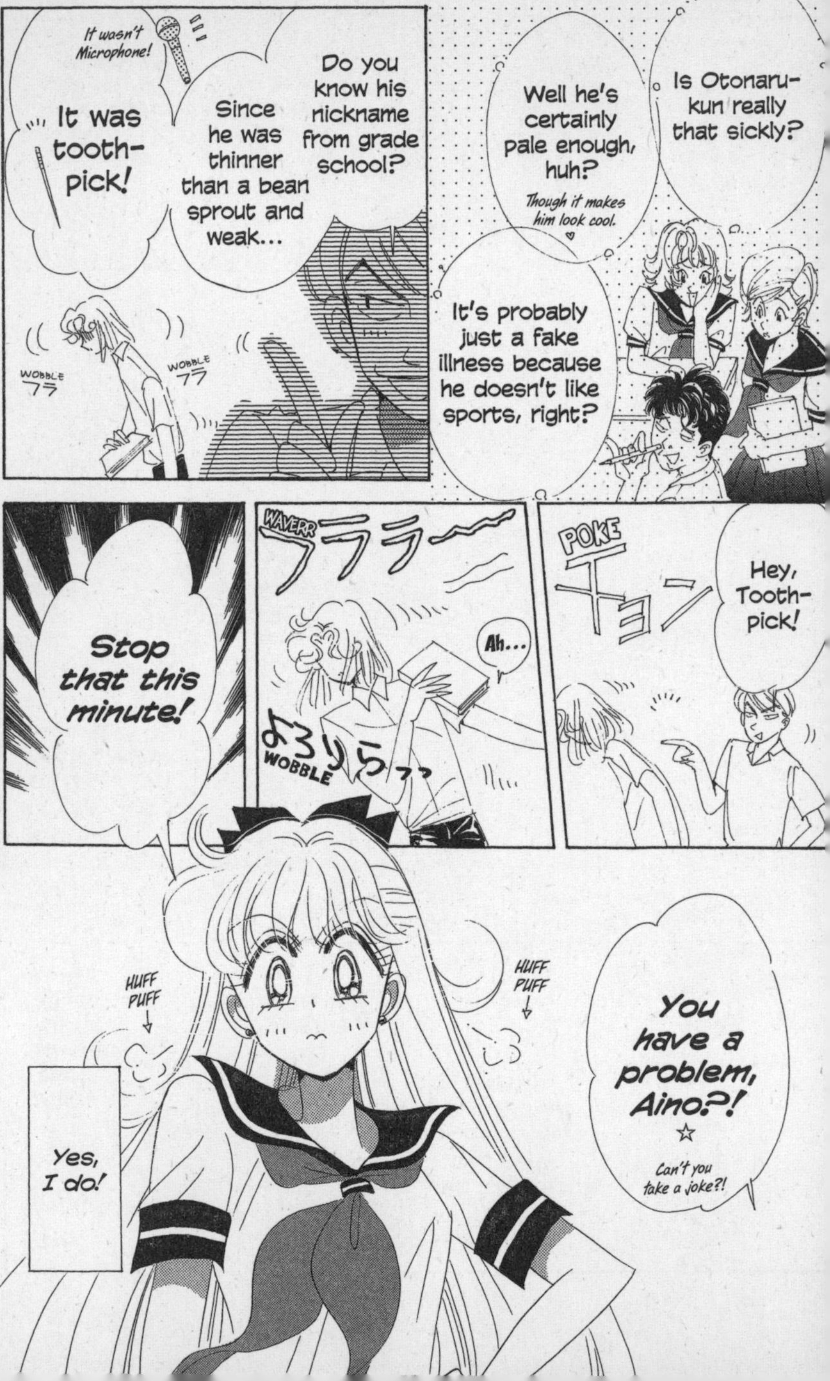

Is Otonaru-kun really that sickly?
Well he's certainly pale enough, huh?
Though it makes him look cool. ♡
It's probably just a fake illness because he doesn't like sports, right?
Do you know his nickname from grade school?
Since he was thinner than a bean sprout and weak...
It was tooth-pick!
It wasn't Microphone!
WOBBLE フラ
WOBBLE フラ
POKE
Hey, Tooth-pick!
WAVERR フララー
Ah...
よろりら
WOBBLE
Stop that this minute!
You have a problem, Aino?! ☆
Can't you take a joke?!
HUFF PUFF
HUFF PUFF
Yes, I do!

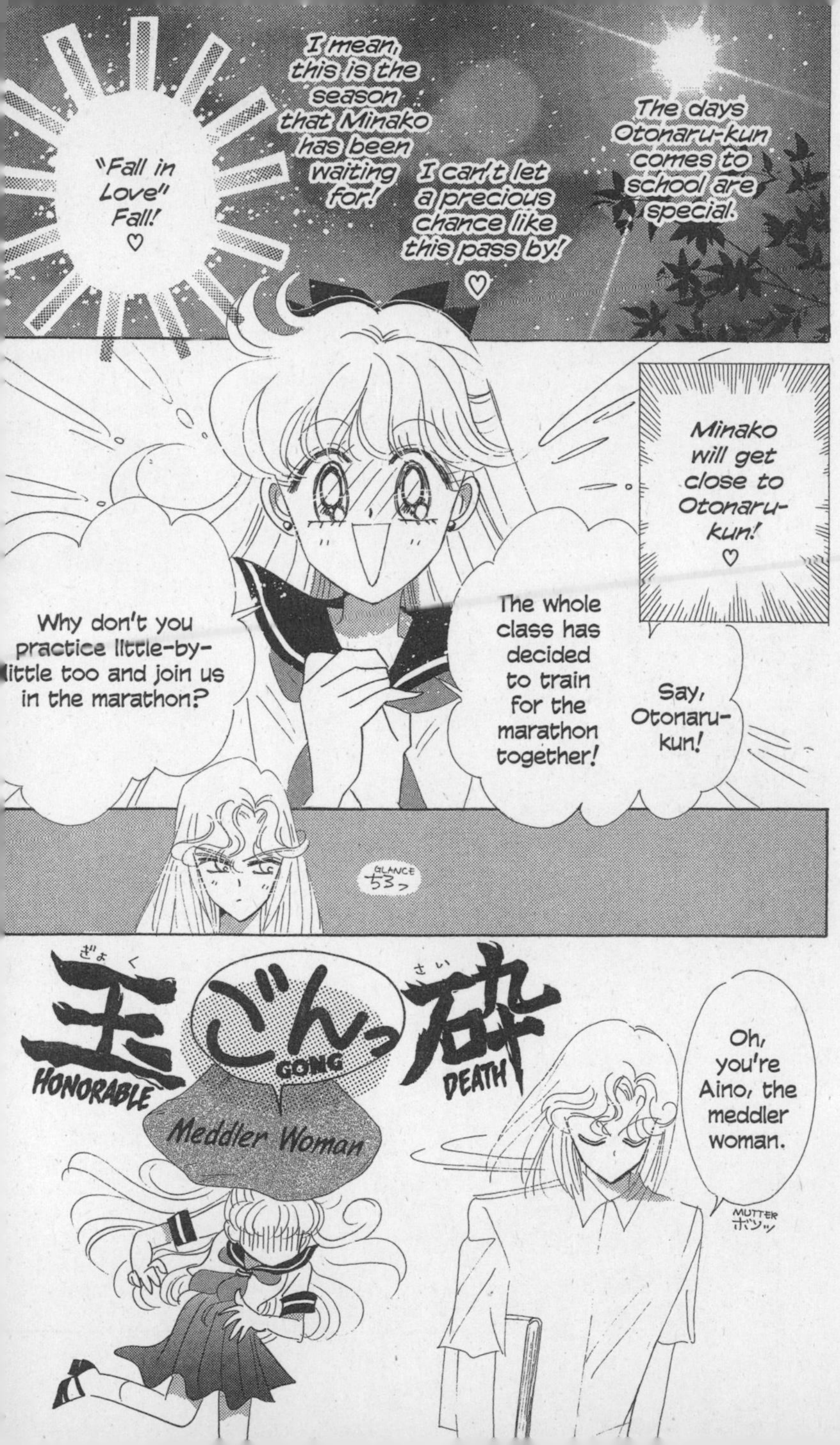
The days Otonaru-kun comes to school are special.
I mean, this is the season that Minako has been waiting for!
I can't let a precious chance like this pass by! ♡
"Fall in Love" Fall! ♡
Minako will get close to Otonaru-kun! ♡
Say, Otonaru-kun!
The whole class has decided to train for the marathon together!
Why don't you practice little-by-little too and join us in the marathon?
GLANCE ちろっ
Oh, you're Aino, the meddler woman.
MUTTER ボソッ
玉ごんっ砕
HONORABLE GONG DEATH
Meddler Woman

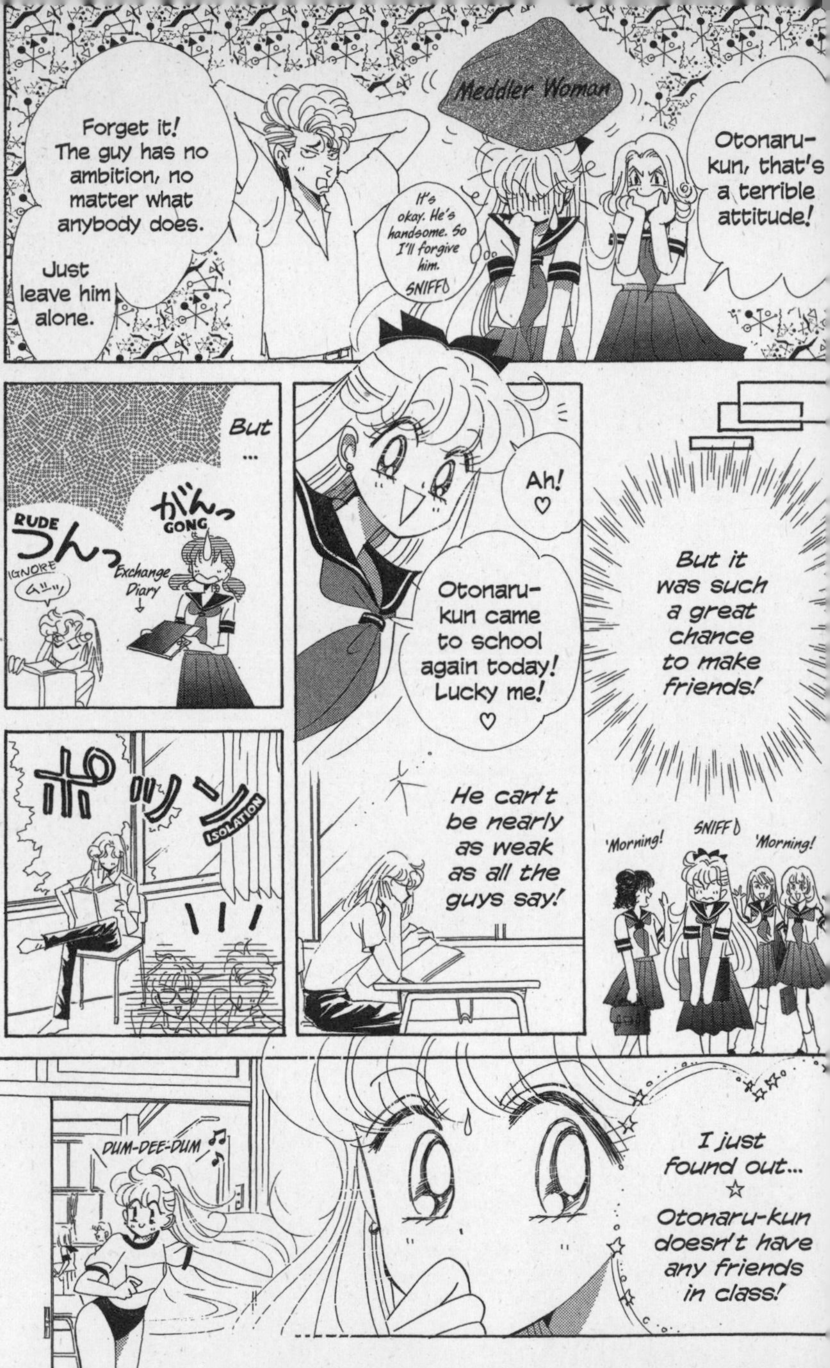
Otonaru-kun, that's a terrible attitude!
Meddler Woman
It's okay. He's handsome. So I'll forgive him.
SNIFF
Forget it! The guy has no ambition, no matter what anybody does.
Just leave him alone.
But it was such a great chance to make friends!
'Morning!
SNIFF
'Morning!
Ah! ♡
Otonaru-kun came to school again today! Lucky me! ♡
He can't be nearly as weak as all the guys say!
But ...
がんっ
GONG
RUDE
つんっ
IGNORE
ムッツ
Exchange Diary
ポツン
ISOLATION
I just found out... ☆ Otonaru-kun doesn't have any friends in class!
DUM-DEE-DUM ♫

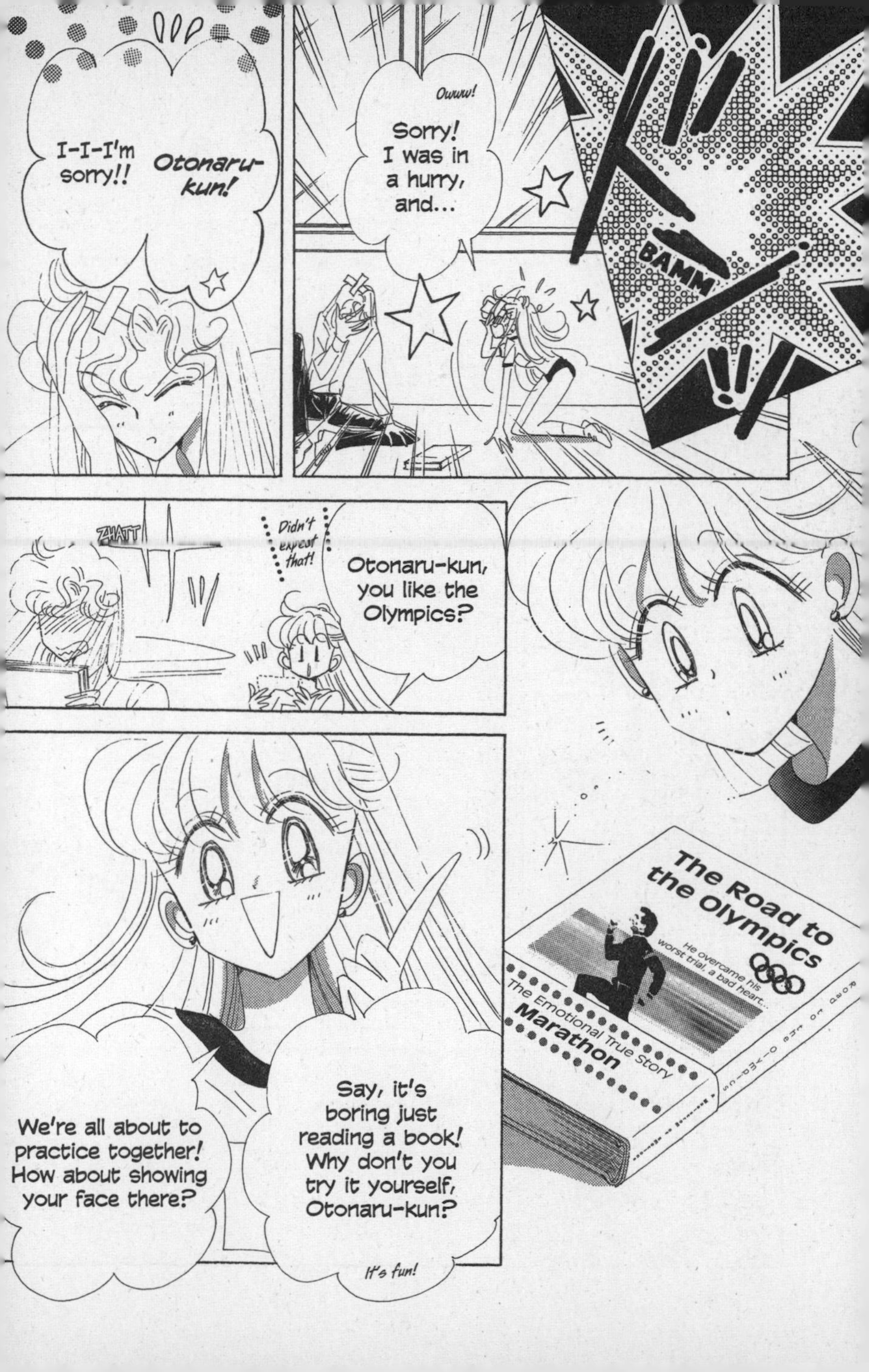
BAMM!!
Owww!
Sorry! I was in a hurry, and...
I-I-I'm sorry!! Otonaru-kun!
The Road to the Olympics
He overcame his worst trial, a bad heart...
The Emotional True Story
Marathon
ZHATT
Didn't expect that!
Otonaru-kun, you like the Olympics?
Say, it's boring just reading a book! Why don't you try it yourself, Otonaru-kun?
It's fun!
We're all about to practice together! How about showing your face there?

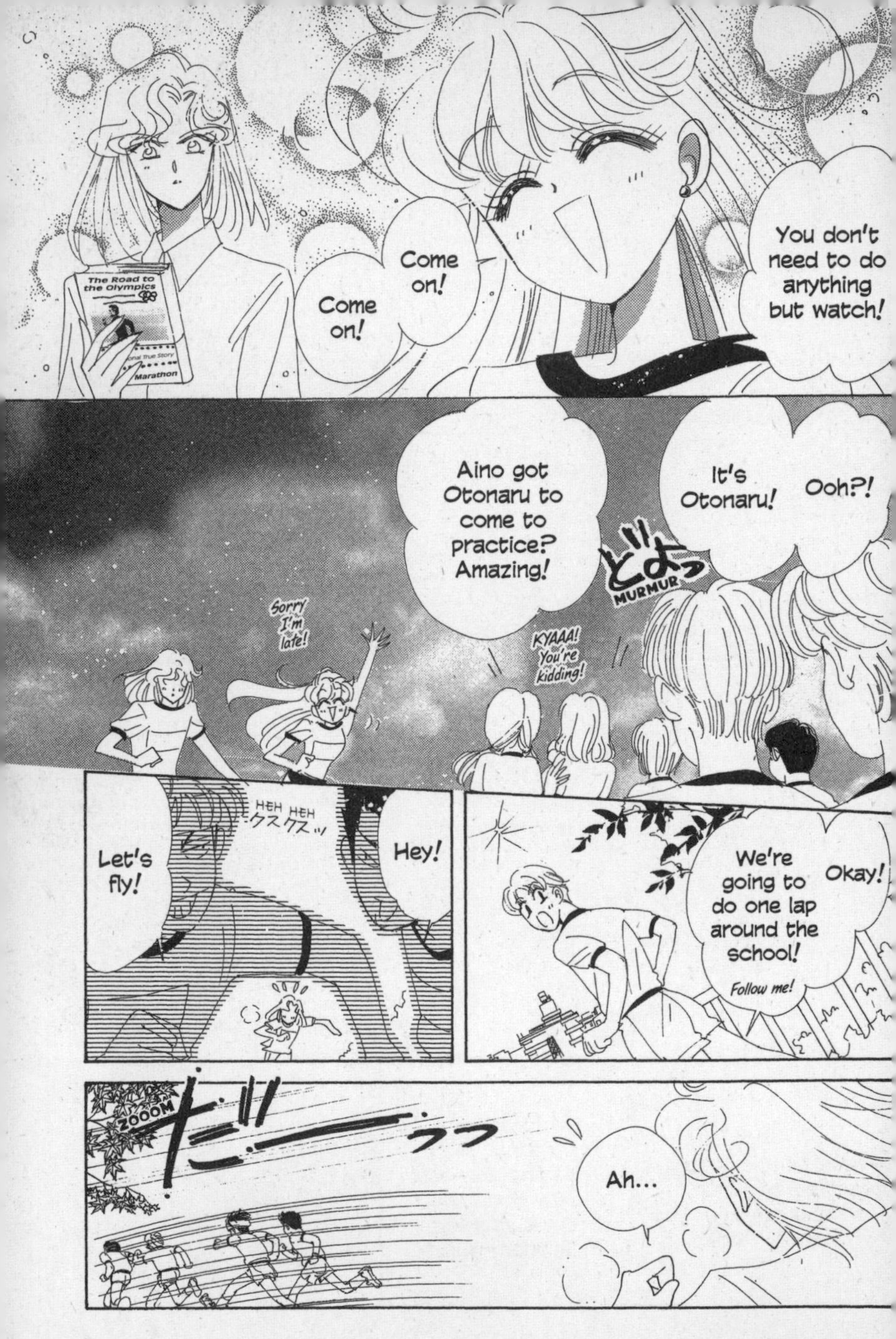
You don't need to do anything but watch!
Come on!
Come on!
The Road to the Olympics
Marathon
Ooh?!
It's Otonaru!
Aino got Otonaru to come to practice? Amazing!
どよっ MURMUR
KYAAA! You're kidding!
Sorry I'm late!
Okay!
We're going to do one lap around the school!
Follow me!
Hey!
HEH HEH クスクスッ
Let's fly!
Ah...
ZOOOM ダーーっっ

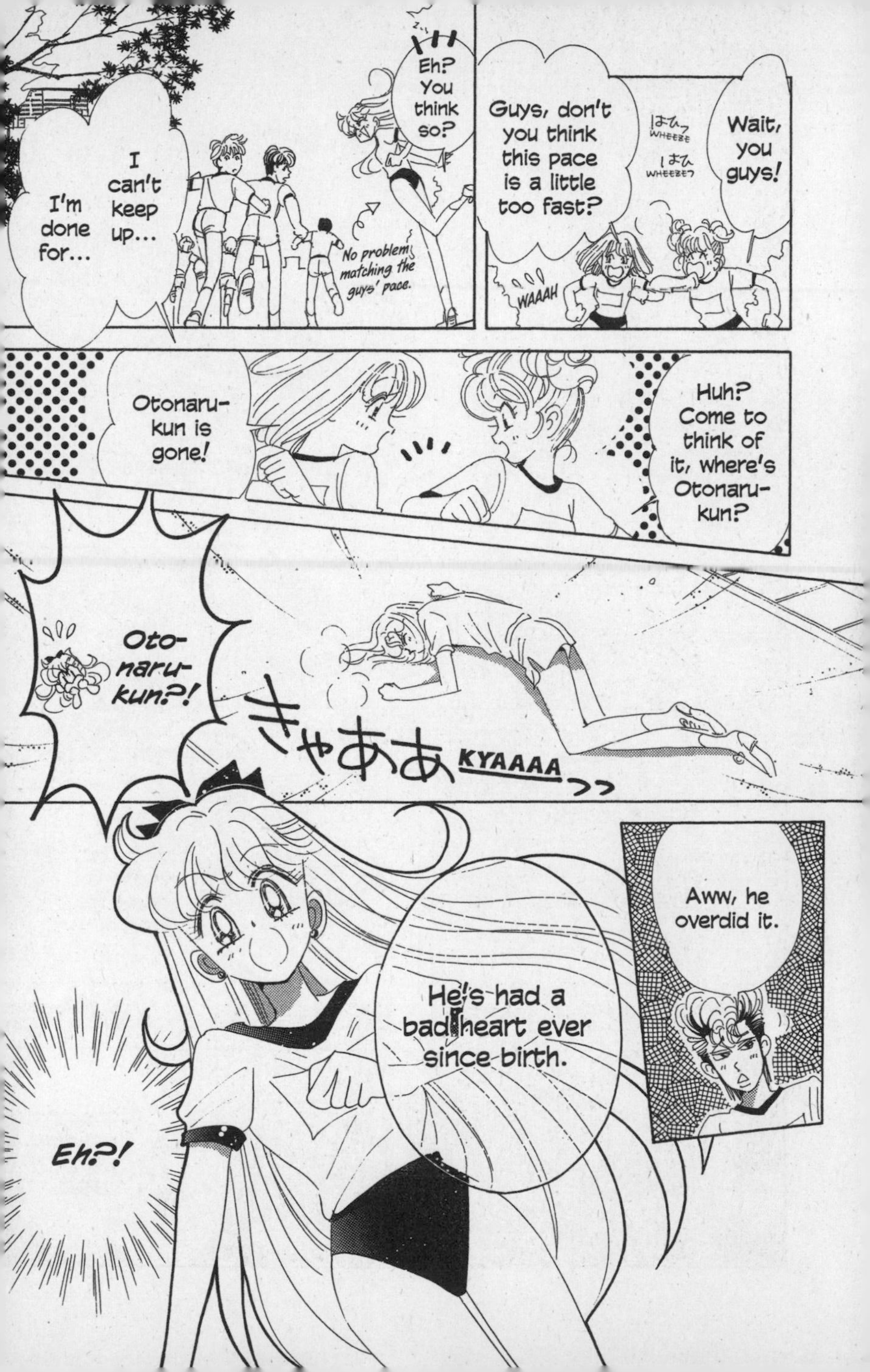
Wait, you guys!
Guys, don't you think this pace is a little too fast?
はひっ WHEEBE
はひ WHEEBE
WAAAH
Eh? You think so?
No problem matching the guys' pace.
I can't keep up...
I'm done for...
Huh? Come to think of it, where's Otonaru-kun?
Otonaru-kun is gone!
きゃあ KYAAAA
Oto-naru-kun?!
Aww, he overdid it.
He's had a bad heart ever since birth.
Eh?!

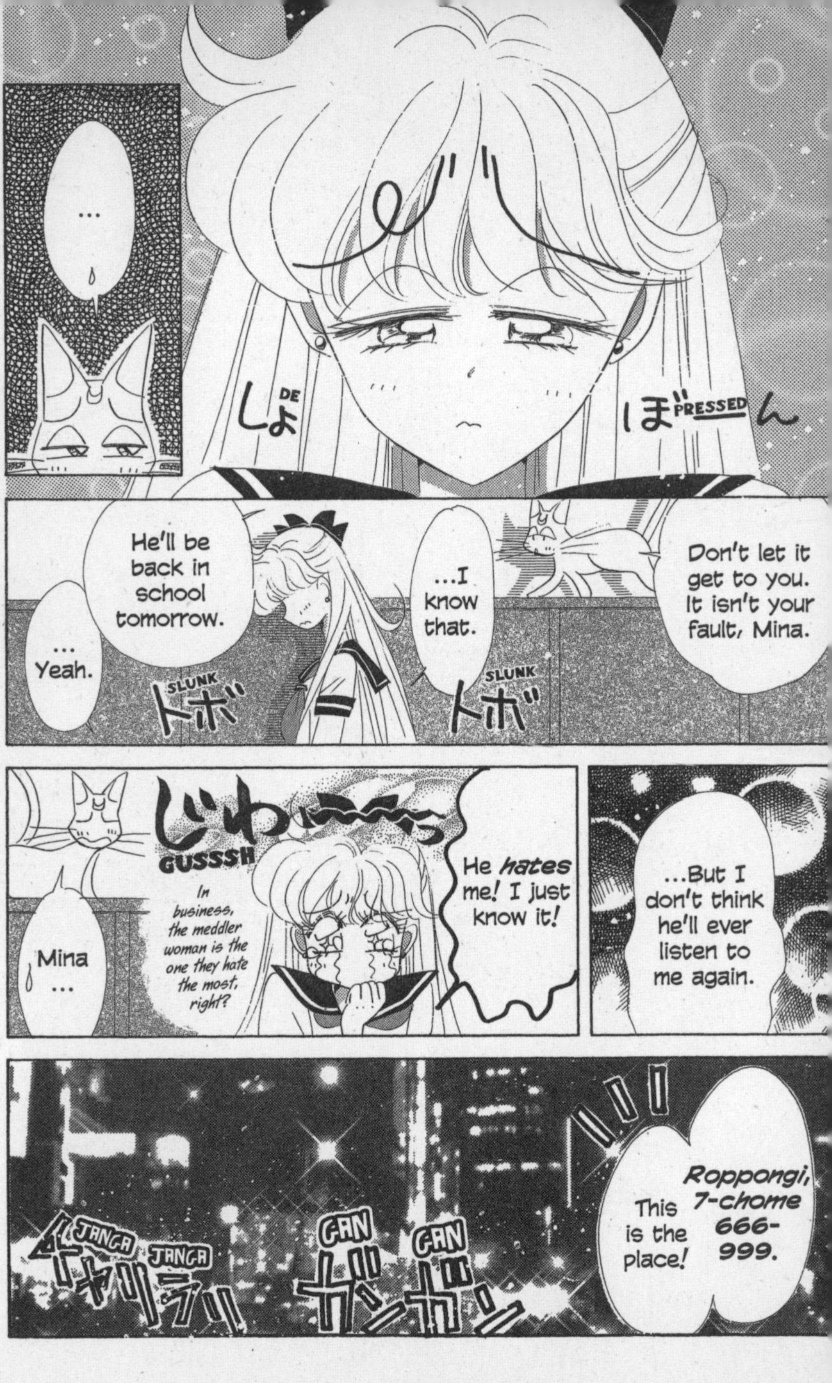
DE
PRESSED
...
Don't let it get to you. It isn't your fault, Mina.
...I know that.
SLUNK
He'll be back in school tomorrow.
... Yeah.
SLUNK
...But I don't think he'll ever listen to me again.
He *hates* me! I just know it!
GUSSSH
In business, the meddler woman is the one they hate the most, right?
Mina ...
Roppongi, 7-chome 666-999.
This is the place!
GAN
GAN
JANGA
JANGA

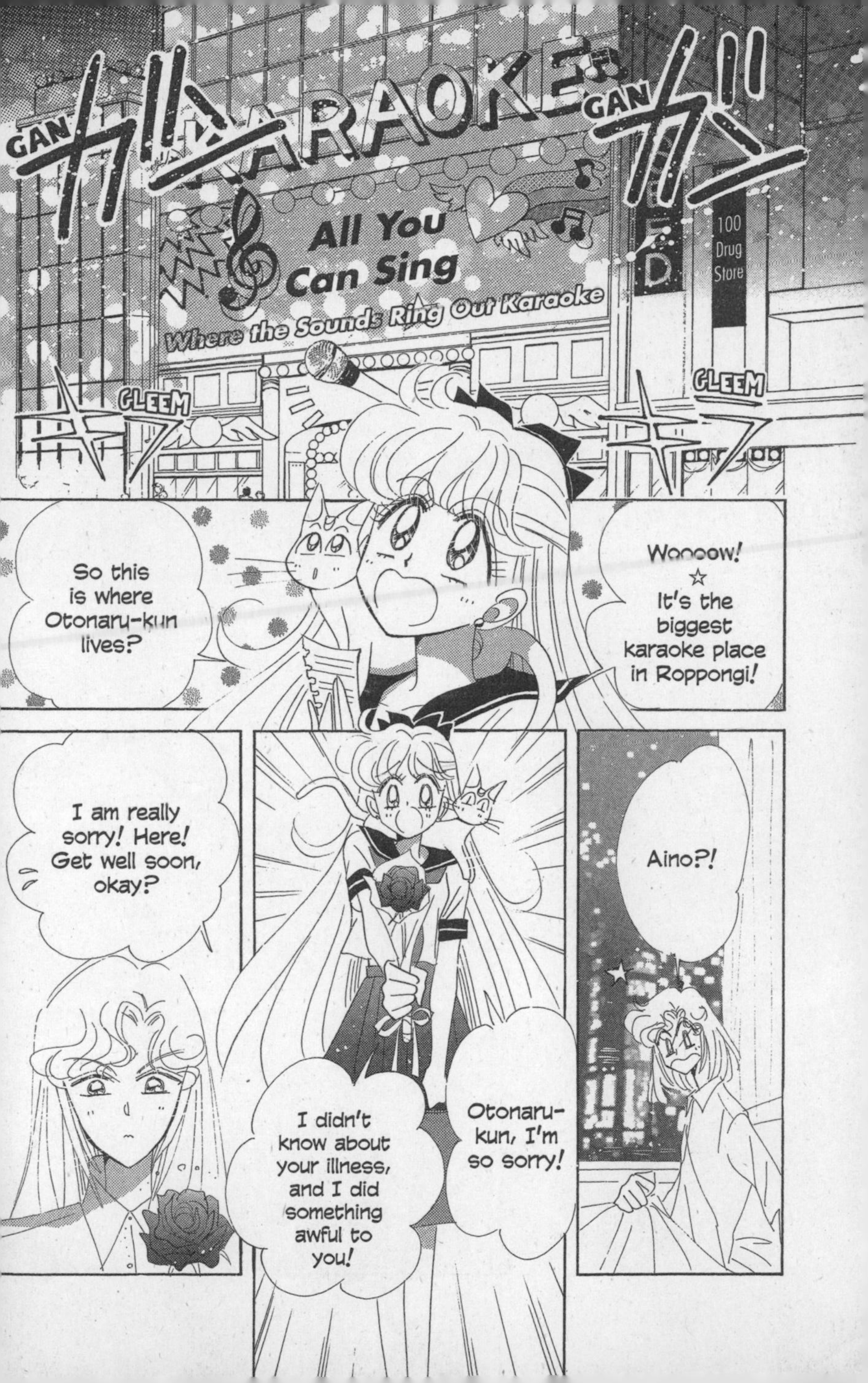
GAN カARAOKE
GAN ガ
All You Can Sing
Where the Sounds Ring Out Karaoke
100 Drug Store
D
GLEEM
GLEEM
Wooow! ☆ It's the biggest karaoke place in Roppongi!
So this is where Otonaru-kun lives?
Aino?!
Otonaru-kun, I'm so sorry!
I didn't know about your illness, and I did something awful to you!
I am really sorry! Here! Get well soon, okay?

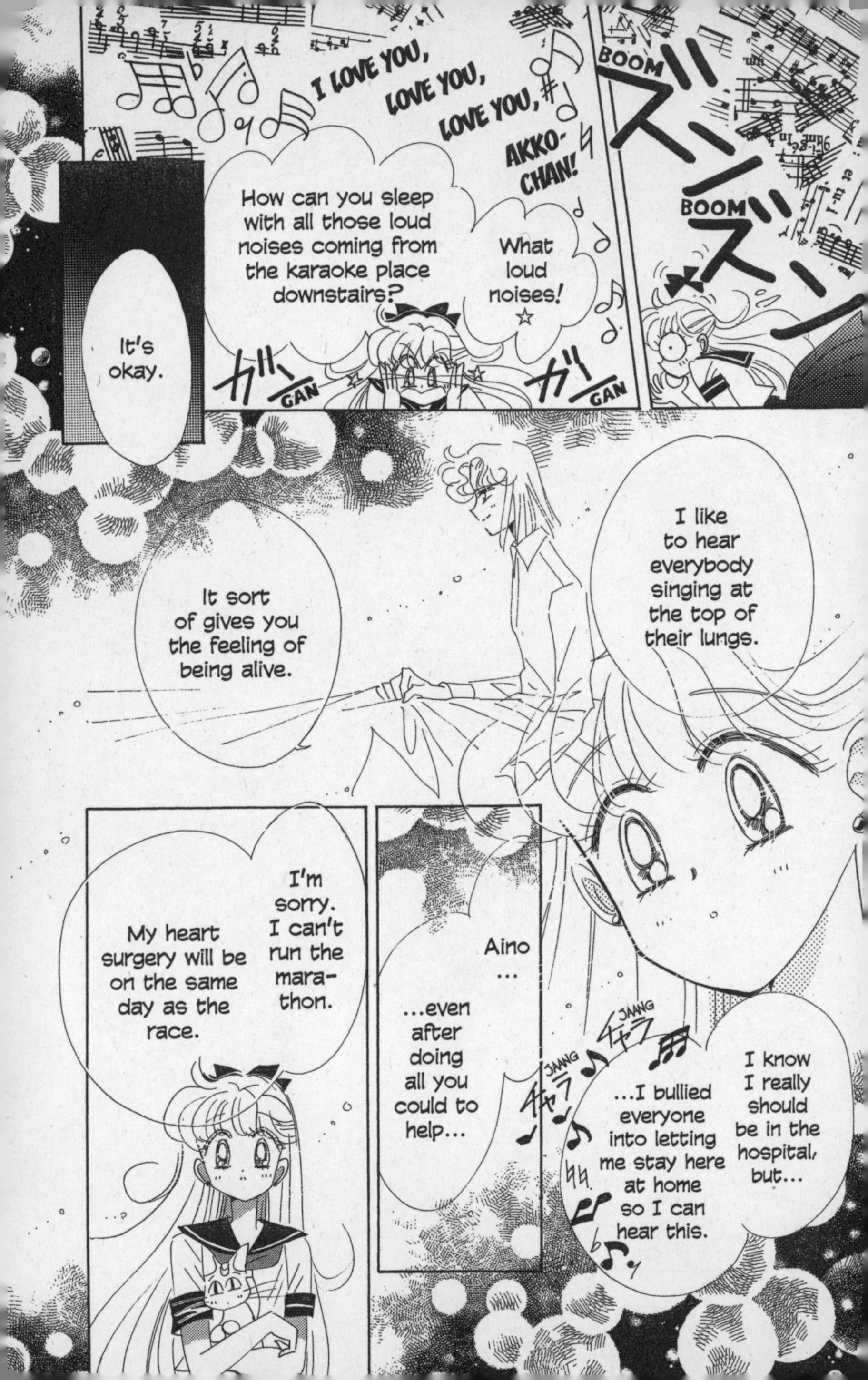
BOOM ズン
BOOM ズン
I LOVE YOU, LOVE YOU, LOVE YOU, AKKO-CHAN!
How can you sleep with all those loud noises coming from the karaoke place downstairs?
What loud noises! ☆
ガン GAN
ガン GAN
It's okay.
I like to hear everybody singing at the top of their lungs.
It sort of gives you the feeling of being alive.
I know I really should be in the hospital, but...
...I bullied everyone into letting me stay here at home so I can hear this.
JAANG チャラ
JAANG チャラ
Aino ...
...even after doing all you could to help...
I'm sorry. I can't run the mara-thon.
My heart surgery will be on the same day as the race.

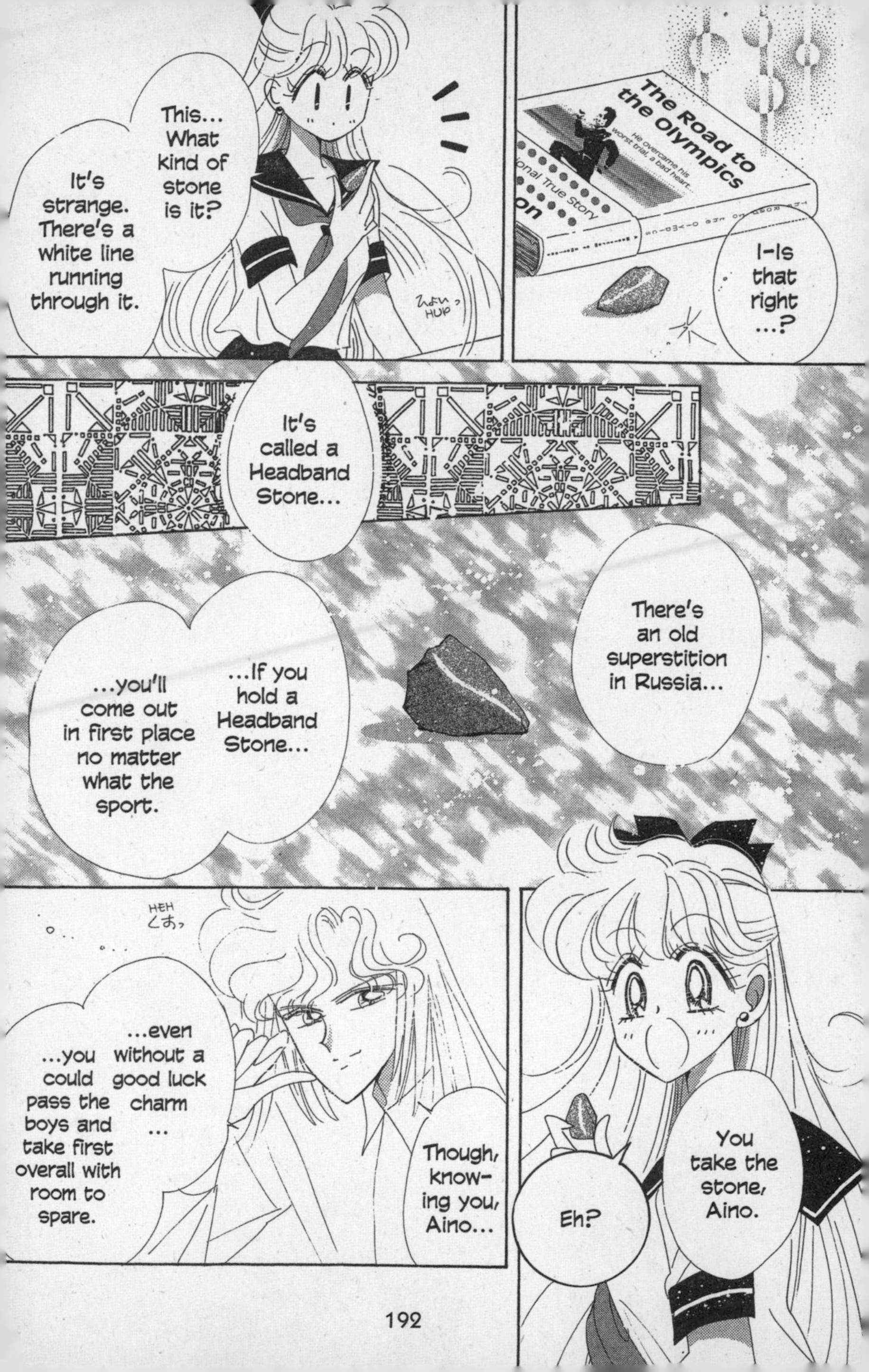
The Road to the Olympics
He overcame his worst trial, a bad heart...
I-Is that right ...?
This... What kind of stone is it?
It's strange. There's a white line running through it.
HUP
It's called a Headband Stone...
There's an old superstition in Russia...
...If you hold a Headband Stone...
...you'll come out in first place no matter what the sport.
You take the stone, Aino.
Eh?
Though, knowing you, Aino...
...even without a good luck charm ...
...you could pass the boys and take first overall with room to spare.
HEH

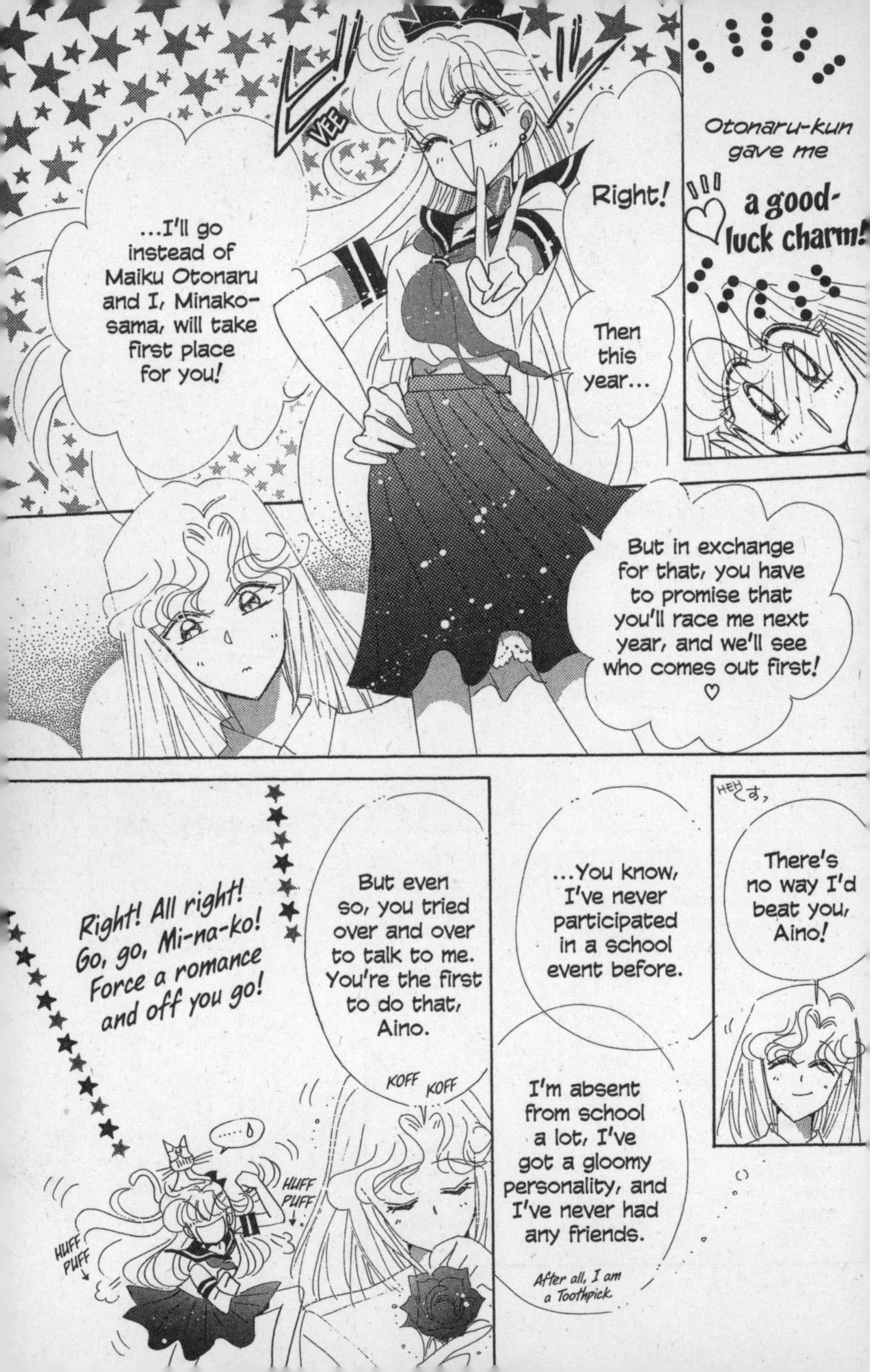
Otonaru-kun gave me a good-luck charm!
VEE
Right!
Then this year...
...I'll go instead of Maiku Otonaru and I, Minako-sama, will take first place for you!
But in exchange for that, you have to promise that you'll race me next year, and we'll see who comes out first! ♡
HEH くす,
There's no way I'd beat you, Aino!
...You know, I've never participated in a school event before.
I'm absent from school a lot, I've got a gloomy personality, and I've never had any friends.
After all, I am a Toothpick.
But even so, you tried over and over to talk to me. You're the first to do that, Aino.
KOFF KOFF
Right! All right! Go, go, Mi-na-ko! Force a romance and off you go!
HUFF PUFF
HUFF PUFF

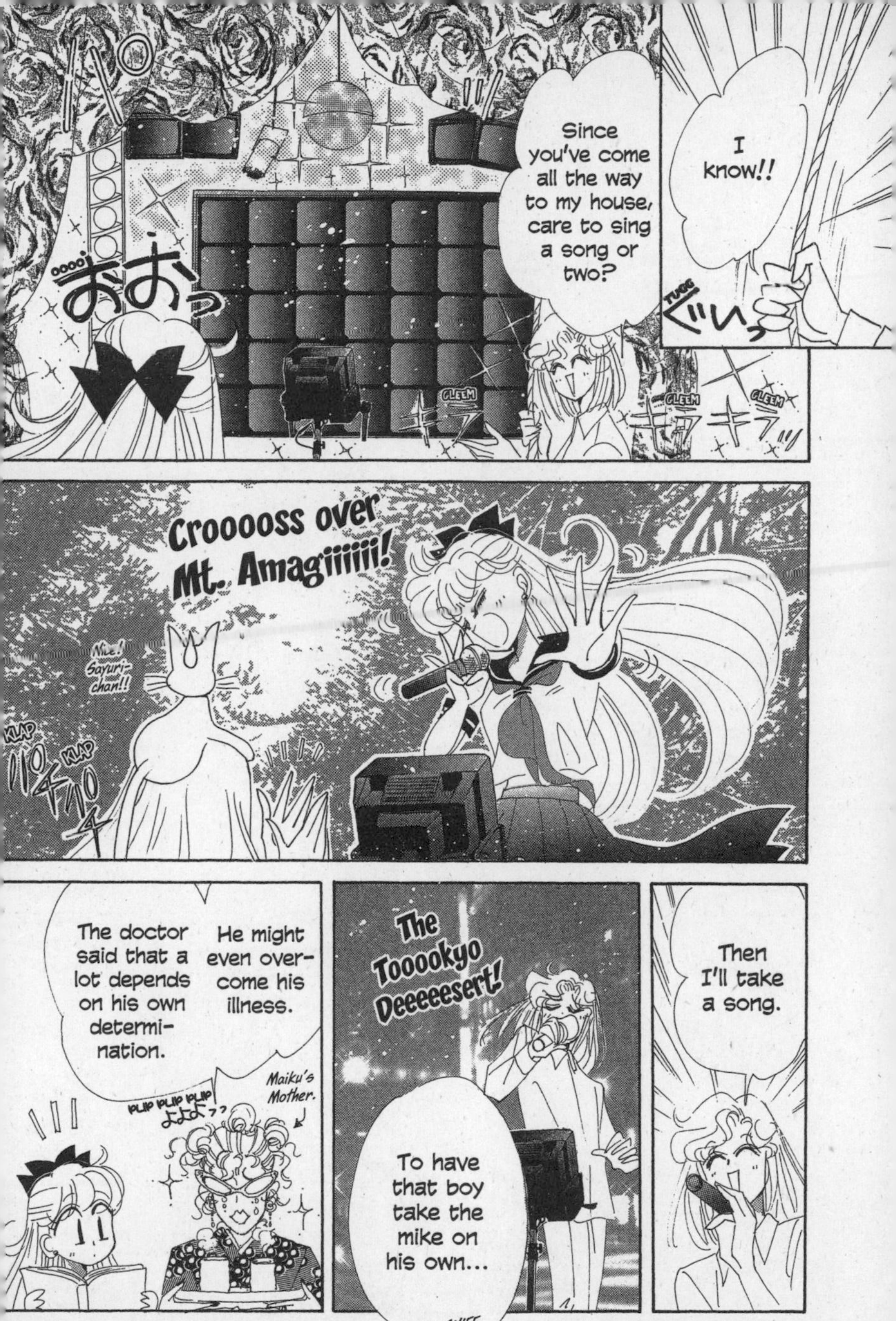
I know!!
TUGG ぐいっ
Since you've come all the way to my house, care to sing a song or two?
GLEEM キラ
GLEEM キラ
GLEEM キラッ
OOOO! おおっ
Croooooss over Mt. Amagiiiiiii!
Nice! Sayuri-chan!!
KLAP
KLAP
Then I'll take a song.
The Tooookyo Deeeeeesert!
To have that boy take the mike on his own...
SNIFF
The doctor said that a lot depends on his own determination.
He might even overcome his illness.
Maiku's Mother.
PLIP PLIP PLIP よよよっ

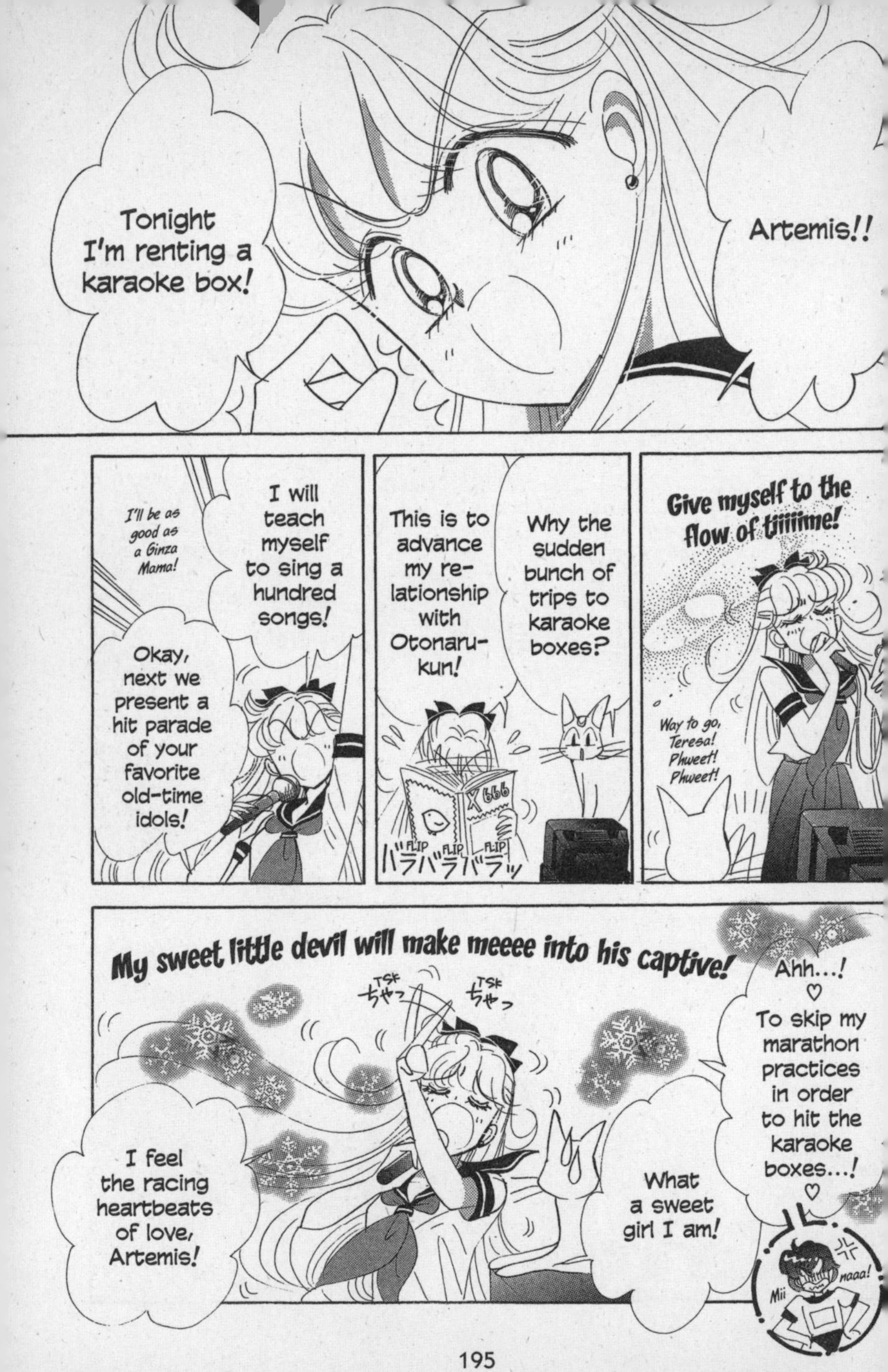
Artemis!!
Tonight I'm renting a karaoke box!
Give myself to the flow of tiiiiime!
Way to go, Teresa! Phweet! Phweet!
Why the sudden bunch of trips to karaoke boxes?
This is to advance my relationship with Otonaru-kun!
X 666
FLIP FLIP FLIP
バラバラバラッ
I will teach myself to sing a hundred songs!
I'll be as good as a Ginza Mama!
Okay, next we present a hit parade of your favorite old-time idols!
My sweet little devil will make meeee into his captive!
TSK ちゃっ
TSK ちゃっ
Ahh...! ♡ To skip my marathon practices in order to hit the karaoke boxes...! ♡
What a sweet girl I am!
I feel the racing heartbeats of love, Artemis!
Mii naaa!

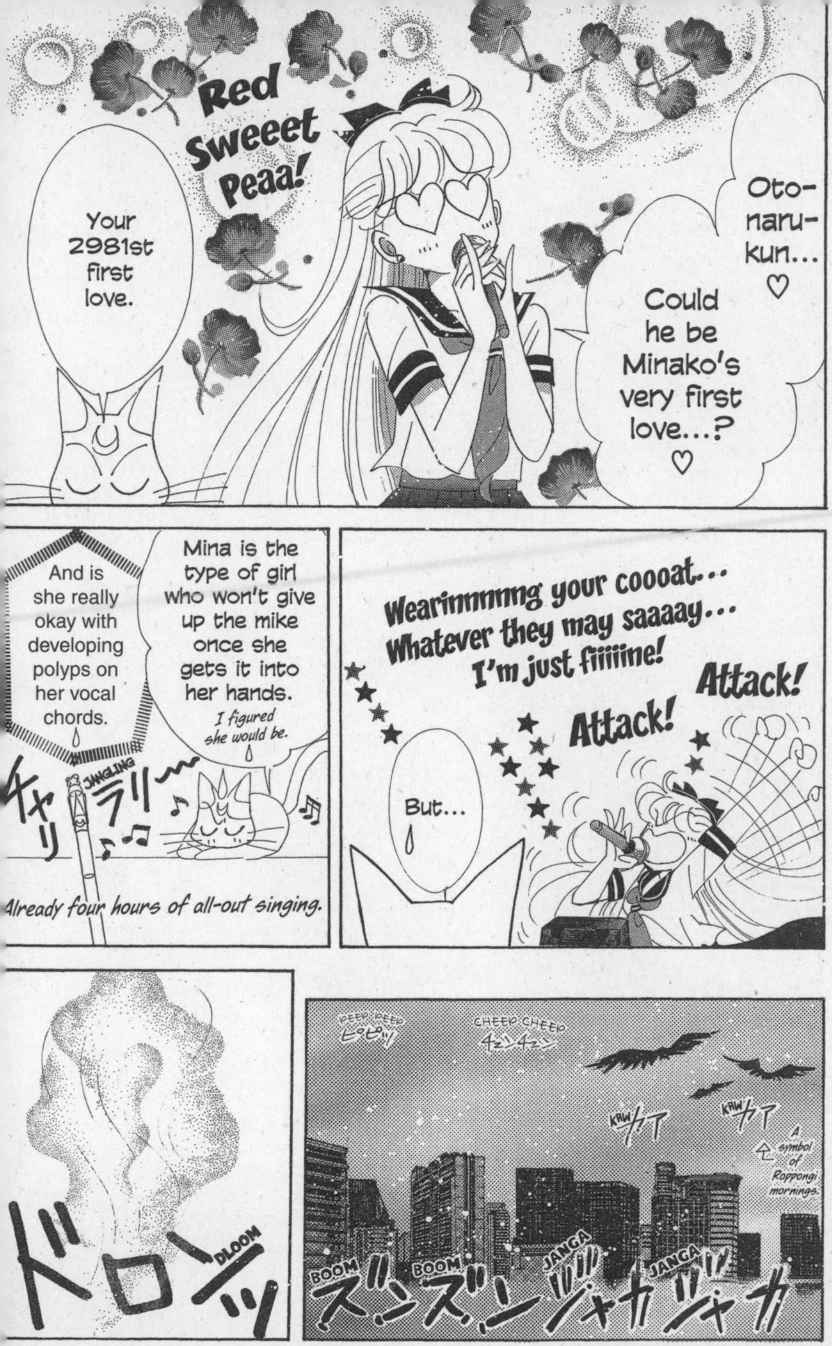
Oto-naru-kun... ♡
Could he be Minako's very first love...? ♡
Red Sweeet Peaa!
Your 2981st first love.
Wearinnnnng your coooat... Whatever they may saaaay... I'm just fiiiiine!
Attack!
Attack!
But...
Mina is the type of girl who won't give up the mike once she gets it into her hands.
I figured she would be.
And is she really okay with developing polyps on her vocal chords.
JANGLING チャリラリ
Already four hours of all-out singing.
PEEP PEEP ピピッ
CHEEP CHEEP チュンチュン
KRAW カア
KRAW カア
A symbol of Roppongi mornings.
BOOM BOOM ズンズン
JANGA JANGA ジャカジャカ
DLOOM ドロッ

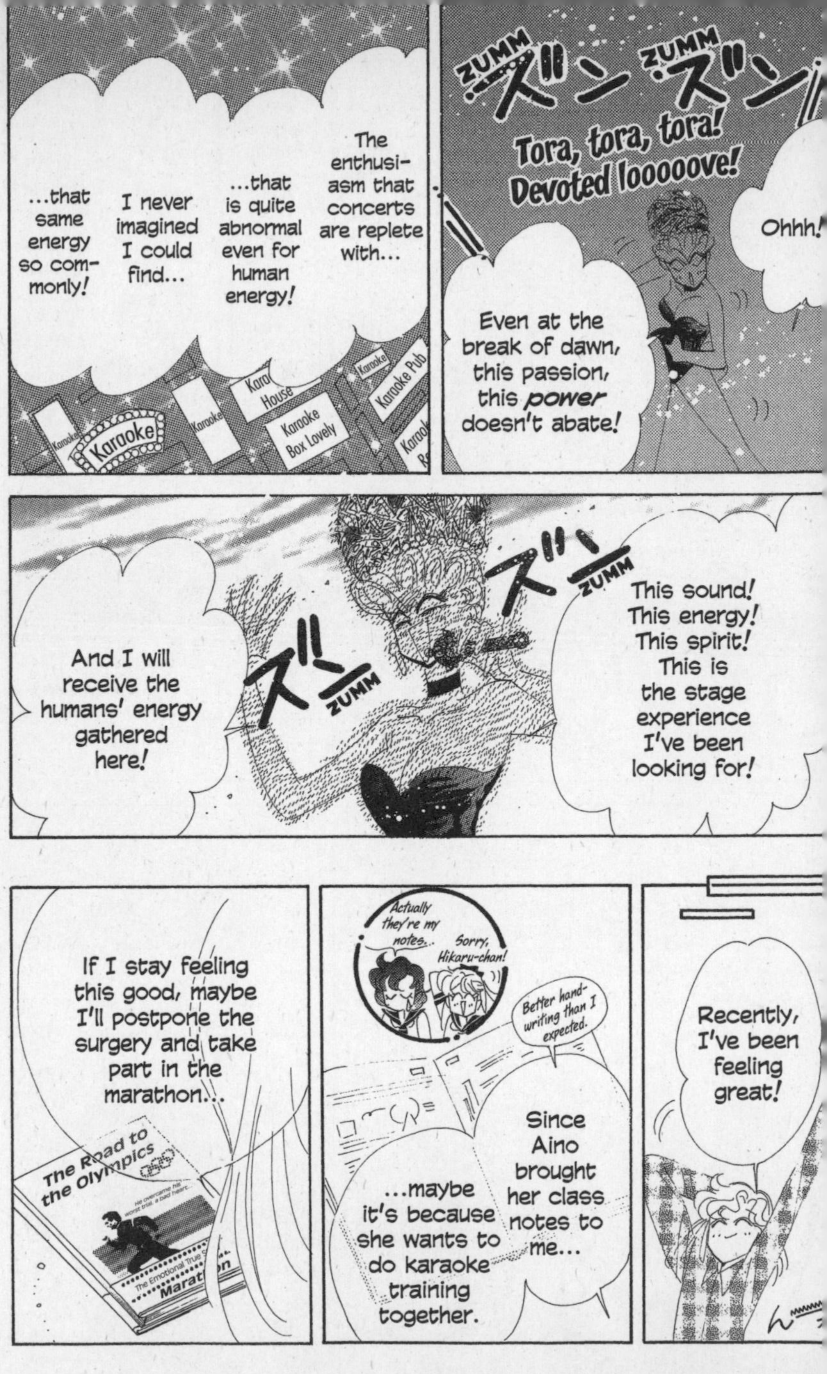
ZUMM
ZUMM
Tora, tora, tora! Devoted looooove!
Ohhh!
Even at the break of dawn, this passion, this *power* doesn't abate!
The enthusi- asm that concerts are replete with...
...that is quite abnormal even for human energy!
I never imagined I could find...
...that same energy so com- monly!
Karaoke Pub
Karaoke
Karaoke Box Lovely
Karaoke
Karaoke
Karaoke
ZUMM
This sound! This energy! This spirit! This is the stage experience I've been looking for!
ZUMM
And I will receive the humans' energy gathered here!
Recently, I've been feeling great!
Actually they're my notes...
Sorry, Hikaru-chan!
Better hand- writing than I expected.
Since Aino brought her class notes to me...
...maybe it's because she wants to do karaoke training together.
If I stay feeling this good, maybe I'll postpone the surgery and take part in the marathon...
The Road to the Olympics
Marathon

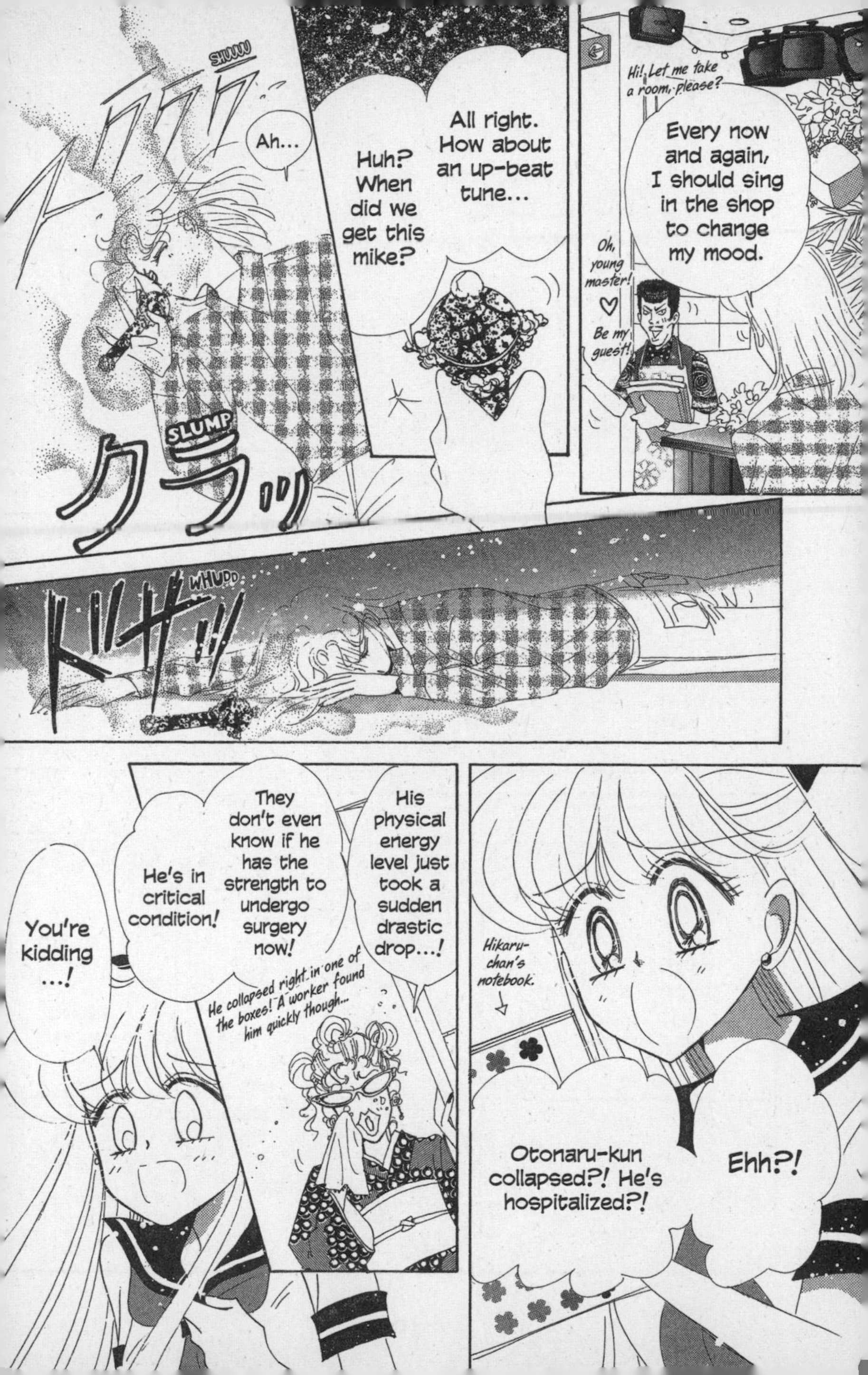
Hi! Let me take a room, please?
Every now and again, I should sing in the shop to change my mood.
Oh, young master! ♥ Be my guest!
All right. How about an up-beat tune...
Huh? When did we get this mike?
SHUUU
Ah...
SLUMP
WHUDD
Ehh?!
Otonaru-kun collapsed?! He's hospitalized?!
Hikaru-chan's notebook.
His physical energy level just took a sudden drastic drop...!
They don't even know if he has the strength to undergo surgery now!
He's in critical condition!
He collapsed right in one of the boxes! A worker found him quickly though...
You're kidding ...!

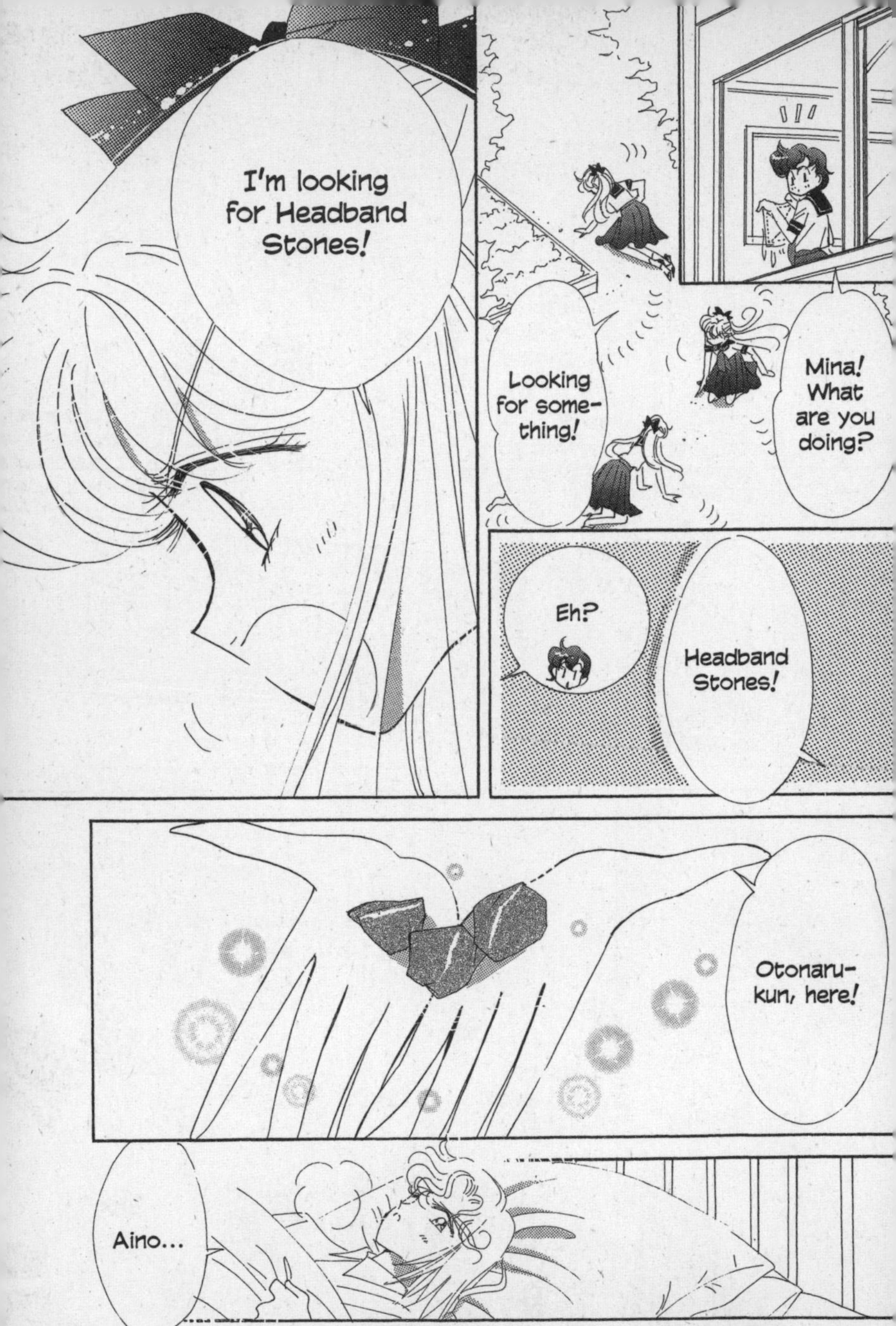

Mina! What are you doing?
Looking for some-thing!
Headband Stones!
Eh?
I'm looking for Headband Stones!
Otonaru-kun, here!
Aino...

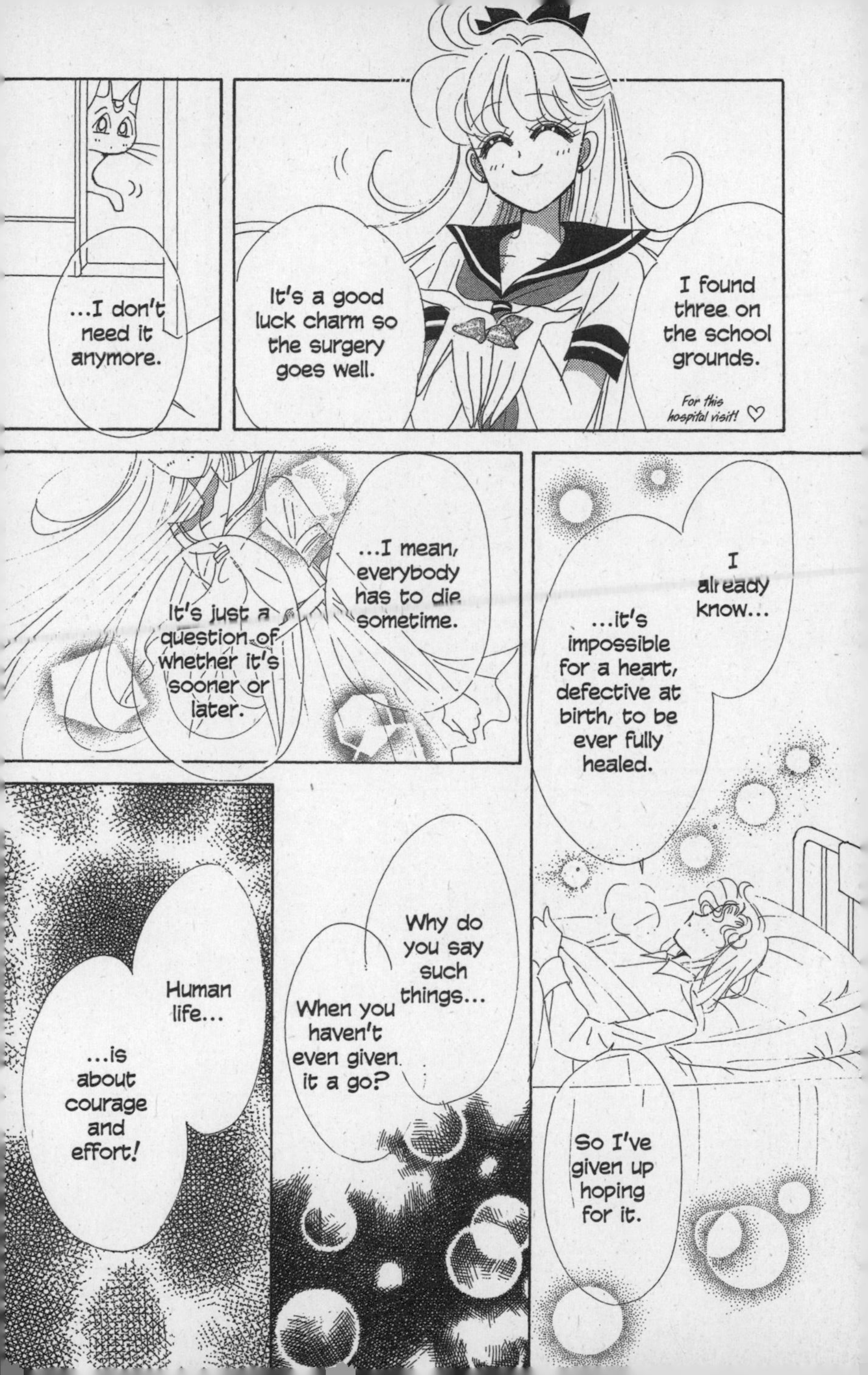
I found three on the school grounds.
For this hospital visit! ♡
It's a good luck charm so the surgery goes well.
...I don't need it anymore.
I already know...
...it's impossible for a heart, defective at birth, to be ever fully healed.
So I've given up hoping for it.
...I mean, everybody has to die sometime.
It's just a question of whether it's sooner or later.
Why do you say such things...
When you haven't even given it a go?
Human life...
...is about courage and effort!

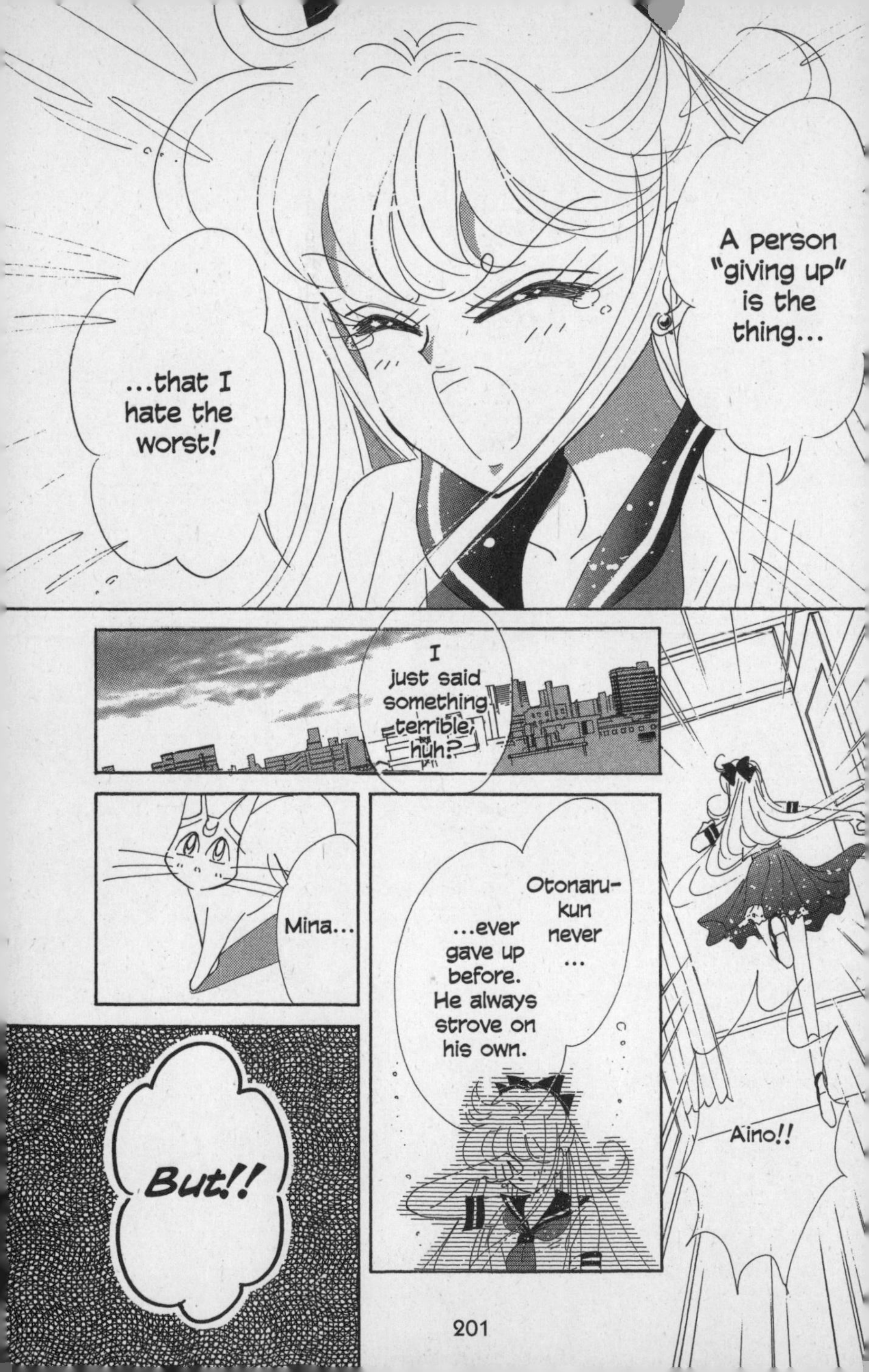
A person "giving up" is the thing...
...that I hate the worst!
Aino!!
I just said something terrible, huh?
Otonaru-kun never ...
...ever gave up before. He always strove on his own.
Mina...
But!!

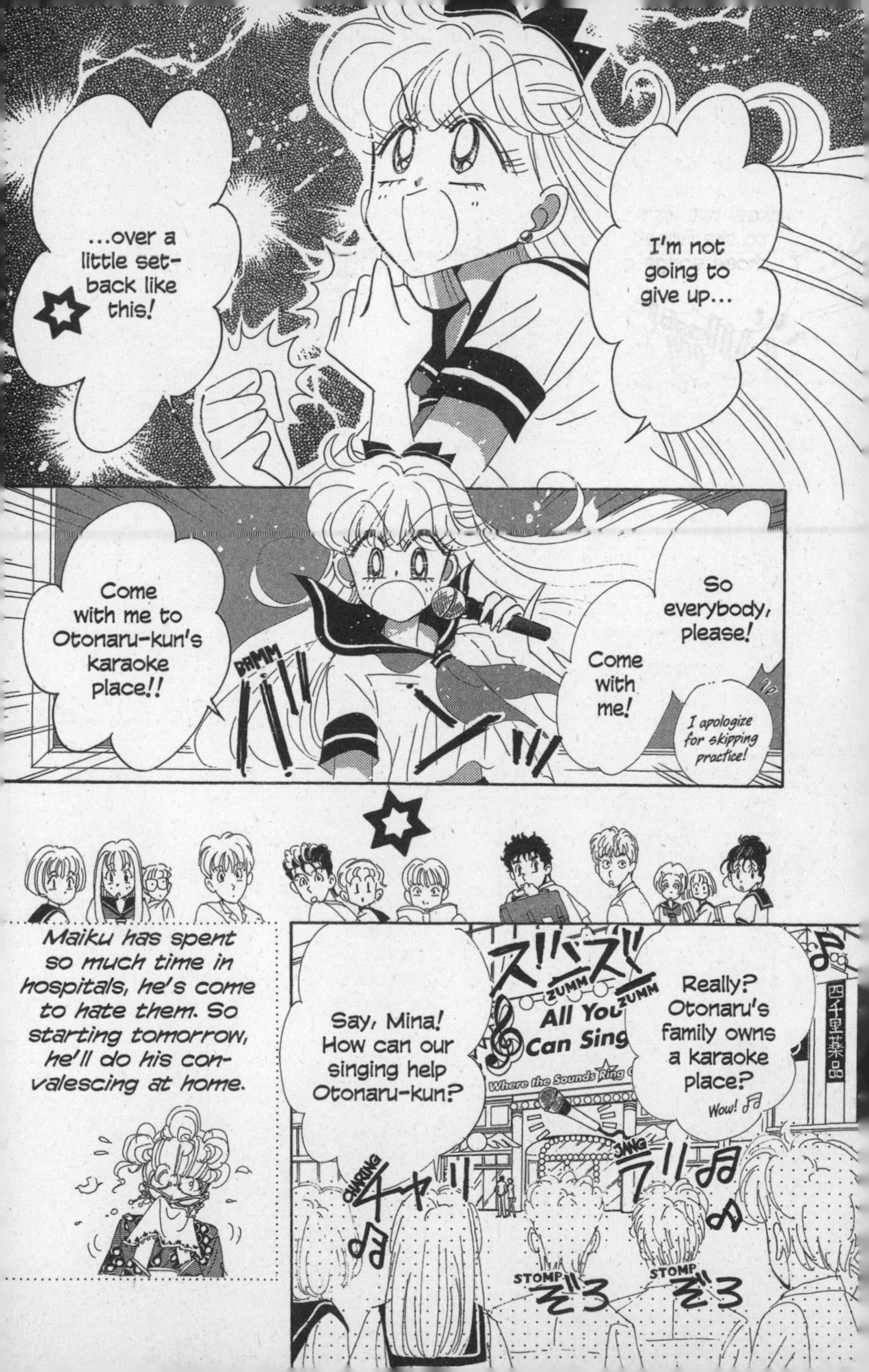
I'm not going to give up...
...over a little set-back like this!
So everybody, please!
I apologize for skipping practice!
Come with me!
Come with me to Otonaru-kun's karaoke place!!
BAMM
Really? Otonaru's family owns a karaoke place?
Wow!
ZUMM
ZUMM
All You Can Sing
Where the Sounds Ring
四千里薬品
Say, Mina! How can our singing help Otonaru-kun?
SING
CHARING
STOMP
STOMP
Maiku has spent so much time in hospitals, he's come to hate them. So starting tomorrow, he'll do his con-valescing at home.

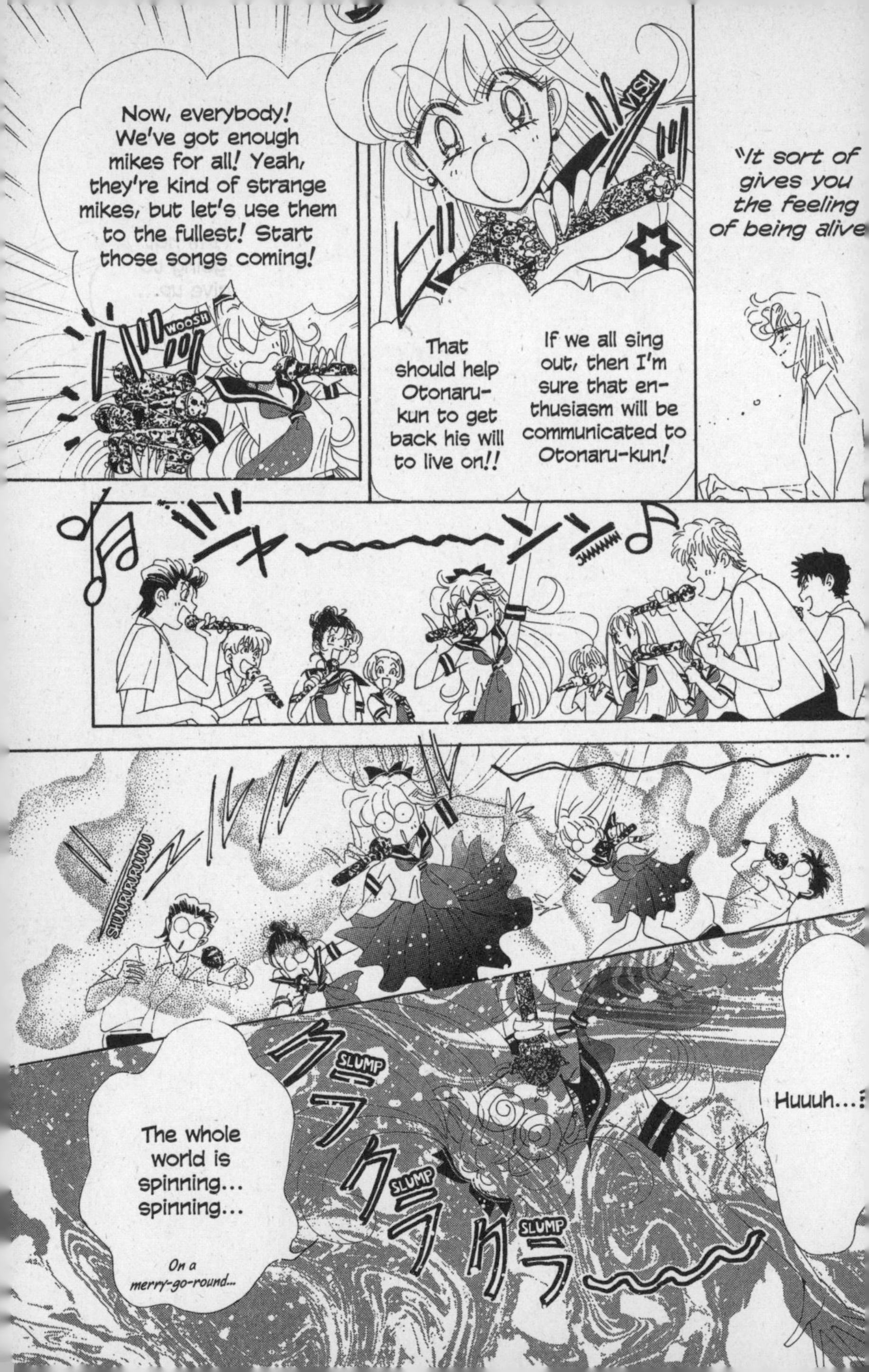
"It sort of gives you the feeling of being alive
VISH
If we all sing out, then I'm sure that enthusiasm will be communicated to Otonaru-kun!
That should help Otonaru-kun to get back his will to live on!!
Now, everybody! We've got enough mikes for all! Yeah, they're kind of strange mikes, but let's use them to the fullest! Start those songs coming!
WOOSH
SHUURURURUUU
Huuuh...?
SLUMP
SLUMP
SLUMP
The whole world is spinning... spinning...
On a merry-go-round...

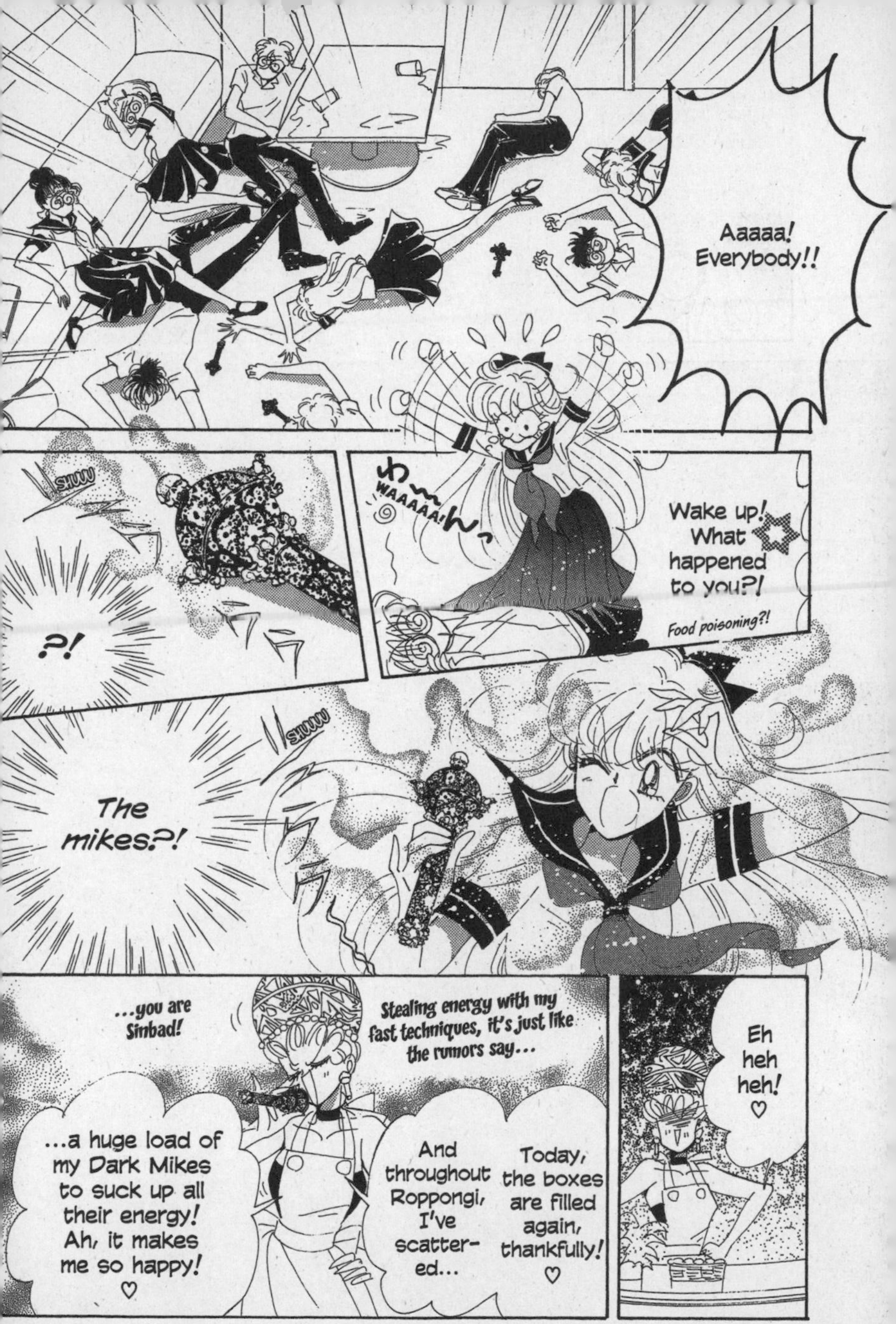
Aaaaa! Everybody!!
わ～ん
WAAAAA!
Wake up! What happened to you?!
Food poisoning?!
SHUUU
?!
SHUUU
The mikes?!
Eh heh heh! ♡
Today, the boxes are filled again, thankfully! ♡
And throughout Roppongi, I've scattered...
...a huge load of my Dark Mikes to suck up all their energy! Ah, it makes me so happy! ♡
Stealing energy with my fast techniques, it's just like the rumors say...
...you are Sinbad!

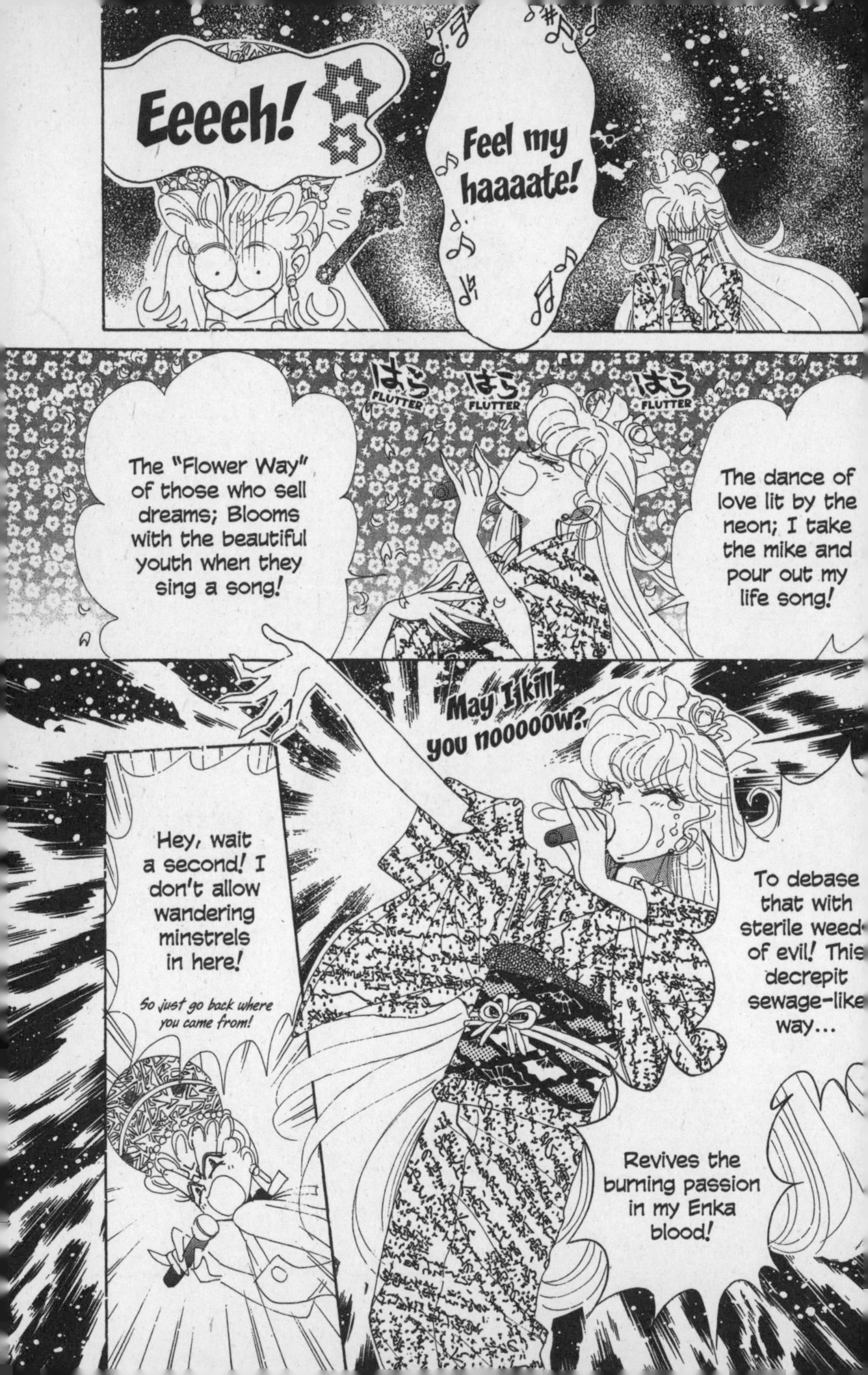

Feel my haaaate!
Eeeeh!
はら FLUTTER
はら FLUTTER
はら FLUTTER
The dance of love lit by the neon; I take the mike and pour out my life song!
The "Flower Way" of those who sell dreams; Blooms with the beautiful youth when they sing a song!
May I kill you nooooow?
To debase that with sterile weed of evil! This decrepit sewage-like way...
Revives the burning passion in my Enka blood!
Hey, wait a second! I don't allow wandering minstrels in here!
So just go back where you came from!

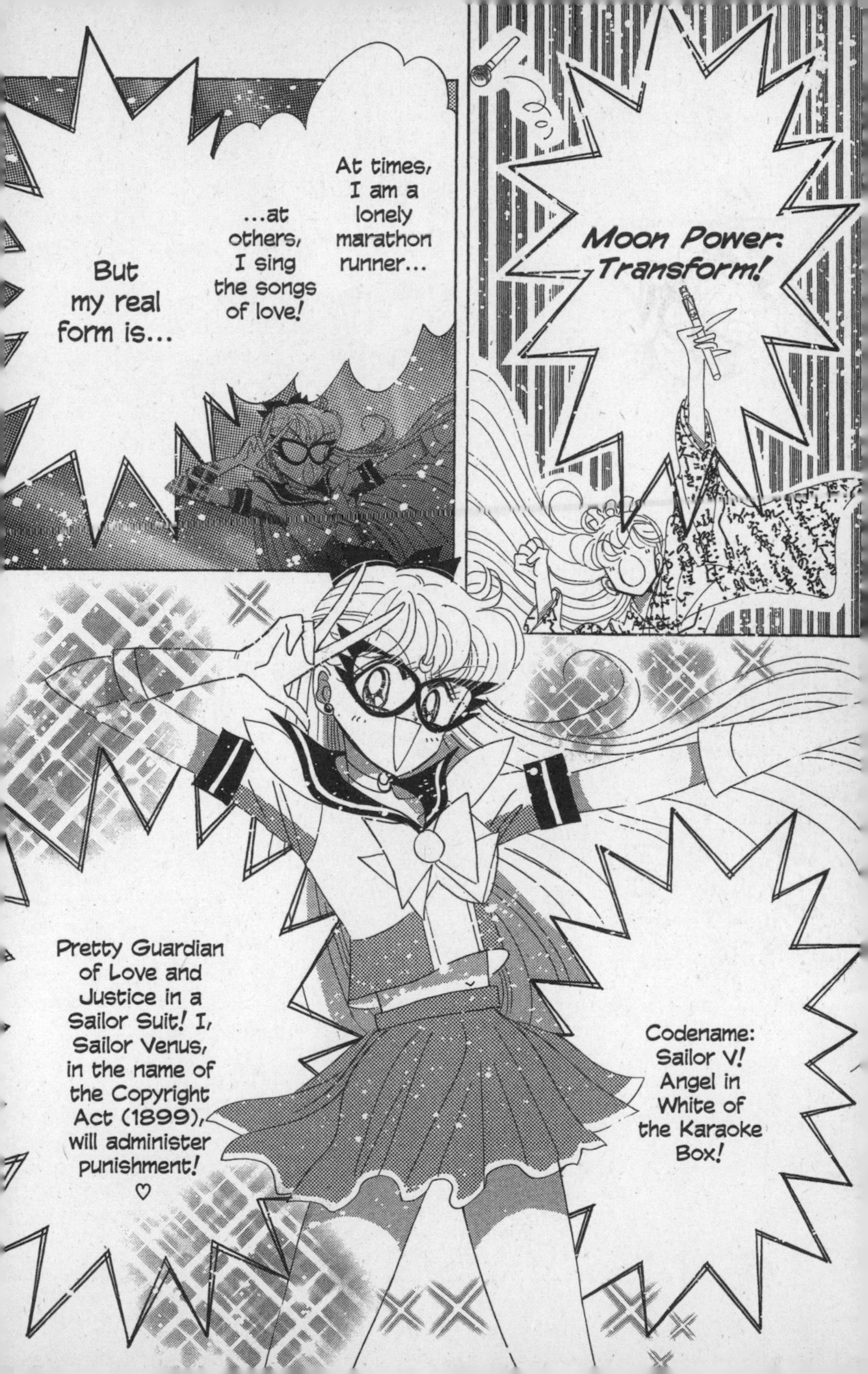

Moon Power: Transform!
At times, I am a lonely marathon runner...
...at others, I sing the songs of love!
But my real form is...
Codename: Sailor V! Angel in White of the Karaoke Box!
Pretty Guardian of Love and Justice in a Sailor Suit! I, Sailor Venus, in the name of the Copyright Act (1899), will administer punishment! ♡

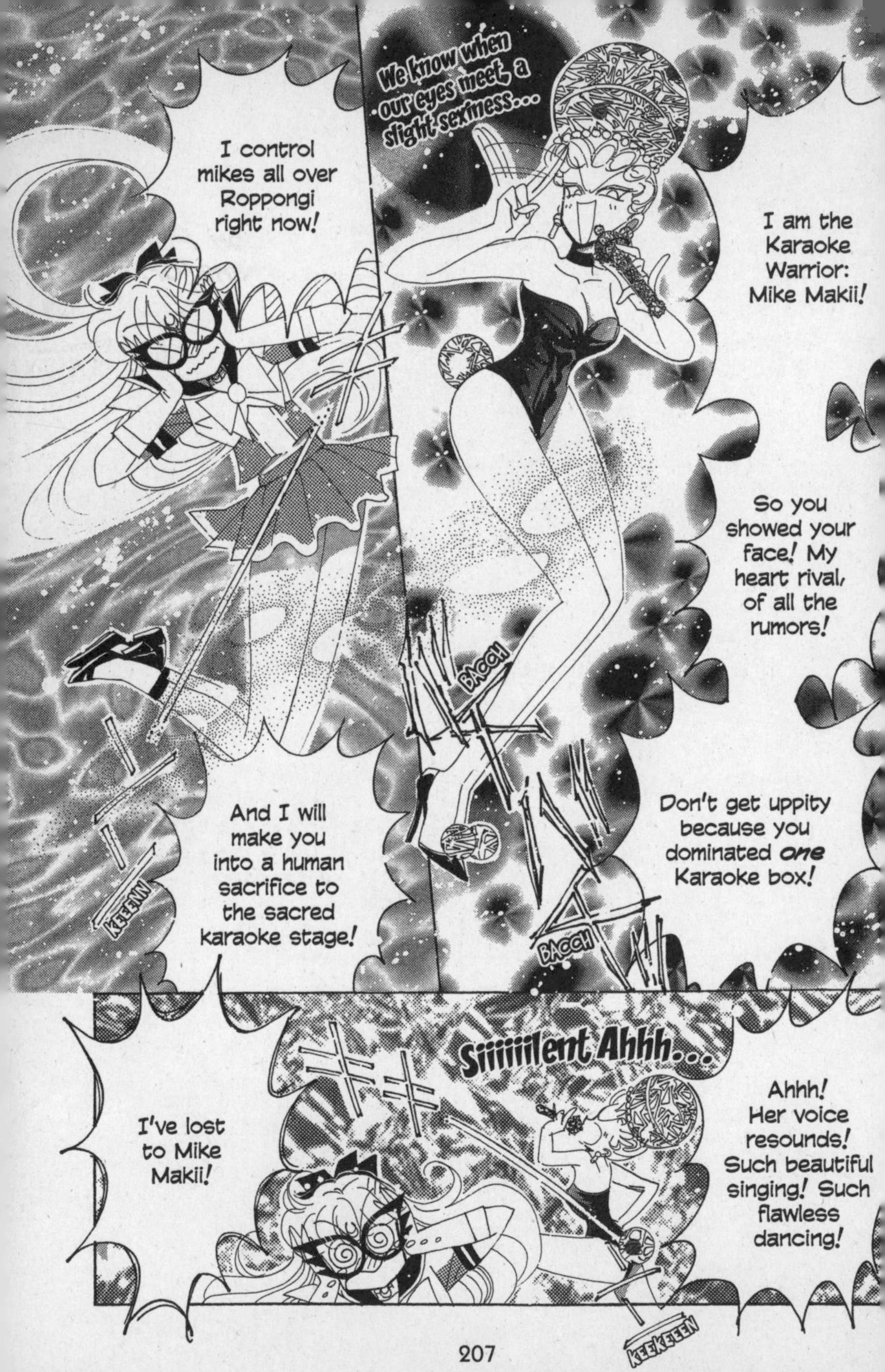

We know when our eyes meet, a slight sexiness...
I am the Karaoke Warrior: Mike Makii!
So you showed your face! My heart rival, of all the rumors!
BACCH
Don't get uppity because you dominated *one* Karaoke box!
BACCH
I control mikes all over Roppongi right now!
And I will make you into a human sacrifice to the sacred karaoke stage!
KEEENN
Siiiiiilent Ahhh...
Ahhh! Her voice resounds! Such beautiful singing! Such flawless dancing!
I've lost to Mike Makii!
KEEKEEEN

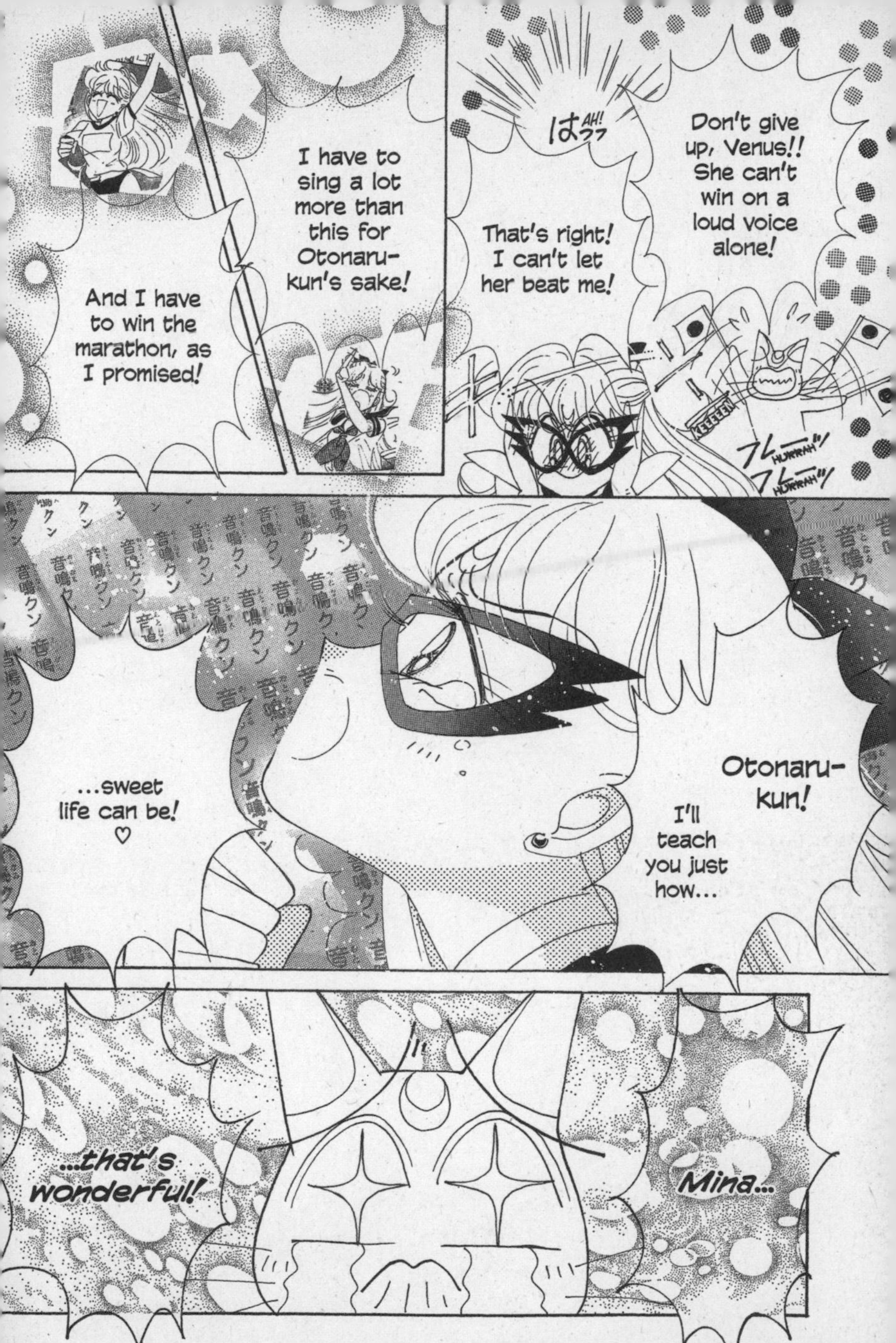
Don't give up, Venus!! She can't win on a loud voice alone!
はAH!ッッ
That's right! I can't let her beat me!
フレーHURRAH!!
フレーHURRAH!!
I have to sing a lot more than this for Otonaru-kun's sake!
And I have to win the marathon, as I promised!
Otonaru-kun!
I'll teach you just how...
...sweet life can be! ♡
Mina...
...that's wonderful!

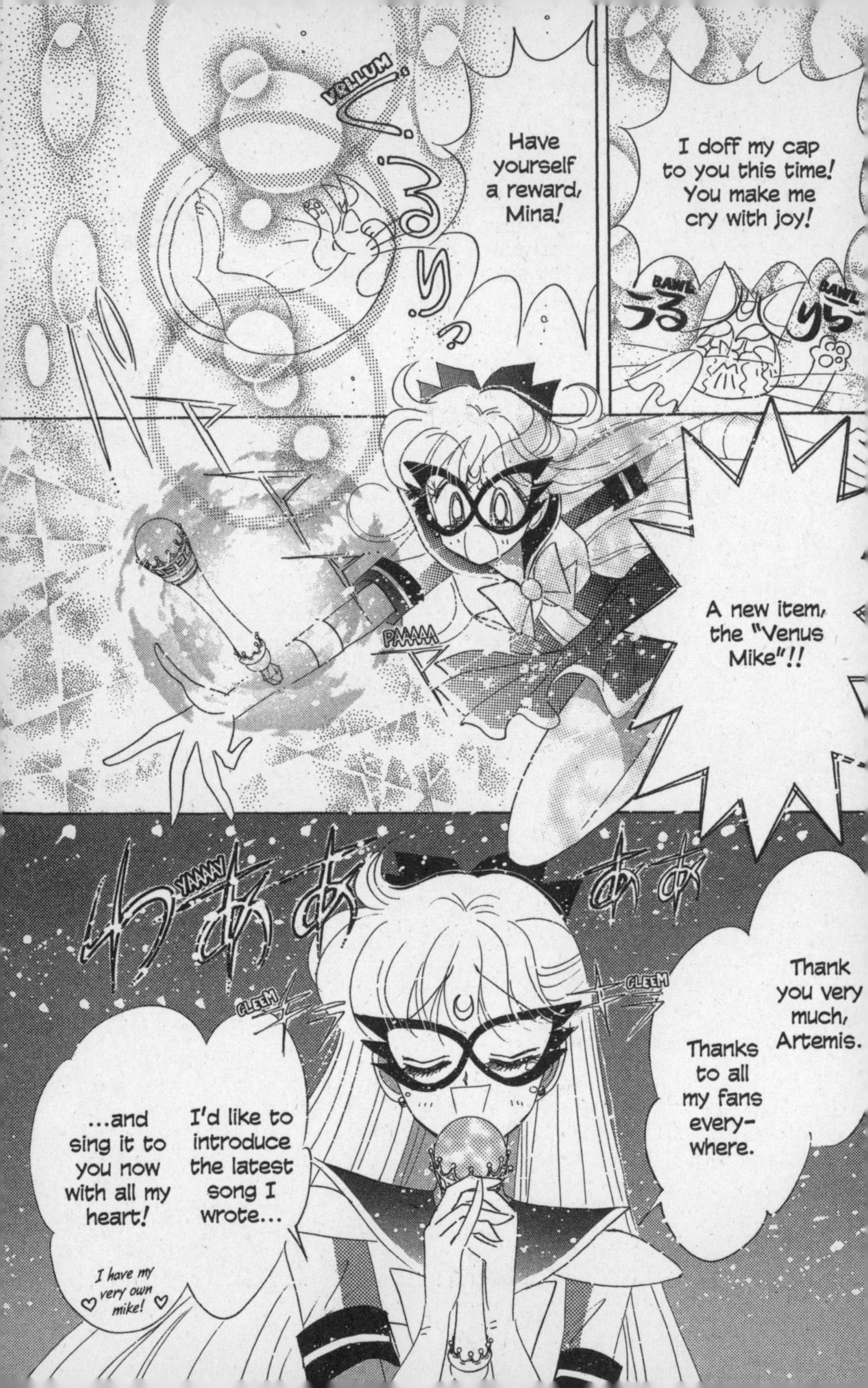
I doff my cap to you this time! You make me cry with joy!
BAWL
BAWL
VELLUM
Have yourself a reward, Mina!
PAAAAA
A new item, the "Venus Mike"!!
YAAAAY
GLEEM
GLEEM
Thank you very much, Artemis.
Thanks to all my fans every-where.
I'd like to introduce the latest song I wrote...
...and sing it to you now with all my heart!
I have my very own mike!

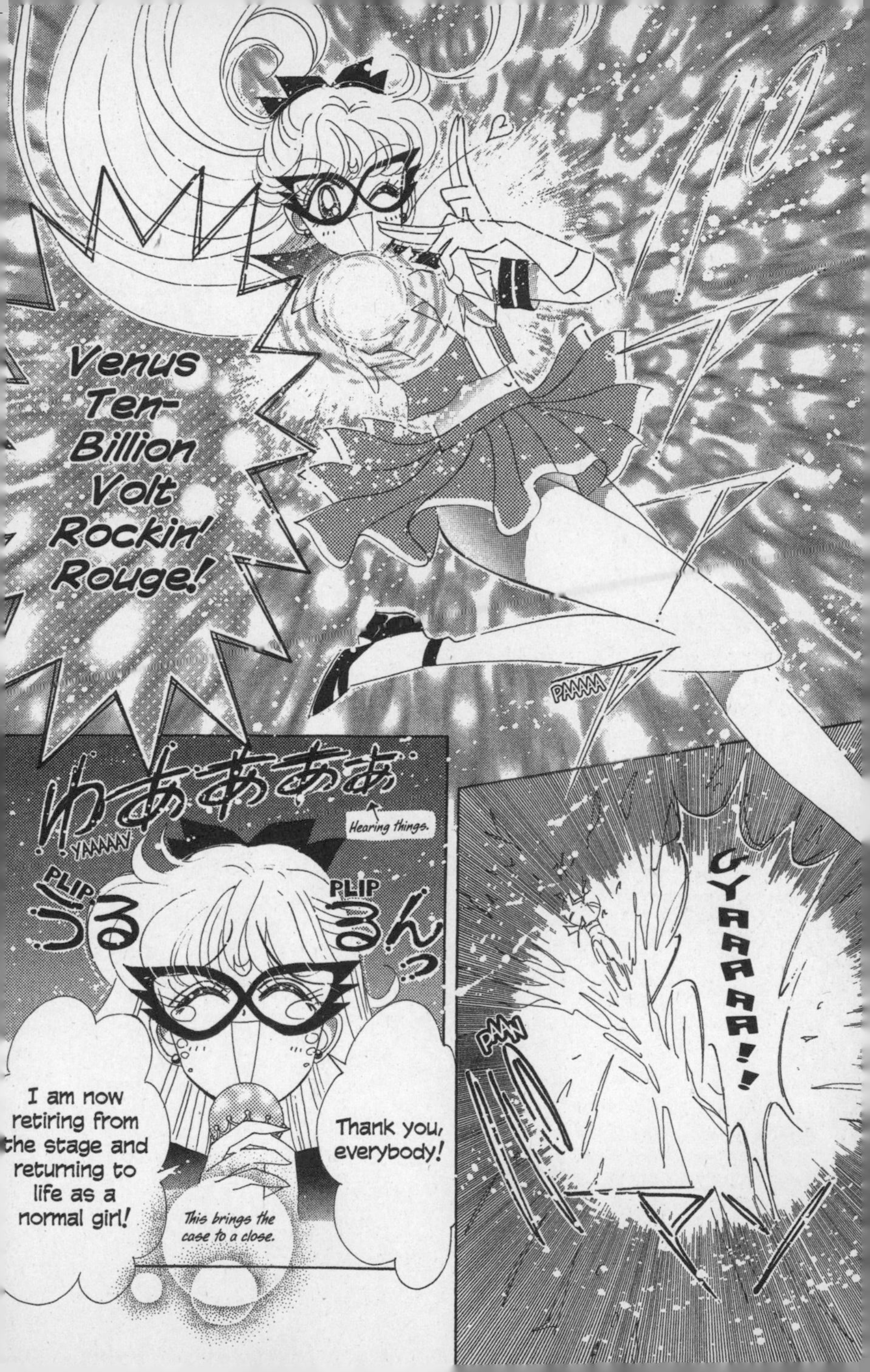
Venus Ten-Billion Volt Rockin' Rouge!
PAAAAA
GYAAAA!!
PAAN
わあああああ!
YAAAAAY
Hearing things.
PLIP
つる
PLIP
るんっ
Thank you, everybody!
I am now retiring from the stage and returning to life as a normal girl!
This brings the case to a close.

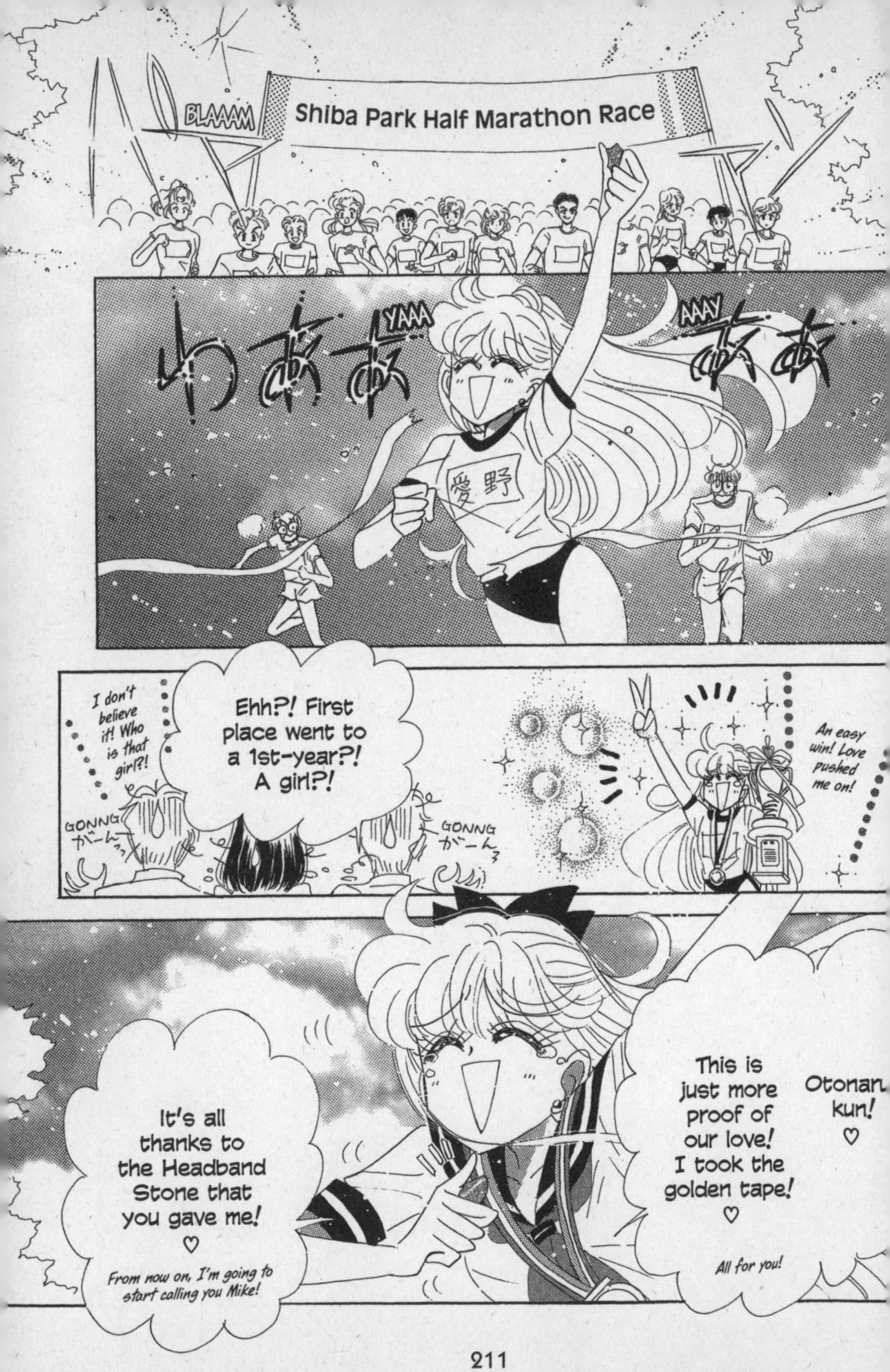
BLAAAM
Shiba Park Half Marathon Race
AAAY
ああ
YAAA
わあああ
愛野
An easy win! Love pushed me on!
I don't believe it! Who is that girl?!
Ehh?! First place went to a 1st-year?! A girl?!
GONNG がーん
GONNG がーん
Otonar kun! ♡
This is just more proof of our love! I took the golden tape! ♡
All for you!
It's all thanks to the Headband Stone that you gave me! ♡
From now on, I'm going to start calling you Mike!

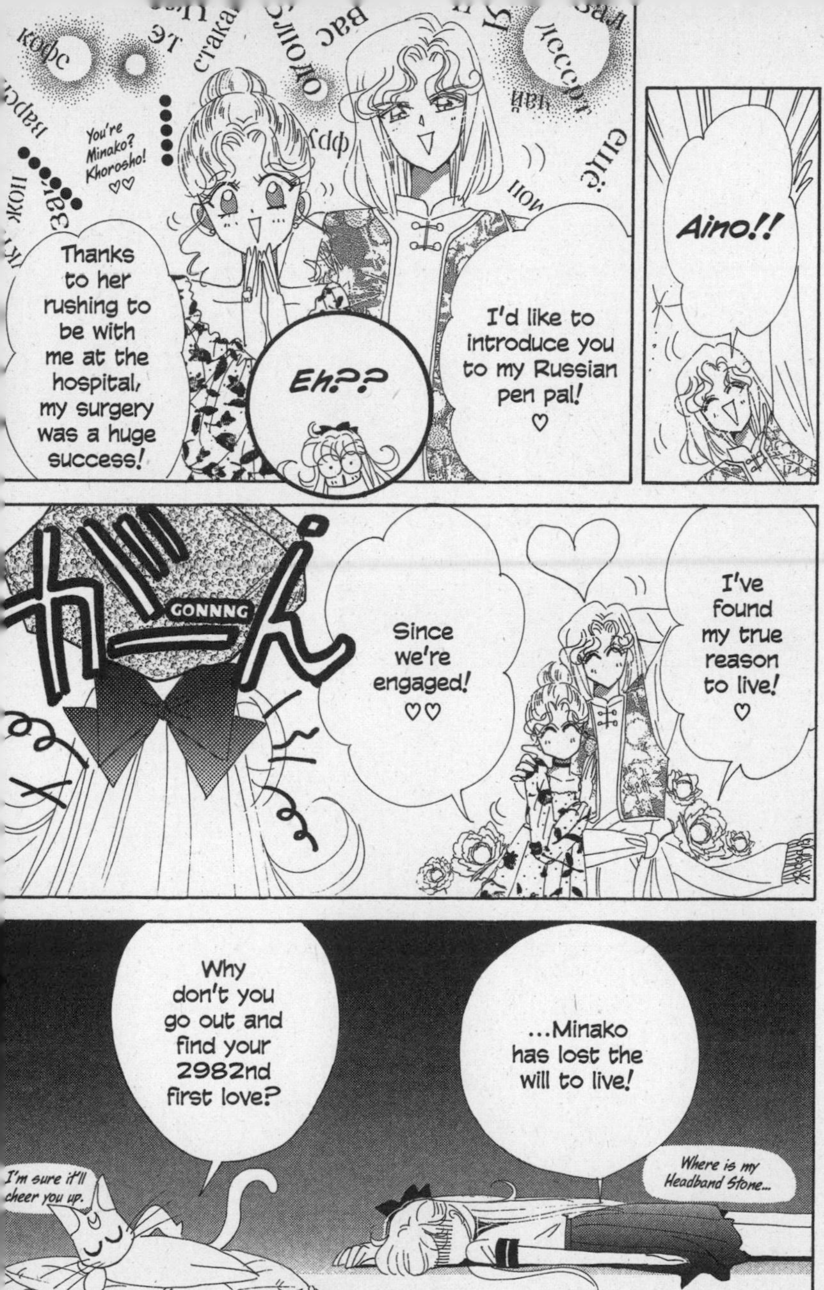

Aino!!
I'd like to introduce you to my Russian pen pal! ♡
You're Minako? Khorosho! ♡♡
Eh??
Thanks to her rushing to be with me at the hospital, my surgery was a huge success!
I've found my true reason to live! ♡
Since we're engaged! ♡♡
GONNNG
...Minako has lost the will to live!
Where is my Headband Stone...
Why don't you go out and find your 2982nd first love?
I'm sure it'll cheer you up.

● *The End* ●

Vol. 15 Setting Out on a New Journey, Part 1

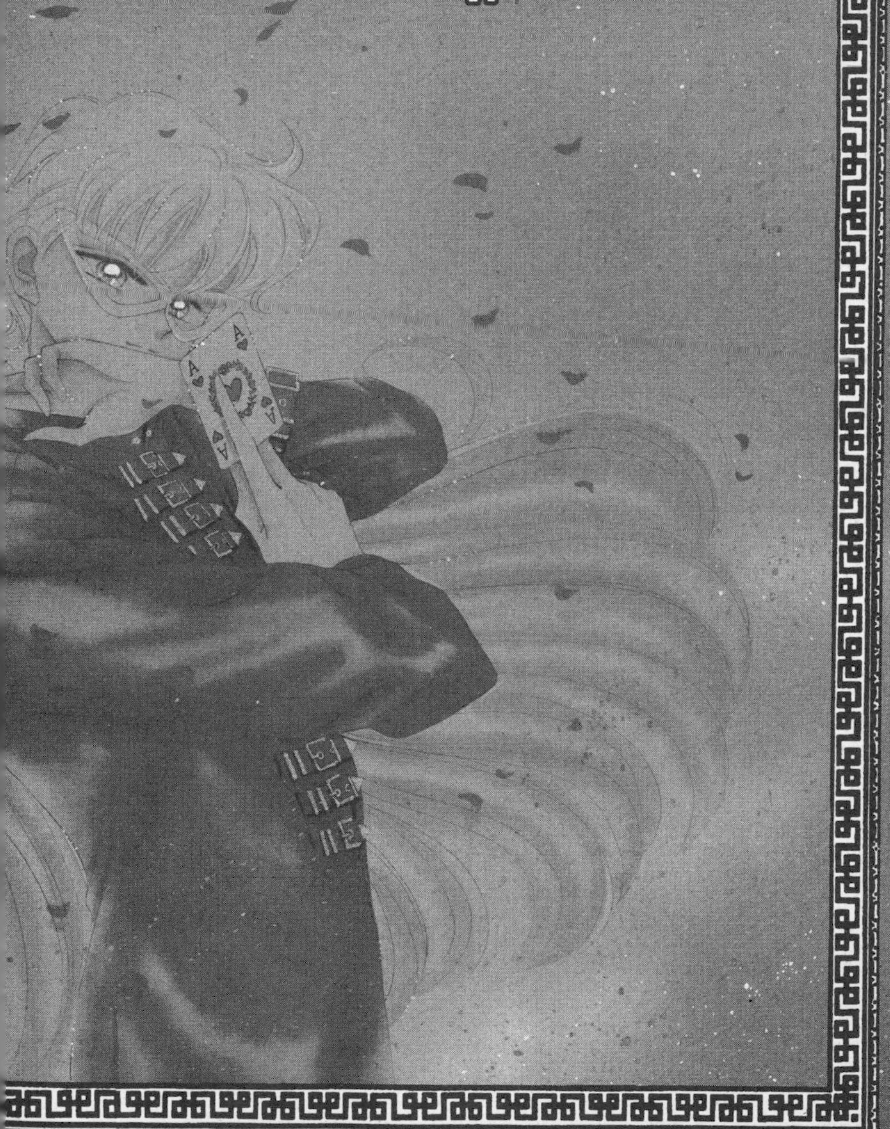

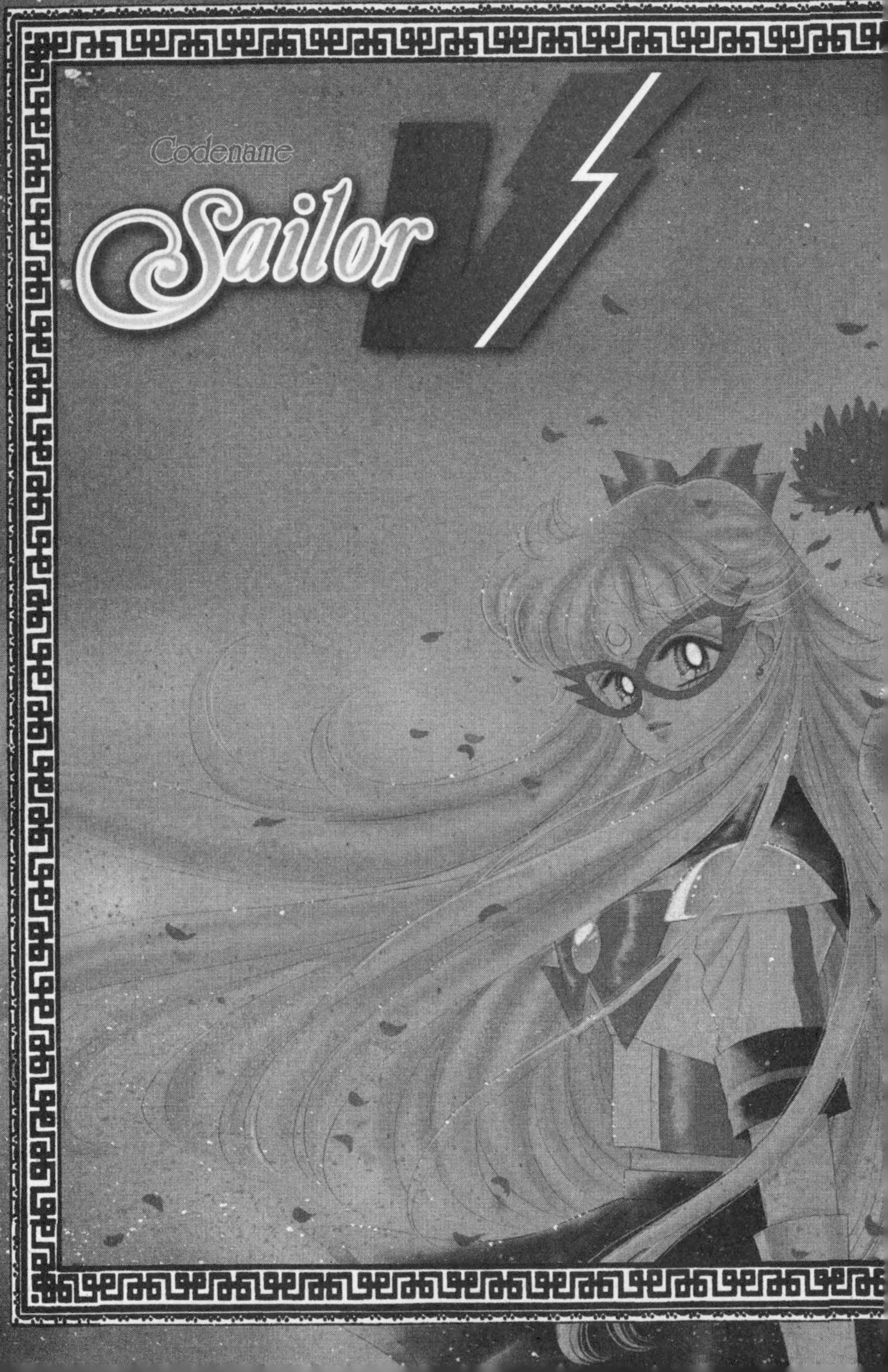
Codename
Sailor V

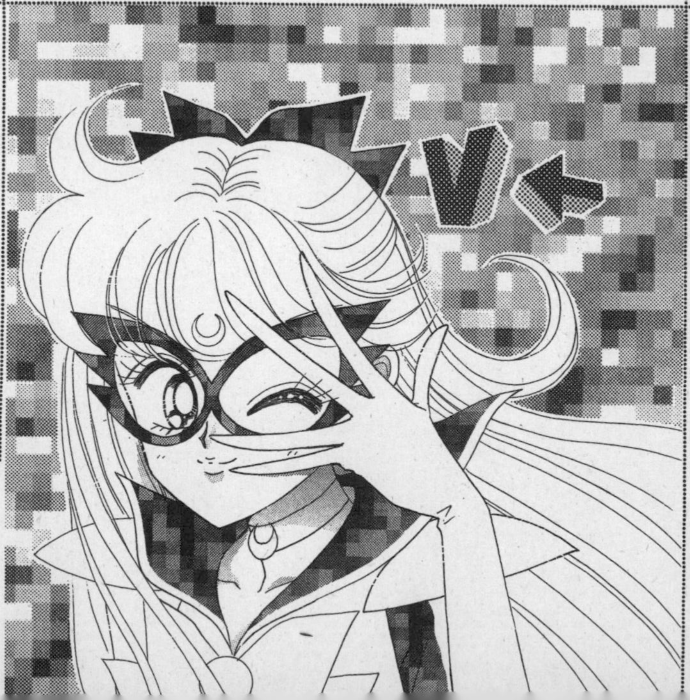
V

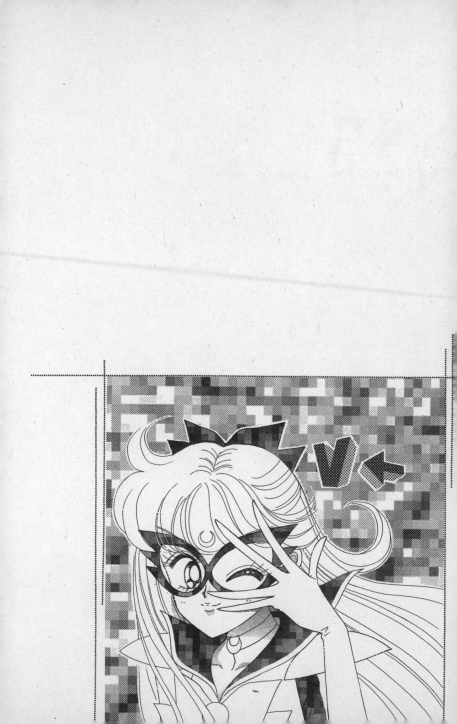

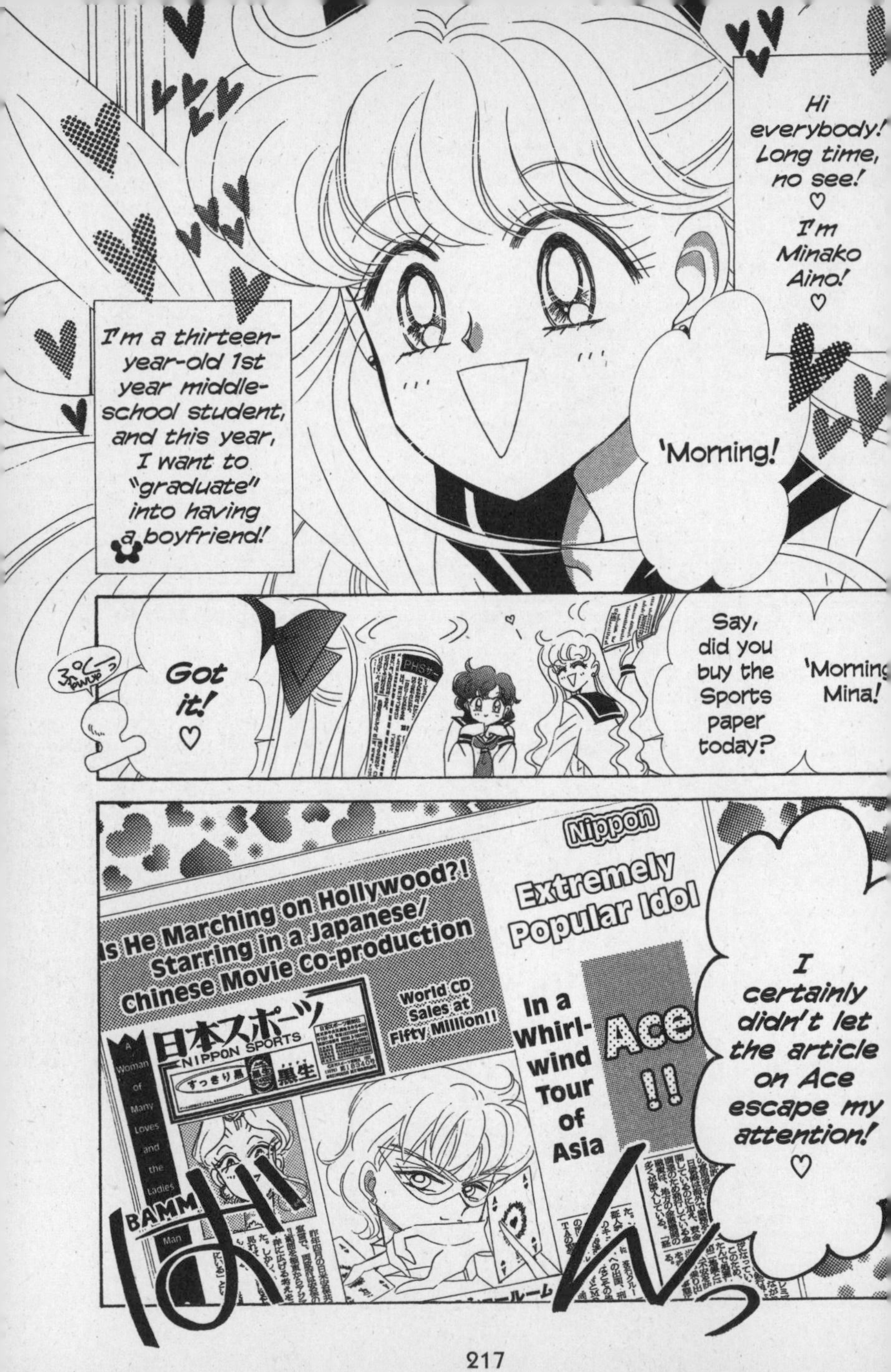
Hi everybody! Long time, no see! ♡ I'm Minako Aino! ♡
'Morning!
I'm a thirteen-year-old 1st year middle-school student, and this year, I want to "graduate" into having a boyfriend!
'Morning Mina!
Say, did you buy the Sports paper today?
Got it! ♡
I certainly didn't let the article on Ace escape my attention! ♡
Nippon
Extremely Popular Idol
Ace !!
In a Whirlwind Tour of Asia
Is He Marching on Hollywood?! Starring in a Japanese/Chinese Movie Co-production
World CD Sales at Fifty Million!!
日本スポーツ
NIPPON SPORTS
A Woman of Many Loves and the Ladies Man
BAMM

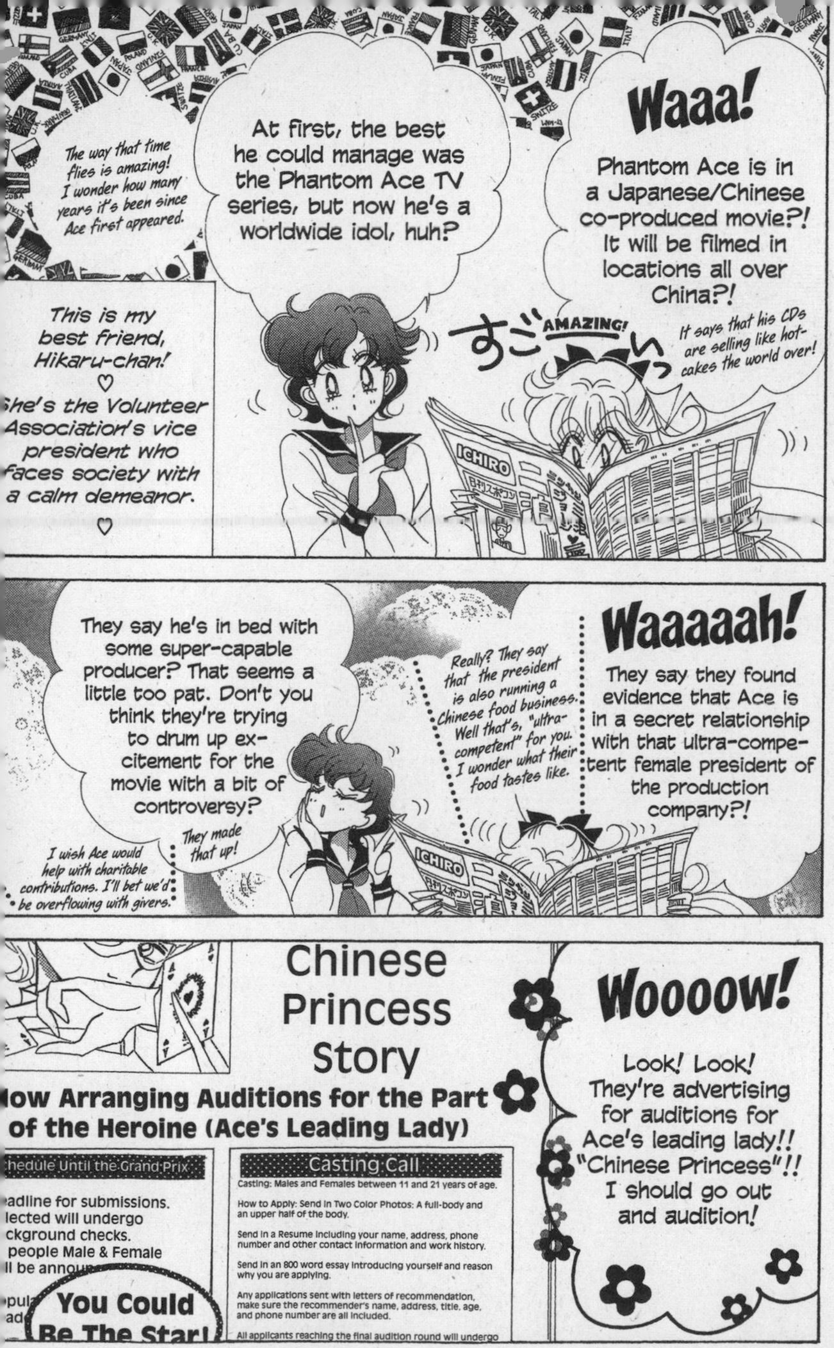

Waaa!
Phantom Ace is in a Japanese/Chinese co-produced movie?! It will be filmed in locations all over China?!
It says that his CDs are selling like hot-cakes the world over!
すごーい AMAZING!
At first, the best he could manage was the Phantom Ace TV series, but now he's a worldwide idol, huh?
The way that time flies is amazing! I wonder how many years it's been since Ace first appeared.
This is my best friend, Hikaru-chan! ♡ She's the Volunteer Association's vice president who faces society with a calm demeanor. ♡
Waaaaah!
They say they found evidence that Ace is in a secret relationship with that ultra-competent female president of the production company?!
Really? They say that the president is also running a Chinese food business. Well that's, "ultra-competent" for you. I wonder what their food tastes like.
They say he's in bed with some super-capable producer? That seems a little too pat. Don't you think they're trying to drum up excitement for the movie with a bit of controversy?
They made that up!
I wish Ace would help with charitable contributions. I'll bet we'd be overflowing with givers.
Wooooow!
Look! Look! They're advertising for auditions for Ace's leading lady!! "Chinese Princess"!! I should go out and audition!
Chinese Princess Story
ow Arranging Auditions for the Part of the Heroine (Ace's Leading Lady)
Casting Call
Casting: Males and Females between 11 and 21 years of age.
How to Apply: Send in Two Color Photos: A full-body and an upper half of the body.
Send in a Resume including your name, address, phone number and other contact information and work history.
Send in an 800 word essay introducing yourself and reason why you are applying.
Any applications sent with letters of recommendation, make sure the recommender's name, address, title, age, and phone number are all included.
All applicants reaching the final audition round will undergo
hedule Until the Grand Prix
adline for submissions.
lected will undergo
ckground checks.
people Male & Female
You Could Be The Star!

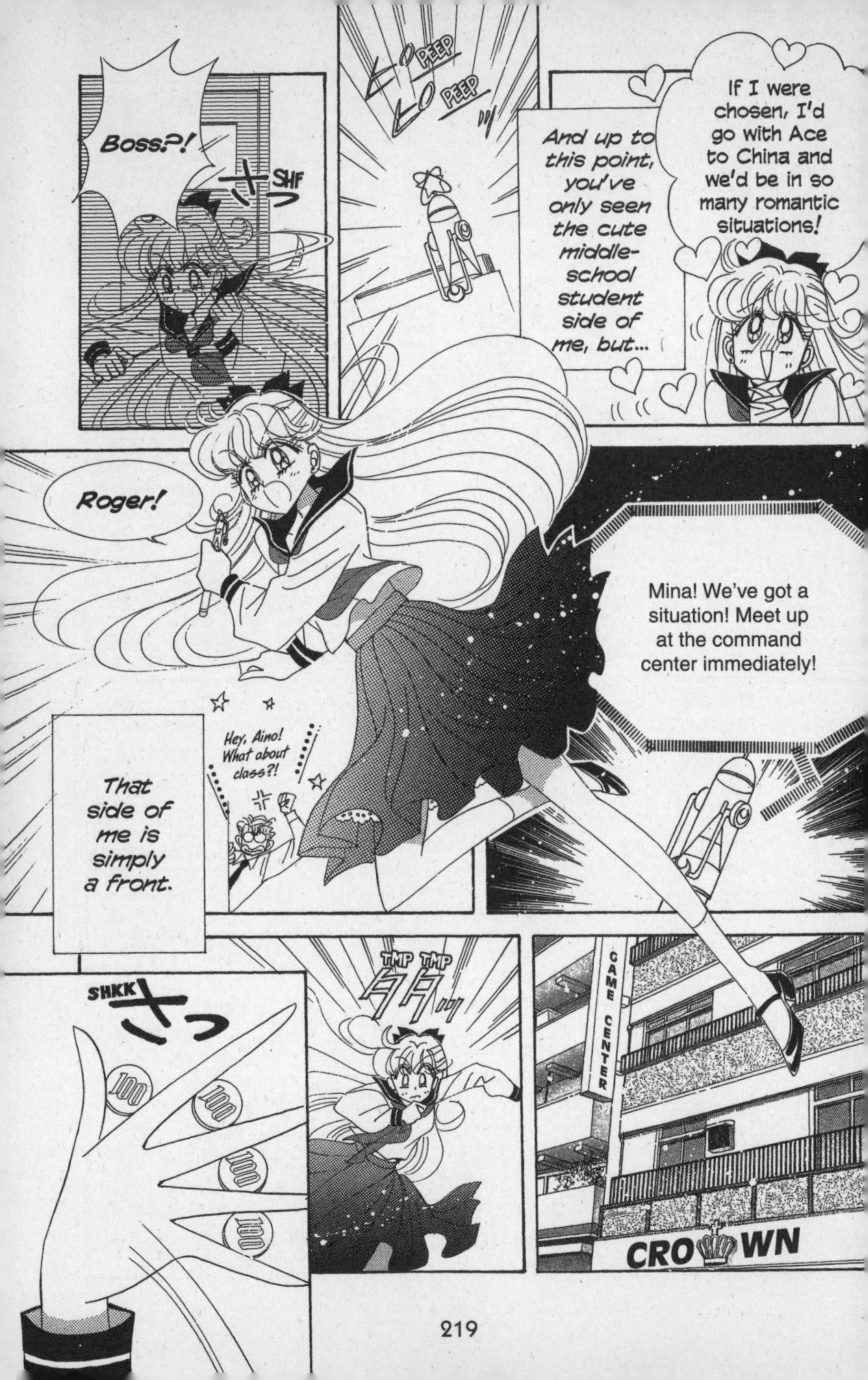
If I were chosen, I'd go with Ace to China and we'd be in so many romantic situations!
PEEP
PEEP
And up to this point, you've only seen the cute middle-school student side of me, but...
Boss?!
SHF
Mina! We've got a situation! Meet up at the command center immediately!
Roger!
Hey, Aino! What about class?!
That side of me is simply a front.
GAME CENTER
CROWN
TMP TMP
SHKK
さっ
100
100
100
100

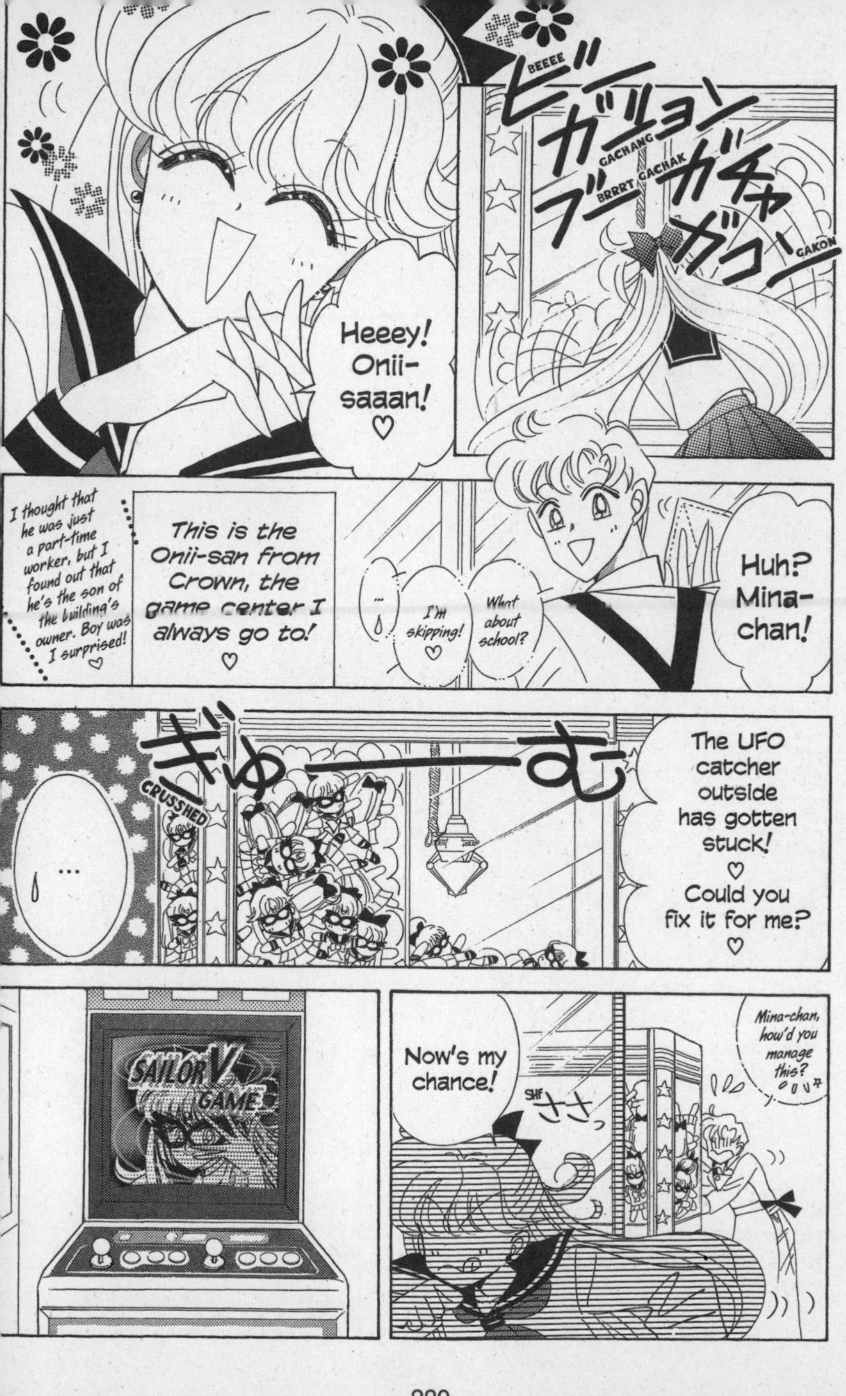
BEEEE
GACHANG
BRRRT GACHAK
GAKON
Heeey! Onii-saaan! ♡
Huh? Mina-chan!
What about school?
...
I'm skipping! ♡
This is the Onii-san from Crown, the game center I always go to! ♡
I thought that he was just a part-time worker, but I found out that he's the son of the building's owner. Boy was I surprised! ♡
The UFO catcher outside has gotten stuck! ♡ Could you fix it for me? ♡
CRUSSHED
ぎゅーーむ
...
Mina-chan, how'd you manage this?
SHF
ささっ
Now's my chance!
SAILOR V GAME

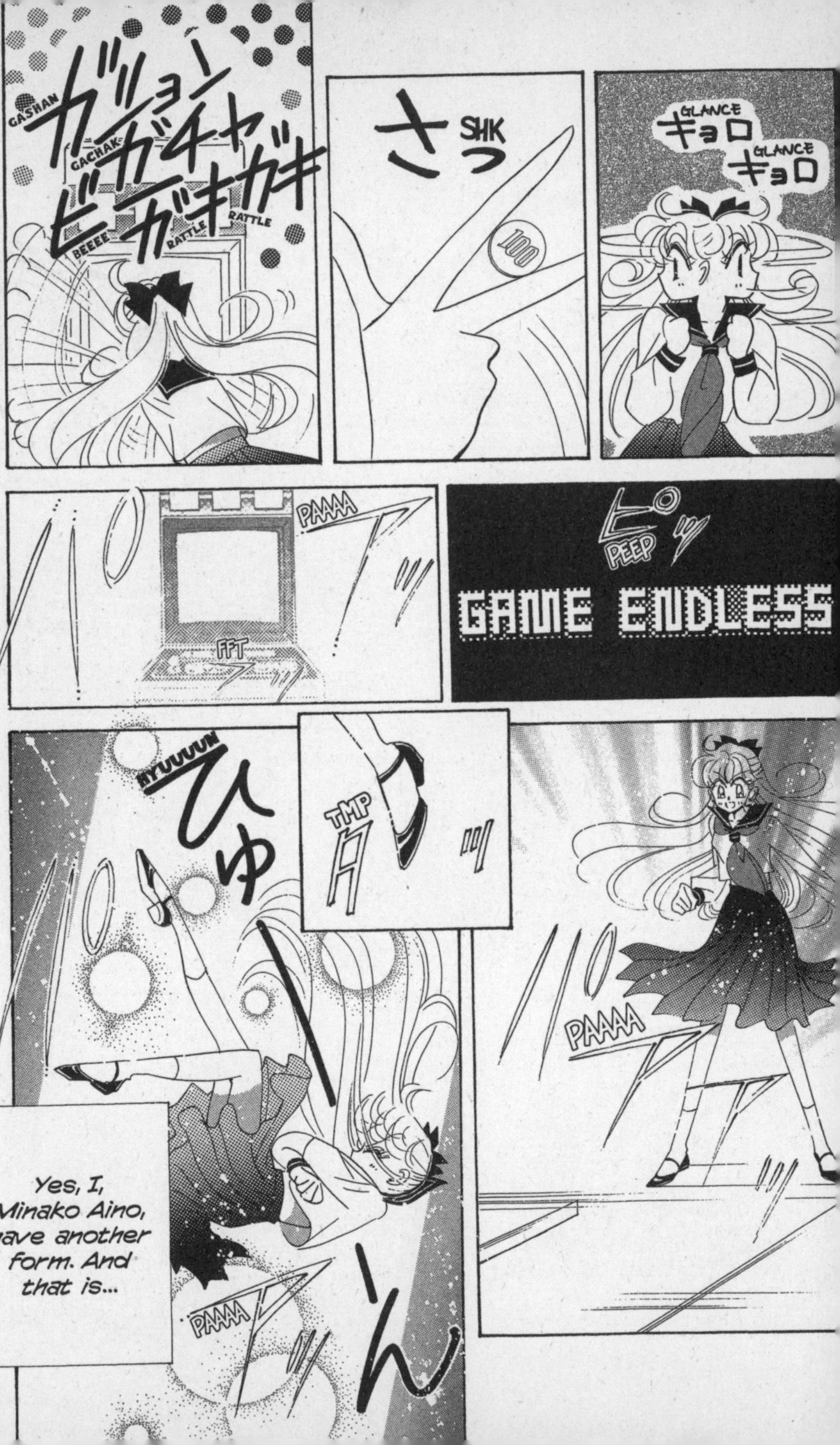
GLANCE
ギョロ
GLANCE
ギョロ
さっ
SHK
GASHAN
GACHAK
BEEEE
RATTLE
RATTLE
ピッ
PEEP
GAME ENDLESS
PAAAA
FFT
PAAAA
TMP
ひゅーん
HYUUUN
PAAAA
Yes, I, Minako Aino, have another form. And that is...

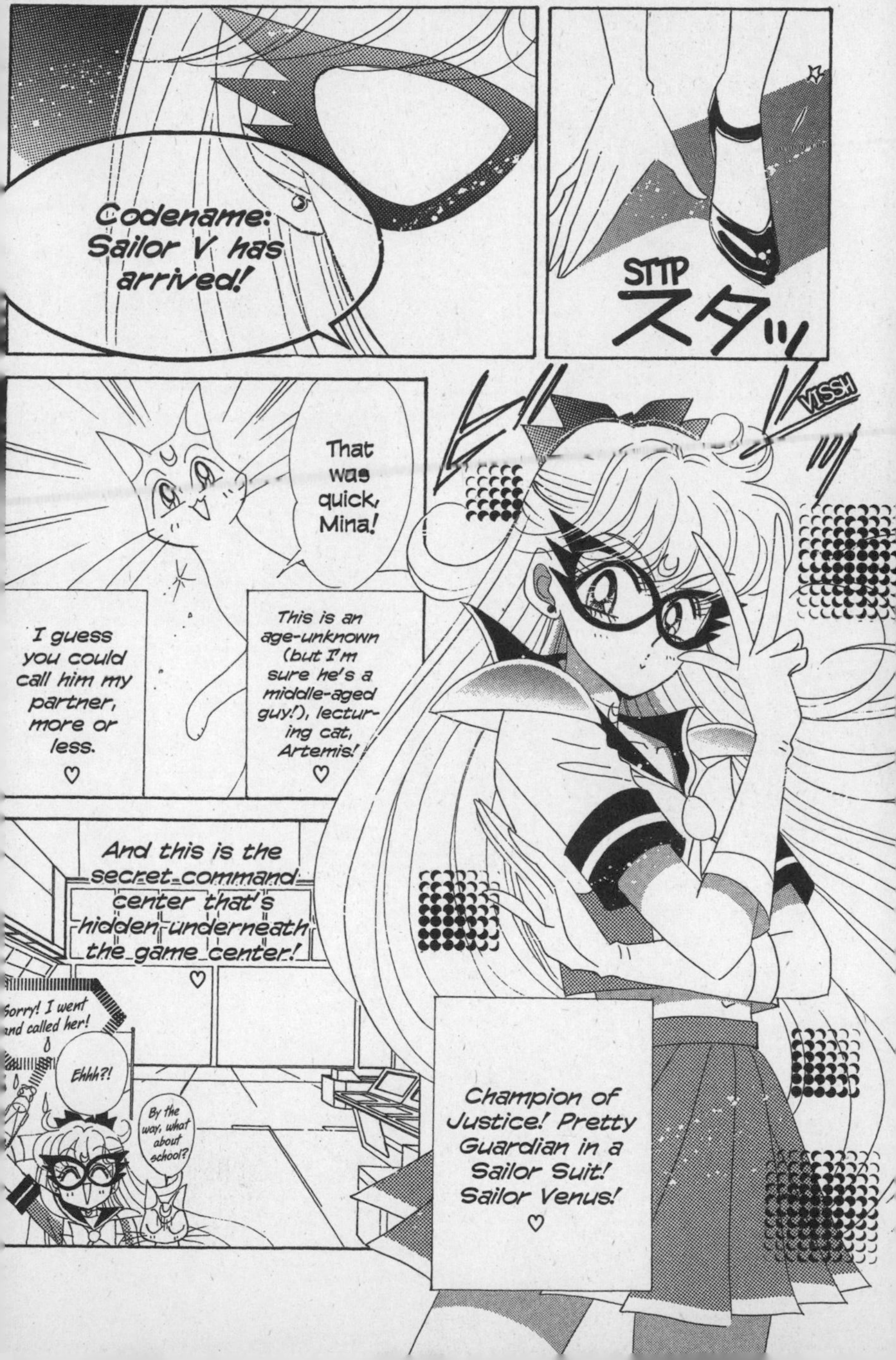

STTP
スタッ
Codename: Sailor V has arrived!
VISSH
Champion of Justice! Pretty Guardian in a Sailor Suit! Sailor Venus!
That was quick, Mina!
This is an age-unknown (but I'm sure he's a middle-aged guy!), lecturing cat, Artemis!
I guess you could call him my partner, more or less.
And this is the secret command center that's hidden underneath the game center!
By the way, what about school?
Ehhh?!
Sorry! I went and called her!

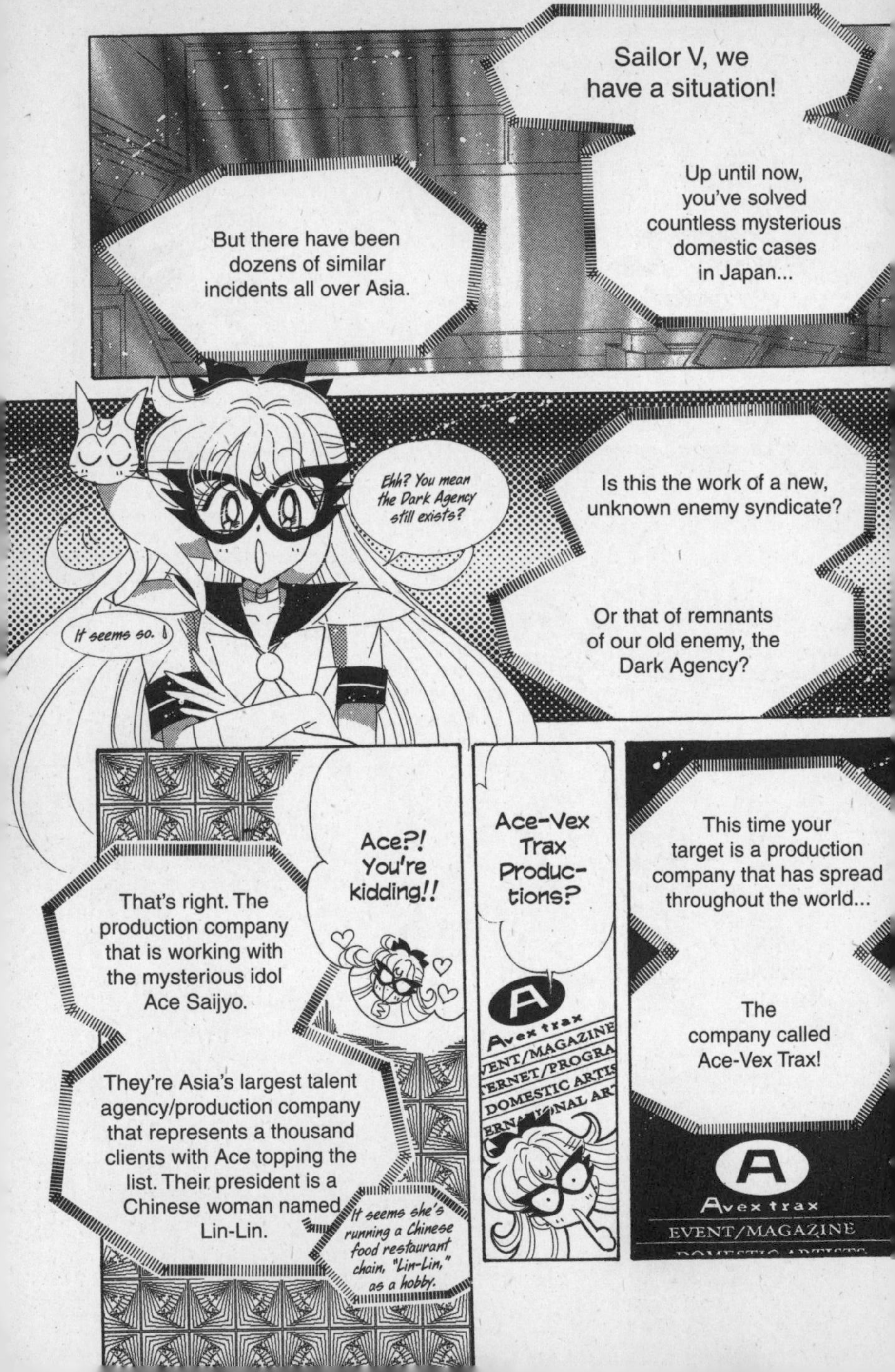

Sailor V, we have a situation!
Up until now, you've solved countless mysterious domestic cases in Japan...
But there have been dozens of similar incidents all over Asia.
Is this the work of a new, unknown enemy syndicate?
Or that of remnants of our old enemy, the Dark Agency?
Ehh? You mean the Dark Agency still exists?
It seems so.
This time your target is a production company that has spread throughout the world...
The company called Ace-Vex Trax!
Avex trax
EVENT/MAGAZINE
Ace-Vex Trax Productions?
Avex trax
DOMESTIC ARTIS
Ace?! You're kidding!!
That's right. The production company that is working with the mysterious idol Ace Saijyo.
They're Asia's largest talent agency/production company that represents a thousand clients with Ace topping the list. Their president is a Chinese woman named Lin-Lin.
It seems she's running a Chinese food restaurant chain, "Lin-Lin," as a hobby.

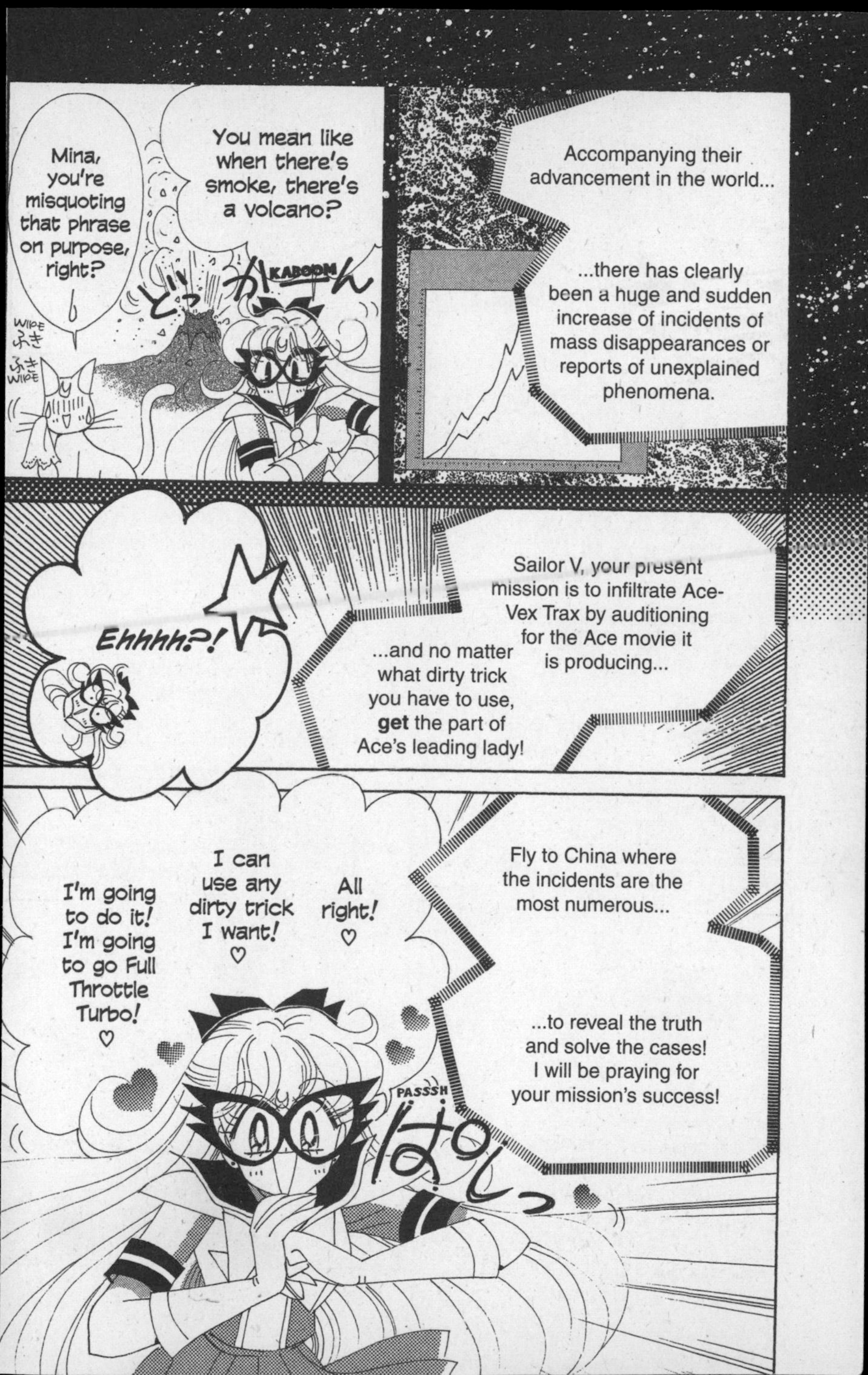
Accompanying their advancement in the world...
...there has clearly been a huge and sudden increase of incidents of mass disappearances or reports of unexplained phenomena.
You mean like when there's smoke, there's a volcano?
KABOOM
Mina, you're misquoting that phrase on purpose, right?
WIPE
WIPE
Sailor V, your present mission is to infiltrate Ace-Vex Trax by auditioning for the Ace movie it is producing...
...and no matter what dirty trick you have to use, **get** the part of Ace's leading lady!
Ehhhh?!
Fly to China where the incidents are the most numerous...
...to reveal the truth and solve the cases! I will be praying for your mission's success!
PASSSH
All right! ♡
I can use any dirty trick I want! ♡
I'm going to do it! I'm going to go Full Throttle Turbo! ♡

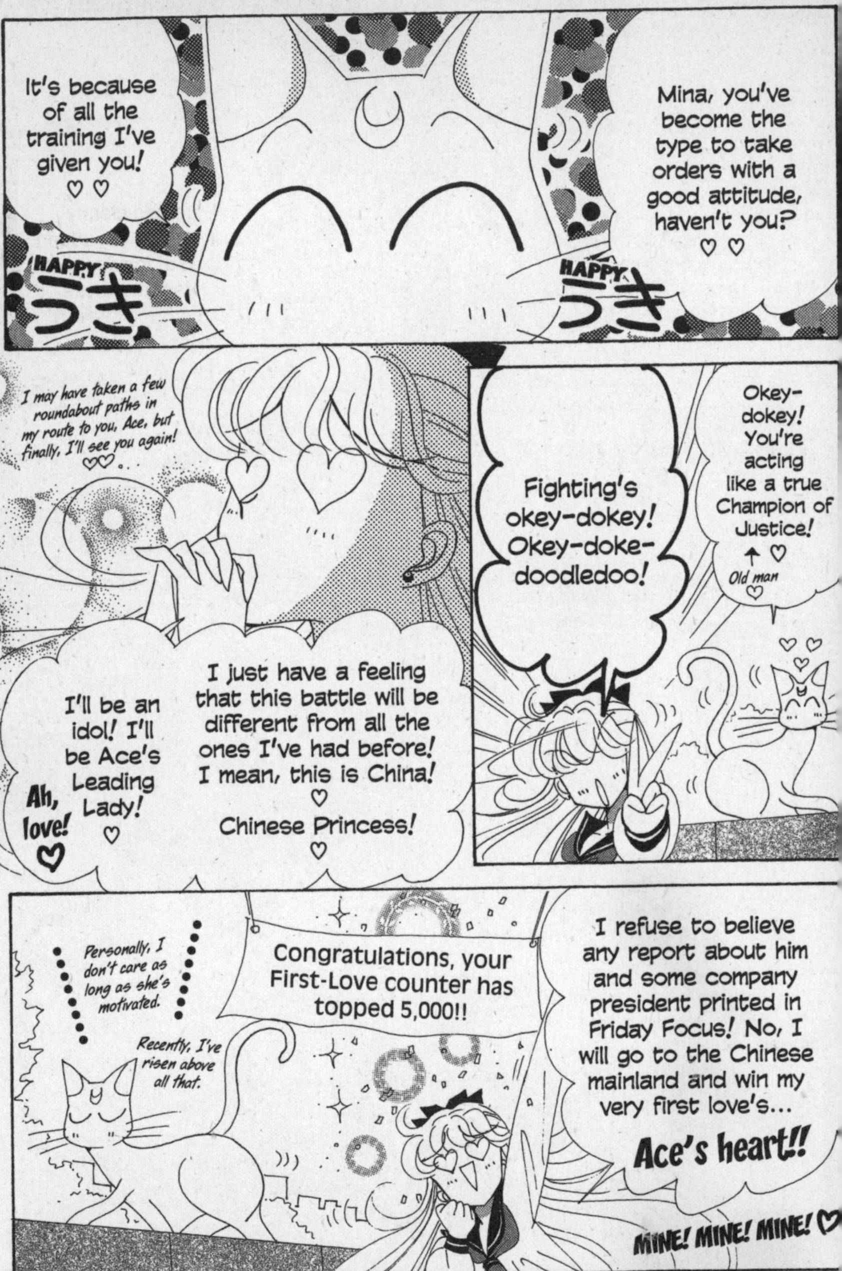
Mina, you've become the type to take orders with a good attitude, haven't you? ♡ ♡
HAPPY
うき
It's because of all the training I've given you! ♡ ♡
HAPPY
うき
Okey-dokey! You're acting like a true Champion of Justice! ↑ ♡
Old man ♡
Fighting's okey-dokey! Okey-doke-doodledoo!
I may have taken a few roundabout paths in my route to you, Ace, but finally, I'll see you again! ♡♡..
I just have a feeling that this battle will be different from all the ones I've had before! I mean, this is China! ♡
Chinese Princess! ♡
I'll be an idol! I'll be Ace's Leading Lady! ♡
Ah, love! ♡
I refuse to believe any report about him and some company president printed in Friday Focus! No, I will go to the Chinese mainland and win my very first love's...
Ace's heart!!
MINE! MINE! MINE! ♡
Congratulations, your First-Love counter has topped 5,000!!
Personally, I don't care as long as she's motivated.
Recently, I've risen above that.

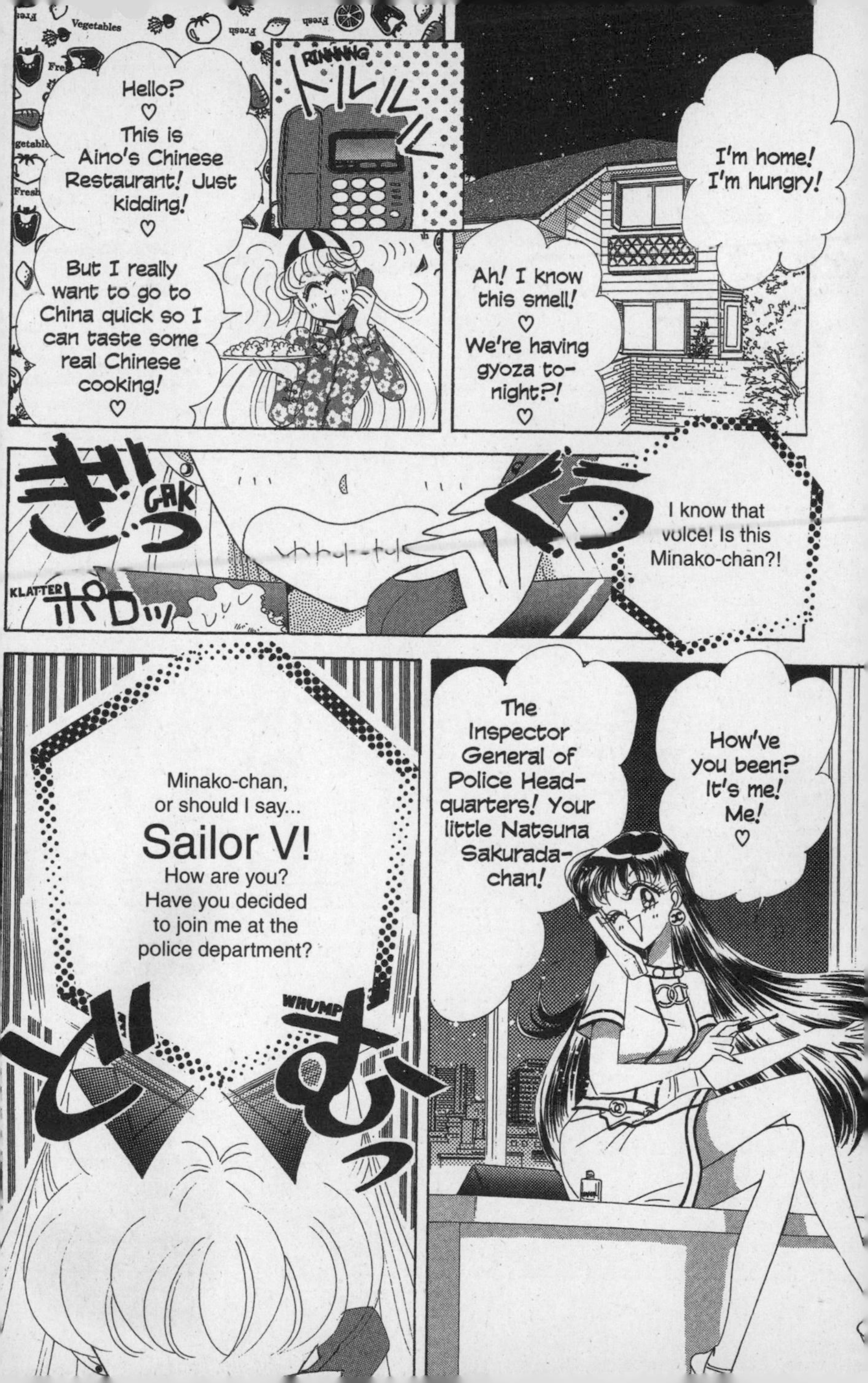
I'm home! I'm hungry!
Ah! I know this smell! ♡ We're having gyoza to-night?! ♡
RINNNNG
トルルル
Hello? ♡ This is Aino's Chinese Restaurant! Just kidding! ♡
But I really want to go to China quick so I can taste some real Chinese cooking! ♡
I know that voice! Is this Minako-chan?!
GAK
ぎっ
KLATTER
ポロッ
How've you been? It's me! Me! ♡
The Inspector General of Police Head-quarters! Your little Natsuna Sakurada-chan!
Minako-chan, or should I say... Sailor V! How are you? Have you decided to join me at the police department?
WHUMP

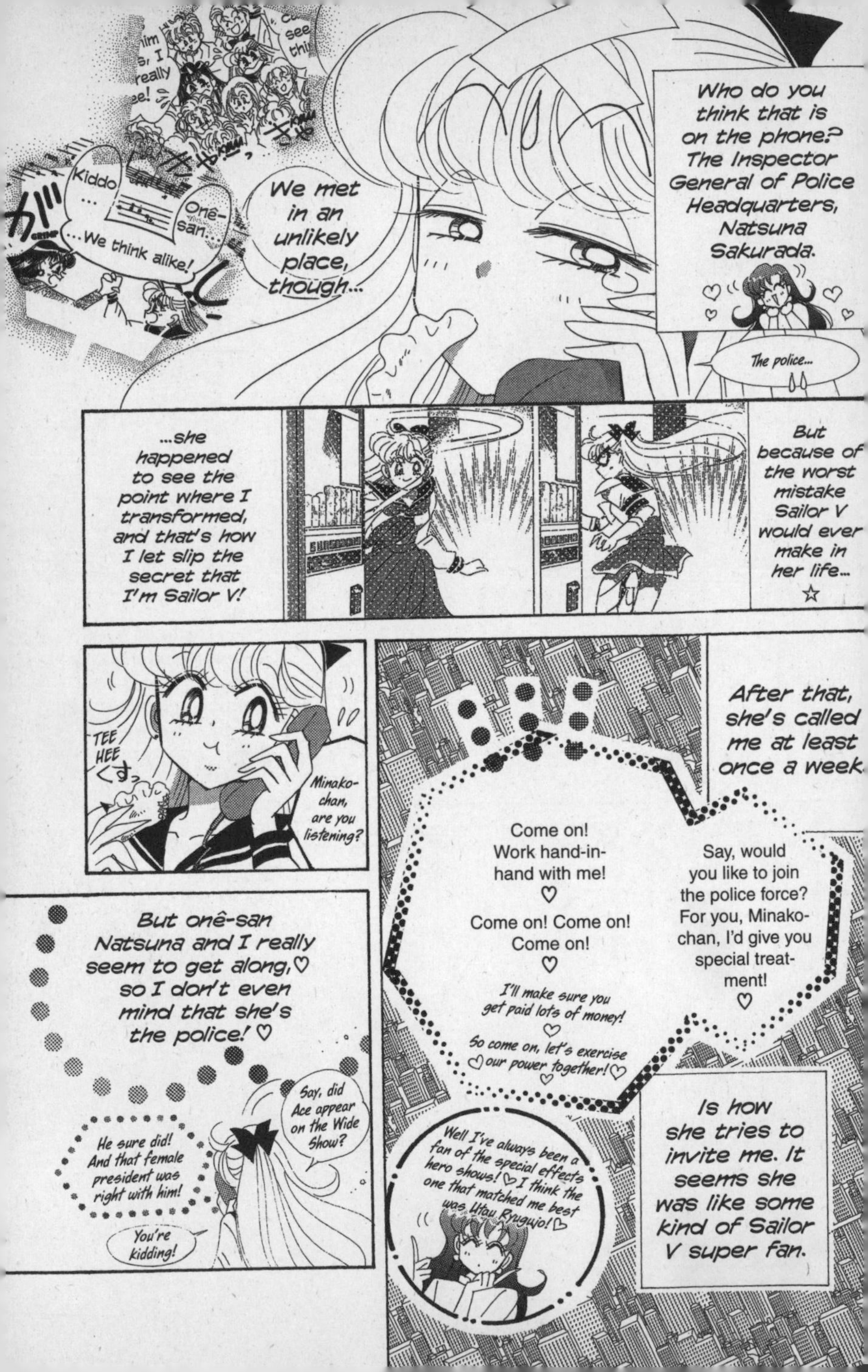
Who do you think that is on the phone? The Inspector General of Police Headquarters, Natsuna Sakurada.
The police...
We met in an unlikely place, though...
Kiddo...
Onê-san...
...We think alike!
But because of the worst mistake Sailor V would ever make in her life... ☆
...she happened to see the point where I transformed, and that's how I let slip the secret that I'm Sailor V!
After that, she's called me at least once a week.
Say, would you like to join the police force? For you, Minako-chan, I'd give you special treatment! ♡
Come on! Work hand-in-hand with me! ♡ Come on! Come on! Come on! ♡
I'll make sure you get paid lots of money! ♡
So come on, let's exercise ♡ our power together! ♡
Well I've always been a fan of the special effects hero shows! ♡ I think the one that matched me best was Utau Ryuguji! ♡
Is how she tries to invite me. It seems she was like some kind of Sailor V super fan.
Minako-chan, are you listening?
TEE HEE くすっ
But onê-san Natsuna and I really seem to get along, ♡ so I don't even mind that she's the police! ♡
Say, did Ace appear on the Wide Show?
He sure did! And that female president was right with him!
You're kidding!

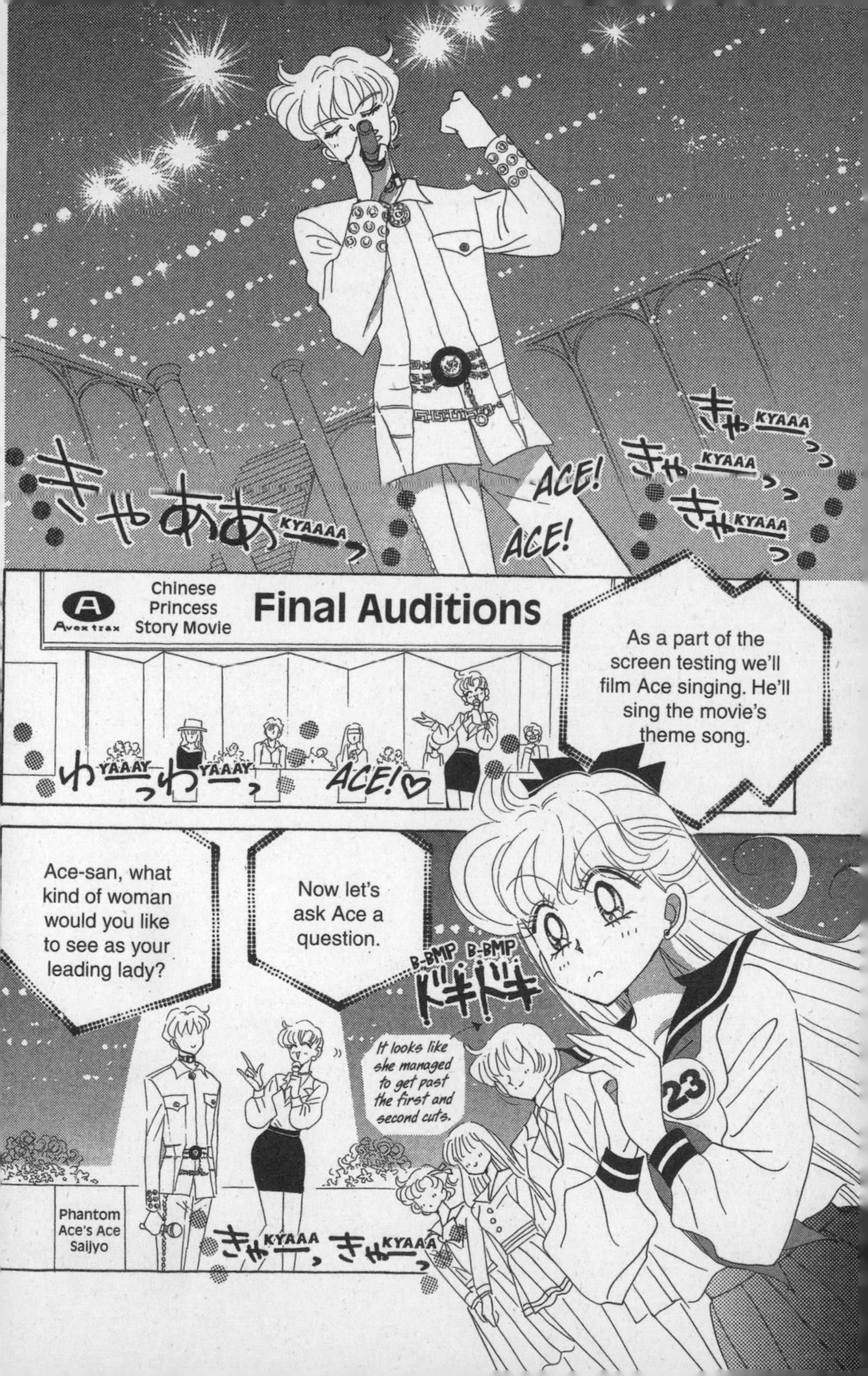

KYAAA
KYAAA
ACE!
KYAAA
ACE!
KYAAAA
As a part of the screen testing we'll film Ace singing. He'll sing the movie's theme song.
Chinese Princess Story Movie Final Auditions
Avex trax
YAAAY YAAAY
ACE!♡
Now let's ask Ace a question.
Ace-san, what kind of woman would you like to see as your leading lady?
B-BMP B-BMP
It looks like she managed to get past the first and second cuts.
23
Phantom Ace's Ace Saijyo
KYAAA KYAAA

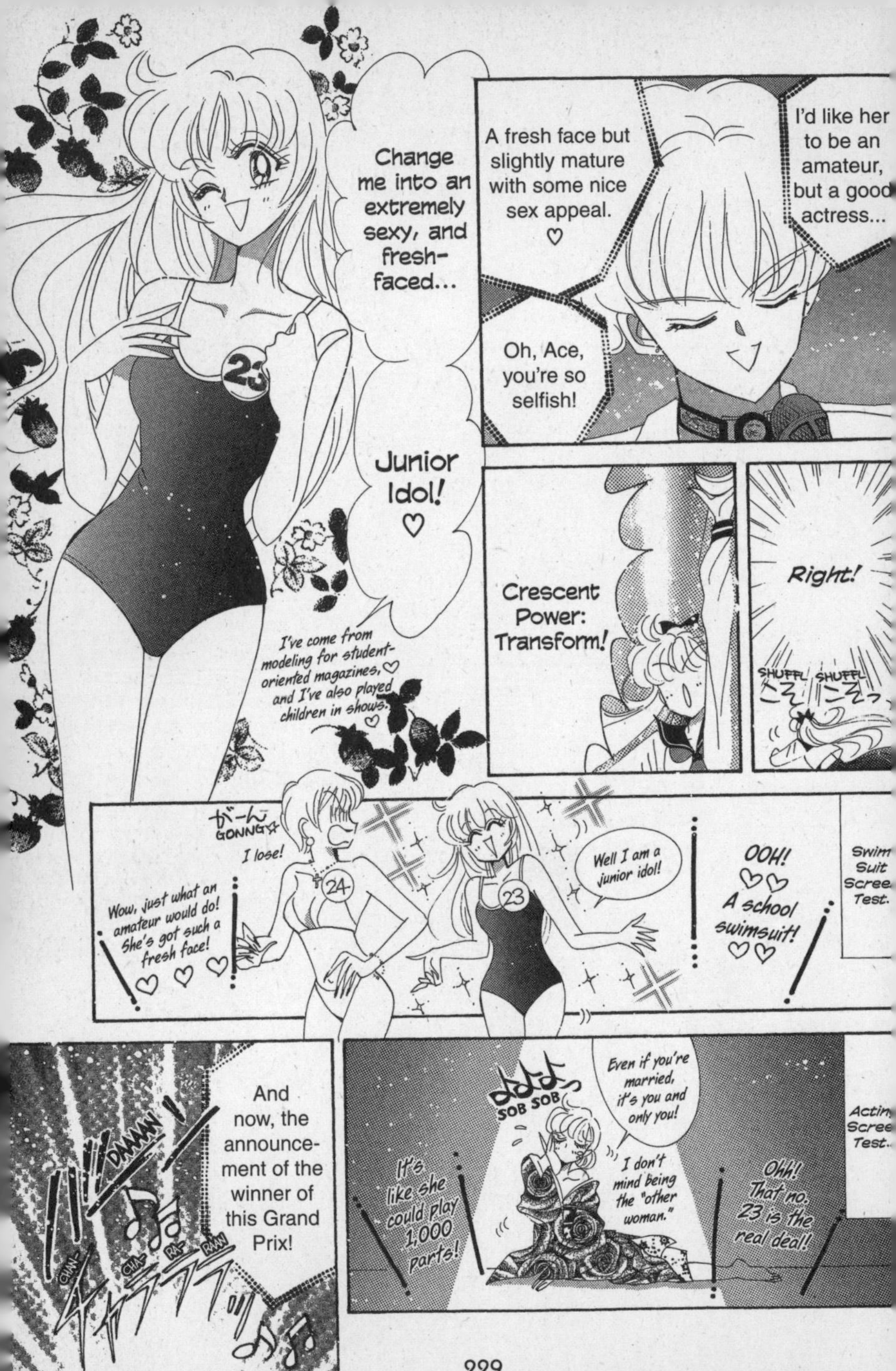
I'd like her to be an amateur, but a good actress...
A fresh face but slightly mature with some nice sex appeal. ♡
Oh, Ace, you're so selfish!
Right!
SHUFFL SHUFFL
こそ こそっ
Crescent Power: Transform!
Change me into an extremely sexy, and fresh-faced...
Junior Idol! ♡
I've come from modeling for student-oriented magazines, ♡ and I've also played children in shows. ♡
Swim Suit Scree Test.
OOH! ♡♡ A school swimsuit! ♡♡
Well I am a junior idol!
がーん
GONNG☆
I lose!
Wow, just what an amateur would do! She's got such a fresh face! ♡ ♡ ♡
Actin Scree Test.
Ohh! That no. 23 is the real deal!
Even if you're married, it's you and only you!
SOB SOB
I don't mind being the "other woman."
It's like she could play 1,000 parts!
And now, the announce-ment of the winner of this Grand Prix!
DAAAN
CHAN CHA RA RAAN

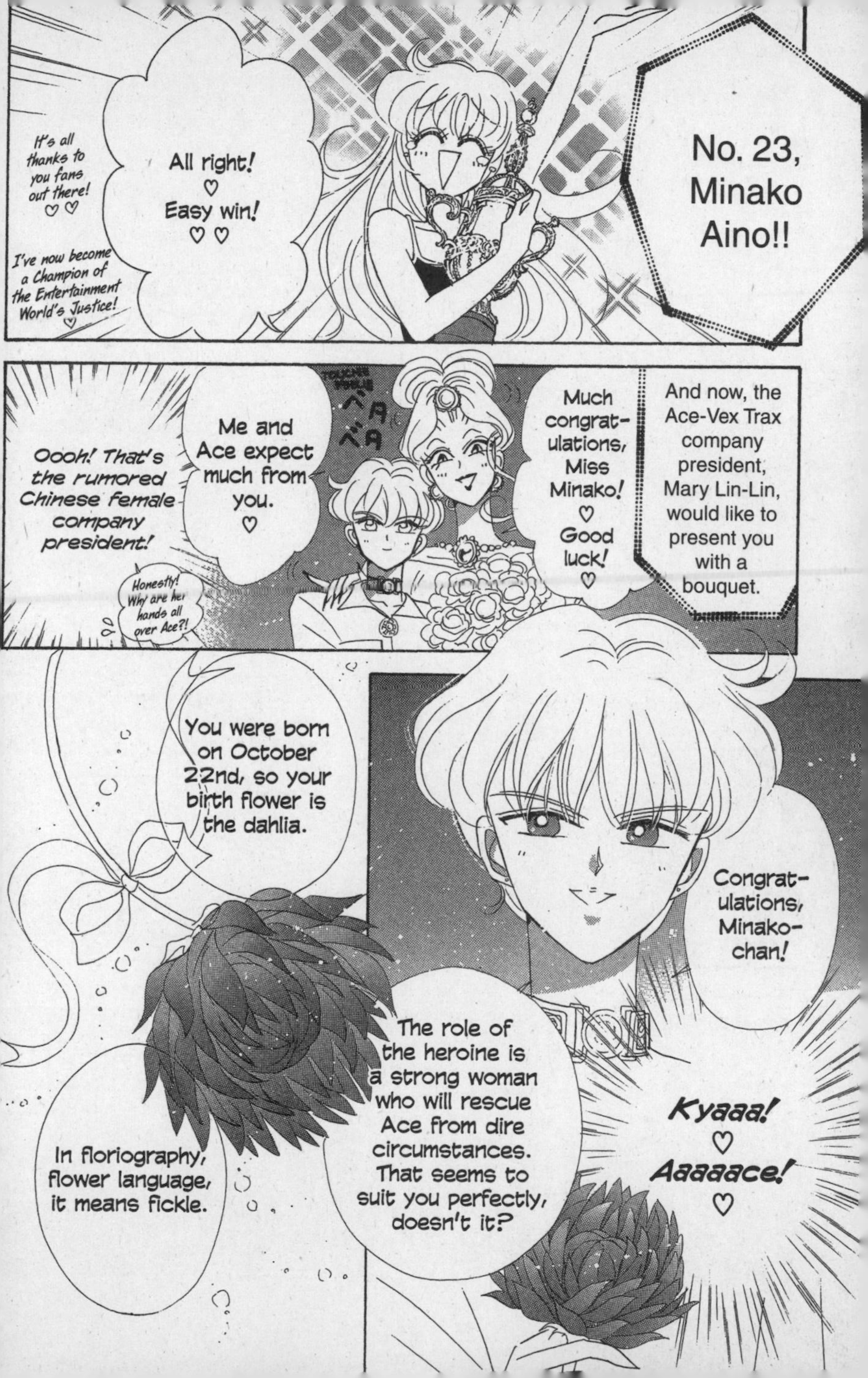
No. 23, Minako Aino!!
All right! ♡ Easy win! ♡ ♡
It's all thanks to you fans out there! ♡ ♡
I've now become a Champion of the Entertainment World's Justice! ♡
And now, the Ace-Vex Trax company president, Mary Lin-Lin, would like to present you with a bouquet.
Much congratulations, Miss Minako! ♡ Good luck! ♡
Me and Ace expect much from you. ♡
Oooh! That's the rumored Chinese female company president!
Honestly! Why are her hands all over Ace?!
Congratulations, Minako-chan!
You were born on October 22nd, so your birth flower is the dahlia.
Kyaaa! ♡ Aaaaace! ♡
The role of the heroine is a strong woman who will rescue Ace from dire circumstances. That seems to suit you perfectly, doesn't it?
In floriography, flower language, it means fickle.

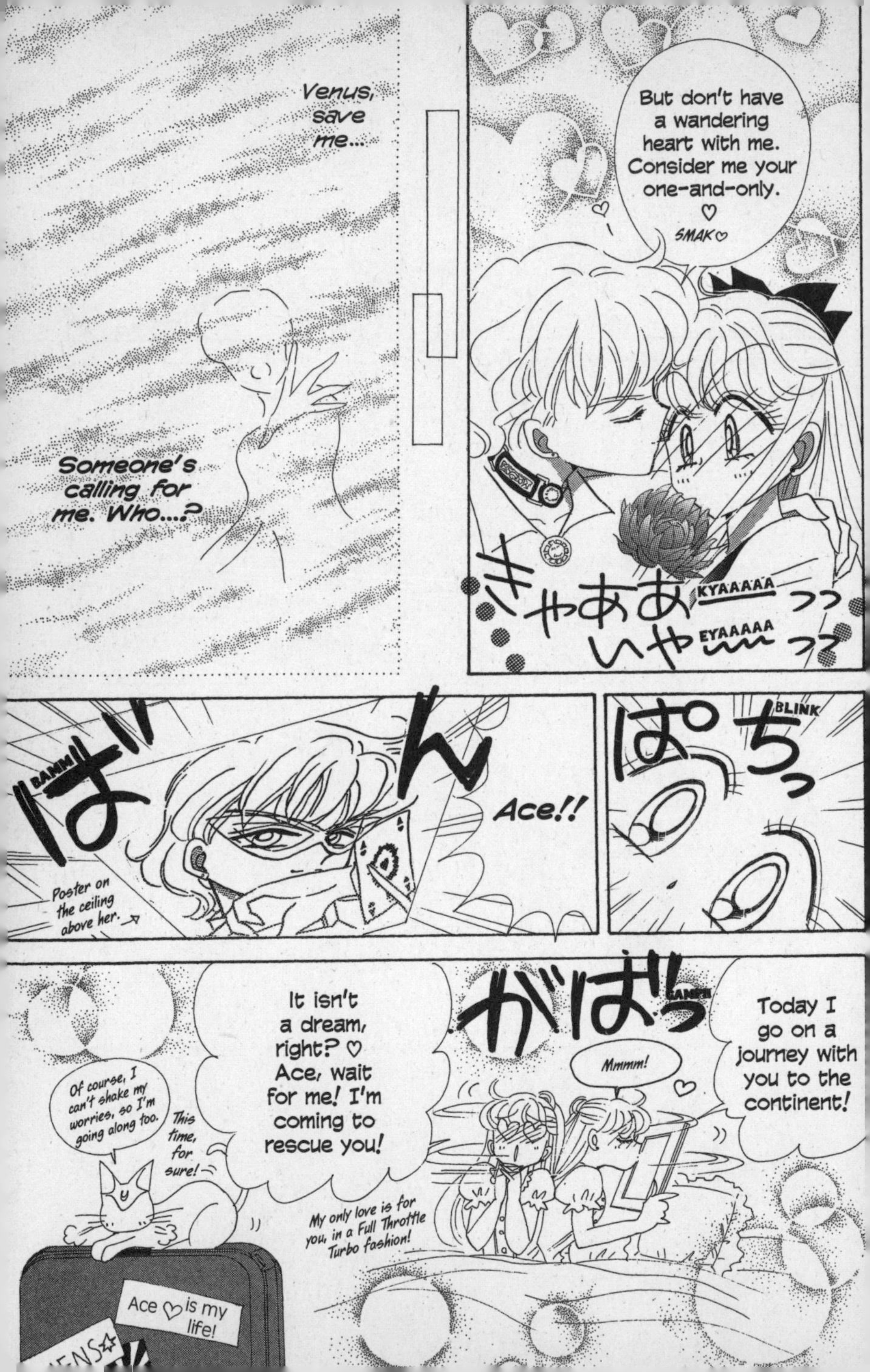

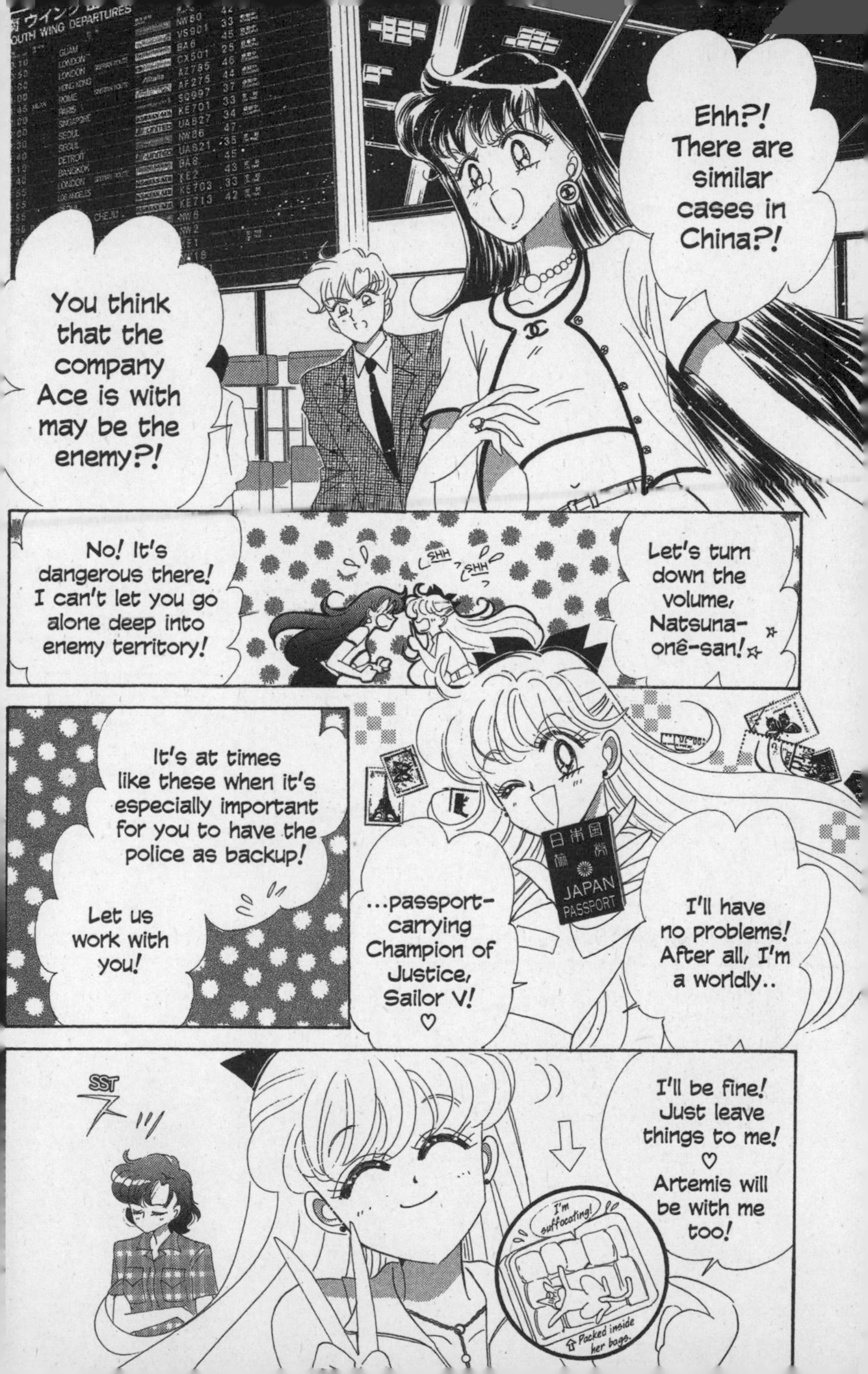
Ehh?! There are similar cases in China?!
You think that the company Ace is with may be the enemy?!
Let's turn down the volume, Natsuna-onê-san! ☆
SHH
SHH
No! It's dangerous there! I can't let you go alone deep into enemy territory!
I'll have no problems! After all, I'm a worldly..
JAPAN PASSPORT
...passport-carrying Champion of Justice, Sailor V! ♡
It's at times like these when it's especially important for you to have the police as backup!
Let us work with you!
I'll be fine! Just leave things to me! ♡ Artemis will be with me too!
I'm suffocating!
Packed inside her bags.
SST

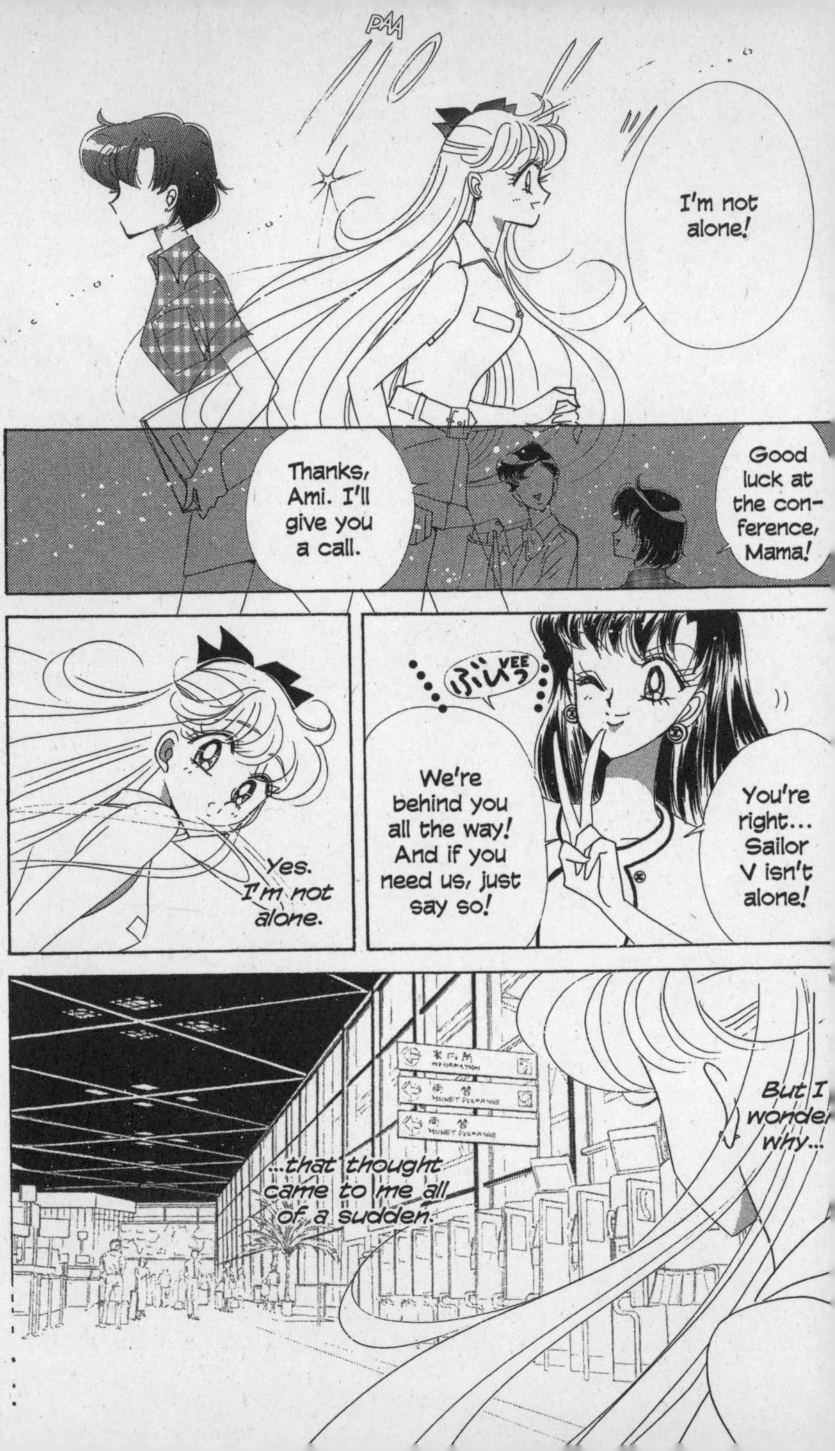
PAA
I'm not alone!
Good luck at the conference, Mama!
Thanks, Ami. I'll give you a call.
You're right... Sailor V isn't alone!
ぶいっ VEE
We're behind you all the way! And if you need us, just say so!
Yes. I'm not alone.
But I wonde why...
...that thought came to me all of a sudden.

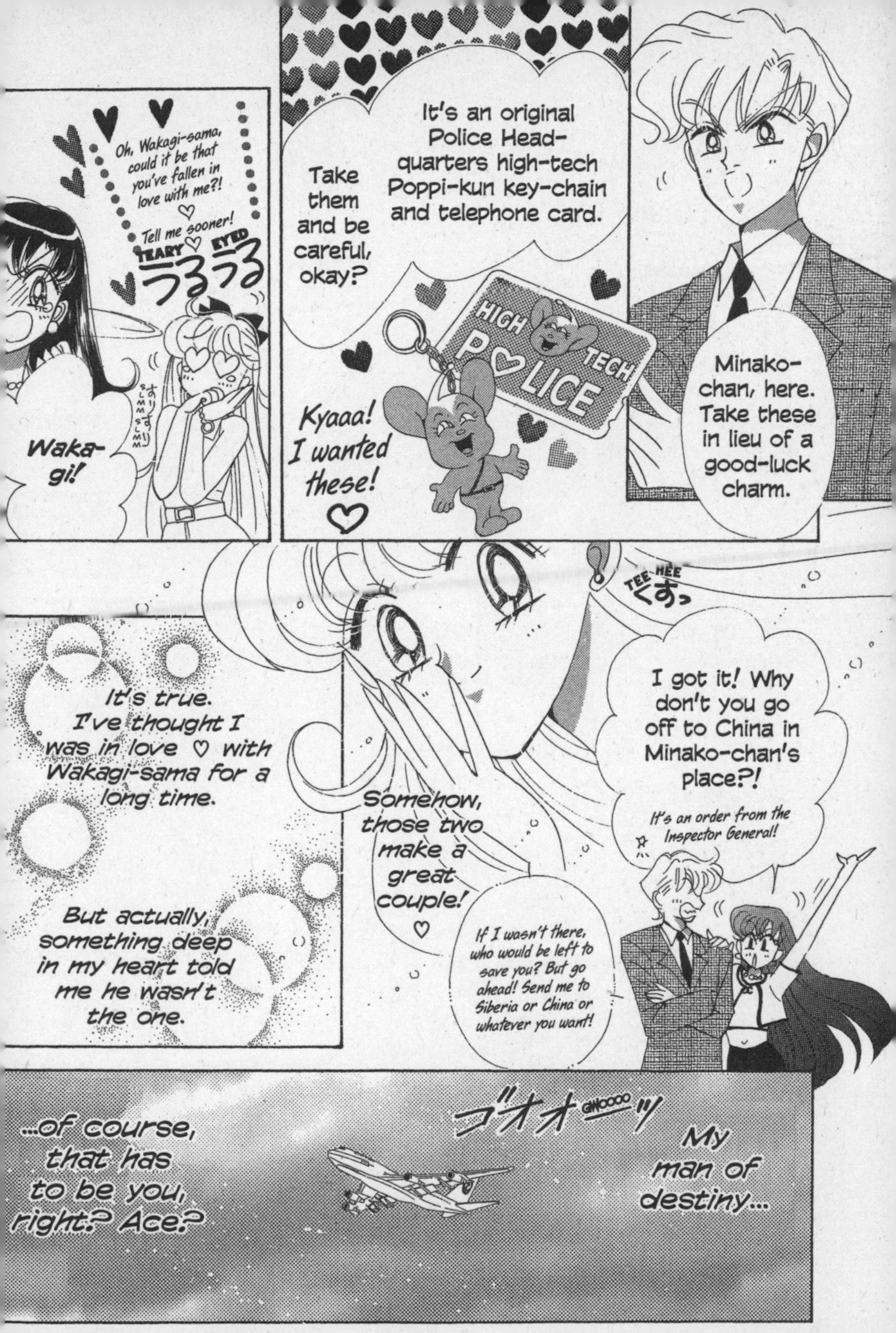
Minako-chan, here. Take these in lieu of a good-luck charm.
It's an original Police Head-quarters high-tech Poppi-kun key-chain and telephone card.
Take them and be careful, okay?
HIGH TECH POLICE
Kyaaa! I wanted these! ♡
Oh, Wakagi-sama, could it be that you've fallen in love with me?! ♡
Tell me sooner!
TEARY ♡ EYED うるうる
Wakagi!
TEE HEE くすっ
I got it! Why don't you go off to China in Minako-chan's place?!
It's an order from the Inspector General!
If I wasn't there, who would be left to save you? But go ahead! Send me to Siberia or China or whatever you want!
Somehow, those two make a great couple! ♡
It's true. I've thought I was in love ♡ with Wakagi-sama for a long time.
But actually, something deep in my heart told me he wasn't the one.
ゴオオ GWOOOO
My man of destiny...
...of course, that has to be you, right? Ace?

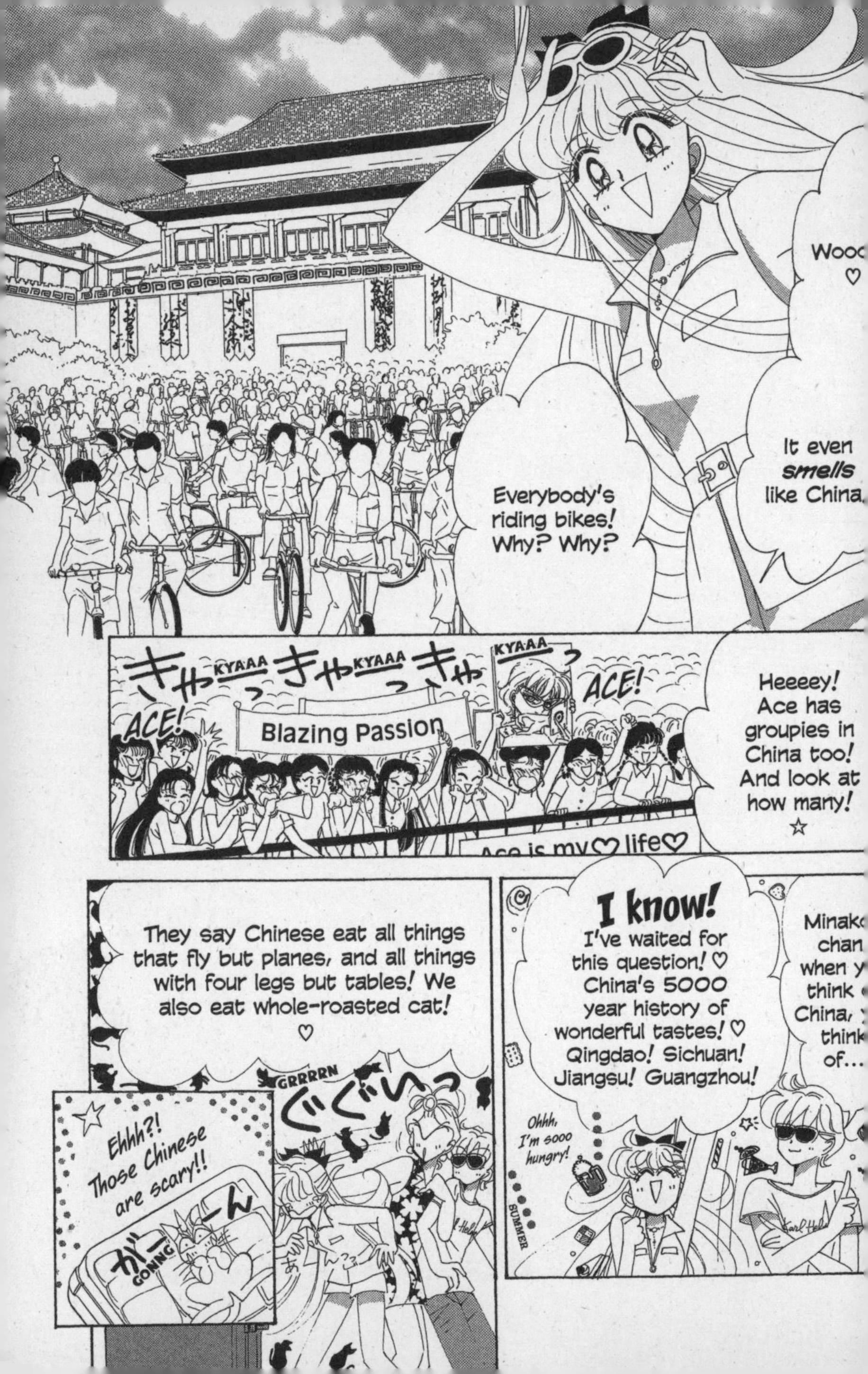
Wooo ♡
It even *smells* like China.
Everybody's riding bikes! Why? Why?
Heeeey! Ace has groupies in China too! And look at how many! ☆
KYA-AA
ACE!
KYAAA
KYAAA
ACE!
Blazing Passion
Ace is my♡ life♡
Minako chan when y think China, think of...
I know!
I've waited for this question! ♡ China's 5000 year history of wonderful tastes! ♡ Qingdao! Sichuan! Jiangsu! Guangzhou!
Ohhh, I'm sooo hungry!
SUMMER
They say Chinese eat all things that fly but planes, and all things with four legs but tables! We also eat whole-roasted cat! ♡
GRRRRN
Ehhh?! Those Chinese are scary!!
GONNG

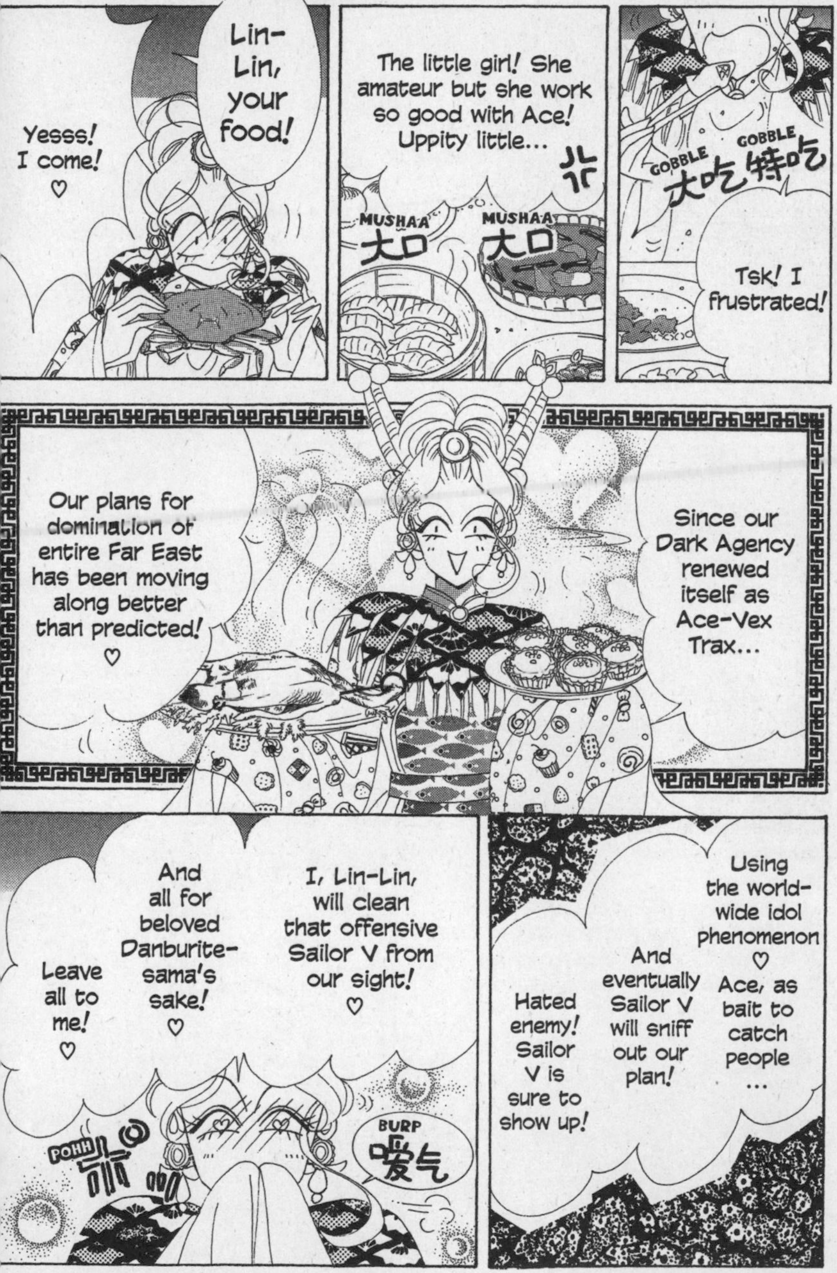
GOBBLE
GOBBLE
大吃特吃
Tsk! I frustrated!
The little girl! She amateur but she work so good with Ace! Uppity little...
MUSHA'A
大口
MUSHA'A
大口
Lin-Lin, your food!
Yesss! I come! ♡
Since our Dark Agency renewed itself as Ace-Vex Trax...
Our plans for domination of entire Far East has been moving along better than predicted! ♡
Using the world-wide idol phenomenon ♡ Ace, as bait to catch people ...
And eventually Sailor V will sniff out our plan!
Hated enemy! Sailor V is sure to show up!
I, Lin-Lin, will clean that offensive Sailor V from our sight! ♡
And all for beloved Danburite-sama's sake! ♡
Leave all to me! ♡
BURP
嗳气
POHH

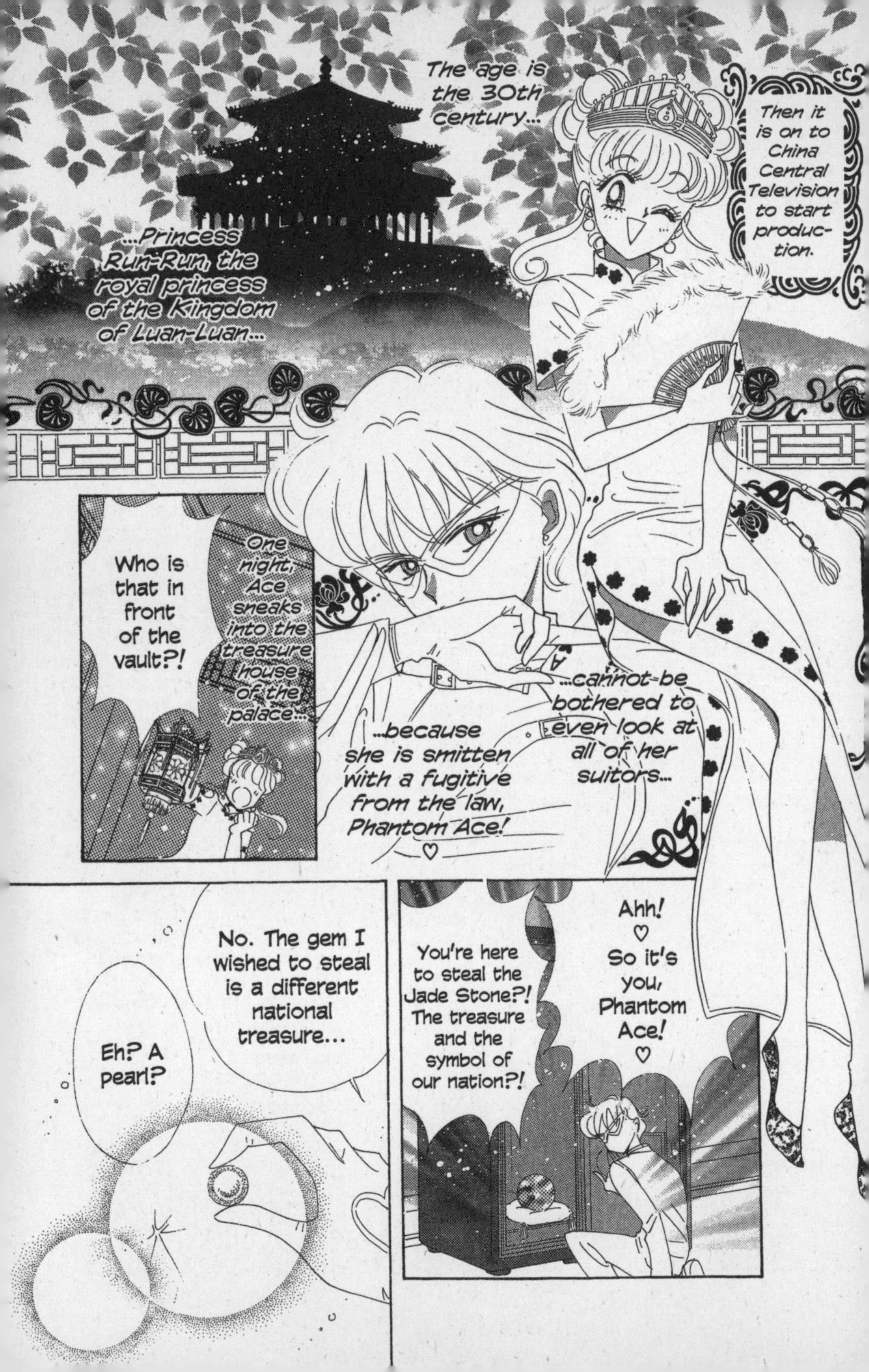
Then it is on to China Central Television to start production.
The age is the 30th century...
...Princess Run-Run, the royal princess of the Kingdom of Luan-Luan...
...cannot be bothered to even look at all of her suitors...
...because she is smitten with a fugitive from the law, Phantom Ace! ♡
One night, Ace sneaks into the treasure house of the palace...
Who is that in front of the vault?!
Ahh! ♡ So it's you, Phantom Ace! ♡
You're here to steal the Jade Stone?! The treasure and the symbol of our nation?!
No. The gem I wished to steal is a different national treasure...
Eh? A pearl?

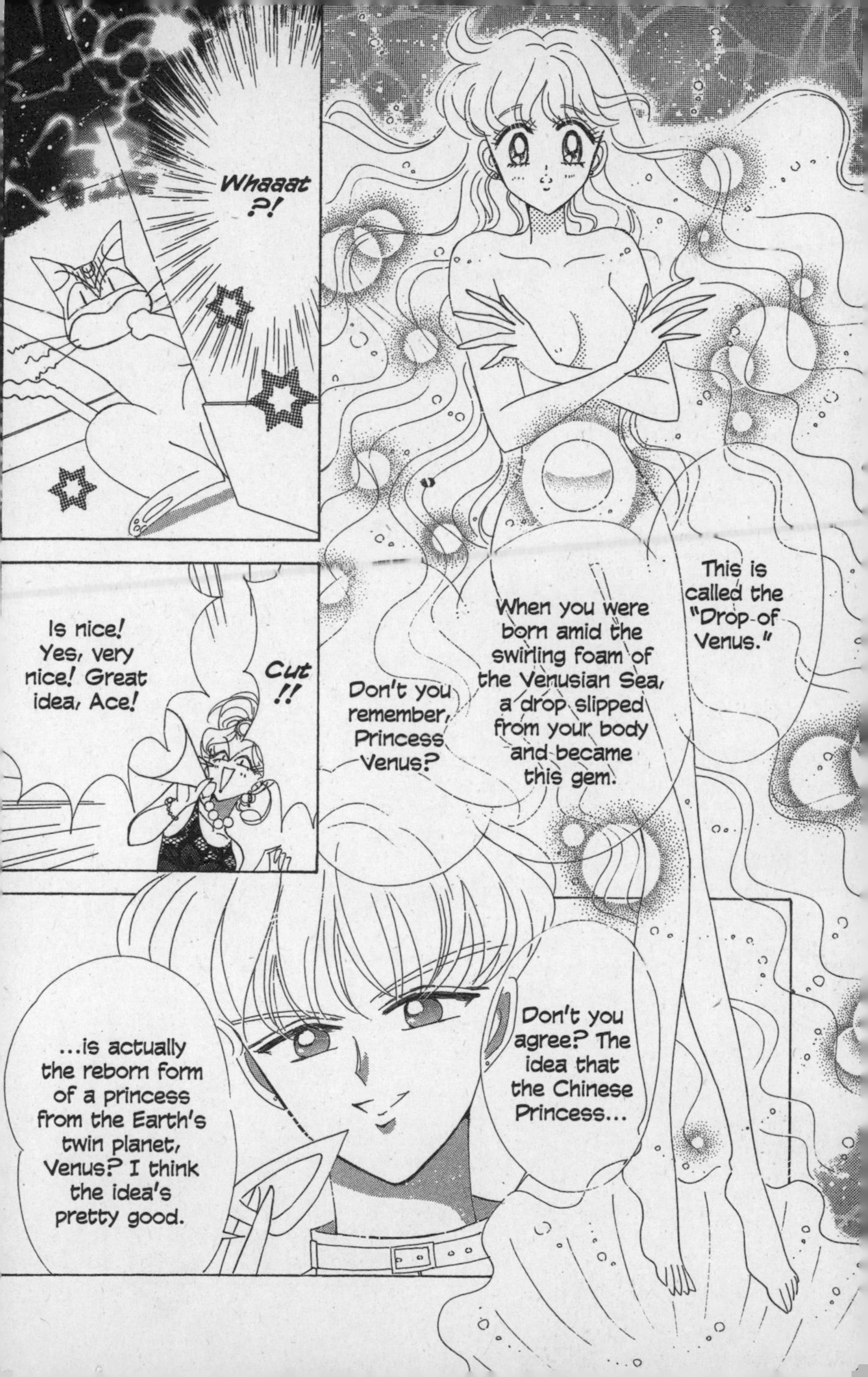
This is called the "Drop of Venus."
When you were born amid the swirling foam of the Venusian Sea, a drop slipped from your body and became this gem.
Don't you remember, Princess Venus?
Whaaat ?!
Cut !!
Is nice! Yes, very nice! Great idea, Ace!
Don't you agree? The idea that the Chinese Princess...
...is actually the reborn form of a princess from the Earth's twin planet, Venus? I think the idea's pretty good.

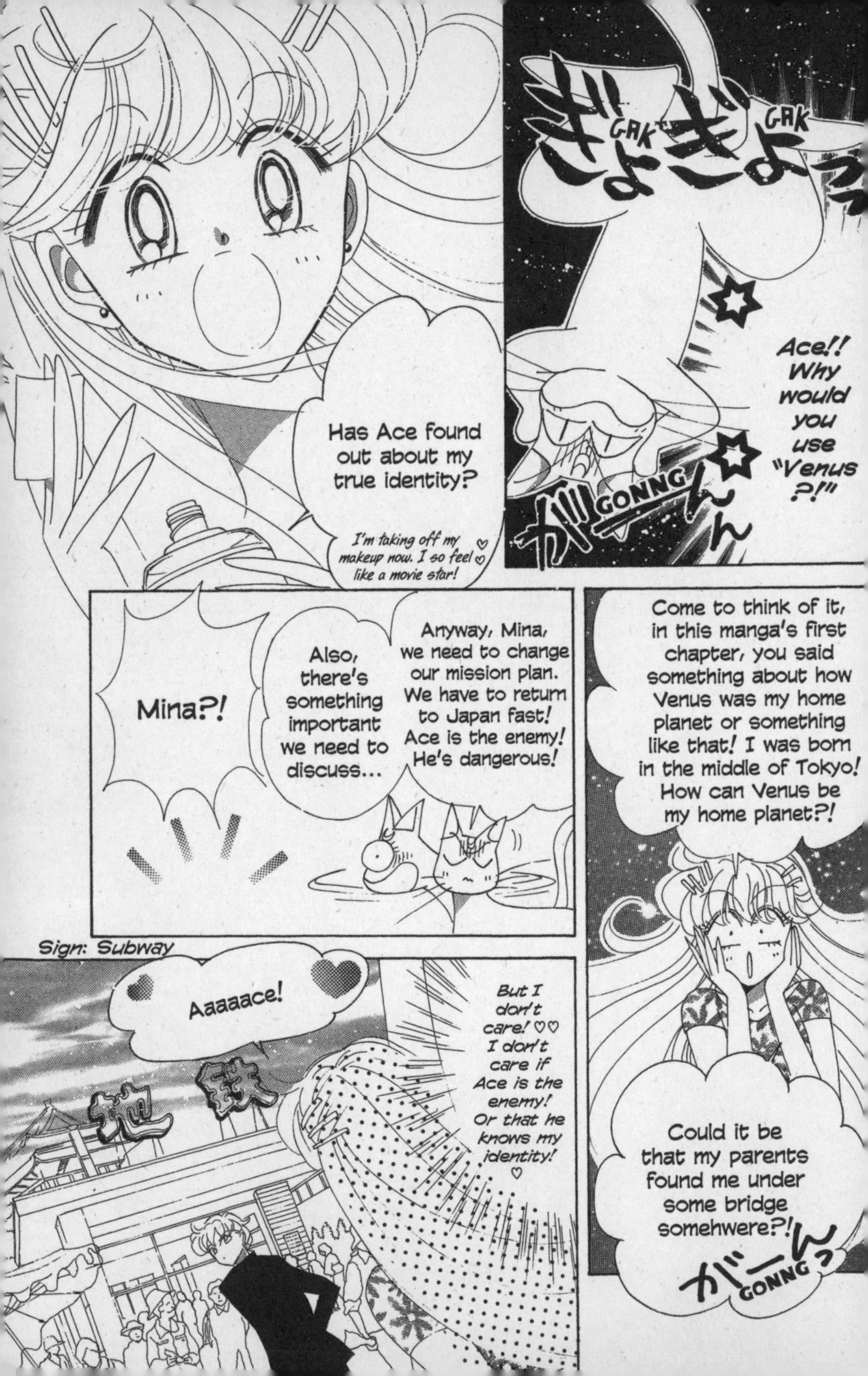

GAK GAK
Ace!! Why would you use "Venus?!"
GONNG
Has Ace found out about my true identity?
I'm taking off my makeup now. I so feel like a movie star! ♡♡
Come to think of it, in this manga's first chapter, you said something about how Venus was my home planet or something like that! I was born in the middle of Tokyo! How can Venus be my home planet?!
Could it be that my parents found me under some bridge somehwere?!
GONNG
Anyway, Mina, we need to change our mission plan. We have to return to Japan fast! Ace is the enemy! He's dangerous!
Also, there's something important we need to discuss...
Mina?!
Sign: Subway
But I don't care! ♡♡ I don't care if Ace is the enemy! Or that he knows my identity! ♡
Aaaaace!

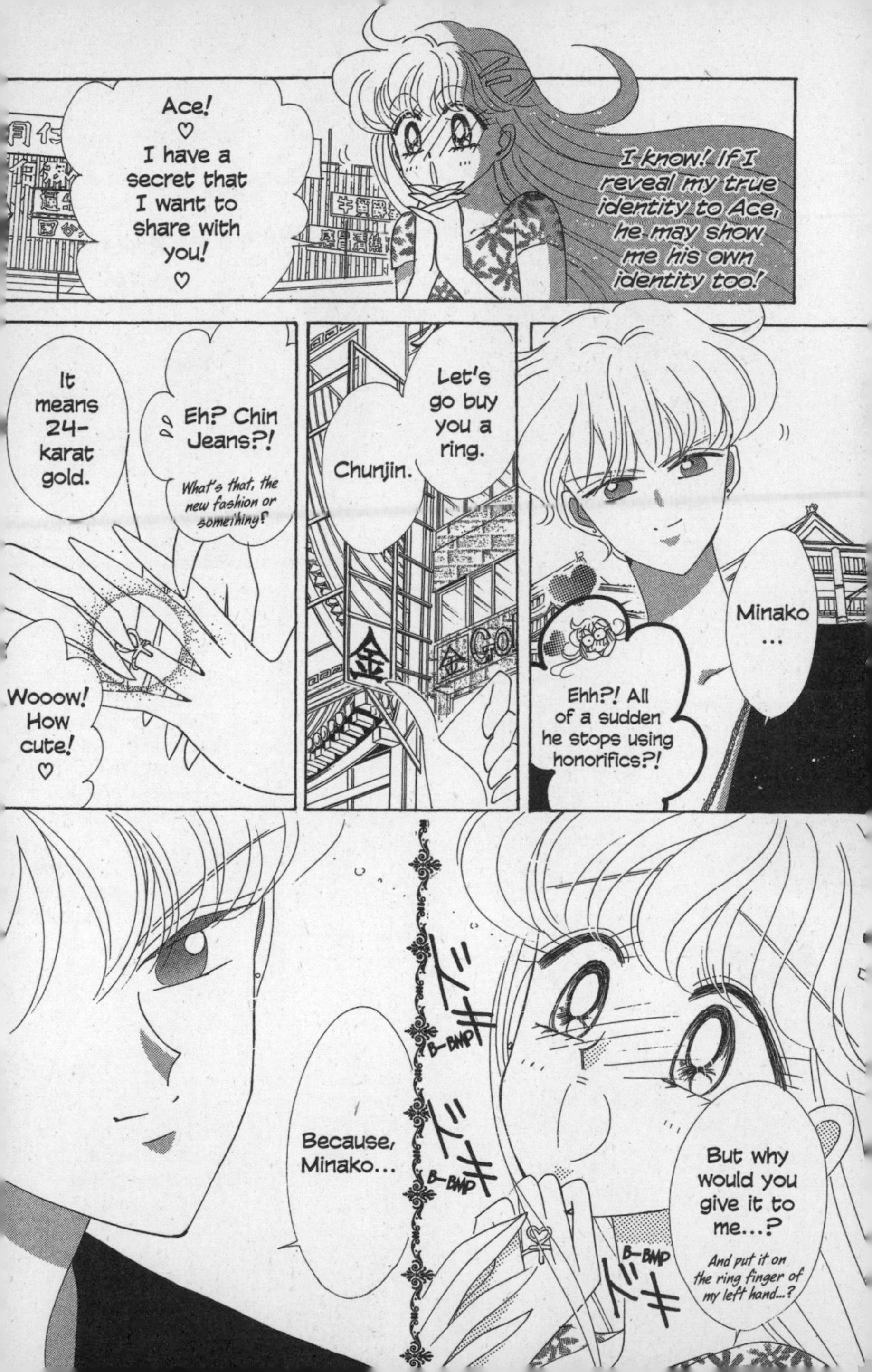
I know! If I reveal my true identity to Ace, he may show me his own identity too!
Ace! ♡ I have a secret that I want to share with you! ♡
Minako...
Ehh?! All of a sudden he stops using honorifics?!
Let's go buy you a ring.
Chunjin.
Eh? Chin Jeans?!
What's that, the new fashion or something?
It means 24-karat gold.
Wooow! How cute! ♡
But why would you give it to me...?
And put it on the ring finger of my left hand...?
B-BMP
B-BMP
B-BMP
Because, Minako...

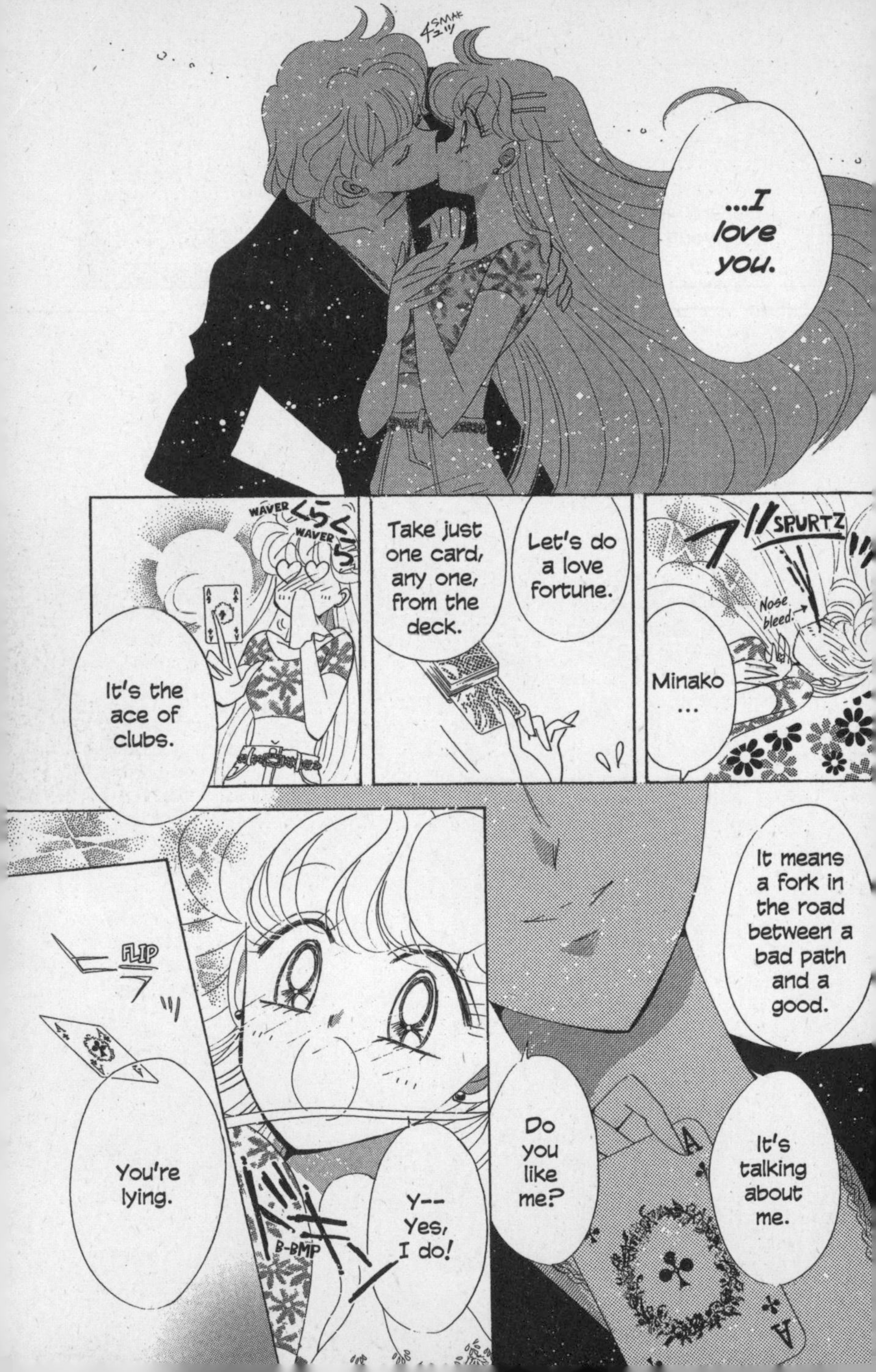
SMAK
...I love you.
SPURTZ
Nose bleed.
Minako ...
Let's do a love fortune.
Take just one card, any one, from the deck.
WAVER WAVER
It's the ace of clubs.
It means a fork in the road between a bad path and a good.
It's talking about me.
Do you like me?
Y-- Yes, I do!
B-BMP
FLIP
You're lying.

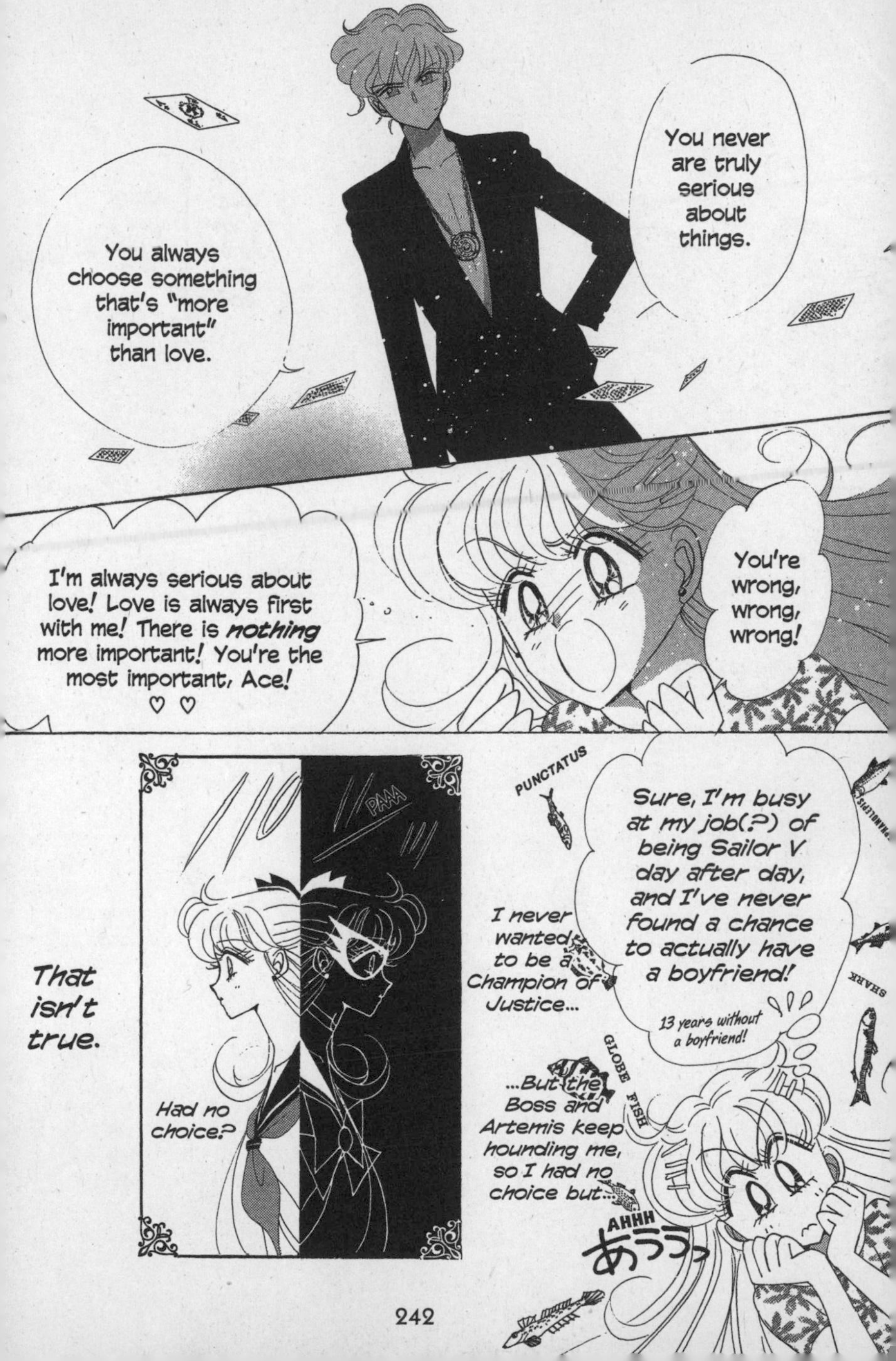
You never are truly serious about things.
You always choose something that's "more important" than love.
You're wrong, wrong, wrong!
I'm always serious about love! Love is always first with me! There is ***nothing*** more important! You're the most important, Ace! ♡ ♡
Sure, I'm busy at my job(?) of being Sailor V day after day, and I've never found a chance to actually have a boyfriend!
13 years without a boyfriend!
PUNCTATUS
SHARK
I never wanted to be a Champion of Justice...
GLOBE FISH
...But the Boss and Artemis keep hounding me, so I had no choice but...
AHHH
あううっ
PAAA
Had no choice?
That isn't true.

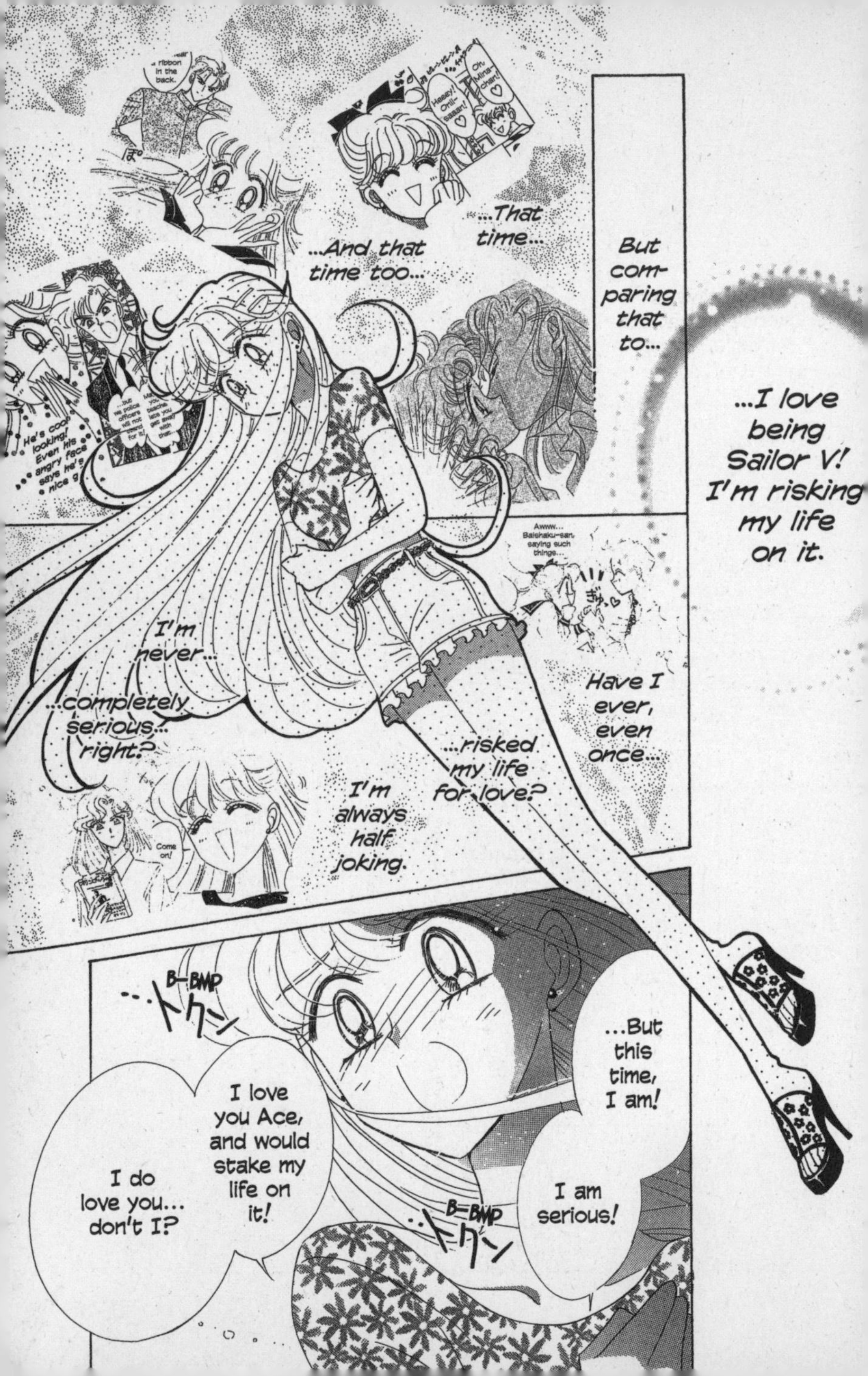
...I love being Sailor V! I'm risking my life on it.
But comparing that to...
...That time...
Heeey! Onii-saaan! ♡
Oh, Mina-chan! ♡
a ribbon in the back.
...And that time too...
He's cool looking! Even his angry face says he's nice g
Have I ever, even once...
Aww... Baishaku-san, saying such things...
...risked my life for love?
I'm never...
...completely serious... right?
I'm always half joking.
Come on!
...But this time, I am!
B-BMP
I am serious!
B-BMP
I love you Ace, and would stake my life on it!
I do love you... don't I?

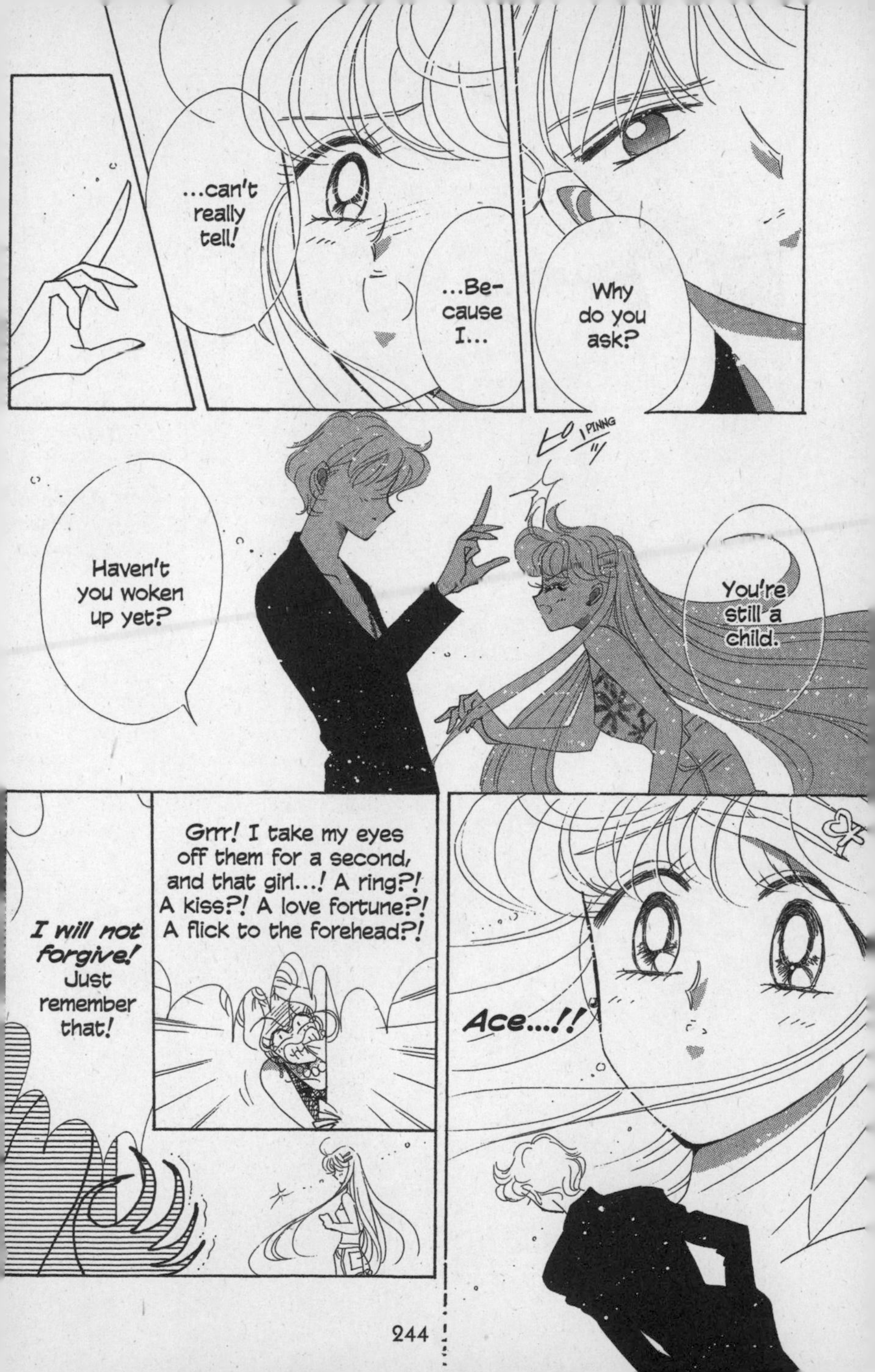
Why do you ask?
...Be-cause I...
...can't really tell!
PINNG
You're still a child.
Haven't you woken up yet?
Ace...!!
Grrr! I take my eyes off them for a second, and that girl...! A ring?! A kiss?! A love fortune?! A flick to the forehead?!
I will not forgive! Just remember that!

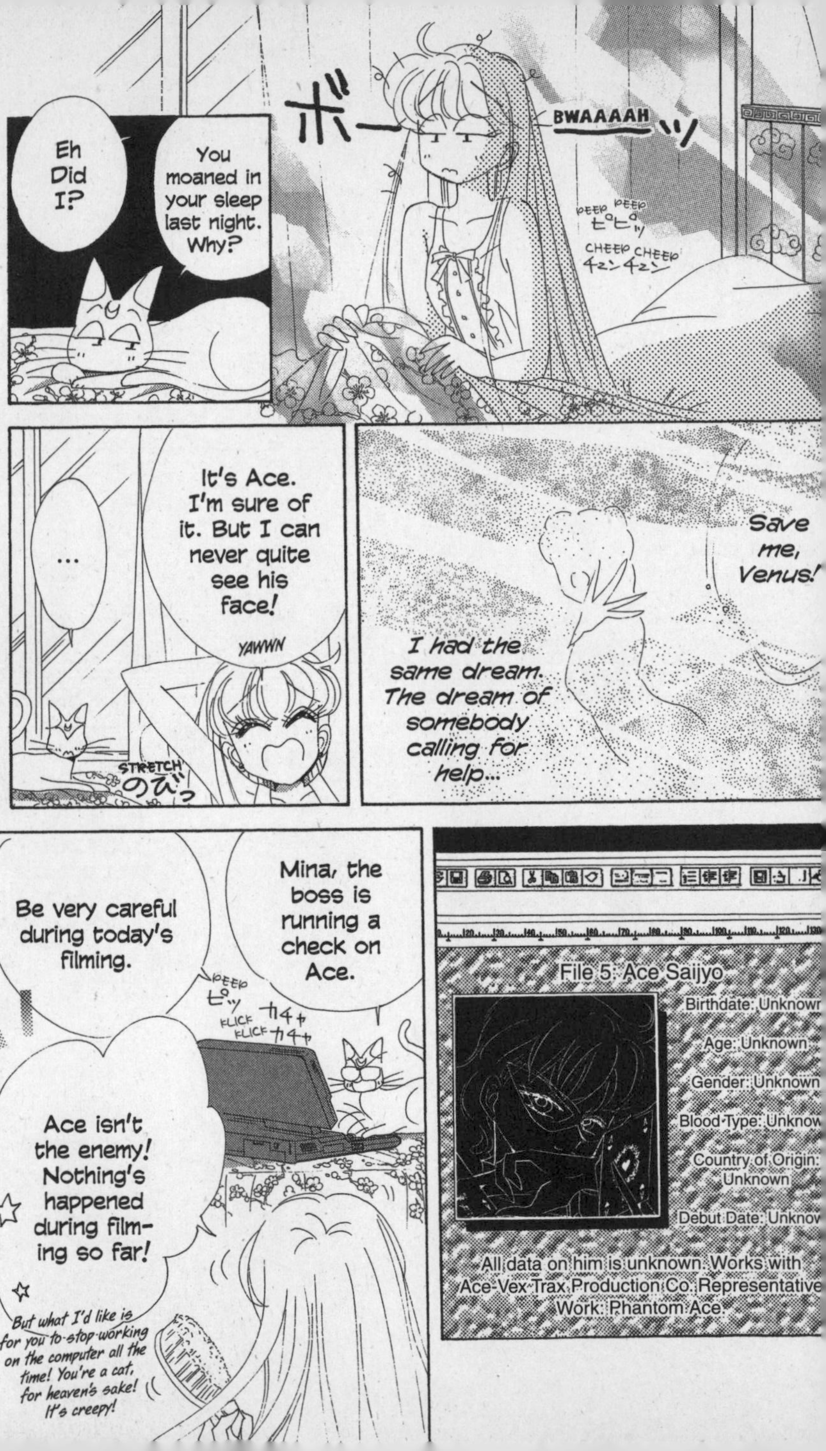

ボー
BWAAAAH ッ
PEEP PEEP ピピッ
CHEEP CHEEP チュンチュン
You moaned in your sleep last night. Why?
Eh Did I?
Save me, Venus!
I had the same dream. The dream of somebody calling for help...
It's Ace. I'm sure of it. But I can never quite see his face!
YAWWN
...
STRETCH のびっ
File 5: Ace Saijyo
Birthdate: Unknow
Age: Unknown
Gender: Unknown
Blood Type: Unknow
Country of Origin: Unknown
Debut Date: Unknow
All data on him is unknown. Works with Ace-Vex Trax Production Co. Representative Work: Phantom Ace.
Mina, the boss is running a check on Ace.
Be very careful during today's filming.
PEEP ピッ
KLICK カチャ KLICK カチャ
Ace isn't the enemy! Nothing's happened during filming so far!
But what I'd like is for you to stop working on the computer all the time! You're a cat, for heaven's sake! It's creepy!

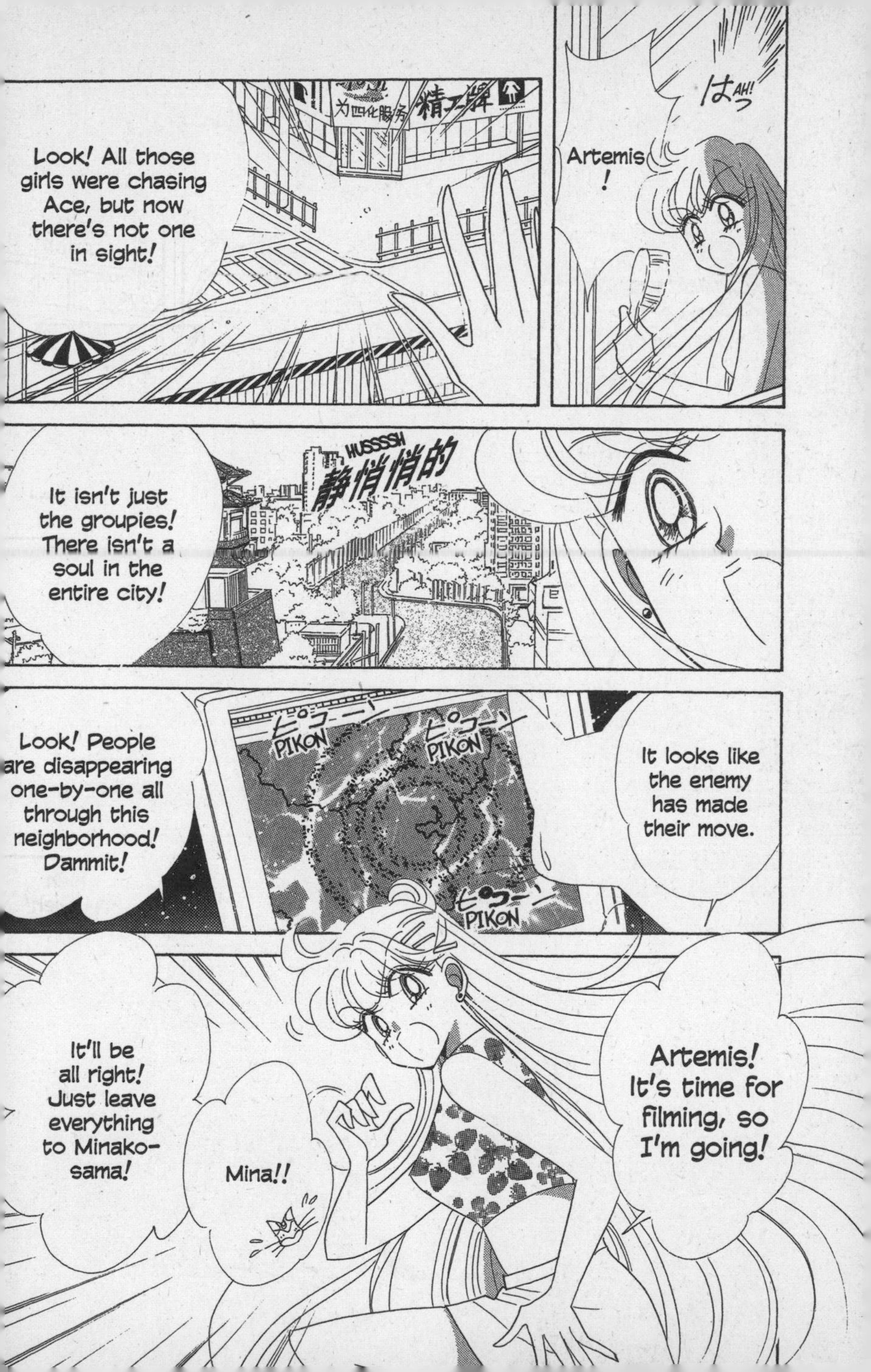

はっ AH!
Artemis!
为四化服务 精工牌
Look! All those girls were chasing Ace, but now there's not one in sight!
HUSSSSH 静悄悄的
It isn't just the groupies! There isn't a soul in the entire city!
It looks like the enemy has made their move.
ピコーン PIKON
ピコーン PIKON
ピコーン PIKON
Look! People are disappearing one-by-one all through this neighborhood! Dammit!
Artemis! It's time for filming, so I'm going!
Mina!!
It'll be all right! Just leave everything to Minako-sama!

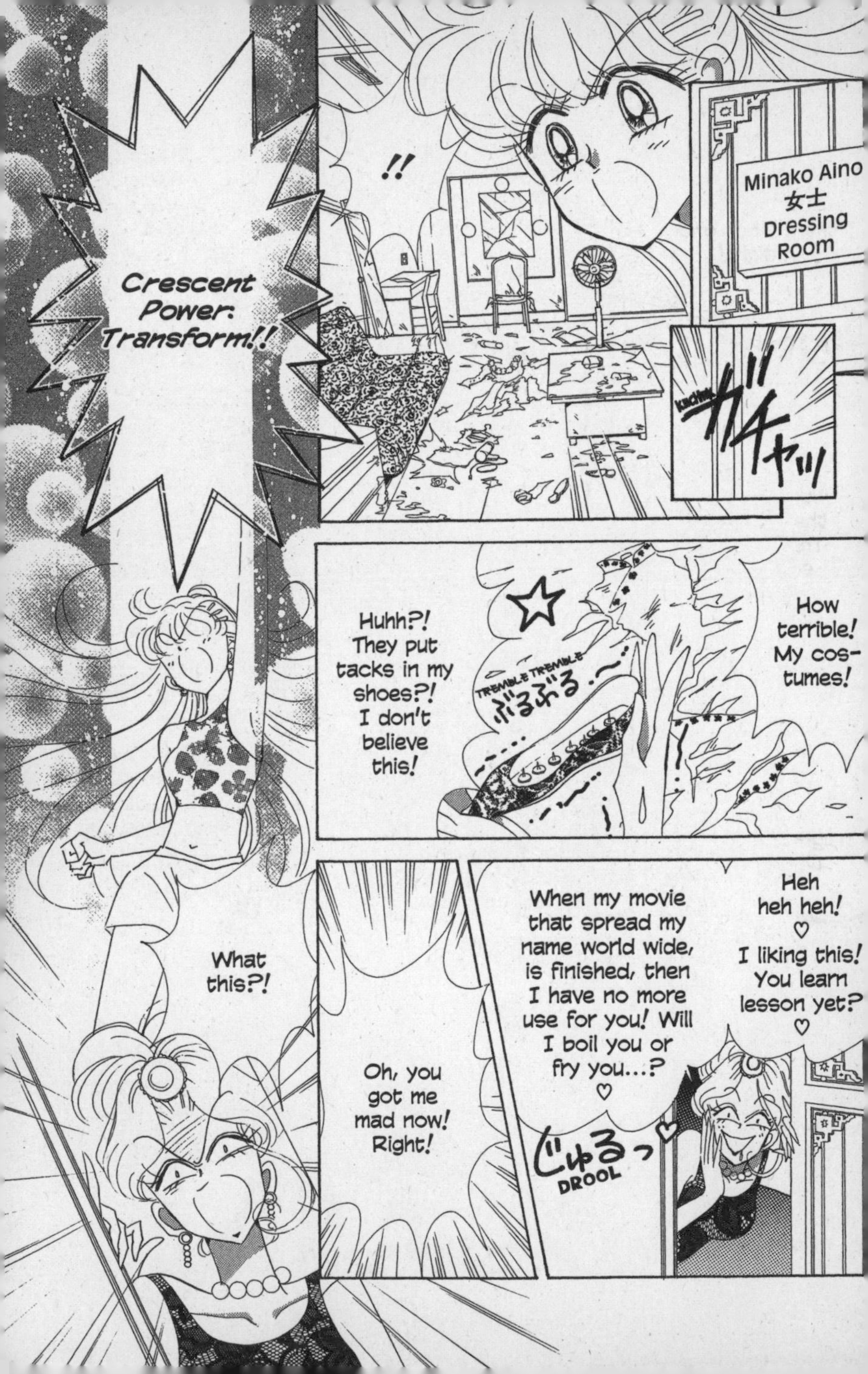

Minako Aino
女士
Dressing
Room
KACHAK
ガチャッ
!!
How terrible! My costumes!
Huhh?! They put tacks in my shoes?! I don't believe this!
TREMBLE TREMBLE
ぶるぶる
Heh heh heh! ♡ I liking this! You learn lesson yet? ♡
When my movie that spread my name world wide, is finished, then I have no more use for you! Will I boil you or fry you...? ♡
じゅるっ
DROOL
Oh, you got me mad now! Right!
What this?!
Crescent Power: Transform!!

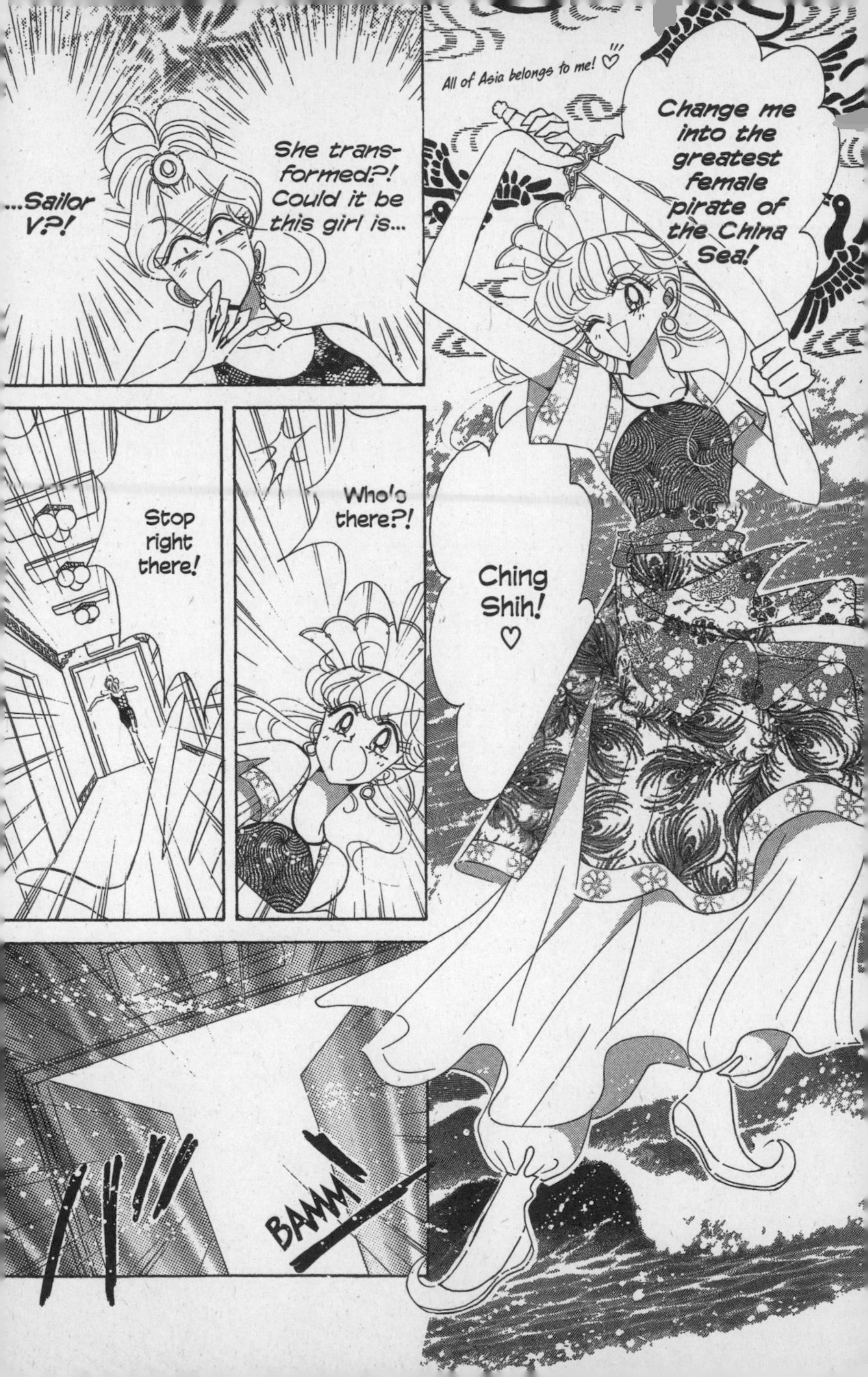
Change me into the greatest female pirate of the China Sea!
All of Asia belongs to me! ♡
Ching Shih! ♡
She transformed?! Could it be this girl is...
...Sailor V?!
Who's there?!
Stop right there!
BAMM

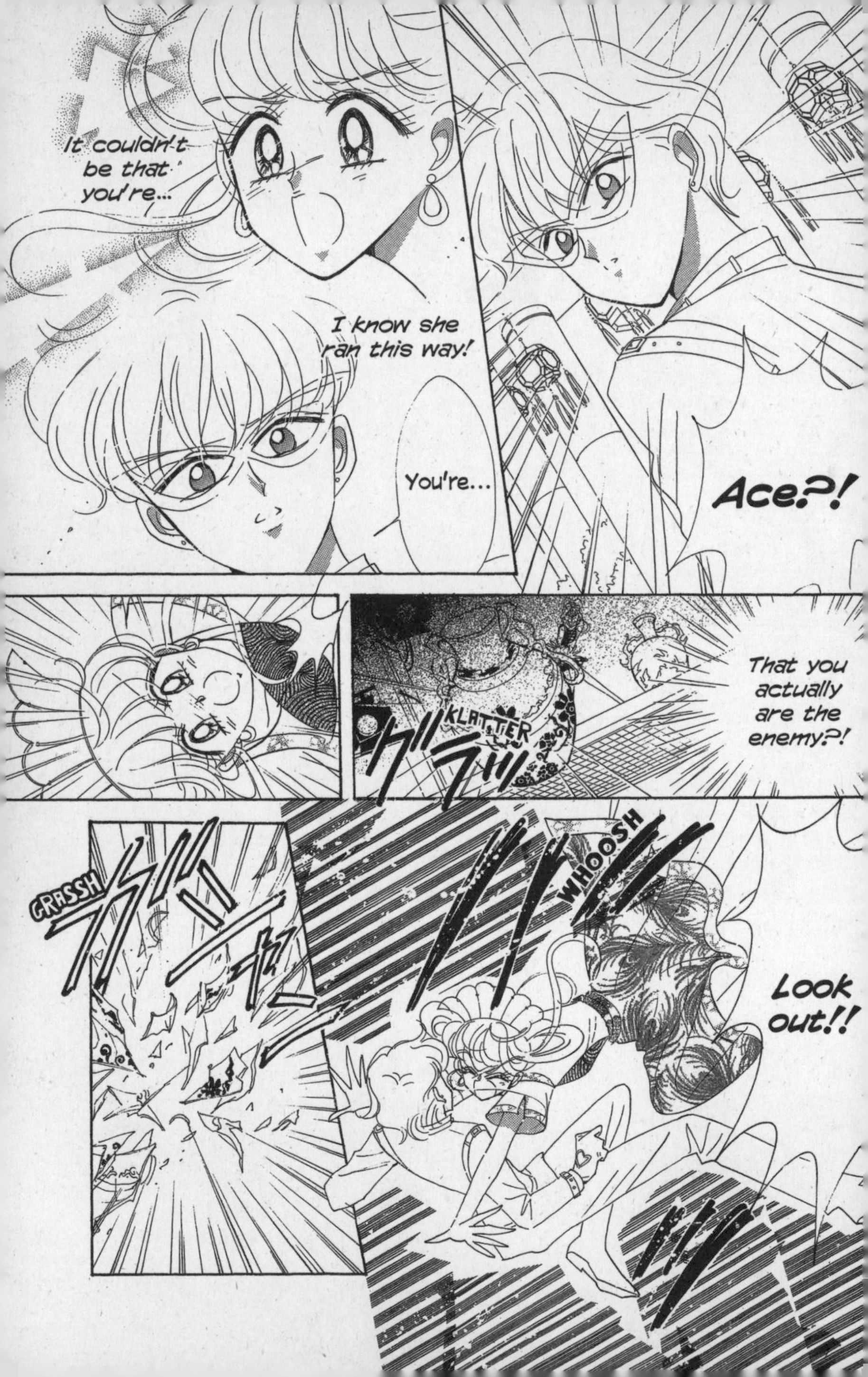
It couldn't be that you're...
I know she ran this way!
You're...
Ace?!
KLATTER
That you actually are the enemy?!
WHOOSH
Look out!!
GRASSH

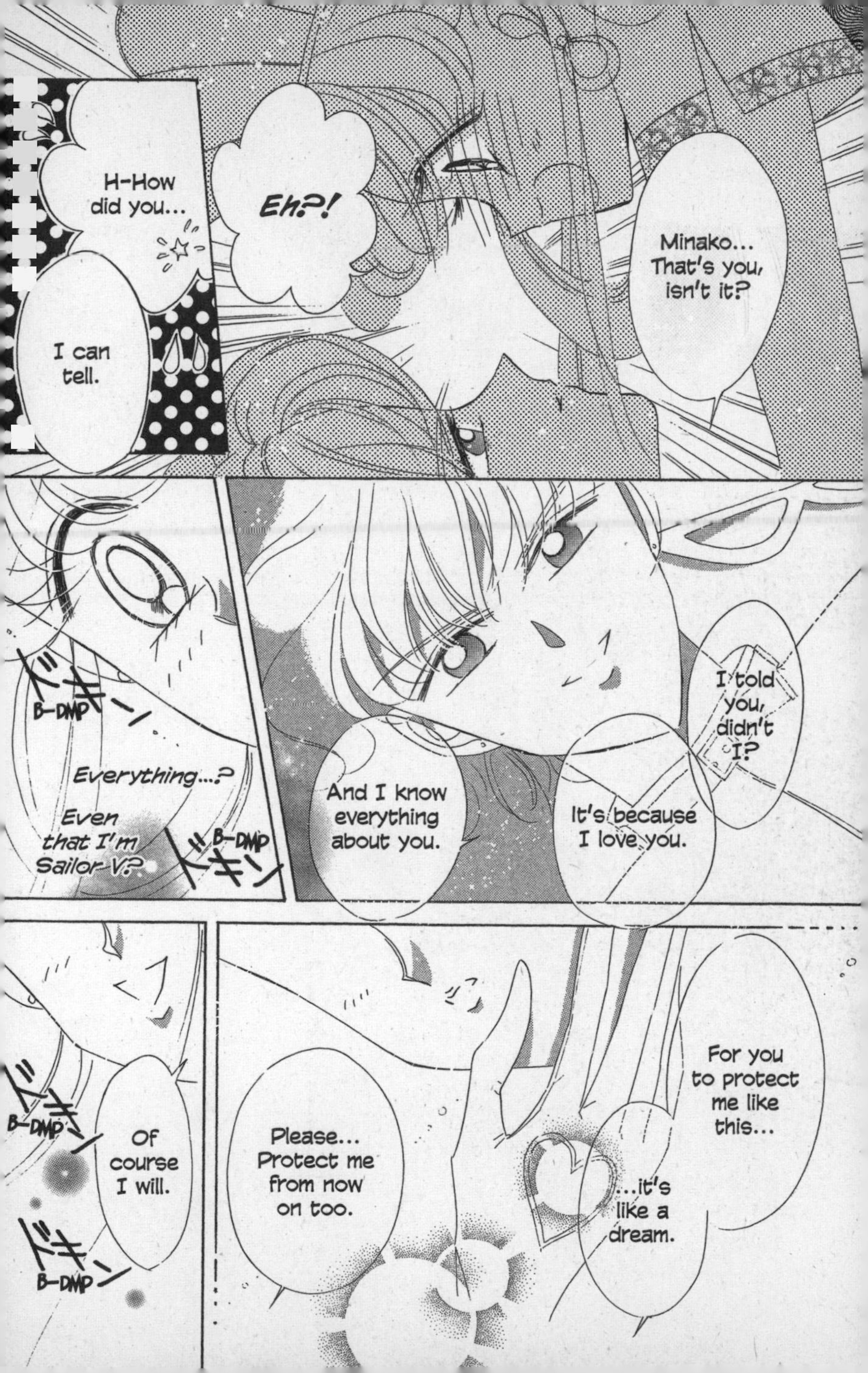
Minako... That's you, isn't it?
Eh?!
H-How did you...
I can tell.
I told you, didn't I?
It's because I love you.
And I know everything about you.
B-DMP
Everything...?
Even that I'm Sailor V?
B-DMP
For you to protect me like this...
...it's like a dream.
Please... Protect me from now on too.
B-DMP
Of course I will.
B-DMP

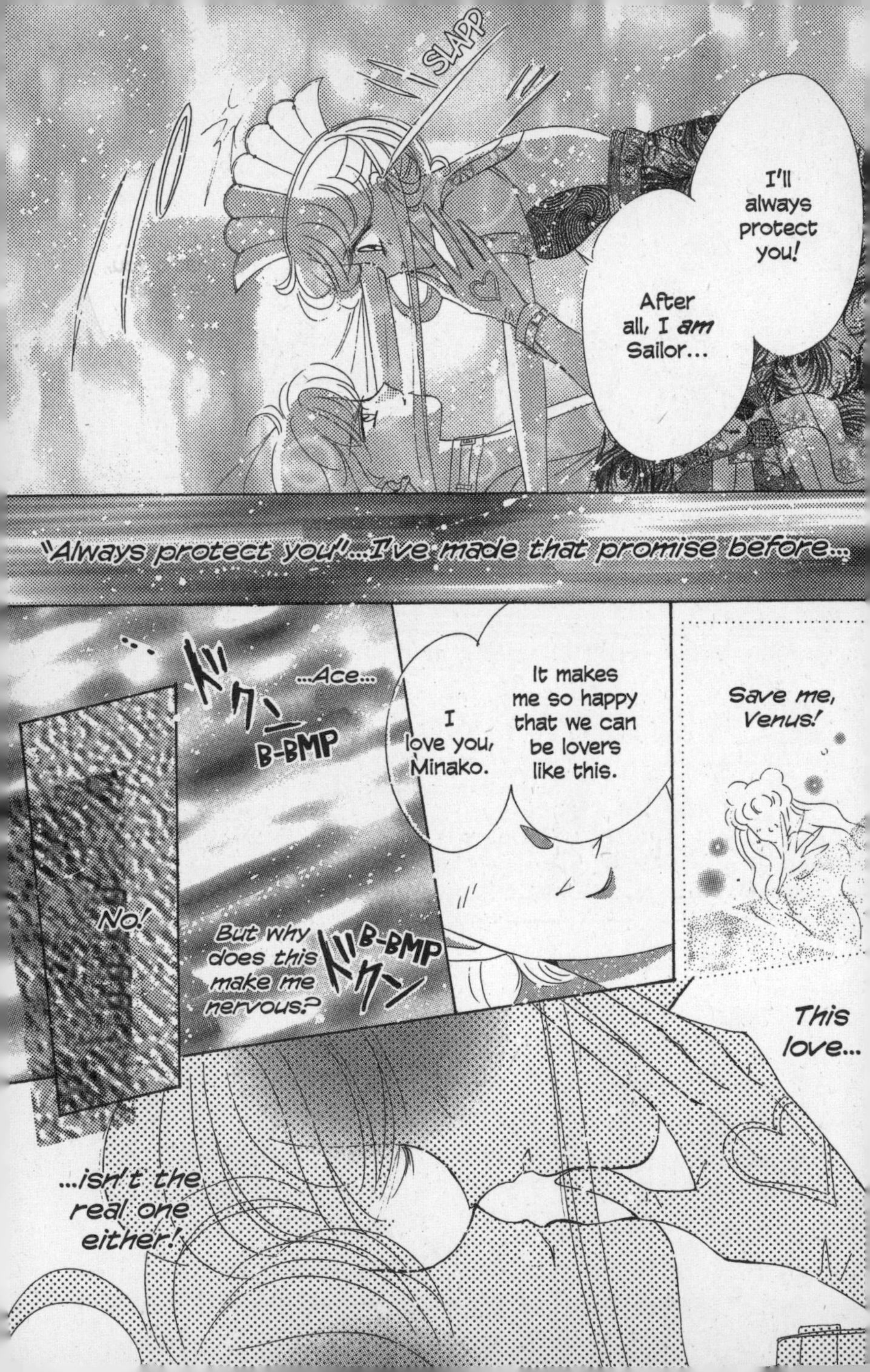
SLAPP
I'll always protect you!
After all, I *am* Sailor...
"Always protect you!"...I've made that promise before...
Save me, Venus!
It makes me so happy that we can be lovers like this.
I love you, Minako.
...Ace...
B-BMP
But why does this make me nervous?
B-BMP
No!
This love...
...isn't the real one either!

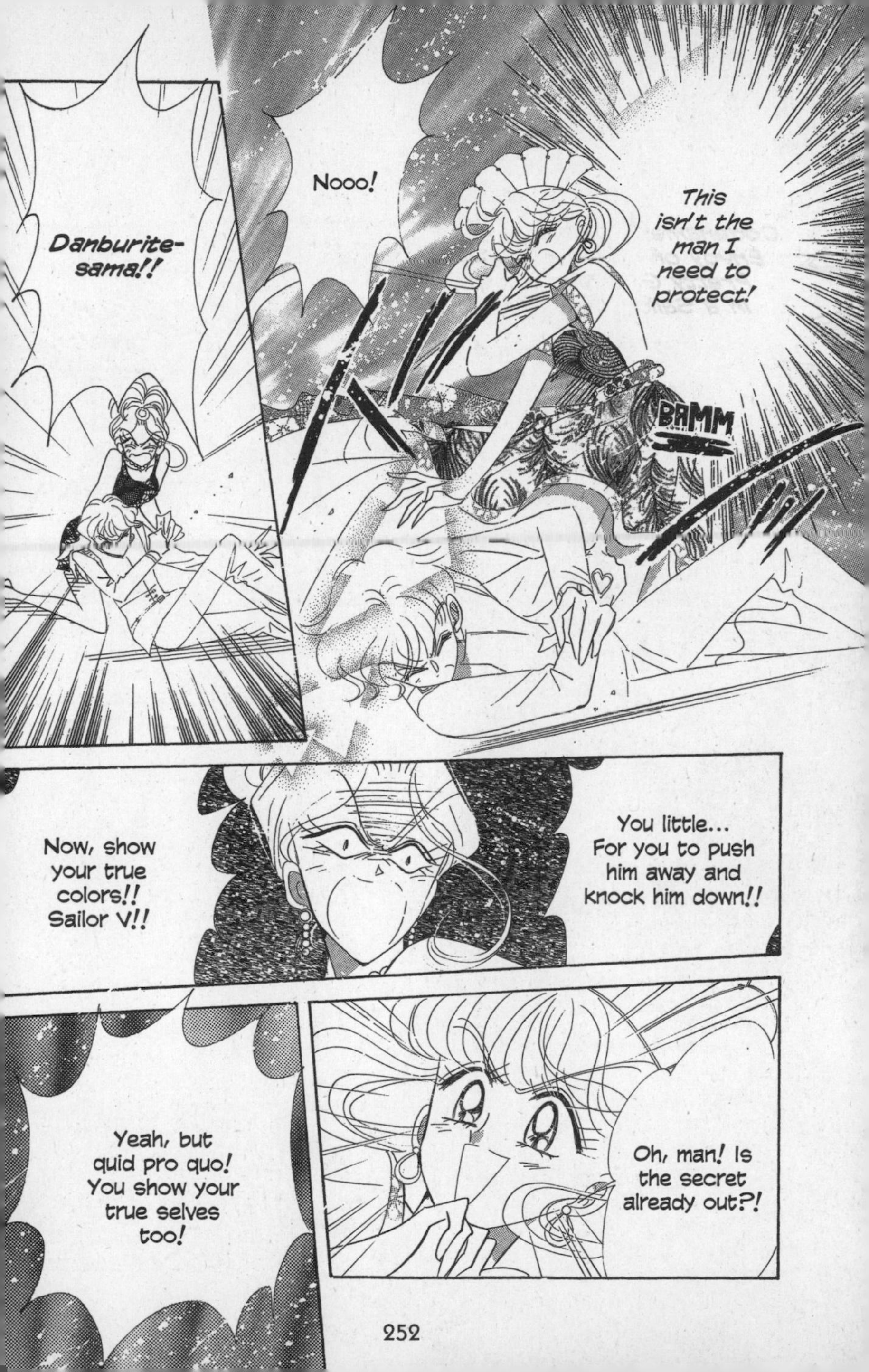
This isn't the man I need to protect!
Nooo!
BAMM
Danburite-sama!!
You little... For you to push him away and knock him down!!
Now, show your true colors!! Sailor V!!
Oh, man! Is the secret already out?!
Yeah, but quid pro quo! You show your true selves too!

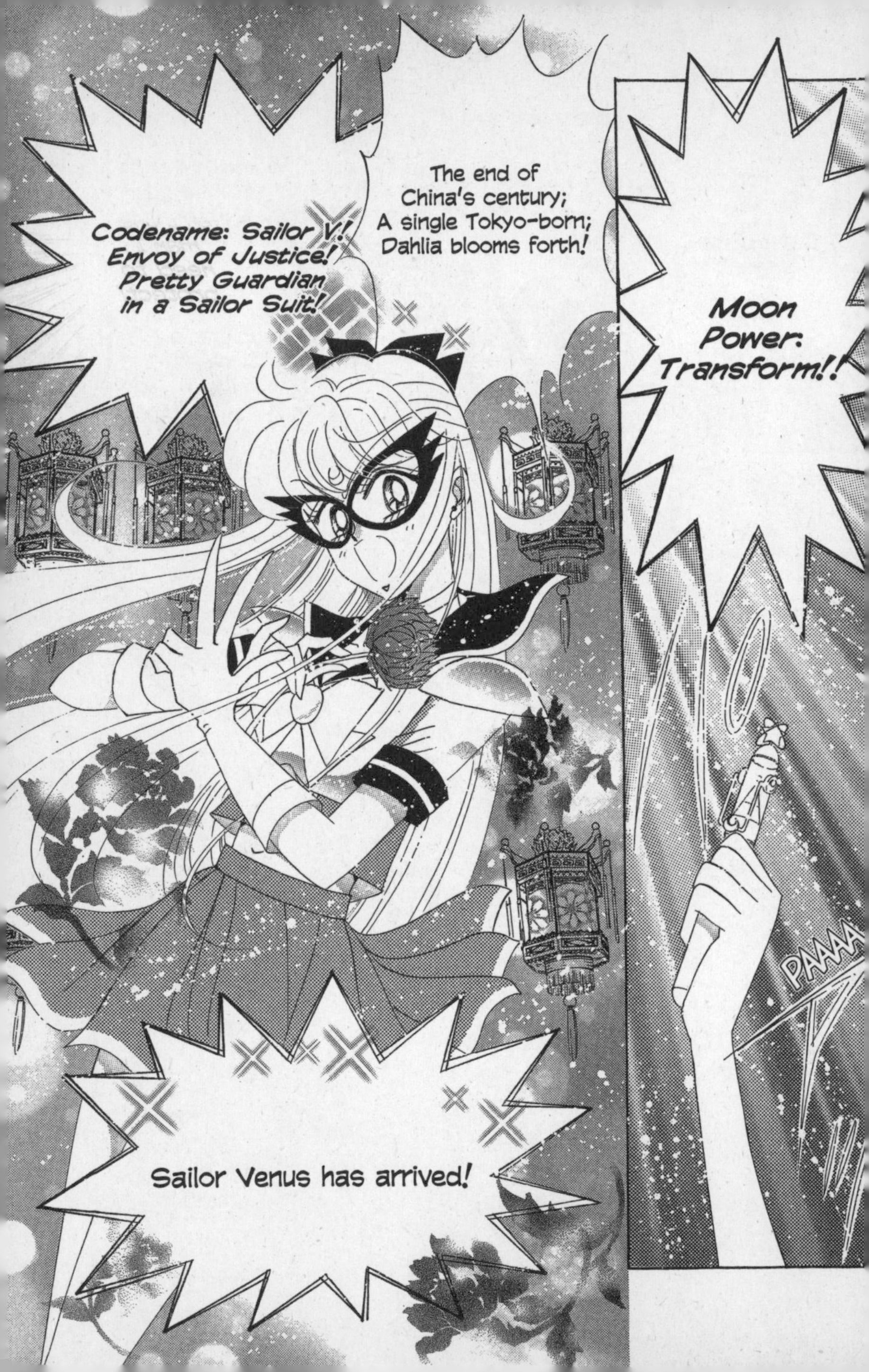
Moon Power: Transform!!
PAAAA
The end of China's century; A single Tokyo-born; Dahlia blooms forth!
Codename: Sailor V! Envoy of Justice! Pretty Guardian in a Sailor Suit!
Sailor Venus has arrived!

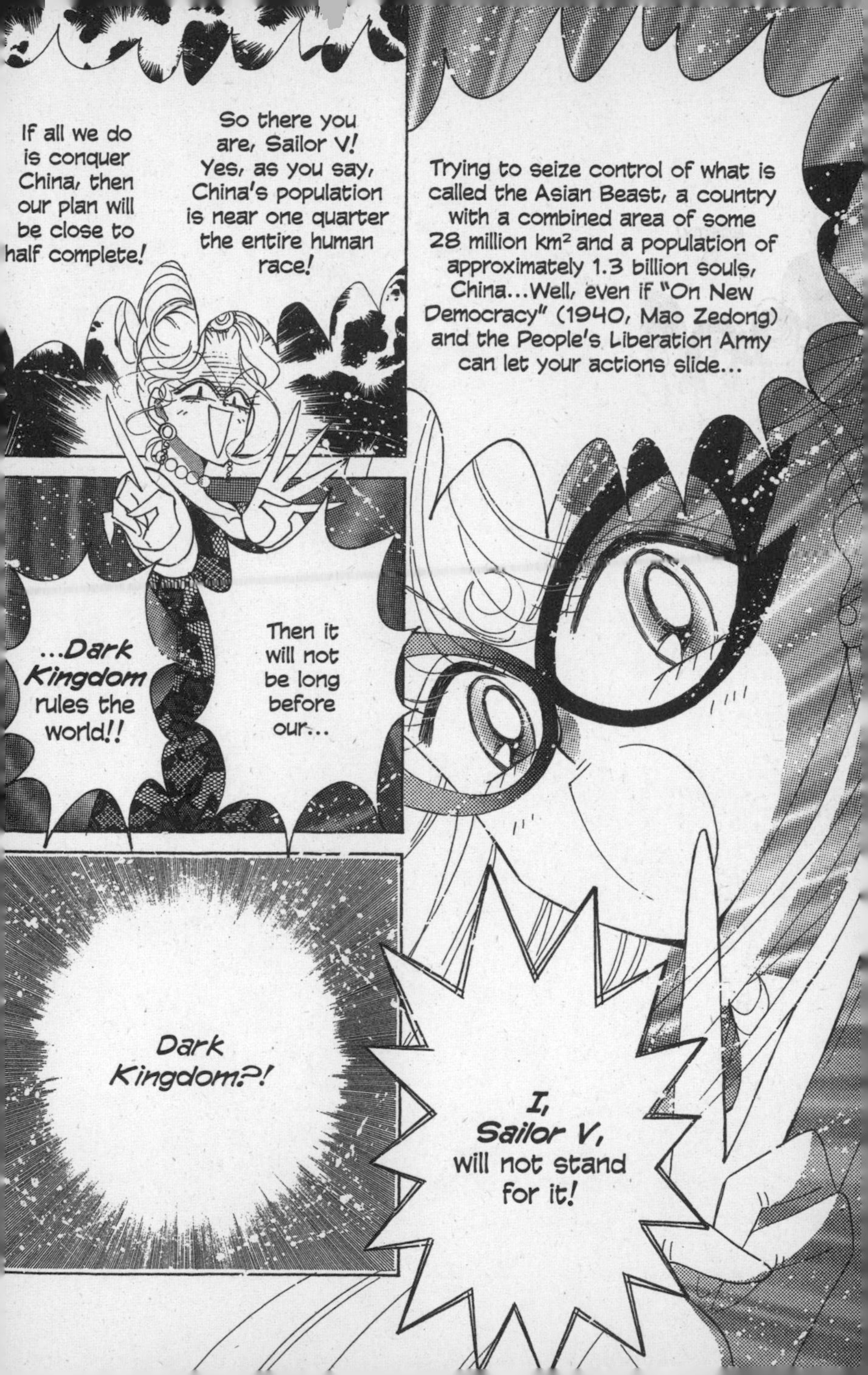
Trying to seize control of what is called the Asian Beast, a country with a combined area of some 28 million km² and a population of approximately 1.3 billion souls, China...Well, even if "On New Democracy" (1940, Mao Zedong) and the People's Liberation Army can let your actions slide...
I, Sailor V, will not stand for it!
So there you are, Sailor V! Yes, as you say, China's population is near one quarter the entire human race!
If all we do is conquer China, then our plan will be close to half complete!
Then it will not be long before our...
...Dark Kingdom rules the world!!
Dark Kingdom?!

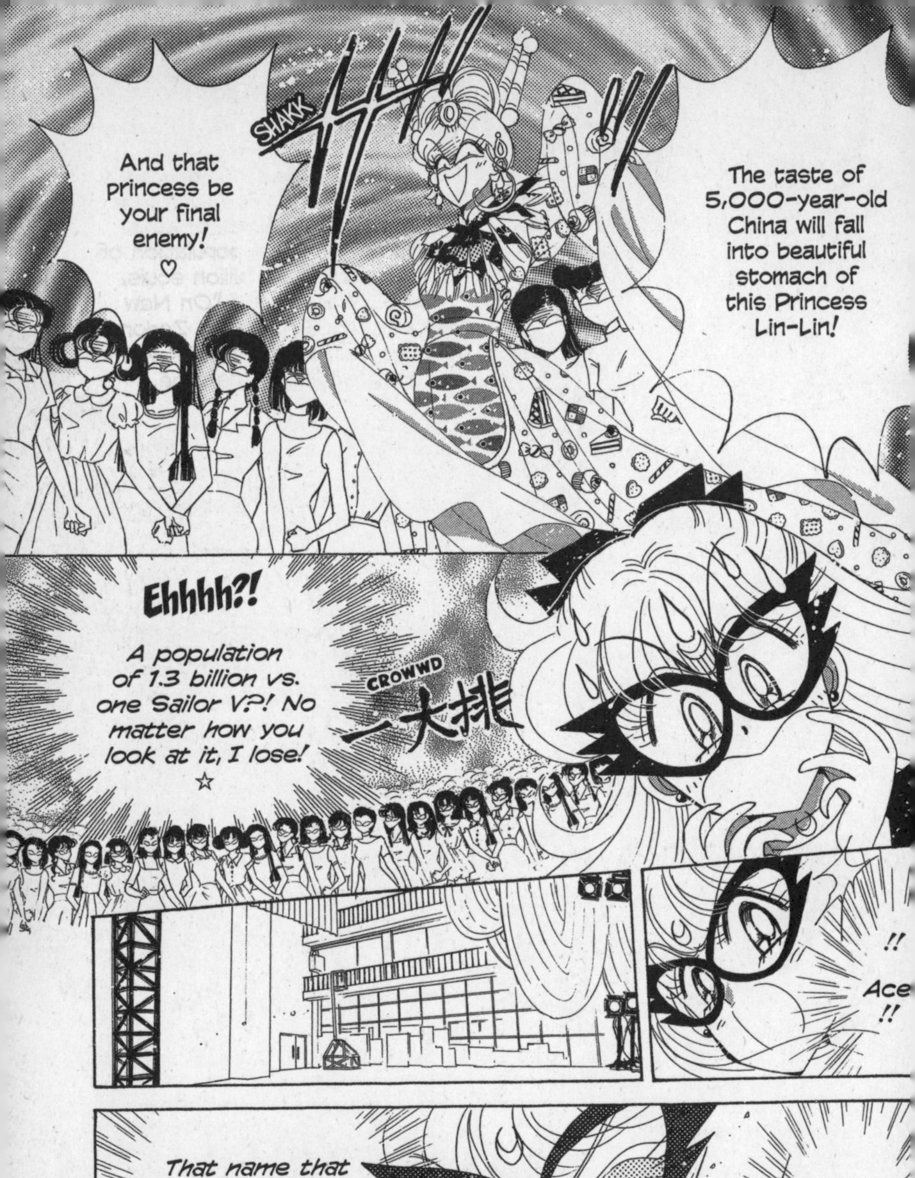
The taste of 5,000-year-old China will fall into beautiful stomach of this Princess Lin-Lin!
SHAKK
And that princess be your final enemy! ♡
CROWWD
一大排
Ehhhh?!
A population of 1.3 billion vs. one Sailor V?! No matter how you look at it, I lose! ☆
!! Ace !!
"Danburite-sama!"
That name that Lin-Lin called you! Is that really your name, or did I just mis-hear it?!

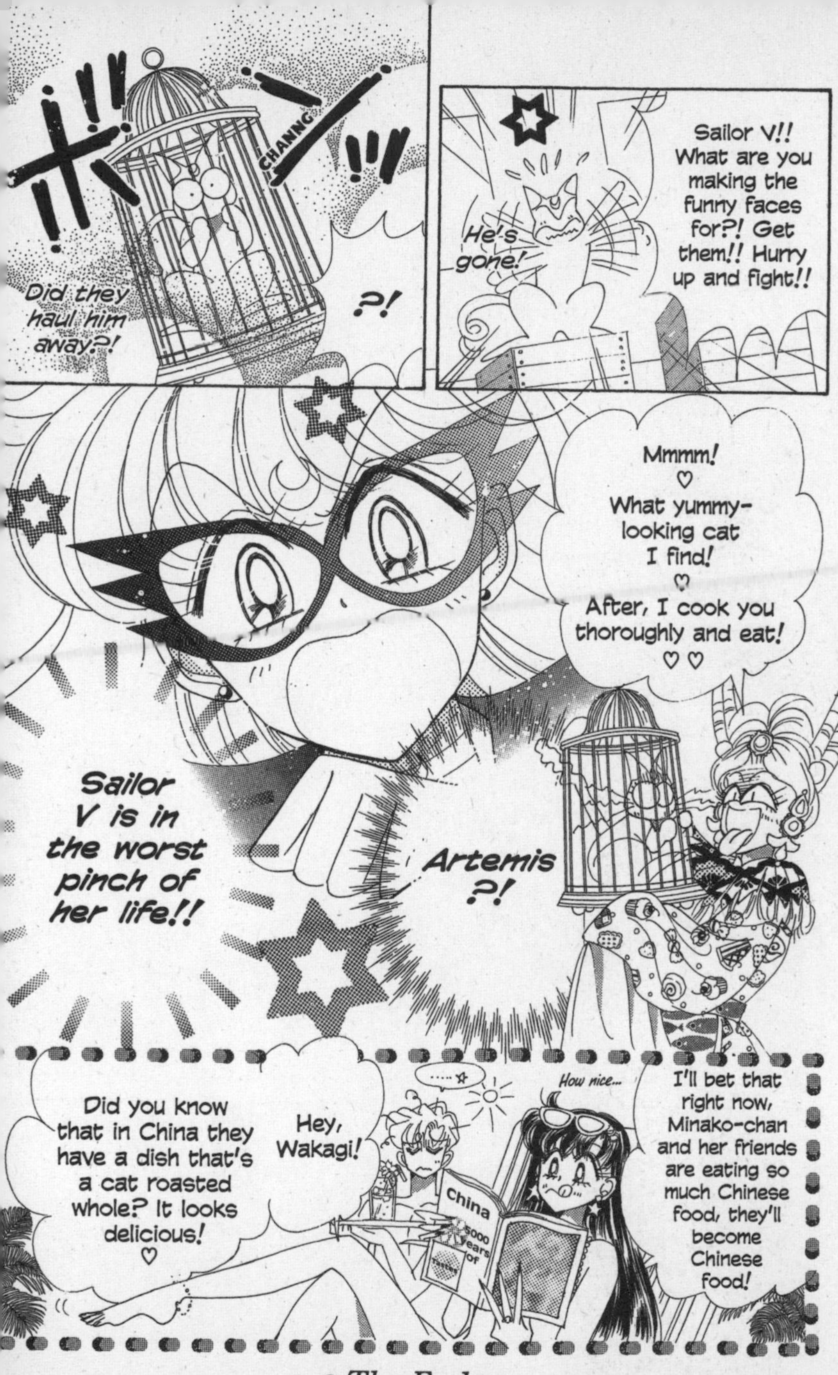
Sailor V!! What are you making the funny faces for?! Get them!! Hurry up and fight!!
He's gone!
CHANNG
Did they haul him away?!
?!
Mmmm! ♡ What yummy-looking cat I find! ♡ After, I cook you thoroughly and eat! ♡ ♡
Artemis ?!
Sailor V is in the worst pinch of her life!!
I'll bet that right now, Minako-chan and her friends are eating so much Chinese food, they'll become Chinese food!
How nice...
.....☆
Hey, Wakagi!
Did you know that in China they have a dish that's a cat roasted whole? It looks delicious! ♡
China
5000 Years of

• The End •

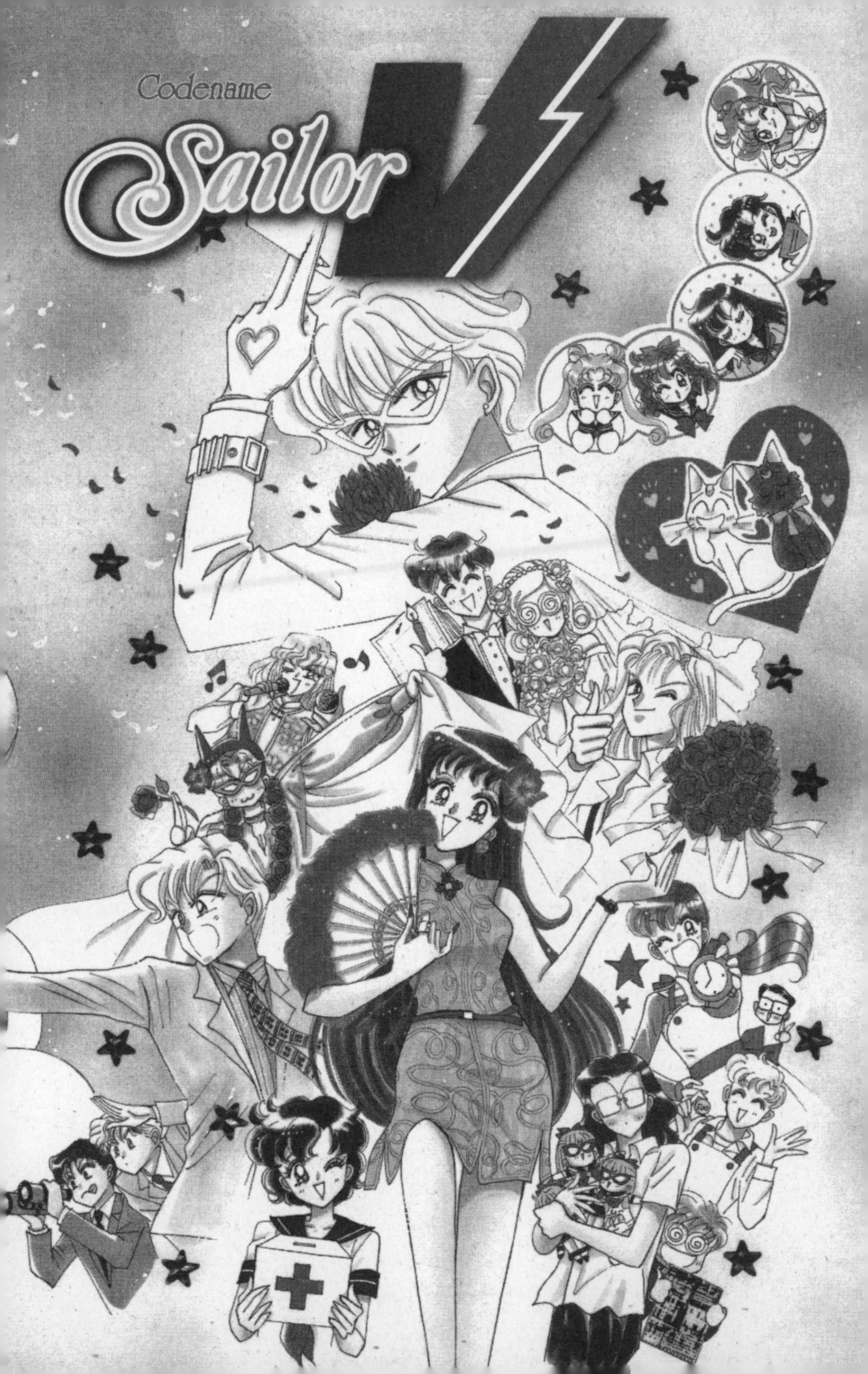
Codename
Sailor V

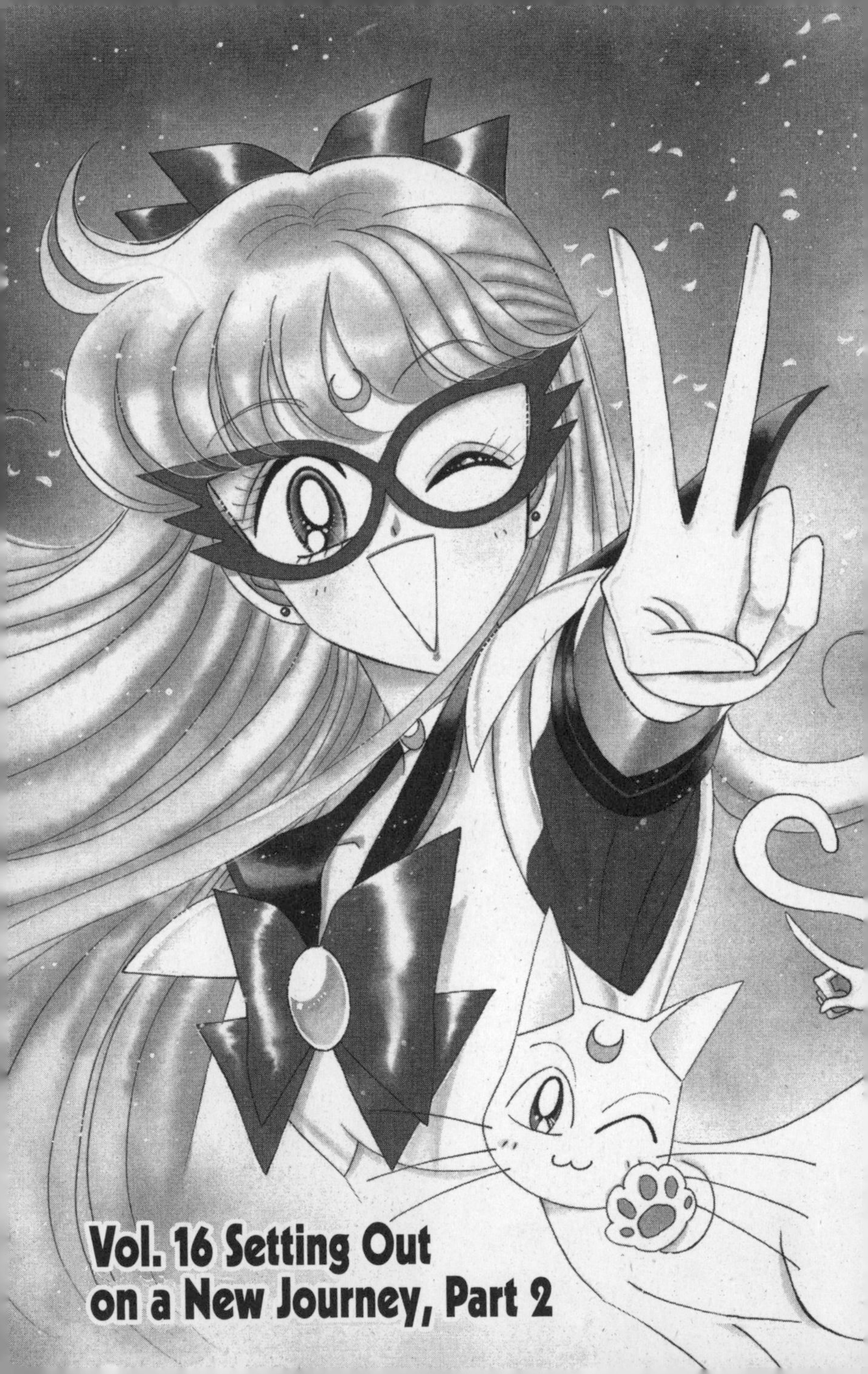

Vol. 16 Setting Out on a New Journey, Part 2

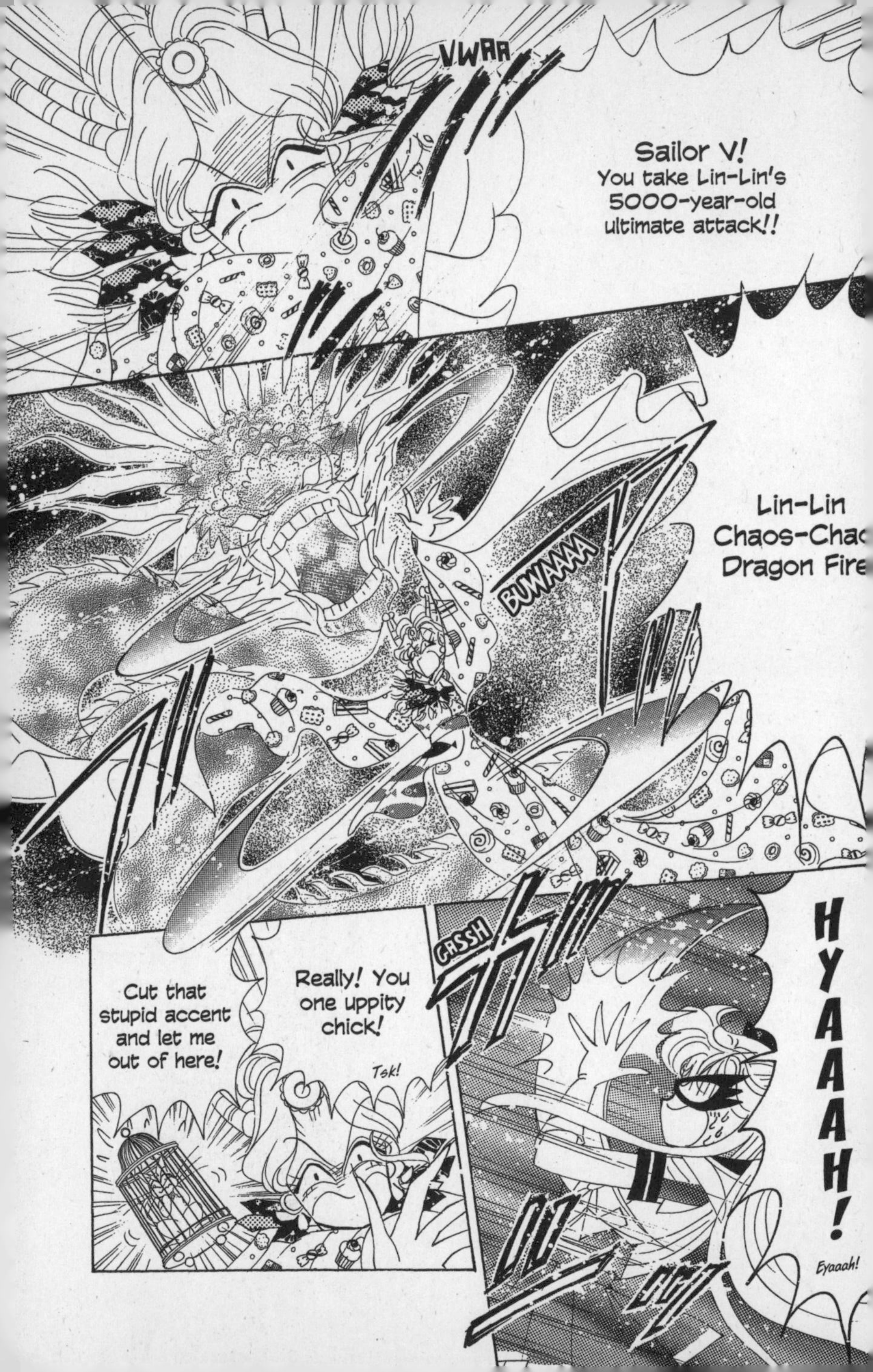
VWAA
Sailor V! You take Lin-Lin's 5000-year-old ultimate attack!!
Lin-Lin Chaos-Cha Dragon Fire
BUWAAAA
GASSH
HYAAAAH!
Eyaaah!
Really! You one uppity chick!
Cut that stupid accent and let me out of here!
Tsk!

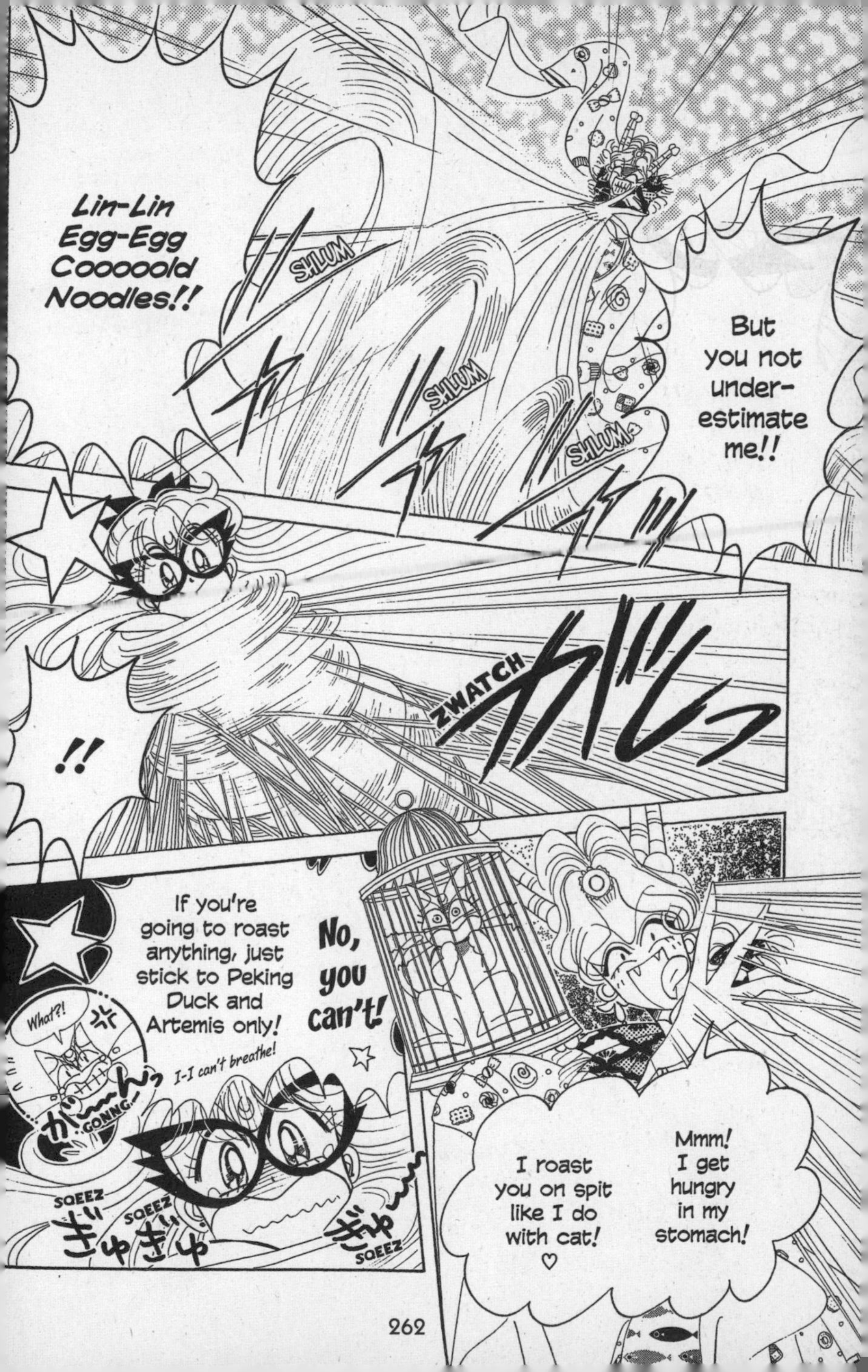
But you not under-estimate me!!
SHLUM
SHLUM
SHLUM
Lin-Lin Egg-Egg Cooooold Noodles!!
ZWATCH
!!
Mmm! I get hungry in my stomach!
I roast you on spit like I do with cat! ♡
No, you can't!
If you're going to roast anything, just stick to Peking Duck and Artemis only!
What?!
I-I can't breathe!
GONNG
SQEEZ
SQEEZ
SQEEZ

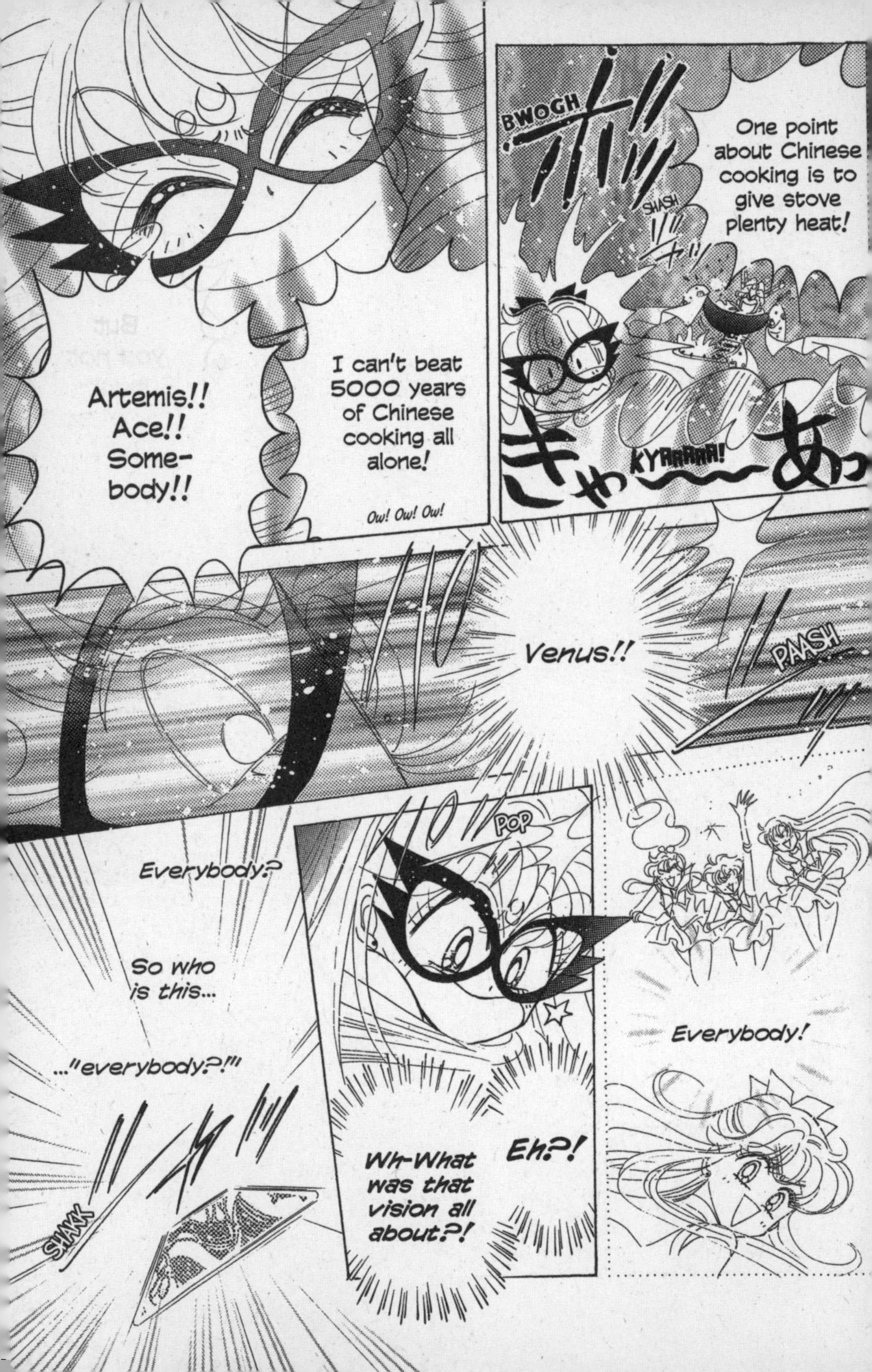
BWOGH
SHASH
One point about Chinese cooking is to give stove plenty heat!
きゃ〜〜あっ
KYAAAAA!
I can't beat 5000 years of Chinese cooking all alone!
Ow! Ow! Ow!
Artemis!! Ace!! Some-body!!
PAASH
Venus!!
Everybody!
POP
Eh?!
Wh-What was that vision all about?!
Everybody?
So who is this...
..."everybody?!"
SHAKK

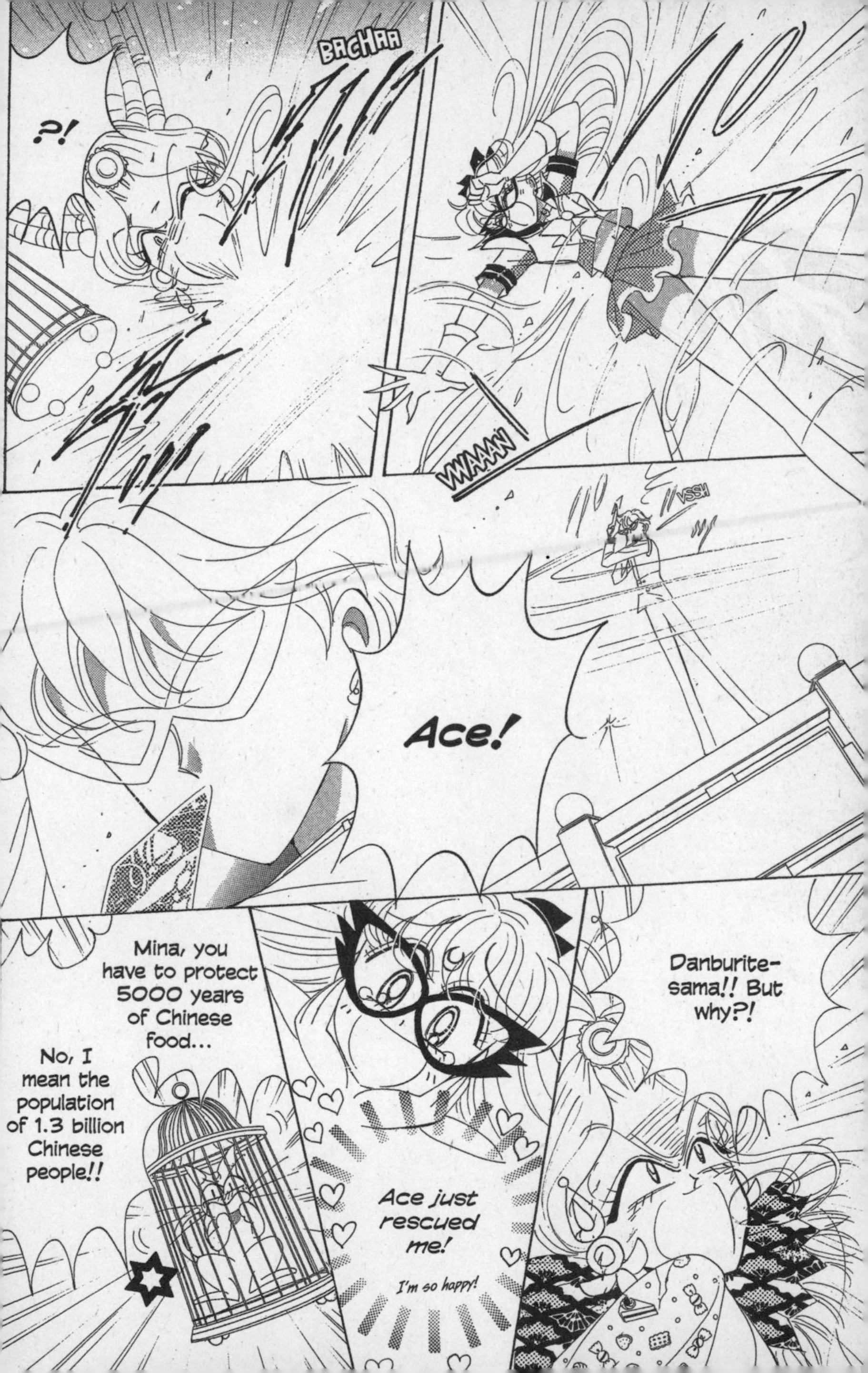
VWAAAN
BACHAA
?!
VSSH
Ace!
Danburite-sama!! But why?!
Ace just rescued me!
I'm so happy!
Mina, you have to protect 5000 years of Chinese food...
No, I mean the population of 1.3 billion Chinese people!!

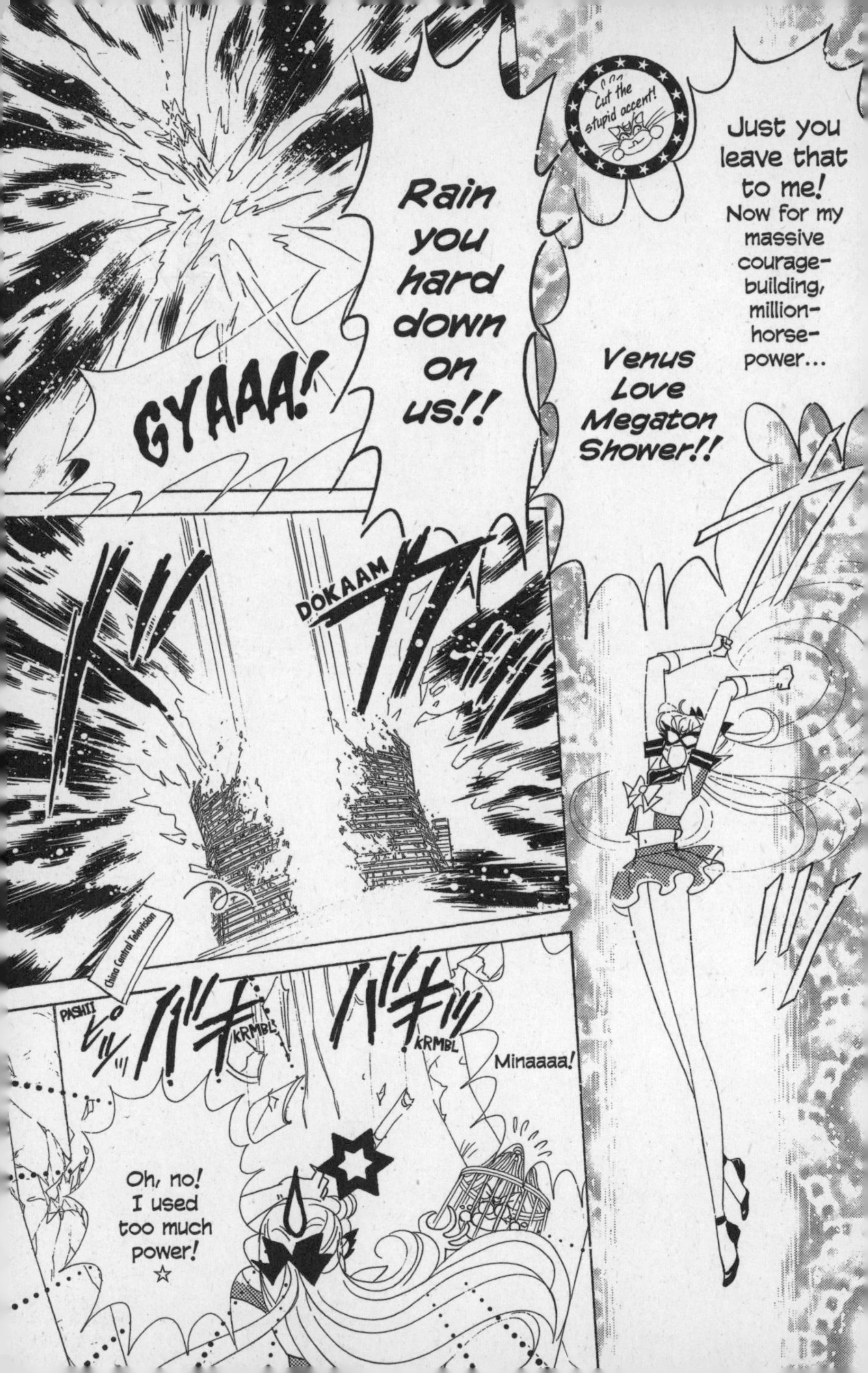

Just you leave that to me! Now for my massive courage-building, million-horse-power...
Venus Love Megaton Shower!!
Cut the stupid accent!
Rain you hard down on us!!
GYAAA!
DOKAAM
China Central Television
Minaaaa!
KRMBL
KRMBL
PASHII
Oh, no! I used too much power! ☆

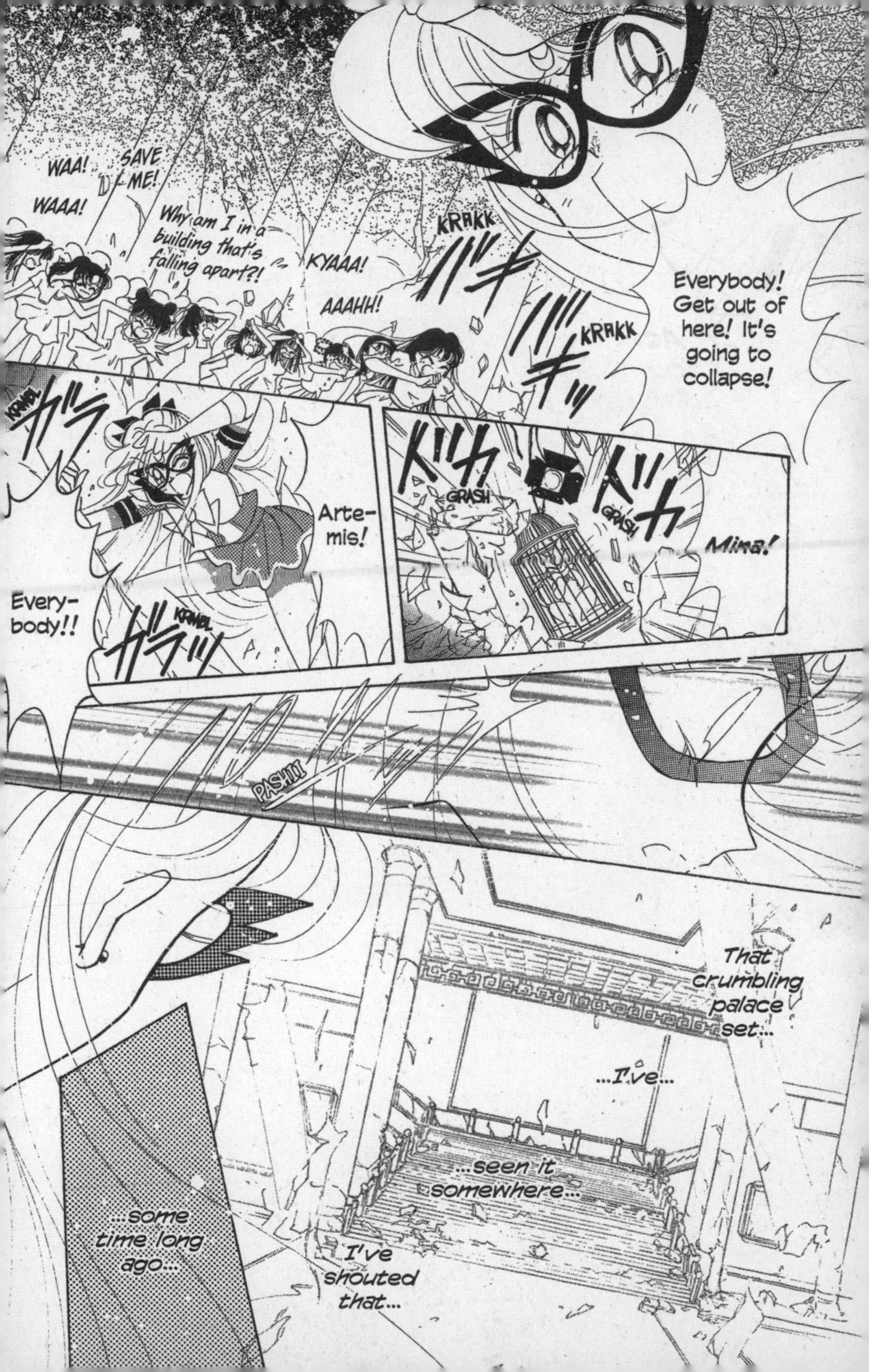

Everybody! Get out of here! It's going to collapse!
KRAKK
KRAKK
KYAAA!
AAAHH!
Why am I in a building that's falling apart?!
SAVE ME!
WAA!
WAAA!
GRASH
GRASH
Mina!
Arte-mis!
KRAKL
Every-body!!
KRAKL
PASHIII
That crumbling palace set...
...I've...
...seen it somewhere...
I've shouted that...
...some time long ago...

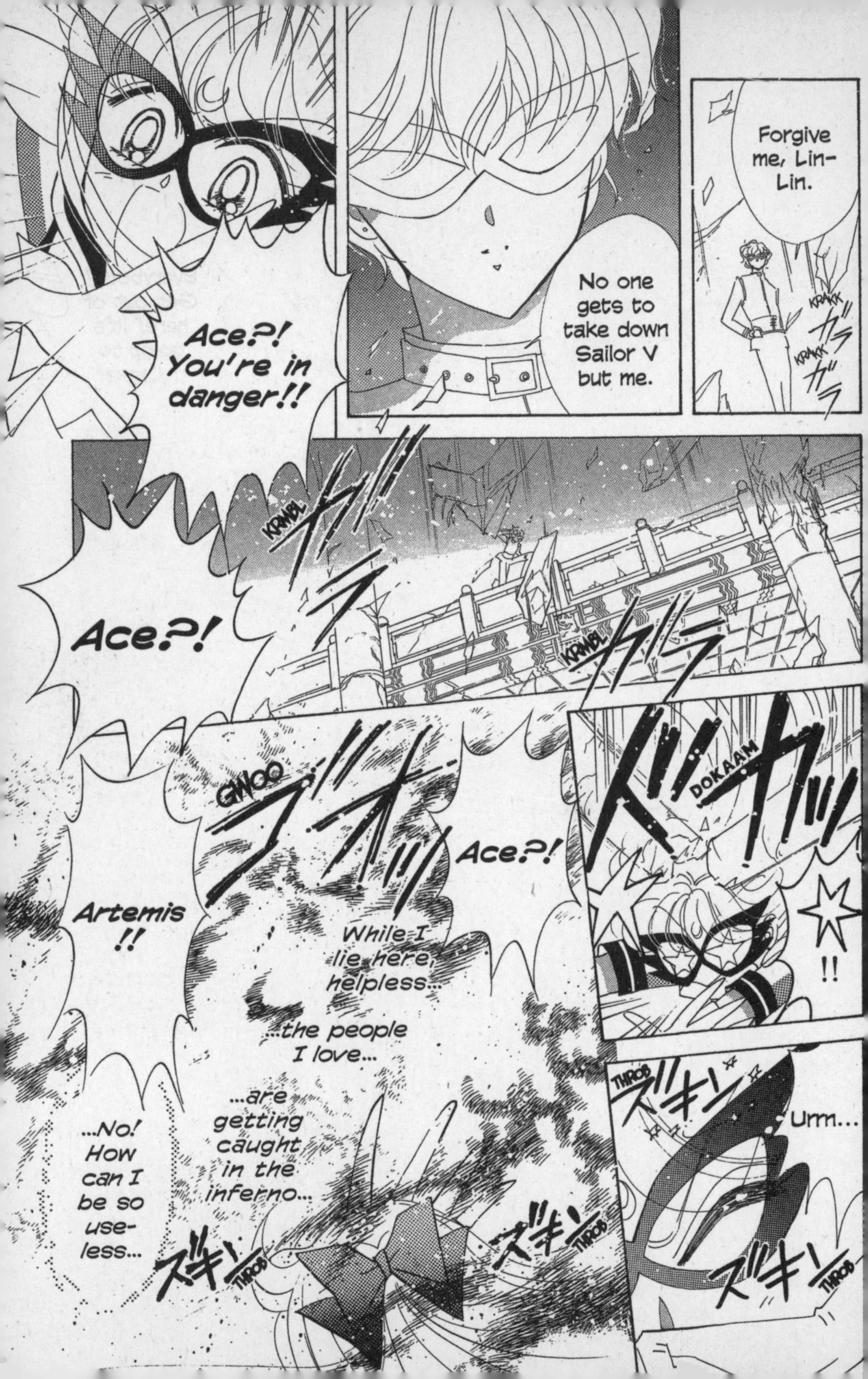
Forgive me, Lin-Lin.
KRAKK
KRAKK
No one gets to take down Sailor V but me.
Ace?! You're in danger!!
KRMBL
KRMBL
Ace?!
DOKAAM
!!
THROB
Urm...
THROB
GWOO
Ace?!
Artemis!!
While I lie here, helpless...
...the people I love...
...are getting caught in the inferno...
...No! How can I be so useless...
THROB
THROB

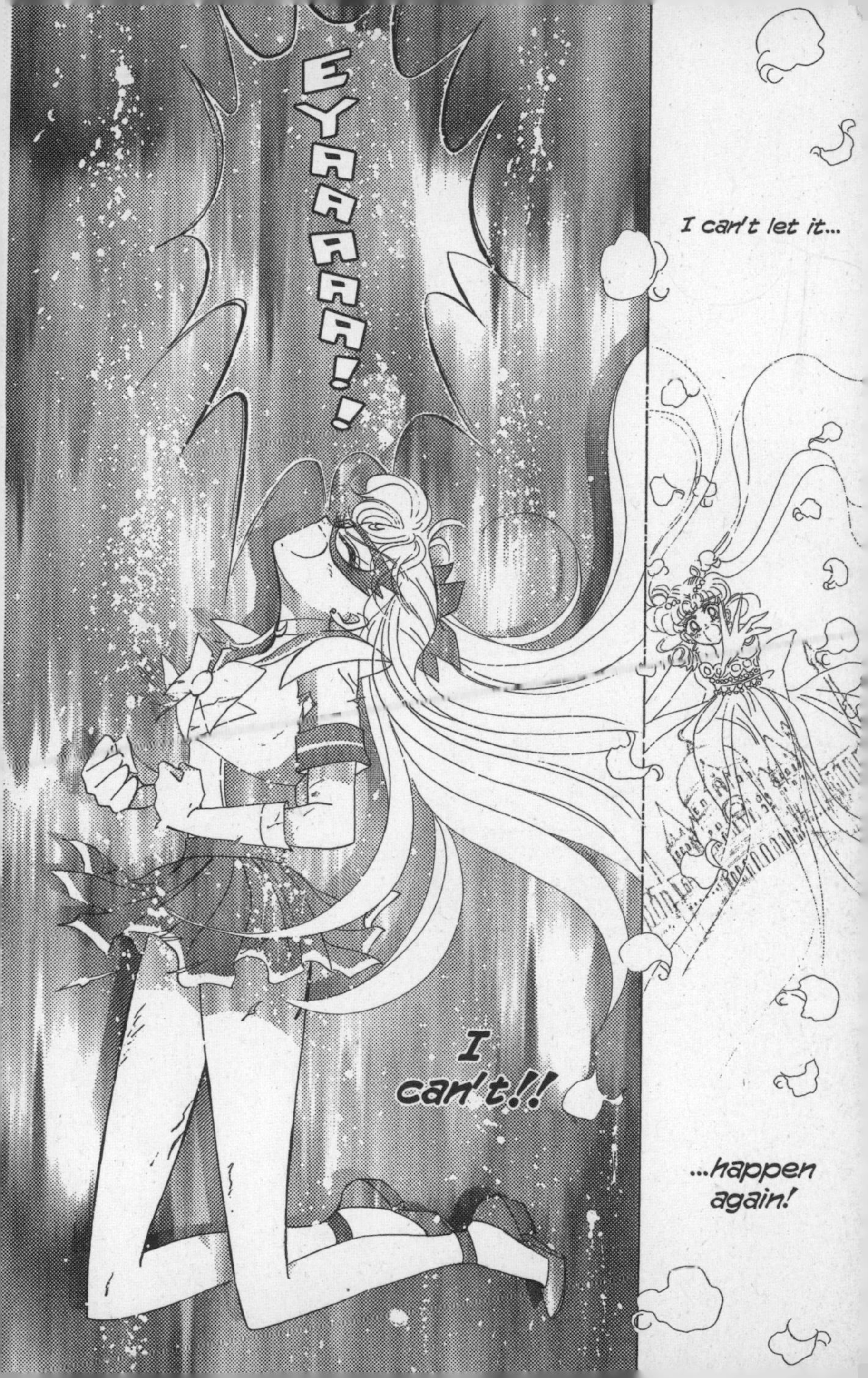
I can't let it...
...happen again!
EYAAAAAA!!
I can't!!

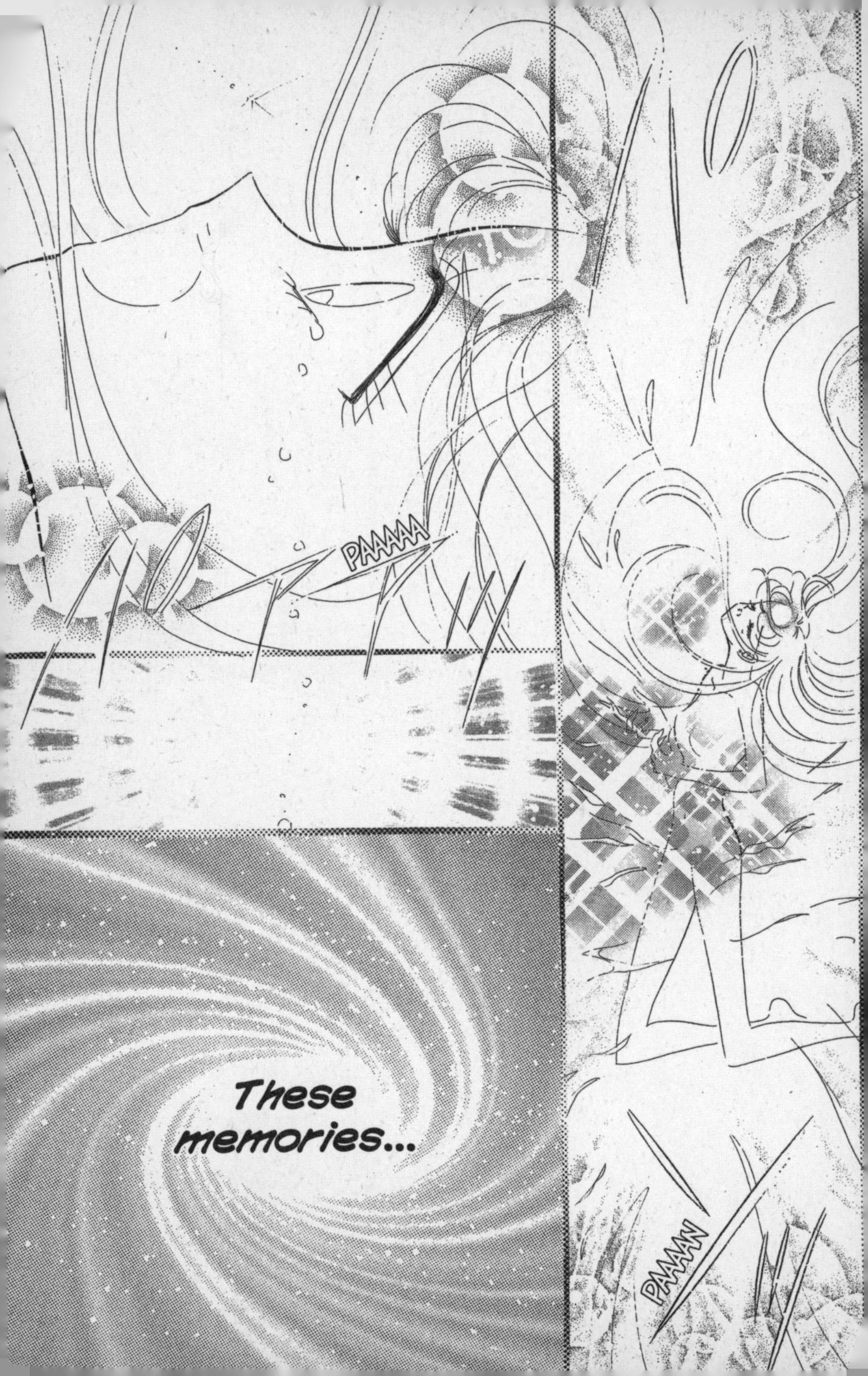
PAAAAN
PAAAAA
These memories...

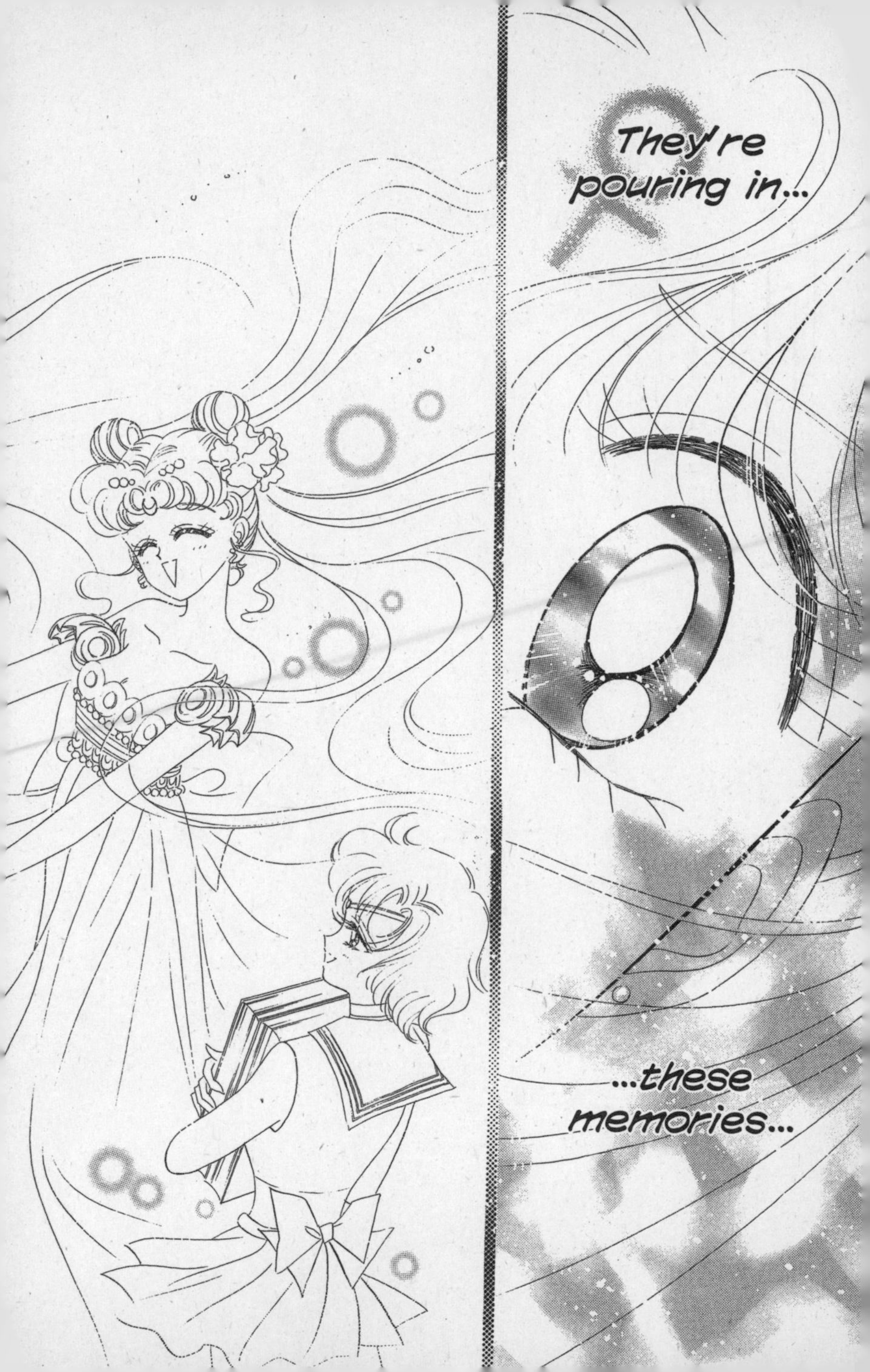
They're pouring in...
...these memories...

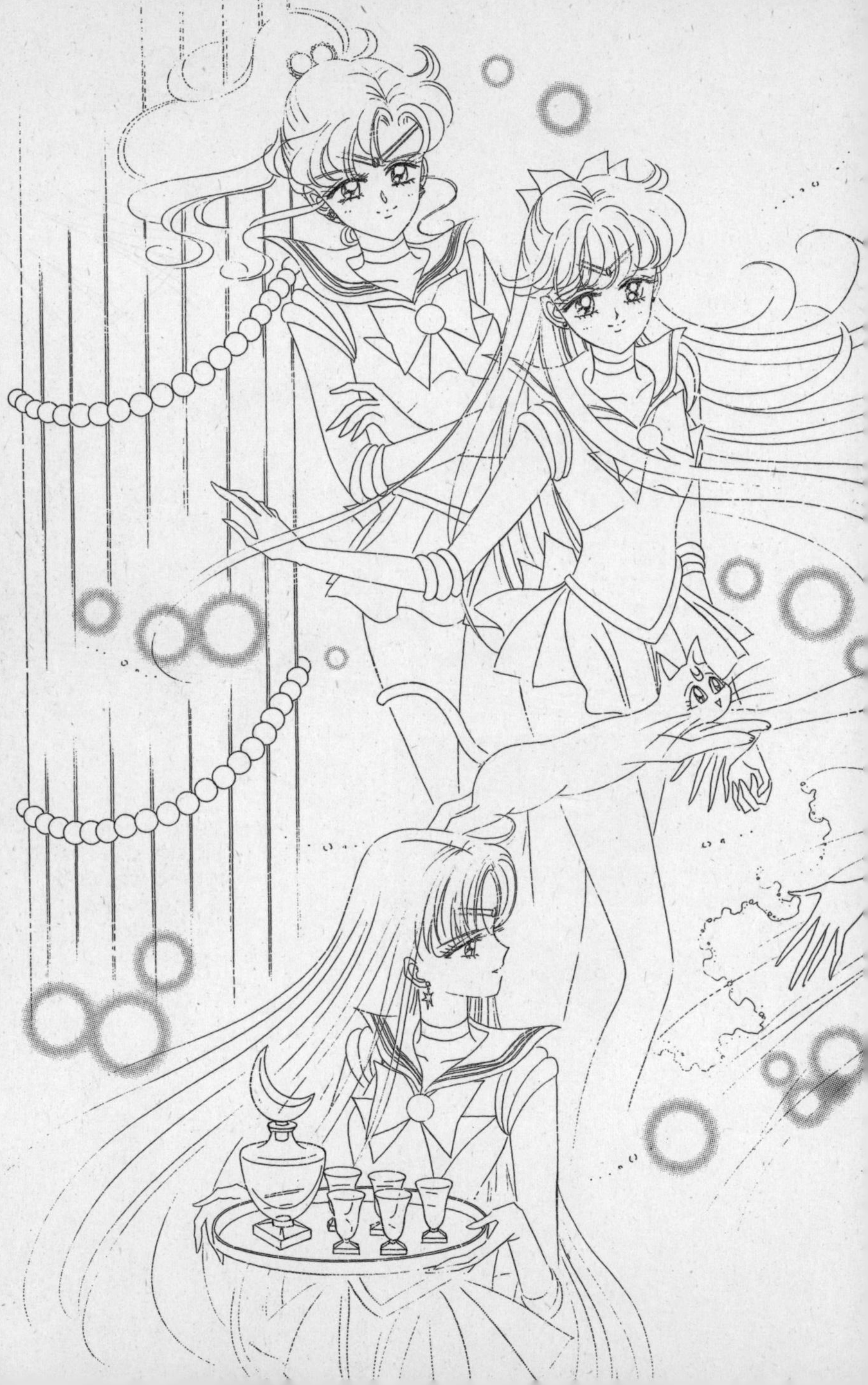

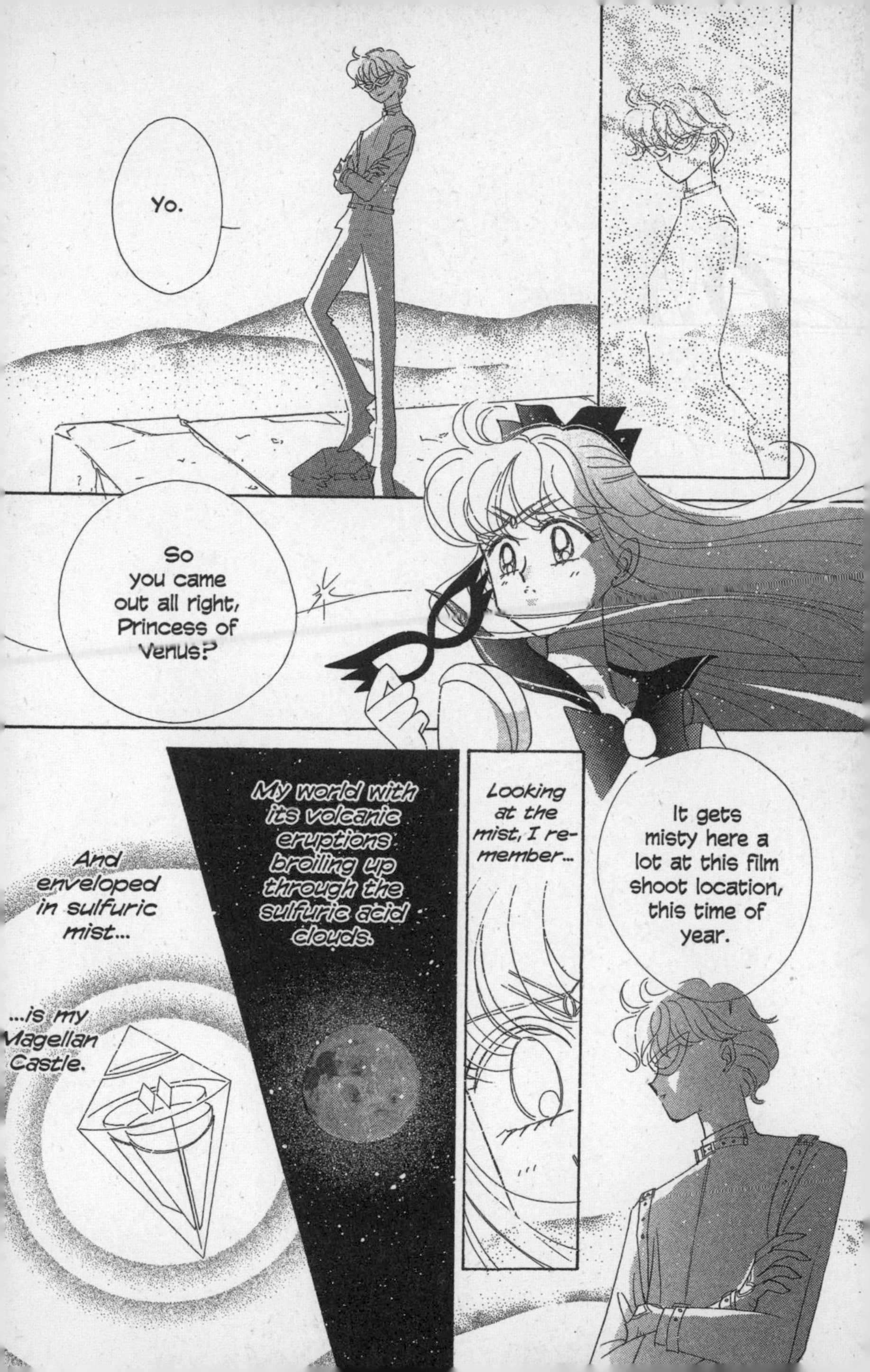
Yo.
So you came out all right, Princess of Venus?
It gets misty here a lot at this film shoot location, this time of year.
Looking at the mist, I remember...
My world with its volcanic eruptions broiling up through the sulfuric acid clouds.
And enveloped in sulfuric mist...
...is my Magellan Castle.

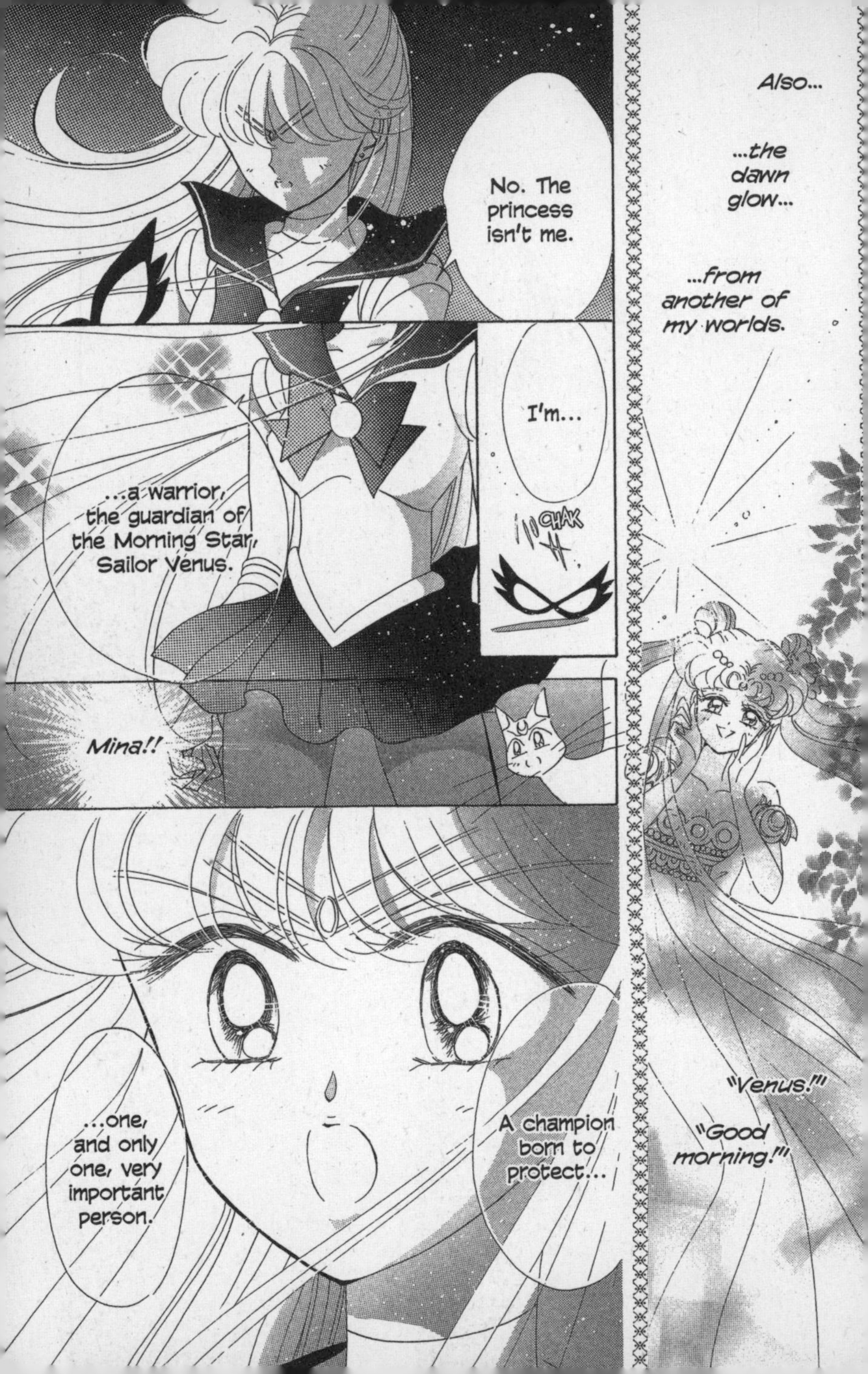
Also...
...the dawn glow...
...from another of my worlds.
"Venus!"
"Good morning!"
No. The princess isn't me.
I'm...
CHAK
...a warrior, the guardian of the Morning Star, Sailor Venus.
Mina!!
A champion born to protect...
...one, and only one, very important person.

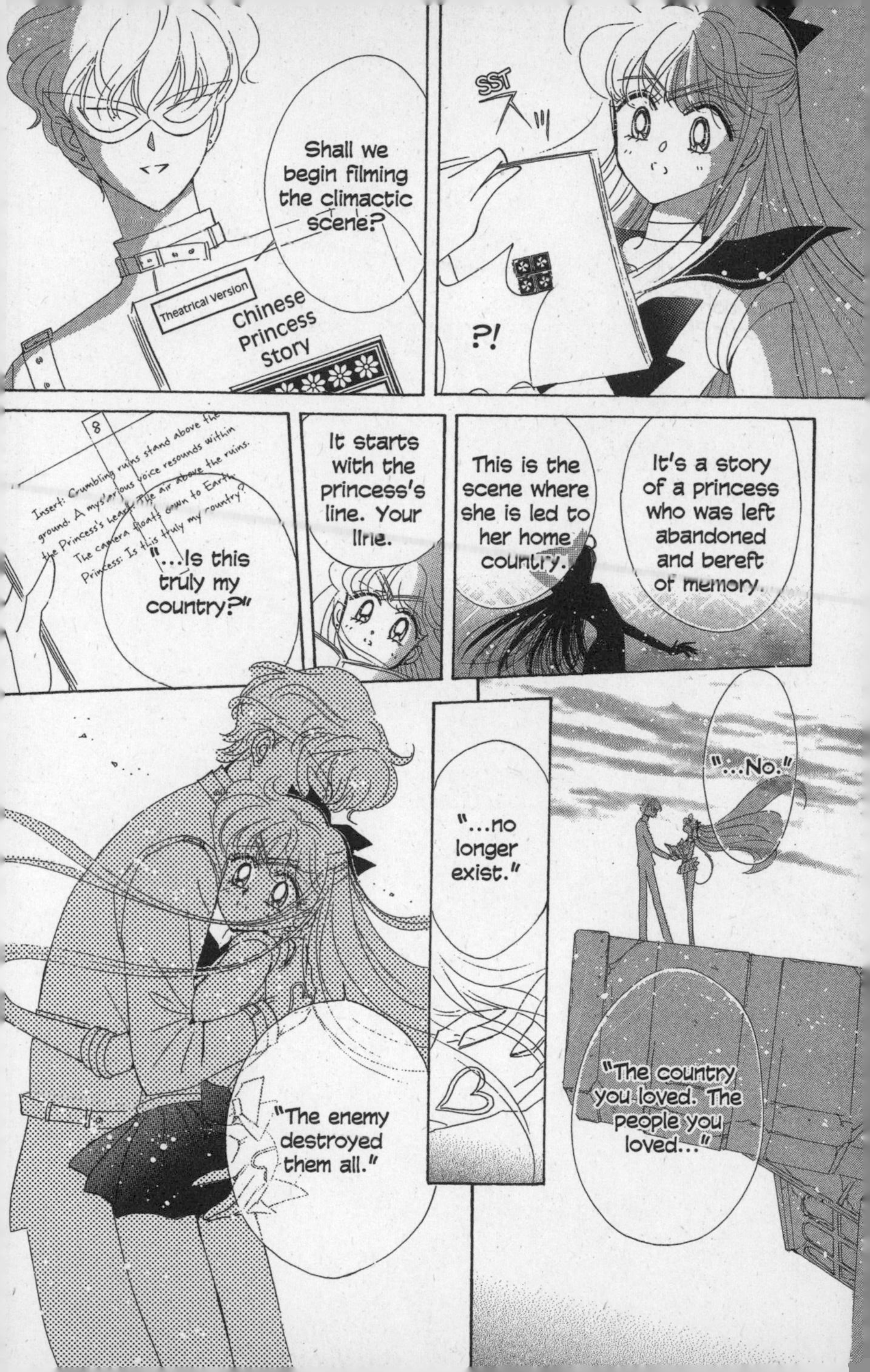
SST
?!
Shall we begin filming the climactic scene?
Theatrical Version
Chinese Princess Story
It's a story of a princess who was left abandoned and bereft of memory.
This is the scene where she is led to her home country.
It starts with the princess's line. Your line.
8
Insert: Crumbling ruins stand above the ground. A mysterious voice resounds within the Princess's heart. The air above the ruins. The camera floats down to Earth.
Princess: Is this truly my country?
"...Is this truly my country?"
"...No."
"The country you loved. The people you loved..."
"...no longer exist."
"The enemy destroyed them all."

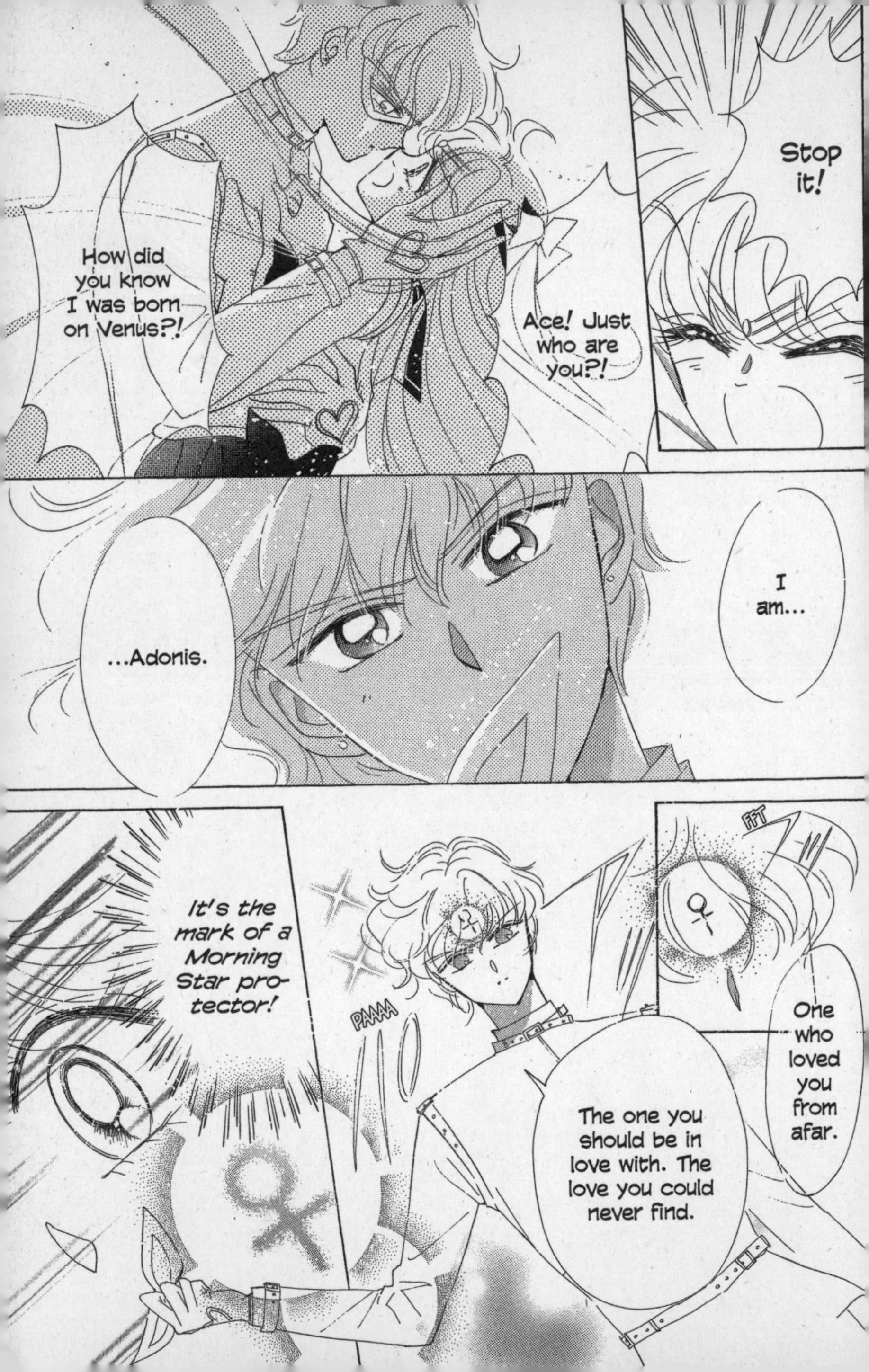

Stop it!
Ace! Just who are you?!
How did you know I was born on Venus?!
I am...
...Adonis.
FFT
One who loved you from afar.
The one you should be in love with. The love you could never find.
PAAAA
It's the mark of a Morning Star protector!

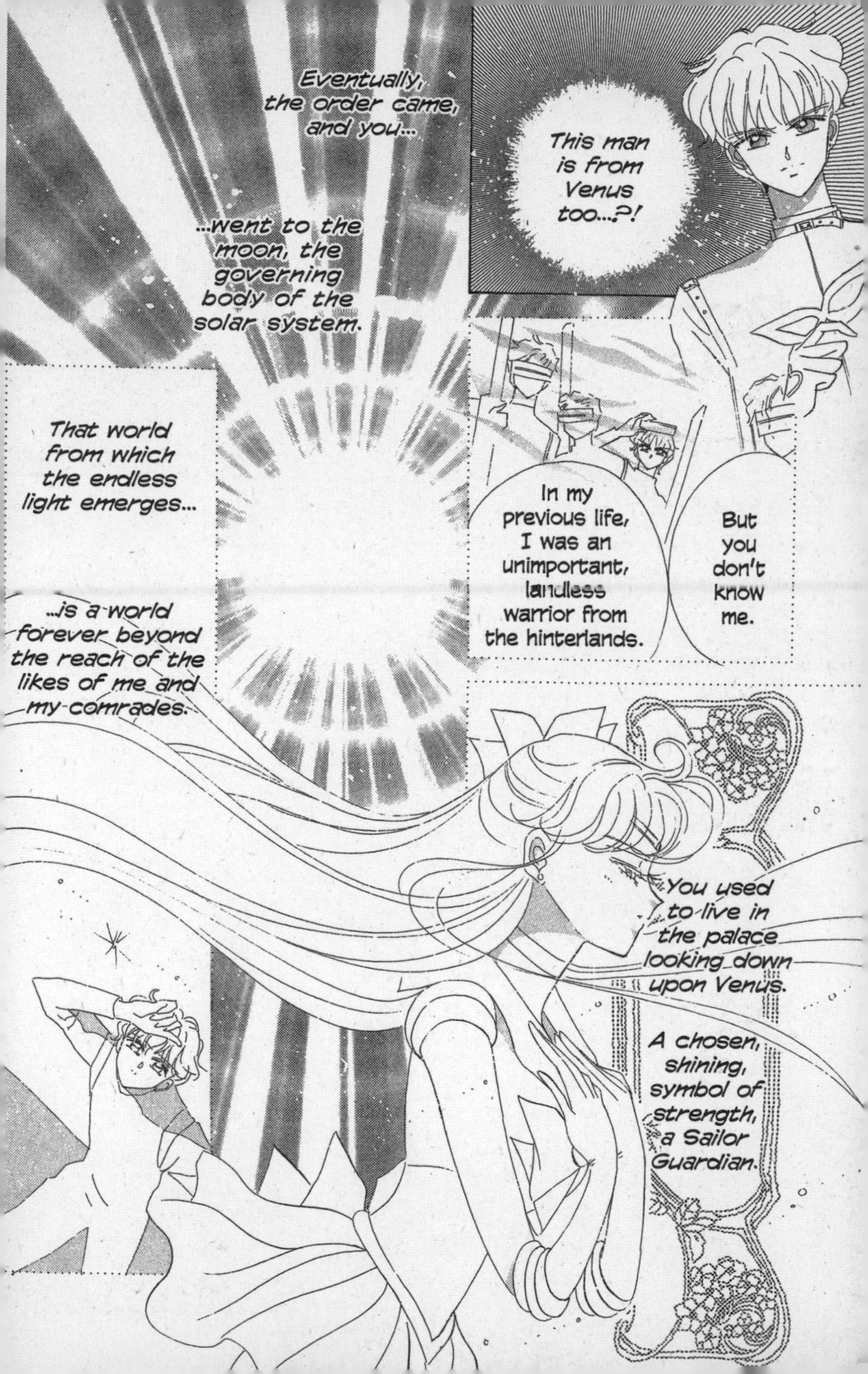
This man is from Venus too...?!
But you don't know me.
In my previous life, I was an unimportant, landless warrior from the hinterlands.
Eventually, the order came, and you...
...went to the moon, the governing body of the solar system.
That world from which the endless light emerges...
...is a world forever beyond the reach of the likes of me and my comrades.
You used to live in the palace looking down upon Venus.
A chosen, shining, symbol of strength, a Sailor Guardian.

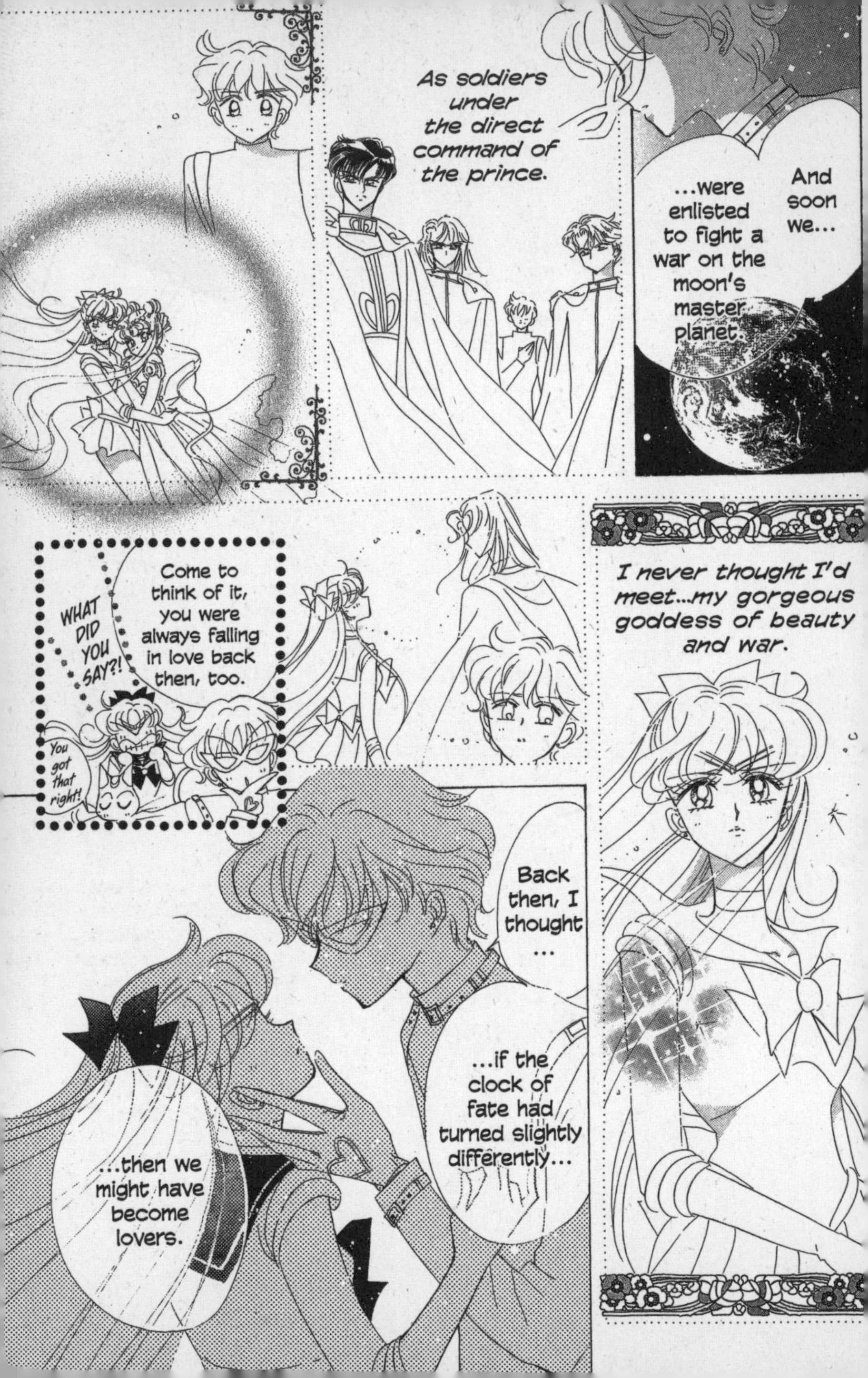
And soon we...
...were enlisted to fight a war on the moon's master planet.
As soldiers under the direct command of the prince.
I never thought I'd meet...my gorgeous goddess of beauty and war.
Come to think of it, you were always falling in love back then, too.
WHAT DID YOU SAY?!
You got that right!
Back then, I thought...
...if the clock of fate had turned slightly differently...
...then we might have become lovers.

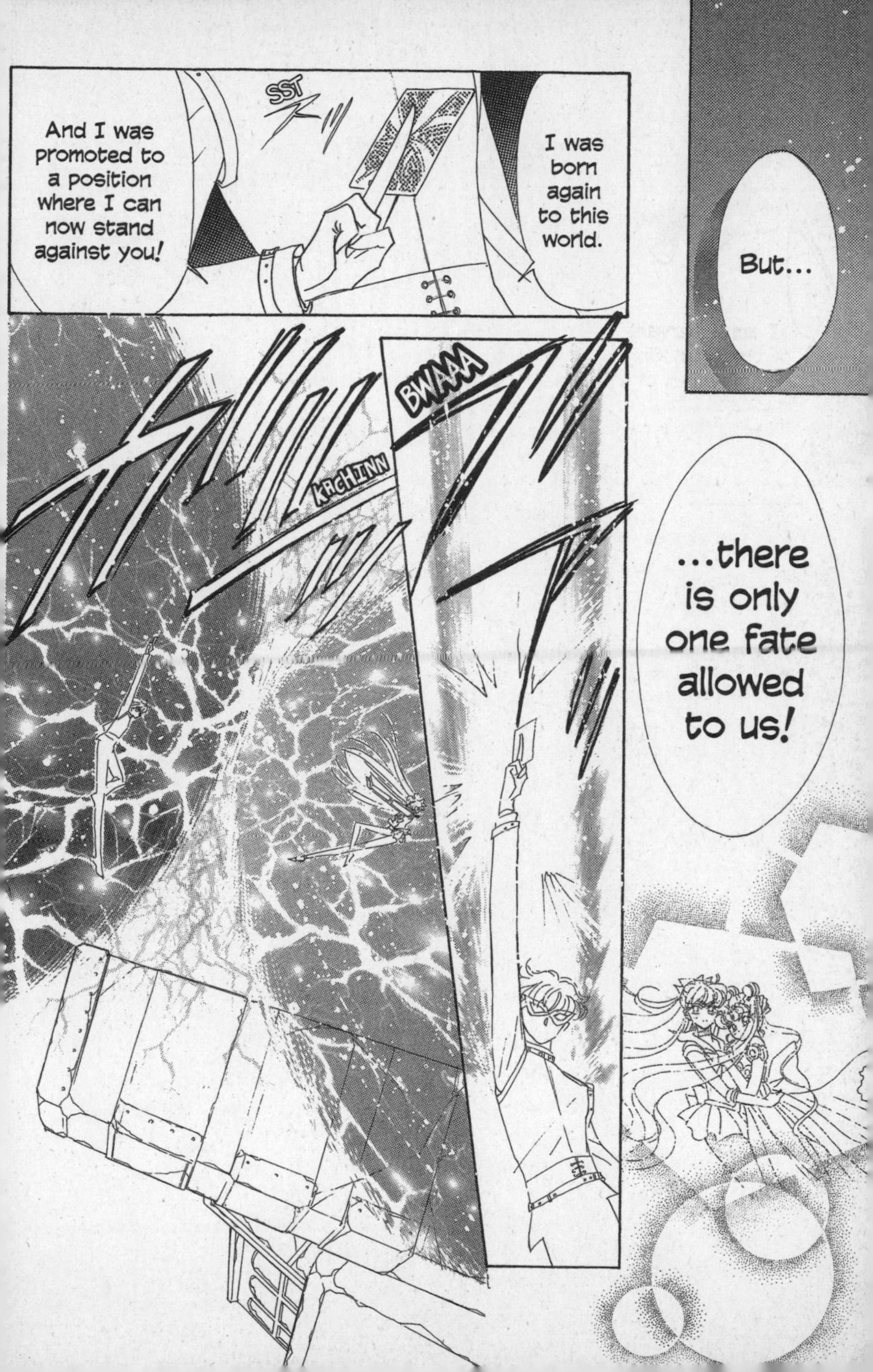

But...
I was born again to this world.
SST
And I was promoted to a position where I can now stand against you!
...there is only one fate allowed to us!
BWAAA
KACHINN

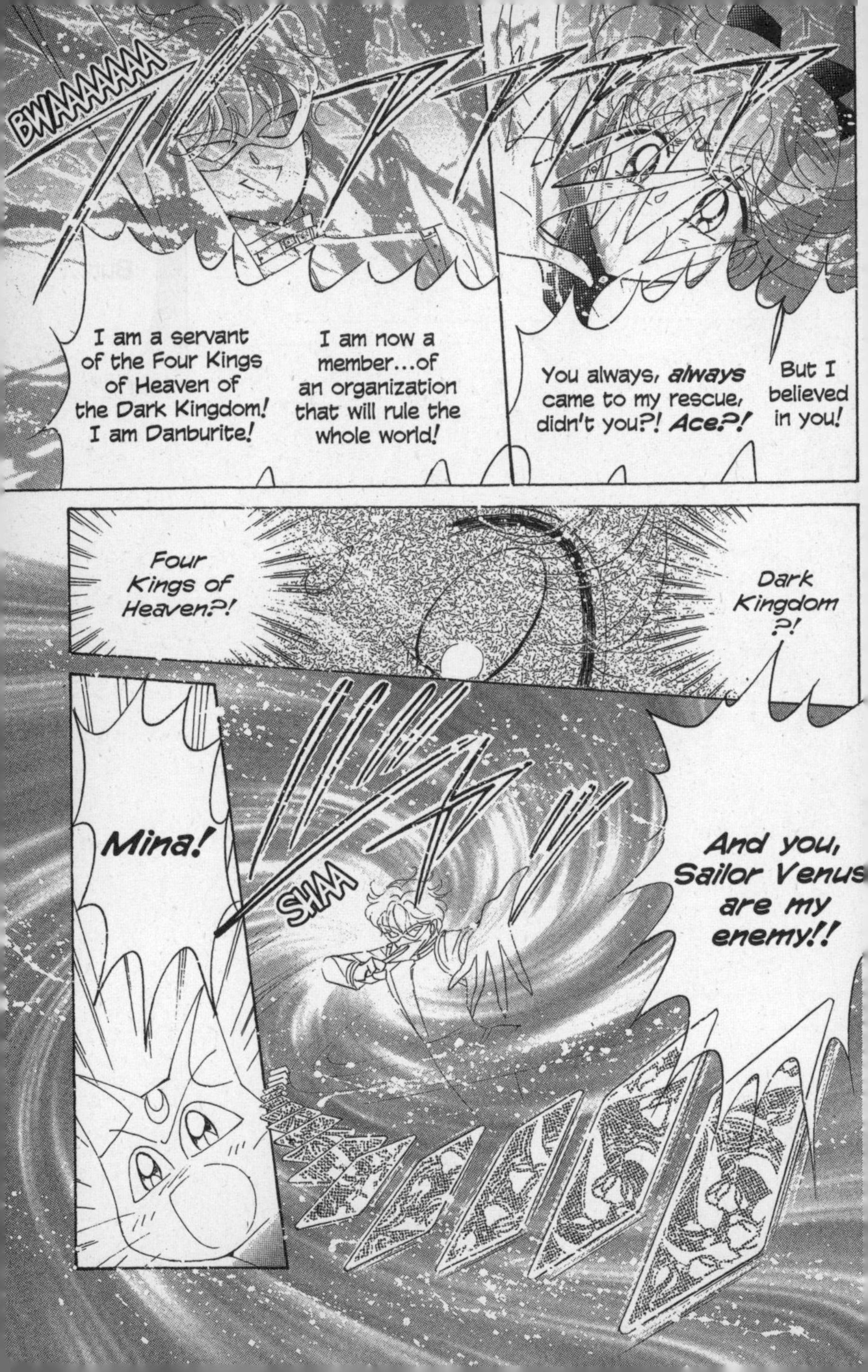
But I believed in you!
You always, *always* came to my rescue, didn't you?! *Ace?!*
BWAAAAAAA
I am now a member...of an organization that will rule the whole world!
I am a servant of the Four Kings of Heaven of the Dark Kingdom! I am Danburite!
Dark Kingdom ?!
Four Kings of Heaven?!
And you, Sailor Venus are my enemy!!
SHAA
Mina!

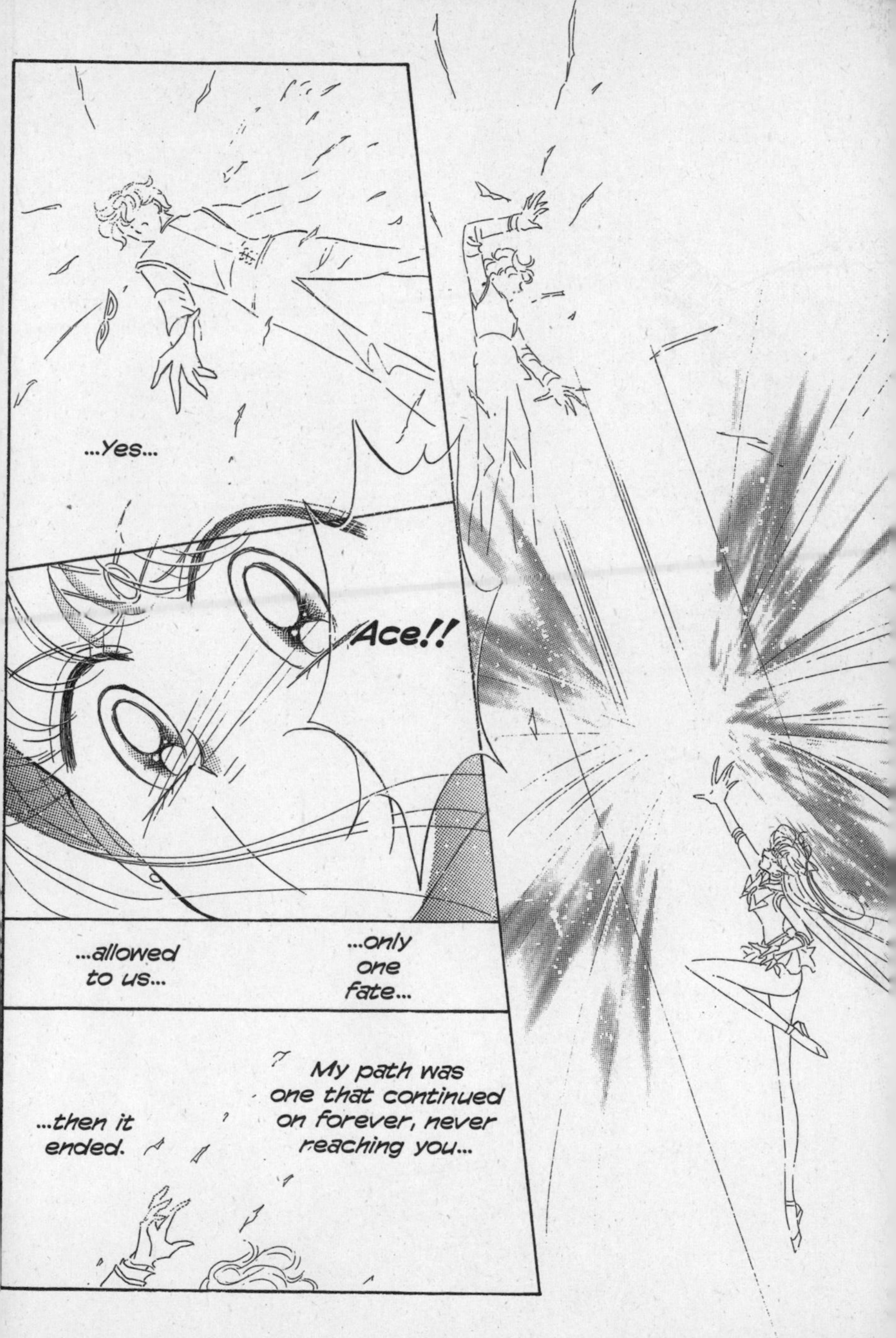
...Yes...
Ace!!
...only one fate...
...allowed to us...
My path was one that continued on forever, never reaching you...
...then it ended.

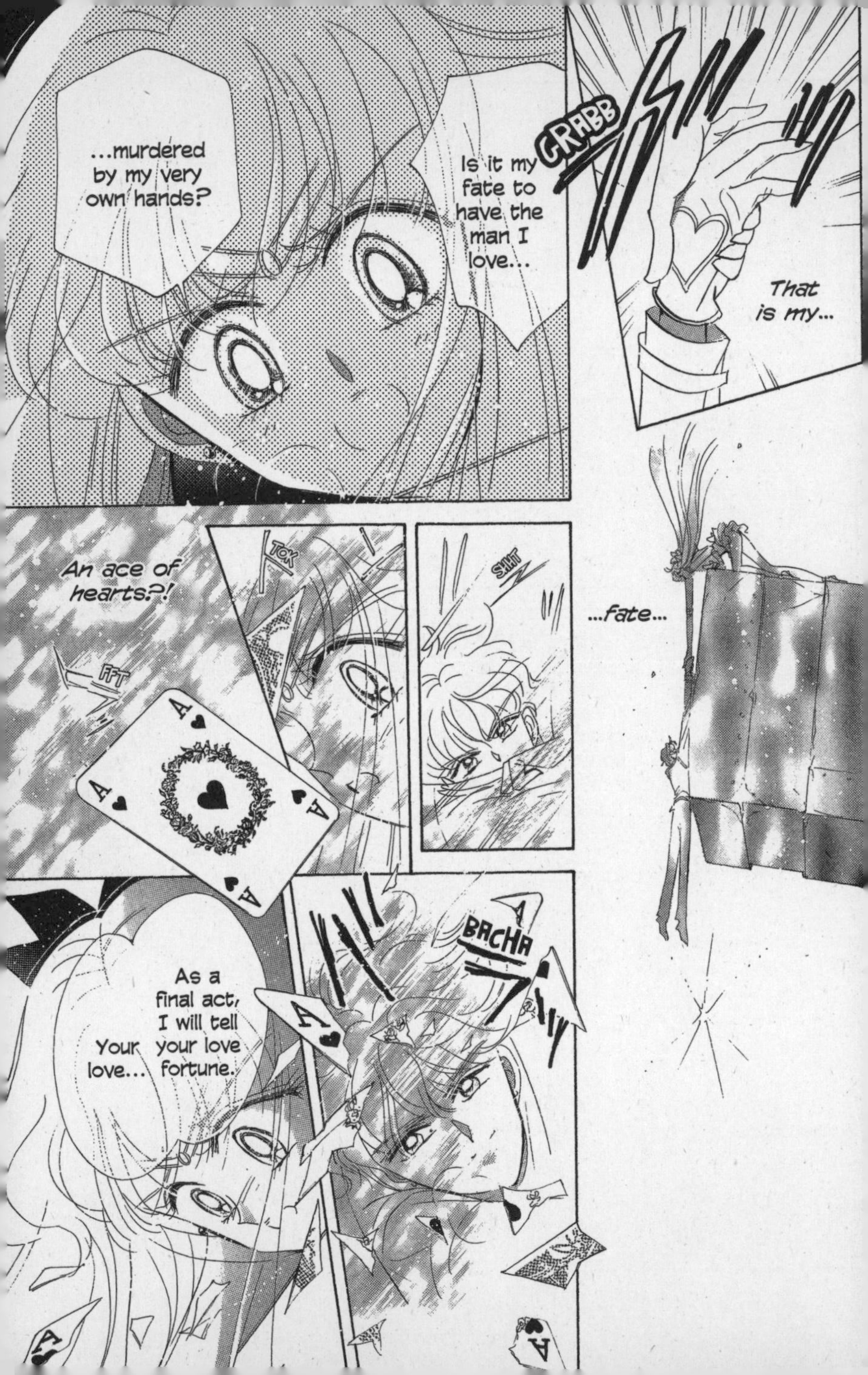
GRABB
That is my...
Is it my fate to have the man I love...
...murdered by my very own hands?
...fate...
SHHT
TOK
An ace of hearts?!
FFT
BACHA
As a final act, I will tell your love fortune.
Your love...

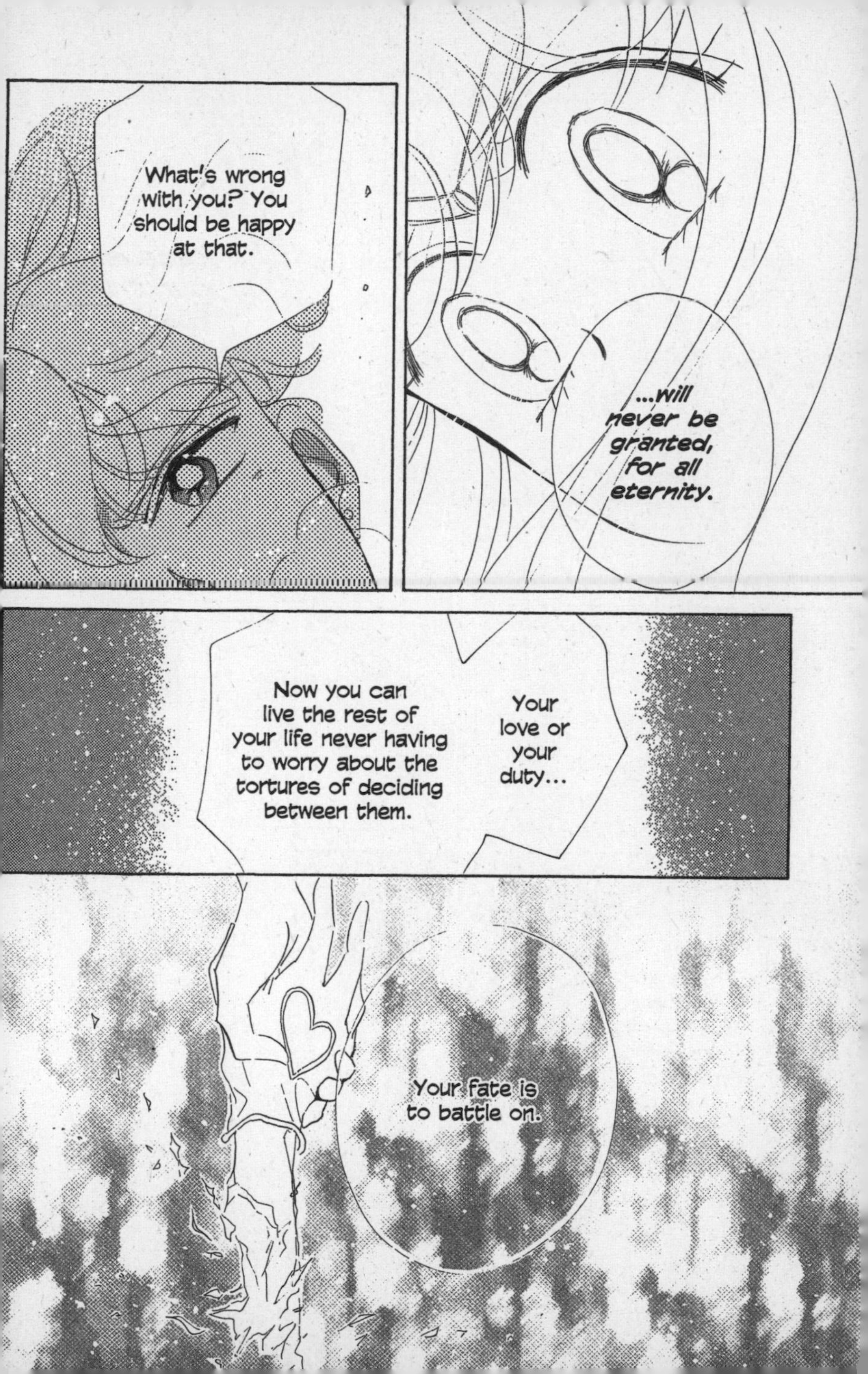
...will never be granted, for all eternity.
What's wrong with you? You should be happy at that.
Your love or your duty...
Now you can live the rest of your life never having to worry about the tortures of deciding between them.
Your fate is to battle on.

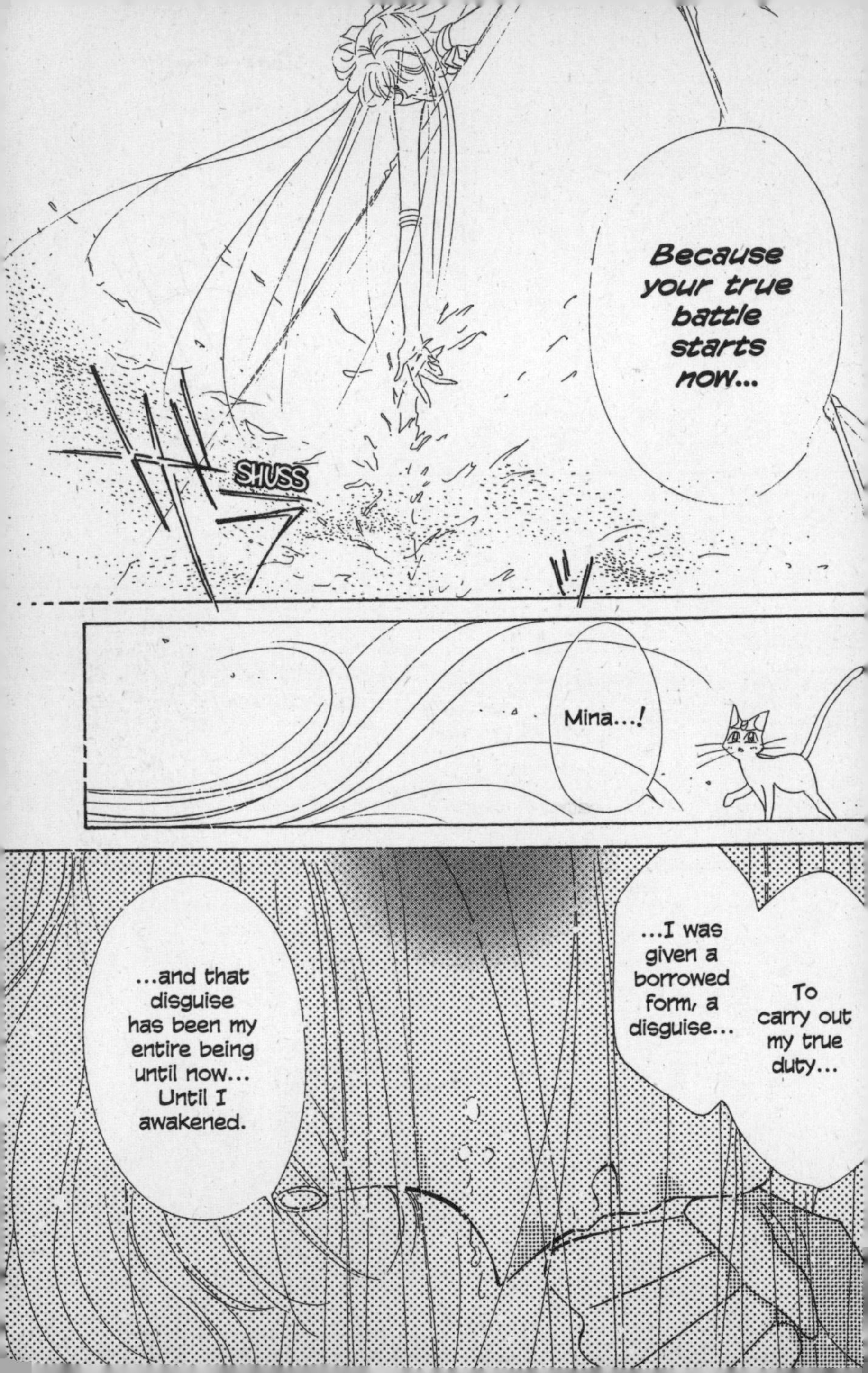
Because your true battle starts now...
SHUSS
Mina...!
To carry out my true duty...
...I was given a borrowed form, a disguise...
...and that disguise has been my entire being until now... Until I awakened.

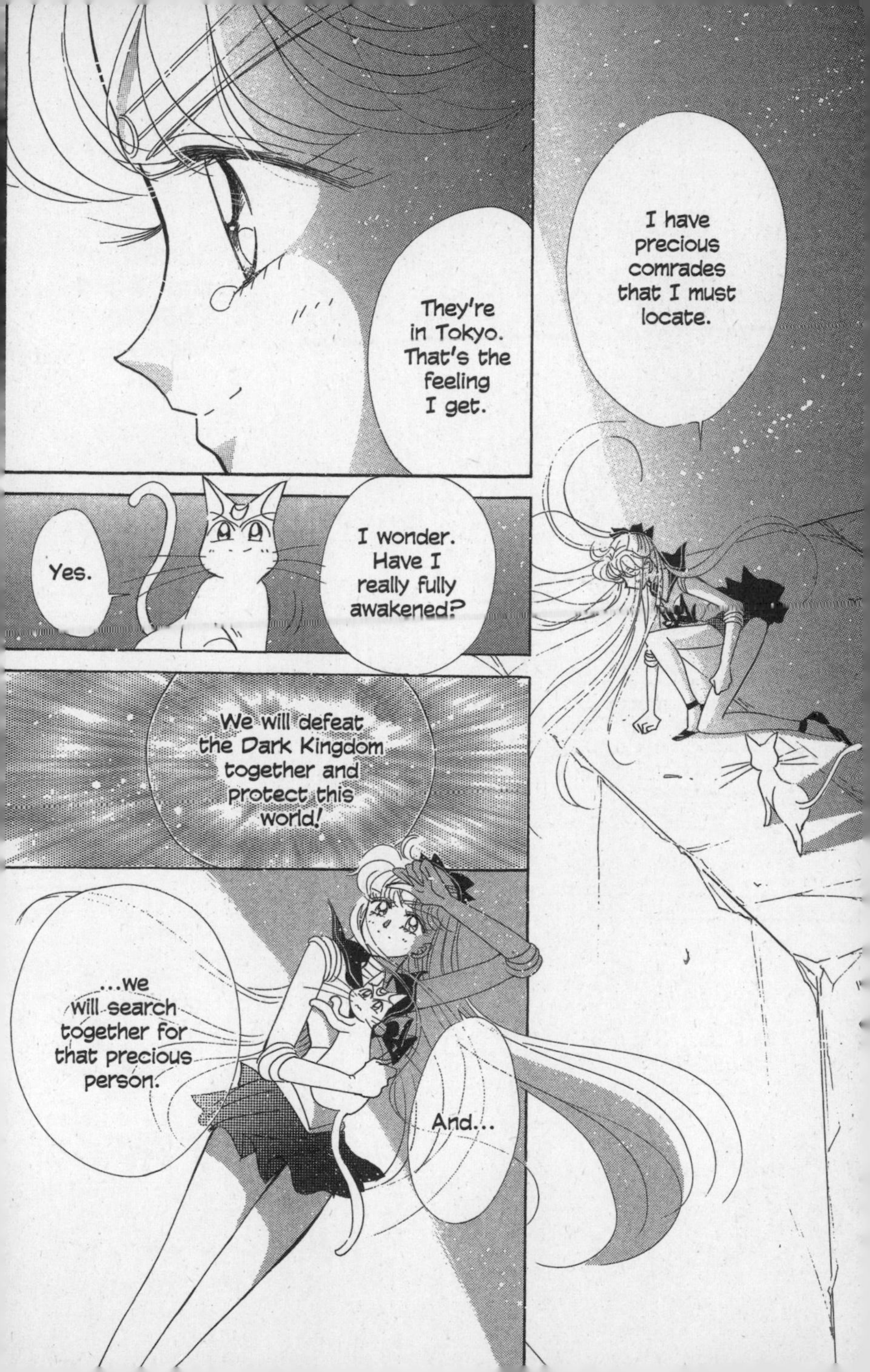

I have precious comrades that I must locate.
They're in Tokyo. That's the feeling I get.
I wonder. Have I really fully awakened?
Yes.
We will defeat the Dark Kingdom together and protect this world!
And...
...we will search together for that precious person.

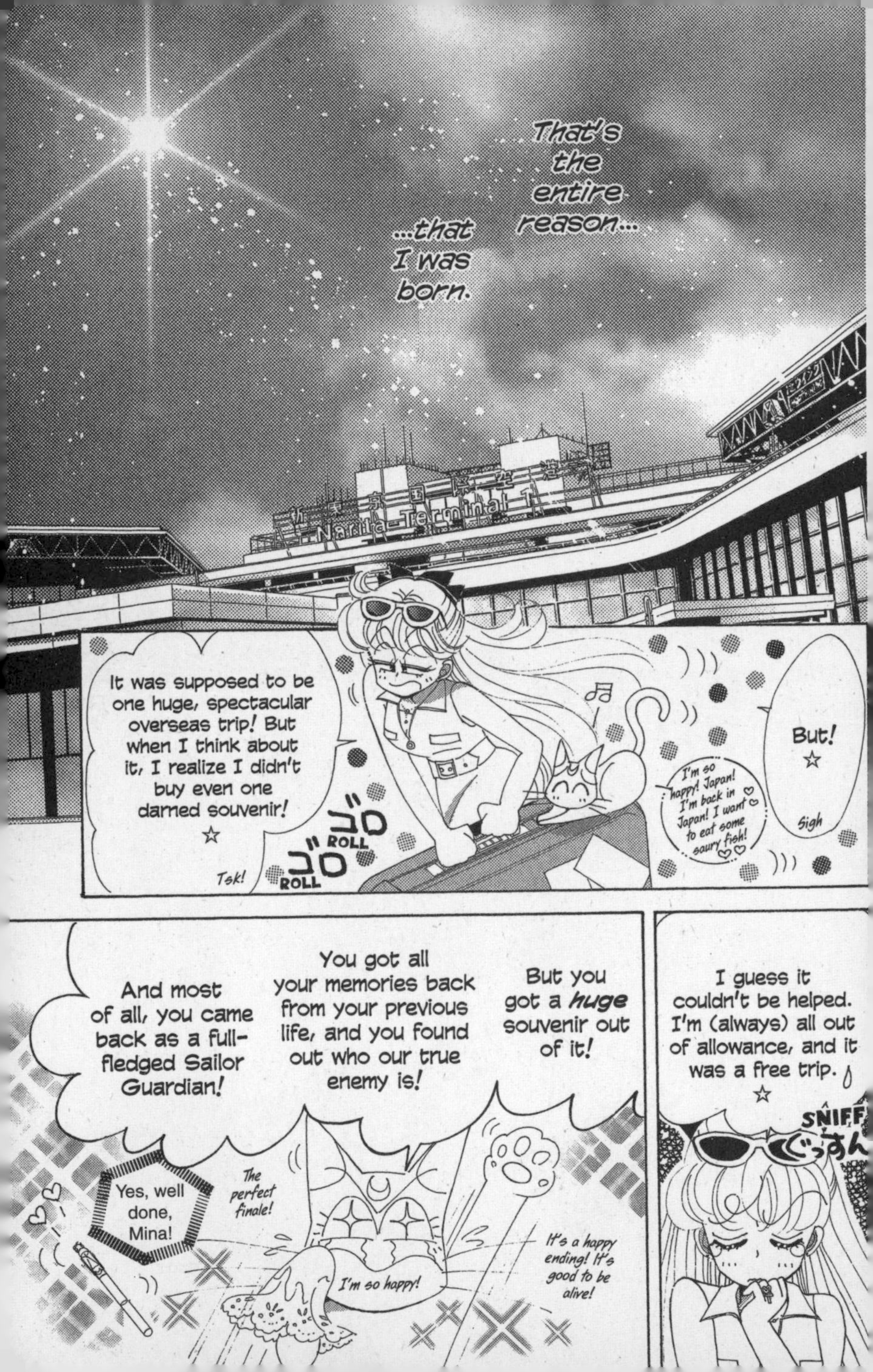
That's the entire reason...
...that I was born.
Narita Terminal 1
But! ☆
I'm so happy! Japan! I'm back in Japan! I want to eat some saury fish! ♡♡
Sigh
It was supposed to be one huge, spectacular overseas trip! But when I think about it, I realize I didn't buy even one darned souvenir! ☆
ゴロ ROLL
ゴロ ROLL
Tsk!
I guess it couldn't be helped. I'm (always) all out of allowance, and it was a free trip. ☆
SNIFF ぐすん
But you got a huge souvenir out of it!
You got all your memories back from your previous life, and you found out who our true enemy is!
And most of all, you came back as a full-fledged Sailor Guardian!
It's a happy ending! It's good to be alive!
The perfect finale!
I'm so happy!
Yes, well done, Mina!

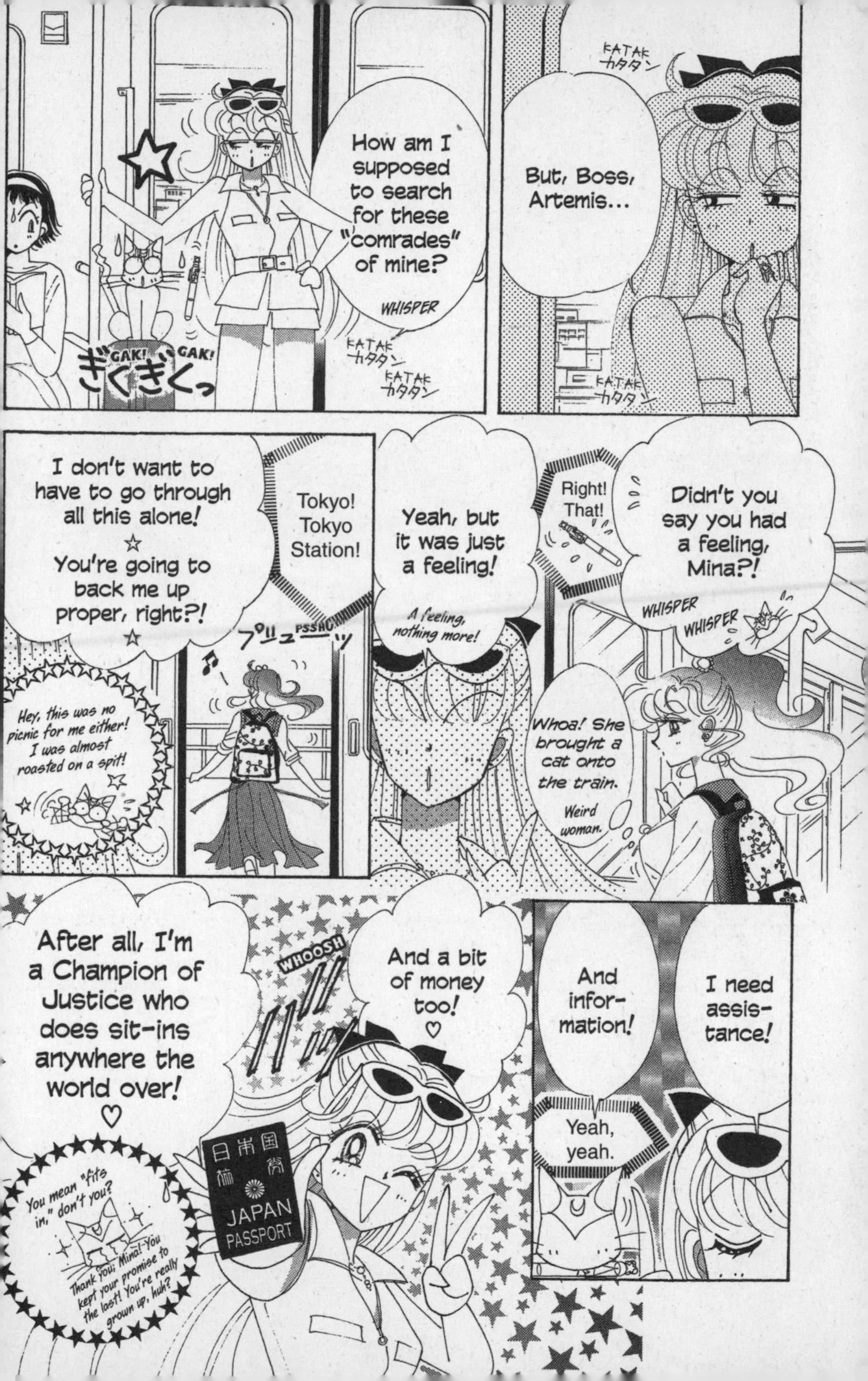
KATAK カタタン
But, Boss, Artemis...
KATAK カタタン
How am I supposed to search for these "comrades" of mine?
WHISPER
KATAK カタタン
KATAK カタタン
GAK! GAK! ぎくぎくっ
Didn't you say you had a feeling, Mina?!
Right! That!
WHISPER WHISPER
Yeah, but it was just a feeling!
A feeling, nothing more!
Whoa! She brought a cat onto the train.
Weird woman.
Tokyo! Tokyo Station!
I don't want to have to go through all this alone! ☆ You're going to back me up proper, right?! ☆
PSSHU プシュー
Hey, this was no picnic for me either! I was almost roasted on a spit!
I need assistance!
And information!
Yeah, yeah.
And a bit of money too! ♡
WHOOSH
After all, I'm a Champion of Justice who does sit-ins anywhere the world over! ♡
日本国 旅券
JAPAN PASSPORT
You mean "fits in," don't you?
Thank you, Mina! You kept your promise to the last! You're really grown up, huh?

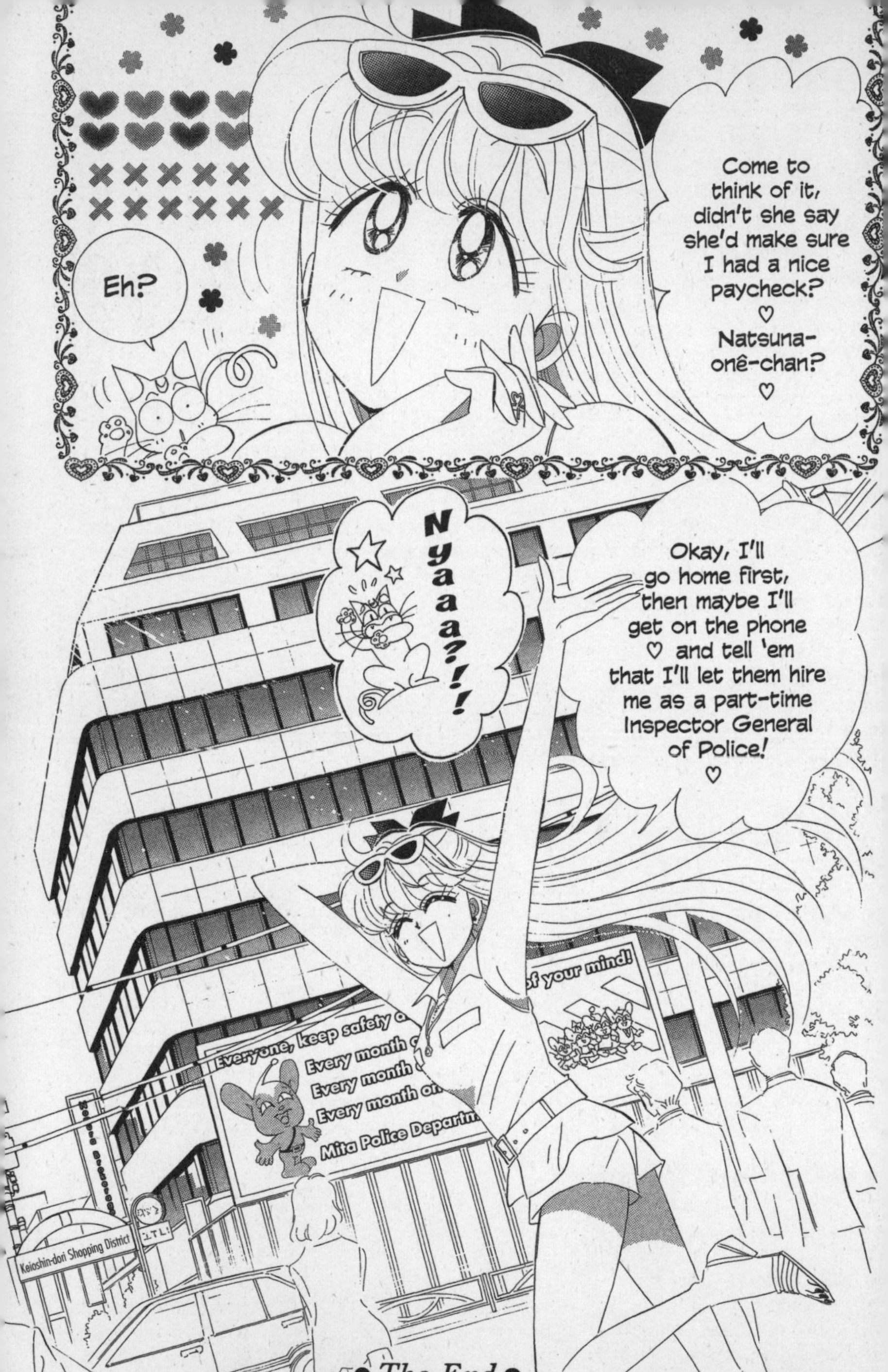
Come to think of it, didn't she say she'd make sure I had a nice paycheck? ♡ Natsuna-onê-chan? ♡
Eh?
Okay, I'll go home first, then maybe I'll get on the phone ♡ and tell 'em that I'll let them hire me as a part-time Inspector General of Police! ♡
Nyaaa?!!
Everyone, keep safety a
of your mind!
Every month o
Every month
Every month on
Mita Police Departm
Keioshin-dori Shopping District

• The End •

Translation Notes

Japanese is a tricky language for most Westerners, and translation is often more art than science. For your edification and reading pleasure, here are notes on some of the places where we could have gone in a different direction with our translation of the work, or where a Japanese cultural reference is used.

Page 9, Valentine's Day

There are very few holidays as associated with a particular product as Valentine's Day is with chocolate in Japan. True, the West has it's chocolate hearts and gifts of assorted chocolate candies, but in Japan, it has taken on a special significance–it has become the "Sadie Hawken's" day of relationships, where girls are encouraged to confess their love" to their sweethearts. The gift of chocolate, and the acceptance of that gift means that the guy is forced to at least consider the girl as a potential girlfriend. As it turns out, Valentine's chocolates are (to the joy of all males) specifically for women to give to men. But guys, don't get too excited, there are obligatory gifts of chocolates, too, that have no more meaning of love than an annual birthday card. For those gifts that do have romantic overtones, there is a particular day where the guy can respond, and that day is White Day.

Page 9, Sembei

In this scene, they're all eating a cooked Japanese snack called sembei. These are made of rice and somewhat resemble crackers–they could be called "rice crackers," but they aren't what Americans normally think of when they hear the words "rice crackers." One does not see individual grains of rice, and sembei flavorings are usually basted onto the cracker while cooking rather than added via powder afterwards.

Page 38, Hurts so good

Whereas a "relaxing massage" is generally considered a nice soothing rubbing of muscles in the West, in Japan, a "relaxing massage," consists of a muscular masseuse performing a workout on one's back. They are considered to be painful but very effective.

Page 53, Panpi

This word is a Japanese contraction of the Japanese word, ippan (normal) and the English word "people."

Page 66, Heroin

In Japanese the drug "heroin" is pronounced heroin, and "heroine" is pronounced hiroin. Minako misreads the sign (written in English even in the Japanese comic) using the pronunciation for the drug.

Page 67 Founde

Although some fan web sites transliterate Founde's name as "Fande," in reality her name is short for the English loan-word, "foundation." Thus the names Liquid Founde for "liquid foundation," Water Founde for "water-based foundation," Powder Founde for "powder foundation," and Solid Founde for "solid foundation."

Page 83, Department Store Worker

Female workers in Japanese department stores who wear uniforms similar to those that the Founde characters are wearing have a reputation for extremely polite customer service.

Page 103, Knight's Rally

This is a game held during athletics fairs in which three students (usually male) form a triangle and act as the "horse," and a "rider" (usually female) rides on their interlocked arms. Each "rider" wears a headband and the object of the game is to capture the headband of all of the "riders" on the opposing side. Once one's headband is taken, the "rider" and "horse" are retired from play.

Page 105 Worry wort fool
In Japanese, Artemis called himself an oyabaka, which literally means "parent fool," but its meaning is closer to "doting parent."

Page 110, Victor Hugo
Victor Hugo, poet and author of *The Hunchback of Notre Dame* and *Les Miserables*, had several quotes regarding cruelty to animals that are still being quoted by animal rights organizations today.

Page 113, Sweet Potatoes
In Japan, sweet potatoes have the same reputation as beans do in the west, as a catalyst for flatulence.

Page 122, Ogai's Dancing Girl
This was a novel of a Japanese man in Germany and the German ballerina who fell in love with him.

Page 143, edicts banning cruelty to animals
This is a page out of Japanese history where the Shogun saw animal abuse and issued an edict to protect animals from cruelty. It was a good thought, but in many cases, people suspected of being cruel to animals (whether true or not) were put to death for their alleged offenses. It was a symbol of good intention overzealously defended, leading to worse cruelty.

Page 146, 30 million koku
A koku was a standardized monetary unit supposedly equivalent to a year's worth of rice for an adult man or about 150 kg of rice. As a monetary unit, it was used to measure the wealth of fiefdoms in the Japanese feudal system. As comparison, the Shogun's property was said to be one million koku. So one can only assume that 30 million koku grudge is a rather big grudge.

Page 150, Merry Married Couple
This was something of a pun in the Japanese. Decades ago, on a television commercial for a company that makes the small shrines found in Japanese homes, they talked about how when one presses the lines (shiwa) in ones palm together (awase) with the lines in the other palm, it makes for shiawase ("happy").

Page 159, The Red Artery Society
This was a pun in Japanese. Since a cross symbol in Japanese looks like the kanji for the number ten, they call any cross symbol (including the Christian symbol) jûji or "ten character." So the Red Cross Society translates out to Sekijûji. The number for 9 is pronounced kyû in Japanese, and a homophone for kyû is to suck as in "sucking blood" and is used in the Japanese word for "vampires." So basically in Japanese, this take on the Red Cross conjures the image of "red blood sucking." Trying to keep with vampire-ish joke, I substituted "arteries" to again conjure up the sucking of blood.

Page 167 Oh my god
Usually, since most Japanese are very non-religious by western standards, I try to avoid religious references in their exclamations. But here, in the Japanese, Artemis said the English words, "Oh my god."

Page 169, Josei Comic
Like seinen manga (comics for adult men), there are manga for adult women as well that illustrate the dramas adult women may come in contact with. And josei comics are subdivided into smaller demographics for housewives, young working women, etc. The one mentioned in the Japanese text was manga for OL (office ladies), a group of professional women, usually in their early twenties, doing office support jobs.

Page 169, Mosquitoes
I certainly didn't notice any specific time of day for mosquitoes to attack when I lived in the States, but in Japan mosquitoes tend to come out with the most force just around dusk. Mosquitoes in the early afternoon are a rarity.

Page 176, Diphenhydramine
Diphenhydramine is an antihistamine that can be taken after a mosquito bite to alleviate the itching and redness

...ge 179, Blood Donation

...mentioned in the author note, the information on this page is based on the Japanese Red Cross blood ...nation rules. The American Red Cross has different rules for donation based on state law. And of course, ...Red Cross of other countries will have their own regulations as well.

...ge 184, Club Sempai

...schools, club have sempai (members from previous years) and kohai (younger members in the club), and ...other institutions, the sempai have the right to order their kohai around (and are expected to offer guidance ...he younger club members in return). So if a club sempai tells the kohai they need to finish in the top twenty, ...an order from one's superior.

...ge 185, It wasn't Microphone

...he Japanese version, Maiku's name is spelled in kanji indicating that it is a traditional Japanese name, and ...refore this translation transliterated it using regular Japanese rules. However, maiku is the way the Japanese ...ell the foreign word "mike" as in microphone. (It is also they way the spell the nickname "Mike" short for ...chael.)

...ge 187 Exchange diary

...exchange diary is one of the symbols of young romance. One member of the couple takes the diary and ...tes in it. Then it is exchanged in school the next day, and the other member of the couple then takes the diary ...ne to write a reply. To refuse someone's exchange diary is the same as rejecting the person as a romantic ...tner.

...ge 191, Roppongi & Chome

...re are many "party spots" in the Tokyo area, but Roppongi has a special reputation for bars, restaurants, ...bs and other adult entertainments. The word chome is sometimes translated as "block." Whereas western ...dresses are based on where one finds a building on a street, Japanese addresses are based on roughly ...arish sections of a city or town. These blocks are numbered and called chome, for example, ichi-chome ...ld be translated as "first block."

...ge 192, Otonaru Karaoke

...re's a pun here. The word for "sound" in Japanese is oto, and the word for "ringing out" is naru. So Otonaru's ...me is on the main Karaoke business's sign.

...ge 196, Cross Over Mt. Amagi

...popular song by the singer Sayuri Ishikawa of the Japanese traditional music style enka. In 2008, Ichiro Suzuki ...he Seattle Mariners chose this song (Japanese title: Amagi Goe) as one of his "at bat" songs.

...ge 196, Tokyo Desert

...is a pop song from 1976 sung by Hiroshi Uchiyamada and the Cool Five. The Japanese name is "Tokyo ...aku."

...ge 197, Karaoke Box

...tern Karaoke tends to come in bars and restaurants, and although Japanese karaoke can also come in bars ...restaurants, a more popular style are the "karaoke boxes." These are small sound-insulated rooms where one ...belt out a song alone or with a small group of friends without feeling the fear of singing in front of strangers.

...ge 197, Give Myself to the Flow of Time

...Japanese name of this 1986 pop single is Toki no Nagare ni Mi wo Makase. It was sung by Chinese star ...sa Teng, and she won the "Gold Award" for it in Japan.

...ge 197, Ginza Mama

...nen who run their own bars are often called "Mama." They are generally known to be good listeners and are ...to entertain their customers with lively conversation and songs. The best of them are found in the ...-priced establishments in the famous shopping district, the Ginza.

Page 197, Sweet Devil
A hit from the three-girl pop vocal group, the Candies, Yasashi Akuma (Sweet Devil) was released in 1977 and charted to no. 4 on the Japanese pop charts.

Page 198, Red Sweet Pea
An early hit by the long-time hit maker female vocalist Seiko Matsuda. The song charted in the Japanese top twenty for seventeen months.

Page 198, Attack Attack
This is the opening theme song for the classic shôjo Volleyball anime Attack No. 1.

Page 199, Tora Tora Tora
The first hit by the four-woman pop group MAX, short for Musical Active eXperience. The group (along with superstar Namie Amuro) used to be members of the group Super Monkey, but when they branched out, Tora Tora Tora gave them their first top-20 hit and placed them on the musical map.

Page 206, You are Sinbad
Okay, so this was a non-sequitur. But it happens, when you say a phrase that is found in a popular song, and that leads to completing the lyric of the song. (It doesn't happen to you?) This is what happened here. Makii i singing about her mikes, but the "just as the rumors say," line leads her into Pink Lady's 1977 no. 1 hit, Nagisa n Sinbad (Sinbad on the Beach).

Page 207, Feel my Hate
The song Urami•masu ("Feel my hate") was a hit on Miyuki Nakajima's 1980 No. 1-charting album, Ikiteitemo Ii Desuka ("Do You Mind if I Go On Living").

Page 207, May I kill you now
This is another lyric from "Cross Over Mt Akagi," noted in a note above.

Page 209, Mike Makii
The name of the villain in this story, Mike Makii, seems to be a parody of the name of a pop star and actor Mik Maki who himself has had several pop singles.

Page 209 What we know from our eyes meeting
These are lyrics from the hit song by Shizuka Kudo, Mugo•n...Iroppoi ("Silen•t Sexy"). A 1988 hit that charted at no. 6 on the Orikon pop charts.

Page 228, Gyoza
Gyoza is the Japanese name for Potstickers, a small Chinese dumpling, usually pan fried for Japanese tastes, that is a common part of Dim Sum dishes.

Page 229, Utau Ryogujo
Was an early '90s live-action magical girl TV show.

Page 241, Under a bridge
One of the pranks played on children is telling them that they were found abandoned under a bridge some-where.

The Pretty Guardians are back!

★

Kodansha Comics is proud to present *Sailor Moon* with all new translations.

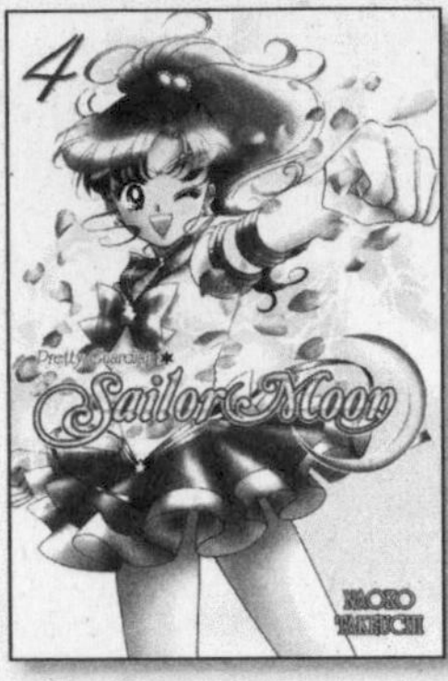
4
Pretty Guardian
Sailor Moon
NAOKO TAKEUCHI
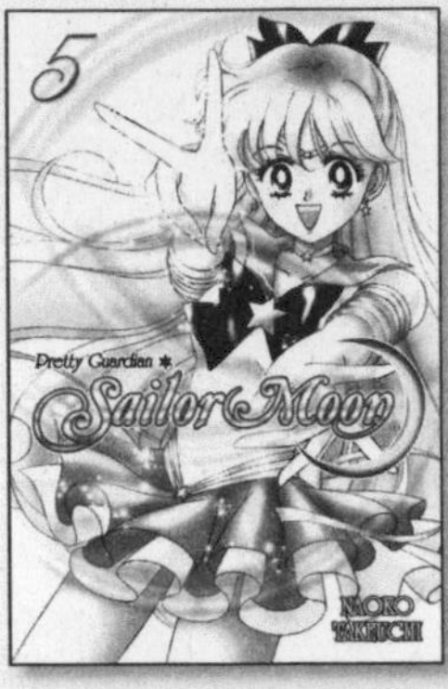
5
Pretty Guardian
Sailor Moon
NAOKO TAKEUCHI
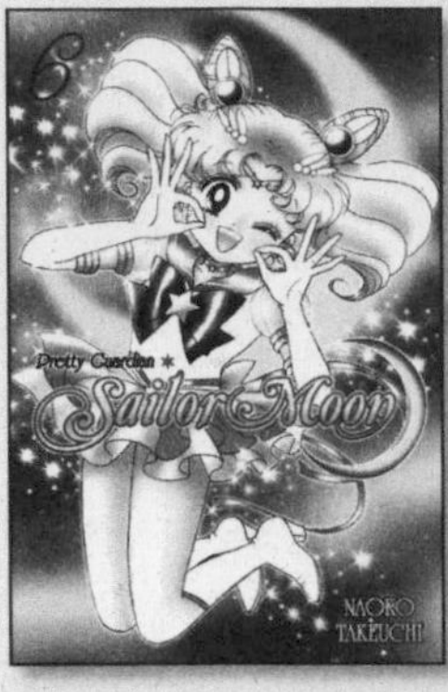
6
Pretty Guardian
Sailor Moon
NAOKO TAKEUCHI
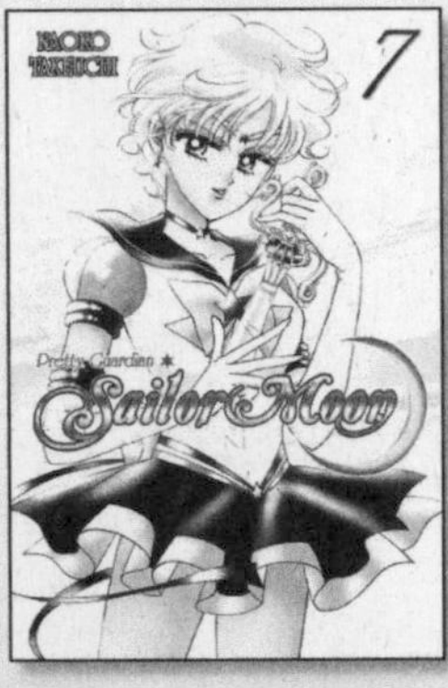
NAOKO TAKEUCHI
7
Pretty Guardian
Sailor Moon
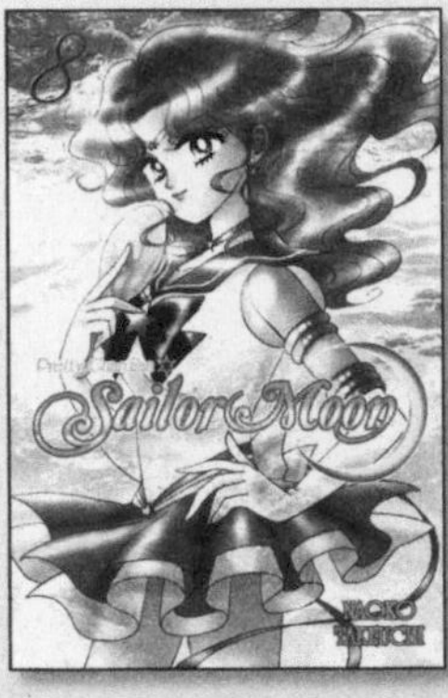
8
Pretty Guardian
Sailor Moon
NAOKO TAKEUCHI
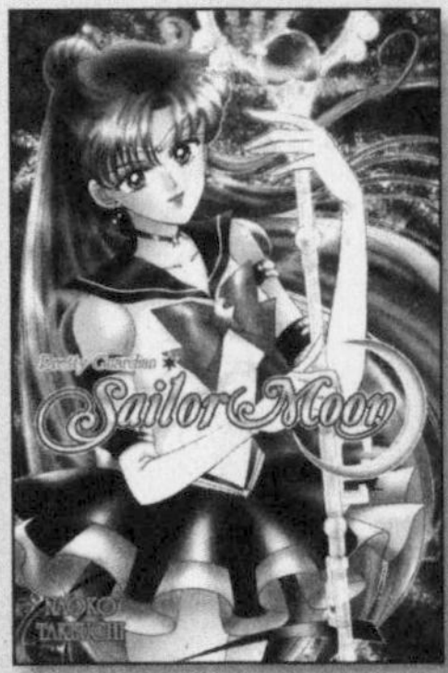
Pretty Guardian
Sailor Moon
NAOKO TAKEUCHI
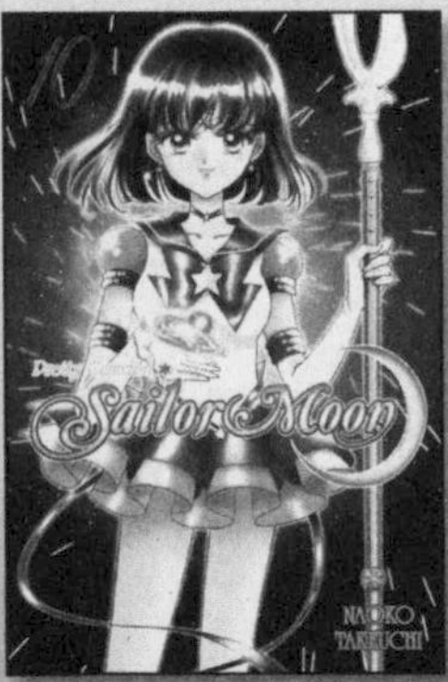
10
Pretty Guardian
Sailor Moon
NAOKO TAKEUCHI
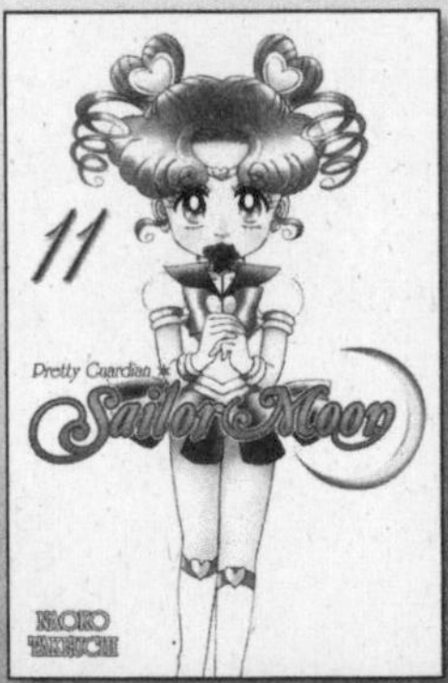
11
Pretty Guardian
Sailor Moon
NAOKO TAKEUCHI
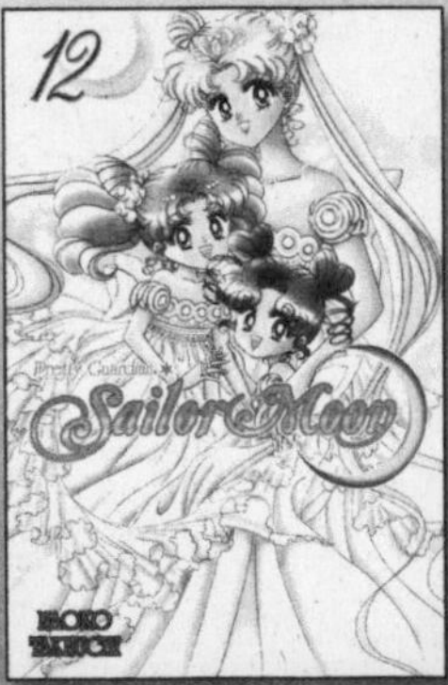
12
Pretty Guardian
Sailor Moon
NAOKO TAKEUCHI

A Kodansha Comics Trade Paperback Original.

Codename: Sailor V volume 2 copyright © 2004 Naoko Takeuchi
English translation copyright © 2011 Naoko Takeuchi

Published in the United States by Kodansha Comics, an imprint
of Kodansha USA Publishing, LLC, New York.

Publication rights for this English edition arranged through
Kodansha Ltd, Tokyo.

First published in Japan in 2004 by Kodansha Ltd., Tokyo, as
Codename wa Sailor V, volume 2.

ISBN 978-1-935-42978-4

Printed in Canada.

www.kodanshacomics.com

9 8 7 6 5 4 3 2 1

Translator/Adapter: William Flanagan
Lettering: Jennifer Skarupa

TOMARE!

STOP

You're going the wrong way!

Manga is a completely different type of reading experience.

To start at the beginning,
Go to the end!

hat's right! Authentic manga is read the traditional Japanese way—
om right to left, exactly the opposite of how American books are
ead. It's easy to follow: Just go to the other end of the book and read
ach page—and each panel—from right side to left side, starting at
e top right. Now you're experiencing manga as it was meant to be!